Global Status Survey and Conservation Action Plan

Microchiropteran Bats

Compiled by Anthony M. Hutson, Simon P. Mickleburgh, and Paul A. Racey

IUCN/SSC Chiroptera Specialist Group

IUCN
The World Conservation Union

Species Survival Commission

Fauna & Flora International

The Bat Conservation Trust

Sultanate of Oman

WWF

Council of Agriculture

DETR
Environment Transport Regions

Center for Marine Conservation

Published by: IUCN, Gland, Switzerland and Cambridge, UK.

Citation: Hutson, A.M., Mickleburgh, S.P., and Racey, P.A. (comp.). (2001). *Microchiropteran bats: global status survey and conservation action plan*. IUCN/SSC Chiroptera Specialist Group. IUCN, Gland, Switzerland and Cambridge, UK. x + 258 pp.

ISBN: 2-8317-0595-9

Cover photo: Brown long-eared bat (*Plecotus auritus*). F.R. Greenaway.

Produced by: The Nature Conservation Bureau Ltd, Newbury, UK.

Printed by: Information Press, Oxford, UK.

Available from: IUCN Publications Services Unit
219c Huntingdon Road, Cambridge CB3 0DL, United Kingdom
Tel: +44 1223 277894, Fax: +44 1223 277175
E-mail: info@books.iucn.org
http://www.iucn.org
A catalogue of IUCN publications is also available.

The text of this book is printed on 115 gsm Zone Silk, which is rated as 4-star under the Eco-Check system and is made from 100% sustainable fibre sources using chlorine-free processes.

This Action Plan is dedicated to four bat experts who contributed to its preparation, but sadly died before seeing the final printed version. John Edwards Hill, Karl Koopman, Frank Ansell, and Arthur Greenhall all made major contributions to the fields of bat biology and conservation over the past decades. Their deaths have left a huge gap in knowledge and expertise. It is hoped that this Plan will go a long way towards helping the cause of bat conservation worldwide and they would have been pleased by its final publication.

Contents

Foreword

In 1992, I wrote the foreword to *Old World Fruit Bats – An Action Plan for their Conservation.* The plan was well received by governments, NGOs, and the conservation community and stimulated a great deal of activity. Fifteen of the 20 major recommendations have been addressed and, as a result, projects on fruit bats have been initiated in many countries of the Old World tropics.

Encouraged by the success of the Old World Fruit Bat Plan, IUCN asked the compilers to produce a quick overview of the remaining 834 bat species, the Microchiroptera. Seven years on, it certainly hasn't been quick, but as successive drafts have been read and commented upon by members of IUCN's Chiroptera Specialist Group and others, the quality of the information it contains has improved.

This is the first attempt at producing a Global Action Plan for a group of animals that occupies every continent (with the exception of polar regions) and many oceanic islands. It is clear from the Plan that bats face a wide range of threats, which have led to precipitous declines. With 834 species, it is impossible to deal with each individually. The compilers have, therefore, written 20 Species Action Plans for a wide diversity of bat species. These aim not only to stimulate action on those species, but also to provide templates from which plans on species facing similar problems can be produced in the countries in which they occur.

Microchiropteran bats have always faced challenges. They have a public relations problem and their roosting habits sometimes bring them into conflict with humans. Nevertheless, the bats covered by this volume are important components of ecosystems mainly as aerial insectivores throughout the world. They also act as pollinators and seed dispersers in the New World tropics. Bats are often major contributors to a country's mammalian diversity and the 1992 Convention on Biological Diversity has led to a new appreciation of the importance of such diversity.

Bats have been the focus of conservation initiatives for many years, some of which have halted or reversed declines in numbers. These initiatives have shown what can be done. The compilers are to be congratulated in producing a comprehensive document that together with the Plan on Old World fruit bats provides the first detailed conservation overview for this highly important group. Stimulated by this plan, I hope the growing community of bat biologists and conservationists will renew their efforts to safeguard this major part of our biological heritage.

The Earl of Cranbrook DSc DL

Acknowledgements

We would like to thank The Bat Conservation Trust and Fauna & Flora International for providing office facilities and financial support, without which it would not have been possible to undertake this project. We also thank the IUCN/SSC Peter Scott Action Plan Fund that provided additional funding.

A large number of people have contributed to this document. Some of them are acknowledged elsewhere in the Plan, but we would like to thank them all here: Gary Ades, Issa Aggundey, Ludmilla Aguiar, L.F. Aguirre, Zubaid Akbar, J. Scott Altenbach, S. Andreev, the late Frank Ansell, Hector Arita, Keith Atkinson, Stephane Aulagnier, Jonathan Baillie, Angela Bakka, Sergey Bakka, Paul Bates, Jackie Belwood, Jesus Benzal, Ric Bernard, Vladimir Beshkov, Frank Bonaccorso, John Borg, Alex Borissenko, Alexandr Botvinkin, Evan Bowen-Jones, Peter Boye, Monika Braun, Anne Brooke, Neil Burgess, John A. Burton, David Butler, Annette Carlstrom, John Collie, Gabor Csorba, D.H.M. Cumming, Geoffrey Davison, Abigail Entwistle, Jacques Fairon, Nina Fascione, Brock Fenton, Tim Flannery, Ted Fleming, Charles Francis, Barbara French, Jiri Gaisler, Justin Gerlach, Anne-Marie Gillesberg, Mariano Gimenez-Dixon, Felix Gonzalez-Alvarez, Steve Goodman, the late Arthur Greenhall, Brian Groombridge, Timothy Gross, Regine Grünmeier, Toni Guillen, S.S. Guitart, Roger Haagenson, Marianne Haffner, Les Hall, David Happold, Meredith Happold, Christine Harbusch, Larry Heaney, Paul Heideman, Gerardo Herrera, the late John Edwards Hill, S. Hoch, Kim Howell, Linette Humphrey, Vladimir Iljin, Nina Ingle, Carlos Iudica, Gareth Jones, C. Joulot, Javier Juste, Tolibjon Khabilov, Jonathan Kingdon, Tigga Kingston, Ronan Kirsch, Dieter Kock, Tomasz Kokurewicz, the late Karl Koopman, Carmi Korine, Irina Kovalyova, Eugenia Kozhurina, Dorothea Krull, Sergey Kruskop, Boris Krystufek, Tom Kunz, Ivan Kuzmin, Ralph Labes, Ya-Fu Lee, Grzegorz Lesinski, Susan Liebermann, Herman Limpens, Peter Lina, Lindy Lumsden, Jader Marinho-Filho, Matti Masing, Didier Masson, Kate McAney, Tim McCarthy, Gary McCracken, Jeff McNeely, Rodrigo Medellin, Jacqui Morris, Sam Morris, Jean Francois Noblet, Colin O'Donnell, D. Ortega, Jorge Palmeirim, Rumiana Pandurska, Milan Paunovic, Dainius-Haroldas Pauza, Gunars Petersons, Dixie Pierson, Jacques Pir, Artiom Polkanov, Bill Rainey, Ana Rainho, Irina Rakhmatulina, Naas Rautenbach, Greg Richards, Klaus Richarz, Mark Robinson, Luisa Rodrigues, Rolando Rodriguez-Munoz, Tamar Ron, Jens Rydell, Rafael Samudio Jr., Julieta de Samudio, Anthony Santana, Dino Scaravelli, Josh Schachter, John Seyjaget, Benny Shalmon, Rebecca Smith, Friederike Spitzenberger, Belinda Stewart-Cox, Torsten Stjernberg, Tor Stormark, Peter Strelkov, Hans-Peter Stutz, Per Ole Syvertsen, Gilberto Silva Taboada, Valdir Taddei, Mikhail Tiunov, R. Tizard, Marcel Uhrin, Zbigniew Urbanczyk, Ruth Utzurrum, Victor van Cakenberghe, Aldo Voute, Sally Walker, Steve Walker, Joe Walston, Gary Wiles, Don Wilson, Eduard Yavrovyan, Derek Yalden, and Szabolcs Zavoczky.

Two workshops were held to help gather information for this Plan. We would particularly like to thank those who helped organise these: the Lubee Foundation, particularly John Seyjaget and Roger Haagenson, for the Neotropical Workshop in Florida in 1993 and Uwe Schmidt for the Palaearctic Workshop in Bonn in 1994.

We would also like to thank Dick Vane-Wright and Paul Williams at the Natural History Museum in London for their invaluable help in the analysis of hotspots presented in Chapter 5 and the regional accounts.

We would also like to thank those who generously provided photographs for the Plan. Paul Bates, Daniel Bennett, Stephen Dalton, C. Ecroyd, Frank Greenaway, Gareth Jones, Ivan Kuzman, Thomas Lemke, Lindy Lumsden, Pat Morris, Jorg Palmeirim, Noel Speechley, Bob Stebbings, Rob Strachan, M. Tuttle, and David Woodfall.

We are responsible for any errors or omissions that may occur in this document. In a few cases, there may have been conflicting views from experts and in such situations we have had to make our own decisions, for which we accept responsibility.

Anthony M. Hutson
Winkfield, Station Road, Plumpton Green,
East Sussex BN7 3BU, UK
Phone: +44 (0)1273 890341
Fax: +44 (0)1273 890859
e-mail: hutsont@pavilion.co.uk
(formerly of the Bat Conservation Trust)

Simon P. Mickleburgh
Fauna & Flora International, Great Eastern House,
Tenison Road, Cambridge CB1 2TT, UK
Phone: +44 (0)1223 579 477
Fax: +44 (0)1223 461 481
e-mail: s.mickleburgh@fauna-flora.org

Paul A. Racey
University of Aberdeen, Department of Zoology,
Tillydrone Avenue, Aberdeen AB24 2TZ, UK
Phone: +44 (0)1224 272 858
Fax: +44 (0)1224 272 396
e-mail: p.racey@abdn.ac.uk

Executive Summary

Following the publication of *Old World Fruit Bats – An Action Plan for their Conservation*, the Chiroptera Specialist Group (CSG) of IUCN's Species Survival Commission offers the results of the first comprehensive review to identify the conservation priorities for the remainder of the bats – the 834 species of Microchiroptera. The CSG makes no attempt to give an account of each of these species but, rather, this volume provides an overview that can be used as a basis for the development of more local or regional action, or actions for particular groups of bat species, by taxon or by habitat.

The Action Plan is divided into two parts. The first gives a brief review of the biology and ecology of the Microchiroptera relevant to their conservation. It also presents the authors' approach to the application of IUCN categories of threat to all species. The list of 834 species in 17 families and 137 genera includes conservation status assessments and broad distribution for all taxa. Where the taxonomic status of a species is not yet agreed, the authors have generally recognized the taxon as a separate species for the purposes of conservation. For this reason, the list includes more species than other world catalogues prepared by individual authorities. Subspecies and other taxa below the species level are not dealt with in this volume. Approximately 22% of bat species are considered threatened and a further 23% as Near Threatened.

The second part of this volume discusses the broad conservation issues and makes general recommendations for conservation action. Some examples of recorded declines are presented and the major threats to bats worldwide are identified.

National legislation for the protection of bats varies greatly, but can benefit from international collaboration through appropriate conventions and other treaties. The Agreement on the Conservation of Bats in Europe (under the Bonn Convention) and the Program for the Conservation of Migratory Bats of Mexico and the United States are examples of international initiatives specifically developed for bats. Other existing international treaties that could be used to benefit the conservation of bats are identified.

Using WORLDMAP to investigate the distribution of bats at the generic level, key areas of diversity are identified at a global and zoogeographic regional level and for the major families of bats. The diversity in Central and northern South America far exceeds anywhere in the Old World, but six areas of major importance to diversity in the Old World are identified. These are found in East Africa, and in areas focussing on Peninsular Malaysia, Sulawesi, around Nepal/NE India to South China and adjacent countries. There is a major need to extend these analyses, particularly at the species level, to assess the degree to which current conservation practice, including the network of protected areas, can ensure the conservation of the world's bat fauna.

General recommendations that can be applied to almost all range states are presented and demonstrate a range of actions from the protection of species and their habitats to the value of education and of underpinning legislation. The general needs for survey and population monitoring are highlighted. More detailed accounts of conservation problems and recommendations are provided for each of the relevant zoogeographic regions: Afrotropical, Australasian, Indomalayan, Nearctic, Neotropical, and Palaearctic. Thus, the conservation of key habitats, such as woodland and underground habitats (e.g., caves) is of concern throughout the world, but regionally particular habitats may be at risk, and particular kinds of land use (especially for agriculture or forestry practices) may threaten bat populations. Key areas for bat diversity in each region are discussed and particular taxa of regional significance are identified. While systematic studies continue in all regions, there are areas where such work at a general level or to resolve particular taxonomic difficulties has a high priority. The same applies to studies of distribution and ecology – there are many species for which almost nothing is known apart from the existence of a few museum specimens. Regional checklists, summaries of conservation status of species for each included nation state, and regional bibliographies are included.

A series of 20 sample summary Species Action Plans are presented. The selected species are not necessarily the rarest or most threatened, but are offered to highlight the range of conservation concerns and potential actions to address these concerns. These are not all top priority species, but are examples of concerns and actions that can be applied to other threatened species and to maintain a favourable conservation status for currently less-threatened species.

This action plan recognises that much has been done and is being done in various parts of the world for the conservation of bats, and a section on recent conservation initiatives highlights examples of the range of local and regional initiatives that can be applied elsewhere to the conservation of bats.

A final chapter gives the IUCN Red List species for each country, with a summary of the number of bat species in each Red List category and reference for the source of such faunal data. For the most part, faunal lists were drawn from major key works and so it is likely that many such lists could be refined by those with specialist knowledge of the countries concerned. Systematic lists are presented of the bat species in each of the IUCN Red List categories of threat: Extinct, Critically Endangered, Endangered, Vulnerable, Data Deficient, and Lower Risk: Near Threatened.

Thus the volume aims to provide a framework for further action for the conservation of bats, which make up a quarter of all mammals, and for which almost half the species can be considered threatened or near threatened at a global level.

PART 1

Biology, Ecology, and Systematics of Microchiropteran Bats

Chapter 1

Biology and Ecology of Microchiropteran Bats

1.1 Background

In 1992, an Action Plan for the Megachiroptera (167 species) was published (Mickleburgh *et al.* 1992). This was the first document of its kind to assemble information about the status of this group, and was compiled with the assistance of over 50 of the world's bat experts, including members of the Chiroptera Specialist Group (CSG) of IUCN – The World Conservation Union's Species Survival Commission. This plan was highly successful in stimulating a range of activities aimed at the conservation of megachiropterans. As a result, IUCN approached the CSG to request the production of an Action Plan for the remaining 834 bat species which comprise the suborder Microchiroptera. A number of authorities had approached some of the issues that would be covered in an Action Plan for the Microchiroptera, from both a national and international perspective. However, this would be the first time that information had been sought from throughout the world community of bat specialists. Both CSG members and others would be asked to identify the many problems that faced the second largest group of mammals, the activities that had been undertaken for their conservation, and broad measures that needed to be taken to halt recorded and implied declines. The aim was to produce a wide-ranging overview that would act as a basis for more specific action directed at regions or at particular faunas, or species at risk.

Lack of information is an overriding problem when compiling documents of this type. In essence, out of the 834 species of microchiropteran bats, only a small number have been well studied and, for some species, there is no information other than an original description. In many areas of the world, even basic distributional information is lacking and knowledge of a species' biology and ecology is vital before effective management decisions can be taken. This plan is an overview of the major issues, but highlights large gaps in knowledge. The issue of information, or lack of it, is discussed further in Chapter 3.

With the Megachiroptera, individual accounts were compiled for every species and subspecies. However, given the number of species involved, the Action Plan for the Microchiroptera needed to take a different approach. This Plan reviews the major threats to microchiropterans and lists recommendations for the conservation of threatened species, sites, and habitats. It was decided first to deal with issues on a regional basis – six zoogeographic regions were chosen (Afrotropical, Australasian, Indomalayan, Nearctic, Neotropical, and Palaearctic – see Map 1 for regional boundaries) and within each of these, threats to taxonomic groups of bats, geographic areas, habitats, feeding areas, and roosts are reviewed. Threats arising through interactions with humans are also highlighted. Within each region, key areas for bat biodiversity are discussed. It was decided to produce Action Plans for 20 species that were chosen to provide a range of examples of the kind of threats facing bats worldwide. Each account also includes recommended actions to help conserve the species. An analysis of the global biodiversity of microchiropteran bat genera was undertaken using the WORLDMAP software developed by R.I. Vane-Wright and P. Williams at The Natural History Museum in London. Finally, recommendations for the conservation of species and their habitats are presented. The Plan will be circulated to individuals and organisations worldwide who are involved in the conservation of microchiropteran bats. It will also be sent to governments to encourage their participation in the process of conserving bats and habitats within their countries.

This introduction discusses the biology and ecology of microchiropteran bats. Conservation issues, including threats, are discussed in Part 2 which provides a range of examples of the threats bats face and identifies some of the measures that have been taken to counter these. An indication of the high status bats should have in considering mammal conservation can be seen in such works as IUCN (2000). More specific reviews of bat conservation issues can be found in Fenton (1992), Mickleburgh *et al.* (1992), Kunz and Pierson (1994), Fenton (1997), Racey (1998a), Kunz and Racey (1998), and Racey and Entwistle (in press). General accounts of bats are given by, amongst others, Wimsatt (1970a,b, 1977), Kunz (1982b), Hill and Smith (1984), Fenton (1992), Richarz and Limbrunner (1992), Kunz and Pierson (1994), Altringham (1996), and Neuweiler (2000).

1.2 Order Chiroptera

At present there are 1,001 recognised species of bats (Chiroptera) worldwide, about a quarter of all known mammal species. The Order Chiroptera is divided into two Suborders, the Megachiroptera (167 species of Old World fruit bats) and the Microchiroptera (834 species).

The Microchiroptera show considerable variation in form and structure. They range in size from very small with forearms of 22.5mm, to moderately large with forearms of 115.0mm. Many species have nose leaves or other dermal outgrowths above the nostrils or on the lips. A tragus (a lobe of skin inside the pinna of the ear) is usually present. The interfemoral membrane is usually well developed and the tail relatively long. The second digit lacks a claw and the eyes are generally small. All microchiropterans orientate, and most seek and capture food, using a system of echolocation which involves ultrasonic sounds being emitted through the mouth or nose.

About 75% of microchiropterans feed on insects, although food sources may include other invertebrates, fish, amphibians, small mammals (including other bats), blood, fruit, and flowers. In the Neotropical family Phyllostomidae, the majority of species feed on fruit, nectar, and pollen, and complement the fruit bats of the Old World (Megachiroptera, family Pteropodidae).

Microchiropteran bats are found throughout the world, except for the Arctic and Antarctic and on some isolated oceanic islands. The general distribution of families, genera, and species is given in Chapter 2. Findley (1993) also examines the distribution of bat faunas in relation to their systematics, physiology, behaviour, and ecology. The largest families are the Vespertilionidae (357 species) with a worldwide distribution and the Phyllostomidae (151 species) found in the Nearctic and Neotropical regions. Eight families are represented by single genera – Rhinopomatidae, Nycteridae, Noctilionidae, Natalidae, Thyropteridae, Mystacinidae, Craseonycteridae, and Myzopodidae, and the latter two families are currently represented by single species.

1.3 Biology and ecology

1.3.1 Habitat use

Microchiropteran bats use a variety of habitats both for roosting and feeding. Forests and woodlands worldwide are key habitats – in tropical areas primary or well-regenerated secondary forest is used by many taxa. In temperate areas, woodlands are equally important. Aquatic habitats (e.g., rivers, streams, lakes, and canals) are favoured as feeding areas as they often attract a rich supply of insects that are the main food source for many species. Some species have adapted well to urban environments and bats can be found feeding and roosting within major conurbations. In temperate areas in recent years, research has shown the importance of linear landscape elements to bats. These may include hedges, woodland edges, tree lines, canals, and other features that provide vital links between feeding and roosting areas.

Map 1. Boundaries of zoogeographic regions.
1. Nearctic; 2. Neotropical; 3. Palaearctic; 4. Afrotropical; 5. Indomalayan; 6. Australasian.

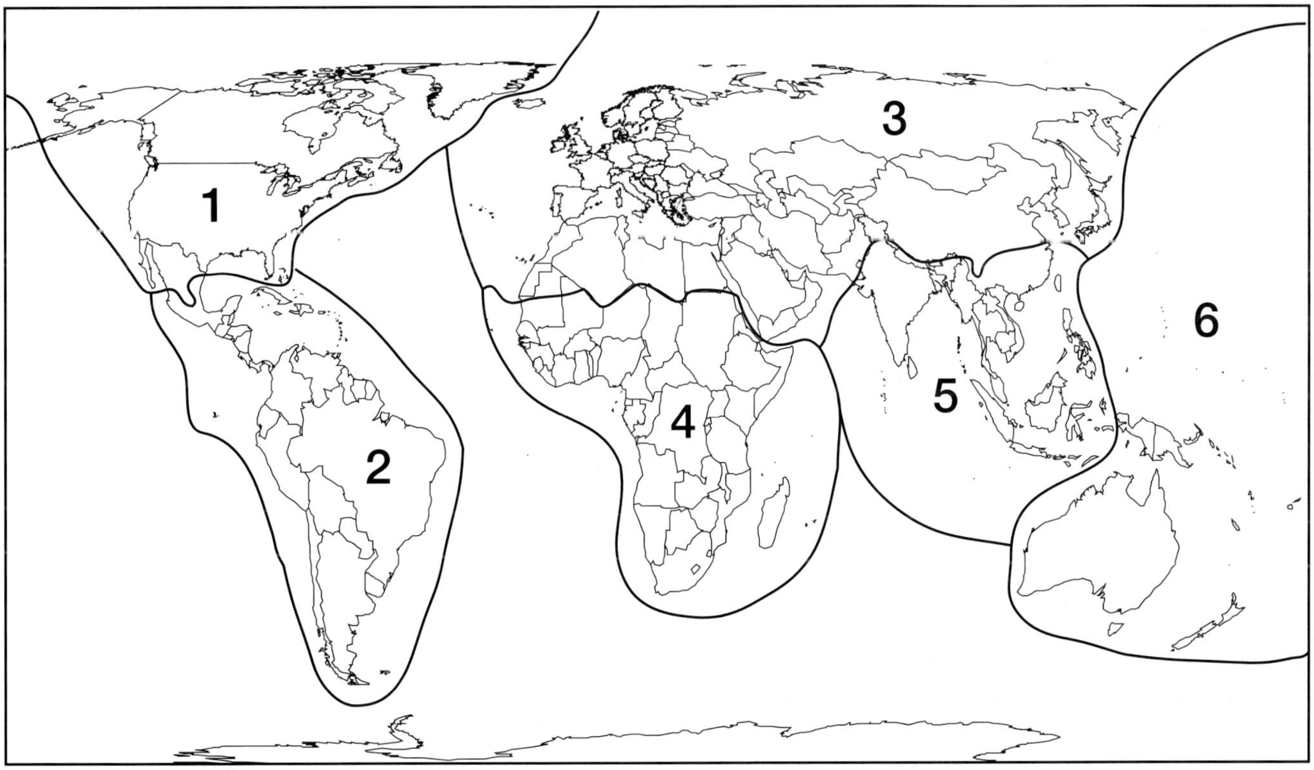

1.3.2 Roosts

A wide variety of sites are used by microchiropteran bats for roosting. A comprehensive review of the roosting ecology of bats is given by Kunz (1982c). Bats may utilise holes in trees that have been created naturally or through the activities of other animals such as birds. Mature trees, including standing dead trees or "snags", tend to have more available holes and thus can be of greater importance for bats. In tropical forests, bats may modify the leaves of some plants to construct tents under which they roost. Some species roost amongst dense foliage, others hang free from branches in both temperate and tropical forests.

In temperate areas, caves and mines provide ideal conditions for hibernation and, in their warmest parts, for nursing. Other smaller underground structures, such as rock crevices or ledges, may also be of importance in some areas. The world's largest aggregations of bats are found in caves in both temperate and tropical regions, where millions of animals may be found in a single site. Abandoned mines may also house hundreds of thousands of bats.

Artificial structures may also be used by bats, including a wide range of buildings such as houses and churches. Within such sites they may, for example, use crevices in walls, attic spaces, chimneys, or be found under tiles or other roofing materials. A range of other structures is used; for example, a bridge in Austin, Texas, in the southern USA is used by over one million *Tadarida brasiliensis*.

Some bats use only one type of roost, for example caves, while others may vary the roost type seasonally. In many cases, even bats that consistently use one type of roost site will frequently change sites.

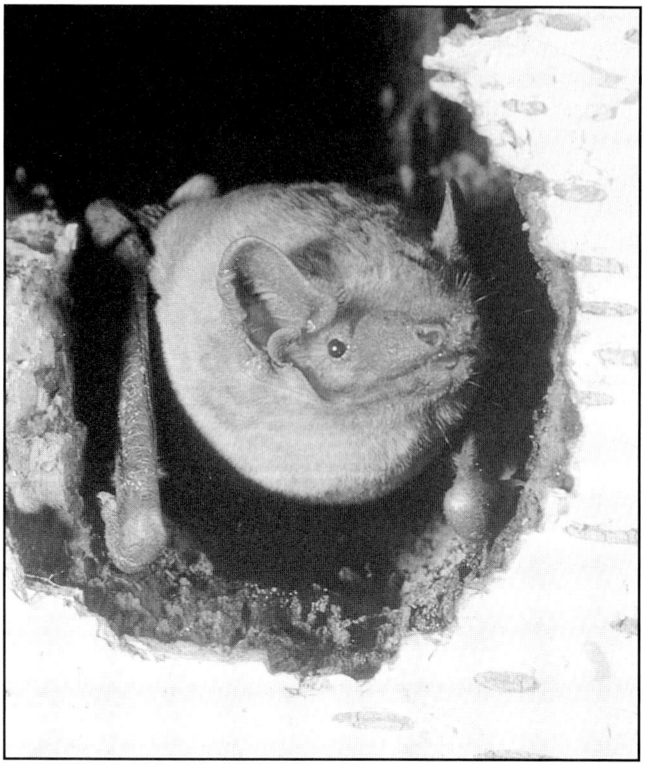

F.R. Greenaway

European tree-roosting noctule bat, *Nyctalus noctula*.

1.3.3 Food

Most microchiropteran bats feed mainly on insects and other invertebrates. A review of the feeding ecology of insectivorous bats is given by Fenton (1982). Fleming (1982) and Dobat and Peikert-Holle (1985) review the foraging strategies of plant-visiting bats. Schnitzler and

R. Strachan

Wrinkle-lipped bats, *Tadarida plicata*, emerging from Khao Yai cave roost in Thailand.

Kalko (1998) and Kalko and Schnitzler (1998) give detailed accounts of how bats use echolocation to search for and acquire food.

Insects may be caught in flight, or taken from vegetation, the ground, or water surfaces in a foraging style referred to as gleaning. Echolocation is generally used to locate prey although some bats use 'passive listening', homing in on the sounds made by the prey themselves. Some insect species, such as some moths and lacewings, have developed means of avoiding capture by detecting the ultrasound of approaching bats and falling to the ground. Food may be consumed on the wing or taken to a perch to be eaten. Such feeding perches may be regularly used and rejected food remains discarded beneath the site may reveal the presence of bats in that area. Some of the larger Microchiroptera are carnivorous, feeding on fish, amphibians, birds, and small mammals, including other bats. The fish-eating *Noctilio leporinus* has greatly elongated feet that are dragged through the water to gaff fish. *Trachops cirrhosus* is able to gauge the size of a frog by listening to its call and can thus select the largest meal. *Vampyrum spectrum* is one of the largest microchiropteran bats with a wingspan of up to 1.0m and feeds on a diet of birds, some almost as large as the bat itself, as well as rodents and smaller bats (Navarro and Wilson 1982). Gardner (1977) gives a detailed account of the feeding habits of phyllostomid bats, many of which feed on flowers and fruits. Three species of microchiropterans (*Desmodus rotundus*, *Diaemus youngi,* and *Diphylla ecaudata*) feed on blood (Greenhall and Schmidt 1988). *Desmodus* feeds mainly on the blood of livestock (cattle, horses, goats, sheep, and pigs), poultry, and occasionally humans. *Diaemus* prefers avian blood, while *Diphylla* seems to feed exclusively on birds (Greenhall and Schmidt 1988). All three species have specialised dentition and are very agile when walking quadrupedally and on their prey.

Lesser horseshoe bat, *Rhinolophus hipposideros*; the majority of Microchiroptera are insectivorous.

F.R. Greenaway

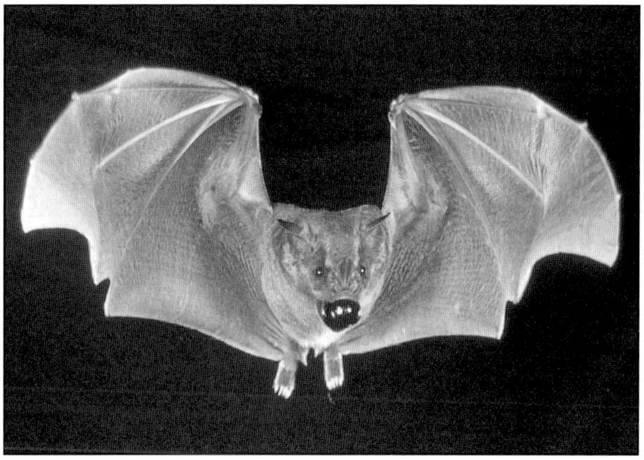

M. Tuttle/BC

Jamaican fruit bat, *Artibeus jamaicensis*; many spear-nosed bats of Central and South America are important for pollination and seed dispersal.

1.3.4 Predators

There are relatively few observations of animals feeding on bats. The main bat predators are owls, hawks, and falcons, and snakes. A few mammals such as raccoons, ringtails, and opposums may also feed on bats, and in the case of raccoons, may be major predators (B. French *pers. comm.*). In Poland and Romania, stone martens (*Martes foina*) take small numbers of bats (Romanowski and Lesinski 1991; Tryjanowski 1997). In New Zealand, *Mystacina tuberculata* is frequently a forest-floor dweller, a habit which has made it especially vulnerable to introduced rats, feral cats, and stoats (Daniel and Williams 1984; Daniel 1990). The largest phyllostomid bats (*Vampyrum spectrum*, *Chrotopterus auritus*, and *Phyllostomus hastatus*) are suspected or known to eat smaller bats (Goodwin and Greenhall 1961; Valdivieso 1964; Greenhall 1968a).

Remains of bats have been found in owl pellets (Krzanowski, 1973). A study in Europe (Lipej and Gjerkes 1992) examined the occurrence of bats in the pellets of three owl species. In no case did the proportion of bats in the diet exceed 3%, thus owls could not be considered a significant predator. In Haiti, 27 of 147 prey items of a Hispaneolan barn owl (*Tyto glaucops*) were phyllostomid bats (Wetmore and Swales 1931). In Poland, tawny owls (*Strix aluco*) were found to feed on seven bat species. One species (*Myotis myotis*) formed about 10% of the diet, but it was felt that the owls were unlikely to be having an impact on bat populations (Kowalski and Lesinski 1990). It has been rumoured that the presence of barn owls (*Tyto alba*) in roost sites of *Coleura seychellensis* in the Seychelles was a factor in the dramatic decline of this species. Gerlach

(1997) considers this only a contributory factor, the main cause of decline being habitat degradation, but Fairon *et al.* (1996) considered that bats could not roost with barn owls. Predation on bats by owls may be patchy in space and time and thus could be easily underestimated. Given the low reproductive rates of bats compared to say rodents, the impact of owl predation on bats may be an underestimate (B. French, *pers. comm.*). In Africa and eastwards to New Guinea, the bat hawk (*Machaerhamphus alcinus*) catches bats as they emerge from caves in the early evening. Bat falcons (*Falco rufigularis*) also occur in Central and South America. There have also been records of birds other than birds of prey feeding on bats (Gillette and Kimborough 1970).

Snakes are regular predators of bats. In Mexico, the northern pine snake (*Pituophis melanoleucus*) has been observed snatching Mexican funnel-eared bats (*Natalus stramineus*) from the air as they flew past. Similarly, in Cuba, the Cuban boa (*Epicrates angulifer*) takes leaf-nosed bats (*Phyllonycteris poeyi*). In Africa, Blanding's cat snake (*Boiga blandingii*) feeds on two common roof-dwelling bats, *Eptesicus tenuipinnis* and *Mops condylurus,* while in Panama, *Boa constrictor* and the puffing snake (*Pseustes poecilonotus*) frequent the roosts of *Myotis nigricans* and are commonly found in attics containing colonies of *Molossus coibensis* (Gillette and Kimborough 1970). It is unlikely that any of these has a very significant impact on the populations of microchiropteran bats.

1.3.5 Movements and migration

Temperate zone bats may undertake a variety of movements ranging from short distances between roosts and foraging areas (Fenton 1997) to long-range migrations between seasonally occupied sites. The daily feeding range of *Tadarida brasiliensis*, up to 60km, is more than the normal annual movements of many species. In temperate and subtropical bats, migration may be to maintain feeding opportunities, e.g., *Lasiurus*, *Tadarida*, or *Leptonycteris*, or to suitable hibernation sites, e.g., *Nyctalus*, *Miniopterus*, *Pipistrellus*, and *Lasionycteris*. In some species, it is mainly females that undertake the spring northerly migration to give birth and rear young, e.g., *Tadarida, Nyctalus,* and *Lasionycteris*. In *Leptonycteris*, the births are in the south of the range, but the volant young move north with the adult females. Even at the same latitude, separate populations of a species may be migratory or non-migratory, e.g., *T. brasiliensis* in the USA. Many of the northern temperate migrants are tree-dwelling species. e.g., *Lasiurus*, *Lasionycteris*, *Nyctalus,* and *Pipistrellus*, but many cave bats also undertake regular seasonal migrations, e.g., *Miniopterus*, and such movements may be in any direction to suitable roosting sites. Movement of 1,304km is recorded for *Miniopterus schreibersii* in Australia (Dwyer 1969). In the USA, movements of more than 500km have been recorded for both *Myotis sodalis* and *M. grisescens* (Myers 1964, Tuttle 1976). In Europe, movements of *Nyctalus noctula* and *Pipistrellus nathusii* of up to 1,600km and 1,800km, respectively, are recorded (Sluiter and van Heerdt 1966, Strelkov 1969) and involve crossing many national borders; the movements of *Lasiurus* in North America are likely to be more extensive.

Transitional roosts on migration routes are known for *Miniopterus*, but poorly known generally, as is the importance of landscape structure for the movements of migrant bats. Even species with wing morphology and flight behaviour apparently not well adapted for migration may regularly undertake greater seasonal movements than has been assumed; *Plecotus*, for which movements of 64km have been recorded in the USA and 62km in Europe, is also regularly recorded at high passes in the European Alps during migration periods (Lehmann *et al.* 1992) and is recorded from oil installations and light ships in the North Sea (Corbet 1970, 1971). In the tropics, there is less clear evidence of migrational movements in Microchiroptera. *Miniopterus schreibersii natalensis* in South Africa undertakes annual migrations between caves situated on the southern Transvaal Highveld and those in the northern Transvaal Bushveld. There are also local inter-cavern migrations (van der Merwe 1973, 1975, 1978). There seems to be good evidence, from capture data in Zimbabwe, of *Hipposideros commersoni* migrating (M.B. Fenton *pers. comm.*). It is likely that the need to follow seasonal flowering and fruiting of food plants results in the migration of some phyllostomids in the Neotropics (Fleming 1991; Fleming *et al.* 1993). The seasonal fluctuations in numbers of many insectivorous species in caves, e.g., *Otomops* in Kenya (Mutere 1973), suggest at least local movements. The possibility of trans-boundary movements and the consequent implications for their conservation is important for species with restricted distribution (e.g., *Ia io* is recorded from 11 localities in six countries of a mountainous part of the Indomalayan region (Bates and Harrison 1997, G. Csorba *pers. comm.*). Little is known of altitudinal

Nathusius's pipistrelle bat, *Pipistrellus nathusii*, is a long-range migrant in Europe.

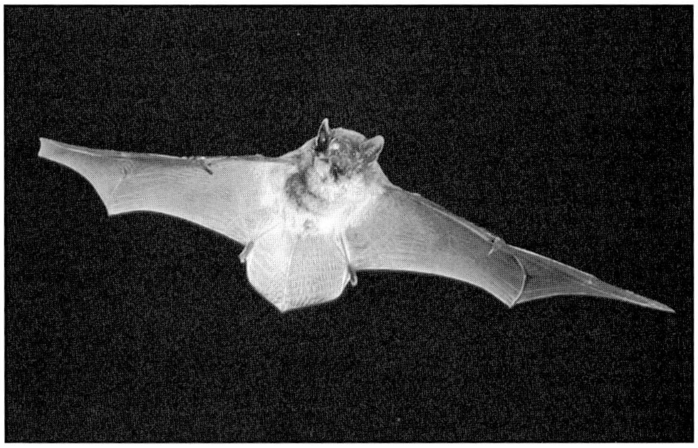

F.R. Greenaway

F.R. Greenaway

Noctule bat, *Nyctalus noctula*, migrates from northern Europe to hibernation roosts further south.

migration, but this may be an important factor in conservation and may particularly affect the flower- and fruit-feeding phyllostomids. It has been shown that hoary bats (*Lasiurus cinereus*) in South America engage in seasonal altitudinal migrations (Sanborn and Crespo 1957). It has been suggested that bats in the Galapagos Islands may similarly undertake seasonal altitudinal migrations, with the result that upland mesic habitats may be critical to the maintenance of viable populations (McCracken *et al.* 1997).

Ringing (banding) has been the traditional method for the study of bat migration, but it is likely that DNA analysis may be a major contributor to future studies. There have been various attempts to classify the movements of bats (e.g., Strelkov 1969, 1997), but none is entirely satisfactory and it is complicated by the intraspecific differences in behaviour depending on sex or provenance of the population under study.

1.3.6 Ecological role

Bats play an important role in the pollination and seed dispersal of many tropical plants. In the Neotropics, phyllostomid bats act as seed dispersal agents for up to 24% of forest tree species at some sites (Humphrey and Bonaccorso 1979). It is thought that phyllostomid bats become increasingly important as dispersal agents in wetter forests (Humphrey and Bonaccorso 1979).

Fruit-eating bats and bat fruits have undergone considerable co-evolution, resulting in a series of adaptations by both species. Thus, bat fruits tend to have strong odours, dull colours, and are presented in exposed positions free of dense foliage. They remain attached to the tree through maturity and have a hard skin or pulp. Fruit-eating bats have a good sense of smell, have large eyes for orientation, approach the fruit from the air, harvest the fruit from the tree rather than the ground, have strong dentition for tearing fruit, and generally carry the fruits from the trees to night roosts (van der Pijl 1972). Frugivorous phyllostomids usually select ripe fruit, which ensures that seeds are protected until they are mature and viable. Most phyllostomids may change their night-feeding roosts every few days (Greenhall 1956, 1965; Nellis 1971). Once taken to the feeding roost, seeds are either discarded as the fruit is eaten or swallowed with the juice and pulp. The dispersal of seeds that are too large to be swallowed is limited by the location of night-feeding roosts, while fruits with seeds that are swallowed are ejected with the bats' faeces and can thus land anywhere the bat travels. Seeds defecated in this way may have a higher germination rate (Humphrey and Bonaccorso 1979). There are over 100 phyllostomid species that are responsible for dispersing seeds or pollinating plants, many of which are commercially valuable (Dobat and Peikert-Holle 1985). For example, Seba's short-tailed fruit bat (*Carollia perspicillata*), one of the commonest bats in Latin America, plays an important functional role in tropical rainforest. The majority of the diet is fruit from shrubs, particularly those of the genus *Piper* and early successional trees such as *Cecropia peltata* and *Muntingia calabura*. *Carollia* is the most important disperser of seeds of the hundreds of *Piper* species in the Neotropics and generally is crucial to pioneer and early successional plants. In a typical night, an individual *Carollia* eats about 35 *Piper* or eight to 10 *Cecropia* fruits. It moves relatively short distances before consuming these fruits, with the result that most seeds are dispersed close to the parent plant. Each bat may eat up to 60,000 seeds a night; a colony of 400 could disperse 146 million seeds annually. Even if only 0.1% of these germinate, that represents 146,000 seedlings (Fleming 1988). Overall, frugivorous bats play an important role in the regeneration of forests in disturbed habitats. In the Neotropics, bat-dispersed plants, such as *Cecropia*, *Piper*, *Muntingia*, *Solanum*, and

Vismia, are among the first and most abundant species to invade natural and human-made clearings.

Bats may also play a key role in pollination of plants. A comprehensive review of the relationship between bats and flowers is given by Dobat and Peikert-Holle (1985). It has been estimated that bats play some part in the pollination of at least 500 Neotropical species of 96 genera (Vogel 1969). The importance of phyllostomids as pollinating agents increases in drier habitats (Humphrey and Bonaccorso 1979). Flowers pollinated by bats characteristically bloom at night, have a strong musty odour, are dull coloured, are in an exposed position outside dense foliage, are large, produce copious quantities of nectar and/or pollen, and are either tube-like with protruding anthers or brush-shaped (Faegri and van der Pijl 1971). Flower-feeding bats characteristically forage at night, have a good sense of smell, have large eyes for orientation, approach flowers from the air, have a high metabolic rate and large body size compared to other pollinators, and have elongate snouts and protrusible tongues for probing deep into flowers (Faegri and van der Pijl 1971). The association between bats and flowers is mutualistic. Plants divert energy into production of odours and floral parts that attract bats, as well as nectar and pollen to feed them. By moving from flower to flower, bats transport pollen that results in fertilisation. Many Neotropical phyllostomids are important pollinators, including the whole of the subfamilies Glossophaginae and Lonchophyllinae. A good example is bats of the genus *Leptonycteris*, which are the main pollinators of century plants (*Agave* spp.), from which tequila is produced. Such bats are probably integral to the maintenance of arid habitats (Arita and Wilson 1987). The threatened *Leptonycteris curasoae* is thought to play an important role in the pollination of cardon (*Pachycereus pringlei*) and organ pipe (*Stenocereus thurberi*) cacti in the Sonoran Desert in Mexico (Fleming 1989). Flower drop-off rates were shown to be particularly high for organ pipe cacti, possibly due to the limited availability of *Leptonycteris* as a nocturnal pollinator. It is believed that the stigmas of organ pipe flowers are only receptive to pollen at night. This suggests a close dependence between the cacti and its bat pollinators (Fleming 1989).

In the Old World, apart from the primarily insectivorous *Mystacina tuberculata* from New Zealand, which is phylogenetically associated with the phyllostomids, there are no fruit- or nectar -feeding microchiropterans (Daniel 1976; Pierson *et al.* 1986); this role is taken by the Megachiroptera (family Pteropodidae).

1.3.7 Economic importance

There are several ways in which bats can be considered to be of economic importance. Pollination and seed dispersal are major ecological services, although there have been no attempts to place a value on them. This is in contrast to the Old World megachiropterans, where a detailed analysis of their economic importance has been made (Fujita and Tuttle, 1991).

The majority of bats are insectivorous, are the primary consumers of nocturnal insects, and probably play an important role in the control of insect numbers in many parts of the world. Some species consume very large quantities of insects. For example, in the USA, *Tadarida brasiliensis*, which can roost in colonies numbering 20 million, may ingest 50–70% of its body mass per night (Kunz *et al.* 1995) and *Myotis lucifugus* as much as 100% (Kurta *et al.* 1989). In Texas, McCracken (1996) estimated that one million nursing *T. brasiliensis* could eat over 10 tonnes of insects each night. At least 100 million bats occupy the major maternity caves of central Texas in summer and thus over 1,000 tonnes of insects are eaten each night. Mosquitoes (Culicidae) are an important dietary item. In a study in southeastern Ontario, Canada, little brown bats (*M. lucifugus*) fed predominantly on mosquitos, with 85% of faecal samples containing mosquito remains, suggesting that this species could play an important role in the biological control of insect pests (Fascione *et al.* 1991). Bats also consume a variety of other insects including Lepidoptera, Coleoptera, Homoptera, Hemiptera, and Trichoptera (Ross 1967; Black 1974; Kunz 1974a; Whitaker and Black 1976; Anthony and Kunz 1977; Whitaker *et al.* 1977; Warner 1984; Swift *et al.* 1985; Dalton *et al.* 1986; Rydell 1986; Kunz *et al.* 1995). Bats are predators on a number of economically important insects, including cucumber bugs (*Diabotrica* species), June bugs (*Phyllophaga* species), and corn borers and Jerusalem crickets, which are important agricultural pests on crops such as corn, cotton, and potatoes (Whitaker 1993). McCracken (1996) details work on the high-altitude feeding of *T. brasiliensis* in Texas. He suggests that bats fly at heights of up to 3,000m and intercept the high-altitude migrations of agricultural pests, particularly the corn earworm moth, which is the most important agricultural pest in America. It is very difficult to calculate the quantities of insects that are consumed by individuals or populations. A conservative estimate for a colony peaking at 50 million *T. brasiliensis* was 6,700 tonnes over a 120-day summer feeding period (Hill and Smith 1984). Another calculation for the same colony put the figure at 13,000 tonnes, though these are much lower than the figures suggested by McCracken (1996). The bat population using Niah Caves in Sarawak on the island of Borneo was estimated to consume 7,500kg of insects every day (MacKinnon *et al.* 1996). What is certain is that bats do consume huge quantities of insects, some of which are considered pests.

Some of the largest bat colonies in caves contain millions of bats, which produce large quantities of guano. In some sites, such as Carlsbad Cavern in New Mexico, guano mining was an economically important activity in the early part of the 20th century. By 1923, it was estimated that 101,600 tonnes of guano had been removed from Carlsbad (Geluso *et al.* 1987). In recent years, the increased use of artificial fertilisers has led to a decline in the use of bat guano in developed countries. It is still, however, an important source of revenue for communities in the developing world.

1.4 Population biology

There is great variation in the timing and number of oestrous cycles in microchiropteran bats (Racey 1982; Racey and Entwistle 2000). Temperate zone species are monoestrus, which is related to their need to hibernate during the winter period of shortage. Young are born and develop during summer, when climate and food resources are optimal. Many tropical species are also monoestrus. For example, rhinopomatids, megadermatids, and some phyllostomids appear to be monoestrus with births occurring just prior to the rainy season. Many other tropical species are polyoestrus. Food and climate are less restrictive in the tropics, but most bats still exhibit some seasonality. One exception is the common vampire bat (*Desmodus rotundus*) that appears to be reproductively active throughout the year and may have up to four oestrous cycles. Most phyllostomids have two oestrous cycles with reproductive peaks just prior to March–April, and at the end of July–August, the rainy season. The timing and regulation of oestrous cycles is determined by factors such as temperature, rainfall, and nutritional state of the individual.

Temperate zone bats are faced with the problem of having to hibernate or migrate during the winter period of food shortage, and their reproductive cycle is interrupted by hibernation. Oestrous begins in late summer or autumn when most copulation occurs, although it is also observed during winter. Spermatozoa are stored in the female reproductive tract and fertilisation is delayed until spring. Occasionally, fertilisation follows insemination and implantation is delayed until conditions become more favourable, or post-implantation development is retarded. In males, sperm production is seasonal and occurs during summer.

In most temperate and some tropical zone species, pregnant females segregate in single-sex groups, while adult males remain isolated or form male-only groups. In spring, females form maternity colonies that may contain a few males. These maternity sites may be used year after year. Most microchiropteran bats give birth to a single young each year. There are, however, species where multiple births have been regularly recorded. In *Leptonycteris* and *Macrotus californicus* (Phyllostomidae), twins are not uncommon. Twins are also usual in several vespertilionids: *Pipistrellus subflavus* and *P. hesperus*, *Nycticeius humeralis*, *Tylonycteris pachypus* and *T. robustula*, *Chalinolobus gouldii*, *Lasionycteris noctivagans*, *Scotophilus kuhlii*, and *Rhogeessa parvula*. The red bat (*Lasiurus borealis*) regularly has four and occasionally five young. In eastern North America, female big brown bats (*Eptesicus fuscus*) commonly have twins, while in the west single young are born (Cockrum 1955; Brenner 1968; Kunz 1974b). The care and feeding of young bats is exclusively the responsibility of the female. From a very young age, baby bats produce vocalisations that can be recognised by the mother. This is particularly important in species such as *Tadarida brasiliensis*, where nursery roosts may number in the millions. Females of smaller species generally leave their young in the nursery roost while they forage, while larger bats may carry them on feeding flights. In most species, lactation lasts from one to three months, and a majority of young adult bats do not reproduce until late in their first or early in their second year.

For their size, bats are relatively long-lived mammals. Some species have been recorded as living at least 30 years (Tuttle and Stevenson 1982 and references therein). Mortality is highest amongst young bats. In Poland, the majority of bats killed on roads were young animals, probably killed during dispersal (G. Lesinski *pers. comm.*). At this time, the greatest threats to young bats include falling from the roost, climate, distance to a feeding area and the fact that the feeding success of young bats is lower than those of adults, and avian predators. In temperate zone species, young bats need to increase fat reserves quickly in order to survive their first hibernation period. Overall mortalities in the first year may be as high as 40–50%. A comprehensive review of the growth and survival of bats is given by Tuttle and Stevenson (1982).

Chapter 2

World List of Microchiroptera with IUCN Red List Categories of Threat and Distribution

2.1 IUCN categories of threat

2.1.1 Definitions

The conservation status of all microchiropteran bats has been assessed using criteria developed by IUCN – The World Conservation Union (IUCN 1994). An explanation of these categories can be found in Appendix 1. In total, there are nine categories used by IUCN. Where the status of a taxon has not been assessed using these criteria, it is listed as Not Evaluated (NE). Where a taxon has been evaluated, but there are inadequate data to make an assessment, it is listed as Data Deficient (DD). The remaining eight categories fall into three groups:

1. Extinct (EX) and Extinct in the Wild (EW);
2. Threatened categories including, in decreasing order of threat, Critically Endangered (CR), Endangered (EN), and Vulnerable (VU);
3. Lower Risk categories including, in decreasing order of threat, Lower Risk: Near Threatened (LR: nt), Lower Risk: Conservation Dependent (LR: cd), and Lower Risk: Least Concern (LR: lc).

The threat categories also include a range of subcriteria used to identify and quantify the kinds of threatening processes affecting taxa. Full details of these are given in Appendix 1.

2.1.2 *The IUCN Red List of Threatened Species*

The assignment of categories of threat follows that presented in *The 2000 IUCN Red List of Threatened Species* (IUCN 2000). It was initiated in consultation with various specialists, when different systems for categorising threat were under discussion. We have changed a number of assigned categories from those given in IUCN (1996) in accordance with fresh data or more authoritative opinion than was available at the time. These changes are asterisked and a source of evidence for changes given in Chapter 6.6. The assigned categories are for global status and do not fully account for local or national status. Since 1996, the IUCN has posted the Red List on its website (www.iucn.org) and regularly updates the entries.

2.1.3 Use of the terms 'threatened' and 'IUCN Red List species'

There is some confusion over the use of the term 'threatened'. As outlined above, strictly speaking, this only includes taxa in the categories CR, EN, and VU. However, *The 2000 IUCN Red List of Threatened Species* includes taxa in **all** categories except NE and LR: lc. To avoid confusion, in this Plan the term 'threatened' is limited to the strict interpretation outlined above (i.e., CR, EN, and VU). The term 'IUCN Red List species' may be used and, in such cases, means all taxa except those in categories NE and LR: lc.

2.1.4 Use of the Data Deficient category

It is fully appreciated that there are very few data available to evaluate the conservation status for the majority of species. It would have been easy, therefore, to assess most species as Data Deficient, but that would not have been useful. Almost all described species were assessed and the category Data Deficient was only applied to species of uncertain status, i.e., some newly described species and species for which systematists consider that there is insufficient material available to be confident that the name applies to a recognisable species, or other reasonable doubt about the validity of the species. IUCN is considering ways of identifying the quality of data that is available for species assessments. We would appreciate receiving information or opinion to improve the list.

2.2 Systematics of microchiropteran bats

The systematics of Microchiroptera is constantly being revised. New species are being described and there are sometimes differences of opinion on the status of certain taxa. A number of major taxonomic works have been published in the past few years, including Corbet and Hill (1991, 1992), Koopman (1993, 1994), and Flannery (1995a,b). No single list of bat species is universally accepted by all authorities. For the most part, we have adopted the higher classification (genus and above) of Koopman (1993) in accordance with the policy of IUCN. At the species level, we have taken greater account of the opinion of

Table 1. Number of microchiropteran bat species in each IUCN category of threat

Category	Number of species
Extinct	4
Critically Endangered	15
Endangered	30
Vulnerable	135
Lower Risk: near threatened	190
Lower Risk: conservation dependent	0
Lower Risk: least concern	404
Data Deficient	56
TOTAL	834

other standard works, have incorporated the results of more recent publications, and have adopted the opinions of a range of specialists.

In summary, the list presented here recognizes 17 families, 137 genera, and 834 species. The number of species in each category of threat is given in Table 1.

Some mistaken or incomplete data on distributions are given in *The 1996 Red List of Threatened Animals*. Revisions have been incorporated into the distributions of IUCN Red List species given in Chapter 6.5, but we would welcome further additions or corrections.

2.3 Definitions of distributional regions

For the purposes of the distributional information presented in this species list, the world has been divided into 11 major regions: 1. North America, 2. Central America, 3. Caribbean, 4. South America, 5. Europe, 6. Africa, 7. Arabian Peninsula, 8. Asia, 9. Australia, 10. New Zealand, and 11. Oceania. Within Asia and Africa, there are further subdivisions; Map 2 shows these regions. Areas where bats have been recorded only as vagrants or where there have never been records of bats have been excluded from this list. Details of these areas are given below. Countries included in each of the regions and sub-regions are as follows:

1. NORTH AMERICA
Canada and the United States

2. CENTRAL AMERICA
Belize, Costa Rica, El Salvador, Guatemala, Honduras, Mexico, Nicaragua, and Panama

3. CARIBBEAN
American Virgin Islands, Anguilla, Antigua and Barbuda, Aruba, Bahamas, Barbados, Bermuda, British Virgin

Map 2. Microchiropteran bat distribution – delineated areas.
1. North America; 2. Central America; 3. Caribbean; . South America; 5. Europe; 6. Africa; 6a. North Africa; 6b. Subsaharan Africa; 6c. Malagasy Subregion; 7. Arabian Peninsula; 8. Asia; 8a. Indian Subcontinent; 8b. Southeast Asia; 8c. New Guinea; 9. Australia; 10. New Zealand; 11. Oceania.

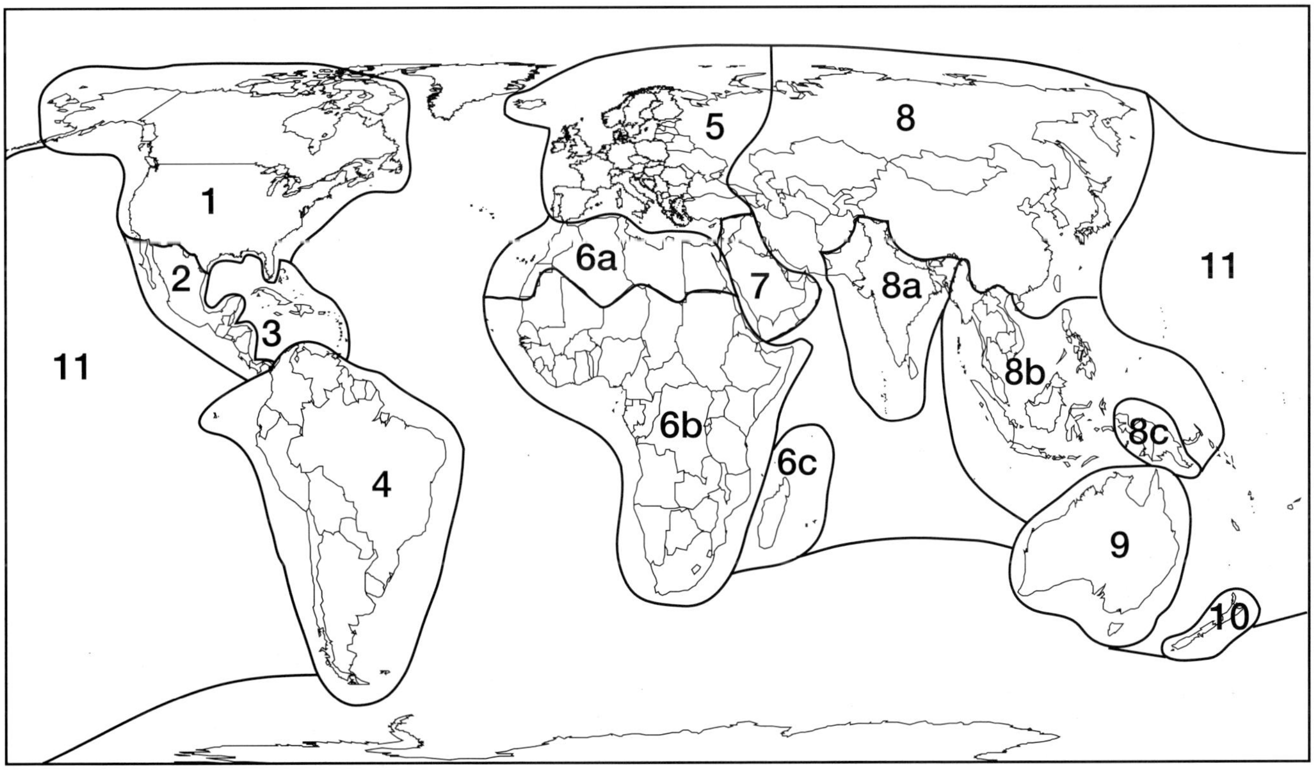

Islands, Cayman Islands, Cuba, Dominica, Dominican Republic, Grenada, Guadeloupe, Haiti, Jamaica, Martinique, Montserrat, Netherlands Antilles, Puerto Rico, St. Kitts and Nevis, St. Lucia, St. Vincent, Trinidad and Tobago, and the Turks and Caicos Islands

4. SOUTH AMERICA
Argentina, Bolivia, Brazil, Chile, Colombia, Ecuador (including Galapagos Islands), French Guiana, Guyana, Paraguay, Peru, Suriname, Uruguay, and Venezuela

5. EUROPE
Albania, Andorra, Austria, Belarus, Belgium, Bosnia-Herzegovina, Bulgaria, Croatia, Cyprus, Czech Republic, Denmark, Estonia, Finland, France, Germany, Gibraltar, Greece, Hungary, Ireland, Italy, Latvia, Liechtenstein, Lithuania, Luxembourg, Macedonia, Malta, Moldova, Monaco, The Netherlands, Norway, Poland, Portugal (including Azores and Madeira), Romania, Russia (west of Urals), San Marino, Slovakia, Slovenia, Spain (including Balearics and Canary Islands), Sweden, Switzerland, Turkey, Ukraine, United Kingdom (including Channel Islands and Isle of Man), Vatican City, and Yugoslavia

6. AFRICA – This is divided into three subregions

6a. North Africa
Algeria, Cape Verde Islands, Egypt, Libya, Morocco, and Tunisia

6b. Subsaharan Africa
Angola, Benin, Botswana, Burkina Faso, Burundi, Cameroon, Central African Republic, Chad, Congo Republic, Côte d'Ivoire, Democratic Republic of Congo, Djibouti, Equatorial Guinea, Eritrea, Ethiopia, Gabon, Gambia, Ghana, Guinea, Guinea-Bissau, Kenya, Lesotho, Liberia, Malawi, Mali, Mauritania, Mozambique, Namibia, Niger, Nigeria, Rwanda, São Tomé and Príncipe, Senegal, Sierra Leone, Somalia, South Africa, Sudan, Swaziland, Tanzania (including Zanzibar and Pemba), Togo, Uganda, Zambia, and Zimbabwe

6c. Malagasy Subregion
Comoros, Madagascar, Mauritius, Mayotte, Réunion, and Seychelles

7. ARABIAN PENINSULA
Bahrain, Iraq, Israel, Jordan, Kuwait, Lebanon, Oman, Qatar, Saudi Arabia, Syria, United Arab Emirates, and Yemen

8. ASIA
Afghanistan, Andaman and Nicobar Islands, Armenia, Azerbaijan, Bangladesh, Bhutan, Brunei, Cambodia, China, Georgia, India, Indonesia, Iran, Japan, Kazakhstan, Kyrgyzstan, Laos, Malaysia, Maldives, Mongolia, Myanmar, Nepal, North Korea, Pakistan, Papua New Guinea, Philippines, Russia (east of Urals), Singapore, South Korea, Sri Lanka, Taiwan, Tajikistan, Thailand, Turkmenistan, Uzbekistan, and Viet Nam

The following subregions are highlighted within the Asia region:

8a. Indian Subcontinent
Bangladesh, Bhutan, India (excluding Andaman and Nicobar Islands), Maldives, Nepal, Pakistan, and Sri Lanka

8b. Southeast Asia
Andaman and Nicobar Islands, Brunei, Cambodia, Indonesia (excluding Irian Jaya), Laos, Malaysia, Myanmar, Papua New Guinea (excluding island of New Guinea), Philippines, Singapore, Thailand, and Viet Nam

8c. New Guinea
The island of New Guinea, which includes part of Indonesia (Irian Jaya) and part of Papua New Guinea

9. AUSTRALIA
Australia

10. NEW ZEALAND
New Zealand

11. OCEANIA
American Samoa, Commonwealth of the Northern Mariana Islands, Cook Islands, Federated States of Micronesia, Fiji, Guam, New Caledonia, Palau, Samoa, Solomon Islands, Tonga, United States (Hawaii), Vanuatu, and Wallis and Futuna Islands

Notes on microchiropteran bat distribution

Bats have been recorded from almost every country in the world. The exceptions are areas of the Arctic and Antarctic, and isolated oceanic islands. In the Northern Hemisphere, Palaearctic bats have been recorded as far north as 70° N (Rydell *et al.* 1994), while in North America one species occurs at a latitude of 65° N (Hall 1981). In the Southern Hemisphere, bats have been found south of Tierra del Fuego in Chile, at a latitude of 65° S (Koopman 1967).

Bats have only been recorded as vagrants in **Iceland** and the **Falkland Islands**; there are no resident populations on these islands. Bats have **never been recorded** from the following islands:

Arctic Ocean Islands – Greenland, Jan Mayen, Svalbard and Bjørnøya (Bear Island), the northern Russian islands (e.g., Zemlya Frantsa Iosifa (Franz Josef Land), Novaya Zemlya, Severnaya Zemlya (North Land),

Novosbirskiyeostrova (New Siberian Islands), Ostrova Vrangelya (Wrangel Island), and the northern Canadian islands (e.g., Banks Island, Parry Island, Melville Island, Victoria Island, Devon Island, Ellesmere Island, and Baffin Island).

Atlantic Ocean Islands – Føroyar (Faeroes), Fernando de Noronha, Ascension, St. Helena, Trinidade, Tristan da Cunha, and Gough Island.

Indian Ocean Islands – Chagos Archipelago, Île Amsterdam (Amsterdam Island), Île St. Paul (St. Paul Island), Prince Edward Islands, Îles Crozet (Crozet Islands), Îles Kerguelen (Kerguelen Islands), and Cocos Islands (Keeling Islands).

Pacific Ocean Islands – Aleutian Islands, the northwestern Hawaiian Islands, U.S. administered islands in the central Pacific (Midway Islands, Wake Island, Johnston Atoll, Kingman Reef, Palmyra Atoll, Howland Island, Baker Island, Jarvis Island), Marshall Islands, Kiribati (including Gilbert, Phoenix, and Line Islands), Nauru, Tuvalu, Tokelau, French Polynesia (including Society Islands, Tuamotu Archipelago, Marquesas Islands, Gambier Islands, and Austral Islands), Pitcairn Islands, Easter Island, Sala y Gomez Island, San Felix Island, San Ambrosio Island, Juan Fernandez Islands, Guadelupe Island, Revillagigedo Islands, Clipperton Island, Cocos Island, Malpelo Island, Kermadec Islands, Norfolk Island, Three Kings Islands, Chatham Islands, Bounty Islands, Antipodes Islands, Campbell Island, Auckland Islands, and Chesterfield Islands.

Antarctica and Antarctic Islands – Antarctica, South Georgia, South Sandwich Islands, South Orkneys, South Shetlands, Bouvet Island, Balleny Islands, Macquarie Island, Campbell Island, and Heard Island.

Box 1. Brief explanation of the IUCN Red List subcategories.

Full details of the IUCN categories of threat are given in Appendix 1. The subcategories of the main threat categories (CR, EN and VU) can be summarised as follows.

For each category there are five subcategories (**A** to **E**) which are used to define the risk of extinction.

A identifies threshold levels of population reduction either in the past (1) or predicted for the future (2).
1. This can be based on any of the following:
   a. direct observation;
   b. an index of abundance;
   c. decline in area of occupancy, extent of occurrence or quality of habitat;
   d. levels of exploitation;
   e. effects of introduced taxa, hybridisation, pathogens, pollutants, competitors or parasites.
2. This can be based on any one of b. to e. outlined under 1. above.

B defines thresholds of the extent of occurrence or area of occupancy. This includes estimates indicating two out of three of the following.
1. Severe fragmentation of the population.
2. Declines in any of the following –
   a. extent of occurrence
   b. area of occupancy
   c. area, extent and/or quality of habitat
   d. number of locations or subpopulations
   e. number of mature individuals
3. Extreme fluctuations in any of the following –
   a. extent of occurrence
   b. area of occupancy
   c. number of locations or subpopulations
   d. number of mature individuals.

C relates to estimates of the number of mature individuals and either:
1. an estimated continuing decline in a given time period or number of generations or
2. a continuing decline in numbers of mature individuals and population structure in terms of either –
   a. severely fragmented or
   b. all individuals in a single subpopulation.

D relates to estimates of the number of mature individuals (where figures are much lower than under **C**). For species in the VU category, **D** refers to a very small or restricted population in the form of either:
1. Less than 1000 mature individuals or
2. Population is very restricted in its area of occupancy (usually less than 100 km^2) or in the number of locations (usually less than five).

E is used where quantitative analysis shows that the probability of extinction is likely at set levels.

2.4 Species list with status assessments and distribution

Status assessments in this list use the categories currently recognised by IUCN (IUCN 1994), outlined above. The subcategories are summarised in Box 1 and included in full in Appendix 1. The status assessments that appear in this list are identical to those presented in *The 2000 IUCN Red List of Threatened Species* (IUCN 2000). Where the status of a species has changed from that shown in the previous Red List (IUCN 1996), the new status is marked with asterisks (**). The previous assessment and the appropriate citations are given in Chapter 6.6. Full country-by-country distributions for all IUCN Red List species (i.e., all except Lower Risk: Least Concern and Not Evaluated) are given in Chapter 6.4.

ORDER CHIROPTERA		
SUB-ORDER MICROCHIROPTERA (17 families, 137 genera, 834 species)		
FAMILY RHINOPOMATIDAE (1 genus, 4 species)		
Africa (North Africa and Subsaharan Africa only), Arabian Peninsula, Asia (Indian Subcontinent, Southeast Asia)		
***Rhinopoma* (4 species)**		
Africa (North Africa and Subsaharan Africa only), Arabian Peninsula, Asia (Indian Subcontinent, Southeast Asia)		
Rhinopoma hardwickei Gray 1831	LR: lc	Africa (North Africa and Subsaharan Africa only), Arabian Peninsula, Asia (Indian Subcontinent, Southeast Asia)
Rhinopoma microphyllum (Brünnich 1782)	LR: lc	Africa (North Africa and Subsaharan Africa only), Arabian Peninsula, Asia (Indian Subcontinent)
Rhinopoma macinnesi Hayman 1937	VU: A2c, D2	Africa (Subsaharan Africa only)
Rhinopoma muscatellum Thomas 1903	LR: lc	Arabian Peninsula, Asia (Indian Subcontinent)
FAMILY CRASEONYCTERIDAE (1 genus, 1 species)		
Asia (Southeast Asia only)		
***Craseonycteris* (1 species)**		
Asia (Southeast Asia only)		
Craseonycteris thonglongyai Hill 1974	EN: B1 + 2c,C2b	Asia (Southeast Asia only)
FAMILY EMBALLONURIDAE (13 genera, 48 species)		
Central America, Caribbean, South America, Europe, Africa (North Africa, Subsaharan Africa, Malagasy Subregion), Arabian Peninsula, Asia (Indian Subcontinent, Southeast Asia, New Guinea), Australia, Oceania		
***Balantiopteryx* (3 species)**		
Central and South America		
Balantiopteryx infusca (Thomas 1897)	EN: B1 + 2c	South America
Balantiopteryx io Thomas 1904	LR: nt	Central America
Balantiopteryx plicata Peters 1867	LR: lc	Central and South America
***Centronycteris* (1 species)**		
Central and South America		
Centronycteris maximiliani (Fischer 1829)	LR: lc	Central and South America
***Coleura* (2 species)**		
Africa (Subsaharan Africa and Malagasy Subregion only), Arabian Peninsula		
Coleura afra (Peters 1852)	LR: lc	Africa (Subsaharan Africa only), Arabian Peninsula
Coleura seychellensis Peters 1868	CR: B1 + 2c,d,e, C2b, D	Africa (Malagasy Subregion only)
***Cormura* (1 species)**		
Central and South America		
Cormura brevirostris (Wagner 1843)	LR: lc	Central and South America
***Cyttarops* (1 species)**		
Central and South America		
Cyttarops alecto Thomas 1913	LR: nt	Central and South America
***Diclidurus* (4 species)**		
Central America, Caribbean, South America		
Diclidurus albus Wied-Neuwied 1820	LR: lc	Central America, Caribbean, South America
Diclidurus ingens Hernandez-Camacho 1955	VU: A2c	South America
Diclidurus isabellus (Thomas 1920)	LR: nt	South America
Diclidurus scutatus Peters 1869	LR: lc	South America

***Emballonura* (9 species)**		
Africa (Malagasy Subregion only), Asia (Southeast Asia, New Guinea), Oceania		
Emballonura alecto (Eydoux and Gervais 1836)	LR: lc	Asia (Southeast Asia only)
Emballonura atrata Peters 1874	VU: A2c	Africa (Malagasy Subregion only)
Emballonura beccarii Peters and Doria 1881	LR: lc	Asia (Southeast Asia and New Guinea only)
Emballonura dianae Hill 1956	VU: A2c	Asia (New Guinea), Oceania
Emballonura furax Thomas 1911	VU: A2c, D2	Asia (New Guinea)
Emballonura monticola Temminck 1838	LR: lc	Asia (Southeast Asia only)
Emballonura raffrayana Dobson 1879	LR: nt **	Asia (Southeast Asia and New Guinea only), Oceania
Emballonura semicaudata (Peale 1848)	EN: A1a,c **	Oceania
Emballonura serii Flannery 1994	DD	Asia (Southeast Asia and New Guinea only)
***Mosia* (1 species)**		
Asia (Southeast Asia and New Guinea only), Oceania		
Mosia nigrescens (Gray 1843)	LR: lc	Asia (Southeast Asia and New Guinea only), Oceania
***Peropteryx* (3 species)**		
Central and South America		
Peropteryx kappleri Peters 1867	LR: lc	Central and South America
Peropteryx leucoptera Peters 1867	LR: lc	South America
Peropteryx macrotis (Wagner 1843)	LR: lc	Central and South America
***Rhynchonycteris* (1 species)**		
Central America, Caribbean, South America		
Rhynchonycteris naso (Wied-Neuwied 1820)	LR: lc	Central America, Caribbean, South America
***Saccolaimus* (4 species)**		
Africa (Subsaharan Africa only), Asia (Indian Subcontinent, Southeast Asia, and New Guinea only), Australia, Oceania		
Saccolaimus flaviventris Peters 1867	LR: nt	Asia (New Guinea only), Australia
Saccolaimus mixtus Troughton 1925	VU: A2c	Asia (New Guinea only), Australia
Saccolaimus peli (Temminck 1853)	LR: nt	Africa (Subsaharan Africa only)
Saccolaimus saccolaimus (Temminck 1838)	LR: lc	Asia (Indian Subcontinent, Southeast Asia, and New Guinea only), Australia, Oceania
***Saccopteryx* (4 species)**		
Central America, Caribbean, South America		
Saccopteryx bilineata (Temminck 1838)	LR: lc	Central America, Caribbean, South America
Saccopteryx canescens Thomas 1901	LR: lc	South America
Saccopteryx gymnura Thomas 1901	VU: A2c, D2 **	South America
Saccopteryx leptura (Schreber 1774)	LR: lc	Central America, Caribbean, South America
***Taphozous* (14 species)**		
Europe, Africa (North Africa, Subsaharan Africa, Malagasy Subregion), Arabian Peninsula, Asia (Indian Subcontinent, Southeast Asia, New Guinea), Australia		
Taphozous achates Thomas 1915	VU: D2	Asia (Southeast Asia only)
Taphozous australis Gould 1854	LR: nt	Asia (New Guinea only), Australia
Taphozous georgianus Thomas 1915	LR: lc	Australia
Taphozous hamiltoni Thomas 1920	VU: A2c	Africa (Subsaharan Africa only)
Taphozous hildegardeae Thomas 1909	VU: A2c	Africa (Subsaharan Africa only)
Taphozous hilli Kitchener 1980	LR: lc	Australia
Taphozous kapalgensis McKean and Friend 1979	VU: A2c	Australia
Taphozous longimanus Hardwicke 1825	LR: lc	Asia (Indian Subcontinent and Southeast Asia only)
Taphozous mauritianus E. Geoffroy 1818	LR: lc	Africa (Subsaharan Africa and Malagasy Subregion only)
Taphozous melanopogon Temminck 1841	LR: lc	Asia (Indian Subcontinent, Southeast Asia)
Taphozous nudiventris Cretzschmar 1830	LR: lc	Europe, Africa (North Africa and Subsaharan Africa only), Arabian Peninsula, Asia (Indian Subcontinent)
Taphozous perforatus E. Geoffroy 1818	LR: lc	Africa (North Africa and Subsaharan Africa only), Arabian Peninsula, Asia (Indian Subcontinent)
Taphozous theobaldi Dobson 1872	LR: lc	Asia (Indian Subcontinent and Southeast Asia only)
Taphozous troughtoni Tate 1952	CR: A1a,c; B1 + 2a,b,c,d,e; D	Australia

FAMILY NYCTERIDAE (1 genus, 14 species)		
Africa (North Africa, Subsaharan Africa and Malagasy Subregion), Arabian Peninsula, Asia (Southeast Asia only)		
***Nycteris* (14 species)**		
Africa (North Africa, Subsaharan Africa and Malagasy Subregion), Arabian Peninsula, Asia (Southeast Asia only)		
Nycteris arge Thomas 1903	LR: lc	Africa (Subsaharan Africa only)
Nycteris aurita K. Andersen 1912	LR: nt	Africa (Subsaharan Africa only)
Nycteris gambiensis (K. Andersen 1912)	LR: lc	Africa (Subsaharan Africa only)
Nycteris grandis Peters 1865	LR: lc	Africa (Subsaharan Africa only)
Nycteris hispida (Schreber 1775)	LR: lc	Africa (Subsaharan Africa only)
Nycteris intermedia Aellen 1959	LR: nt	Africa (Subsaharan Africa only)
Nycteris javanica E. Geoffroy 1813	VU: A1c	Asia (Southeast Asia only)
Nycteris macrotis Dobson 1876	LR: lc	Africa (Subsaharan Africa only)
Nycteris madagascariensis Grandidier 1937	DD**	Africa (Malagasy Subregion only)
Nycteris major (K. Andersen 1912)	VU: A2c, D2	Africa (Subsaharan Africa only)
Nycteris nana (K. Andersen 1912)	LR: lc	Africa (Subsaharan Africa only)
Nycteris thebaica E. Geoffroy 1818	LR: lc	Africa (North Africa and Subsaharan Africa only), Arabian Peninsula
Nycteris tragata (K. Andersen 1912)	LR: lc	Asia (Southeast Asia only)
Nycteris woodi K. Andersen 1914	LR: nt	Africa (Subsaharan Africa only)
FAMILY MEGADERMATIDAE (4 genera, 5 species)		
Africa (Subsaharan Africa only), Asia (Indian Subcontinent, Southeast Asia), Australia		
***Cardioderma* (1 species)**		
Africa (Subsaharan Africa only)		
Cardioderma cor (Peters 1872)	LR: nt	Africa (Subsaharan Africa only)
***Lavia* (1 species)**		
Africa (Subsaharan Africa only)		
Lavia frons (E. Geoffroy 1810)	LR: lc	Africa (Subsaharan Africa only)
***Macroderma* (1 species)**		
Australia		
Macroderma gigas (Dobson 1880)	VU: A2c	Australia
***Megaderma* (2 species)**		
Asia (Indian Subcontinent, Southeast Asia)		
Megaderma lyra E. Geoffroy 1810	LR: lc	Asia (Indian Subcontinent, Southeast Asia)
Megaderma spasma (Linnaeus 1758)	LR: lc	Asia (Indian Subcontinent, Southeast Asia)
FAMILY HIPPOSIDERIDAE (9 genera, 75 species)		
Africa (North Africa, Subsaharan Africa, Malagasy Subregion), Arabian Peninsula, Asia (Indian Subcontinent, Southeast Asia, New Guinea), Australia, Oceania		
***Anthops* (1 species)**		
Oceania		
Anthops ornatus Thomas 1888	VU: A2c, D2	Oceania
***Asellia* (2 species)**		
Africa (North Africa and Subsaharan Africa only), Arabian Peninsula, Asia (Indian Subcontinent)		
Asellia patrizii DeBeaux 1931	VU: A2c, D2	Africa (Subsaharan Africa only), Arabian Peninsula
Asellia tridens (E. Geoffroy 1813)	LR: lc	Africa (North Africa and Subsaharan Africa only), Arabian Peninsula, Asia (Indian Subcontinent)
***Asselliscus* (2 species)**		
Asia (Southeast Asia and New Guinea only), Oceania		
Aselliscus stoliczkanus (Dobson 1871)	LR: lc	Asia (Southeast Asia only)
Aselliscus tricuspidatus (Temminck 1835)	LR: lc	Asia (Southeast Asia and New Guinea only), Oceania
***Cloeotis* (1 species)**		
Africa (Subsaharan Africa only)		
Cloeotis percivali Thomas 1901	LR: nt	Africa (Subsaharan Africa only)
***Coelops* (3 species)**		
Asia (Indian Subcontinent, Southeast Asia)		
Coelops frithi Blyth 1848	LR: lc	Asia (Indian Subcontinent, Southeast Asia)
Coelops hirsutus (Miller 1911)	DD	Asia (Southeast Asia only)
Coelops robinsoni Bonhote 1908	LR: nt	Asia (Southeast Asia only)

***Hipposideros* (60 species)**

Africa (North Africa, Subsaharan Africa, Malagasy Subregion), Arabian Peninsula, Asia (Indian Subcontinent, Southeast Asia, New Guinea), Australia, Oceania

Hipposideros abae J. A. Allen 1917	LR: lc	Africa (Subsaharan Africa only)
Hipposideros armiger (Hodgson 1835)	LR: lc	Asia (Indian Subcontinent, Southeast Asia)
Hipposideros ater Templeton 1848	LR: lc	Asia (Indian Subcontinent, Southeast Asia and New Guinea only), Australia
Hipposideros beatus K. Andersen 1906	LR: lc	Africa (Subsaharan Africa only)
Hipposideros bicolor (Temminck 1834)	LR: lc	Asia (Southeast Asia only)
Hipposideros breviceps Tate 1941	VU: D2	Asia (Southeast Asia)
Hipposideros caffer (Sundevall 1846)	LR: lc	Africa (North Africa and Subsaharan Africa only), Arabian Peninsula
Hipposideros calcaratus (Dobson 1877)	LR: lc	Asia (New Guinea), Oceania
Hipposideros camerunensis Eisentraut 1956	LR: nt	Africa (Subsaharan Africa only)
Hipposideros cervinus (Gould 1863)	LR: lc	Asia (Southeast Asia and New Guinea only), Australia, Oceania
Hipposideros cineraceus Blyth 1853	LR: lc	Asia (Indian Subcontinent and Southeast Asia only)
Hipposideros commersoni (E. Geoffroy 1813)	LR: lc	Africa (Subsaharan Africa and Malagasy Subregion only)
Hipposideros coronatus (Peters 1871)	LR: nt	Asia (Southeast Asia only)
Hipposideros corynophyllus Hill 1985	VU: A2c, D2	Asia (New Guinea only)
Hipposideros coxi Shelford 1901	VU: D2	Asia (Southeast Asia only)
Hipposideros crumeniferus Lesueur and Petit 1807	DD	Asia (Southeast Asia only)
Hipposideros curtus G. M. Allen 1921	LR: nt	Africa (Subsaharan Africa only)
Hipposideros cyclops (Temminck 1853)	LR: lc	Africa (Subsaharan Africa only)
Hipposideros demissus K. Andersen 1909	VU: A2c, D2	Oceania
Hipposideros diadema (E. Geoffroy 1813)	LR: lc	Asia (Southeast Asia and New Guinea only), Australia, Oceania
Hipposideros dinops K. Andersen 1905	LR: nt	Asia (Southeast Asia only), Oceania
Hipposideros doriae (Peters 1871)	DD	Asia (Southeast Asia only)
Hipposideros durgadasi Khajuria 1970	VU: B1 + 2c, D2	Asia (Indian Subcontinent only)
Hipposideros dyacorum Thomas 1902	LR: lc	Asia (Southeast Asia only)
Hipposideros edwardshilli Flannery and Colgan 1993	LR: nt	Asia (New Guinea only)
Hipposideros fuliginosus (Temminck 1853)	LR: nt	Africa (Subsaharan Africa only)
Hipposideros fulvus Gray 1838	LR: lc	Asia (Indian Subcontinent and Southeast Asia only)
Hipposideros galeritus Cantor 1846	LR: lc	Asia (Indian Subcontinent and Southeast Asia only)
Hipposideros halophyllus Hill and Yenbutra 1984	LR: nt	Asia (Southeast Asia only)
Hipposideros hypophyllus Kock and Bhat 1994	VU: B1 + 2c, D2**	Asia (Indian Subcontinent only)
Hipposideros inexpectatus Laurie and Hill 1954	VU: A2c	Asia (Southeast Asia only)
Hipposideros jonesi Hayman 1947	LR: nt	Africa (Subsaharan Africa only)
Hipposideros lamottei Brosset 1984	DD	Africa (Subsaharan Africa only)
Hipposideros lankadiva Kelaart 1850	LR: lc	Asia (Indian Subcontinent only)
Hipposideros larvatus (Horsfield 1823)	LR: lc	Asia (Indian Subcontinent, Southeast Asia)
Hipposideros lekaguli Thonglongya and Hill 1974	LR: nt	Asia (Southeast Asia only)
Hipposideros lylei Thomas 1913	LR: nt	Asia (Southeast Asia only)
Hipposideros macrobullatus Tate 1941	LR: nt	Asia (Southeast Asia only)
Hipposideros madurae Kitchener and Maryanto 1993	LR: nt	Asia (Southeast Asia only)
Hipposideros maggietaylorae Smith and Hill 1981	LR: lc	Asia (Southeast Asia and New Guinea only)
Hipposideros marisae Aellen 1954	VU: A2c	Africa (Subsaharan Africa only)
Hipposideros megalotis (Heuglin 1862)	LR: nt **	Africa (Subsaharan Africa only), Arabian Peninsula
Hipposideros muscinus (Thomas and Doria 1886)	VU: D2	Asia (New Guinea only)
Hipposideros nequam K. Andersen 1918	CR: B1 + 2c	Asia (Southeast Asia only)
Hipposideros obscurus (Peters 1861)	LR: nt	Asia (Southeast Asia only)
Hipposideros papua (Thomas and Doria 1886)	VU: A2c	Asia (Southeast Asia and New Guinea only)
Hipposideros pomona K. Andersen 1918	LR: lc**	Asia (Indian Subcontinent, Southeast Asia)
Hipposideros pratti Thomas 1891	LR: nt	Asia (Southeast Asia)
Hipposideros pygmaeus (Waterhouse 1843)	LR: nt	Asia (Southeast Asia only)
Hipposideros ridleyi Robinson and Kloss 1911	VU: B1 + 2c	Asia (Southeast Asia only)
Hipposideros ruber (Noack 1893)	LR: lc	Africa (Subsaharan Africa only)
Hipposideros sabanus Thomas 1898	LR: lc	Asia (Southeast Asia only)
Hipposideros schistaceus K. Andersen 1918	DD**	Asia (Indian Subcontinent only)
Hipposideros semoni Matschie 1903	LR: nt	Asia (New Guinea only), Australia
Hipposideros sorenseni Kitchener and Maryanto 1993	LR: nt	Asia (Southeast Asia only)
Hipposideros speoris (Schneider 1800)	LR: lc	Asia (Indian Subcontinent only)
Hipposideros stenotis Thomas 1913	LR: nt	Australia
Hipposideros sumbae (Oei 1960)	LR: nt	Asia (Southeast Asia only)
Hipposideros turpis Bangs 1901	EN: A2c	Asia (Southeast Asia)
Hipposideros wollastoni Thomas 1913	LR: nt	Asia (New Guinea only)

***Paracoelops* (1 species)** Asia (Southeast Asia only)		
Paracoelops megalotis Dorst 1947	CR: B1 + 2c	Asia (Southeast Asia only)
***Rhinonicteris* (1 species)** Australia		
Rhinonicteris aurantia (Gray 1845)	VU: A1c	Australia
***Triaenops* (4 species)** Africa (Subsaharan Africa and Malagasy Subregion only), Arabian Peninsula, Asia (Indian Subcontinent)		
Triaenops auritus Grandidier 1912	DD**	Africa (Malagasy Subregion only)
Triaenops furculus Trouessart 1906	VU: A2c	Africa (Malagasy Subregion only)
Triaenops persicus Dobson 1871	LR: lc	Africa (Subsaharan Africa and Malagasy Subregion only) Arabian Peninsula, Asia (Indian Subcontinent)
Triaenops rufus Milne-Edwards 1881	DD**	Africa (Malagasy Subregion only)
FAMILY RHINOLOPHIDAE (1 genus, 66 species) Europe, Africa (North Africa and Subsaharan Africa only), Arabian Peninsula, Asia (Indian Subcontinent, Southeast Asia, New Guinea), Australia		
***Rhinolophus* (66 species)** Europe, Africa (North Africa and Subsaharan Africa only), Arabian Peninsula, Asia (Indian Subcontinent, Southeast Asia, New Guinea), Australia		
Rhinolophus acuminatus Peters 1871	LR: lc	Asia (Southeast Asia only)
Rhinolophus adami Aellen and Brosset 1968	DD	Africa (Subsaharan Africa only)
Rhinolophus affinis Horsfield 1823	LR: lc	Asia (Indian Subcontinent, Southeast Asia)
Rhinolophus alcyone Temminck 1852	LR: nt	Africa (Subsaharan Africa only)
Rhinolophus anderseni Cabrera 1909	DD	Asia (Southeast Asia only)
Rhinolophus arcuatus Peters 1871	LR: lc	Asia (Southeast Asia and New Guinea only)
Rhinolophus beddomei K. Andersen 1905	LR: nt**	Asia (Indian Subcontinent only)
Rhinolophus blasii Peters 1866	LR: nt	Europe, Africa (North Africa and Subsaharan Africa only), Arabian Peninsula, Asia (Indian Subcontinent)
Rhinolophus bocharicus Kastschenko and Akimov 1917	LR: lc	Asia
Rhinolophus borneensis Peters 1861	LR: lc	Asia (Southeast Asia only)
Rhinolophus canuti Thomas and Wroughton 1909	LR: nt	Asia (Southeast Asia only)
Rhinolophus capensis Lichtenstein 1823	VU: A2c, D2	Africa (Subsaharan Africa only)
Rhinolophus celebensis K. Andersen 1905	LR: nt	Asia (Southeast Asia only)
Rhinolophus clivosus Cretzschmar 1828	LR: lc	Africa (North Africa and Subsaharan Africa only), Arabian Peninsula, Asia
Rhinolophus coelophyllus Peters 1867	LR: lc	Asia (Southeast Asia only)
Rhinolophus cognatus K. Andersen 1906	VU: A2c, D2	Asia (Indian Subcontinent only)
Rhinolophus convexus Csorba 1997	CR: D **	Asia (Southeast Asia only)
Rhinolophus cornutus Temminck 1835	LR: nt	Asia
Rhinolophus creaghi Thomas 1896	LR: nt	Asia (Southeast Asia only)
Rhinolophus darlingi K. Andersen 1905	LR: lc	Africa (Subsaharan Africa only)
Rhinolophus deckenii Peters 1867	DD	Africa (Subsaharan Africa only)
Rhinolophus denti Thomas 1904	LR: lc	Africa (Subsaharan Africa only)
Rhinolophus eloquens K. Andersen 1905	LR: lc	Africa (Subsaharan Africa only)
Rhinolophus euryale Blasius 1853	VU: A2c	Europe, Africa (North Africa only), Arabian Peninsula, Asia
Rhinolophus euryotis Temminck 1835	LR: lc	Asia (Southeast Asia and New Guinea only)
Rhinolophus ferrumequinum (Schreber 1774)	LR: nt**	Europe, Africa (North Africa only), Arabian Peninsula, Asia (Indian Subcontinent)
Rhinolophus fumigatus Rüppell 1842	LR: lc	Africa (Subsaharan Africa only)
Rhinolophus guineensis Eisentraut 1960	LR: nt	Africa (Subsaharan Africa only)
Rhinolophus hildebrandti Peters 1878	LR: lc	Africa (Subsaharan Africa only)
Rhinolophus hipposideros (Bechstein 1800)	VU: A2c	Europe, Africa (North Africa and Subsaharan Africa only), Arabian Peninsula, Asia (Indian Subcontinent)
Rhinolophus imaizumii Hill and Yoshiyuki 1980	EN: A2c, B1 + 2a,b,c,d,e	Asia
Rhinolophus inops K. Andersen 1905	DD	Asia (Southeast Asia only)
Rhinolophus keyensis Peters 1871	EN: C2a	Asia (Southeast Asia only)
Rhinolophus landeri Martin 1838	LR: lc	Africa (Subsaharan Africa only)
Rhinolophus lepidus Blyth 1844	LR: lc	Asia (Indian Subcontinent, Southeast Asia)
Rhinolophus luctus Temminck 1835	LR: lc	Asia (Indian Subcontinent, Southeast Asia)
Rhinolophus maclaudi Pousargues 1897	LR: nt	Africa (Subsaharan Africa only)
Rhinolophus macrotis Blyth 1844	LR: lc	Asia (Indian Subcontinent, Southeast Asia)
Rhinolophus malayanus Bonhote 1903	LR: lc	Asia (Southeast Asia only)

Rhinolophus marshalli Thonglongya 1973	LR: nt **	Asia (Southeast Asia only)
Rhinolophus megaphyllus Gray 1834	LR: lc	Asia (New Guinea), Australia
Rhinolophus mehelyi Matschie 1901	VU: A2c	Europe, Africa (North Africa only), Arabian Peninsula, Asia
Rhinolophus mitratus Blyth 1844	DD	Asia (Indian Subcontinent only)
Rhinolophus monoceros K. Andersen 1905	LR: nt	Asia
Rhinolophus nereis K. Andersen 1905	LR: nt	Asia (Southeast Asia only)
Rhinolophus osgoodi Sanborn 1939	DD	Asia
Rhinolophus paradoxolophus (Bourret 1951)	VU: B1 + 2c	Asia (Southeast Asia only)
Rhinolophus pearsoni Horsfield 1851	LR: lc	Asia (Indian Subcontinent, Southeast Asia)
Rhinolophus philippinensis Waterhouse 1843	LR: nt	Asia (Southeast Asia and New Guinea only), Australia
Rhinolophus pusillus Temminck 1834	LR: lc	Asia (Indian Subcontinent and Southeast Asia only)
Rhinolophus rex G. M. Allen 1923	VU: B1 + 2c	Asia
Rhinolophus rouxi Temminck 1835	LR: lc	Asia (Indian Subcontinent, Southeast Asia)
Rhinolophus rufus Eydoux and Gervais 1836	LR: nt	Asia (Southeast Asia only)
Rhinolophus sedulus K. Andersen 1905	LR: lc	Asia (Southeast Asia only)
Rhinolophus shameli Tate 1943	LR: nt	Asia (Southeast Asia only)
Rhinolophus silvestris Aellen 1959	LR: nt	Africa (Subsaharan Africa only)
Rhinolophus simulator K. Andersen 1904	LR: lc	Africa (Subsaharan Africa only)
Rhinolophus sinicus K. Andersen 1905	LR: lc **	Asia (Southeast Asia)
Rhinolophus stheno K. Andersen 1905	LR: lc	Asia (Southeast Asia only)
Rhinolophus subbadius Blyth 1844	DD	Asia (Indian Subcontinent and Southeast Asia only)
Rhinolophus subrufus K. Andersen 1905	VU: A2c	Asia (Southeast Asia only)
Rhinolophus swinnyi Gough 1908	LR: lc	Africa (Subsaharan Africa only)
Rhinolophus thomasi K. Andersen 1905	LR: nt	Asia (Southeast Asia)
Rhinolophus trifoliatus Temminck 1834	LR: lc	Asia (Indian Subcontinent and Southeast Asia only)
Rhinolophus virgo K. Andersen 1905	LR: nt	Asia (Southeast Asia only)
Rhinolophus yunanensis Dobson 1872	LR: nt	Asia (Indian Subcontinent, Southeast Asia)
FAMILY NOCTILIONIDAE (1 genus, 2 species) Central America, Caribbean, South America		
***Noctilio* (2 species)** Central America, Caribbean, South America		
Noctilio albiventris Desmarest 1818	LR: lc	Central and South America
Noctilio leporinus (Linnaeus 1758)	LR: lc	Central America, Caribbean, South America
FAMILY MORMOOPIDAE (2 genera, 8 species) North and Central America, Caribbean, South America		
***Mormoops* (2 species)** North and Central America, Caribbean, South America		
Mormoops blainvillii Leach 1821	LR: nt	Caribbean
Mormoops megalophylla (Peters 1864)	LR: lc	North America, Central America, Caribbean, South America
***Pteronotus* (6 species)** Central America, Caribbean, South America		
Pteronotus davyi Gray 1838	LR: lc	Central America, Caribbean, South America
Pteronotus gymnonotus Natterer 1843	LR: lc	Central and South America
Pteronotus macleayii (Gray 1839)	VU: A2c	Caribbean
Pteronotus parnellii (Gray 1843)	LR: lc	Central America, Caribbean, South America
Pteronotus personatus (Wagner 1843)	LR: lc	Central America, Caribbean, South America
Pteronotus quadridens (Gundlach 1840)	LR: nt	Caribbean
FAMILY PHYLLOSTOMIDAE (49 genera, 151 species) North and Central America, Caribbean, South America		
Subfamily Phyllostominae		
***Chrotopterus* (1 species)** Central and South America		
Chrotopterus auritus (Peters 1856)	LR: lc	Central and South America
***Lonchorhina* (5 species)** Central America, Caribbean, South America		
Lonchorhina aurita Tomes 1863	LR: lc	Central America, Caribbean, South America
Lonchorhina fernandezi Ochoa and Ibanez 1982	VU: A2c	South America
Lonchorhina inusitata Handley and Ochoa 1997	DD**	South America
Lonchorhina marinkellei Hernandez-Camacho and Cadena-G. 1978	VU: A2c	South America
Lonchorhina orinocensis Linares and Ojasti 1971	LR: nt	South America

***Macrophyllum* (1 species)** Central and South America		
Macrophyllum macrophyllum (Schinz 1821)	LR: lc	Central and South America
***Macrotus* (2 species)** North and Central America, Caribbean		
Macrotus californicus Baird 1858	VU: A2c	North and Central America
Macrotus waterhousii Gray 1843	LR: lc	Central America, Caribbean
***Micronycteris* (12 species)** Central America, Caribbean, South America		
Micronycteris behnii (Peters 1865)	VU: A2c	South America
Micronycteris brachyotis (Dobson 1879)	LR: lc	Central America, Caribbean, South America
Micronycteris brosseti Simmons and Voss 1998	DD **	South America
Micronycteris daviesi (Hill 1964)	LR: nt	Central and South America
Micronycteris hirsuta (Peters 1869)	LR: lc	Central America, Caribbean, South America
Micronycteris megalotis (Gray 1842)	LR: lc	Central America, Caribbean, South America
Micronycteris minuta (Gervais 1856)	LR: lc	Central America, Caribbean, South America
Micronycteris nicefori Sanborn 1949	LR: lc	Central America, Caribbean, South America
Micronycteris pusilla Sanborn 1949	VU: A2c	South America
Micronycteris sanborni Simmons 1996	DD **	South America
Micronycteris schmidtorum Sanborn 1935	LR: lc	Central and South America
Micronycteris sylvestris (Thomas 1896)	LR: nt	Central America, Caribbean, South America
***Mimon* (2 species)** Central America, Caribbean, South America		
Mimon bennettii (Gray 1838)	LR: lc	Central and South America
Mimon crenulatum (E. Geoffroy 1810)	LR: lc	Central America, Caribbean, South America
***Phylloderma* (1 species)** Central and South America		
Phylloderma stenops Peters 1865	LR: lc	Central and South America
***Phyllostomus* (4 species)** Central America, Caribbean, South America		
Phyllostomus discolor Wagner 1843	LR: lc	Central America, Caribbean, South America
Phyllostomus elongatus (E. Geoffroy 1810)	LR: lc	South America
Phyllostomus hastatus (Pallas 1767)	LR: lc	Central America, Caribbean, South America
Phyllostomus latifolius (Thomas 1901)	LR: nt	South America
***Tonatia* (7 species)** Central America, Caribbean, South America		
Tonatia bidens (Spix 1823)	LR: lc	Central America, Caribbean, South America
Tonatia brasiliense (Peters 1866)	LR: lc	Central America, Caribbean, South America
Tonatia carrikeri (J. A. Allen 1910)	VU: A2c	South America
Tonatia evotis Davis and Carter 1978	LR: nt	Central America
Tonatia saurophila Koopman and Williams 1951	LR: lc	Central and South America
Tonatia schulzi Genoways and Williams 1980	VU: A2c	South America
Tonatia silvicola (d'Orbigny 1836)	LR: lc	Central and South America
***Trachops* (1 species)** Central America, Caribbean, South America		
Trachops cirrhosus (Spix 1823)	LR: lc	Central America, Caribbean, South America
***Vampyrum* (1 species)** Central America, Caribbean, South America		
Vampyrum spectrum (Linnaeus 1758)	LR: nt	Central America, Caribbean, South America
Subfamily Lonchophyllinae ***Lionycteris* (1 species)** Central and South America		
Lionycteris spurrelli Thomas 1913	LR: lc	Central and South America
***Lonchophylla* (7 species)** Central and South America		
Lonchophylla bokermanni Sazima *et al.* 1978	VU: A2c	South America

Lonchophylla dekeyseri Taddei *et al.* 1983	VU: A2c	South America
Lonchophylla handleyi Hill 1980	VU: A2c, D2	South America
Lonchophylla hesperia G. M. Allen 1908	VU: A2c, D2	South America
Lonchophylla mordax Thomas 1903	LR: lc	Central and South America
Lonchophylla robusta Miller 1912	LR: lc	Central and South America
Lonchophylla thomasi J. A. Allen 1904	LR: lc	Central and South America
***Platalina* (1 species)** South America		
Platalina genovensium Thomas 1928	VU: D2	South America
Subfamily Brachyphyllinae ***Brachyphylla* (2 species)** Caribbean		
Brachyphylla cavernarum Gray 1834	LR: lc	Caribbean
Brachyphylla nana Miller 1902	LR: nt	Caribbean
Subfamily Phyllonycterinae ***Erophylla* (1 species)** Caribbean		
Erophylla sezekorni (Gundlach 1860)	LR: lc	Caribbean
***Phyllonycteris* (3 species)** Caribbean		
Phyllonycteris aphylla (Miller 1898)	EN: B1 + 2c	Caribbean
Phyllonycteris major Anthony 1917	EX	Caribbean
Phyllonycteris poeyi Gundlach 1860	LR: nt	Caribbean
Subfamily Glossophaginae ***Anoura* (5 species)** Central America, Caribbean, South America		
Anoura caudifer (E. Geoffroy 1818)	LR: lc	South America
Anoura cultrata Handley 1960	LR: lc	Central and South America
Anoura geoffroyi Gray 1838	LR: lc	Central America, Caribbean, South America
Anoura latidens Handley 1984	LR: nt	South America
Anoura luismanueli Molinari 1994	DD	South America
***Choeroniscus* (4 species)** Central America, Caribbean, South America		
Choeroniscus godmani (Thomas 1903)	LR: nt	Central and South America
Choeroniscus intermedius (J. A. Allen and Chapman 1893)	LR: nt	Caribbean, South America
Choeroniscus minor (Peters 1868)	LR: lc	South America
Choeroniscus periosus Handley 1966	VU: D2	South America
***Choeronycteris* (1 species)** North and Central America		
Choeronycteris mexicana Tschudi 1844	LR: nt	North and Central America, ?South America
***Glossophaga* (5 species)** Central America, Caribbean, South America		
Glossophaga commissarisi Gardner 1962	LR: lc	Central and South America
Glossophaga leachii Gray 1844	LR: lc	Central America
Glossophaga longirostris Miller 1898	LR: lc	Caribbean, South America
Glossophaga morenoi Martinez and Villa 1938	LR: nt	Central America
Glossophaga soricina (Pallas 1766)	LR: lc	Central America, Caribbean, South America
***Hylonycteris* (1 species)** Central America		
Hylonycteris underwoodi Thomas 1903	LR: nt **	Central America
***Leptonycteris* (2 species)** North and Central America, Caribbean, South America		
Leptonycteris curasoae Miller 1900	VU: A1c **	North and Central America, Caribbean, South America
Leptonycteris nivalis (Saussure 1860)	EN: A1c **	North and Central America

***Lichonycteris* (1 species)** Central and South America		
Lichonycteris obscura Thomas 1895	LR: lc	Central and South America
***Monophyllus* (2 species)** Caribbean		
Monophyllus plethodon Miller 1900	LR: nt	Caribbean
Monophyllus redmani Leach 1821	LR: lc	Caribbean
***Musonycteris* (1 species)** Central America		
Musonycteris harrisoni Schaldach and McLaughlin 1960	VU: A2c	Central America
***Scleronycteris* (1 species)** South America		
Scleronycteris ega Thomas 1912	VU: A2c, D2	South America
Subfamily Carolliinae ***Carollia* (4 species)** Central America, Caribbean, South America		
Carollia brevicauda (Schinz 1821)	LR: lc	Central and South America
Carollia castanea H. Allen 1890	LR: lc	Central and South America
Carollia perspicillata (Linnaeus 1758)	LR: lc	Central America, Caribbean, South America
Carollia subrufa (Hahn 1905)	LR: lc	Central and South America
***Rhinophylla* (3 species)** South America		
Rhinophylla alethina Handley 1966	LR: nt	South America
Rhinophylla fischerae Carter 1966	LR: nt	South America
Rhinophylla pumilio Peters 1865	LR: lc	South America
Subfamily Stenodermatinae ***Ametrida* (1 species)** Caribbean, Central and South America		
Ametrida centurio Gray 1847	LR: lc	Caribbean, Central and South America
***Ardops* (1 species)** Caribbean		
Ardops nichollsi (Thomas 1891)	LR: nt	Caribbean
***Ariteus* (1 species)** Caribbean		
Ariteus flavescens (Gray 1831)	VU: A2c, D2	Caribbean
***Artibeus* (21 species)** North and Central America, Caribbean, South America		
Artibeus amplus Handley 1987	LR: nt	South America
Artibeus anderseni Osgood 1916	LR: lc	South America
Artibeus aztecus K. Andersen 1906	LR: lc	Central America
Artibeus cinereus (Gervais 1856)	LR: lc	South America
Artibeus concolor Peters 1865	LR: nt	South America
Artibeus fimbriatus Gray 1838	LR: nt	South America
Artibeus fraterculus Anthony 1924	VU: A2c	South America
Artibeus glaucus Thomas 1893	LR: lc	Central America, Caribbean, South America
Artibeus gnomus Handley 1987	LR: lc	South America
Artibeus hartii Thomas 1892	LR: lc	North and Central America, Caribbean, South America
Artibeus hirsutus K. Andersen 1906	VU: A2c **	Central America
Artibeus incomitatus Kalko and Handley 1994	DD	Central America
Artibeus inopinatus Davis and Carter 1964	VU: A2c **	Central America
Artibeus intermedius Allen 1897	LR: lc	Central and South America
Artibeus jamaicensis Leach 1821	LR: lc	?North America, Central America, Caribbean, South America
Artibeus lituratus (Olfers 1818)	LR: lc	Central America, Caribbean, South America
Artibeus obscurus Schinz 1821	LR: nt	South America
Artibeus phaeotis (Miller 1902)	LR: lc	Central and South America

Artibeus planirostris (Spix 1823)	LR: lc	South America
Artibeus toltecus (Saussure 1860)	LR: lc	Central America
Artibeus watsoni Thomas 1901	LR: lc	Central and South America
***Centurio* (1 species)** Central America, Caribbean		
Centurio senex Gray 1842	LR: lc	Central America, Caribbean
***Chiroderma* (5 species)** Central America, Caribbean, South America		
Chiroderma doriae Thomas 1891	VU: A2c, D2	South America
Chiroderma improvisum Baker and Genoways 1976	EN: A2c, B1 + 2c	Caribbean
Chiroderma salvini Dobson 1878	LR: lc	Central and South America
Chiroderma trinitatum Goodwin 1958	LR: lc	Central America, Caribbean, South America
Chiroderma villosum Peters 1860	LR: lc	Central America, Caribbean, South America
***Ectophylla* (1 species)** Central and South America		
Ectophylla alba H. Allen 1892	LR: nt **	Central and South America
***Mesophylla* (1 species)** Central America, Caribbean, South America		
Mesophylla macconnelli Thomas 1901	LR: lc	Central America, Caribbean, South America
***Phyllops* (1 species)** Caribbean		
Phyllops falcatus (Gray 1839)	LR: nt	Caribbean
***Platyrrhinus* (10 species)** Central America, Caribbean, South America		
Platyrrhinus aurarius (Handley and Ferris 1972)	LR: nt	South America
Platyrrhinus brachycephalus (Rouk and Carter 1972)	LR: lc	South America
Platyrrhinus chocoensis Alberico and Velasco 1991	VU: A2c, D2	South America
Platyrrhinus dorsalis (Thomas 1900)	LR: lc	Central and South America
Platyrrhinus helleri (Peters 1866)	LR: lc	Central America, Caribbean, South America
Platyrrhinus infuscus (Peters 1880)	LR: nt	South America
Platyrrhinus lineatus (E. Geoffroy 1810)	LR: lc	South America
Platyrrhinus recifinus (Thomas 1901)	VU: A2c, D2	South America
Platyrrhinus umbratus (Lyon 1902)	LR: nt	Caribbean, South America
Platyrrhinus vittatus (Peters 1860)	LR: lc	Central and South America
***Pygoderma* (1 species)** South America		
Pygoderma bilabiatum (Wagner 1843)	LR: nt **	South America
***Sphaeronycteris* (1 species)** South America		
Sphaeronycteris toxophyllum Peters 1882	LR: lc	South America
***Stenoderma* (1 species)** Caribbean		
Stenoderma rufum Desmarest 1820	VU: A1c **	Caribbean
***Sturnira* (12 species)** Central America, Caribbean, South America		
Sturnira aratathomasi Peterson and Tamsitt 1968	LR: nt	South America
Sturnira bidens Thomas 1915	LR: nt	South America
Sturnira bogotensis Shamel 1927	LR: lc	South America
Sturnira erythromos (Tschudi 1844)	LR: lc	South America
Sturnira lilium (E. Geoffroy 1810)	LR: lc	Central America, Caribbean, South America
Sturnira ludovici Anthony 1924	LR: lc	Central and South America
Sturnira luisi Davis 1980	LR: lc	Central and South America
Sturnira magna de la Torre 1966	LR: nt	South America
Sturnira mordax (Goodwin 1938)	LR: nt	Central America
Sturnira nana Gardner and O'Neill 1971	VU: D2	South America

Sturnira thomasi de la Torre and Schwartz 1966	EN: B1 + 2c	Caribbean
Sturnira tildae de la Torre 1959	LR: lc	Caribbean, South America
***Uroderma* (2 species)** Central America, Caribbean, South America		
Uroderma bilobatum Peters 1866	LR: lc	Central America, Caribbean, South America
Uroderma magnirostrum Davis 1968	LR: lc	Central and South America
***Vampyressa* (5 species)** Central and South America		
Vampyressa bidens (Dobson 1878)	LR: nt	South America
Vampyressa brocki Peterson 1968	LR: nt **	South America
Vampyressa melissa Thomas 1926	LR: nt	South America
Vampyressa nymphaea Thomas 1909	LR: lc	Central and South America
Vampyressa pusilla (Wagner 1843)	LR: lc	Central and South America
***Vampyrodes* (1 species)** Central America, Caribbean, South America		
Vampyrodes caraccioli (Thomas 1889)	LR: lc	Central America, Caribbean, South America
Subfamily Desmodontinae ***Desmodus* (1 species)** Central America, Caribbean, South America		
Desmodus rotundus (E. Geoffroy 1810)	LR: lc	Central America, Caribbean, South America
***Diaemus* (1 species)** Central America, Caribbean, South America		
Diaemus youngi (Jentink 1893)	LR: lc	Central America, Caribbean, South America
***Diphylla* (1 species)** North, Central and South America		
Diphylla ecaudata Spix 1823	LR: nt	North, Central and South America
FAMILY NATALIDAE (1 genus, 5 species) Central America, Caribbean, South America ***Natalus* (5 species)** Central America, Caribbean, South America		
Natalus lepidus (Gervais 1837)	LR: nt	Caribbean
Natalus micropus Dobson 1880	LR: lc	Caribbean, South America
Natalus stramineus Gray 1838	LR: lc	Central America, Caribbean, South America
Natalus tumidifrons (Miller 1903)	VU: D2	Caribbean
Natalus tumidirostris Miller 1900	LR: lc	Caribbean, South America
FAMILY FURIPTERIDAE (2 genera, 2 species) Central America, Caribbean, South America ***Amorphochilus* (1 species)** South America		
Amorphochilus schnablii Peters 1877	VU: A2c	South America
***Furipterus* (1 species)** Central America, Caribbean, South America		
Furipterus horrens (F. Cuvier 1828)	LR: lc	Central America, Caribbean, South America
FAMILY THYROPTERIDAE (1 genus, 3 species) Central America, Caribbean, South America ***Thyroptera* (3 species)** Central America, Caribbean, South America		
Thyroptera discifera (Lichtenstein and Peters 1855)	LR: lc	Central and South America
Thyroptera lavali Pine 1993	VU: B1 + 2c, D2	South America
Thyroptera tricolor Spix 1823	LR: lc	Central America, Caribbean, South America
FAMILY MYZOPODIDAE (1 genus, 1 species) Africa (Malagasy Subregion only) ***Myzopoda* (1 species)** Africa (Malagasy Subregion only)		
Myzopoda aurita Milne-Edwards and A. Grandidier 1878	VU: A2c	Africa (Malagasy Subregion only)

FAMILY VESPERTILIONIDAE (37 genera, 357 species)
North and Central America, Caribbean, South America, Europe, Africa (North Africa, Subsaharan Africa, Malagasy Subregion), Arabian Peninsula, Asia (Indian Subcontinent, Southeast Asia, New Guinea), Australia, New Zealand, Oceania

Subfamily Kerivoulinae

***Kerivoula* (21 species)**
Africa (Subsaharan Africa only), Asia (Indian Subcontinent, Southeast Asia, New Guinea), Australia

Kerivoula aerosa (Tomes 1858)	DD	?Africa (Subsaharan Africa only)
Kerivoula africana Dobson 1878	DD	Africa (Subsaharan Africa only)
Kerivoula agnella Thomas 1908	VU: D2	Asia (Southeast Asia only)
Kerivoula argentata Tomes 1861	LR: lc	Africa (Subsaharan Africa only)
Kerivoula atrox Miller 1905	LR: lc	Asia (Southeast Asia only)
Kerivoula cuprosa Thomas 1912	LR: nt	Africa (Subsaharan Africa only)
Kerivoula flora Thomas 1914	LR: lc	Asia (Southeast Asia)
Kerivoula hardwickei (Horsfield 1824)	LR: lc	Asia (Indian Subcontinent, Southeast Asia)
Kerivoula intermedia Hill and Francis 1984	LR: nt	Asia (Southeast Asia only)
Kerivoula jagori (Peters 1866)	LR: lc	Asia (Southeast Asia only)
Kerivoula lanosa (A. Smith 1847)	LR: lc	Africa (Subsaharan Africa only)
Kerivoula minuta Miller 1898	LR: nt	Asia (Southeast Asia only)
Kerivoula muscina Tate 1941	VU: D2	Asia (New Guinea only)
Kerivoula myrella Thomas 1914	VU: A2c	Asia (Southeast Asia only)
Kerivoula papillosa (Temminck 1840)	LR: lc	Asia (Indian Subcontinent and Southeast Asia only)
Kerivoula papuensis (Dobson 1878)	LR: lc	Asia (New Guinea only), Australia
Kerivoula pellucida (Waterhouse 1845)	LR: lc	Asia (Southeast Asia only)
Kerivoula phalaena Thomas 1912	LR: lc	Africa (Subsaharan Africa only)
Kerivoula picta (Pallas 1767)	LR: lc	Asia (Indian Subcontinent, Southeast Asia)
Kerivoula smithi Thomas 1880	LR: nt	Africa (Subsaharan Africa only)
Kerivoula whiteheadi Thomas 1894	LR: lc	Asia (Southeast Asia only)

Subfamily Vespertilioninae

***Antrozous* (2 species)**
North and Central America, Caribbean

Antrozous dubiaquercus Van Gelder 1959	VU: A2c, D2	Central America
Antrozous pallidus (Le Conte 1856)	LR: lc	North and Central America, Caribbean

***Arielulus* (5 species)**
Asia (Indian Subcontinent and Southeast Asia)

Arielulus aureocollaris (Kock and Storch 1996)	DD **	Asia (Southeast Asia only)
Arielulus circumdatus (Temminck 1840)	LR: lc	Asia (Indian Subcontinent, Southeast Asia)
Arielulus cuprosus (Hill and Francis 1984)	VU: A2c	Asia (Southeast Asia only)
Arielulus societatis (Hill 1972)	DD	Asia (Southeast Asia only)
Arielulus torquatus Csorba and Lee 1999	DD**	Asia

***Barbastella* (2 species)**
Europe, Africa (North Africa and Subsaharan Africa only), Asia (Indian Subcontinent, ?Southeast Asia)

Barbastella barbastellus (Schreber 1774)	VU: A2c	Europe, Africa (North Africa only), Asia
Barbastella leucomelas (Cretzschmar 1826)	LR: lc	Africa (North Africa and Subsaharan Africa only), Asia (Indian Subcontinent, ?Southeast Asia)

***Chalinolobus* (16 species)**
Africa (Subsaharan Africa only), Asia (New Guinea only), Australia, New Zealand, Oceania

Chalinolobus alboguttatus (J. A. Allen 1917)	VU: D2	Africa (Subsaharan Africa only)
Chalinolobus argentatus (Dobson 1875)	LR: lc	Africa (Subsaharan Africa only)
Chalinolobus beatrix (Thomas 1901)	LR: nt	Africa (Subsaharan Africa only)
Chalinolobus dwyeri Ryan 1966	VU: A2c	Australia
Chalinolobus egeria (Thomas 1913)	LR: nt	Africa (Subsaharan Africa only)
Chalinolobus gleni (Peterson and Smith 1973)	LR: nt	Africa (Subsaharan Africa only)
Chalinolobus gouldii Gray 1841	LR: lc	Australia, Oceania
Chalinolobus kenyacola (Peterson 1982)	DD	Africa (Subsaharan Africa only)
Chalinolobus morio Gray 1841	LR: lc	Australia
Chalinolobus neocaledonicus Revilliod 1913–1914	EN: B1 + 2c	Oceania
Chalinolobus nigrogriseus Gould 1852	LR: lc	Asia (New Guinea only), Australia
Chalinolobus picatus Gould 1852	LR: nt	Australia
Chalinolobus poensis (Gray 1842)	LR: nt	Africa (Subsaharan Africa only)
Chalinolobus superbus (Hayman 1939)	VU: D2	Africa (Subsaharan Africa only)
Chalinolobus tuberculatus (Forster 1844)	VU: A2b,c**	New Zealand
Chalinolobus variegatus (Tomes 1861)	LR: lc	Africa (Subsaharan Africa only)

***Eptesicus* (39 species)** Central America, Caribbean, South America, Europe, Africa (North Africa, Subsaharan Africa, Malagasy Subregion), Arabian Peninsula, Asia (Indian Subcontinent, Southeast Asia), Australia		
Eptesicus andinus (J. A. Allen 1914)	LR: lc	Central and South America
Eptesicus baverstocki Kitchener, Jones, and Caputi 1987	LR: lc	Australia
Eptesicus bobrinskoi Kuzyakin 1935	LR: lc **	Asia
Eptesicus bottae (Peters, 1869)	LR: lc	Europe, Africa (North Africa only), Arabian Peninsula, Asia (Indian Subcontinent)
Eptesicus brasiliensis (Desmarest 1819)	LR: lc	Central America, Caribbean, South America
Eptesicus brunneus (Thomas 1880)	LR: nt	Africa (Subsaharan Africa only)
Eptesicus capensis (A. Smith 1829)	LR: lc	Africa (Subsaharan Africa and Malagasy Subregion only)
Eptesicus caurinus Thomas 1914	LR: nt	Australia
Eptesicus darlingtoni Allen 1933	LR: lc	Australia
Eptesicus demissus Thomas 1916	VU: A2c	Asia (Southeast Asia only)
Eptesicus diminutus Osgood 1915	LR: lc	South America
Eptesicus douglasorum Kitchener 1976	LR: nt	Australia
Eptesicus finlaysoni Kitchener, Jones, and Caputi 1987	LR: lc	Australia
Eptesicus flavescens (Seabra 1900)	DD	Africa (Subsaharan Africa only)
Eptesicus floweri (de Winton 1901)	LR: nt	Africa (Subsaharan Africa only)
Eptesicus furinalis (d'Orbigny 1847)	LR: lc	Central and South America
Eptesicus fuscus (Beauvois 1796)	LR: lc	North and Central America, Caribbean, South America
Eptesicus gobiensis Bobrinsky 1926	LR: lc	Asia (Indian Subcontinent)
Eptesicus guadeloupensis Genoways and Baker 1975	EN: B1 + 2c	Caribbean
Eptesicus guineensis (Bocage 1889)	LR: nt	Africa (Subsaharan Africa only)
Eptesicus hottentotus (A. Smith 1833)	LR: lc	Africa (Subsaharan Africa only)
Eptesicus innoxius (Gervais 1841)	VU: A2c	South America
Eptesicus kobayashii Mori 1928	DD	Asia
Eptesicus matroka (Thomas and Schwann 1905)	DD **	Africa (Malagasy Subregion only)
Eptesicus melckorum Roberts 1919	LR: lc	Africa (Subsaharan Africa only)
Eptesicus nasutus (Dobson 1877)	VU: A2c	Arabian Peninsula, Asia (Indian Subcontinent)
Eptesicus nilssonii (Keyserling and Blasius 1839)	LR: lc	Europe, Asia (Indian Subcontinent)
Eptesicus pachyotis (Dobson 1871)	LR: nt	Asia (Indian Subcontinent and Southeast Asia only)
Eptesicus platyops (Thomas 1901)	VU: D2	Africa (Subsaharan Africa only)
Eptesicus pumilus Gray 1841	LR: lc	Australia
Eptesicus regulus (Thomas 1906)	LR: lc	Australia
Eptesicus rendalli (Thomas 1889)	LR: lc	Africa (Subsaharan Africa only)
Eptesicus serotinus Schreber 1774	LR: lc	Europe, Africa (North Africa only), Asia (Indian Subcontinent, Southeast Asia)
Eptesicus somalicus (Thomas 1901)	LR: lc	Africa (Subsaharan Africa only)
Eptesicus tatei Ellerman and Morrison-Scott 1951	DD	Asia (Indian Subcontinent only)
Eptesicus tenuipinnis (Peters 1872)	LR: lc	Africa (Subsaharan Africa only)
Eptesicus troughtoni Kitchener, Jones, and Caputi 1987	LR: lc	Australia
Eptesicus vulturnus Thomas 1914	LR: lc	Australia
Eptesicus zuluensis Roberts 1924	LR: nt **	Africa (Subsaharan Africa only)
***Euderma* (1 species)** North and Central America		
Euderma maculatum (J. A. Allen 1891)	LR: lc	North and Central America
***Eudiscopus* (1 species)** Asia (Southeast Asia only)		
Eudiscopus denticulus (Osgood 1932)	LR: nt	Asia (Southeast Asia only)
***Glischropus* (2 species)** Asia (Southeast Asia only)		
Glischropus javanus Chasen 1939	EN B1 + 2d **	Asia (Southeast Asia only)
Glischropus tylopus (Dobson 1875)	LR: lc	Asia (Southeast Asia only)
***Hesperoptenus* (5 species)** Asia (Indian Subcontinent, Southeast Asia)		
Hesperoptenus blanfordi (Dobson 1877)	LR: lc	Asia (Southeast Asia only)
Hesperoptenus doriae (Peters 1868)	EN: B1 + 2c	Asia (Southeast Asia only)

Hesperoptenus gaskelli Hill 1983	VU: B1 + 2c	Asia (Southeast Asia only)
Hesperoptenus tickelli (Blyth 1851)	LR: lc	Asia (Indian Subcontinent, Southeast Asia)
Hesperoptenus tomesi Thomas 1905	LR: lc	Asia (Southeast Asia only)
***Histiotus* (5 species)** South America		
Histiotus alienus Thomas 1916	VU: A2c	South America
Histiotus humboldti Handley 1996	DD **	South America
Histiotus macrotus (Poeppig 1835)	LR: nt	South America
Histiotus montanus (Philippi and Landbeck 1861)	LR: lc	South America
Histiotus velatus (I. Geoffroy 1824)	LR: lc **	South America
***Ia* (1 species)** Asia (Indian Subcontinent, Southeast Asia)		
Ia io Thomas,1902	LR: nt	Asia (Indian Subcontinent, Southeast Asia)
***Idionycteris* (1 species)** North and Central America		
Idionycteris phyllotis (G. M. Allen 1916)	LR: lc	North and Central America
***Laephotis* (4 species)** Africa (Subsaharan Africa only)		
Laephotis angolensis Monard 1935	LR: nt	Africa (Subsaharan Africa only)
Laephotis botswanae Setzer 1971	LR: nt	Africa (Subsaharan Africa only)
Laephotis namibensis Setzer 1971	EN: A2c	Africa (Subsaharan Africa only)
Laephotis wintoni Thomas 1901	LR: nt	Africa (Subsaharan Africa only)
***Lasionycteris* (1 species)** North and Central America, Caribbean		
Lasionycteris noctivagans (Le Conte 1831)	LR: lc	North and Central America, Caribbean
***Lasiurus* (11 species)** North and Central America, Caribbean, South America, Oceania		
Lasiurus atratus Handley 1996	DD **	South America
Lasiurus blossevillii (Lesson and Garnet 1826)	LR: lc	North, Central and South America
Lasiurus borealis (Müller 1776)	LR: lc	North and Central America, Caribbean, South America
Lasiurus castaneus Handley 1960	VU: D2	Central America
Lasiurus cinereus (Beauvois 1796)	LR: lc	North and Central America, Caribbean, South America, Oceania
Lasiurus ebenus Fazzolari and Corrca 1994	VU: B1 + 2c, D2	South America
Lasiurus ega (Gervais 1856)	LR: lc	North and Central America, Caribbean, South America
Lasiurus egregius (Peters 1870)	LR: nt	South America
Lasiurus intermedius H. Allen 1862	LR: lc	North and Central America, Caribbean
Lasiurus seminolus (Rhoads 1895)	LR: lc	North America, ?Central America, Caribbean
Lasiurus xanthinus (Thomas 1897)	LR: lc	North and Central America
***Mimetillus* (1 species)** Africa (Subsaharan Africa only)		
Mimetillus moloneyi (Thomas 1891)	LR: lc	Africa (Subsaharan Africa only)
***Myotis* (92 species)** North and Central America, Caribbean, South America, Europe, Africa (North Africa, Subsaharan Africa, Malagasy Subregion), Arabian Peninsula, Asia (Indian Subcontinent, Southeast Asia, New Guinea), Australia, Oceania		
Myotis abei Yoshikura 1944	DD	Asia
Myotis adversus (Horsfield,1824)	LR: lc	Asia (Southeast Asia, New Guinea), Australia, Oceania
Myotis aelleni Baud 1979	VU: A2c, D2	South America
Myotis albescens (E. Geoffroy 1806)	LR: lc	Central and South America
Myotis altarium Thomas 1911	LR: lc	Asia (Southeast Asia)
Myotis annectans (Dobson 1871)	LR: nt	Asia (Indian Subcontinent and Southeast Asia only)
Myotis atacamensis (Lataste 1892)	VU: A2c, D2	South America
Myotis ater (Peters 1866)	LR: lc	Asia (Southeast Asia)
Myotis auriculus Baker and Stains 1955	LR: lc	North and Central America
Myotis australis (Dobson 1878)	DD	Australia
Myotis austroriparius (Rhoads 1897)	LR: lc	North America
Myotis bechsteinii (Kuhl 1817)	VU: A2c	Europe, Asia
Myotis blythii (Tomes 1857)	LR: lc	Europe, Africa (North Africa only), Arabian Peninsula, Asia (Indian Subcontinent)

Myotis bocagei (Peters 1870)	LR: lc	Africa (Subsaharan Africa only), Arabian Peninsula
Myotis bombinus Thomas 1906	LR: nt	Asia
Myotis brandtii (Eversmann 1845)	LR: lc	Europe, Asia
Myotis californicus (Audubon and Bachman 1842)	LR: lc	North and Central America
Myotis capaccinii (Bonaparte 1837)	VU: A2c	Europe, Africa (North Africa only), Arabian Peninsula, Asia
Myotis chiloensis (Waterhouse 1840)	LR: nt	South America
Myotis chinensis (Tomes 1857)	LR: lc	Asia (Southeast Asia)
Myotis ciliolabrum (Merriam 1886)	LR: lc	North America
Myotis cobanensis Goodwin 1955	CR: B1 + 2c	Central America
Myotis csorbai Topal 1998	DD**	Asia (Indian Subcontinent only)
Myotis dasycneme (Boie 1825)	VU: A2c	Europe, Asia
Myotis daubentonii (Kuhl 1817)	LR: lc	Europe, Asia (Indian Subcontinent)
Myotis dominicensis Miller 1902	VU: A2c, D2	Caribbean
Myotis elegans Hall 1962	LR: nt **	Central America
Myotis emarginatus (E.Geoffroy 1806)	VU: A2c	Europe, Africa (North Africa only), Arabian Peninsula, Asia
Myotis evotis (H. Allen 1864)	LR: lc	North and Central America
Myotis fimbriatus (Peters 1871)	LR: nt **	Asia
Myotis findleyi Bogan 1978	EN: B1 + 2c	Central America
Myotis formosus (Hodgson 1835)	LR: lc	Asia (Indian Subcontinent and Southeast Asia)
Myotis fortidens Miller and Allen 1928	LR: nt	Central America
Myotis frater G. M. Allen 1923	LR: nt	Asia
Myotis gomatongensis Francis and Hill 1998	DD**	Asia (Southeast Asia only)
Myotis goudoti (A. Smith 1834)	LR: nt	Africa (Malagasy Subregion only)
Myotis grisescens A. H. Howell 1909	EN: A1c	North America
Myotis hasseltii (Temminck 1840)	LR: lc	Asia (Indian Subcontinent and Southeast Asia only)
Myotis hermanni Thomas 1923	DD	?Asia (Southeast Asia only)
Myotis horsfieldii (Temminck 1840)	LR: lc	Asia (Indian Subcontinent, Southeast Asia)
Myotis hosonoi Imaizumi 1954	VU: A2c, B1 + 2c **	Asia
Myotis ikonnikovi Ognev 1912	LR: lc	Asia
Myotis insularum (Dobson 1878)	DD	Oceania
Myotis keaysi J. A. Allen 1914	LR: lc	Central America, Caribbean, South America
Myotis keenii (Merriam 1895)	LR: lc	North America
Myotis leibii (Audubon and Bachman 1842)	LR: lc	North and Central America
Myotis lesueuri Roberts 1919	VU: A2c, D2	Africa (Subsaharan Africa only)
Myotis levis (I. Geoffroy 1824)	LR: lc	South America
Myotis longipes (Dobson 1873)	VU B1 + 2c, D2**	Asia (Indian Subcontinent)
Myotis lucifugus (Le Conte 1831)	LR: lc	North and Central America
Myotis macrodactylus (Temminck 1840)	LR: lc **	Asia
Myotis macrotarsus (Waterhouse 1845)	LR: nt	Asia (Southeast Asia only)
Myotis martiniquensis LaVal 1973	LR: nt	Caribbean
Myotis milleri Elliot 1903	EN: A2c **	Central America
Myotis montivagus (Dobson 1874)	LR: nt	Asia (Indian Subcontinent, Southeast Asia)
Myotis morrisi Hill 1971	VU: D2	Africa (Subsaharan Africa only)
Myotis muricola (Gray 1846)	LR: lc	Asia (Indian Subcontinent and Southeast Asia only)
Myotis myotis (Borkhausen 1797)	LR: nt	Europe, Africa (North Africa only), Arabian Peninsula, Asia
Myotis mystacinus (Kuhl 1817)	LR: lc	Europe, Africa (North Africa only), Arabian Peninsula, Asia
Myotis nattereri (Kuhl 1817)	LR: lc	Europe, Africa (North Africa only), Arabian Peninsula, Asia
Myotis nesopolus Miller 1900	LR: nt	Caribbean, South America
Myotis nigricans (Schinz 1821)	LR: lc	Central America, Caribbean, South America
Myotis oreias (Temminck 1840)	DD	Asia (Southeast Asia only)
Myotis oxyotus (Peters 1867)	LR: lc	Central and South America
Myotis ozensis Imaizumi 1954	EN: A2c, B1 + 2c **	Asia
Myotis peninsularis Miller 1898	VU: A1c **	Central America
Myotis pequinius Thomas 1908	LR: nt	Asia
Myotis planiceps Baker 1955	CR: B1 + 2c **	Central America
Myotis pruinosus Yoshiyuki 1971	EN: B1 + 2c	Asia
Myotis ricketti (Thomas 1894)	LR: nt	Asia
Myotis ridleyi Thomas 1898	LR: nt	Asia (Southeast Asia only)
Myotis riparius Handley 1960	LR: lc	Central America, Caribbean, South America
Myotis rosseti (Oey 1951)	LR: nt	Asia (Southeast Asia only)

Myotis ruber (E. Geoffroy 1806)	VU: A2c	South America
Myotis schaubi Kormos 1934	EN: B1 + 2c, C2a, D **	Europe, Asia
Myotis scotti Thomas 1927	VU: A2c, D2	Africa (Subsaharan Africa only)
Myotis seabrai Thomas 1912	VU: A2c, D2	Africa (Subsaharan Africa only)
Myotis septentrionalis (Trouessart 1897)	LR: lc	North America
Myotis sicarius Thomas 1915	VU: A2c, D2	Asia (Indian Subcontinent only)
Myotis siligorensis (Horsfield 1855)	LR: lc	Asia (Indian Subcontinent, Southeast Asia)
Myotis simus Thomas 1901	LR: lc	South America
Myotis sodalis Miller and Allen 1928	EN: A1c	North America
Myotis stalkeri Thomas 1910	EN: B1 + 2c	Asia (Southeast Asia only)
Myotis thysanodes Miller 1897	LR: lc	North and Central America
Myotis tricolor (Temminck 1832)	LR: lc	Africa (Subsaharan Africa only)
Myotis velifer (J. A. Allen 1890)	LR: lc	North and Central America
Myotis vivesi Menegaux 1901	VU: A2c	Central America
Myotis volans (H. Allen 1866)	LR: lc	North and Central America
Myotis welwitschii (Gray 1866)	LR: lc	Africa (Subsaharan Africa only)
Myotis yanbarensis Maeda and Matsumara 1998	DD**	Asia
Myotis yesoensis Yoshiyuki 1984	VU: A2c	Asia
Myotis yumanensis (H. Allen 1864)	LR: lc	North and Central America
***Nyctalus* (6 species)**		
Europe, Africa (North Africa and ?Subsaharan Africa only), Asia (Indian Subcontinent, Southeast Asia)		
Nyctalus aviator (Thomas 1911)	LR: nt	Asia
Nyctalus azoreum (Thomas 1901)	VU: A2c, B1 + 2c **	Europe
Nyctalus lasiopterus (Schreber 1780)	LR: nt	Europe, Africa (North Africa only), Asia
Nyctalus leisleri (Kuhl 1817)	LR: nt	Europe, Africa (North Africa only), Asia (Indian Subcontinent)
Nyctalus montanus (Barrett-Hamilton 1906)	LR: nt	Asia (Indian Subcontinent)
Nyctalus noctula (Schreber 1774)	LR: lc	Europe, Africa (North Africa and ?Subsaharan Africa only), Asia (Indian Subcontinent, Southeast Asia)
***Nycticeinops* (1 species)**		
Africa (North Africa and Subsaharan Africa only), Arabian Peninsula		
Nycticeinops schlieffeni (Peters 1859)	LR: lc	Africa (North Africa and Subsaharan Africa only), Arabian Peninsula
***Nycticeius* (6 species)**		
North and Central America, Caribbean, Asia (New Guinea only), Australia		
Nycticeius balstoni (Thomas 1906)	LR: lc	Australia
Nycticeius greyii (Gray 1842)	LR: lc	Australia
Nycticeius humeralis (Rafinesque 1818)	LR: lc	North and Central America, Caribbean
Nycticeius orion (Troughton 1937)	LR: lc	Australia
Nycticeius rueppellii (Peters 1866)	LR: nt	Australia
Nycticeius sanborni (Troughton 1937)	LR: lc	Asia (New Guinea only), Australia
***Nyctophilus* (12 species)**		
Asia (Southeast Asia, New Guinea), Australia, Oceania		
Nyctophilus arnhemensis Johnson 1959	LR: lc	Australia
Nyctophilus bifax (Thomas 1915)	LR: lc	Asia (New Guinea only), Australia
Nyctophilus daedalus (Thomas 1915)	LR: nt	Australia
Nyctophilus geoffroyi Leach 1821	LR: lc	Australia
Nyctophilus gouldi Tomes 1858	LR: lc	Asia (New Guinea only), Australia
Nyctophilus heran Kitchener, How, and Maharadatunkamsi 1991	EN: B1 + 2c	Asia (Southeast Asia only)
Nyctophilus howensis McKean 1973	EX	Australia
Nyctophilus microdon Laurie and Hill 1954	VU: D2	Asia (New Guinea only)
Nyctophilus microtis Thomas 1888	LR: lc	Asia (New Guinea only)
Nyctophilus sherrini (Thomas 1915)	LR: nt	Australia
Nyctophilus timoriensis E. Geoffroy 1806	VU: A2c	Asia (New Guinea), Australia
Nyctophilus walkeri Thomas 1892	LR: nt	Australia
***Otonycteris* (1 species)**		
Africa (North Africa and Subsaharan Africa only), Arabian Peninsula, Asia (Indian Subcontinent)		
Otonycteris hemprichii Peters 1859	LR: lc	Africa (North Africa and Subsaharan Africa only), Arabian Peninsula, Asia (Indian Subcontinent)

***Pharotis* (1 species)** Asia (New Guinea only)		
Pharotis imogene Thomas 1914	CR: B1 + 2c, C2b	Asia (New Guinea only)
***Philetor* (1 species)** Asia (Indian Subcontinent, Southeast Asia and New Guinea only)		
Philetor brachypterus (Temminck 1840)	LR: lc	Asia (Indian Subcontinent, Southeast Asia and New Guinea only)
***Pipistrellus* (53 species)** North and Central America, Europe, Africa (North Africa, Subsaharan Africa, Malagasy Subregion), Arabian Peninsula, Asia (Indian Subcontinent, Southeast Asia, New Guinea), Australia, Oceania		
Pipistrellus abramus (Temminck 1840)	LR: lc	Asia (Southeast Asia)
Pipistrellus adamsi Kitchener, Caputi, and Jones 1986	LR: lc	Australia
Pipistrellus aegyptius (Fischer 1829)	LR: lc	Africa (North Africa and Subsaharan Africa only)
Pipistrellus aero Heller 1912	DD	Africa (Subsaharan Africa only)
Pipistrellus affinis (Dobson 1871)	LR: lc	Asia (Indian Subcontinent, Southeast Asia)
Pipistrellus anchietai (Seabra 1900)	VU: A2c	Africa (Subsaharan Africa only)
Pipistrellus angulatus (Peters 1880)	LR: lc	Asia (Southeast Asia and New Guinea only), ?Australia, Oceania
Pipistrellus anthonyi Tate 1942	CR: B1 + 2c	Asia (Southeast Asia only)
Pipistrellus arabicus Harrison 1979	VU: D2	Arabian Peninsula
Pipistrellus ariel Thomas 1904	VU: D2 **	Africa (North Africa and Subsaharan Africa only), Arabian Peninsula
Pipistrellus bodenheimeri Harrison 1960	LR: nt	Arabian Peninsula
Pipistrellus cadornae Thomas 1916	LR: nt	Asia (Indian Subcontinent and Southeast Asia only)
Pipistrellus ceylonicus (Kelaart 1852)	LR: lc	Asia (Indian Subcontinent, Southeast Asia)
Pipistrellus collinus Thomas 1920	LR: lc	Asia (New Guinea only)
Pipistrellus coromandra (Gray 1838)	LR: lc	Asia (Indian Subcontinent, Southeast Asia)
Pipistrellus crassulus Thomas 1904	LR: lc	Africa (Subsaharan Africa only)
Pipistrellus dormeri (Dobson 1875)	LR: lc	Asia (Indian Subcontinent)
Pipistrellus eisentrauti Hill 1968	LR: lc	Africa (Subsaharan Africa only)
Pipistrellus endoi Imaizumi 1959	EN: B1 + 2c **	Asia
Pipistrellus hesperus (H. Allen 1864)	LR: lc	North and Central America
Pipistrellus imbricatus (Horsfield 1824)	LR: lc	Asia (Southeast Asia only)
Pipistrellus inexpectatus Aellen 1959	LR: lc	Africa (Subsaharan Africa only)
Pipistrellus javanicus (Gray 1838)	LR: lc	Asia (Indian Subcontinent and Southeast Asia), ?Australia
Pipistrellus joffrei (Thomas 1915)	CR: B1 + 2c	Asia (Southeast Asia only)
Pipistrellus kitcheneri Thomas 1916	LR: nt	Asia (Southeast Asia only)
Pipistrellus kuhlii (Kuhl 1817)	LR: lc	Europe, Africa (North Africa and Subsaharan Africa only), Arabian Peninsula, Asia (Indian Subcontinent)
Pipistrellus lophurus Thomas 1915	DD	Asia (Southeast Asia only)
Pipistrellus macrotis (Temminck 1840)	LR: nt	Asia (Southeast Asia only)
Pipistrellus maderensis (Dobson 1878)	VU: A2c, B1 + 2c	Europe
Pipistrellus mckenziei (Kitchener, Caputi, and Jones 1986)	VU: A2c	Australia
Pipistrellus minahassae (Meyer 1899)	DD	Asia (Southeast Asia only)
Pipistrellus mordax (Peters 1866)	LR: nt	Asia (Southeast Asia only)
Pipistrellus musciculus Thomas 1913	LR: nt	Africa (Subsaharan Africa only)
Pipistrellus nanulus Thomas 1904	LR: lc	Africa (Subsaharan Africa only)
Pipistrellus nanus (Peters 1852)	LR: lc	Africa (Subsaharan Africa and Malagasy Subregion only)
Pipistrellus nathusii (Keyserling and Blasius 1839)	LR: lc	Europe, Asia
Pipistrellus papuanus (Peters and Doria 1881)	LR: nt	Asia (Southeast Asia and New Guinea only)
Pipistrellus paterculus Thomas 1915	LR: nt	Asia (Indian Subcontinent, Southeast Asia)
Pipistrellus peguensis Sinha 1969	DD	Asia (Southeast Asia only)
Pipistrellus permixtus Aellen 1957	DD	Africa (Subsaharan Africa only)
Pipistrellus petersi (Meyer 1899)	LR: lc	Asia (Southeast Asia only)
Pipistrellus pipistrellus (Schreber 1774)	LR: lc	Europe, Africa (North Africa only), Arabian Peninsula, Asia (Indian Subcontinent)
Pipistrellus pulveratus (Peters 1871)	LR: nt	Asia (Southeast Asia)

Pipistrellus rueppelli (Fischer 1829)	LR: lc	Africa (North Africa and Subsaharan Africa only)
Pipistrellus rusticus (Tomes 1861)	LR: lc	Africa (Subsaharan Africa only)
Pipistrellus savii (Bonaparte 1837)	LR: lc	Europe, Africa (North Africa only), Asia (Indian Subcontinent, Southeast Asia)
Pipistrellus stenopterus (Dobson 1875)	LR: lc	Asia (Southeast Asia only)
Pipistrellus sturdeei Thomas 1915	EX **	Asia
Pipistrellus subflavus (F. Cuvier 1832)	LR: lc	North and Central America
Pipistrellus tasmaniensis (Gould 1858)	LR: lc	Australia
Pipistrellus tenuis (Temminck 1840)	LR: lc	Asia (Indian Subcontinent, Southeast Asia and New Guinea only), Australia, Oceania
Pipistrellus wattsi Kitchener, Caputi, and Jones 1986	LR: nt	Asia (New Guinea only)
Pipistrellus westralis Koopman 1984	LR: lc	Australia
***Plecotus* (7 species)** North and Central America, Europe, Asia (Indian Subcontinent)		
Plecotus auritus (Linnaeus 1758)	LR: lc	Europe, Asia (Indian Subcontinent)
Plecotus austriacus (Fischer 1829)	LR: lc	Europe, Asia (Indian Subcontinent)
Plecotus mexicanus (G. M. Allen 1916)	LR: lc	Central America
Plecotus rafinesquii Lesson 1827	VU: A2c	North America
Plecotus taivanus Yoshiyuki 1991	VU: A2c	Asia
Plecotus teneriffae Barret-Hamilton 1907	VU: A2c, D2	Europe
Plecotus townsendii Cooper 1837	VU: A2c	North and Central America
***Rhogeessa* (7 species)** Central America, Caribbean, South America		
Rhogeessa alleni Thomas 1892	LR: nt	Central America
Rhogeessa genowaysi Baker 1984	VU: A2c, D2 **	Central America
Rhogeessa gracilis Miller 1897	LR: nt	Central America
Rhogeessa minutilla Miller 1897	LR: nt	South America
Rhogeessa mira LaVal 1973	EN: A2c, B1 + 2c,d **	Central America
Rhogeessa parvula H. Allen 1866	LR: nt	Central America
Rhogeessa tumida H. Allen 1866	LR: lc	Central America, Caribbean, South America
***Scotoecus* (3 species)** Africa (Subsaharan Africa only), Asia (Indian Subcontinent only)		
Scotoecus albofuscus Thomas 1890	LR: nt	Africa (Subsaharan Africa only)
Scotoecus hirundo de Winton 1899	LR: lc	Africa (Subsaharan Africa only)
Scotoecus pallidus Dobson 1876	LR: lc	Asia (Indian Subcontinent only)
***Scotomanes* (2 species)** Asia (Indian Subcontinent and Southeast Asia only)		
Scotomanes emarginatus (Dobson 1871)	DD	Asia (Indian Subcontinent only)
Scotomanes ornatus (Blyth 1851)	LR: nt	Asia (Indian Subcontinent and Southeast Asia only)
***Scotophilus* (10 species)** Africa (Subsaharan Africa and Malagasy Subregion only), Asia (Indian Subcontinent, Southeast Asia)		
Scotophilus borbonicus (E. Geoffroy 1803)	CR: A1c	Africa (Malagasy Subregion only)
Scotophilus celebensis Sody 1928	DD	Asia (Southeast Asia only)
Scotophilus dinganii (A. Smith 1833)	LR: lc	Africa (Subsaharan Africa only)
Scotophilus heathi (Horsfield 1831)	LR: lc	Asia (Indian Subcontinent, Southeast Asia)
Scotophilus kuhlii Leach 1821	LR: lc	Asia (Indian Subcontinent, Southeast Asia)
Scotophilus leucogaster (Cretzschmar 1826)	LR: lc	Africa (Subsaharan Africa and Malagasy Subregion only)
Scotophilus nigrita (Schreber 1774)	LR: nt	Africa (Subsaharan Africa and Malagasy Subregion only)
Scotophilus nux Thomas 1904	LR: lc	Africa (Subsaharan Africa only)
Scotophilus robustus Milne-Edwards 1881	LR: nt	Africa (Malagasy Subregion only)
Scotophilus viridis (Peters 1852)	LR: lc	Africa (Subsaharan Africa only)
***Tylonycteris* (2 species)** Asia (Indian Subcontinent, Southeast Asia)		
Tylonycteris pachypus (Temminck 1840)	LR: lc	Asia (Indian Subcontinent, Southeast Asia)
Tylonycteris robustula Thomas 1915	LR: lc	Asia (Indian Subcontinent)

***Vespertilio* (2 species)**		
Europe, Asia		
Vespertilio murinus Linnaeus 1758	LR: lc	Europe, Asia
Vespertilio superans Thomas 1899	LR: lc	Asia
Subfamily Murininae		
***Harpiocephalus* (2 species)**		
Asia (Indian Subcontinent, Southeast Asia)		
Harpiocephalus harpia (Temminck 1840)	LR: lc	Asia (Indian Subcontinent, Southeast Asia)
Harpiocephalus mordax Thomas 1923	LR: nt	Asia (Southeast Asia only)
***Murina* (16 species)**		
Asia (Indian Subcontinent, Southeast Asia, New Guinea), Australia		
Murina aenea Hill 1964	LR: nt	Asia (Southeast Asia only)
Murina aurata Milne-Edwards 1872	LR: nt	Asia (Indian Subcontinent, Southeast Asia)
Murina cyclotis Dobson 1872	LR: lc	Asia (Indian Subcontinent, Southeast Asia)
Murina florium Thomas 1908	LR: lc	Asia (Southeast Asia and New Guinea only), Australia
Murina fusca Sowerby 1922	DD	Asia
Murina grisea Peters 1872	EN: B1 + 2c	Asia (Indian Subcontinent)
Murina huttoni (Peters 1872)	LR: nt	Asia (Indian Subcontinent, Southeast Asia)
Murina leucogaster Milne-Edwards 1872	LR: lc	Asia (Indian Subcontinent, Southeast Asia)
Murina puta Kishida 1924	VU: A2c	Asia
Murina rozendaali Hill and Francis 1984	LR: nt	Asia (Southeast Asia only)
Murina ryukyuana Maeda and Matsumara 1998	DD**	Asia
Murina silvatica Yoshiyuki 1983	LR: nt	Asia
Murina suilla (Temminck 1840)	LR: lc	Asia (Southeast Asia only)
Murina tenebrosa Yoshiyuki 1970	CR: B1 + 2c, D **	Asia
Murina tubinaris (Scully 1881)	LR: lc	Asia (Indian Subcontinent and Southeast Asia only)
Murina ussuriensis Ognev 1913	EN: A2c	Asia
Subfamily Miniopterinae		
***Miniopterus* (14 species)**		
Europe, Africa (North Africa, Subsaharan Africa, Malagasy Subregion), Arabian Peninsula, Asia (Indian Subcontinent, Southeast Asia, New Guinea), Australia, Oceania		
Miniopterus australis Tomes 1858	LR: lc	Asia (Southeast Asia and New Guinea only), Australia, Oceania
Miniopterus fraterculus Thomas and Schwann 1906	LR: nt	Africa (Subsaharan Africa only)
Miniopterus fuscus Bonhote 1902	VU: A2c	Asia (Southeast Asia, New Guinea)
Miniopterus gleni Peterson, Eger, and Mitchell 1995	LR: nt**	Africa (Malagasy Subregion only)
Miniopterus inflatus Thomas 1903	LR: lc	Africa (Subsaharan Africa only)
Miniopterus magnater Sanborn 1931	LR: lc	Asia (Indian Subcontinent, Southeast Asia, New Guinea)
Miniopterus majori Thomas 1906	DD**	Africa (Malagasy Subregion only)
Miniopterus manavi Thomas 1906	DD**	Africa (Malagasy Subregion only)
Miniopterus medius Thomas and Wroughton 1909	LR: lc	Asia (Southeast Asia and New Guinea only)
Miniopterus minor Peters 1866	LR: nt	Africa (Subsaharan Africa and Malagasy Subregion only)
Miniopterus pusillus Dobson 1876	LR: lc	Asia (Indian Subcontinent, Southeast Asia, ? New Guinea), Oceania
Miniopterus robustior Revilliod 1914	EN: B1 + 2c	Oceania
Miniopterus schreibersii (Kuhl 1817)	LR: nt	Europe, Africa (North Africa, Subsaharan Africa, Malagasy Subregion), Arabian Peninsula, Asia (Indian Subcontinent, Southeast Asia, New Guinea), Australia
Miniopterus tristis (Waterhouse 1845)	LR: lc	Asia (Southeast Asia and New Guinea only), Oceania
Subfamily Tomopeatinae		
***Tomopeas* (1 species)**		
South America		
Tomopeas ravus Miller 1900	VU: A2c, D2	South America
FAMILY MYSTACINIDAE (one genus, two species)		
New Zealand		
***Mystacina* (2 species)**		
New Zealand		
Mystacina robusta Dwyer 1962	EX	New Zealand
Mystacina tuberculata Gray 1843	VU: A2c, C2a	New Zealand

FAMILY MOLOSSIDAE (12 genera, 90 species)
North and Central America, Caribbean, South America, Europe, Africa (North Africa, Subsaharan Africa, Malagasy Subregion), Arabian Peninsula, Asia (Indian Subcontinent, Southeast Asia, New Guinea), Australia, Oceania

Chaerephon **(18 species)**
Africa (Subsaharan Africa and Malagasy Subregion only), Arabian Peninsula, Asia (Indian Subcontinent, Southeast Asia, New Guinea), Australia, Oceania

Chaerephon aloysiisabaudiae (Festa 1907)	LR: lc	Africa (Subsaharan Africa only)
Chaerephon ansorgei (Thomas 1913)	LR: lc	Africa (Subsaharan Africa only)
Chaerephon bemmeleni (Jentink 1879)	LR: lc	Africa (Subsaharan Africa only)
Chaerephon bivittata (Heuglin 1861)	LR: lc	Africa (Subsaharan Africa only)
Chaerephon bregullae (Felten 1964)	LR: nt	Oceania
Chaerephon chapini J. A. Allen 1917	LR: nt	Africa (Subsaharan Africa only)
Chaerephon gallagheri (Harrison 1975)	CR: B1 + 2c	Africa (Subsaharan Africa only)
Chaerephon jobensis (Miller 1902)	LR: lc	Asia (?Southeast Asia and New Guinea only), Australia, Oceania
Chaerephon johorensis (Dobson 1873)	LR: nt	Asia (Southeast Asia only)
Chaerephon leucogaster (Grandidier 1869)	DD**	Africa (Malagasy Subregion only)
Chaerephon major (Trouessart 1897)	LR: lc	Africa (Subsaharan Africa only)
Chaerephon nigeriae Thomas 1913	LR: lc	Africa (Subsaharan Africa only), Arabian Peninsula
Chaerephon plicata (Buchanan 1800)	LR: lc	Asia (Indian Subcontinent, Southeast Asia)
Chaerephon pumila (Cretzschmar 1826)	LR: lc	Africa (Subsaharan Africa and Malagasy Subregion only), Arabian Peninsula
Chaerephon pusilla (Miller 1902)	VU: D1 + 2	Africa (Malagasy Subregion only)
Chaerephon russata J. A. Allen 1917	LR: lc	Africa (Subsaharan Africa only)
Chaerephon solomonis Troughton 1931	LR: nt	Oceania
Chaerephon tomensis Juste and Ibanez 1993	VU: A2c, D2	Africa (Subsaharan Africa only)

Cheiromeles **(2 species)**
Asia (Southeast Asia only)

Cheiromeles parvidens Miller and Hollister 1921	LR: nt	Asia (Southeast Asia only)
Cheiromeles torquatus Horsfield 1824	LR: nt	Asia (Southeast Asia only)

Eumops **(8 species)**
North and Central America, Caribbean, South America

Eumops auripendulus (Shaw 1800)	LR: lc	Central America, Caribbean, South America
Eumops bonariensis (Peters 1874)	LR: lc	Central and South America
Eumops dabbenei Thomas 1914	LR: lc	South America
Eumops glaucinus (Wagner 1843)	LR: lc	North and Central America, Caribbean, South America
Eumops hansae Sanborn 1932	LR: lc	Central and South America
Eumops maurus (Thomas 1901)	VU: A2c, D2	South America
Eumops perotis (Schinz 1821)	LR: lc	North and Central America, Caribbean, South America
Eumops underwoodi Goodwin 1940	LR: nt	North and Central America

Molossops **(7 species)**
Central America, Caribbean, South America

Molossops abrasus (Temminck 1827)	LR: nt	South America
Molossops aequatorianus Cabrera 1917	VU: A2c, D2	South America
Molossops greenhalli (Goodwin 1958)	LR: lc	Central America, Caribbean, South America
Molossops mattogrossensis Vieira 1942	LR: nt	South America
Molossops neglectus Williams and Genoways 1980	LR: nt **	South America
Molossops planirostris (Peters 1865)	LR: lc	Central and South America
Molossops temminckii (Burmeister 1854)	LR: lc	South America

Molossus **(7 species)**
Central America, Caribbean, South America

Molossus ater E. Geoffroy 1805	LR: lc	Central America, Caribbean, South America
Molossus aztecus Saussure 1860	LR: nt	Central America
Molossus bondae J. A. Allen 1904	LR: lc	Central and South America
Molossus coibensis J. A. Allen 1904	LR: nt	Central and South America
Molossus molossus (Pallas 1766)	LR: lc	Central America, Caribbean, South America
Molossus pretiosus Miller 1902	LR: lc	Central and South America
Molossus sinaloae J. A. Allen 1906	LR: lc	Central America, Caribbean, South America

Mops **(15 species)**
Africa (Subsaharan Africa and Malagasy Subregion only), Arabian Peninsula, Asia (Southeast Asia only)

Mops brachypterus (Peters 1852)	LR: lc	Africa (Subsaharan Africa only)
Mops condylurus (A. Smith 1833)	LR: lc	Africa (Subsaharan Africa and ?Malagasy Subregion only)
Mops congicus J. A. Allen 1917	LR: nt	Africa (Subsaharan Africa only)

Mops demonstrator (Thomas 1903)	LR: nt	Africa (Subsaharan Africa only)
Mops leucostigma (Allen 1918)	DD**	Africa (Malagasy Subregion only)
Mops midas (Sundevall 1843)	LR: lc	Africa (Subsaharan Africa and Malagasy Subregion only), Arabian Peninsula
Mops mops (de Blainville 1840)	LR: lc	Asia (Southeast Asia only)
Mops nanulus J. A. Allen 1917	LR: lc	Africa (Subsaharan Africa only)
Mops niangarae J. A. Allen 1917	CR: B1 + 2c	Africa (Subsaharan Africa only)
Mops niveiventer Cabrera and Ruxton 1926	LR: lc	Africa (Subsaharan Africa only)
Mops petersoni (El Rayah 1981)	LR: nt	Africa (Subsaharan Africa only)
Mops sarasinorum (Meyer 1899)	LR: nt	Asia (Southeast Asia only)
Mops spurrelli (Dollman 1911)	LR: lc	Africa (Subsaharan Africa only)
Mops thersites (Thomas 1903)	LR: lc	Africa (Subsaharan Africa only)
Mops trevori J. A. Allen 1917	LR: nt	Africa (Subsaharan Africa only)

***Mormopterus* (11 species)**

Caribbean, South America, Africa (Subsaharan Africa and Malagasy Subregion only), Asia (Southeast Asia and New Guinea only), Australia, ?Oceania

Mormopterus acetabulosus (Hermann 1804)	VU: B1 + 2c	Africa (Subsaharan Africa and Malagasy Subregion only)
Mormopterus beccarii Peters 1881	LR: lc	Asia (Southeast Asia and New Guinea only), Australia
Mormopterus doriae K. Andersen 1907	VU: A2c	Asia (Southeast Asia only)
Mormopterus jugularis (Peters 1865)	VU: A2c	Africa (Malagasy Subregion only)
Mormopterus kalinowskii (Thomas 1893)	VU: A2c, D2	South America
Mormopterus minutus (Miller 1899)	VU: A2c	Caribbean
Mormopterus norfolkensis (Gray 1840)	LR: lc	Australia, ?Oceania
Mormopterus petrophilus (Roberts 1917)	LR: lc	Africa (Subsaharan Africa only)
Mormopterus phrudus (Handley 1956)	EN: B1 + 2c	South America
Mormopterus planiceps (Peters 1866)	LR: lc	Asia (New Guinea only), Australia
Mormopterus setiger Peters 1878	LR: lc	Africa (Subsaharan Africa only)

***Myopterus* (2 species)**

Africa (Subsaharan Africa only)

Myopterus daubentonii Desmarest 1820	DD	Africa (Subsaharan Africa only)
Myopterus whitleyi (Scharff 1900)	LR: lc	Africa (Subsaharan Africa only)

***Nyctinomops* (4 species)**

North and Central America, Caribbean, South America

Nyctinomops aurispinosus (Peale 1848)	LR: lc	Central and South America
Nyctinomops femorosaccus (Merriam 1889)	LR: lc	North and Central America
Nyctinomops laticaudatus (E. Geoffroy 1805)	LR: lc	Central America, Caribbean, South America
Nyctinomops macrotis (Gray 1840)	LR: lc	North and Central America, Caribbean, South America

***Otomops* (6 species)**

Africa (Subsaharan Africa and Malagasy Subregion only), Asia (Indian Subcontinent, Southeast Asia and New Guinea only)

Otomops formosus Chasen 1939	VU: A2c	Asia (Southeast Asia only)
Otomops johnstonei Kitchener, How, and Maryanto 1992	VU: D2	Asia (Southeast Asia only)
Otomops martiensseni (Matschie 1897)	VU: A2c	Africa (Subsaharan Africa and Malagasy Subregion only), Arabian Peninsula.
Otomops papuensis Lawrence 1948	VU: D2	Asia (New Guinea only)
Otomops secundus Hayman 1952	VU: D2	Asia (New Guinea only)
Otomops wroughtoni (Thomas 1913)	CR: B1 + 2c	Asia (Indian Subcontinent only)

***Promops* (2 species)**

Central America, Caribbean, South America

Promops centralis Thomas 1915	LR: lc	Central America, Caribbean, South America
Promops nasutus (Spix 1823)	LR: lc	Caribbean, South America

***Tadarida* (8 species)**

North and Central America, Caribbean, South America, Europe, Africa (North Africa and Subsaharan Africa only), Arabian Peninsula, Asia (Indian Subcontinent, New Guinea), Australia

Tadarida aegyptiaca (E. Geoffroy 1818)	LR: lc	Africa (North Africa and Subsaharan Africa only), Arabian Peninsula, Asia (Indian Subcontinent)
Tadarida australis (Gray 1839)	LR: nt	Asia (New Guinea only), Australia
Tadarida brasiliensis (I. Geoffroy 1824)	LR: nt	North and Central America, Caribbean, South America
Tadarida fulminans (Thomas 1903)	LR: nt	Africa (Subsaharan Africa only)
Tadarida latouchei Thomas 1920	DD **	Asia (Southeast Asia only)
Tadarida lobata (Thomas 1891)	VU: D2	Africa (Subsaharan Africa only)
Tadarida teniotis (Rafinesque 1814)	LR: lc	Europe, Asia
Tadarida ventralis (Heuglin 1861)	LR: nt	Africa (Subsaharan Africa only)

PART 2

Conservation Issues

Chapter 3

Threats to Microchiropteran Bats

3.1 Population declines

Bat populations in many countries are thought to have declined over the past 50–100 years, although the evidence for such reductions is often circumstantial (Stebbings 1988). There are cases, however, where declines have been well documented. Three examples are the declines in *Rhinolophus* species in Europe, in several species in the USA, and in cave-dwelling *Tadarida brasiliensis* in Mexico.

3.1.1 *Rhinolophus* species in Europe

A total of five *Rhinolophus* species have been recorded in Europe, all of them threatened in some part of their range. *Rhinolophus* species are heavily reliant on caves for at least part of their life cycle and such sites have been subject to increasing disturbance. In the UK, *Rhinolophus ferrumequinum* is reliant on caves for winter hibernation and on buildings with large open roof spaces for breeding. Such buildings are often derelict or semi-derelict and may deteriorate further, or are restored to the detriment of resident bats. The range of *R. ferrumequinum* has contracted over the past 100 years and, although the full extent of the decline is disputed, the population decline is probably over 90% (Stebbings 1988). This species was recorded in southeast England in the early part of the 20th century but is now confined mainly to southwest Britain. However, there have been recent records of isolated individuals that have extended the range eastwards again. In mainland Europe, *R. ferrumequinum* is now rare in many countries. For example, fewer than 250 individuals are thought to occur in Belgium, it is considered critically endangered in Israel, only one nursery colony remains in Luxembourg, and it is probably the most endangered species in Hungary. The species is the subject of a European Action Plan prepared under the Bern Convention. There are similar concerns about *Rhinolophus hipposideros*, although in the UK the population appears to be stable or increasing. *R. hipposideros* is thought to be extinct in The Netherlands and Luxembourg, and critically endangered in Germany. In Switzerland, a drastic decline has been seen since 1940. The three remaining *Rhinolophus* species (*R. blasii*, *R. euryale,* and *R. mehelyi*) are similarly thought to be extinct or seriously threatened in a number of countries.

3.1.2 Declines in the USA

The southern USA and Mexico have some of the largest bat colonies in the world. In some cases, however, the current populations are only a fraction of those thought to have been present in the recent past. *Tadarida brasiliensis* forms the largest known mammalian aggregations, with colonies in Texas currently reaching 20 million (McCracken 1986). However, at some known roost caves, populations declined in the 1950s and 1960s by as much as 99% (Mohr 1972).

In the USA, there are also documented cases of range contraction. The Ozark big-eared bat (*Plecotus townsendii ingens*), which was known from four states including Missouri, is no longer found in that state (Harvey 1980; Hensley and Scott 1995), and *Myotis occultus*, considered in this document to be a synonym of *M. lucifugus*, known originally in California and from a single colony along the Colorado River (Stager 1943), has not been seen in this state since 1967.

Bats may sometimes undergo severe local declines while still maintaining their overall distribution. In the 1950s, population declines in cave-dwelling bats in the eastern USA (Mohr 1952, 1953, 1972) led to the protection of *Myotis grisescens*, *M. sodalis,* and the two eastern subspecies of *Plecotus townsendii* under the US Endangered Species Act. Although each of these species maintained their historic distributions, censuses in the 1970s showed overall declines of 76–89% at *M. grisescens* maternity caves (Tuttle 1979; Rabinowitz and Tuttle 1980), and up to 73% at *M. sodalis* hibernacula (Humphrey 1978). An apparent decline of 50% was recorded for *Myotis austroriparius* in Florida with only five out of a previously known 15 maternity caves occupied in 1991 (Gore and Hovis 1992). Similar declines have been reported for the migrant nectarivorous bats *Leptonycteris* and *Choeronycteris*.

3.1.3 Cave populations in Mexico

Dramatic evidence of declines is provided by a survey of roosts of the Mexican free-tailed bat (*Tadarida brasiliensis*) in northern Mexico in 1991. The information is summarised in Table 2 (information from S. Walker *pers. comm.*).

3.2 Threats

3.2.1 Increasing human population

Most of the threats to bats are directly related to the increasing human population worldwide. An increasing population brings with it extra demands for land, resources, and food, which often results in the degradation or destruction of certain habitat types with a concomitant

Table 2. Declines in populations of cave-dwelling bats in northern Mexico.
*** All estimates of historical populations are very conservative.**

Cave Name	State	Historical Population*	1991 Population	Decline	Cause
La Ojuela	Durango	184,000	0	100%	burning, dynamite, exclusion
Tio Bartola	Nuevo Leon	4,000,000	30,000	99%	burning, mining
La Boca	Nuevo Leon	millions	100,000	95%	mining, tourism
Del Marviri	Sinaloa	940,000	250,000	73%	burning, mining
Del Tigre	Sonora	2,000,000	2,000,000	0%	
El Olmo	Tamaulipas	millions	0	100%	mining, pesticides
El Abra	Tamaulipas	76,000	76,000	0%	
Del Guano	Tamaulipas	440,000	125,000	78%	mining
Quintero	Tamaulipas	567,000	30,000	95%	burning, mining
La Mula	Tamaulipas	303,000	100,000	67%	burning

effect on bat populations. The greatest pressure is often in tropical countries where a large proportion of the human population live in rural areas and have incomes below the poverty line.

In Africa, the human population was estimated at 647 million in 1990 (UN 1989) and this is projected to rise to 1,581 million by the year 2025. Better health care provision in Africa has led to a decline in death rates, but there has not been a corresponding decrease in birth rates. In consequence, the annual percentage increase in population has risen from 2.2% in the period 1950–55 to 3.0% in 1985–90 (UN Department of International Economic and Social Affairs 1989), and is currently increasing more rapidly than that of any other continent. All African countries bar four (Egypt, Morocco, South Africa, and Tunisia) are predicted to at least double their population between 1990 and 2025 (World Resources Institute 1992). The population in five countries (Cameroon, Côte d'Ivoire, Kenya, Tanzania, and Zambia) is predicted to at least triple over the same period. In the Indian Subcontinent the total population is currently 1,160 million (about 20% of the total world population) and this is expected to rise to 2,100 million by 2025 (World Resources Institute 1992). In India alone the population is expected to reach 1,442 million by 2025. In India, the population is very unevenly distributed with over 25% living in two states – Uttar Pradesh and Bihar in the north of the country. The situation is similar in China where the population was estimated at 1,139 million in 1990, growing to an estimated 1,512 million by 2025. Much of the population is concentrated in certain areas, in this case the plains and riverine valleys of the southeast, with the result that 90% of the population inhabits only 15% of the land area (Europa Publications 1987). This results in very heavy pressure on natural resources. Even in the Middle East, populations are estimated to double in the next 20 to 30 years with many countries having growth rates in excess of 3% per year (World Resources Institute 1992).

The rapid increase in human populations in many areas of the world poses the single most serious threat to bat populations. Fenton and Rautenbach (1998) use the example of Zimbabwe to illustrate the consequences of rapidly increasing human populations; since 1900, the population has increased from 0.5 million to over 10 million (Cumming 1991) and in the last 40 years, the rate of land clearance in the Sebungwe District has been about 4% per annum (D.H.M. Cumming *pers. comm.*). This type of increase is likely to have a serious impact on bat populations in this area.

In Central and South America, forested areas are cleared for agriculture. Shifting cultivation has been identified as the major cause of forest loss in this area. Trans-migration, particularly in Brazil, has compounded the effects of shifting cultivation. Large landowners have moved in after shifting cultivators and cleared the land for cattle ranching. Cattle ranching in Latin America is estimated to have occupied 20,000km^2 of forest per year in the late 1970s. Such forest clearance brings with it problems of soil erosion and degradation. Introduction of cattle to large areas of Central and South America has provided vampire bats with a ready food source. As a result, populations have increased bringing with them a range of problems. This is discussed in more detail later in this Chapter.

In Spain, there are examples of the effects of increasing human populations on bats (T. Guillen *pers. comm.*). The Mediterranean lowlands of Spain are the most populated areas of the country and all the river valleys and coastal plains are heavily used for agriculture and industry; these are also favoured bat-foraging habitat. A good example of the threats to bats are in the Mediterranean coastal plains of Valencia and the lowland part of the Jucar River valley. The climate is warm and humid, and the area has a rich abundance of insects. There are also many warm limestone caves. These factors result in a high density of bat colonies in the area. The rich agricultural lands and tourism in this region have produced a very economically active society with intense industrial development. This has, in turn, resulted in heavy pollution, deforestation, and loss of natural lowland vegetation, particularly in the last 20 years. Evidence suggests a severe decline in the local bat fauna. There is a trend towards habitat simplification and a reduction in the diversity and abundance of insects. This may threaten the survival of Spanish populations of *Myotis capaccinii* that are limited mainly to the highly populated Mediterranean lowlands of Valencia. This area contains four of the five known breeding colonies of *M. capaccinii* in Spain. This species is also threatened by other factors, such as disturbance of cave sites and heavy pesticide use in their feeding habitats. These factors are also affecting southern Andalucian populations of *Myotis daubentonii*, particularly those in isolated, drought-affected river valleys.

3.2.2 Habitat destruction and modification

Loss of forests

An additional effect of increasing human populations is increased habitat destruction, most particularly in forested areas. Forests are a key habitat for bats throughout the world. While major areas of forest, such as in Amazonia, remain relatively intact, destruction of rainforest is widespread and many forested areas worldwide are severely threatened. Much attention has been focused on tropical moist forests, but there are similar problems in other tropical and temperate forests. For example, dry forests in the Neotropical region that are found from Mexico to Argentina may be the most threatened of all habitats in this area. In parts of central and eastern Europe, economic pressures have increased the exploitation of old-growth woodlands.

Amazonia is the largest area of tropical moist forest in the world. Most of Amazonia is found within the borders of Brazil, and deforestation has been measured precisely in 1978, 1988, 1989, 1990, and 1991 by Brazil's Instituto Nacional de Pesquisas Espaciais (National Space Research Institute) (INPE) (Fearnside *et al.* 1990, INPE 1992). Overall, over 10% of the approximately four million km^2 of Amazonian forest has been cleared and deforestation has continued at a rate of more than 10,000km^2 per year (Fearnside 1990; Brown and Brown 1992). While these figures are worrying, other areas within South America have suffered even greater losses. In coastal Ecuador, 96% of the forests have been destroyed and only 1% of the coastal dry forest remains. The Atlantic forest region of Brazil is the country's agricultural and industrial heart, and is home to about 43% of the population. It may be the most threatened area of its type in the world (Mittermeier 1988). Originally, the Atlantic forest covered about 1.2 million km^2, but by 1990 over one million km^2 had been lost. Most of the remaining forest is highly fragmented.

In Africa, the loss of tropical moist forest has varied enormously from country to country. The largest remaining area of forest is in the Democratic Republic of Congo where the 1.19 million km^2 represents 67% of the original forest cover. In Gabon, 88% (227,500km^2) of original forest cover still remains, while at the other end of the scale, the 80km^2 in Zimbabwe is only 1% of the original cover. Areas with less than 5% of their original forest cover also include Benin (2.5%), Djibouti and Malawi (3.0%), Burundi and Mozambique (3.9%), and Guinea (4.1%). Countries with more than 50% of their original forest cover include Gabon (88.2%), Somalia (69.8%), Democratic Republic of Congo (66.7%), Equatorial Guinea (65.4%), and Congo (62.4%) (FAO 1988; Sayer *et al.* 1992). Overall, West Africa's forests are being lost at a greater rate than those of any other region (2.1% per annum – World Resources Institute 1992).

In other areas of the world, losses have been equally, if not more dramatic. For example, the forests of Southwest Asia have been exploited for timber for thousands of years. The forests of the East Mediterranean were largely cleared in ancient times and those in Afghanistan in medieval times. It is estimated that the Levantine forests now cover less than 5% of their original area. In the Pacific Northwest of North America, clear-cutting is a common occurrence and less than 10% of the old-growth rainforests survive in small fragments scattered throughout the area. In Mexico, there are no definitive statistics on deforestation rates, but a recent review gives some information (Masera *et al.* 1992). In the mid-1980s, over 8,000km^2 of closed forests were lost each year – an overall rate of 1.56% per year. This makes Mexico the country with the world's third highest rate of deforestation, behind Brazil and Indonesia. Forest loss has impacted temperate coniferous and broad-leaved, and tropical evergreen and deciduous forests. In Australia, approximately 40% of forests have been cleared since European settlement in 1788 and a further 40% have been modified by logging (State of the Environment Advisory Council 1996). Large tracts of woodland and forest have been cleared for agriculture and, at current logging rates, it has been suggested that no unlogged forest will be left in timber production tenures by 2015 (Resource Assessment Commission 1991). The area of forest remaining is approximately 400,000km^2, about 80,000km^2 of which is in conservation reserves (Lunney 1991). In southeast Alaska, over 42% of the most productive forests had been logged by 1990 (United States Department of Agriculture 1991, 1993) and extensive harvesting continues. Five species of bats occur in southeastern Alaska's coniferous rainforests and studies of bat activity make it clear that conservation of old-growth forest and riparian habitats is essential for the continued viability of the bat community (Parker *et al.* 1995). In these areas, neither clearcuts nor second-growth forests provide the necessary habitat characteristics essential for most bats in the summer. Even selective logging operations can be very problematic, with the extraction process more damaging than the felling operation itself (Crome *et al.* 1991). In Spain, old riparian forests are the only woodlands left in the heavily deforested areas that are now mainly used for agriculture. There is now great pressure to use these riverine lands for *Populus* forestry and there is no legislation protecting these areas. The old riparian forests are vital for bats in these areas, as they are the only source of roosts for tree-dwelling species (T. Guillen *pers. comm.*).

The above figures do not necessarily tell the whole story. While the results of clear-felling are obvious, other forms of degradation can have equally damaging effects, even though the forest cover may broadly remain. Mechanical harvesting techniques may target particular trees, but in the process may damage much surrounding vegetation. For example, in eastern Pará State in Brazil, although only four to eight trees per hectare are saleable, mechanised logging kills or damages 26% of pre-harvest standing trees (Uhl and Viera 1989). So-called selective logging in primary forest can leave between one-third and two-thirds of the residual trees severely damaged if logging operations are not done with adequate care. The opening up of tropical forests can result in the introduction of non-rainforest bat species (Crome and Richards 1988). In temperate eucalypt forests, such as in Australia, the effects are apparently mixed (Richards 1994). From the foraging point of view, the removal of forest or even selective logging may favour species that feed in more open areas to the detriment of those that prefer to feed in more enclosed habitat. This reduces the potential natural faunal diversity of these areas.

Logging activities, particularly the construction of access routes, can open up previously inaccessible sites to a range of groups such as hunters, settlers, and miners, as well as providing areas for agricultural expansion. In Amazonia, road access along the southern and eastern rim almost always sets off an acceleration of deforestation for pastures and subsistence farming.

Loss of key landscape elements

Recent research, particularly in The Netherlands, has highlighted the importance of certain landscape features for bats. Tree lines, hedgerows, and canals are used regularly by bats during flight (Limpens *et al.* 1989; Limpens and Kapteyn 1991; Verboom 1998). Where such elements are abundant there is a dense network of flight paths, whereas in areas with few such features there are few flight paths. Some species, such as *Myotis daubentonii* and *Rhinolophus hipposideros*, will make detours to follow hedgerows rather than cross an open area on the shortest route to a feeding area (Racey 1998). It is possible that this allows feeding en route, as well as acting as an anti-predator strategy. Windbreaks may be particularly attractive as they may provide shelter for insects (Gaisler and Kolibac 1992).

This highlights the importance of an integrated approach to bat conservation. Bats clearly use a range of feeding sites and habitats at different times of the year. Although protecting individual roost sites is important, it is equally important to protect foraging habitats and the landscape elements used by bats for commuting (Racey 1998, 2000).

Such landscape features are threatened mainly through changes in agricultural practices. In the UK, for example, many miles of hedgerows have been lost through intensification of agricultural activities. In countries where, until now, agriculture has been practised at a much less intensive level (such as in central and eastern Europe), cultural landscape features may come under threat as agriculture becomes more intensified.

Aquatic habitats

Aquatic features are vital to bats in a number of ways (Racey 1998b). Some species, such as Daubenton's bats (*Myotis daubentonii*), spend much of their time feeding over water. Species such as *Noctilio leporinus* feed on fish, while other species use water features as navigational aids during flight (Verboom 1998). Alteration or complete loss of aquatic habitats is an almost universal threat. Pollution alters the aquatic ecosystem and the insects that associate with it, and thus may affect bats. In some cases, this may actually benefit bats. It has, for example, been suggested that the increase in *M. daubentonii* in Europe can be attributable to a level of eutrophication of waterways, which increases the number of chironomid midges (Kokurewicz 1995). There is some evidence to support this hypothesis (Racey *et al.* 1998). Generally though, pollution is detrimental to bats. Activities such as removal of bankside vegetation from rivers and canalisation may also adversely affect the diversity of insects available as food for bats. In arid and semi-arid regions, the loss of open-water drinking sites and the use of cattle troughs that trap bats are key factors affecting the survival of populations (B. French *pers. comm.*).

Agriculture

Worldwide, agriculture has had a major impact on many habitats. The increasing human population has meant ever increasing demands on agriculture to produce more food. In many countries, this has led to a change from traditional to more intensive agricultural techniques, with greater use of artificial chemicals as fertilisers and pesticides. In Europe, for example, about 50% of the land surface is occupied by arable land, and many habitats have been lost through expanding and developing more efficient agricultural systems. In other areas, land has been cleared to make way for domestic livestock, often resulting in over-grazing of habitats.

Shifting Cultivation

In many tropical countries, the traditional method of farming involves shifting cultivation. A small area of land is cleared and cultivated for a short period, typically two to three years, until the fertility of the plot decreases. The area is then left fallow while the process is repeated elsewhere. Cleared areas are allowed to regenerate before they are cultivated again making the whole process ecologically sustainable. Fallow periods are generally at least 10–15 years. This kind of cultivation is well adapted to tropical moist forest environments and results in a mosaic of habitats from cultivated land to secondary and primary forest patches. However, with increasing human population, fallow periods have shortened and areas that are unsuitable for agriculture have been cleared. The so-called "slash and burn" approach has resulted in the degradation of large areas of land. A recent example of this that has been investigated with respect to bats is in Laos (T. Guillen *pers. comm.*). The nomadic peoples of the Nam Et Highlands burn primary forest in order to plant food crops, and move on to other areas when the primary forest has been exhausted around their settlements. This threatens many of the sensitive and endangered species of bats. Slash and burn practices not only destroy vegetation cover but also kill many individual bats that use tree crevices as roost sites. Dramatic differences were recorded between sites with good vegetation cover and those recently burnt or in secondary cover, with much higher bat abundance and diversity in the former (T. Guillen *pers. comm.*). The highland forest habitats of Southeast Asia are favoured by endemic species such as *Rhinolophus paradoxolophus*, *Myotis annectans*, and *Arielulus aureocollaris*. These kinds of habitats are attractive for human communities as they are suitable for long-term sustainable use for agriculture and grazing, and, as a consequence, are rapidly disappearing. On Madagascar, the slash and burn methods are particularly destructive and it has been calculated that between 1950 and 1985 deforestation in the eastern rainforests amounted to 1,100km² per year (Green and Sussman 1990).

Cultivation of cash crops

The replacement of natural vegetation with cash crops such as oil palm, cocoa, rubber, and coffee is widespread in many tropical countries. These result in monoculture plantations with very low species diversity, which affects the insect fauna available for feeding bats. In Peninsular Malaysia, much of the original forest has been cleared for rubber plantations. Oil palm is now replacing rubber as a leading plantation crop, while in Papua New Guinea coffee is more important. In Africa, vast areas of countries such as Liberia, Ghana, and Nigeria have been planted in this way. In western Ecuador, forests have been devastated by the environmental impacts from large-scale commercial oil-palm and banana plantations. In certain areas of South America, the cash crop is somewhat different. In the cloud forests of Bolivia and Peru, coca is grown, mostly to produce cocaine for the illegal North American and European markets. Similarly, marijuana and opium poppies are grown in Colombia for the export market. This has led to the destruction of huge areas of forest. Attempts to control this activity have had a devastating effect on natural ecosystems both directly by indiscriminate spraying of chemicals from aircraft, and indirectly, since drug growers merely clear more forest for cultivation on steeper slopes in more inaccessible sites.

Overgrazing

The introduction of domestic livestock can have a dramatic effect on ecosystems. In North America, the grasslands that once dominated the central areas have been greatly reduced through overgrazing, agricultural development, and fire suppression. These grasslands are the primary agricultural land in North America and only about 1% of the original prairie ecosystem is still intact (Barbour and Christensen 1993). In the Middle East, overgrazing by goats, sheep, cattle, and camels is one of the principal causes of desertification in the region. In Central and Northern Asia, over-grazing is a serious threat in semi-arid regions, where most of the pasture has been degraded and lost to erosion. In South America, huge areas of the cerrado have been devastated in the last decade by cattle ranching and mechanised agriculture. In 1990, an estimated 56% of the original two million km² was in managed use and 37% under cultivation (Dias 1990). In Africa, large herds of cattle and goats are maintained, and their grazing has a major impact in many areas of woodland, wooded grassland, shrubland, and grassland. Restrictions of movement of animals, along with increases in numbers, have led to severe environmental degradation in some areas. Successful tsetse fly eradication campaigns, such as in the Zambezi Valley, have led to uncontrolled settlement and introduction of domestic cattle, causing the rapid degradation of previously almost untouched vegetation. On small islands, over-grazing can be a major threat to the survival of native ecosystems. For example, on the Canary Islands, over-grazing is the second most important threat in some parts of Gran Canaria and particularly on the island of Fuerteventura, where original forest landscape has been reduced to desert over the centuries.

Collection of fuelwood

In some areas, fuelwood and charcoal provide the major source of domestic energy. In Uganda, 96% of total energy usage is from fuelwood (530,000 m³ of wood and 73,000 tons of charcoal per annum) (ODA 1992a), while in Ghana it is more than 75% (12 million m³ of wood and charcoal in 1985, rising to 15.9 million m³ in 1988 and predicted to reach 17 million m³ by the year 2000) (World Bank 1988; FAO 1991; ODA 1992b). While some of this wood comes from plantations and plots, most comes from natural woodland and forest. As the population increases, collection of fuelwood becomes less selective and, in many areas, this kind of harvesting is unsustainable. In Ghana, according to a World Bank (1988) estimate, fuelwood consumption was predicted to grow by approximately 2.8% between 1986 and 2000. Setting this figure against a decline in wood availability of 0.7%, gave a predicted fuelwood deficit of 11.6 million m^3 by the year 2000. Most of this wood comes from natural ecosystems. In India, more than 80% of the firewood is gathered illegally and increased needs have led to deforestation in some areas. In the Middle East, wood and charcoal are the main energy sources and there is now a major shortage in some areas, such as southwest Arabia and northeastern Afghanistan. The demand, particularly for charcoal, has led to rapid deforestation around towns and cities (World Conservation Monitoring Centre 1988).

Pesticides

While insecticides with low mammalian toxicity have now been produced, such toxic chemicals as DDT (dichloro-diphenyl-trichloroethane) are still widely used in the developing world. Pesticides may also be carried by air to countries no longer applying such chemicals. In Canada, for example, there is evidence of DDT being deposited in lakes from airborne sources (M.B. Fenton *pers. comm.*). There is little information on the effects of these chemicals on bats, but there may be sub-lethal effects that could impair breeding performance (T. Guillen *pers. comm.*). Pesticides aim to reduce insect numbers and diversity, and this may have implications for bat populations.

Continuous declines in numbers, combined with poisoning incidents in colonies of the endangered *Myotis grisescens* located close to areas treated with organochlorine pesticides, have been reported in the USA (Clark *et al.* 1978, 1980; Clark 1981; Clawson and Clark 1989). The impact of insecticides on bat populations in the USA is discussed by Cockrum (1969, 1970) and Reidinger and Cockrum (1978). The use of DDT was implicated in dramatic declines in numbers of Mexican free-tailed bats (*Tadarida brasiliensis*) in the southern USA, though use of this chemical has been banned since 1972. In Australia, build-up of DDT was thought to have been responsible for massive die-offs of *Miniopterus schreibersii*.

In Spain, organochlorine pesticides were heavily used prior to their being banned in the 1970s. Bat research at this time was almost non-existent, so the impacts of such use were unknown. Current studies on *Pipistrellus pipistrellus* show residue levels that may have sub-lethal effects on the animals (T. Guillen *pers. comm.*). There is little information on the sub-lethal or chronic effects of pesticide residues on bats (Clark 1988; Swanepoel *et al.* 1999), but there is evidence of debilitating effects in other mammal groups, such as seals (Reijnders 1986). Since the 1960s, other pesticides such as organophosphates, carbamates, and, more recently, pyrethroids and benzoyl-ureas, have been replacing organochlorines in agricultural use. In Spain, organophosphates are the most widely used pesticides. Theoretically these chemicals degrade rapidly, but adverse effects have been reported in wild birds (Busby *et al.* 1990) and small mammals (Crick 1986). In The Netherlands, pesticide residues are implicated in the decline of pond bats (*Myotis dasycneme*) (Leeuwangh and Voûte 1985).

In many areas of Africa, the prevalence of insect-borne diseases, such as malaria and sleeping sickness, means that pesticides such as DDT are still used (Fenton and Rautenbach 1998). Until recently in Zimbabwe, DDT was used to control tsetse flies, malarial mosquitoes, and agricultural pests. By comparing sprayed with unsprayed areas, McWilliam (1994) showed that spraying increased the mortality in some bats. There were differences in the vulnerability of species related to their roosting habits and foraging behaviour. In affected areas, species such as *Nycteris thebaica* that roosted in large hollow trees and gleaned prey on the ground were more at risk than species such as *Scotophilus* that roosted in small hollows and took airborne prey.

Other agricultural practices may adversely affect bats. In the UK, avermectin anthelminthics and other endectocides used for cattle and sheep may reduce the insect fauna found in dung (Strong 1992). Scaraboid and geotrupid dung beetles are a dominant part of the diet during the summer, autumn, and winter months of the endangered *Rhinolophus ferrumequinum,* and other large bats such as *Nyctalus* and *Eptesicus* species. Juveniles forage independently both before and after weaning, and cattle-grazed permanent pasture close to ancient woodland and adjacent to the roost is probably important for juvenile survival. The use of endectocides in cattle pastured in the vicinity of such roosts could be particularly detrimental to juvenile bats (Duvergé and Jones 1994). Widespread concern about the effects of endectocides on dung fauna and its predators has led to the drafting of a Recommendation to the Bern Convention for further research with a view to restrictions or banning of some types of use.

Fire

Fire plays an important role in some ecosystems, such as African woodlands, wooded grasslands, and grasslands. In Africa, humans have used fire as an ecological tool for at least 150,000 years. Here there are many fire-tolerant species, and many savanna and fynbos species are dependent on fire for their survival in competition with larger species. Occasional fires may also be necessary for the germination of some species. Fire is now commonly used in agriculture as a way of clearing vegetation. While most burning is controlled, some fires can burn unchecked with the result that much of Africa outside the forests, deserts, and areas of densest settlement is regularly burnt. Even moist forests can be burnt, particularly during periods of drought. In India, annual fires are a severe threat to habitat in some areas, such as in *Pinus wallichiana* forest in Bhutan and in subtropical pine forest in Arunachal Pradesh. Similarly, although fire is a major factor in the drier Mediterranean ecosystems in Europe, uncontrolled or deliberately provoked fires destroy large areas each year. The use of pines and *Eucalyptus* in plantations increases this threat, for example in the Serra da Estrêla and elsewhere in Portugal. In Spain, fire is one of the greatest threats to forest cover. In 1994, around 350,000ha, mostly in the Mediterranean regions, were affected by fire. In Valencia, the area most affected in the last 20 years, practically all the important bat roosts have suffered through the burning of surrounding vegetation. This included four out of the five known colonies of *Myotis capaccinii* in Spain (T. Guillen *pers. comm.*). In the West Indies, many plants are not fire-tolerant, so fires are generally more destructive. In these areas, fire is used to clear land for agriculture and settlements, to "clean" undergrowth in forests, and to encourage new growth in savannas and bushland in the dry season for pasturage. Often fires are allowed to spread unchecked. The long-term effect of recent massive forest fires in Indonesia has yet to be appreciated.

In Australia, wildfires are a serious problem. To help manage the intensity of these fires, foresters undertake 'controlled burning', especially in winter. These fires burn at low intensity and reduce the availability of fuel that would otherwise burn during vulnerable periods. These practices appear to rapidly modify the habitat for bats and can have a variety of effects, given that the density and height of understorey influences habitat utilisation by some forest species (Richards 1994).

The use of fire in "slash and burn" agriculture is discussed elsewhere. It should also be stressed that there are natural causes of fire, such as lightning strikes in dry ecosystems. These events are obviously exacerbated in periods of drought, such as during El Niño events. Also, in some cases the methods used to suppress the spread of fire, while effective at reducing the risk, have resulted in loss of biodiversity.

Industrial activities

A range of industrial activities may specifically threaten bat habitats and populations. Quarrying for limestone may result in disturbance to, or destruction of, caves used by bats. Abandoned mines are used as roost sites by bats in many areas of the world. Renewed mining activity may involve the destruction of such sites. Mining techniques generally are environmentally destructive and can involve the use of chemicals, such as mercury, that are highly toxic. In South America, there is increasing concern about the effects of mining for precious metals. Apart from the obvious physical destruction, the chemicals used during the extraction process, such as cyanide, are highly toxic to wildlife. Gold mining is a widespread, though generally small-scale, activity in Amazonia. While direct impact on the forest is small, the process involves the use of mercury, which can cause serious pollution problems in aquatic ecosystems. In the Atacama Desert in Chile, there has been a long history of mining, with current activities concentrating on copper. As well as the disturbance of the land surface and vegetation cover, the dumping of tailings on the coast has led to dramatic decreases in biodiversity in this area. Similar concerns have been expressed in North America, where the creation of large, toxin-laden pools have been responsible for substantial wildlife mortality (Clark and Hothem 1991). In April 1998, the Doñana National Park in southern Spain, one of the most important wetland sites in Europe, was threatened after a dam burst releasing four million m^3 of toxic mining waste, containing heavy metals such as cadmium, mercury, and arsenic, into the ecosystem around the Park. Emergency earthworks prevented much of the waste from entering the Park, but a 2,000ha area adjacent was contaminated (Anon. 1998).

Oil exploration has also caused problems of pollution. The spillage and leakage of oil and creation of sludge ponds is a particular concern, especially in dry areas. There are large reserves of oil as yet untapped and, in areas such as the Andean rainforest, prospecting has already begun. The potential threat from large-scale oil exploration is a cause for serious concern.

The construction of dams for hydroelectric schemes may dramatically alter large areas of habitat, as well as having impacts on river systems. In South America, there is increasing pressure to harness the capacity of rivers such as the Amazon and the Orinoco. In China, the Three Gorges Dam will have a major impact on the ecology of the region with unknown consequences for bat populations.

3.2.3 Roost site disturbance

Loss of trees

The loss of forests and woodlands is a worldwide threat to bats. While clear-felling is an obvious threat, other woodland management techniques can have damaging impacts. The removal of larger, older trees can deprive a woodland of valuable roosting sites for bats. Similarly, the removal of dead or decaying branches from trees can make them less attractive to bats. Initiatives in North America and Europe have designated 'veteran' or 'wildlife' trees to highlight their conservation interest. Different species of trees attract different varieties and numbers of insects. In the UK, a National Bat Habitat Survey in the early 1990s showed that bats tended to forage in edge and linear habitats, and avoided more open and intensively managed habitat types. In woodlands, edges were more strongly selected than openings, and semi-natural broadleaved woodland was more strongly selected than either mixed or coniferous woodland. Although vespertilionid bats in the UK use a variety of habitats, riparian and woodland areas are particularly important (Walsh *et al.* 1995; Walsh and Harris 1996a,b). Woodland cover in the UK declined to around 5% of the total land surface in 1920, but has since increased to around 10% following large reforestation programmes (Racey 1998a). Most of the increase has been in the form of conifers, though broadleaved species have formed an increasing proportion in recent years. The latter increase has mainly come about through financial incentives and a greater appreciation of the value of such trees to insects (Osborne and Krebs 1981; Kennedy and Southwood 1984). There are suggestions that upland forest areas may be more important than previously thought. A good example is shown by *Myotis sodalis* in the USA. In this case, the key habitat was thought to be riparian forest, but the species also relies on upland forest areas which are being lost and thus threatening the long-term survival of the species (G. McCracken *pers. comm.*).

The importance of tree cavities for bats is not always fully appreciated. In North America, for example, most bat species make use of trees, including those commonly associated with buildings. It has been suggested that tree roost fidelity is directly related to roost permanency and inversely related to roost availability (Lewis 1995; Barclay and Brigham 1996). Bats may not be loyal to a specific tree, but to an area containing several roosts. Thus, even trees not heavily used by bats may be important to them.

Loss of buildings or alterations to such sites

Buildings of all types can be crucial to the life histories of some species at all times of year. Species such as the serotine (*Eptesicus serotinus*) roost almost exclusively in houses. In the UK, greater and lesser horseshoe bats (*Rhinolophus ferrumequinum* and *R. hipposideros*) rely on buildings with large open roof spaces to act as nursery sites. In the case of lesser horseshoe bats, preferred buildings tend to be 19th Century with stone walls and slate roofs (Schofield 1996). The destruction or refurbishment of such buildings can affect the survival of local bat populations. Brown long-eared bats (*Plecotus auritus*) roost in buildings more than 100 years old (Entwistle *et al.* 1997). The use of timber treatment chemicals in the roof spaces of buildings is also thought to have had a severe impact on some populations. Such chemicals are used to control various types of wood-boring insects and fungi, and those containing chlorinated hydrocarbons, such as lindane and pentachlorophenol, resulted in the death of bats (Racey and Swift 1986). However, recent formulations use pyrethroids and other chemicals less toxic to mammals. Fear, prejudice, and, sometimes, genuine problems arising from the presence of bats in a building can also result in their destruction or exclusion.

Underground habitats

Underground sites, both natural (e.g., caves) and artificially created (e.g., mines and fortifications), are crucial to the survival of many bat species worldwide. In temperate areas, caves, mines, and other underground structures provide conditions suitable for hibernation, as well as being breeding sites. In tropical areas, the largest aggregations of bats occur in caves. Underground sites are very vulnerable to a range of threats. These include closure, quarrying, guano mining, swiftlet nest collection, caving, tourism, and deliberate disturbance. The threats to karst ecosystems, which are characterised by the presence of caves, has led to the drafting of Guidelines for Cave and Karst Protection under the IUCN World Commission on Protected Areas (Watson *et al.* 1997).

In the past, mineral extraction activities have produced underground sites that are now of key importance to the survival of many species, some highly threatened. Some countries, such as the USA, have large numbers of abandoned mines that provide refuges for bat species and are used all year round (Tuttle and Taylor 1998). Loss of and disturbance to traditional roost sites such as caves, buildings, and trees, has meant that bats have gradually moved into abandoned mines. Current rates of mine closure threaten many summer colonies of bats that may use individual sites for hibernation. Surveys of 6,000 mines in the states of Arizona, California, Colorado, and New Mexico showed between 30% and 70% used by bats, with 10% containing significant colonies (Tuttle and Taylor 1998). In Australia, where there are few natural caves, abandoned mines are important alternative underground roost sites. For example, the endemic and vulnerable ghost bat (*Macroderma gigas*) is heavily reliant on mines, with one site in Northern Territory containing around 15% of the total population. In central Poland, limestone exploitation in one cave has produced a site that is much more suitable for bat hibernation and which is used by 1,500 bats (G. Lesinski *pers. comm.*).

A range of other artificially created underground sites may be used by bats. In western Poland, for example, a series of underground fortifications built in the 1930s has become one of the most important bat hibernation sites in Europe, used by around 30,000 bats. This site now forms the Nietoperek Bat Reserve. In the UK, abandoned railway and canal tunnels are used by hibernating bats, with one canal tunnel containing the largest winter aggregation in the country.

Mining and quarrying activities

Current mining activities may often be highly detrimental to bats. A colony of the vulnerable ghost bat (*Macroderma gigas*) in an abandoned gold mine at Pine Creek in Northern Territory in Australia is threatened as the area had been earmarked for open cut mining; only the low value of the ore has prevented this from taking place. However, this situation could easily change in the future (Richards and Hall 1998). Two type localities for species in Australia (*Taphozous troughtoni* and *Chalinolobus dwyeri*) have been lost through mining or other activities. In the USA, current mining practices destroy old mines and create open pits as opposed to underground workings. Closure of abandoned mines, for example for safety reasons, may have serious consequences for bat populations. In Wisconsin in the USA, more than 600,000 bats of four species were saved because two mines were surveyed and protected from closure (Tuttle and Taylor 1998). Conversely, in New Jersey, the state's largest population of hibernating bats was inadvertently trapped in Hibernia Mine when it was capped. Thankfully, pressure from biologists ensured it was immediately re-opened. The colonial habits of many bat species makes them especially vulnerable to mine closures. Some threatened species in the USA have been found in mines in numbers of up to 100,000. The danger of killing very large numbers of bats through mine closure is greatest in the northern Midwest from the Dakotas to Wisconsin and Michigan, as well as farther north into Canada (Tuttle and Taylor 1998).

Quarrying activities are one of the main threats to caves. For example, Samanar Hill near Madurai in southern India is honeycombed with caves that are used by many species of bats. Years of nearby stone quarrying and dynamiting has altered the rainfall catchment area, with the result that the water table has receded. Only the cancelling of new quarrying leases has saved the site (Murphy 1987a). In Australia, quarrying activities have threatened a number of species (Richards and Hall 1998). Large colonies of the ghost bat have been threatened by limestone quarrying in Queensland.

Guano mining

The larger cave roosts of bats produce substantial quantities of guano. This can be a valuable resource, particularly in developing communities, where it is collected and used as fertiliser. For example, at Niah Cave in Sarawak on the island of Borneo, the Sarawak Museum operates a guano cooperative. The guano is used on Sarawak's black pepper fields. With the availability of more reliable commercial fertilisers, the large-scale commercial use of bat guano has declined in Sarawak and probably other areas of Borneo (MacKinnon *et al.* 1996). The careless collection of guano and cave swiftlet nests at Niah Cave has damaged the archaeological potential of the cave, and has affected the invertebrate fauna (Francis 1987). Unless it is properly controlled, the process of collecting can also disturb bat communities, as has been shown at Carlsbad Cavern in New Mexico (Geluso *et al.* 1987).

Bird nest collection

In some areas, bats share caves with cave swiftlets. For example, in Borneo at least four species of swiftlets breed in caves. Bornean cave swiftlets live in colonies of up to one million or more and build their cup-shaped nests on rocky ledges. Edible nests are produced by the black-nest and white-nest swiftlets. The hardened saliva used in these nests is highly prized for the famous bird's nest soup and Chinese traders have been visiting Borneo for over 1,000 years to buy bird's nests (Medway 1957). Though nests are collected only at certain times of the breeding season, there is considerable loss of young and eggs. Nests are collected by climbing bamboo poles or ladders and removing the nests with knives, the whole activity illuminated by flaming torches (Medway 1960, Francis 1987). The nests of the less common white-nest swiftlet are most prized and can command a price of $1,200 per kg. Edible bird's nests are a valuable export from Indonesia, with more than 62,000 kg exported in 1983 (de Beer and McDermott 1989). The value of the trade in exported bird's nests from Sabah has been estimated at $1 million a year (Francis 1987). Though nest collecting should be sustainable, there is evidence from caves, such as Gomantong and Niah, that swiftlet populations are declining (Francis 1987). The total harvest of nests of black-nest swiftlets from Gomantong, Batu Timbang, and Madai, the only Sabah caves to produce significant numbers, is now only about 15,000 kg, whereas the total exports of nests of black-nest swiftlets from Sabah in 1977 and 1978 reached 24,000 kg per year (Francis 1987). Since 1987, all nest collecting at Niah has been banned, though it continues virtually unmonitored in other areas of Borneo (MacKinnon *et al.* 1996). Efforts to restrict the trade have been addressed through CITES (Convention on International Trade in Endangered Species of Wild Fauna and Flora).

Bats sharing caves with swiftlets may be disturbed through nest-collecting activities and increasing pressure on this valuable resource may seriously threaten bat populations. In Sarawak, there has been a dramatic decline in the size and number of colonies of naked bats (*Cheiromeles torquatus*). A survey of seven colonies identified through museum specimens and old publications showed that five had been abandoned. The two extant colonies (Niah and Mulu) had reduced numbers. Niah had gone from 30,000 in the 1950s (Medway 1958) to just over 1,000 in 1992, while evidence suggested that only a small colony of less than 50 still existed at Mulu (L.S. Hall *pers. comm.*). The cave sites where these bats had disappeared were shared with cave swiftlets. Despite attempts to control the harvest of nests, the current over-exploitation will eventually lead to the collapse of the swiftlet nest industry. The collectors of nests also harvest naked bats for human consumption at a higher rate than the population can sustain. The five out of seven sites from which naked bats have disappeared now only support small numbers of swiftlets (L.S. Hall *pers. comm.*).

Caving

Caving is becoming an increasingly popular sport, and regular discoveries of new caves or extensions to current systems may increase the potential of disturbance to bats using such sites. While there are large numbers of caving groups which could be involved in attempts at controlling disturbance to key sites, there are also many individuals who do not belong to such groups. This can make the control of disturbance a difficult task. In the UK, collaboration between bat conservation groups and those involved in caving and underground archaeology led to the publication of a code of conduct for all visitors to underground sites (Hutson *et al.* 1995). This suggested the grading of sites according to their importance for bats and threat from disturbance. Similar agreements have been made in Switzerland and the USA. In Australia, there is a Minimal Impact Caving Code, formulated by the Australian Speleological Foundation in 1985 (Watson *et al.* 1997). In Spain, as in other countries, speleology has become more popular over the last 20 years. There are now hundreds of speleological groups in the country (T. Guillen *pers. comm.*). The number of occasional speleologists exceeds those registered with societies, and wild cave tours are offered by some tourism companies. Few of these activities are controlled, with the result that there is an almost continuous human presence in sites throughout Spain leading to disturbance threats to bats that use caves. In Basaura cave, a popular caving destination in Navarra in north-central Spain, a survey of usage showed that at least 1,000 people a year visited the site (T. Guillen *pers. comm.*).

Tourism

Some of the more spectacular caves worldwide have been affected through development for tourism. About 20 million people visit tourist caves globally every year. Mammoth Cave in Kentucky in the USA alone receives two million visitors a year. There are around 650 tourist caves worldwide not counting those used for 'wild' tours (Watson *et al.* 1997). Often economic factors underlay the development of these sites and efforts to preserve the habitat within them is minimal. Air currents may be modified, doors and lights installed, and the frequency of visits is high (T. Guillen *pers. comm.*). This can lead to an extreme modification of the cave environment and exclusion of bats. In Spain, touristic developments of caves have, in general, been disastrous for bats. At least 10 large caves containing bats have been lost in Andalucia and Valencia in the last 20 years. If carried out sympathetically, touristic developments can be compatible with conservation of the cave environment. In Spain, Pileta Cave in Cadiz Province is a rare example of this (T. Guillen *pers. comm.*). In the tropics, cave exploitation for tourism has caused abandonment or severe reduction in bat numbers, and this has sometimes occurred where bats were the object of the tourism. The emergence period of bats from Khao Luuk Chang Bat Cave in Thailand was reduced from 20–40 minutes to about seven minutes during a period when the guides were entering the cave to demonstrate the bats, but the bat population has recovered following better control of tourist activity. Carlsbad Cavern, New Mexico, is an example of carefully controlled tourism and an arena has been built outside the cave to allow tourists to watch the evening emergence. In Texas, Bat Conservation International and the Texas Nature Conservancy collaborated to develop a management plan for Eckert James River Cave to ensure the long-term survival of the resident population of Mexican free-tailed bats (*Tadarida brasiliensis*), one of the top 10 sites for this species. This included a nature trail and provision of educational materials (Morton 1990).

Deliberate disturbance

Bats using underground sites may be deliberately disturbed during eradication campaigns, such as those against vampire bats in South America. In Israel, caves containing fruit bats were fumigated following the bats' implication in incidences of damage to fruit orchards (Makin and Mendelssohn 1986, 1987). This resulted in deaths of fruit bats, as well as many insectivorous species using the sites. Acts of vandalism against bats are relatively rare, but can be very destructive. In the USA, four men in Kentucky were convicted for the deliberate killing of several hundred bats in Thornhill Cave in 1987. The dead bats included 66 endangered Indiana bats (*Myotis sodalis*) (Murphy 1987b). Declines in populations of *Tadarida brasiliensis* in Eagle Creek Cave in Arizona may have been partially attributable to deliberate disturbance. The cave is accessible to those with four-wheel-drive vehicles, horses, or the energy to walk four miles, and the cave entrance and trail leading to it are conspicuous and littered with shell cases (McCracken 1986).

Sealing of caves and mines

Concerns over public safety or a desire to protect important artefacts have led to the sealing of underground sites. In most cases, such action is not a deliberate attempt to exclude bats since their presence may not be known. The construction of concrete walls, doors, grilles with vertical bars may all exclude bats, either through the provision of a physical barrier or through alterations to the internal environment. In Spain, archaeological activities have resulted in exclusions of bats in at least five caves in Valencia and Andalucia (T. Guillen *pers. comm.*). Also in Spain (as in the UK and the USA), there are laws that force landowners to seal mines that are no longer in use for safety reasons. This may take place many years after mining has ceased, when the sites are occupied by bats. A recent project to halt the leaching of metallic and sulphur residues from old mines into rivers in the north of Huelva Province in Spain resulted in the blocking of some very important roosts of the endangered *Rhinolophus mehelyi*. Strategies for the treatment of disused mines to take bat use into account have been developed in the USA and UK. In the USA, Bat Conservation International's Bats and

Mines Project explains the importance of abandoned mines as roosting sites for bats, and provides practical information on mine assessment techniques and closure methods that protect both bats and people. BCI has held a number of regional workshops where participants can learn gating techniques, how to assess mines for the presence of bats, and such workshops provide an important opportunity for networking. BCI has also signed a Memorandum of Understanding with the U.S. Bureau of Mines to ensure long-term protection of sites (Taylor 1995).

The protection of caves and mines with grilles, even when undertaken for the conservation of their bats, at times has itself led to declines or abandonment. Such activities have to be done with careful consideration of the nature of the site and the requirements of the bat species using it (Rodrigues 1996, Tuttle and Taylor 1998).

3.2.4 Health issues

Rabies

A comprehensive review of bats and rabies is given by Brass (1994), while Greenhall and Schutt (1996), Greenhall and Schmidt (1988), Greenhall *et al.* (1983, 1984) and Turner (1975) focus specifically on vampire bats. The phylogeny of rabies viruses in the USA and the human incidents attributable to different strains is discussed in Smith *et al.* (1995).

The rabies virus has been recorded in most areas of the world. It is most regularly recorded in wild and domestic carnivores such as dogs, foxes, raccoons, and skunks. Worldwide, more than 30,000 human deaths a year are attributable to rabies, principally following bites from rabid dogs in Asia (Brass 1994). Insectivorous bats may also act as vectors of the rabies virus, though they are of minor significance when compared to carnivores. In Latin America, vampire bats are significant vectors of the rabies virus and may have considerable local impact on livestock populations. Their impact on humans is greater than for insectivorous bats, though still minor in terms of overall cases from other sources. Rabies in insectivorous bats is widespread in the USA and Canada, and infection with European Bat lyssaviruses (rabies-related viruses) has recently been recognised widely in Europe. Limited reports exist from Africa and Asia. Australian Bat lyssavirus has recently been described from fruit bats and a sac-winged bat in Australia (Fraser *et al.* 1996; Hooper *et al.* 1997; Gould *et al.* 1998).

The significance of human rabies of bat origin can be gauged by examining certain figures. Between 1953, when rabies was first confirmed in bats in the USA, and 1990, there were only 20 cases of rabies attributed to a virus of bat origin. A further eight cases in the rest of the world could be attributed to insectivorous bats. In Latin America, a total of 471 cases of human rabies following the bite of a vampire bat were recorded between 1929 and 1990, an average of seven to eight cases a year. Thus, between 1929 and 1990 around 500 deaths from rabies worldwide could be attributable to bats and this should be compared to the figure of 30,000 deaths *per year* given above.

The implications for livestock are more serious and economically more significant. Rabies in livestock has often led to ill-conceived and highly damaging vampire-bat control programmes that have impacted many non-target species. These issues are discussed in more detail below.

Vampire bats

There are only three species of vampire bats and all occur in Latin America. *Desmodus rotundus*, the common vampire bat, is the most common and widespread species, occurring from eastern and western Mexico southward through Central America and much of South America to Uruguay, northern Argentina, and central Chile. In the West Indies, it is only found on Trinidad. This species feeds mainly on the blood of livestock (cattle, equines, goats, sheep, and pigs), poultry, and occasionally humans. It is the species of most significance in terms of rabies. The other two vampire bats are much rarer. *Diaemus youngi*, the white-winged vampire bat, has been recorded from northeastern Mexico south through eastern Mexico, Central America, and Panama. In South America, its range extends across the Amazon Basin and the Guianas south to northern Argentina and southwestern Brazil. It does not occur west of the Andes south of Colombia. In the West Indies, it is found on Trinidad and Margarita. Its primary food source is avian blood, though mammalian blood is sometimes taken. *Diphylla ecaudata*, the hairy-legged vampire bat, is recorded from the southern USA southward through eastern Mexico and most of Central America, to South America at least as far as Peru and southern Brazil. This species appears to feed only on avian blood.

Vampire bats and threats to livestock

Populations of vampire bats have increased sharply in areas of Latin America to which European livestock have been introduced. For example, in northeast Argentina, vampire bat populations are almost twice as large in cattle-raising ecosystems as in natural ecosystems (Delpietro *et al.* 1992). Turner (1975) observed that the average cow received visits from 10.5 bats per evening, with the resultant loss of at least 0.25 litre of blood. According to Goodwin and Greenhall (1961), a vampire bat may be responsible for as much as 26 litre of blood loss annually. This is potentially very debilitating. Vampire bats also have the potential to spread disease, most significantly bovine paralytic rabies. An estimated population of approximately 70 million head of cattle exist within the range of vampire bats (Acha 1986). Recent estimates are that an average of 100,000 head of cattle (0.15%) die from rabies annually, representing an economic loss of about $30 million (Acha and Arambulo 1985).

Wounds caused by vampire bats may also be vulnerable to secondary infections, particularly by screw-worm (*Cochliomyia hominivorax*).

This economic impact together with the small, but significant, threat to humans from rabies carried by bats has led to a range of control methods being implemented.

Vampire bat control methods

Vampire bat control programmes have involved a range of methods, including: protective measures to prevent vampire bites; pre-exposure rabies prophylaxis in the case of animals and humans at risk (e.g., bat workers, control operators, and vets); post-exposure prophylaxis in the case of humans; and destruction of bats in the wild, both in their natural habitats and in the vicinity of livestock.

The prophylatic vaccination of cattle can be very effective at protecting animals against rabies. Some vaccines protected 100% of immunised cattle three years after vaccination (Arellano-Sota 1988). However, cost and a reluctance from farmers to use vaccines until cattle have been infected, have limited the effectiveness of such schemes.

Reduction of vampire bat populations has been approached in one of two principal ways. These have centred either on the destruction of bats in their wild environment or on poisoning bats in the vicinity of cattle. Population reduction takes advantage of the low reproductive potential of vampire bats, which have a gestation of about seven months and give birth to a single offspring. A variety of techniques have been used, some more effective than others (Greenhall, 1963, 1970, 1974, 1985; Linhart, 1975). These have included: 1. the use of firearms with scatter-shot cartridges; 2. electrocution of bats in caves; 3. smoke and fire, often effective at driving bats from hollow trees and caves (e.g., during World War II, American armed forces used flame-throwers to kill cave-dwelling bats in Trinidad); 4. dynamite, gasoline bombs, and poison gas – especially Rhodiatrox (a phosphorus-based compound) and cyanide gas; and 5. biological warfare – Abello Fernandez (1966) reported the destruction of 5,000 vampire bats in Colombia by infecting them with Newcastle disease via airborne instillation of atomised virus. Such an approach is highly indiscriminate and potentially dangerous to humans and poultry. All of these methods share the disadvantage of being non-selective. Greenhall (1970) identified several species of bats that roost in association with vampires. The needless destruction of these species may have far-reaching ecological and public-health ramifications.

Other methods have targeted bats while they are in the process of attacking cattle. These have principally involved the use of poisons, such as strychnine and arsenic, and various anti-coagulants.

Poisons can be applied directly to wounds to take advantage of vampire bats' habit of returning to old wounds. Strychnine has been used effectively in this manner on cattle, goats, sheep, mules, donkeys, and poultry (de Verteuil and Urich 1936; Greenhall 1963). Arsenic has been used in a similar fashion. Although thc method is effective, it can pose serious health risks to both livestock and workers applying the poisons.

Vampire bats are very sensitive to anti-coagulants, such as diphenadione, which can be injected directly into the rumen of adult cattle at doses that have little observable effect on the animal, but are sufficient to kill bats. In one large herd in Nicaragua, such administration of anticoagulants reduced the number of bites sustained by the herd of 212 head of cattle by more than 99%, from 1,560 to seven per day (Brass 1994). The disadvantages of this method include its short period of effectiveness (three days), its toxicity to calves, and the fact that only ruminants can be treated. Intramuscular administration of warfarin, a potent anti-coagulant found in rat poisons, has also proven effective. Because of its ease of administration, it may be the most practical method of control.

Anti-coagulants may be applied directly to vampire bats in their roosts and are rapidly spread through the colony by mutual grooming. However, this method can affect non-target species and it has been recommended that its use be discontinued (T.J. McCarthy *pers. comm.*). Anticoagulants may also be applied in the form of a paste to the open wounds of cattle or to the backs of individual vampires. Under field conditions, the application of paste to wounds significantly reduced the number of vampire bites sustained by cattle in three heavily attacked herds after 15 days (Flores-Crespo and Arellano-Sota 1991). The use of anti-coagulant pastes applied to a bat's back is very efficacious in reducing vampire bat populations, and T.J. McCarthy (*pers. comm.*) recommends the concurrent use of this and systemic treatments.

The success of a vampire-bat control programme lies in predicting the path of a 'migrating' epizootic of vampire bat rabies. Such 'migrations' often move along paths dictated by ecological, topographical, and geological features. Once the path is known, the propagation of the rabies epizootic can be interrupted by selective destruction of vampire bats between 10–20km ahead of the last known case of bovine paralytic rabies. This method has been successful in several countries, notably Brazil and Venezuela. While anti-coagulants are very effective and generally target only vampires, their potential effect on other species is not fully understood and needs further investigation.

The use of genetically engineered vaccines shows promise. These could be applied orally to vampire bats. Their efficacy in vampires awaits testing.

The possible impact of vampire-bat control methods on non-target species has often not been considered. For example, an estimated 900,000 bats of various species were gassed annually in Venezuela from 1964 to 1966. Pint

(1994) reported that the entrances to various caves in Mexico, which harboured populations of non-vampire species, had been barricaded with chicken wire in attempts to seal in and destroy vampire bats presumed to be present inside. Trees are also used by vampire bats as roosts, and fear has led to the selective burning of old hollow trees, again with the consequent loss of non-target species. It is likely that localised destruction campaigns also take place. McCarthy (1978) recounted that anti-coagulant paste was smeared on randomly collected bats of many species by untrained collectors in Belize, resulting in the needless deaths of many bats. The potentially damaging effects on tropical ecosystems of these types of campaigns need to be appreciated. Many bats play a crucial role in tropical ecosystems and their wholesale loss could have far-reaching effects. It should be stressed that while reducing vampire populations may be acceptable in certain areas, the aim should not be to completely eradicate the species. Greenhall (1968a) stressed that the two major aims of vampire control should be: 1. regulation of population levels of the offending species, rather than indiscriminate destruction of individuals; and 2. protection of non-target species. Lord (1988) takes a similar approach.

Threats to humans from bat-related rabies

Canine rabies poses the most significant threat to humans. In comparison, the threat from bats is relatively minor, but that does not imply it can be ignored. There are several possible routes of transmission of bat rabies. Primary transmission may result directly from a bite (or possibly a scratch) or from inhalation of an infectious aerosol. Secondary transmission may occur following exposure to a terrestrial animal itself infected by a bat, via corneal transplantation from an undiagnosed rabid donor, or possibly by mechanical transmission of short-lived virus in the saliva of a cat or dog that has just had a rabid bat in its mouth.

There have only been four cases of rabies contracted through the inhalation of an infectious aerosol, and this is only likely to be of very minor concern in a few unique underground environments; indeed, authorities still question whether aerosol transmission was the actual mechanism for infection in these cases (Brass 1994). Similarly, there has been only one case of transmission of a non-terrestrial variant of the rabies virus following a corneal transplant. There have been no cases of human rabies following mechanical transfer of the virus.

Primary transmission via a bite is, by far, the most significant route of human exposure to a rabies virus. There are three probable patterns of exposure: 1. the vast majority of bites have occurred when people have handled sick or moribund bats; 2. less common are reports of encounters with bats that have wandered into homes or even been brought in by a family pet; 3. least common are reports of deranged behaviour and seemingly unprovoked aggression.

While there is a threat to human health from bat-inflicted rabies, as mentioned above, this should be put into context. Although the total number of bats reported rabid annually has continued to rise dramatically each year, the percentage of specimens that are confirmed rabid has remained essentially unchanged (Brass 1994). Although the prevalence of the disease may be relatively high (5–10% or more) among suspect submissions, it is generally extremely low (less than 1%) in randomly collected, healthy-looking specimens that have been adequately sampled. Thus, the human health hazards posed by rabid insectivorous bats are extremely low (Brass 1994). In the western Palaearctic, an increase in the recording of rabies-related viruses in bats has caused some concern. However, the recognition of these as separate from terrestrial rabies (the much more prevalent form found particularly in foxes and dogs) and the very low public health risk, coupled with targeted education campaigns, has resulted in minimal adverse reaction from the general public.

The most significant method of transmission of rabies from bats is through bites. In most circumstances, the risk to the public from bat bites is very small. However, it is recommended that those who handle bats regularly should take necessary precautions against being bitten, and should undergo pre-exposure rabies prophylaxis. The general public should be advised to avoid handling bats; this is particularly important if the animal looks sick or is grounded. This advice would be the same for any wild animal. In countries where bat rabies has been recorded or is suspected to occur, anyone being bitten by a bat should seek medical advice.

Vampire bats pose a greater threat to humans than insectivorous species, though again this has to be put into context. Human deaths from vampire-inflicted rabies have been reported from 11 Latin American countries (Trinidad, Mexico, Guyana, Brazil, Suriname, Colombia, Argentina, Bolivia, Peru, El Salvador, and Venezuela). There are an average of seven to eight cases a year (Brass, 1994). These figures are only approximations and an accurate assessment is not available. In recent years, there has been a marked increase in the number of persons bitten by vampire bats, particularly in Peru and Brazil. This, in part, is thought to be associated with clearing of forests, which results in significant ecological disruption of resident wildlife populations (Schneider 1991; Schneider and Uieda 1998). Some activities, such as mining, deforestation, road and dam construction, development of human settlements, and military and guerilla activity, may lead to an increase in human exposure to vampire attacks (Ruiz and Diaz 1990). Areas of forest cleared for the introduction of livestock may attract vampire bats that feed on the cattle and also secondarily expose human populations to greater incidence of bat attacks. Removal, control, or loss of livestock through disease may result in increased human attacks. The feasibility of introducing preventative health measures for populations at risk needs to be assessed. The Pan American World Health Organisation has made recommendations to deal with this issue (PAHO/WHO 1991) which include: 1. delineation of risk factors that would allow identification of human populations at high risk; 2. establishing a surveillance programme in order to systematise the application of pre-exposure rabies prophylaxis in those populations at high risk; 3. investigation of cost/benefit and cost/efficiency models of public health assistance; 4. evaluation of the efficacy of pre- and post-exposure rabies prophylaxis in populations at high risk; 5. ongoing study of vampire bat ecology to help identify human populations at high risk; 6. development of education programmes and investigation of means to disseminate information to isolated communities; and 7. development of educational programmes for health-care workers.

Some of these issues are already being tackled, such as through Bat Conservation International's vampire bat educational programmes. The vampire bat symposium held at the 11th International Bat Research Conference in Brazil in 1998 recognised the importance of many of these issues and issued a Vampire Bat Resolution, described in Chapter 5.

Histoplasmosis

Histoplasmosis is a group of diseases resulting from inhalation of the spores of *Histoplasma capsulatum* , the imperfect state of a fungus of the Ascomycotina (Schwarz 1981; Sacks *et al.* 1986). It occurs in soil, including that with a high nitrogen content such as from the guano of bats and birds. It has been recorded from over 50 countries around the world, with a high incidence of a positive reaction to skin tests in some areas. It has been associated with caves, particularly in the New World and Africa. It has been recorded rarely in Europe and the Middle East (records from Romania, Cyprus, and Israel), Asia (records only from Malaysia), and Australia. It is found principally in dusty bat caves. It may frequently give rise to mild respiratory disorders and is rarely fatal. It is likely that histoplasmosis is the 'cave disease' or 'mine fever' contracted by Mexican guano diggers in the past. A simple precaution is the use of a respirator or mask that can remove particles as small as two microns in diameter.

3.2.5 Persecution

In most cultures bats are frequently considered to be objects of fear. A combination of inaccurate information coupled with perceived risks of damage or disease can lead to deliberate persecution.

House-dwelling species

Buildings, particularly houses, are used by many species of bats worldwide. This can result in conflicts with humans. In Africa, for example, molossid bats (such as *Mops condylurus*, *Chaerephon pumila*, and *Tadarida aegyptiaca*) regularly roost in houses where their presence is frequently not welcomed. Destructive methods, such as fumigation, may be used to deal with such roosts. In North America, the presence of bats in houses may trigger fears about possible risk from diseases such as rabies, though the risk is tiny. In The Netherlands, where a rabies-related virus has been recorded in *Eptesicus serotinus*, successful education campaigns have ensured that roosts of this species have been left undisturbed, even when the bats have tested positive for the rabies virus. Often, however, the concerns are of a more mundane nature concerning smell, noise, and accumulation of droppings. In these cases, a sympathetic approach coupled with education about bats can lead to a positive outcome for both home owner and bats.

Bats in folklore and mythology

Bats appear in the folklore and mythology of many cultures worldwide. There are many folktales around the world relating the cleverness (or deceit) of bats and the uncertainty about their status as birds or mammals. Detailed analyses of the relationships between bats and humans is given in Allen (1939b) and Tupinier (1989). Frequently, they are portrayed in a negative manner. Most commonly, bats have been associated with vampires and witches. The publication of Bram Stoker's *Dracula* in 1897 reinforced the association between bats and vampirism in Europe. In India, there is a very strong vampire tradition with stories of vampire-like creatures wandering between midnight and the early hours of the morning. Though bats are not specifically mentioned in this case, there is an Indian superstition in which bats flying around a house supposedly foretell a death. In the New World, bats were associated with death and darkness by the Mayans. Depictions of bat deities in Mayan culture bear a striking resemblance to leaf-nosed bats of the family Phyllostomidae. Even today, there is continued worship of bat gods in certain areas of Mexico. In South America, there are several stories involving bats sucking blood or eating humans. However, the long-established tradition of a fear of bats influences general perception of their value and can thus be a considerable threat. In other cases, bats are considered symbols of good luck. In the Balkans, dried fragments of bats are carried as talismans. In China, they symbolise happiness or good luck.

3.2.6 Lack of information

Lack of information is one of the greatest, but perhaps least appreciated, threats to bats. Of the 834 species of microchiropteran bats, only a few have been well studied. In Southeast Asia, for example, there is little information about distribution, roosting, and habitat requirements for most bats, and this makes judging which species are threatened or in need of special conservation measures very difficult. Sufficient is known about some species to indicate that they are not endangered (i.e., those that are abundant), but the status of those that are rarely found is hard to judge. Very little is known about species' requirements. Equally little is known about the geographic distribution of bats even in relatively well-studied countries such as Malaysia. For example, there are not yet sufficient data to say whether the bat fauna in primary forest in the south is the same as that in the north (C.M. Francis *pers. comm.*). In some countries, such as Myanmar, Laos, Cambodia, and Viet Nam, information on bats is still limited. There have been recent surveys in Laos (Francis *et al.* 1996, 1997a,b, 1999, Francis and Vonghamheng 1998, Robinson 1997, Robinson and Webber 1998) that have found large numbers of bats of a variety of species, some of which are new records for the country. This suggests that the country is important for bat biodiversity, which would probably be confirmed by more detailed survey work. In Cambodia and Myanmar, political problems within the countries have made it almost impossible to undertake any form of detailed survey work. In Viet Nam, recent surveys have identified sites that are globally important and have provided records of species previously unrecorded in the country (Bates *et al.* 1997). It is likely that further surveys in all these countries will uncover many new records and probably new species. In Africa, many species are rarely recorded and it is impossible to assess reliably the status of species that have only a few records of occurrence. The biology and ecology of most species in Africa is poorly known and there are too few bat biologists who are either interested or properly equipped to undertake such work. Similarly, bats are rarely considered in either environmental policies or educational projects.

In many cases, the only information about a species is based on the original description since it has not been collected subsequently. This naturally makes any conservation planning impossible. Other species, because of their behaviour, are rarely captured during survey work and an assessment of their status is thus very difficult. For example, tree-dwelling species are difficult to study. There is little information on numbers that use such sites, what type of trees are preferred, or their frequency of usage. Frequently, assessment of the status of species has been made in relation to their occurrence in museum collections. This may not reflect the status in the wild, especially for species whose behaviour makes them difficult to sample. Also, museum collections reflect where survey work has taken place. The absence of species in collections may simply reflect a lack of survey work in areas where they occur. For example, *Chaerephon chapini* is a small African molossid that appears to occur widely in savanna woodlands in Ghana, Uganda, Zimbabwe, and Namibia. It is uncommon in museum collections, but at some sites in Zimbabwe, correctly set mist nets regularly produce large numbers of this species. If their status were assessed on the basis of occurrences in museum collections they would be considered rare, but if collection data from Zimbabwe were representative, they would be amongst the most numerous of the molossids (M.B. Fenton *pers. comm.*). Conservation efforts also often focus on species with limited distributions. However, the apparently broad distributions of some species may mask serious local declines, such as with *Miniopterus schreibersii*. Also such species may have large, but patchy distributions because of reliance on particular roost types. In many areas, knowledge of species is patchy across their ranges with no data on viable population levels.

Bats may also undergo seasonal movements, which in some species result in their concentration in a small number of sites at certain times of year. There may also be altitudinal migrations or movements across political boundaries. More information is required about key migration routes and the areas used by bats as stopping-off or resting places. In temperate regions, such studies would help identify key winter hibernation sites. Such issues are being addressed in North America (under the Program for the Conservation of Migratory Bats of Mexico and the United States – PCMM) and Europe (under the Bonn Convention).

Taxonomic uncertainties also make conservation planning difficult. With some families and genera, there are considerable differences of opinion about their taxonomic status. Clearly, whether a taxon is a species or subspecies may have far-reaching implications in terms of planning and legislation. Fenton and Rautenbach (1998) highlight the problem in Africa, where even in common and widespread genera, such as *Pipistrellus* and *Eptesicus,* there are questions about the number of species and their distributions. In Australia, the bat fauna contains a number of 'species' that have been identified in the field, but await formal description. For planning purposes, 'Conservation Units' rather than species are used.

Novel techniques are already being used in systematics to separate taxa that are not separable by traditional methods. For example, mitochondrial DNA and analysis of echolocation calls have been used to establish that one of the most widespread species in Europe, *Pipistrellus pipistrellus*, actually comprises two species, the nominate species and *P. pygmaeus* (Barrett *et al.* 1997; Jones and Barrett 1999). These and other techniques may have far-reaching effects on species recognition and the clarification of higher classification.

Status assessments are a crucial part of assigning categories of threat to bat species, and the current IUCN Red List Categories (IUCN 1994) have introduced a greater degree of quantitative evaluation of species population sizes and recorded or potential declines. As noted by Fenton and Rautenbach (1998), on the African mainland most bat species could be listed as Data Deficient. They give examples of the difficulty of assessing status for African bats. *Chaerephon chapini*, since its original discovery in Uganda, has been found in a progressively wider range of localities suggesting a pattern of distribution typical of woodland bats. But virtually nothing is known of its roosting habits and it is still rare in collections. It may yet prove to be both widely distributed and locally abundant. Even in North America, distribution of bats in many areas is poorly known and when surveys of previously understudied areas are undertaken, new records emerge (Pierson 1998). For example, recent surveys in British Columbia in Canada have extended the known range of several species, most notably *Antrozous pallidus*, *Plecotus townsendii*, *Myotis evotis*, and *M. thysanodes* (Nagorsen and Brigham 1993; Roberts and Roberts 1993; Rasheed *et al.* 1995). The roosting habits of species may also influence the level of knowledge of their status. The status of species that tend to aggregate in very large colonies in caves, such as *Tadarida brasiliensis*, is easier to assess than for those that aggregate in small numbers and whose populations are well dispersed (McCracken 1989).

Fenton and Rautenbach (1998) also pointed out that captures do not necessarily reflect habitat preferences of bats, since they may roost and forage in different areas. As an example, radio-tracking of *Rhinolophus hildebrandti* showed that they roosted in woodland and foraged along rivers (Fenton and Rautenbach 1986). Similarly, while there is extensive literature on the feeding habits of bats, there is little on how specific they are in their feeding requirements and the extent to which they adapt to changes in the landscape.

3.2.7 Introduced predators

There are few natural predators of bats, mostly these are either snakes or birds of prey. However, in some countries the introduction of predators by colonisers has been implicated in the decline or extinction of bat populations. The accidental introduction of rats and then owls to control the rats is thought to have led to the extinction of *Nyctophilus howensis* on Lord Howe Island. In New Zealand, *Mystacina tuberculata* is significantly ground-dwelling, and rats again are implicated in its decline. Australia has suffered from the introduction of a range of predators, such as European fox (*Vulpes vulpes*), feral cats (*Felis catus*), and cane toads (*Bufo marinus*), with possible detrimental effects on bats (Dwyer 1964, L.S. Hall unpub. data).

3.2.8 Over-exploitation for food

The threat to microchiropteran bat populations from their use as a source of food for local communities is not clear. Because of their size and often very visible roosting habits, megachiropteran bats, particularly those from the genera *Pteropus* and *Acerodon*, have long been used as a source of protein for local communities. It is certain that many communities do consume other bats, though some, such as Muslim cultures, consider them 'unclean'. For example, there are records of direct consumption of microchiropteran bats in Africa (A. Entwistle *pers. comm.*), Viet Nam (J. Walston *pers. comm.*), and the Solomon Islands (E. Bowen-Jones *pers. comm.*). In none of these cases is there any suggestion that such consumption is having a detrimental impact on populations as a whole. However, in Laos it is suggested that exploitation for food may be a serious threat to bats (Francis *et al.* 1999). In all areas surveyed in Laos, bats were eaten by local villagers. On many occasions, villagers reported that many bats were in a particular cave, but subsequent surveys found few if any bats. The only large colony of bats seen in a town (a maternity colony of *Scotophilus kuhlii*) was being harvested by young boys using sling shots. Over 40 bats were killed in 20 minutes and it was indicated that up to 100 had been killed on the previous several nights. The explanation was that the villagers had trapped the bats until there were too few left to be worth trapping. Bats were also seen for sale in markets in a number of areas of Laos and Thailand. In one case, very large numbers of bats were seen for sale in northern Laos, including vats containing hundreds of small bats being cooked for sale in north Vientaine (R. Tizard *pers. comm.*). Thousands of *Tadarida plicata* were being smoked in April/May 1999 at Ban Phoulan, a village in the vicinity of Louang-Namtha. Over 3,000 were sold to a single passing truck. In another case, bats were being harvested using a form of funnel trap, which caught them as they emerged from a cave site. It was suggested that even a very large colony could not withstand such harvesting on a continual basis. The level of exploitation of bats worldwide and the possible impacts on populations thus remains to be assessed.

Chapter 4

Legal Protection

4.1 Legal protection

There are many international treaties protecting fauna and flora – for a detailed summary see van Heijnsbergen (1997). Some of these indirectly protect bats or their habitats. The international legislation specifically targeting bats is discussed below. The main treaties that are of particular relevance to bats include:

- *Convention on Wetlands of International Importance Especially as Waterfowl Habitat 1971 (Ramsar Convention)*. This Convention allows for the designation and protection of wetlands that are of international importance. As aquatic areas are important as feeding habitats for bats, the designation of many Ramsar sites undoubtedly benefits bats indirectly.
- *Programme on Man and the Biosphere 1971*. This allows for the creation of a separate category of protected areas known as 'biosphere reserves'. The objective of these reserves is to conserve the diversity and integrity of communities of plants and animals within natural ecosystems and to safeguard the genetic diversity of species on which their continuing evolution depends; provide areas for ecological and environmental research; provide facilities for education and training. Many of these are likely to protect significant bat populations.
- *Convention Concerning the Protection of the World Cultural and Natural Heritage 1972 (World Heritage Convention)*. This Conventions allows for the designation of natural features as World Heritage Sites based on their aesthetic or scientific value, for their geological or physiographical formations, their importance for the conservation of threatened species, or their importance in terms of science conservation or natural beauty. Many of the World Heritage Sites are likely to support significant bat populations.
- *Convention on International Trade in Endangered Species of Wild Fauna and Flora 1973 (CITES)*. This covers trade in endangered species. While this currently has no relevance for microchiropteran bats, it is of importance for megachiropterans that have been traded for food, particularly in the Pacific. Currently all *Pteropus* and *Acerodon* species (64 in total) are listed on Appendix I or II of CITES.
- *Convention on the Conservation of Migratory Species of Wild Animals 1979 (Bonn Convention)*. This Convention covers migratory species and those that regularly cross political boundaries. Appendix I species are those considered 'endangered' while Appendix II species are those with an 'unfavourable conservation status' or 'which would significantly benefit from the international cooperation that could be achieved by an international agreement'. The Convention allows for the conclusion of Agreements or Memoranda of Understanding to protect species. The Agreement on the Conservation of Bats in Europe 1991 is one such instrument so far agreed and covers all European Microchiroptera.
- *Convention on the Conservation of European Wildlife and Natural Habitats 1979 (Bern Convention)*. This Convention provides for general protection, but also has three Appendices that accord extra protection to some species. Appendix I concerns strictly protected flora species, Appendix II strictly protected fauna species, and Appendix III protected fauna species. All bats are included in Appendix III.
- *European Communities Council Directive on the Conservation of Natural Habitats and of Wild Fauna and Flora 1992 (The EEC Habitats and Species Directive)*. This lists two categories of protected species. Annex II includes animal species of community interest and in need of strict protection including 13 European bat species. The Directive allows for the designation of 'special areas of conservation' to protect these species. Annex IV includes animal and plant species of community interest whose taking in the wild and exploitation may be subject to management measures (including all European bat species), and the populations of which should be maintained at a 'favourable' status.
- *Convention on Biological Diversity 1992 (The Rio Convention)*. Under this Convention signatories are required to take measures to rehabilitate and restore degraded ecosystems, and promote the recovery of threatened species through the development and implementation of plans and other management strategies for the conservation and sustainable use of biological diversity. Parties must also develop the necessary legislation and/or other regulatory provisions for the protection of threatened species and populations. Parties must also adopt measures for the recovery and rehabilitation of threatened species and for their reintroduction into their natural habitats under appropriate conditions.

The national legal protection afforded to bats is very varied. In some countries, bats receive no protection at all, while in others, such as India, they are classed as vermin.

In some cases, the bats themselves may be protected but not where they roost or feed. Problems also arise within countries such as Australia and the USA, where each state has its own wildlife laws and can result in species receiving adequate protection in one state, but not in another. In other countries, blanket legislation nominally protecting all wildlife may result in inadequate protection for species with special requirements.

Though legislation may in theory be adequate, often the resources are not available to ensure proper policing. For example, naked bats, *Cheiromeles torquatus*, are on the list of totally protected animals of Sarawak in Malaysia and there is a $25,000 fine for killing them. The legislation, however, is almost impossible to police and naked bats are harvested occasionally even within the Niah National Park (L.S. Hall *pers. comm.*).

The IUCN's Environmental Law Centre in Bonn, Germany, maintains a comprehensive library of environmental legal instruments worldwide (website: www.iucn.org/themes/law).

4.2 Agreement on Conservation of Bats in Europe

The Agreement on the Conservation of Bats in Europe is an Agreement under the Bonn Convention. The Agreement came into force in January 1994 and currently has 23 signatories. A Secretariat is established in Bonn, Germany. The Agreement has an agreed Action Plan with priorities for implementation. It has agreed strategies for the monitoring of populations of selected species in Europe, and is developing international transboundary programmes for the study of selected migratory species in order to develop appropriate conservation measures, and to identify best practice for the management of woodland and underground habitats. Its Secretariat coordinates a public awareness initiative through an annual European Bat Night. Its Advisory Committee assists in the development of activities between sessions of the Meeting of the Parties, which occur at least every three years. The geographical scope of the Agreement extends eastwards to the Caucasus states and southwards to the Mediterranean Sea (including Malta and Cyprus).

4.3 Program for the Conservation of Migratory Bats of Mexico and the United States (PCMM)

An agreement between the USA and Mexico, the Program for the Conservation of Migratory Bats of Mexico and the United States (Programa para la Conservación de Murciélagos Migratorios de México y Estados Unidos de América) was established in 1994 (Walker 1995). The Program has focused on migratory species. Many of North America's most ecologically and economically important bats migrate seasonally across the USA-Mexico border. These include *Tadarida brasiliensis*, *Choeronycteris mexicana*, *Leptonycteris curasoae,* and *L. nivalis*. PCMM has strong government, private, and academic support in both countries and is implementing a multi-faceted programme of research, education, and conservation action designed to reverse the alarming declines in migratory bats and establish a new conservation ethic among citizens in Mexico and the USA. The Program has three main components: research, environmental education; and cave conservation. Research programmes concentrate on monitoring population trends, studying bat/plant relationships, analysing foraging and mating behaviour, learning about the migratory routes and documenting the economic values of these bats. Population research has been initiated in caves in several Mexican states. A project, Bats Aloft, aims to gather information on feeding behaviour and diet of *T. brasiliensis* to assess its economic importance for agriculture (McCracken 1996). An education initiative targets rural communities and schools near key roosting caves in north and central Mexico, and is linked with detailed management plans to permanently protect these sites through formal legislation and local community stewardship (Navarro *et al.* 1996). A general education campaign in Mexico is also being developed. As part of this, a test programme was run at a cave in Nuevo Leon (Walker 1997). This will provide a model for other cave sites. Plans are also being developed for a programme aimed at urban populations and bats living in cities. In terms of cave protection, the Program has been successful in lobbying at the Ministry level for adding addenda to the Environmental Protection Law that states that caves are sites that could be protected.

The European Bats Agreement and PCMM's organisation and programmes provide models for other countries with limited financial resources to develop international collaboration on important bat conservation matters.

Chapter 5

Conservation Recommendations

5.1 Layout of chapter

This chapter presents a range of conservation recommendations for bats worldwide. Recommendations can be easily identified by their presentation in shaded boxes. It is divided into five major sections.

1. General recommendations. This presents general recommendations that address the threats described in Chapter 3. It is expected that these will be applicable to most, if not all, countries worldwide and all governments should aim to address these issues.

2. Centres of bat biodiversity. An analysis of centres of bat biodiversity using WORLDMAP is divided into two sections. The first deals with the results of an analysis of hotspots of generic bat biodiversity worldwide and of separate analyses of several of the major bat families. The second half of the analysis is in the form of identifying hotspots at a regional level and this is presented in each of the relevant regional accounts. In all cases, the results of these analyses are intended to provide an indication of the areas thought to be of particular importance for bat diversity. This section also reviews some of the other approaches to methods of assessment of measuring biodiversity and assesses their possible importance for bats.

3. Regional accounts. The world has been divided into six zoogeographic regions (see Map 1), the boundaries of which are described in each regional account. The major threats within each region are discussed and key areas for bat biodiversity highlighted (including through the results of the WORLDMAP analysis). A series of general recommendations are then presented along with a list of key references. Within each account, a list of species found in the region is given, along with their status.

4. Species Action Plans. Summary Action Plans have been produced for 20 species. The species have been chosen to represent the full range of conservation problems faced by microchiropteran bats. The species are not necessarily the most threatened, simply those where sufficient information is available to make a detailed analysis. The wider application of each plan is discussed.

5. Conservation initiatives. A review of some of the recent bat conservation initiatives worldwide is presented.

5.2 General recommendations

Over 170 nation states have signed the Convention on Biological Diversity 1992 (Rio Convention). This provides a mechanism for developing wildlife conservation, including that of bats, to be integrated with human needs on a global front. At the same time, Agenda 21 was developed to encourage conservation at all levels to be programmed into action that relates the needs of biological and environmental conservation with economic and social needs at local, regional, and national levels. Statements of Principle were agreed for the Sustainable Management of Forests and for Sustainable Development. International treaties for the conservation of bats exist in Europe under the Bonn Convention on the Conservation of Migratory Species of Wild Animals (which could act as a basis for other international collaboration) and between the USA and Mexico (see Chapter 4). At the national level, the conservation status afforded to bats varies greatly. It is certain that, in most countries, bats would benefit from a higher profile in legislation and wider policy issues in recognition of both their contribution to biodiversity, especially of mammals, and in their contribution to the maintenance of ecosystems.

Bats worldwide face a number of common threats. The following recommendations recognise this fact and could be applicable to most countries of the world. In developing activity under these recommendations, nation states should recognise their role in contributing to international conservation initiatives.

Recommendations:
- implement the principles of appropriate international treaties, including the Convention on Biological Diversity (Rio, 1992) and the Convention of the Conservation of Migratory Species of Wild Animals (Bonn, 1979);
- relate bat conservation activities to the wider issues of conservation, and the aims and objectives of IUCN and its Commissions.

5.2.1 Threatened species

Out of the 834 species of microchiropteran bats, over 21% are threatened. A further 23% are considered Near Threatened and are thus of conservation concern. These are identified in *The 2000 IUCN Red List of Threatened Species* and in this volume in Chapter 2. These classifications provide a first attempt to assess the status of all bat species, although the status of many species is based on very limited information. A listing of the Red List species by individual country is presented in Chapter 6.

Recommendations:
- review knowledge of the species listed in *The 2000 IUCN Red List of Threatened Species* and in this volume, and develop Action Plans that will ensure a favourable conservation status for listed species;
- review species within territory, but not listed in the above, with a view to developing conservation policy for those species that are locally rare or threatened and maintaining the status of others, especially endemic species;
- direct particular attention to areas showing high diversity at the generic level (see WORLDMAP analysis and regional accounts in this Chapter) and where centres of species diversity have been identified in the regional accounts or could be identified from further research;
- provide the Chiroptera Specialist Group of IUCN/SSC with any information that will help in the continuing reassessment of the status of threat of all species.

5.2.2 Threatened habitats

Bats use a variety of habitats for both roosting and feeding. Some of these are threatened globally. Woodlands, whether temperate or tropical, deciduous or evergreen, are key habitats for a range of species. In the tropics, rainforest is a critical habitat for a majority of bat species. The loss of forest in the tropics has, justifiably, received much attention from conservationists, but in temperate areas woodlands are also being lost; in some cases, the rate of loss is thought to be higher than that in the tropics.

Aquatic habitats are key feeding areas for many species. Such areas are threatened by a variety of human activities. Pollution of lakes and rivers along with physical alterations to habitats, such as through damming and canalisation, alter the fauna and flora of such ecosystems, which, in turn, affects the range of food available for bats. Riverine habitat loss is also a widely recognised concern.

In some areas of the world, for example Central and Eastern Europe, there have been recent dramatic changes to cultural landscapes associated with intensification of agriculture. Often this is accompanied by an increased use of pesticides, some of which have been withdrawn from use in more developed countries. Cultural landscapes have provided a rich diversity of habitats and prey for bats.

Recommendation:
- recognise the importance to bats of key habitats and, where necessary, incorporate habitat requirements for bats into local, national, or regional management plans and policies. This should include threatened cultural landscapes.

5.2.3 Underground habitats

Caves, mines, and other artificial underground habitats, such as abandoned fortifications, are critical sites for bats throughout the world. Some species rely almost exclusively on such sites for roosting and breeding. The largest aggregations of bats occur in caves, sometimes 20 million animals in one site. Underground habitats are particularly vulnerable to the effects of a range of activities including tourism, caving, guano collection, and quarrying.

Recommendations:
- compile (if not already available) an inventory of underground habitats. This should include information on site suitability for bats, current or potential threats, and management recommendations;
- establish long-term monitoring programmes for sites that are known to be used by bats;
- draw up detailed management plans for key bat roosts, where necessary;
- initiate education programmes to explain the importance of caves and abandoned mines for bats, in particular for people involved in mineral extraction, safety concerns, and leisure activities related to the use of underground habitats (see, for example, Bern Convention Recommendation 36 (1992) on the Conservation of Underground Habitats);
- adopt the Guidelines for Cave and Karst Protection developed by IUCN (Watson *et al.* 1997).

5.2.4 Survey and monitoring

Large areas of the world remain little surveyed or completely unsurveyed for bats. In particular, parts of West and Central Africa, Central Asia, the former Soviet Republics, and many countries in Southeast Asia have little information on the status and distribution of bats. Although some localities of South America may be considered well known in terms of species composition, vast areas of the continent, including some unique ecosystems, are still unsurveyed.

Recommendations:
- ensure an up-to-date species list is available for each nation state, which should identify species and areas in need of further survey work, taking account of the world status of species and areas important for biodiversity conservation;
- establish monitoring of key sites and species;
- establish training programmes for survey work, especially for surveys involving the use of specialist equipment such as bat detectors.

5.2.5 Systematics

The systematics of a number of families and genera of Microchiroptera remains in a state of flux. Also, there are taxa that still remain to be formally described. As explained below, the problem of undescribed taxa in Australia is delaying the implementation of some conservation plans.

Recommendations:
- carry out systematic reviews of families and genera of Microchiroptera where these are required, including at the national/regional level;
- use modern systematic techniques, including DNA analysis, in an attempt to resolve the status of questionable taxa.

5.2.6 Biology and ecology

The biology and ecology of many species remains poorly understood. Little or no information is available for many of the species listed in *The 2000 IUCN Red List of Threatened Species*.

Recommendations:
- initiate research to target primarily threatened species in areas where little or no research has been undertaken;
- initiate research on many aspects of the biology and ecology of bats, including: echolocation studies to assist survey and monitoring; studies of foraging requirements; population studies to assess trends and limits of viable populations; migrations; the role of bats in ecosystem maintenance; roost requirements to ensure appropriate roost management, enhancement, or creation.

5.2.7 Legislation

The legislation pertaining to bats varies from country to country – in many cases bats receive no protection, while elsewhere they are classed as vermin.

Recommendations:
- make efforts to include at least the internationally threatened species on any appropriate national legislation where bats are not protected. Such legislation should reflect the special needs of bat species, as well as the wider concerns of biodiversity conservation;
- make efforts to remove bats from legislation which classifies them as vermin or pests, whilst recognising that some bat species may conflict with socio-economic needs.

5.2.8 Education

This is an almost universal requirement. Threats to bats are often related to ignorance of their lifestyles and roles in ecosystem maintenance. Education should be aimed at a variety of groups, such as government officials, land managers, cavers, tourists, and schoolchildren, as well as the general public.

Recommendations:
- develop educational programmes to encourage an understanding of bats, their diversity, their role in the environment, and conservation concerns. Some countries have already produced a considerable amount of educational material aimed at many of the above interest groups; these should be used as a basis for material for other countries;
- compile a catalogue of currently available educational materials;
- develop more specific educational programmes for trades and industries whose activities have the greatest effect on bat populations.

5.2.9 Vampire bats

At the 11th International Bat Research Conference held in Pirenopolis in Brazil in 1998, a symposium was held on vampire bat biology, control, and conservation.

The meeting formulated a *Resolution on Vampire Bats from the 11th International Bat Research Conference, Pirenopolis, Brazil, 3–6 August 1998*. The Resolution recognises the following factors:

- that Latin America harbours some of the richest biodiversity, including by far the richest bat biodiversity in the world;
- that bats provide a wide variety of ecologically significant roles, including pest insect population control, pollination and seed dispersal for many important plants, and ecosystem recovery through seed dispersal;
- that vampire bats occupy a unique position within this biodiversity and are of value for medical research;
- that there have been serious declines in bat populations over the past few decades, and the halting of such declines requires the recovery and conservation of bat species throughout Latin America;
- that vampire bats have been widely identified as a threat to human, animal, and economic health owing to bites and the transmission of rabies, and that inadequate, ill-conceived methods of control serve only to compound such problems by destroying ecologically valuable populations of beneficial or harmless bat species and their habitats;
- that there exists the need for further research, training, and public awareness initiatives to ensure effective and environmentally sound conservation and management of ecologically important species, while simultaneously addressing the needs of human, animal, and economic health to assist in vampire bat management;
- that there are advantages of addressing these issues through international collaboration.

The Resolution then makes the following recommendations.

RECOMMENDATIONS OF THE RESOLUTION ON VAMPIRE BATS FROM 11TH INTERNATIONAL BAT RESEARCH CONFERENCE

The Resolution urges governments with indigenous vampire bat populations to apply vampire bat control activities only when there is a problem, such as bites on humans or high incidence of bites on domestic animals, and/or when there is a vampire bat-related outbreak of rabies, and further urges these governments that they pursue the priority objectives outlined below.

1. Adoption, for the purpose of control of vampire bats, of agreed species-specific control methods that are harmless to the environment;
2. Prohibition of the application of all other destructive methods of control (such as fumigating, dynamiting, burning, sealing, or otherwise destroying caves and other roost sites);
3. Application of controls appropriate to the incident, dependent on an evaluation, carried out with the assistance of academic institutions and non-governmental organisations, of the conditions of the particular situation;
4. Pursuit of concrete measures to support the development of a system for the international exchange of information relating to vampire bat control;
5. Establishment of programmes of outreach and education in bat biology, their importance, positive impact and vampire bat control;
6. Collaboration on sponsoring an international training course on vampire bat biology and control for Latin America;
7. Establishment or improvement, with the active assistance of academic institutions and non-governmental organisations, of a governmental program to detect and report vampire bat bites inflicted upon people and animals;
8. Development of a model to enable prediction of circumstances where vampire bat management may be required;
9. Recommendation of pre-exposure treatment to, and subsequent monitoring of antibody levels, in all those involved in vampire bat control programmes;
10. Encouragement and support for research on the following to assist vampire bat management:
    a. vampire bat ecology and behaviour both in natural habitats and those altered by human activity;
    b. evolution and ecology of the rabies virus and its relationship with vampire bat population biology;
    c. quantification of the economic, public-health and environmental impact (direct and indirect) of vampire bats and their control;
    d. national assessments and monitoring of the distribution of major vampire bat-related problems.

5.3 Key areas for bat biodiversity

With limited resources available for the conservation of species and habitats, it is important to be able to assess which are the key sites and species worldwide. A range of methods of assessment has been developed, some of which have concentrated on a specific group of species such as birds or plants. In the case of birds, good information on the status of many species has allowed detailed analysis of key areas, particularly for endemic species. Other approaches focus on habitats and attempt to identify the areas which, if conserved, would ensure the maintenance of a representation of all key habitats worldwide. Key countries in terms of their overall biodiversity have been identified, though the data sets for these analyses are limited. All these approaches may have some relevance in terms of identifying key areas and habitats for bats. Up to this point, however, there have been very few attempts to evaluate centres of biodiversity for microchiropteran bats.

A WORLDMAP analysis of bat biodiversity at the generic level is presented below. Some of the other measures used to pinpoint key areas and habitats are also discussed; in particular, their likely relevance for bat conservation.

5.3.1 WORLDMAP analysis of key areas for bat biodiversity

WORLDMAP is a computer programme developed at The Natural History Museum in London by R.I. Vane-Wright, P.H. Williams, C.J. Humphries, and colleagues (Williams 1994). It can be used to identify areas of high diversity (richness hotspots). It can also be used to undertake a step-wise priority analysis to produce a set of areas which, if protected, would conserve the largest number of taxa. This uses the concept of complementarity that refers to the degree to which an area contributes otherwise unrepresented taxa to a set of areas (Vane-Wright *et al.* 1991). In such an analysis, the first step would select any grid cells that include taxa that only occur in that cell. The next stage selects a series of grid cells chosen to give, at each step, the maximum range-size rarity score (a measure of the degree of restriction in the distribution of taxa) from the remaining taxa. The analysis continues until all taxa are represented. The resulting data represents the minimum set of areas that includes representatives of all taxa within a group. It can also be used to target areas that would conserve the most taxa. This is of particular relevance where limited resources are available for conservation and thus where difficult choices need to be made. The analysis can use a range of diversity measures. Simple species richness is the most obvious, but the data can, for example, be weighted to take account of the taxonomic distinctiveness of a fauna. In bats, this would give more priority to areas such as New Zealand, which currently has only two bat species, but one being from a monotypic family (Mystacinidae) that is endemic to that country.

The main difficulty in using the WORLDMAP programme with microchiropteran bats is the lack of detailed information on the distribution of species. Distribution or range maps for most species are not available. For the purposes of this document, therefore, a WORLDMAP analysis was undertaken at the generic level by R.I. Vane-Wright. The distribution of genera was plotted at a global scale using the grid-cell areas (squares) shown in Map 3. The bats provided 4,986 records in 341 squares. There were some difficulties in fitting limited distributional data to these squares and it is likely that closer examination of the data could address these problems. It should be noted that the grid-cell area system used for this analysis does not follow range state boundaries, and that individual squares may link mainland and island elements (e.g., Central America to Caribbean islands) or even distinct larger land masses (e.g., Australia and Papua New Guinea).

Maps are presented for the world, for the Old and New World as separate entities, and for five separate families (Emballonuridae, Hipposideridae, Phyllostomidae, Vespertilionidae, and Molossidae); other families comprise too few genera to produce meaningful maps. Each zoogeographic region has also been examined individually and the results are presented in the relevant sections of this Chapter. The numbers in the squares of these maps indicate the number of genera present in that square and a gradation of tone assists in the identification of the more diverse areas.

WORLDMAP was also used to identify the minimum set of squares that would ensure representation of all genera within a given region or family. Where more than one square can contribute the same genera to the minimum set, the programme automatically selects the northwesterly square. In Map 21, for example, the square selected at the northwest of North America contributes the genus *Lasionycteris* to the minimum set, but many other squares in North America could make the same contribution. The numbers in the squares indicate the number of genera within that square that uniquely contribute to the minimum set; that is, those genera that do not occur in any of the other identified squares. Squares in black cannot be replaced since they include genera not found in other squares and, as such, are essential contributors to the minimum set. Thus, in Map 29, the black square of southern Thailand contributes the genus *Craseonycteris* to the minimum set; since no other square can contribute this genus, this square cannot be replaced by any alternative.

Overall biodiversity

Overall diversity of world genera is shown in Map 4, with a marked centre of diversity in Central and northern South America, the highest diversity being in the grid-cell area of 'Nicaragua', where 58 genera are recorded. Other key areas outside the Neotropical region, are in eastern Africa (23–25 genera), 'Peninsula Malaysia' (23 genera), 'Sulawesi' (22 genera), 'South Yunnan' (23 genera), 'Nepal' (23 genera), and 'Northeast India' (24 genera). Map 5 illustrates the same diversity, but with the data smoothed once (i.e., each square incorporates data from all its adjacent squares) to give a more general pattern of distribution.

In Map 6, the degree of restriction in the distribution of the genera occurring in each area (the range-size rarity) is assessed. Thus, areas containing only widespread genera (e.g., UK) receive a low score (pale coloured), while areas with a high proportion of genera of restricted distribution (e.g., Madagascar and New Zealand) receive a high score (dark coloured).

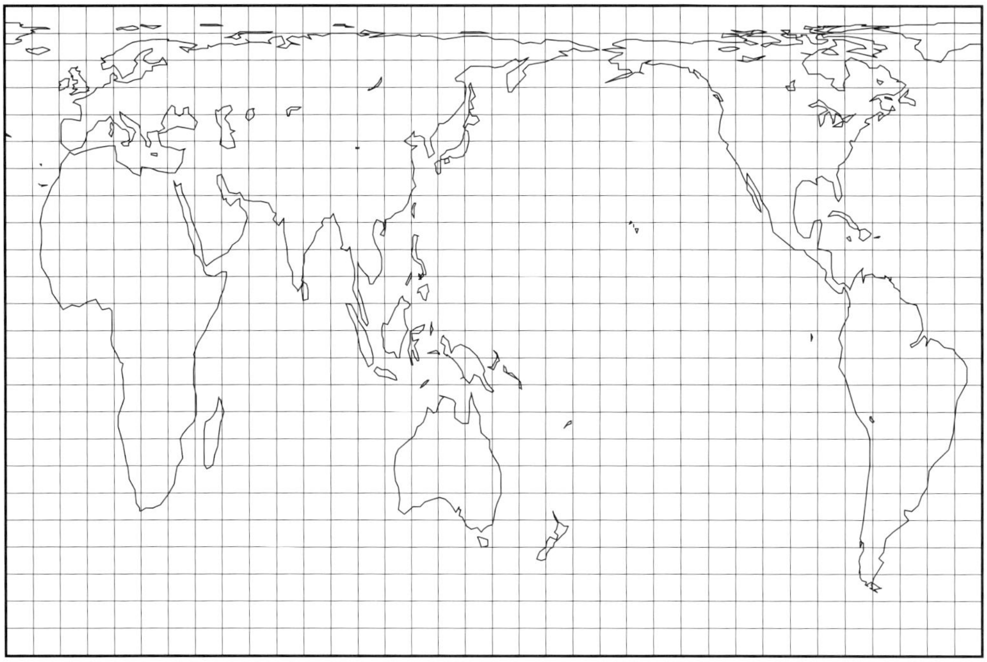

Map 3. World map to show grid-cell areas used in WORLDMAP diversity analysis.
The bats provided 4,986 records in 341 squares. It should be noted that the grid-cell area system used for this analysis does not follow range state boundaries and that individual squares may link mainland and island elements (e.g., Central America to Caribbean islands) or even distinct larger land masses (e.g., Australia and Papua New Guinea). Minor adjustment to the allocation of grid cells was made in considering the zoogeographical regions separately.

There is remarkably little overlap down to the generic level between Old World and New World faunas. Of 17 families of Microchiroptera, only three (Emballonuridae, Vespertilionidae, and Molossidae) occur in both. Of 137 genera, only seven occur in both (*Eptesicus*, *Myotis*, *Pipistrellus*, *Plecotus*, and *Nycticeius* in the Vespertilionidae, and *Mormopterus* and *Tadarida* in the Molossidae – and the New World species here included in *Plecotus* are often assigned to the separate genus *Corynorhinus*).

The richness of genera in the New World is demonstrated in Map 7, which identifies the generic richness per square until the point where the next richest square falls outside of the New World. Thus, 43 areas of the New World (comprising 19.2% of the total area occupied by Microchiroptera) hold a richer generic complement than anywhere else in the world. The rest of the map shows the diversity of the remaining genera endemic to the Old World.

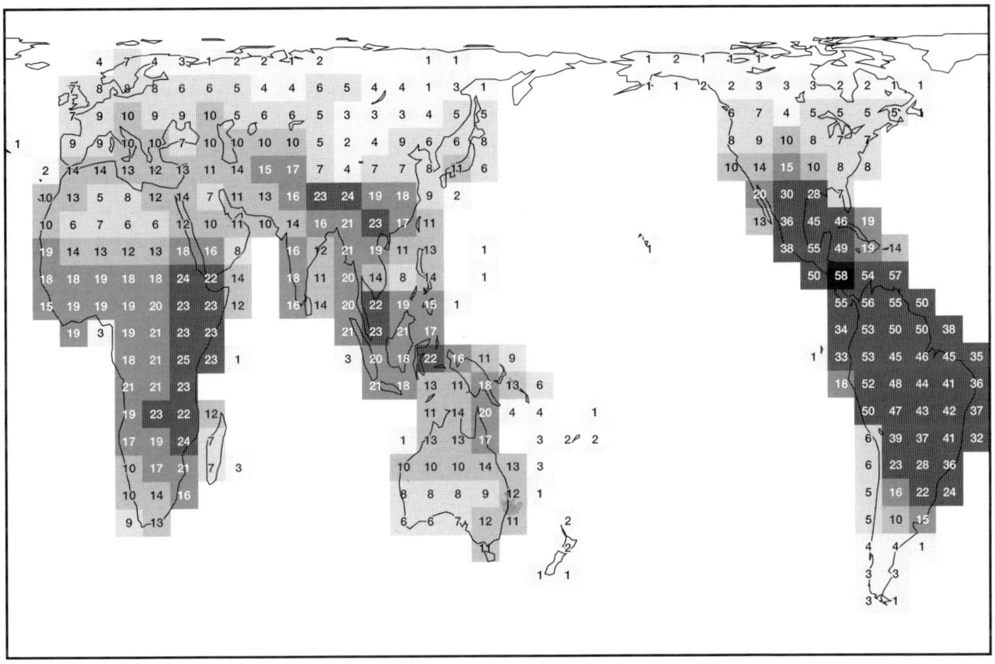

Map 4. Generic richness per grid-cell area for all Microchiroptera.
The numbers in the squares indicate the number of genera present in that square and a gradation of tone assists in the identification of the more diverse areas. Darker areas are more diverse and lighter areas less diverse.

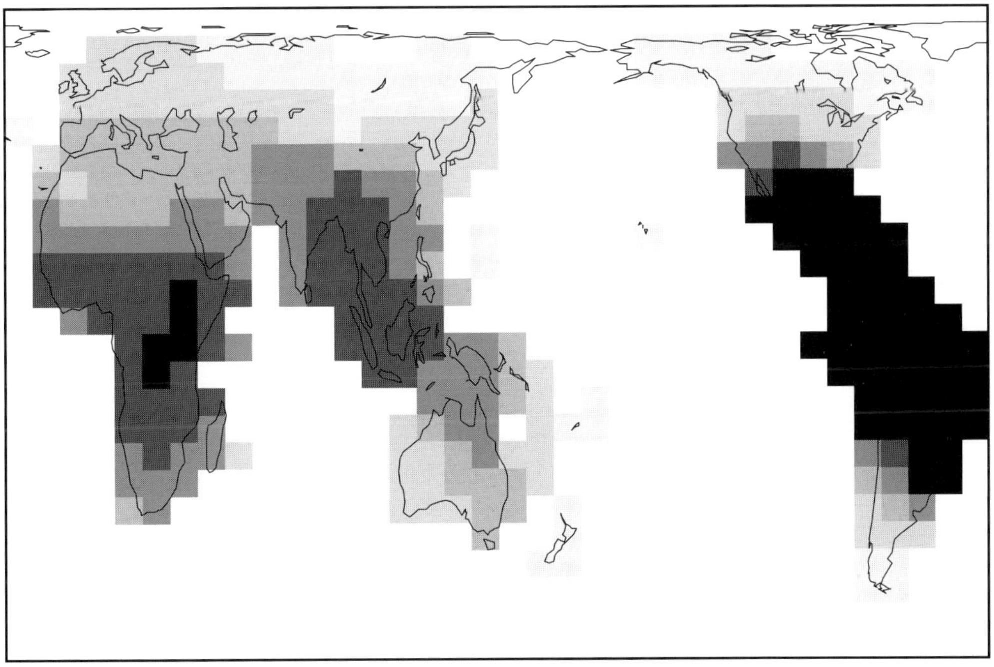

Map 5. Generic richness per grid-cell area for all Microchiroptera smoothed once.
Each square incorporates data from all its adjacent squares. Gradation of tone assists in the identification of the more diverse areas. Darker areas are more diverse and lighter areas less diverse.

The minimum number of squares required to conserve all genera is 19 (Map 8). The numbers in the squares represent the number of genera uniquely contributing to this minimum set. Alternative squares can be identified to cover the full complement of most (but not all) of these 'unique' genera and are shown in Map 9, but the use of any of these alternatives ('fully flexible areas') may not provide the same total generic coverage.

If two squares are identified (where possible) for each genus, the number of squares required for a minimum set is increased to 37 (Map 10).

Biodiversity by zoogeographic region

Clearly the Neotropical region is by far the most diverse. The richness of genera occurring in the New World is shown in Map 11 and more clearly demonstrates the

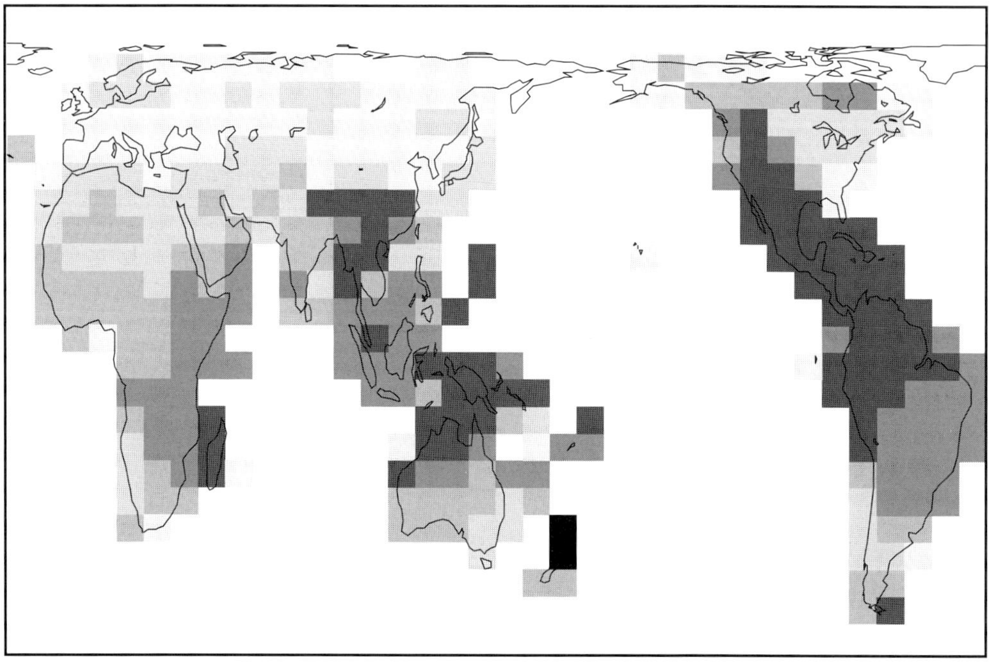

Map 6. Mean range-size rarity for all Microchiroptera.
The degree of restriction in the distribution of the genera occurring in each area (the range-size rarity) is assessed. Thus, areas containing only widespread genera (e.g., UK) receive a low score (light coloured), while areas with a high proportion of genera of restricted distribution (e.g., Madagascar and New Zealand) receive a high score (dark coloured).

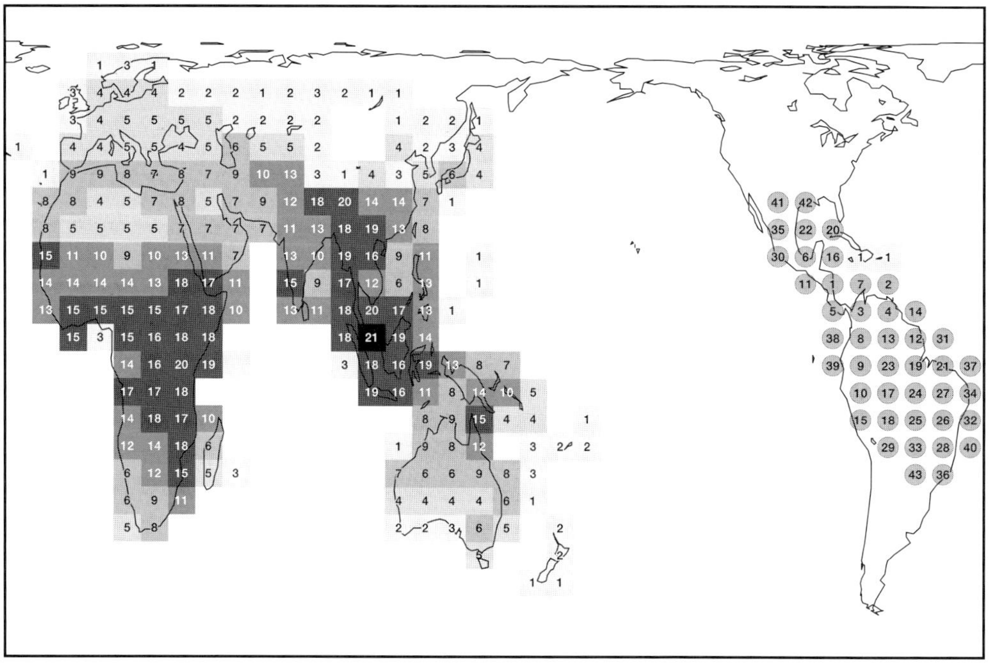

Map 7. Generic richness concentration in the New World.
Generic richness per square is significantly greater in the New World. Squares with the greatest generic diversity are numbered until the point where the next richest square falls outside the New World. Thus, 43 areas of the New World hold a richer generic complement than anywhere else in the world. The 43 areas in the New World, in order of decreasing diversity, are indicated by the numbers in circles. The rest of the map shows the diversity of the remaining genera endemic to the Old World. The numbers in the squares represent the generic diversity once the 43 New World areas have been removed from the analysis.

remarkably little overlap with Old World fauna. The principal areas for generic diversity are in Central America, the Caribbean, northern South America, and extending southwards along the Andes. The richness of genera occurring in the Old World is shown in Map 12, again with little overlap with the New World. Here, hotspots are more widely dispersed, relating to the restricted distribution of many genera and, similarly, the minimum set of 11 squares is widely dispersed (Map 13). In Chapter 5.4 each zoogeographical region has been analysed separately to give a clearer indication of the important areas within each region.

Biodiversity within families

The five families with the greater generic diversity were examined individually. These are Emballonuridae (13

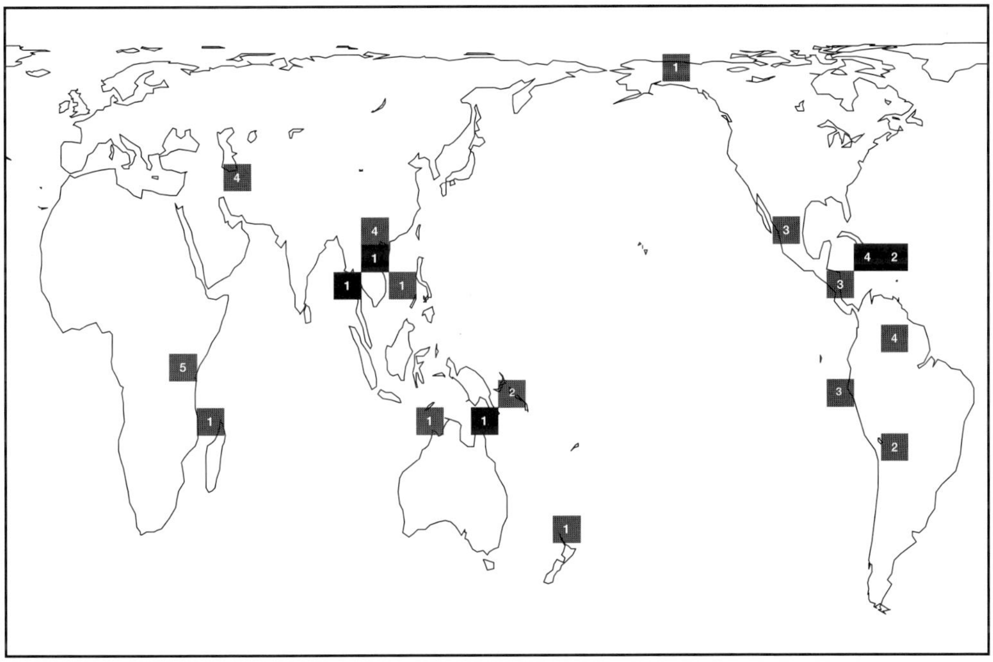

Map 8. Minimum set of squares required to maintain all genera of Microchiroptera.
The minimum number of squares required to conserve all genera is 19. The numbers in the squares represent the number of genera uniquely contributing to this minimum set.

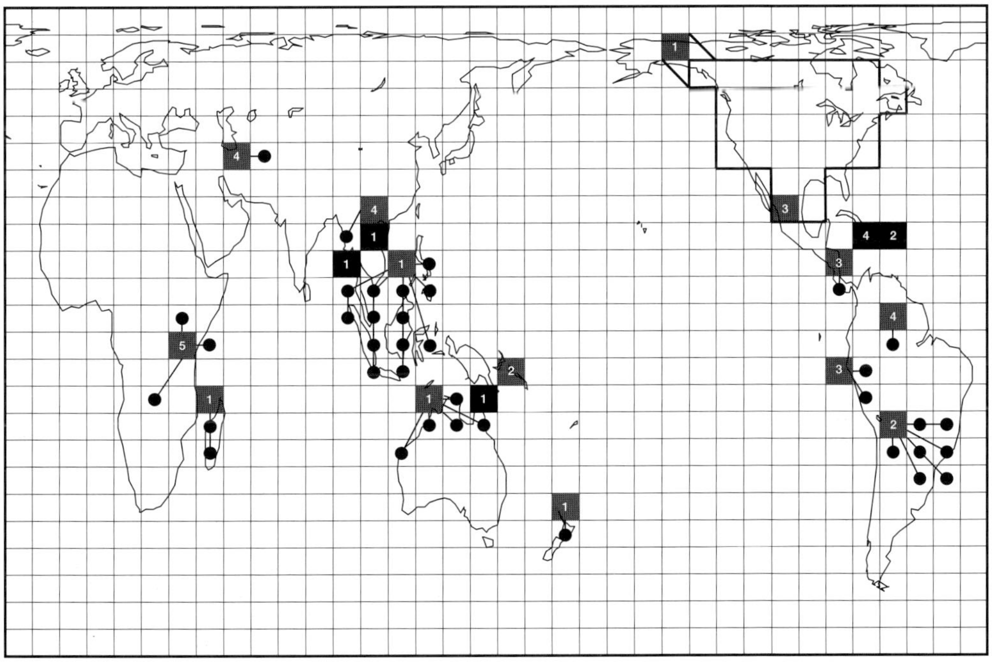

Map 9. Minimum set plus fully flexible areas.
The numbers in the squares represent the number of genera uniquely contributing to this minimum set. Alternative squares can be identified to cover the full complement of most (but not all) of these unique genera and are shown as black circles. The use of any of these alternatives ('fully flexible areas') may not, however, provide the same total generic coverage.

genera), Hipposideridae (nine genera), Phyllostomidae (49 genera), Vespertilionidae (37 genera), and Molossidae (12 genera). All other families include between one and four genera only; the distribution of these families and their constituent genera can be found in Chapter 2.

Emballonuridae

The generic diversity per area is highest in parts of Central America and adjacent areas (Map 14). There is no overlap of genera between the Old and New Worlds and the highest diversities in the Old World are in Southeast Asia. Map 15 plots a minimum set for Emballonuridae as three areas of Central America, Southeast Asia, and Africa. Particularly for Southeast Asia and Africa, many alternative areas would be available while still confining the minimum set to three areas.

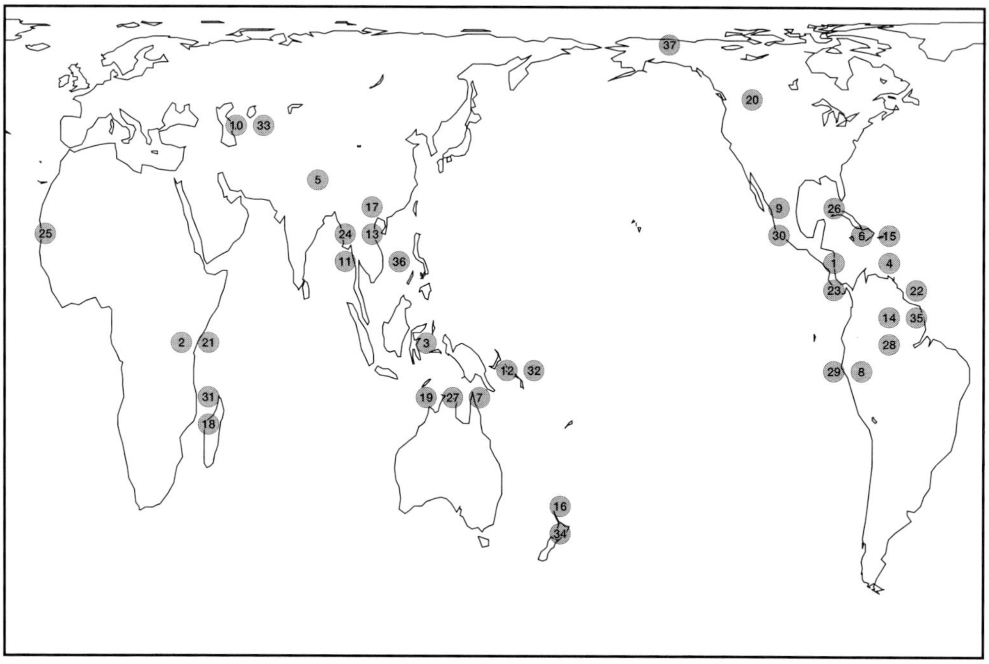

Map 10. Minimum set with two representatives for each genus.
If two squares are identified (where possible) for each genus, the number of squares required for a minimum set is increased to 37.

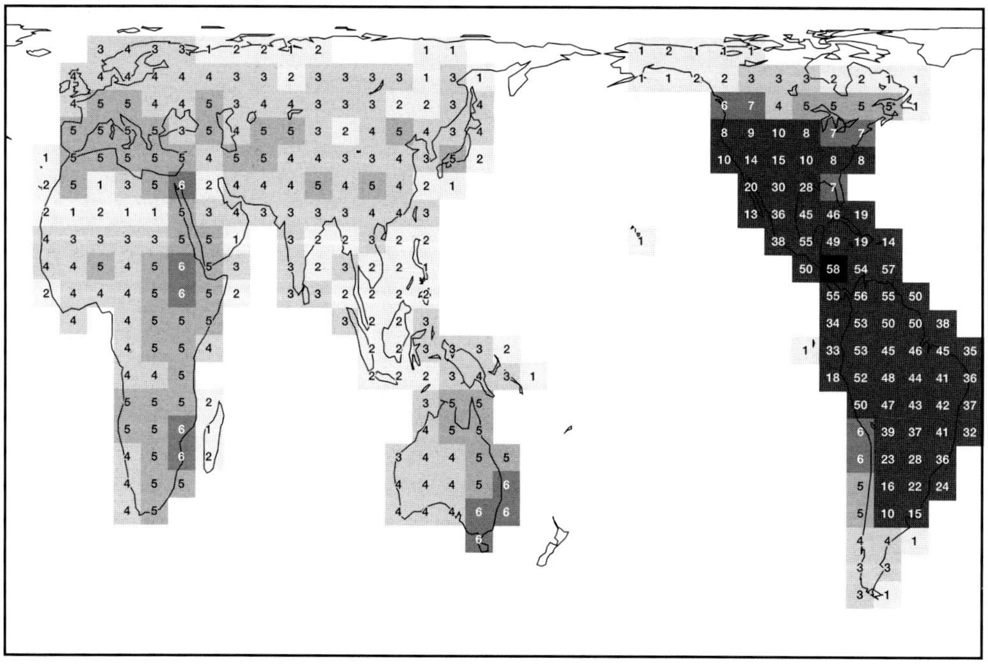

Map 11. Generic richness per grid-cell area for genera occurring in the New World.
The number in each square represents the number of genera occuring in the New World per unit area. New World genera that are also found in the Old World are shown, but the low numbers in the Old World squares show there is little overlap between genera in these two regions.

Hipposideridae

The highest generic diversity occurs in the Afrotropical region and Southeast Asia (Map 16). The genus *Hipposideros* occurs more or less throughout the range of the family and is species rich (60 species). The other eight genera all include between one and four species only, and some are of very restricted distribution. Thus, the minimum set is four areas (Map 17) with no alternatives for two genera: *Anthops* (Solomon Islands) and *Paracoelops* (Viet Nam).

Phyllostomidae

The highest generic diversities are concentrated in Central America, the Caribbean, and northern South America, with Peru/North Bolivia also important (Map 18). The minimum set map (Map 19) identifies seven

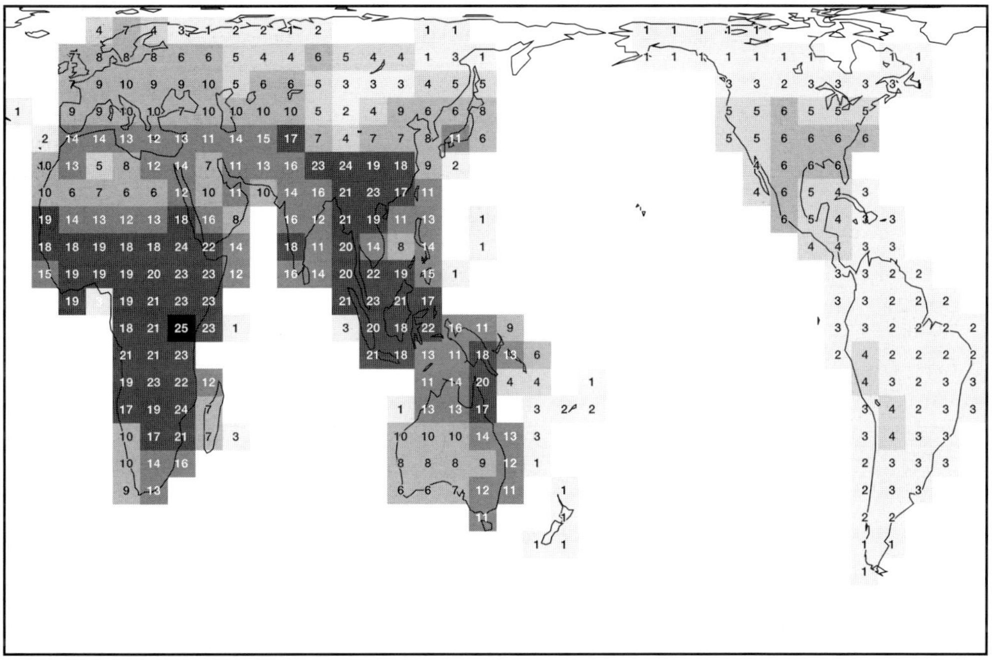

Map 12. Generic richness per grid-cell area for genera occurring in the Old World.
The number in each square represents the number of genera occuring in the Old World per unit area. Old World genera that are also found in the New World are shown, but the low numbers in the New World squares show there is little overlap between genera in these two regions.

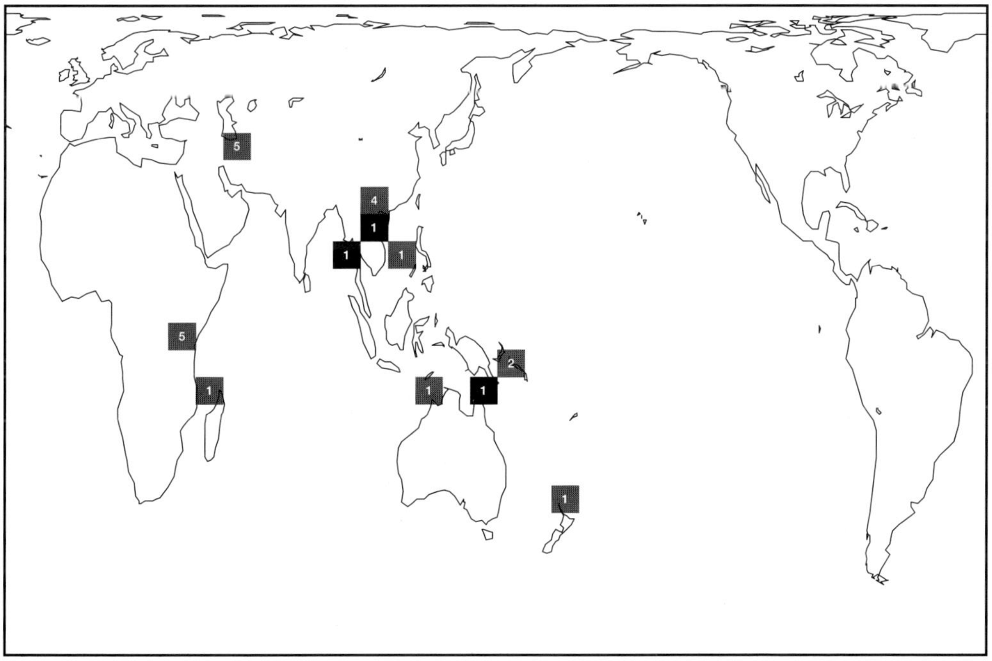

Map 13. Minimum set of squares required to maintain all genera occurring in the Old World.
The minimum number of squares required to conserve all genera is 11. The numbers in the squares represent the number of genera uniquely contributing to this minimum set.

areas that would incorporate all genera, although apart from areas with Caribbean island endemics, alternatives could be identified for most of these squares. The pattern of diversity of this family matches very well with the pattern of diversity of flowering plants.

Vespertilionidae

This is the dominant family in temperate latitudes and a number of genera are restricted to these latitudes. This is reflected in the relatively high diversity in North America and northern Europe (Map 20). Nevertheless, principal areas of diversity are in Asia, especially Southeast Asia, and to a lesser extent in the Afrotropical region. This broad distribution is also reflected in the identification of the minimum set of six areas (Map 21), but it is likely that an identification of fully flexible areas would greatly increase the number of areas available for the conservation of the diversity of this family.

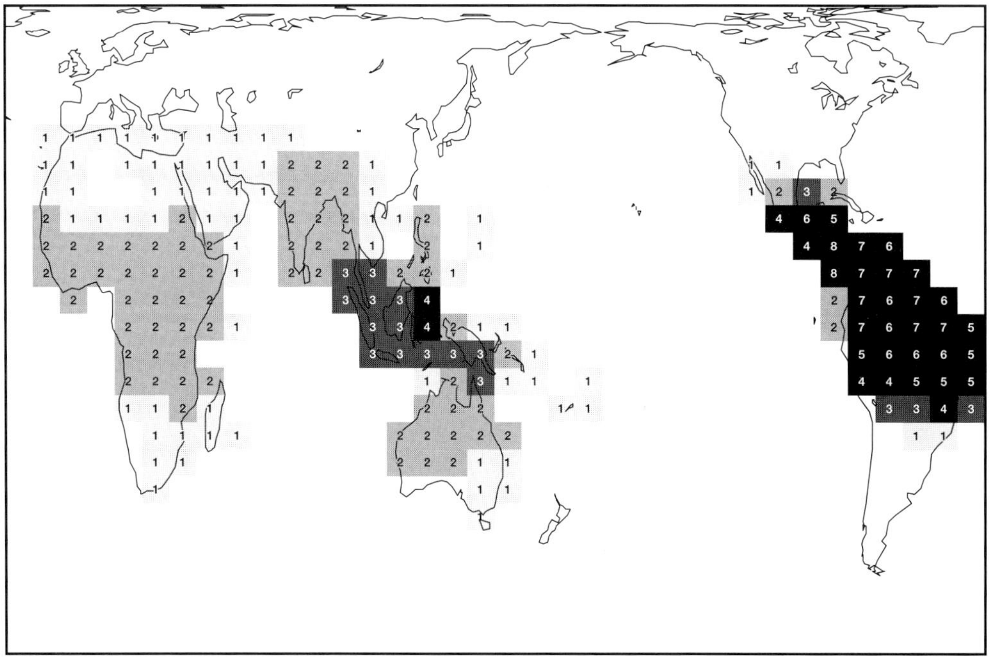

Map 14. Generic richness per grid-cell area for family Emballonuridae.
The numbers in the squares represent the number of emballonurid genera per unit area.

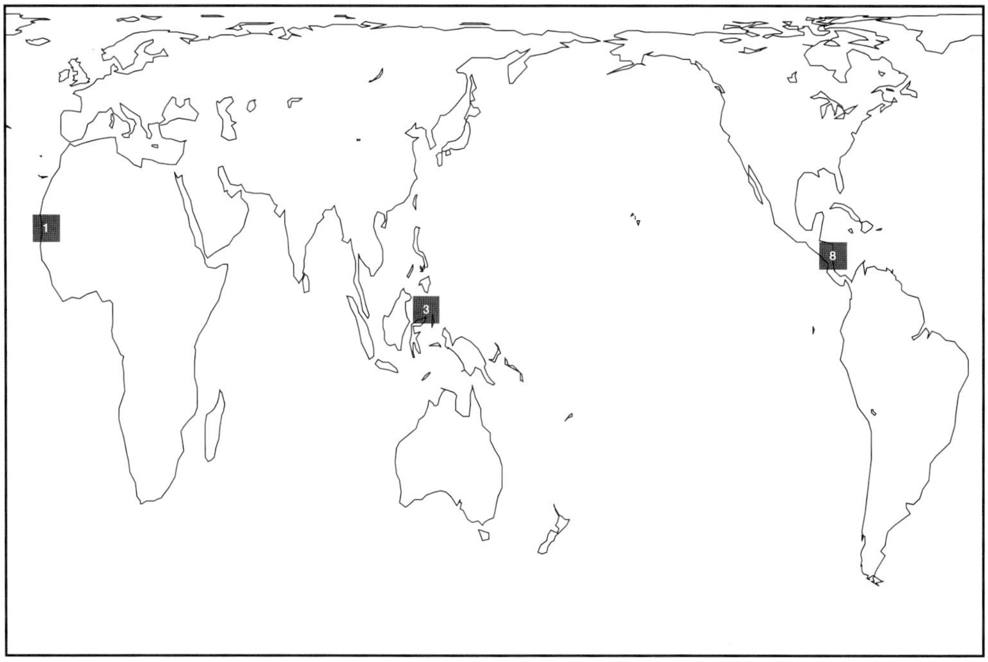

Map 15. Minimum set of grid-cell areas required to maintain all genera of Emballonuridae.
The minimum number of squares required to conserve all genera is three. The numbers in the squares represent the number of genera uniquely contributing to this minimum set.

Molossidae

This is a mainly tropical family with some genera extending into the lower temperate latitudes (Map 22). The highest diversity occurs in the Neotropics, closely followed by parts of the Afrotropical region. Two genera, *Mormopterus* and *Tadarida*, occur in both the Old and New Worlds, while one, *Cheiromeles*, is restricted to Southeast Asia and one, *Myopterus*, to Subsaharan Africa, the latter making the requirement for three areas to supply a minimum set (Map 23).

5.3.2 Other measures of key areas for biodiversity and their likely relevance for bat biodiversity

A number of other measures have been used to identify key areas for biodiversity both at a habitat and a species level. Their relevance for bat biodiversity is as yet unclear, but their possible contribution in this respect is discussed.

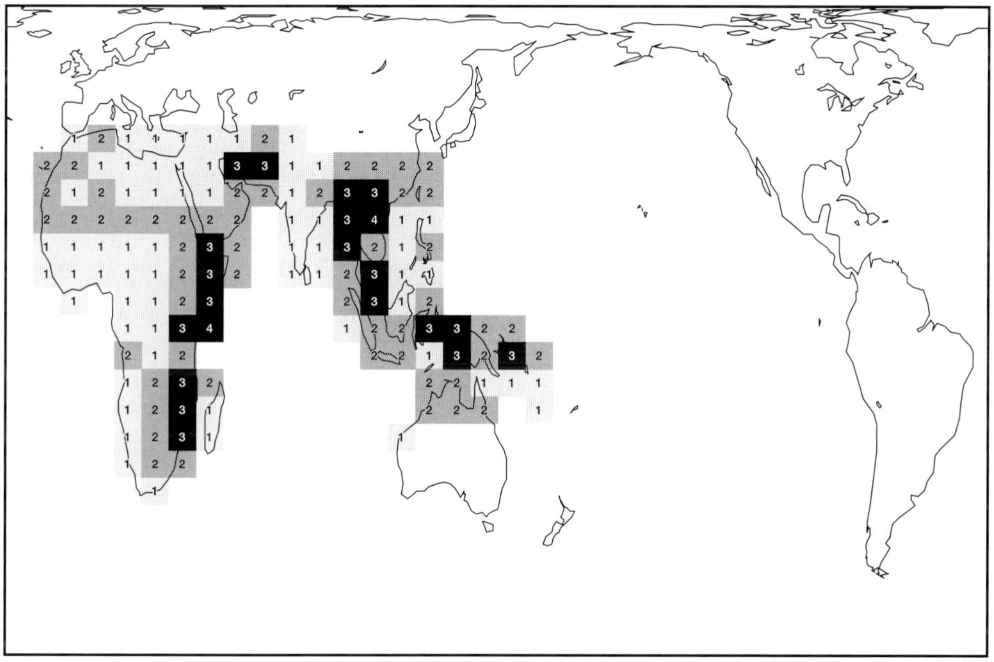

Map 16. Generic richness per grid-cell area for family Hipposideridae.
The numbers in the squares represent the number of hipposiderid genera per unit area.

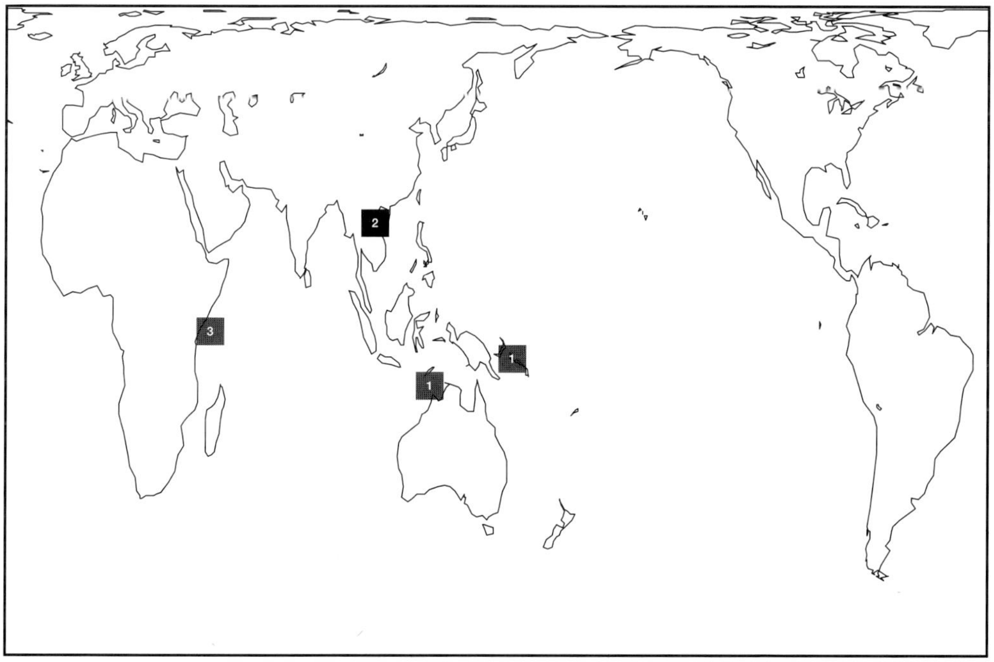

Map 17. Minimum set of grid-cell areas required to maintain all genera of Hipposideridae.
The minimum number of squares required to conserve all genera is four. The numbers in the squares represent the number of genera uniquely contributing to this minimum set.

Megadiversity Countries

This approach focuses on those countries with exceptional levels of biodiversity and endemism on a global scale. It recognises that biodiversity is not evenly distributed worldwide and that areas of high biodiversity also often suffer greater threats. It suggests that efforts should concentrate heavily (though not exclusively) on such areas. The main criterion for inclusion in this list is the level of species endemism. Species diversity is also a criterion, with countries being included if they have more than 2,000 non-fish vertebrate species or 10,000 plant species within their geographical borders. Generic and family diversity and endemism are also assessed. Ecosystem diversity both in terms of the number of different vegetation types, as well as the presence of marine and tropical rainforest ecosystems is a final criterion.

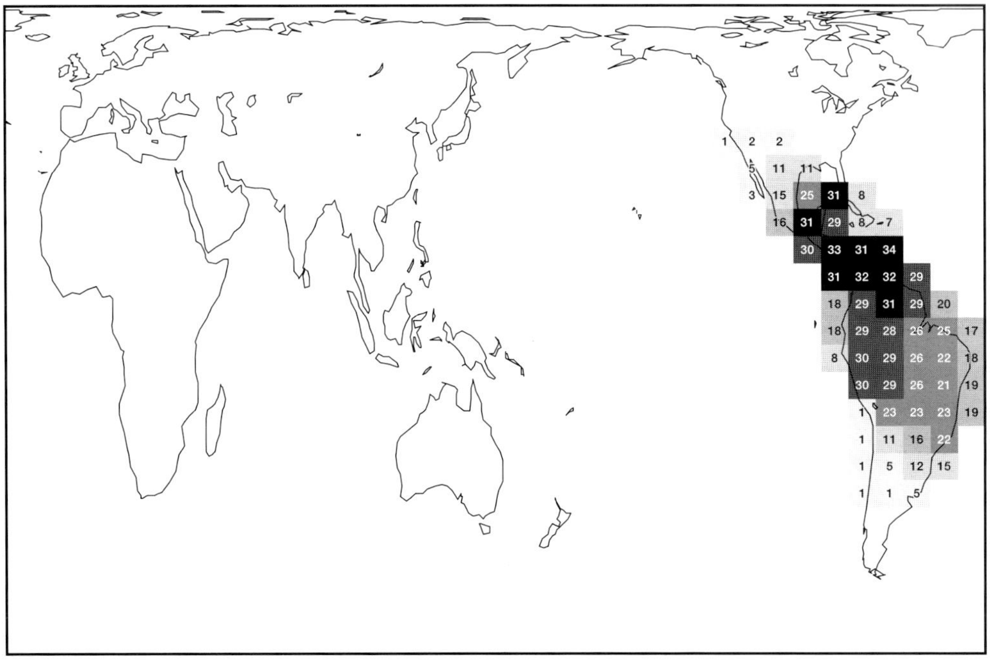

Map 18. Generic richness per grid-cell area for family Phyllostomidae.
The numbers in the squares represent the number of phyllostomid genera per unit area.

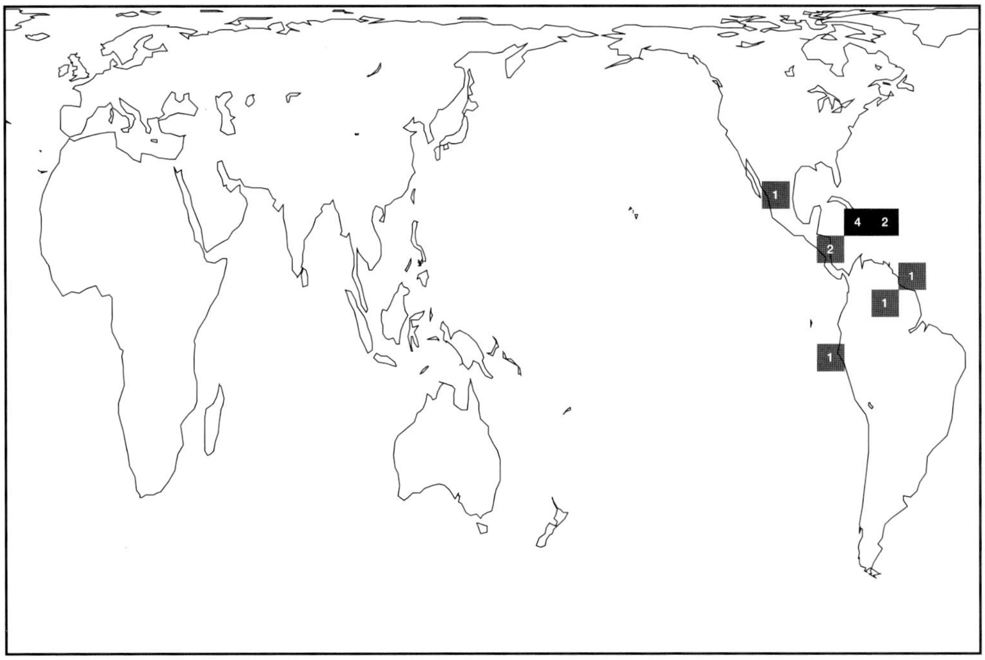

Map 19. Minimum set of grid-cell areas required to maintain all genera of Phyllostomidae.
The minimum number of squares required to conserve all genera is seven. The numbers in the squares represent the number of genera uniquely contributing to this minimum set.

A total of 17 countries have been recognised as Megadiversity Countries (Mittermeier *et al.* 1997) . Many are large with land areas in excess of one million km², including some of the world's largest countries (China, USA, Brazil, and Australia). A majority of the countries would be considered "tropical" – Brazil, Democratic Republic of Congo, Indonesia, Peru, Colombia, Venezuela, Madagascar, Papua New Guinea, Malaysia, Philippines, and Ecuador. Four would be considered 'subtropical' – Australia, India, Mexico, and South Africa; the remaining two would be considered 'temperate' – China and the USA.

In terms of bats, all of the Megadiversity Countries are important. Some of the largest bat faunas occur in these countries, and Australia and Madagascar have high levels of bat endemism. The criterion of presence of tropical

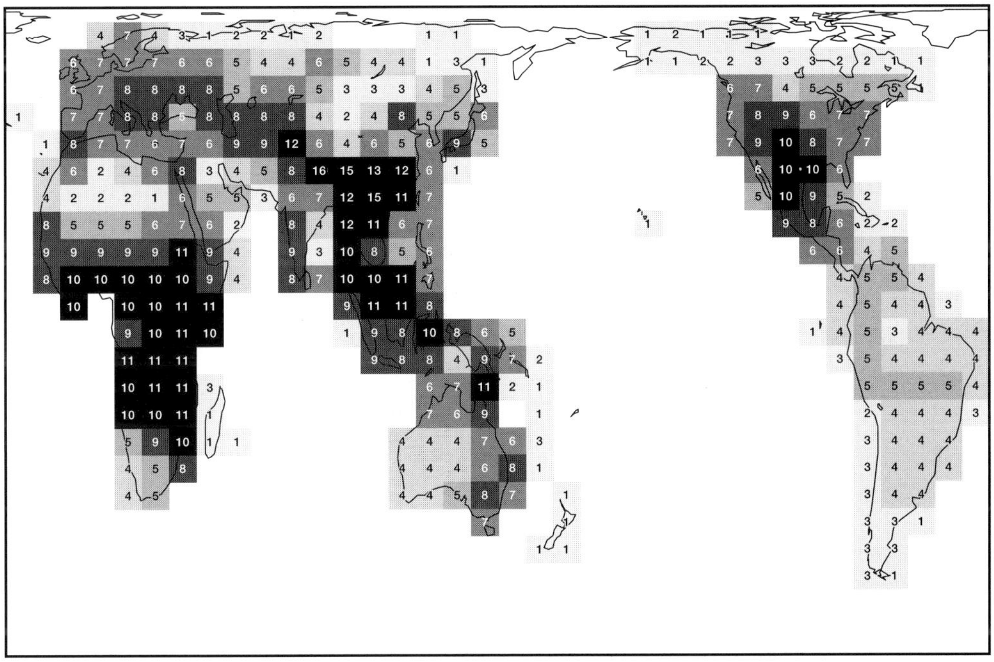

Map 20. Generic richness per grid-cell area for family Vespertilionidae.
The numbers in the squares represent the number of vespertilionid genera per unit area.

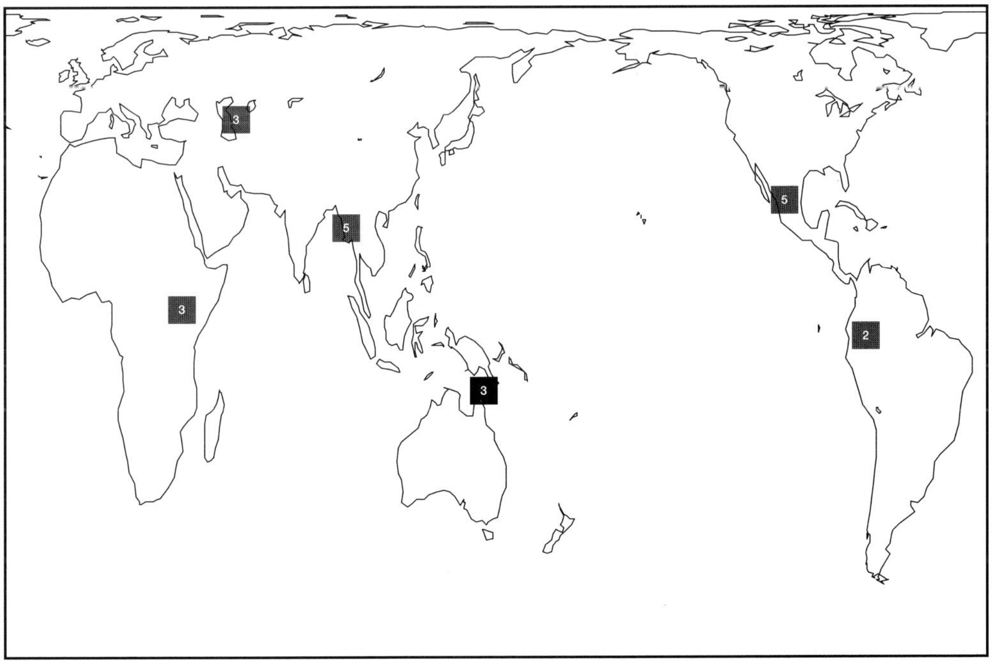

Map 21. Minimum set of grid-cell areas required to maintain all genera of Vespertilionidae.
The minimum number of squares required to conserve all genera is six. The numbers in the squares represent the number of genera uniquely contributing to this minimum set.

rainforest ecosystems is of critical importance as many bat species are heavily reliant on such habitats. One of the drawbacks of focusing attention on these countries is the degree of overlap in the bat faunas of the South American and Southeast Asian countries. For example, while Brazil has a large bat fauna, many species are also found in other countries, including the Megadiversity Countries of Venezuela, Colombia, Ecuador, and Peru. Similarly there is considerable overlap in the bat faunas of Malaysia, Indonesia, and Papua New Guinea. Also, based on the results of the WORLDMAP analysis given above, this approach misses out on some of the centres of bat diversity, such as East Africa, Southeast Asia, and the Caribbean. This approach also excludes the many smaller countries with relatively depauperate faunas and floras, which nevertheless may be important for bats. In particular,

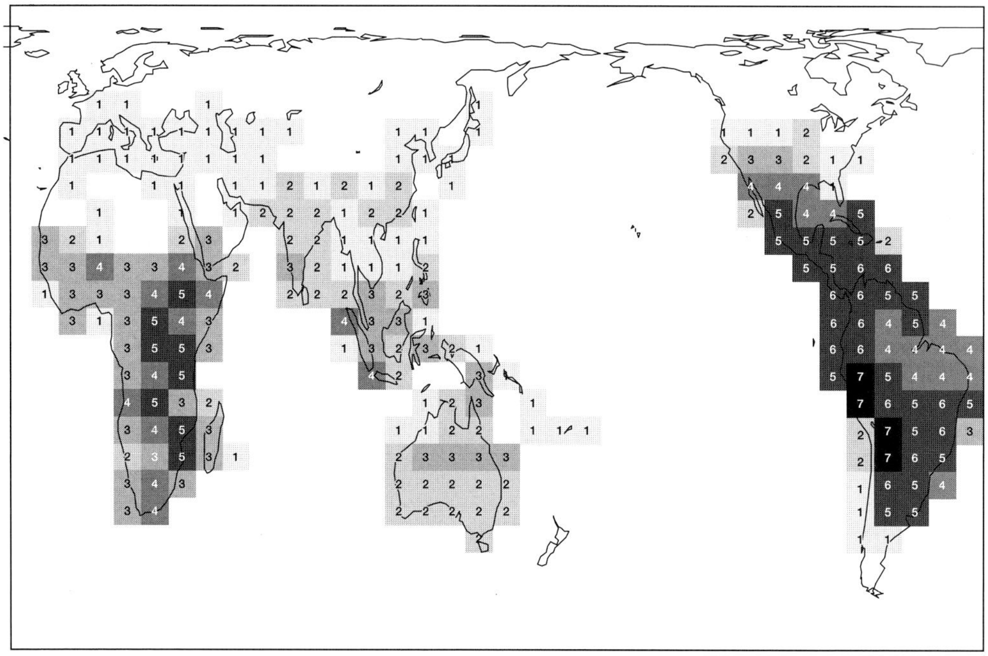

Map 22. Generic richness per grid-cell area for family Molossidae.
The numbers in the squares represent the number of molossid genera per unit area.

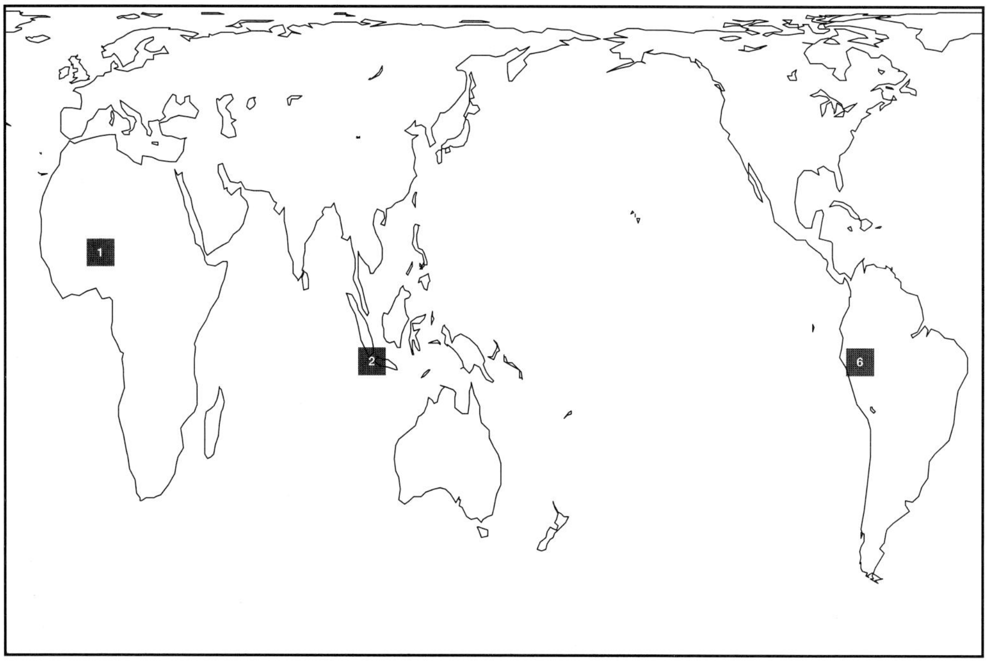

Map 23. Minimum set of grid-cell areas required to maintain all genera of Molossidae.
The minimum number of squares required to conserve all genera is three. The numbers in the squares represent the number of genera uniquely contributing to this minimum set.

island nations are largely excluded. In these situations, bats may represent a significant proportion or even the total mammal fauna, and thus are likely to play a vital role in the ecosystem. Islands are also often under the heaviest threat, mainly from expanding human populations.

Major Tropical Wilderness Areas

This approach focuses on areas of habitat that are still largely intact, where more than 75% of the original pristine vegetation remains and where human population density is low (less than five people per km^2) (Myers 1988, 1990; Conservation International 1990). Three areas have been identified – the Amazon Basin, the Congo Basin, and the island of New Guinea and adjacent archipelagos.

As with the Megadiversity Countries, all three Major Tropical Wilderness Areas are important to bats. However, focusing on these areas would exclude a large number of countries with important and/or threatened bat faunas.

Biodiversity Hotspots

This approach is similar to that of the Major Tropical Wilderness Areas, though it also includes areas outside the tropics. The analysis is based primarily on species numbers using plants as an indicator of species diversity (Mittermeier *et al.* 1998). Hotspots were identified using the criteria of plant endemism and degree of threat. Areas were included that contained more than 0.5% of total global plant diversity represented as endemic species, a minimum of 1,350 species. The degree of threat to habitats was assessed using digitised forest cover data and information on past and present trends in the distribution of original pristine vegetation. Thus, unlike the Major Tropical Wilderness Areas, the Biodiversity Hotspots are areas that have lost much of their original pristine vegetation.

The Tropical Andes tops the list of Biodiversity Hotspots, followed by the Mediterranean Basin, Madagascar and the Indian Ocean Islands, Mesoamerican Forests, and the Caribbean Islands. The list has a wide geographic spread, including many non-tropical ecosystems. So far, 24 Biodiversity Hotspots have been identified that together harbour over 124,000 endemic plant species, representing almost 46% of the world's local endemics.

For bats, this analysis is potentially more useful since it includes areas that do not necessarily have a high mammal diversity, but are still of importance. The inclusion of island nations in the Caribbean, Polynesia, and Micronesia ensures that the small but significant bat faunas of these areas are highlighted. Although the number of bat species in such areas as the Mediterranean Basin, southwestern Australia, and Polynesia/Micronesia is not large, many are threatened by human activities. Indeed, the focus on degree of threat may ensure that a significant proportion of the most threatened bat species are included in this analysis.

Global 200

The Global 200 list identifies the world's most outstanding examples of each major habitat type (Olson and Dinerstein 1998). It recognises that whilst more than half the world's species are found in tropical moist forests, the rest are found elsewhere and to conserve these species requires the conservation of a whole range of habitats. The unit of analysis is the so-called ecoregion. This is defined as a relatively large unit of land or water containing a characteristic set of natural communities that share a large majority of their species, dynamics, and environmental conditions (Dinerstein *et al.* 1995; The Nature Conservancy 1997). Ecoregions are divided initially by realm (terrestrial, freshwater, and marine), then by Major Habitat Types (MHTs) that are roughly equivalent to biomes. MHTs are listed by biogeographic realm to ensure global coverage. The boundaries of ecoregions have been determined following extensive regional analyses. Ecoregions within each biogeographic realm were chosen on the basis of their biological distinctiveness based on the following parameters: species richness, endemism, taxonomic uniqueness, unusual ecological or evolutionary phenomena (such as migrations or exceptional adaptive radiation), and global rarity of MHT (Olson and Dinerstein 1998). Finally the conservation status of terrestrial ecoregions was assessed using regional information. Three broad categories were recognised: critical/endangered (CE), vulnerable (V), and relatively stable/relatively intact (RS).

A total of 233 ecoregions are listed in this analysis – 136 (58%) terrestrial, 36 (16%) freshwater, and 61 (26%) marine. Predictably, the tropical moist forests of South America, Africa, and Southeast Asia are well represented. Other, less well-known habitats such as the dry forests of Mexico, the moist forests of Sulawesi, and the Congolian coastal forests in West Africa are also listed. Among the terrestrial ecoregions, 47% are considered critical or endangered, 29% vulnerable, and only 24% relatively stable or intact. The most threatened MHTs are within tropical dry forests, temperate grasslands, Mediterranean shrublands, and temperate broad-leaf forests. Island ecoregions are particularly vulnerable to species extinction.

For bats, important habitat types are covered in this analysis. The inclusion of freshwater ecosystems is valuable since these may provide important feeding habitats for bats. Riverine vegetation may also be important as both feeding and roosting habitat. The inclusion of less obviously important habitats, such as dry forests, is also key. The highest diversity of bats at a generic level is in the Neotropics and it is likely that such dry habitats play an important role in maintaining this diversity. The inclusion of many habitat types from temperate areas emphasises that threats to bat species in these areas can be as great, if not greater, than in tropical areas. Finally, the emphasis on threat to island ecosystems is crucial in terms of conserving many bat species, genera, and families that are restricted to island states.

Endemic Bird Areas

Of all the analyses of the areas of importance for biodiversity, this is one of the most detailed and comprehensive and has taken 10 years to complete (Stattersfield *et al.* 1998). It focuses on the 2,623 restricted-range landbird species that have had a breeding range of less than 50,000km^2 throughout historical times (since 1800). An Endemic Bird Area (EBA) is defined as an area that encompasses the overlapping breeding ranges of restricted-range bird species, such that the complete ranges of two or more restricted-range species are entirely included within the boundary of the EBA. Seabirds have been excluded from this analysis. The estimated range size of species was based on the "extent of occurence", which encompasses all the known, inferred, or projected sites of current occurence. The strength of the analysis comes from the provision of detailed maps based on 50,000 individual species records.

A total of 218 EBAs have been identified, the majority of which (77%) are found in the tropics and subtropics. There are approximately equal numbers of island EBAs (105) and continental EBAs (113). Seventy percent of island EBAs are on oceanic islands, the rest on the larger continental islands. Of the continental EBAs, 42% are largely in montane areas, 35% in lowland areas, and 24% embrace both these habitats. The key habitat in the majority (83%) of EBAs is forest, mostly tropical lowland and montane moist forest. Temperate and subalpine forest, and tropical dry forest may also be important. Nearly half of all EBAs are estimated to have lost more than 50% of their key habitat and more than 10% have lost over 90% of their key habitat. Most EBAs (85%) have one or more threatened or extinct restricted-range species, and in 23 EBAs all the restricted-range species are threatened. The countries with the most EBAs are Indonesia, Mexico, Peru, Brazil, Colombia, Papua New Guinea, and China. It is an interesting aside that all of these are also listed as Megadiversity Countries and that there is a high overlap with areas that are important for plants. An attempt has been made to rank EBAs in terms of their biological importance and current threat level. Overall, 76 EBAs are Critical priority, 62 are Urgent, and 80 are High priority.

Some habitats of importance to bats, such as caves, will not be targeted in this analysis. On the other hand, some habitats of importance to bird species, such as deserts, high altitude areas, and many oceanic islands may be of lesser significance for bats. However, bats and birds have similar dispersal abilities and it is important to note that on many isolated oceanic islands, bats are the only native mammal species.

Birds are probably the only group where information is currently available to undertake a detailed analysis of endemic areas. One crucial aspect of the EBA analysis is that it provides a methodology that could be followed for other groups. There are insufficient data to determine the levels of overlap between EBAs and areas of endemicity for bats. It has been shown that fewer than half of the most important areas of endemism for birds are also the most important areas for mammals in Afrotropical forests, though these results are preliminary (N. Burgess *pers. comm.*). However, birds and bats do share many biological and ecological attributes (e.g., flight, feeding habits, dispersal), which would suggest the level of congruence might be greater. Until more information is available on the distribution, biology, and ecology of bats, the EBAs may provide a good indication of many areas that are important for bat species.

Centres of Plant Diversity

A full list of Centres of Plant Diversity is given in WWF and IUCN (1994). The concept of identifying Centres of Plant Diversity (CPDs) originated in the early 1980s. There are around 250,000 higher plant species worldwide, an estimated 170,000 of which grow in the tropics. South America is especially rich: between 40–80,000 plant species occur in Brazil, while more than 40,000 are found in Colombia, Ecuador, and Peru. The above figure for total number of higher plant species is almost certainly a considerable underestimate since the World Conservation Monitoring Centre in Cambridge, UK, estimates that there are almost 176,000 single country endemics, and this figure excludes Brazil, Paraguay, and Papua New Guinea. This is supported by the fact that there are incomplete floral inventories for many tropical countries and reflects the situation for many animal groups.

The CPD project aims to: 1) identify which areas of the world, if conserved, would safeguard the greatest number of plant species; 2) document the many benefits, both economic, and scientific, that conservation of those areas would bring to society and to outline the potential value of each for sustainable development; and 3) outline a strategy for the conservation of the areas selected. Areas were selected if they fulfilled either of the following criteria: 1) the area is evidently species-rich, even though the number of species present may not be accurately known; or 2) the area is known to contain a large number of species endemic to it. Other criteria that were also taken into account include the existence of: 1) an important gene pool of plants of value to humans or that are potentially useful; 2) a diverse range of habitat types; 3) a significant proportion of species adapted to special edaphic conditions; and 4) current or imminent threat of large-scale devastation. A total of 490 sites have been identified as Centres of Plant Diversity and Endemism worldwide.

The close relationship between bats and plants is well recorded, particularly in the tropics where many species are thought to rely heavily on primary tropical forest. In South and Central America, bats of the family Phyllostomidae play a key role in the pollination and seed dispersal of a wide variety of plants, many of which are economically important to humans. In the Old World, this role is played largely by fruit bats of the family Pteropodidae. Even species that do not feed on plants still rely on vegetation that supports insects, which is the other major food source for bats worldwide. Vegetation also provides roosting habitat for many bat species. The relationship between endemic plants and bats is less well defined, though it is likely to be more important on islands where bats are often the major or only mammalian pollinator and seed disperser. The protection of CPDs will almost certainly benefit some bat species, particularly on islands.

5.4 Regional accounts and recommendations

5.4.1 Afrotropical Region

This account was compiled using contributions from the following people: Issa Aggundey; the late W.F.H Ansell; Paul Bates; R.T.F. Bernard; Neil Burgess; Annette Carlstrom; John Collie; Brock Fenton; Steve Goodman; David C.D. Happold; Meredith Happold; Kim Howell; Javier Juste; Dieter Kock; the late Karl F. Koopman; Ignatius L. Rautenbach; Victor van Cakenberghe; Don E. Wilson; and Derek Yalden

Geographical boundaries of region

The region includes all of mainland Africa south of the Sahara, together with the island of Madagascar, the oceanic islands of the western Indian Ocean (Mascarenes, Comoros, Seychelles, and Aldabra), and Socotra off the Horn of Africa. The whole of the Arabian Peninsula is excluded. The Cape Verde Islands are included. In North Africa, the boundary begins in the west at 21°30'N, i.e., between Rio de Oro and Mauritania, continues across Mauritania and Mali at the same latitude and thereafter follows the political boundaries, such as to exclude in their entirety Algeria, Libya, and Egypt and to include the whole of Niger, Chad, and Sudan – the Hoggar Mountains are, therefore, excluded and the Tibesti included (see Map 1).

Number of species in the region

A total of 178 microchiropteran bat species have been recorded from the Afrotropical Region. Of these, 31 are threatened – four Critically Endangered, one Endangered, and 26 Vulnerable. A total of 129 species are listed in the Lower Risk categories – 45 as Near Threatened and 84 as Least Concern. A further 18 species are listed as Data Deficient. A full list of species is given at the end of this regional account.

Major threats to bats

The rapidly increasing human population in Africa is the most significant threat to bats. This puts greater pressure on natural resources, such as forests, that are key habitats for many species. Caves are important roost sites and are threatened by disturbance or destruction.

Threats to habitats and roosts

- **Forests** Forests are key habitats for both feeding and roosting. They are threatened by encroachment, shifting agriculture, and logging activities throughout Africa. In some countries, such as Madagascar, all forest types are considered threatened by human incursion. In other areas, such as Ethiopia, Kenya, and especially Tanzania and Malawi, the destruction of montane forest is a major concern.

  Malawi provides a good example of the threat to montane forests. Unlike the national parks and game reserves in Malawi, the forest reserves are not well protected and the future of natural habitats within them is far from secure. Of particular immediate concern is Ntchisi Forest Reserve (13°23'S, 34°00'E), which includes a small area of montane evergreen forest on top of Ntchisi Mountain surrounded by *Brachystegia* woodland savanna. Ntchisi Forest Reserve is listed as one of Malawi's principal timber plantations. This reserve is noted for its unique flora and is frequently mentioned as one of the "special" and important areas of evergreen forest in Malawi. It contains one of the patches of montane forest characteristic of the isolated high plateaux rising from the Central Plateau in the northern half of the country. Some of these are known to have unique mammal faunas because of their isolation from each other. The indigenous forest, especially the montane forest, is being cut down and replaced by plantations of exotic *Pinus*. Also, all of the woodland on the steep hills surrounding the reserve has been removed with consequent erosion. In view of this, it is recommended that the remaining montane forest on Ntchisi Mountain, and a surrounding belt of *Brachystegia* woodland, be protected from further destruction and interference.

  In Kenya, coastal forests are particularly threatened not only by the demand for land to grow food and for materials for building poles and fuelwood, but by the rapidly expanding tourist industry. This increases demand for wood for hotel construction, furniture, and carvings. In other areas of Kenya, commercial activities threaten forests. These include lead ore mining at Kaya Kauma, marble quarrying at Pangani and Kambe, a proposed lime factory at Pangani, and the planned reopening of the rare earth mines on Mrima Hill.

  In South Africa, riparian forests that are key feeding areas for bats have been adversely affected by drought and over-utilisation. Elsewhere, deforestation (of native trees), afforestation (with exotic trees), and swamp drainage will affect important bat-feeding habitat.

The effects of shifting agriculture are widespread, as shown by the example in the mainland area of Equatorial Guinea. On São Tomé and Príncipe, lowland rainforest is threatened by agriculture and land privatisation of the small areas that remain.

- **Grasslands and savanna** In South Africa, highveld grasslands are being replaced by grain monocultures and montane sour grasslands by silviculture of exotic species. Woodland savanna is being threatened by drought, fire, and the removal of trees for use as firewood. In other areas, such as São Tomé, savanna is threatened by increasing development of agriculture and associated human settlements. In some areas, elephants may be a threat to remnant savanna woodland. Permanent and seasonal swamps are being converted to agriculture, for example, for the cultivation of cotton and millet in Malawi.

  In Malawi, woodland savannas with *Hyphaene* palms are considered to be of key importance for bats. In the Lower Shire Valley such palms are used as roosts by bats. *Scotoecus albofuscus* has been rarely collected throughout its geographical range, and only recorded roosting among the leaves of young, low *Hyphaene* palms in forest. *Scotophilus nigrita*, also rarely collected throughout its geographical range, is only found in hollow or large holes in *Hyphaene* palms. It is recommended, therefore, that woodland savannas with *Hyphaene* palms in the Lower Shire Valley need conserving. With species of genera such as *Kerivoula*, *Chalinolobus*, and *Laephotis*, which mainly roost in foliage or bark of open miombo (*Brachystegia/Julbernadia*) or mopane woodland, and perhaps naturally live at low density, increasing encroachment on such woodland for agriculture, grazing, and firewood are potential threats.

Chapin's free-tailed bat, *Tadarida chapini*, a scarce bat of Central and East African dry woodland.

A.M. Hutson

- **Caves** Caves are key roosting sites for many bat species. They are, however, threatened. In coastal areas in Kenya there are many caves that are used by bats. Bats which roost in caves along the coastal shorelines are threatened by developers who acquire the land for the construction of tourist hotels. Some developers, in liaison with local people, would like to develop the caves as tourist attractions to the detriment of bats and the environment. Elsewhere, mining and use of caves by a variety of interest groups, including for guano harvesting and tourism, threaten bat roosts.

Threats to geographical areas

- **Mainland Africa** Whilst threats to bat populations occur throughout mainland Africa, a number of areas have been highlighted because of particular issues. It is likely that these issues will also be relevant in other areas.

  In Southern Africa, the grain belt of South Africa (Orange Free State, southern Transvaal) is an area of extensive monoculture with concomitant use of pesticides. This use of pesticides and habitat loss will inevitably threaten the survival of bat species that use this area. Deforestation for fuel and afforestation of grasslands threatens bat populations. In Zambia, pesticide use has been low and there is a good network of national parks, although the latter may be poorly staffed or resourced.

  The East African area from Ethiopia to Tanzania, in particular the coastal and high altitude forests, is considered to be particularly threatened by, amongst other things, increasing population and deforestation. In Ethiopia, bats are strongly associated with death and thus are killed indiscriminately by most villagers (P.J.J. Bates, *pers. comm.*).

  In Central Africa, Malawi has a rich diversity of bat species and habitats, many of which are threatened by land-use changes, including the cutting of indigenous forest (particularly the remnant high-altitude forest) and conversion of savanna woodland (especially those with *Hyphaene* palm) and permanent and seasonal swamps to agricultural land.

  Little has been reported concerning problems related particularly to bats in West and Equatorial Africa. The area has a very high species diversity. Increasing reliance on shifting agriculture and logging are serious concerns in forested areas such as Rio Muni (Equatorial Guinea). Such problems must be widespread in the region, as must be changes to savanna areas that are likely to mirror those further south, but bats have been subject to limited conservation research in the area in recent decades.

  In some countries, governmental priorities are the welfare of their population, which may mean less resources available for conservation. On the other hand, this can have advantages. For example, in South Africa much effort has been made to protect water resources through improved legislation; this includes the protection of catchments and riparian woodlands. The aim is to ensure a water supply for the people, but the environment benefits indirectly (R.T.F. Bernard *pers. comm.*).

- **Seychelles** The granitic Seychelles have a single endemic microchiropteran, the emballonurid *Coleura seychellensis*, one of two species in the genus. Originally reported as common, this species was recently thought to be possibly extinct. However, two groups totalling 25 animals were found on Silhouette in 1995. The species is still regarded as Critically Endangered. A management plan directs efforts to protect forest and marshland areas that are likely to benefit this species. It roosts in boulder caves that are generally remote and difficult to access. There are also reports of recent sightings of individuals foraging on Mahé and La Digue. Bat detector surveys are required to clarify the status of this species. The low-lying, arid atoll of Aldabra is not facing any major threat as a National Special Reserve and World Heritage Site, but the endemic molossid, *Chaerephon pusilla*, must be regarded as Vulnerable in view of its restriction to this one island.
- **Madagascar** A review published in 1995 (Peterson *et al.* 1995) lists 16 species as endemic, including the monotypic family Myzopodidae. *Myzopoda aurita* is listed as Vulnerable in *The 2000 IUCN Red List of Threatened Species* and the subject of an Action Plan in this volume. As with many other areas, the most serious threats are identified as increasing human population and associated deforestation. In limestone areas of western Madagascar, human predation of *Hipposideros* and *Triaenops* species presents a considerable risk to some colonies. During some seasons near Tsimanampetsotsa, large numbers of *Hipposideros commersoni* are captured on balls of plant burrs attached to sticks (S. Goodman *pers. comm.*)
- **Gulf of Guinea Islands** On the Gulf of Guinea Islands (Bioko and São Tomé and Príncipe), there is a greatly expanding population and this, coupled with the collapse of the local cocoa economy, threatens habitats and ultimately bats on these islands. There is very little information available about the status and ecology of bats on the Gulf of Guinea Islands, about 50% of which are endemic at least at the subspecies level.

Threats to higher taxa

- **Genus *Coleura* (Family Emballonuridae)** The genus includes two species, one widespread and not apparently threatened on the African mainland, the other Critically Endangered in the Seychelles.
- **Family Myzopodidae** The single species of the family is found only in Madagascar, which appears to be restricted to the eastern rainforests. It can be found both in forests or in marshes with extensive tracts of *Ravenala*. Little is known of its requirements or status, but it is likely to be affected by continued forest clearance. An Action Plan for this species is presented in this volume.
- **Subfamily Kerivoulinae (Family Vespertilionidae)** The subfamily Kerivoulinae is represented by seven species of *Kerivoula* in the Afrotropical Region. Two (*K. aerosa* and *K. africana*) are listed as Data Deficient in *The 2000 IUCN Red List of Threatened Species*; *K. aerosa*, although described from South Africa, may be an Asian species. Two further species are sufficiently rarely recorded and restricted in distribution to be of conservation concern. The species are apparently thinly distributed with low population densities. They are possibly vulnerable to the impacts of agriculture through clearance of scrub, overgrazing, and other activities. The species roost in such situations as in deserted weaver bird nests in open woodland, and thus may be threatened through destruction of natural vegetation. On the other hand, they do not form large colonies and, therefore, lack the vulnerability of highly colonial species. Also, their slow and highly manoeuvrable flight, coupled with the acuity of their echolocation system, may result in low catch rates in mist-nets and traps.
- **Genus *Chalinolobus* (Family Vespertilionidae)** There are nine Afrotropical species of *Chalinolobus*, only two of which (*C. argentatus* and *C. variegatus*) can be considered safe. Most species are rarely caught and, hence, poorly known. They generally roost in small groups, usually less than 10, but up to 30 in *C. argentatus*. As with *Kerivoula,* they most commonly roost in open woodland vegetation so that destruction of natural vegetation may be a major threat. No other specific threats have been suggested.
- **Genus *Myotis* (Family Vespertilionidae)** Only three of eight species (*M. bocagei*, *M. tricolor*, and *M. welwitschii*) are widely distributed in the region and even these are poorly known. This genus, the most species-rich amongst bats, is poorly represented in Africa and most of the species are rare.
- **Genus *Otomops* (Family Molossidae)** Although widespread on the African mainland and also in Yemen on the Arabian Peninsula, the single species, *O. martiensseni*, is far from common and the only known sizeable colonies have undergone severe reduction in numbers within the last 25 years. The population on Madagascar has recently been separated as *O. madagascariensis*, but is only known from a few specimens. The three Indomalayan species are all very poorly known and the genus is discussed in the Species Action Plan for *O. martiensseni*.

Other issues

House-dwelling species

A range of species roost in houses and thus come into direct contact, and sometimes conflict with humans.

Molossids, such as *Mops condylurus* and *Chaerephon pumila* use the roofs of houses and other buildings. Residents are very aware of their presence as a result of smell, noise, and faeces. In South Africa, where *Tadarida aegyptiaca* is the most common house bat, such species are indiscriminately fumigated or otherwise destroyed. In Malawi, however, rarely is any action taken to exclude or exterminate the bats. Other house-dwelling species, such as *Scotophilus* spp. are usually less noticeable and often ignored because they do not create the same problems. In South Africa, and probably the rest of the continent, bats that roost in houses are not afforded the same protection as in Europe.

Poisoning

Bats are threatened by poisoning, both directly and indirectly. In Africa, some weaver birds are controlled by the use of avicides. Some of these are toxic to bats and can affect animals that use weaver bird nests as roosts. In some cases, bats that roost in houses are deliberately poisoned by commercial firms. The use of pesticides in areas that are affected by locust migrations has an indirect effect on bats by damaging their feeding areas. They may also directly poison the bats themselves. In South Africa, as in other countries, bats are considered at worst vermin and at best as pests. The public's awareness of the ecological significance of bats needs to be developed through public education.

Lack of knowledge

Many species are rarely recorded and this makes status assessments difficult. The biology and ecology of most species in Africa is poorly known. A concerted and coordinated effort is required to document basic information on bat biology. It is important to ensure that policy- and decision-makers are made fully aware of the importance of bats and their role in African ecosystems.

Key areas for bat biodiversity

Hotspots at a generic level

Centres of diversity at the generic level were assessed using a WORLDMAP analysis (see Chapter 5.3 for further details). For much of mainland Africa the level of diversity is fairly even, but with a peak in generic diversity in the East (Map 24). The minimum set of grid-cell areas required to maintain all genera is four, but none of those given on Map 25 is unique and for most there are several alternatives.

Species richness and endemism

Neil Burgess of the University of Copenhagen, working with Dieter Kock and Jakob Fahrs, has compiled a provisional series of distribution maps for African microchiroptera. Using these, information on species richness and endemism has been assessed. It is important to stress that this is a preliminary analysis and the results may change as more information is added.

The map for species richness shows centres of richness in the following areas:

1. Rift Valley around Lake Albert (Democratic Republic of Congo and Uganda);
2. Eastern African mountain and coastal lowland forests (Kenya, Tanzania, and Uganda);
3. Ethiopia;
4. Border of Zambia and Zimbabwe;
5. West African Guinea savanna.

The last area may be a result of mapping problems with savanna and forest maps overlapping, or may be because the forest and savanna bats are actually both found in rather dense and somewhat forest-like Guinea savanna.

The following areas are centres of endemism:

1. Liberia;
2. Mountains of Cameroon;
3. Albertine Rift Mountains (Democratic Republic of Congo and Uganda), though the evidence for this is rather weak;

Map 24. Generic richness per grid-cell area for genera occurring in the Afrotropical Region.
The numbers in the squares represent the number of genera per unit area.

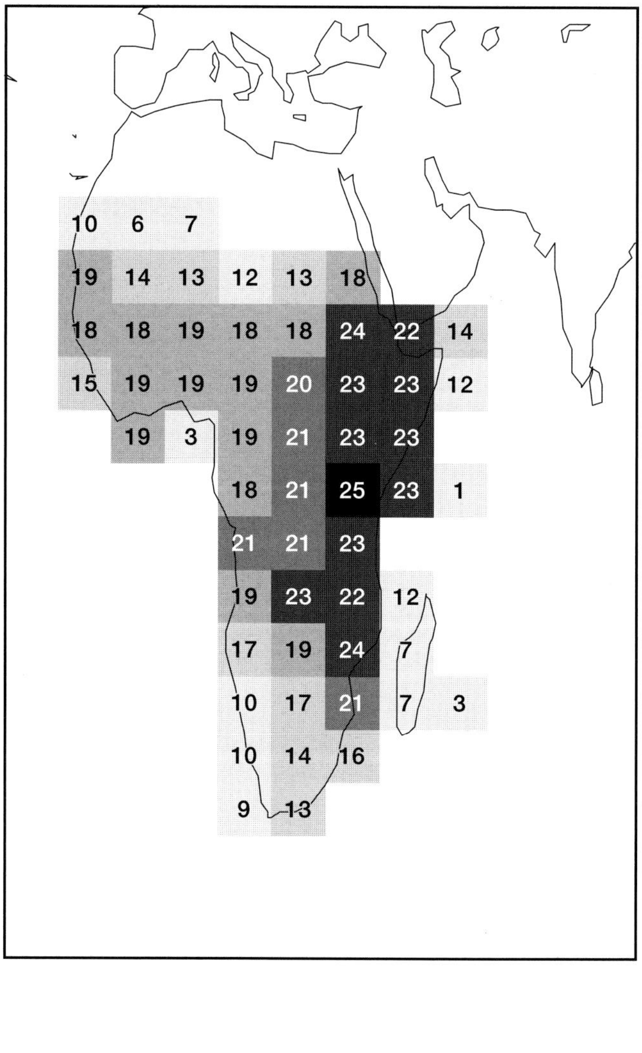

4. Northern Eritrea;
5. Southern Ethiopia;
6. Eastern arc and coastal forests of eastern Africa (Kenya, Tanzania, and Uganda);
7. Border of Zambia and Zimbabwe;
8. Coast of South Africa.

This analysis will improve as more information becomes available, but these broad trends are probably accurate at present. Centres of endemism for bats coincide with those for many other mammal groups.

Ethiopia

Key areas include Bale Province and Awash National Park. In addition, the Sof Omar cave complex east of Bale, and the western forests and grasslands near Gambela on the Sudanese border are key habitats for bats. There are seven globally threatened species in Ethiopia, all of them Vulnerable.

Map 25. Minimum set of grid-cell areas required to maintain all genera occurring in the Afrotropical Region.

The minimum number of squares required to conserve all genera is four. The numbers in the squares represent the number of genera uniquely contributing to this minimum set.

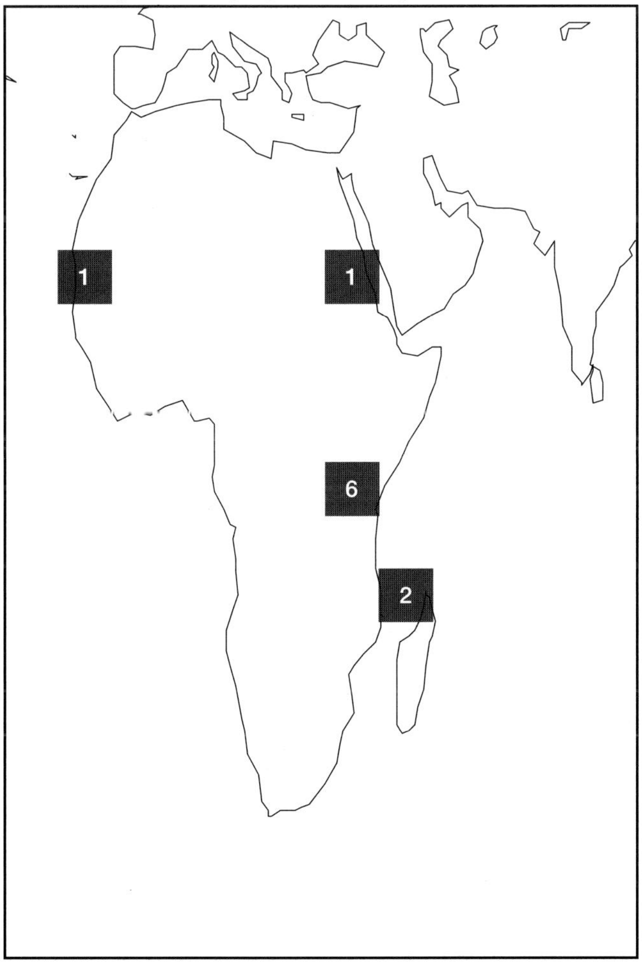

Malawi

Three areas have been identified as of importance for bats (Chiromo, the Shire Highlands, and Liwonde National Park) and have bat faunas with over 25 species.

Kenya

The areas in Kenya that have been pinpointed as being of importance to bats include the coastal area forests, the southwest Mau Forest, the Kakamega Forest and Mt. Elgon, and the Cherangani Hills. Five globally threatened species have been recorded from Kenya, all of them Vulnerable.

South Africa

Two areas of South Africa have been highlighted as being of particular importance for bats. These are northeast Transvaal, particularly along rivers in *Acacia* or mopane woodlands, and the coastal plains on northern Natal. There are five globally threatened species recorded from South Africa, all of them Vulnerable.

Gulf of Guinea Islands

This is an area of high bat biodiversity. The mainland area from southern Nigeria to northern Gabon has a diversity that includes more than 100 species and subspecies of bats. Almost nothing is known of the distribution, population status, habitat requirements, and reproductive biology or ecology of any of the bats of the Gulf of Guinea Islands. The scarce data indicate low population levels of all endemic species and striking seasonal changes in the distribution and behaviour of others. A number of species have only been recorded at a very few locations and are considered rare. The impact of ongoing human activities needs to be assessed and more information must be gathered to plan strategies for the conservation of this unique bat fauna, which should be included in the country's nature protection policies. The islands of São Tomé, Príncipe, and Annobón are important because of their high levels of endemism. Bioko has the richest bat biodiversity with at least 26 species. São Tomé has nine species (five endemic), Príncipe has four (two endemic subspecies), and Annobón two. One species in São Tomé and Príncipe is globally threatened.

Madagascar

A revision of the bat fauna of Madagascar (Peterson *et al.* 1995) listed 26 species of Microchiroptera, including the endemic monotypic family Myzopodidae. In this volume, one of these is considered a synonym. Over half the species are regarded as endemic to Madagascar, including two species also on the Comoros and one also recorded from Aldabra. Bayliss and Hayes (1999) report on the results of a detailed bat survey that showed Makira and Masoala to probably have the highest density of bat species on Madagascar. Seven globally threatened species have been recorded from Madagascar – one Critically Endangered and six Vulnerable.

Recommendations

The following recommendations are based upon information provided by the contributors to this section. They include both general recommendations applicable to the whole area, as well as specific ones relating to particular species, areas, or habitats.

Habitats

Of particular concern are wetlands, forest, riparian woodland, and savanna woodland. Semidesert areas may also be threatened. Use of pesticides, including avicides and insecticides, is also considered a threat.

Recommendations:
- instigate further survey work and research to identify key areas and habitat requirements for integrated management of threatened habitats;
- protect high altitude forests;
- protect montane forests, particularly in Ethiopia, Kenya, Tanzania, and Malawi;
- protect coastal forests in Kenya;
- protect lowland forests on São Tomé and Príncipe;
- protect riparian forest;
- protect highveld grasslands in South Africa;
- protect savanna and savanna woodland;
- control conversion of savanna woodlands to agricultural lands;
- control draining of permanent and seasonal swamps for agriculture.

Roost types

Threats to caves include tourism and development. A range of other concerns about caves have been identified and boulder jumbles may also be included here. Bats using buildings are heavily persecuted and this particularly affects a range of molossids, as well as rhinolophid, hipposiderid, and *Scotophilus* species.

Recommendations:
- identify and protect key sites, create management agreements for other sites as appropriate, develop educational programmes;
- protect coastal caves in Kenya;
- protect house bat roosts where appropriate;
- develop programmes of education regarding bats in houses where appropriate;
- develop systems to resolve conflicts between humans and bats.

Geographical areas

Deforestation of Madagascar, and forest and savanna degradation in the Gulf of Guinea Islands and the adjacent mainland are specific concerns. The grain belt of South Africa, with large-scale monoculture and heavy use of pesticides, threatens resident bat populations.

Recommendations:
- adopt Agenda 21 principles of sustainable development;
- conduct further studies of status and ecology of bats on Madagascar;
- study status and ecology of bats on the Gulf of Guinea Islands;
- control pesticide usage in grain belt of South Africa.

Taxa

Taxa highlighted include the family Myzopodidae, subfamily Kerivoulinae, *Chalinolobus*, and *Myotis*, which all comprise poorly known and rarely encountered species.

Recommendations:
- investigate distribution, status, and threats from changing land use, including loss of natural vegetation, and develop appropriate action;
- assess status of *Coleura seychellensis*, including bat detector surveys;
- assess status and ecological requirements of *Myzopoda aurita*;
- assess status of Vulnerable and Data Deficient *Kerivoula* species;
- assess status of *Myotis* species;
- assess status of *Otomops martiensseni* and *O. madagascariensis*;
- assess status and threats to threatened *Chalinolobus* species;
- assess status of *Chaerephon pusilla* on Aldabra.

Education

Recommendations:
- develop public awareness campaign on ecological significance of bats;
- inform policy and decision makers of role of bats in African ecosystems.

Research

Recommendations:
- document information on basic bat biology;
- assess bat conservation issues in West and equatorial Africa;
- assess threats from mining activities, particularly in Malawi;
- assess threat to bat populations by human predation, particularly in Madagascar;
- assess impact of avicides on bat populations;
- assess impact of ongoing human activities in Gulf of Guinea Islands.

Miscellaneous

Recommendation:
- strengthen national park infrastructure.

Checklist of Afrotropical bats

A total of 178 species are recorded from the Afrotropical Region. The full list is given below.

Species	Status
FAMILY RHINOPOMATIDAE	
Rhinopoma	
Rhinopoma hardwickei Gray 1831	LR: lc
Rhinopoma microphyllum (Brünnich 1782)	LR: lc
Rhinopoma macinnesi Hayman 1937	VU: A2c, D2
FAMILY EMBALLONURIDAE	
Coleura	
Coleura afra (Peters 1852)	LR: lc
Coleura seychellensis Peters 1868	CR: B1 + 2cde, C2b, D
Emballonura	
Emballonura atrata Peters 1874	VU: A2c
Saccolaimus	
Saccolaimus peli (Temminck 1853)	LR: nt
Taphozous	
Taphozous hamiltoni Thomas 1920	VU: A2c
Taphozous hildegardeae Thomas 1909	VU: A2c
Taphozous mauritianus E. Geoffroy 1818	LR: lc
Taphozous nudiventris Cretzschmar 1830	LR: lc
Taphozous perforatus E. Geoffroy 1818	LR: lc
FAMILY NYCTERIDAE	
Nycteris	
Nycteris arge Thomas 1903	LR: lc
Nycteris aurita K. Andersen 1912	LR: nt
Nycteris gambiensis (K. Andersen 1912)	LR: lc
Nycteris grandis Peters 1865	LR: lc
Nycteris hispida (Schreber 1775)	LR: lc
Nycteris intermedia Aellen 1959	LR: nt
Nycteris macrotis Dobson 1876	LR: lc
Nycteris madagascariensis Grandidier 1937	DD
Nycteris major (K. Andersen 1912)	VU: A2c, D2
Nycteris nana (K. Andersen 1912)	LR: lc
Nycteris thebaica E. Geoffroy 1818	LR: lc
Nycteris woodi K. Andersen 1914	LR: nt
FAMILY MEGADERMATIDAE	
Cardioderma	
Cardioderma cor (Peters 1872)	LR: nt
Lavia	
Lavia frons (E. Geoffroy 1810)	LR: lc
FAMILY HIPPOSIDERIDAE	
Asellia	
Asellia patrizii DeBeaux 1931	VU: A2c, D2
Asellia tridens (E. Geoffroy 1813)	LR: lc
Cloeotis	
Cloeotis percivali Thomas 1901	LR: nt
Hipposideros	
Hipposideros abae J. A. Allen 1917	LR: lc
Hipposideros beatus K. Andersen 1906	LR: lc
Hipposideros caffer (Sundevall 1846)	LR: lc
Hipposideros camerunensis Eisentraut 1956	LR: nt
Hipposideros commersoni (E. Geoffroy 1813)	LR: lc
Hipposideros curtus G. M. Allen 1921	LR: nt

Species	Status
Hipposideros cyclops (Temminck 1853)	LR: lc
Hipposideros fuliginosus (Temminck 1853)	LR: nt
Hipposideros jonesi Hayman 1947	LR: nt
Hipposideros lamottei Brosset 1984	DD
Hipposideros marisae Aellen 1954	VU: A2c
Hipposideros megalotis (Heuglin 1862)	LR: nt
Hipposideros ruber (Noack 1893)	LR: lc
Triaenops	
Triaenops auritus Grandidier 1912	DD
Triaenops furculus Trouessart 1906	VU: A2c
Triaenops persicus Dobson 1871	LR: lc
Triaenops rufus Milne-Edwards 1881	DD
FAMILY RHINOLOPHIDAE	
Rhinolophus	
Rhinolophus adami Aellen and Brosset 1968	DD
Rhinolophus alcyone Temminck 1852	LR: nt
Rhinolophus blasii Peters 1866	LR: nt
Rhinolophus capensis Lichtenstein 1823	VU: A2c, D2
Rhinolophus clivosus Cretzschmar 1828	LR: lc
Rhinolophus darlingi K. Andersen 1905	LR: lc
Rhinolophus deckenii Peters 1867	DD
Rhinolophus denti Thomas 1904	LR: lc
Rhinolophus eloquens K. Andersen 1905	LR: lc
Rhinolophus fumigatus Rüppell 1842	LR: lc
Rhinolophus guineensis Eisentraut 1960	LR: nt
Rhinolophus hildebrandti Peters 1878	LR: lc
Rhinolophus hipposideros (Bechstein 1800)	VU: A2c
Rhinolophus landeri Martin 1838	LR: lc
Rhinolophus maclaudi Pousargues 1897	LR: nt
Rhinolophus silvestris Aellen 1959	LR: nt
Rhinolophus simulator K. Andersen 1904	LR: lc
Rhinolophus swinnyi Gough 1908	LR: lc
FAMILY MYZOPODIDAE	
Myzopoda	
Myzopoda aurita Milne-Edwards and A. Grandidier 1878	VU: A2c
FAMILY VESPERTILIONIDAE	
Subfamily Kerivoulinae	
Kerivoula	
?*Kerivoula aerosa* (Tomes 1858)	DD
Kerivoula africana Dobson 1878	DD
Kerivoula argentata Tomes 1861	LR: lc
Kerivoula cuprosa Thomas 1912	LR: nt
Kerivoula lanosa (A. Smith 1847)	LR: lc
Kerivoula phalaena Thomas 1912	LR: lc
Kerivoula smithi Thomas 1880	LR: nt
Barbastella	
Barbastella leucomelas (Cretzschmar 1826)	LR: lc
Chalinolobus	
Chalinolobus alboguttatus (J. A. Allen 1917)	VU: D2
Chalinolobus argentatus (Dobson 1875)	LR: lc
Chalinolobus beatrix (Thomas 1901)	LR: nt
Chalinolobus egeria (Thomas 1913)	LR: nt
Chalinolobus gleni (Peterson and Smith 1973)	LR: nt

Species	Status
Chalinolobus kenyacola (Peterson 1982)	DD
Chalinolobus poensis (Gray 1842)	LR: nt
Chalinolobus superbus (Hayman 1939)	VU: D2
Chalinolobus variegatus (Tomes 1861)	LR: lc
Eptesicus	
Eptesicus brunneus (Thomas 1880)	LR: nt
Eptesicus capensis (A. Smith 1829)	LR: lc
Eptesicus flavescens (Seabra 1900)	DD
Eptesicus floweri (de Winton 1901)	LR: nt
Eptesicus guineensis (Bocage 1889)	LR: nt
Eptesicus hottentotus (A. Smith 1833)	LR: lc
Eptesicus matroka (Thomas and Schwann 1905)	DD
Eptesicus melckorum Roberts 1919	LR: lc
Eptesicus platyops (Thomas 1901)	VU: D2
Eptesicus rendalli (Thomas 1889)	LR: lc
Eptesicus somalicus (Thomas 1901)	LR: lc
Eptesicus tenuipinnis (Peters 1872)	LR: lc
Eptesicus zuluensis Roberts 1924	LR: nt
Laephotis	
Laephotis angolensis Monard 1935	LR: nt
Laephotis botswanae Setzer 1971	LR: nt
Laephotis namibensis Setzer 1971	EN: A2c
Laephotis wintoni Thomas 1901	LR: nt
Mimetillus	
Mimetillus moloneyi (Thomas 1891)	LR: lc
Myotis	
Myotis bocagei (Peters 1870)	LR: lc
Myotis goudoti (A. Smith 1834)	LR: nt
Myotis lesueuri Roberts 1919	VU: A2c, D2
Myotis morrisi Hill 1971	VU: D2
Myotis scotti Thomas 1927	VU: A2c, D2
Myotis seabrai Thomas 1912	VU: A2c, D2
Myotis tricolor (Temminck 1832)	LR: lc
Myotis welwitschii (Gray 1866)	LR: lc
Nyctalus	
?*Nyctalus noctula* (Schreber 1774)	LR: lc
Nycticeinops	
Nycticeinops schlieffeni (Peters 1859)	LR: lc
Otonycteris	
Otonycteris hemrichii Peters 1859	LR: lc
Pipistrellus	
Pipistrellus aegyptius (Fischer 1829)	LR: lc
Pipistrellus aero Heller 1912	DD
Pipistrellus anchietai (Seabra 1900)	VU: A2c
Pipistrellus ariel Thomas 1904	VU: D2
Pipistrellus crassulus Thomas 1904	LR: lc
Pipistrellus eisentrauti Hill 1968	LR: lc
Pipistrellus inexpectatus Aellen 1959	LR: lc
Pipistrellus kuhlii (Kuhl 1817)	LR: lc
Pipistrellus musciculus Thomas 1913	LR: nt
Pipistrellus nanulus Thomas 1904	LR: lc
Pipistrellus nanus (Peters 1852)	LR: lc
Pipistrellus permixtus Aellen 1957	DD
Pipistrellus rueppelli (Fischer 1829)	LR: lc
Pipistrellus rusticus (Tomes 1861)	LR: lc
Scotoecus	
Scotoecus albofuscus Thomas 1890	LR: nt
Scotoecus hirundo de Winton 1899	LR: lc
Scotophilus	
Scotophilus borbonicus (E. Geoffroy 1803)	CR: A1c
Scotophilus dinganii (A. Smith 1833)	LR: lc
Scotophilus leucogaster (Cretzschmar 1826)	LR: lc
Scotophilus nigrita (Schreber 1774)	LR: nt
Scotophilus nux Thomas 1904	LR: lc
Scotophilus robustus Milne-Edwards 1881	LR: nt
Scotophilus viridis (Peters 1852)	LR: lc
Subfamily Miniopterinae	
Miniopterus	
Miniopterus fraterculus Thomas and Schwann 1906	LR: nt
Miniopterus gleni Peterson, Eger, and Mitchell 1995	LR: nt
Miniopterus inflatus Thomas 1903	LR: lc
Miniopterus majori Thomas 1906	DD
Miniopterus menavi Thomas 1906	DD
Miniopterus minor Peters 1866	LR: nt
Miniopterus schreibersii (Kuhl 1817)	LR: nt
FAMILY MOLOSSIDAE	
Chaerephon	
Chaerephon aloysiisabaudiae (Festa 1907)	LR: lc
Chaerephon ansorgei (Thomas 1913)	LR: lc
Chaerephon bemmeleni (Jentink 1879)	LR: lc
Chaerephon bivittata (Heuglin 1861)	LR: lc
Chaerephon chapini J. A. Allen 1917	LR: nt
Chaerephon gallagheri (Harrison 1975)	CR: B1 + 2c
Chaerephon leucogaster (Grandidier 1869)	DD
Chaerephon major (Trouessart 1897)	LR: lc
Chaerephon nigeriae Thomas 1913	LR: lc
Chaerephon pumila (Cretzschmar 1826)	LR: lc
Chaerephon pusilla (Miller 1902)	VU: D1 + 2
Chaerephon russata J. A. Allen 1917	LR: lc
Chaerephon tomensis Juste and Ibanez 1993	VU: A2c, D2
Mops	
Mops brachypterus (Peters 1852)	LR: lc
Mops condylurus (A. Smith 1833)	LR: lc
Mops congicus J. A. Allen 1917	LR: nt
Mops demonstrator (Thomas 1903)	LR: nt
Mops leucostigma (Allen 1918)	DD
Mops midas (Sundevall 1843)	LR: lc
Mops nanulus J. A. Allen 1917	LR: lc
Mops niangarae J. A. Allen 1917	CR: B1 + 2c
Mops niveiventer Cabrera and Ruxton 1926	LR: lc
Mops petersoni (El Rayah 1981)	LR: nt
Mops spurrelli (Dollman 1911)	LR: lc
Mops thersites (Thomas 1903)	LR: lc
Mops trevori J. A. Allen 1917	LR: nt
Mormopterus	
Mormopterus acetabulosus (Hermann 1804)	VU: B1 + 2c
Mormopterus jugularis (Peters 1865)	VU: A2c
Mormopterus petrophilus (Roberts 1917)	LR: lc
Mormopterus setiger Peters 1878	LR: lc
Myopterus	
Myopterus daubentonii Desmarest 1820	DD
Myopterus whitleyi (Scharff 1900)	LR: lc
Otomops	
Otomops martiensseni (Matschie 1897)	VU: A2c
Tadarida	
Tadarida aegyptiaca (E. Geoffroy 1818)	LR: lc
Tadarida fulminans (Thomas 1903)	LR: nt
Tadarida lobata (Thomas 1891)	VU: D2
Tadarida ventralis (Heuglin 1861)	LR: nt

Table 3. Number of IUCN Red List species for countries in the Afrotropical region.
The table also includes information on numbers of endemics and the estimated size of the bat fauna. For sources of the figures for size of faunas see Chapter 6. Full lists of IUCN Red List species per country are given in the same Chapter. **Countries not listed here do not have a recorded bat fauna.**

	IUCN RED LIST SPECIES								ENDEMICS	TOTAL NO. OF SPECIES		
Country	**CR**	**EN**	**VU**	**LRcd**	**LRnt**	**EX**	**DD**	***Total***	***Total***	**Mega**	**Micro**	***Total***
Angola	0	0	3	0	6	0	2	11	0	15	43	58
Benin	0	0	1	0	0	0	0	1	0	4	21	25
Botswana	0	0	0	0	5	0	1	6	0	2	28	30
Burkina Faso	0	0	0	0	2	0	0	2	0	5	25	30
Burundi	0	0	0	0	0	0	1	1	0	5	17	22
Cameroon	0	0	2	0	16	0	0	18	0	14	57	71
Cape Verde Is.	0	0	0	0	0	0	0	0	0	0	2	2
Central African Republic	0	0	1	0	1	0	0	2	0	10	16	26
Chad	0	0	1	0	0	0	0	1	0	4	17	21
Comoros	0	0	0	0	2	0	0	2	0	3	2	5
Congo Rep.	0	0	1	0	7	0	1	9	1	12	36	48
Côte d'Ivoire	0	0	3	0	4	0	1	8	0	12	34	46
D.R.C.(1)	2	0	5	0	25	0	1	33	2	17	78	95
Djibouti	0	0	1	0	1	0	0	2	0	0	2	2
Eq. Guinea	0	0	1	0	8	0	0	9	0	9	39	48
Eritrea	0	0	2	0	0	0	0	2	0	0	11	11
Ethiopia	0	0	7	0	12	0	1	20	1	8	58	66
Gabon	0	0	1	0	5	0	0	6	0	9	23	32
Gambia	0	0	0	0	1	0	0	1	0	4	23	27
Ghana	0	0	2	0	16	0	1	19	0	13	71	84
Guinea	0	0	1	0	6	0	1	8	1	9	28	37
Guinea-Bissau	0	0	0	0	5	0	0	5	0	7	28	35
Kenya	0	0	5	0	17	0	2	24	1	10	72	82
Lesotho	0	0	0	0	0	0	0	0	0	0	4	4
Liberia	0	0	2	0	8	0	1	11	0	12	35	47
Madagascar	1	0	6	0	7	0	8	22	14	3	25	28
Malawi	0	0	0	0	8	0	1	9	0	6	51	57
Mali	0	0	0	0	3	0	0	3	0	3	15	18
Mauritania	0	0	0	0	0	0	0	0	0	0	13	13
Mauritius	0	0	1	0	0	0	0	1	0	1	2	3
Mayotte	0	0	0	0	0	0	0	0	0	1	1	2
Mozambique	0	0	0	0	7	0	1	8	0	5	41	46
Namibia	0	1	1	0	3	0	1	6	1	3	23	26
Niger	0	0	0	0	0	0	0	0	0	2	19	21
Nigeria	0	0	2	0	11	0	0	13	0	12	59	71
Réunion	1	0	1	0	0	0	0	2	0	2	3	5
Rwanda	0	0	1	0	3	0	0	4	0	8	33	41
São Tomé and Príncipe	0	0	1	0	1	0	0	2	1	3	6	9
Senegal	0	0	2	0	5	0	1	8	0	5	36	41
Seychelles	1	0	2	0	0	0	0	3	2	1	3	4
Sierra Leone	0	0	0	0	9	0	1	10	0	10	46	56
Somalia	0	0	1	0	6	0	0	7	0	2	35	37
South Africa	0	0	5	0	10	0	2	17	3	4	47	51
Sudan	0	0	3	0	10	0	0	13	0	9	58	67
Swaziland	0	0	0	0	1	0	0	1	0	1	10	11
Tanzania	0	0	2	0	13	0	3	18	2	13	66	79
Togo	0	0	0	0	3	0	0	3	0	9	31	40
Uganda	0	0	1	0	13	0	0	14	0	11	51	62
Zambia	0	0	2	0	8	0	0	10	0	11	54	65
Zimbabwe	0	0	2	0	8	0	1	11	0	6	41	47

Note:
1. Democratic Republic of Congo (formerly Zaire)

Table 3 shows the number of IUCN Red List species recorded from each country together with information on numbers of endemics and the size of the total bat fauna.

Key references

The following is a list of important references relating to bats in the Afrotropical region. It is by no means an exhaustive list and concentrates mainly on distributional studies at a national or regional level.

Aellen, V. 1952. Contribution à l'étude des chiroptères du Cameroun. *Mémoires de la Société des Sciences Naturelles de Neuchâtel*, 8, 1–121.

Aggundey, I.R. and Schlitter, D.A. 1985. Annotated checklist of the mammals of Kenya. I. Chiroptera. *Annals of the Carnegie Museum*, 53 (5), 119–158.

Allen, G.M. 1939. A checklist of African mammals. *Bulletin of the Museum of Comparative Zoology, Harvard College*, 83, 1–763.

Allen, G.M. and Coolidge, H.J. 1930. Mammals of Liberia. *In: The African Republic of Liberia and the Belgian Congo. Based on observations made and material collected during the Harvard East African Expedition 1926–1927.* (ed. R.P. Strong). Harvard University Press, Cambridge.

Ansell, W.F.H. 1960. *Mammals of Northern Rhodesia.* Lusaka.

Ansell, W.F.H. 1978. *The mammals of Zambia.* National Parks and Wildlife Service, Chilanga.

Ansell, W.F.H. and Dowsett, R.J. 1988. *The mammals of Malawi.* The Trendrine Press, Trendrine.

Baeten, B., van Cakenberghe, V., and de Vree, F. 1984. An annotated inventory of a collection of bats from Rwanda. *Revue de Zoologie et de Botanique Africaines*, 98, 183–196.

Barnett, A.A. and Prangley, M.L. 1997. Mammalogy in the Republic of Guinea: An overview of research from 1946 to 1996, a preliminary check-list and a summary of research recommendations for the future. *Mammal Review*, 27 (3), 115–164.

Cabrera, A. 1929. Catalogo descriptivo de los mammiferos de la Guinea Espanola. *Memorias de la Real Sociedad Espãnola de Historia Natural*, 16, 1–121.

Cansdale, G.S. 1948. *Provisional checklist of Gold Coast mammals.* Government Printing Department, Accra.

Cheke, A.S. and Dahl, A.F. 1981. The status of bats on western Indian Ocean islands, with special reference to *Pteropus*. *Mammalia*, 45, 205–238.

De Beaux, O. 1924. Mammiferi della Somalia Italiana. *Atti della Societá Ligustica di Scienze Naturali e Geograpfiche*, 1, 149–168.

Dekeyser, P.L. 1955. *Les mammifères de l'Afrique Française*. Dakar.

Dowsett, R.J. and Granjon, L. 1991. Liste préliminaire des mammifères du Congo. *Tauraco Research Report*, 4, 297–310.

Eisentraut, M. 1964. La faune de chiroptères de Fernando-Po. *Mammalia*, 28, 529–552.

Ellerman, J.R., Morrison-Scott, T.C.S., and Hayman, R.W. 1953. *Southern African mammals 1758 to 1951: A reclassification.* British Museum (Natural History), London.

Fenton, M.B. 1975. Observations on the biology of some Rhodesian bats, including a key to the Chiroptera of Rhodesia. *Life Sciences Contributions, Royal Ontario Museum*, 104, 1–27.

Fenton, M.B. and Rautenbach, I.L. 1998. Impacts of ignorance and human and elephant populations on the conservation of bats in African woodlands. Pp. 261–270 *in: Bat biology and conservation* (eds. T.H. Kunz and P.A. Racey). Smithsonian Institution Press, Washington DC.

Funaioli, G. and A.M. Simonetta 1966. The mammalian fauna of the Somali Republic: Status and conservation problems. *Monitore Zoologico Italiano (Supplement)*, 74, 285–347.

Garbutt, N. 1999. *Mammals of Madagascar.* Pica Press, East Sussex.

Gerlach, J. (ed.) 1997. *Seychelles red data book – 1997*. The Nature Protection Trust of Seychelles, Victoria, Mahé.

Grubb, P., Jones, T.S., Davies, A.G., Edberg, E., Starin, A.D., and Hill, J.E. 1998. *Mammals of Ghana, Sierra Leone and The Gambia.* Trendrine Press, Zennor.

Happold, D.C.D. 1987. *The mammals of Nigeria.* Clarendon Press, Oxford.

Happold, D.C.D, Happold, M., and Hill, J. Edwards, 1987. The bats of Malawi. *Mammalia*, 51 (3), 337–414.

Harrison, D.L. 1960. A checklist of the bats (Chiroptera) of Kenya Colony. *Journal of the East African Natural History Society and National Museum*, 23 (7), 286–295.

Hayman, R.W. 1967. *Preliminary identification manual for African mammals. 2. Chiroptera.* U.S. National Museum, Washington DC.

Hayman, R.W. and Hill, J. Edwards 1971. Order Chiroptera. Pp. 1–73 *in: The mammals of Africa. An identification manual. Part 2.* (eds. J. Meester and H.W. Setzer). Smithsonian Institution Press, Washington DC.

Hayman, R.W., Misonne, X., and Verheyen, W. 1966. The bats of the Congo and of Rwanda and Burundi. *Annales. Musée Royal de l'Afrique Centrale*, 154, 1–105.

Hill, J. Edwards 1971. The bats of Aldabra Atoll, western Indian Ocean. *Philosophical Transactions of the Royal Society London B* 260, 573–576.

Hill, J. Eric and Carter, T.D. 1941. The mammals of Angola, Africa. *Bulletin of the American Museum of Natural History*, 78 (1), 1–212.

Hutton, J.M. 1986. The status and distribution of bats in Zimbabwe. *Cimbebasia, (Series A)*, 8 (26), 219–236.

Juste, J. and Ibanez, C. 1993. Bats of the Gulf of Guinea Islands: Faunal composition and origins. *Biodiversity and Conservation*, 3 (9), 837–850.

Kingdon, J. 1974. *East African mammals. An atlas of evolution in Africa, Volume 2A (Insectivores and bats).* Academic Press, New York and London.

Kingdon, J. 1997. *The Kingdon field guide to African mammals.* Academic Press, London.

Koch-Weser, S. 1984. Fledermäuse aus Obervolta, W-Afrika. *Senckenbergiana Biologica*, 64 (4/6), 255–311.

Kock, D. 1969. Die Fledermaus-Fauna des Sudan (Mammalia, Chiroptera). *Abhandlungen der Senckenbergischen Naturforschenden Gesellschaft*, 521, 1–238.

Kock, D., 1981. Zur Chiropteren-Fauna von Burundi (Mammalia). *Senckenbergiana Biologica*, 61 (5/6), 329–336.

Koopman, K.F. 1975. Bats of the Sudan. *Bulletin of the American Museum of Natural History*, 154 (4), 353–444.

Koopman, K.F., Kofron, C.P., and Chapman, A. 1995. The bats of Liberia: Systematics, ecology and distribution. *American Museum Novitates*, 3148, 1–24.

Kuhn, H.J. 1965. A provisional check-list of the mammals of Liberia. *Senckenbergiana Biologica*, 46 (5), 321–340.

Kulzer, E. 1962. Fledermäuse aus Tanganyika. *Zeitschrift für Säugetierkunde*, 27 (2), 164–181.

Largen, M.J., Kock, D., and Yalden, D.W. 1974. Catalogue of the mammals of Ethiopia. 1. Chiroptera. *Monitore Zoologico Italiano, (Supplement V)*, 16, 221–298.

Malbrant, R. and Maclatchy, A. 1949. *Faune de l'équateur Africain Français. Tome II. Mammifères.* Lechevalier, Paris.

Meester, J. and Setzer, H.W. (eds.) 1971. *The mammals of Africa: An identification manual.* Smithsonian Institution Press, Washington DC.

Meester, J.A.J., Rautenbach, I.L., Dippenaar, N.J., and Baker, C.M. 1986. Classification of southern African mammals. *Transvaal Museum Monographs*, 5, 1–359.

Meirte, D. 1984. De vleermuizen van de Comoren. *Africa-Tervuren*, 30 (1–4), 49–57.

Pakenham, R.H.W. 1984. *The mammals of Zanzibar and Pemba Islands.* Privately published, Harpenden.

Panouse, J.B. 1951. Les chauves-souris du Maroc. *Travaux de l'Institut Scientifique Chérifan*, 1, 1–120.

Peterson, R.L., Eger, J.L., and Mitchell, L. 1995. Chiroptères. *Faune de Madagascar*, 84, 1–204.

Racey, P.A. and Nicoll, M.E. 1984. Mammals of the Seychelles. Pp. 607–626 *in: Biogeography and ecology of the Seychelles Islands* (ed. D.R. Stoddart). Junk, Den Haag.

Robbins, C.B. 1980. Small mammals of Togo and Benin. I. Chiroptera. *Mammalia*, 44 (1), 83–88.

Roberts, A. 1951. *The mammals of South Africa.* Trustees of the Mammals of South Africa Bookfund, Johannesburg.

Rosevear, D. 1953. *Checklist and atlas of Nigerian mammals, with a foreword on vegetation.* Government Printer, Lagos.

Rosevear, D. 1965. *Bats of West Africa.* British Museum (Natural History), London.

Schlitter, D.A., Robbins, L.W., and Buchanan, S.A. 1983. Bats of the Central African Republic (Mammalia: Chiroptera). *Annals of the Carnegie Museum*, 51 (8), 133–155.

Sclater, W.L. 1900. *The mammals of South Africa.* I and II. Trustees of the British Museum (Natural History), London.

Shortridge, G.C. 1934. *The mammals of South West Africa.* Heinemann, London.

Skinner, J.D. and Smithers, R.H.N. 1990. *Mammals of the southern African subregion,* Second edition. University of Pretoria Press, Pretoria.

Smithers, R.H.N. 1971. *The mammals of Botswana.* Museum Memoir 4. Trustees National Museum Rhodesia, Salisbury.

Smithers, R.H.N. 1983. *Mammals of the southern African subregion.* University of Pretoria Press, Pretoria.

Smithers, R.H.N. and Tello, J.L.P.L. 1976. *Checklist and atlas of the mammals of Mocambique.* Museum Memoir No. 8. Trustees National Museums and Monuments, Salisbury.

Smithers, R.H.N. and Wilson, V.J. 1979. *Checklist and atlas of the mammals of Zimbabwe Rhodesia.* Trustees National Museums and Monuments, Salisbury.

Sweeney, R.C.H. 1959. *A preliminary annotated checklist of the mammals of Nyasaland.* The Nyasaland Society, Blantyre.

Swynnerton, G.H. and Hayman, R.W. 1951. Checklist of the land mammals of the Tanganyika Territory and the Zanzibar Protectorate. *Journal of the East African Natural History Society*, 20 (6/7), 274–392.

Taylor, P.J. 2000. *Bats of Southern Africa; Guide to biology, identification, and conservation.* University of Natal Press, Pietermaritzburg. 206pp.

Vielliard, J. 1974. Les Cheiroptères du Tchad. *Revue Suisse de Zoologie*, 81 (4), 975–991.

Yalden, D.W., Largen, M.J., Kock, D., and Hillman, J.C. 1996. Catalogue of the mammals of Ethiopia and Eritrea. 7. Revised checklist, zoogeography and conservation. *Tropical Ecology*, 9, 73–164.

5.4.2 Australasian Region

This account was compiled using contributions from the following: David Butler; Tim Flannery; Les Hall; the late Karl F. Koopman; Lindy Lumsden; Colin O'Donnell; Greg Richards; and Don E. Wilson.

Geographical boundaries of region

The region includes the major land areas of Australia, New Guinea, and New Zealand, plus islands to the east of the Philippines and the Moluccas (see Map 1). The Galapagos Islands and Hawaii are thus excluded.

Number of species in the region

A total of 106 species are recorded from the Australasian Region. Of these, two are Extinct and 26 threatened – two Critically Endangered, three Endangered, and 21 Vulnerable. A total of 76 species are listed in the Lower Risk categories – 22 as Near Threatened and 53 as Least Concern. A further three species are listed as Data Deficient. A full list of species is given below at the end of this regional account.

Major threats to bats

In Australia and New Zealand, pressure from increasing human populations is not a major issue as in other areas of the world. However, the loss of native forests is a major concern. In many Pacific islands, human populations are increasing rapidly, threatening species, many of which are endemics. As with other areas, caves are key habitats threatened by a variety of human activities. In Australia, mines rather than caves are the main concern. Threats on islands in the Pacific are also compounded by natural events such as cyclones.

Threats to habitats and roosts

- **Forest** Duncan *et al.* (1999) identified habitat loss and forest harvesting as major threats to Australian bats. Approximately 20% of the forest on the Australian continent has been cleared or thinned since the country was settled by Europeans in 1788 (Graetz *et al.* 1992). Of the forest present in 1788, 40% has been modified by logging (State of the Environment Advisory Council 1996). Broadscale clearing has actually increased in the past fifty years, with as much land cleared between 1945 and 1995 as was cleared between 1795 and 1945 (Duncan *et al.* 1999). The Resource Assessment Commission (1991) concluded that at current logging rates there would be very little unlogged forest remaining in forest production tenures by 2015. There remains approximately 400,000km^2 of forest in Australia, about 80,000km^2 of which is in conservation reserves. Foresters manage the intensity of wildfires by 'controlled burning', particularly in winter, and this can rapidly modify habitats for bats (Richards 1994). The selective removal of trees during felling operations can be more damaging than the felling operation itself. Massive forest clearance has taken place in New Zealand in the last 100 years and has destroyed a vast amount of suitable bat habitat. While the rate of clearance has declined dramatically, ongoing selective logging and deforestation programmes may threaten bat populations in some areas. Both species of bat in New Zealand (*Mystacina tuberculata* and *Chalinolobus tuberculatus*) often use the largest and oldest trees, which are often targeted by selective logging operations (Molloy 1995). Deforestation would also appear to be the greatest threat throughout the rest of the region.

  Trees are important as roost sites for many bat species throughout the region and forest clearance or current management practices are likely to be affecting a wide range of species. Loss of forests reduces the number of foraging areas, as well as reducing the number of tree hollows available for bats. In grazed woodland, the loss of sapling trees will reduce the future availability of hollows for bats (Bennett *et al.* 1994). It is suspected that the removal of emergent trees that provide roosts with an uncluttered exit area may have a proportionately greater effect on fast-flying forest bats (G.C. Richards *unpublished*). There are no quantitative data on the effects of land clearance on insectivorous bats, but the negative effects upon populations of the grey-headed flying fox (*Pteropus poliocephalus*) indicate what may be happening. Forest fragmentation and removal of areas with traditional bat roost sites has caused colonies to break into smaller camps in the southern half of Australia and indicates likely problems for microchiropteran bats.
- **Caves and mines** Caves and mines in Australia are important as roost sites for a variety of species, including many that are threatened (Richards and Hall 1998). During the 1960s and 1970s, tens of thousands of cave bats in southeastern Australia were banded. Some of these colonies have since declined or disappeared, and it is important to identify whether such a reduction in numbers is a general or isolated trend (Richards and Hall 1998). There are few natural caves in Australia and abandoned mines are important alternative underground roost sites. Mines may also provide links to roost sites in isolated cave areas, such as Chillagoe, Queensland, which were not previously used by bats (Richards and Hall 1998). *The Action Plan for Australian Bats* (Duncan *et al.* 1999) lists eight Australian microchiropteran taxa considered threatened and 10 as Data Deficient. Nine of these are threatened by collapse, closure, or re-working of old mines. Improved extraction techniques have meant that some formerly abandoned mines have been re-opened, threatening bats that may use such sites. For example, Troughton's sheath-tail bat (*Taphozous troughtoni*) was originally recorded from Native Bee Mine, near Mt Isa, Queensland. This site was bulldozed and the species is now only known from one other roost site nearby, which could suffer the same fate. Similarly, the large-eared pied bat (*Chalinolobus dwyeri*) was originally described from a mine that was later flooded following construction of a reservoir. The endemic ghost bat (*Macroderma gigas*), listed as Vulnerable, is heavily reliant on mines as roost sites. Its population is thought to number less than 10,000 (Phillips 1990). Approximately 1,500 bats roost in an abandoned gold mine at Pine Creek in Northern Territory. Recent plans to renew mining operations have been dropped, but the situation could easily change. Currently, there is no national policy for managing bat populations that use mines. Mines that are considered unsafe are bulldozed with no concern for bats that may use such sites.

  While the region provides examples of many of the difficulties encountered elsewhere, there are also problems particular to this area such as the natural loss of small sea caves, important on many of the smaller oceanic islands, through blocking by beach debris during storms (e.g., Samoa), and heavy harvesting of insectivorous bats for human food (e.g., Solomon Islands).

Threats to higher taxa

- **Family Emballonuridae** This family includes 15 species recorded from this region, of which six are considered globally threatened. These include island endemics, such as *Emballonura semicaudata*, threatened by development and the effects of cyclone damage, and also mainland species, such as *Taphozous troughtoni* in Australia, where only six specimens have ever been collected. For further information see the Species Action Plan for *Emballonura semicaudata* in this volume
- **Family Mystacinidae** The family includes the single extant species, *Mystacina tuberculata*, and is endemic to New Zealand. Until recently, the species has been regarded as severely threatened, but more intensive work, particularly with the use of bat detectors, has located further populations. Nevertheless, it is the subject of considerable conservation effort and a Recovery Plan (Molloy 1995). For further information see the Species Action Plan in this volume.
- **Family Megadermatidae** Of this family of five species, the single member recorded from this region, *Macroderma gigas*, is endemic to Australia, where it is considered Vulnerable. For further information see the Species Action Plan for this species in this volume.
- **Genus *Kerivoula* (Family Vespertilionidae)** As with other regions, the species of this genus are poorly known and one of the two species recorded from this region is considered Vulnerable.
- **Genera *Pharotis* and *Nyctophilus* (Family Vespertilionidae)** The single species of the genus *Pharotis*, *P. imogene*, was described from Papua New Guinea in 1914. It has not been seen since the original specimens were collected in 1890. The related genus, *Nyctophilus* with 11 species, is endemic to this Region and adjacent parts of the Indomalayan Region. Three species are considered threatened. One, *N. howensis*, has only ever been recorded from Lord Howe Island and is thought to be extinct. The only record was of an incomplete skull, thought to be of sub-fossil origin. Recent re-examination has suggested this material was no more than 100 years old. Surveys of all the caves on the island, as well as mist-netting and trapping has failed to locate any further specimens (L.S. Hall and G. Hoye *unpublished*).

Threats to geographical areas

- **Pacific islands** All have high human population pressure that has led to habitat loss, which, with the additional effects of cyclones, causes many problems. The Solomon Islands have a very diverse bat fauna and high levels of endemism. However, many of the islands suffer from logging and habitat degradation.
- **Australia and New Zealand** Both countries have prepared detailed Action Plans for their bat faunas, discussing the local problems and identifying proposed action. That for New Zealand (with two species, both endemic – Molloy 1995) is well in hand. That for Australia (with 90 taxa) was published in 1999 (Duncan *et al.* 1999).

Other issues

Identification problems

Richards and Hall (1998) highlight the taxonomic problems in Australian bats. The Australian bat fauna contains taxa that have been identified, or are being identified, as distinct in the field, but are awaiting formal description. In *The Action Plan for Australian Bats*, Duncan *et al.* (1999) detail the many taxonomic issues relating to the Australian bat

N. Speechley

Lesser long-eared bat, *Nyctophilus geoffroyi*, one of a small group of species that is restricted to the Australasian region.

fauna that remain to be resolved. Few Australian biologists have the necessary taxonomic expertise and, as a result, many new taxa remain undescribed. As a consequence, important ecological projects that could contribute vital information for conservation planning are rendered inadequate. Parnaby (1991) considered that two-thirds of Australian bat species required taxonomic clarification. The need for clarification of taxonomy is a major recommendation of this Action Plan.

Almost one-third of Australia's insectivorous bats are supra-canopy species that are difficult to capture and can only be identified through their echolocation calls (G.C Richards and L.S Hall *pers. comm.*). The need for regional libraries of reference echolocation calls, which could be compiled as part of regional surveys, was another recommendation of *The Action Plan for Australian Bats*.

Introduced predators, competitors, and pollutants

There is circumstantial evidence that introduced predators caused the extinction of the Lord Howe Island bat (*Nyctophilus howensis*) in the early 1900s (Richards and Hall 1998). Rats (*Rattus norvegicus*) were inadvertently introduced to the island causing the demise of the species, assisted by the owls introduced to control the rats. Similarly, in New Zealand, colonies of *Mystacina tuberculata* and, in particular, the now extinct *M. robusta*, are believed to have been eliminated by introduced rats, as well as feral cats and stoats (Molloy 1995). Short-tailed bats (*Mystacina* spp.) may be vulnerable to predation while feeding on the forest floor or on tree trunks. Males may undertake prolonged singing displays at leks and may thus attract mammalian predators. The presumed extinction of both *Mystacina* species on Big South Cape and Solomon Islands after the introduction of ship rats gives an indication of the severity of predation on these species (Molloy 1995). Predation is likely to be a widespread problem for island populations of bats, especially those with restricted distributions. Predators of Australian bats include introduced species, such as the European fox (*Vulpes vulpes*), feral cats (*Felis catus*), and cane toads (*Bufo marinus*) that hunt at cave entrances or within caves (Dwyer 1964; L.S. Hall *unpublished*). There is also evidence that English starlings (*Sturnus vulgaris*) evict species such as Gould's wattled bat (*Chalinolobus gouldii*) from tree hollows.

The build-up of DDT in the tissues of bent-wing bats (*Miniopterus schreibersii*) in Australia was the suspected cause of several mass die-offs involving thousands of animals. Though DDT is now banned as an agricultural chemical, these incidents highlight risks from insecticides (Richards and Hall 1998). In New Zealand, toxins such as cyanide, 1080, phosphorus, and anti-coagulants are used in a variety of forms to control or eliminate browsers and rodents in localities where bats are also present. One case of a short-tailed bat dying as a result of eating cyanide possum bait is documented (Daniel and Williams 1984). As these bats spend a proportion of their time foraging on the forest floor, they are likely to encounter ground-laid poison baits (Molloy 1995).

Key areas for bat biodiversity

Hotspots at a generic level

Centres of diversity at the generic level were assessed using a WORLDMAP analysis (see Chapter 5.3 for further details). There is a distinct concentration in the Northern Queensland/eastern New Guinea area (Map 26), with adjacent areas also demonstrating strong generic diversity. The minimum set of grid-cell areas required to maintain all genera is five (Map 27) and most of these have little or no flexibility in view of the restricted distribution of a number of genera.

Australia

Assessing bat biodiversity in Australia is complicated by taxonomic problems that await resolution. Currently bats comprise almost one-third of the extant land mammal fauna. A database of around 60,000 bat records has allowed the pinpointing of 11 hotspots of species diversity (G.C. Richards and L.S. Hall *pers. comm.*). Northern Queensland, tropical areas of Northern Territory, and north coastal New South Wales are particularly species-rich. Australia has eight globally threatened bat species –

Map 26. Generic richness per grid-cell area for genera occurring in the Australasian Region.

The numbers in the squares represent the number of genera per unit area.

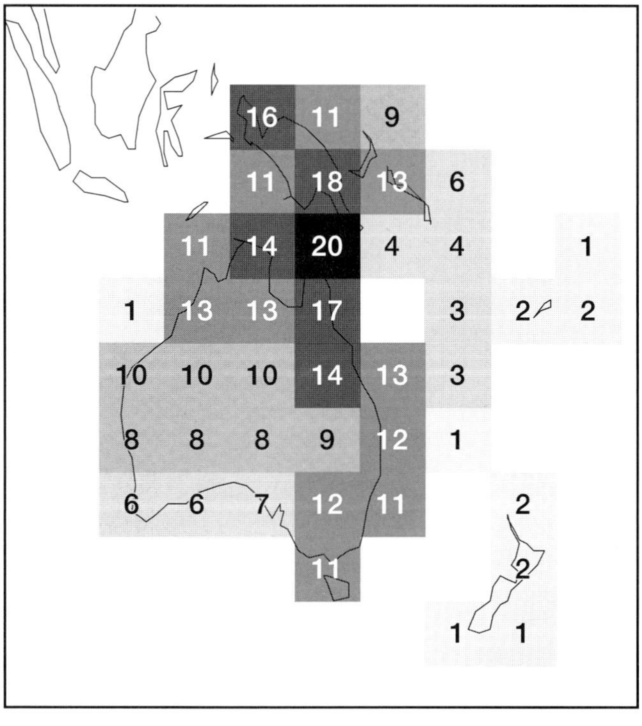

one Critically Endangered and seven Vulnerable. All these factors combine to make Australia a key site for bats within this region.

New Zealand

Although only three species are found in New Zealand, all are endemic. One species (*Mystacina robusta*) is thought to be extinct and the other two (*M. tuberculata* and *Chalinolobus tuberculatus*) are considered threatened. There is evidence of a recent decline in *Chalinolobus* populations (C. O'Donnell *pers. comm.*). This is based on recent index counts that indicate significant declines in populations on the South Island. This species was frequently recorded in the period 1930–1960, and was found in moderate numbers in the late 1970s and early 1980s. There were few or even no records between 1995 and 1998, despite the inclusion of bat detectors in surveys. The uniqueness of the bats in New Zealand (the family Mystacinidae and its sole genus *Mystacina* are found only in New Zealand) give it an importance that far outweighs the size of its chiropteran fauna.

Solomon Islands

The Solomon Islands chain, including Bougainville and Buka (politically part of Papua New Guinea), has a rich microchiropteran bat fauna – Choiseul, Gaudalcanal, and Santa Isabel all have 10 or more species. An expedition to Choiseul found seven species that were new to the island (Bowen-Jones *et al.* 1997). The islands also have significant numbers of megachiropteran bats. In many cases, bats make up 100% of the native mammal fauna. Many of the islands need detailed bat surveys and, as with Choiseul, this may increase the number of known bat species. There are three globally threatened bat species.

Map 27. Minimum set of grid-cell areas required to maintain all genera occurring in the Australasian Region.
The minimum number of squares required to conserve all genera is five. The numbers in the squares represent the number of genera uniquely contributing to this minimum set.

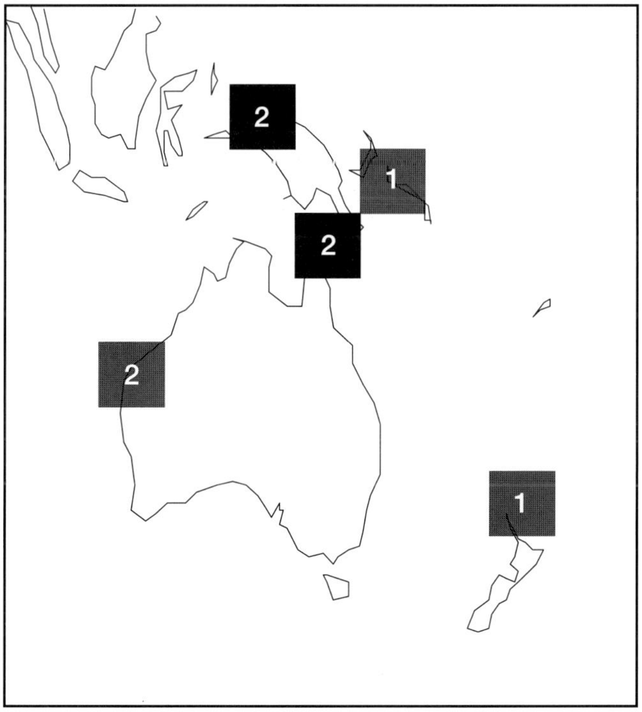

New Guinea

The island of New Guinea has an exceptionally rich bat fauna with 20 megachiropteran and 51 microchiropteran bat species (Flannery 1995a). Thirteen of the microchiropteran species are endemic. The island has extensive tracts (approximately 700,000km^2) of relatively undisturbed forest. The southern fringe of the island, at an elevation of 200–400m, is thought to be of particular importance for bats (T. Flannery *pers. comm.*). Twelve globally threatened species occur on New Guinea –one Critically Endangered and 11 Vulnerable.

Recommendations

New Zealand has published a Bat Recovery Plan (Molloy 1985), and its current work programme and recommendations are well developed. *The Action Plan for Australian Bats* was published in 1999 (Duncan *et al.* 1999).

The Action Plan for Australian Bats

This includes a review of the major conservation issues, threats to taxa, and status assessments for all species, subspecies, and forms in Australia using the latest IUCN criteria (IUCN 1994). It includes Recovery Outlines for all Extinct and threatened taxa (Critically Endangered, Endangered, and Vulnerable) and Taxon Summaries for the remaining Lower Risk: Near Threatened and Data Deficient taxa. There are individual recommendations for all Extinct and threatened taxa. The recommendations that are relevant to microchiropteran bats are summarised below.

Habitat clearance

Recommendation:
- maintain or increase funding for programmes, such as Bushcare, designed to halt the clearance of land and revegetate cleared land.

Survey and research

Recommendations:
- give high priority to survey work and ecological research necessary to clarify the distribution, abundance, and conservation status of Australian bats, in particular threatened, near threatened, and data deficient species;
- identify threats and develop management prescriptions for their mitigation as an integral part of all ecological studies;

- encourage forestry agencies to carry out further research on the impact of logging on tree-dwelling bats. In particular, studies should identify:
  - the sensitivity of bat species to different intensities of logging (e.g., clear-felling vs selective logging);
  - the impact of forest fragmentation on bats at a landscape scale;
  - which species are affected by current forestry practices;
  - the effectiveness of current management prescriptions; and
  - improvements or modifications to existing management actions if required;
- develop and maintain a national atlas of Australian bats using existing and incoming data;
- establish a national library of echolocation calls to assist in ecological research and survey work.

Taxonomy

Recommendation:

- give high priority to providing adequate resources to resolve taxonomic problems of Australian bats. This needs to be recognised by conservation agencies with fauna management responsibilities as an integral part of ensuring the effective conservation of bats in Australia.

Roost protection

Recommendation:

- give high priority to garnering funding from State conservation and other land management agencies for on-the-ground management actions to protect roosts of threatened, near threatened, and data deficient bat species.

Diseases

Recommendation:

- develop a national education programme to address the public health risks associated with contact with bats, as well as the important ecological role of bats and the need to ensure their conservation.

Bat fauna in mines

Recommendation:

- encourage development of guidelines for management and conservation of bat fauna in mines proposed for closure, destruction, or re-working by State conservation agencies in consultation with the mining industry, and government departments responsible for mining and workplace health and safety. Such guidelines could identify potential species in different areas and include options for protection of roosts and prevention of roost disturbance, such as the installation of bat gates and erection of fencing to prevent human access.

National coordination

Recommendations:

- establish a national advisory group to facilitate recovery of threatened bat species (and management of other species) whose distribution and, therefore, management needs extend across Commonwealth, State, and Territory jurisdictions;
- establish a national bat advisory group to advise on the implementation of the national Action Plan; in particular:
  - advise on priorities for survey, research, and taxonomy;
  - set standards for survey work and monitoring;
  - facilitate establishment of an Australian bat atlas and call library;
  - facilitate communication between researchers and managers;
  - advise on/coordinate national issues e.g., handling protocols required due to Australian bat Lyssavirus and other emerging viral diseases; and
  - identify and facilitate projects of broader national significance (e.g., education, public awareness).

New Zealand Bat Recovery Plan

A detailed Recovery Plan for the three species of bats in New Zealand has been published (Molloy 1995). Its long-term goal is to ensure the perpetuation of all extant bat species and subspecies throughout their present ranges and, where feasible, establish new populations within their historical ranges.

The major recommendations of the recovery strategy are given below.

Recommendations:

- undertake or promote research on bats which will assist in their management;
- evaluate the status of both short-tailed (*Mystacina* spp.) and long-tailed bats (*Chalinolobus tuberculatus*);
- establish populations of short-tailed bats on suitable islands;
- select, protect, and monitor populations of short-tailed and long-tailed bats throughout their geographical range;
- raise public awareness of bats and involve the public in bat conservation.

General recommendations

The following recommendations are based upon information provided by the contributors to this section. They include both general recommendations applicable to the whole area, as well as specific ones relating to particular species, areas, or habitats.

Habitats The effects of cyclones exacerbates forest loss through human activity in many islands of Oceania. Pesticide use for disease and pest control is recognised as a likely problem for foraging bats in New Zealand and Australia, as is pollution from, for example, heavy metals.

Recommendations:

- make allowance for additional pressures from natural perturbations, such as cyclones or fire, when considering exploitation of habitats;
- take account of habitat requirements of threatened bat species when developing policies for the control of pollution and use of pesticides;
- obtain quantitative data on the effects of land clearance on insectivorous bats;
- assess impact of pesticide residues on bats;
- assess impact of controlled burning on bat habitats;
- assess impact of selective logging on bat faunal diversity.

Roost types Modern techniques allow the re-exploitation of old mineral workings and greater disturbance to natural cave areas in Australia. The selective logging of larger trees more likely to contain bat roosts in already heavily exploited areas is a major concern.

Recommendations:

- consider important roost types, such as older trees and underground habitats, in practices affecting their sustainability;
- implement recommendations from *The Action Plan for Australian Bats* concerning bats and mines;
- assess impact of introduced predators on bat populations;
- assess threats to cave populations of natural events and harvesting by humans in Oceania.

Geographical areas Deforestation is a general problem, but is of particular concern in northern Queensland, Australia, the Solomon Islands, and other islands of Oceania. In New Zealand, and perhaps Australia, predation by introduced animals is suspected of being a major threat to some species. In New Zealand, the endemic family Mystacinidae may be further threatened by poisoning from baits used to control introduced mammals.

Recommendations:

- give threatened bat species and their habitats greater consideration in general land-use and management policies;
- conduct detailed bat surveys of islands in the Solomons chain.

Taxa Taxa identified as of concern include *Macroderma*, *Kerivoula*, *Murina,* and *Rhinolophus*. In Australia, a number of taxa recognised by bat biologists await formal description. Some genera, such as *Mormopterus*, include unresolved species complexes, and the status of *Miniopterus schreibersii* as a single species or a species complex is under review.

Recommendations:

- conduct studies on biology and ecology of *Macroderma*, *Kerivoula*, *Murina,* and *Rhinolophus* species;
- resolve key taxonomic issues.

Checklist of Australasian bats

A total of 106 species are recorded from the Australasian Region. The full list is given below.

Species	Status	Species	Status
FAMILY EMBALLONURIDAE		**FAMILY MEGADERMATIDAE**	
Emballonura		***Macroderma***	
Emballonura beccarii Peters and Doria 1881	LR: lc	*Macroderma gigas* (Dobson 1880)	VU: A2c
Emballonura dianae Hill 1956	VU: A2c	**FAMILY HIPPOSIDERIDAE**	
Emballonura furax Thomas 1911	VU: A2c, D2	***Anthops***	
Emballonura raffrayana Dobson 1879	LR: nt	*Anthops ornatus* Thomas 1888	VU: A2c, D2
Emballonura semicaudata (Peale 1848)	EN: A1ac	***Aselliscus***	
Emballonura serii Flannery 1994	DD	*Aselliscus tricuspidatus* (Temminck 1835)	LR: lc
Mosia			
Mosia nigrescens (Gray 1843)	LR: lc	***Hipposideros***	
Saccolaimus		*Hipposideros ater* Templeton 1848	LR: lc
Saccolaimus flaviventris Peters 1867	LR: nt	*Hipposideros calcaratus* (Dobson 1877)	LR: lc
Saccolaimus mixtus Troughton 1925	VU: A2c	*Hipposideros cervinus* (Gould 1863)	LR: lc
Saccolaimus saccolaimus (Temminck 1838)	LR: lc	*Hipposideros corynophyllus* Hill 1985	VU: A2c, D2
		Hipposideros demissus K. Andersen 1909	VU: A2c, D2
Taphozous		*Hipposideros diadema* (E. Geoffroy 1813)	LR: lc
Taphozous australis Gould 1854	LR: nt	*Hipposideros dinops* K. Andersen 1905	LR: nt
Taphozous georgianus Thomas 1915	LR: lc	*Hipposideros edwardshilli* Flannery and Colgan 1993	LR: nt
Taphozous hilli Kitchener 1980	LR: lc		
Taphozous kapalgensis McKean and Friend 1979	VU: A2c	*Hipposideros maggietaylorae* Smith and Hill 1981	LR: lc
Taphozous troughtoni Tate 1952	CR: A1ac, B1 + 2abcde, D	*Hipposideros muscinus* (Thomas and Doria 1886)	VU: D2

Species	Status
Hipposideros papua (Thomas and Doria 1886)	VU: A2c
Hipposideros semoni Matschie 1903	LR: nt
Hipposideros stenotis Thomas 1913	LR: nt
Hipposideros wollastoni Thomas 1913	LR: nt
Rhinonicteris	
Rhinonicteris aurantia (Gray 1845)	VU: A1c
FAMILY RHINOLOPHIDAE	
Rhinolophus	
Rhinolophus arcuatus Peters 1871	LR: lc
Rhinolophus euryotis Temminck 1835	LR: lc
Rhinolophus megaphyllus Gray 1834	LR: lc
Rhinolophus philippinensis Waterhouse 1843	LR: nt
FAMILY VESPERTILIONIDAE	
Subfamily Kerivoulinae	
Kerivoula	
Kerivoula muscina Tate 1941	VU: D2
Kerivoula papuensis (Dobson 1878)	LR: lc
Subfamily Vespertilioninae	
Chalinolobus	
Chalinolobus dwyeri Ryan 1966	VU: A2c
Chalinolobus gouldii Gray 1841	LR: lc
Chalinolobus morio Gray 1841	LR: lc
Chalinolobus neocaledonicus Revilliod 1913–1914	EN: B1 + 2c
Chalinolobus nigrogriseus Gould 1852	LR: lc
Chalinolobus picatus Gould 1852	LR: nt
Chalinolobus tuberculatus (Forster 1844)	VU: A2bc
Eptesicus	
Eptesicus baverstocki Kitchener, Jones, and Caputi 1987	LR: lc
Eptesicus caurinus Thomas 1914	LR: nt
Eptesicus darlingtoni Allen 1933	LR: lc
Eptesicus douglasorum Kitchener 1976	LR: nt
Eptesicus finlaysoni Kitchener, Jones, and Caputi 1987	LR: lc
Eptesicus pumilus Gray 1841	LR: lc
Eptesicus regulus (Thomas 1906)	LR: lc
Eptesicus troughtoni Kitchener, Jones, and Caputi 1987	LR: lc
Eptesicus vulturnus Thomas 1914	LR: lc
Myotis	
Myotis adversus (Horsfield 1824)	LR: lc
Myotis australis (Dobson 1878)	DD
Myotis insularum (Dobson 1878)	DD
Nycticeius	
Nycticeius balstoni (Thomas 1906)	LR: lc
Nycticeius greyii (Gray 1842)	LR: lc
Nycticeius orion (Troughton 1937)	LR: lc
Nycticeius rueppellii (Peters 1866)	LR: nt
Nycticeius sanborni (Troughton 1937)	LR: lc
Nyctophilus	
Nyctophilus arnhemensis Johnson 1959	LR: lc
Nyctophilus bifax (Thomas 1915)	LR: lc
Nyctophilus daedalus (Thomas 1915)	LR: nt
Nyctophilus geoffroyi Leach 1821	LR: lc
Nyctophilus gouldi Tomes 1858	LR: lc
Nyctophilus howensis McKean 1973	EX
Nyctophilus microdon Laurie and Hill 1954	VU: D2
Nyctophilus microtis Thomas 1888	LR: lc
Nyctophilus sherrini (Thomas 1915)	LR: nt
Nyctophilus timoriensis E. Geoffroy 1806	VU: A2c
Nyctophilus walkeri Thomas 1892	LR: nt
Pharotis	
Pharotis imogene Thomas 1914	CR: B1+2c, C2b
Philetor	
Philetor brachypterus (Temminck 1840)	LR: lc
Pipistrellus	
Pipistrellus adamsi Kitchener, Caputi, and Jones 1986	LR: lc
Pipistrellus angulatus (Peters 1880)	LR: lc
Pipistrellus collinus Thomas 1920	LR: lc
?*Pipistrellus javanicus* (Gray 1838)	LR: lc
Pipistrellus mckenziei (Kitchener, Caputi, and Jones 1986)	VU: A2c
Pipistrellus papuanus (Peters and Doria 1881)	LR: nt
Pipistrellus tasmaniensis (Gould 1858)	LR: lc
Pipistrellus tenuis (Temminck 1840)	LR: lc
Pipistrellus wattsi Kitchener, Caputi, and Jones 1986	LR: nt
Pipistrellus westralis Koopman 1984	LR: lc
Murina	
Murina florium Thomas 1908	LR: lc
Subfamily Miniopterinae	
Miniopterus	
Miniopterus australis Tomes 1858	LR: lc
Miniopterus fuscus Bonhote 1902	VU: A2c
Miniopterus magnater Sanborn 1931	LR: lc
Miniopterus medius Thomas and Wroughton 1909	LR: lc
Miniopterus pusillus Dobson 1876	LR: lc
Miniopterus robustior Revilliod 1914	EN: B1 + 2c
Miniopterus schreibersii (Kuhl 1817)	LR: nt
Miniopterus tristis (Waterhouse 1845)	LR: lc
FAMILY MYSTACINIDAE	
Mystacina	
Mystacina robusta Dwyer 1962	EX
Mystacina tuberculata Gray 1843	VU: A2c, C2a
FAMILY MOLOSSIDAE	
Chaerephon	
Chaerephon bregullae (Felten 1964)	LR: nt
Chaerephon jobensis (Miller 1902)	LR: lc
Chaerephon solomonis Troughton 1931	LR: nt
Mormopterus	
Mormopterus beccarii Peters 1881	LR: lc
Mormopterus norfolkensis (Gray 1840)	LR: lc
Mormopterus planiceps (Peters 1866)	LR: lc
Otomops	
Otomops papuensis Lawrence 1948	VU: D2
Otomops secundus Hayman 1952	VU: D2
Tadarida	
Tadarida australis (Gray 1839)	LR: nt

Table 4. Number of IUCN Red List species for countries in the Australasian Region.
The table also includes information on numbers of endemics and the estimated size of the bat fauna. For information on the compilation of the figures for size of faunas see Chapter 6. Full lists of IUCN Red List species per country are given in the same Chapter. **Countries not listed here do not have a recorded bat fauna.** Where a country overlaps more than one region, the fauna for the whole country is included.

	IUCN RED LIST SPECIES								ENDEMICS	TOTAL NO. OF SPECIES		
Country	**CR**	**EN**	**VU**	**LRcd**	**LRnt**	**EX**	**DD**	***Total***	***Total***	**Mega**	**Micro**	***Total***
American Samoa	0	1	0	0	0	0	1	2	0	2	2	4
Australia	1	0	7	0	14	1	1	24	15	12	63	75
C.N.M.I. (1)	0	1	0	0	0	0	0	1	0	1	1	2
Cook Islands	0	0	0	0	0	0	0	0	0	1	0	1
F.S M. (2)	0	1	0	0	0	0	0	1	0	4	1	5
Fiji	0	1	0	0	1	0	0	2	0	4	2	6
Guam	0	1	0	0	0	0	0	1	0	1	1	2
Indonesia	0	4	14	0	25	0	4	47	24	63	112	175
New Caledonia	0	2	0	0	0	1	0	3	2	4	4	8
New Zealand	0	0	2	0	0	1	0	3	3	0	3	3
Niue	0	0	0	0	0	0	0	0	0	1	0	1
Palau	0	1	0	0	0	0	0	1	0	2	1	3
Papua New Guinea	1	0	13	0	12	0	1	27	10	34	57	91
Samoa	0	1	0	0	0	0	1	2	0	2	2	4
Solomon Is.	0	0	3	0	4	0	0	7	3	20	13	33
Tonga	0	1	0	0	0	0	0	1	0	1	1	2
Vanuatu	0	1	0	0	1	0	0	2	0	4	7	11
Wallis & Futuna Islands	0	0	0	0	0	0	0	0	0	1	0	1

Notes:
1. Commonwealth of the Northern Mariana Islands
2. Federated States of Micronesia

Table 4 shows the number of IUCN Red List species recorded from each country together with information on numbers of endemics and the size of the total bat fauna.

Key references

The following is a list of important references relating to bats in the Australasian Region. It is by no means an exhaustive list and concentrates mainly on distributional studies at a national or regional level.

Bonaccorso, F. 1998. *Bats of Papua New Guinea.* Conservation International, Washington DC.

Churchill, S. 1998. *Australian bats.* New Holland Publishers, Sydney.

Duncan, A., Baker, G.B., and Montgomery, N. (eds.) 1999. *The action plan for Australian bats.* Environment Australia, Canberra.

Flannery, T. 1990. *The mammals of New Guinea.* Robert Brown and Associates, Carina.

Flannery, T. 1995a. *Mammals of New Guinea.* Revised and expanded edition. Reed Books, Chatswood.

Flannery, T. 1995b. *Mammals of the south-west Pacific and Moluccan Islands.* Australian Museum and Reed Books, Chatswood.

Hall, L.S. and Richards, G.C. 1979. *The bats of eastern Australia.* Queensland Museum Booklet Number 12, Brisbane.

Hill, J. Edwards 1983. Bats (Mammalia: Chiroptera) from Indo-Australia. *Bulletin of the British Museum (Natural History), Zoology*, 45, 103–208.

King, C.M. (ed.) 1995. *The handbook of New Zealand mammals.* Oxford University Press, Oxford.

Menkhorst, P. (ed.) 1995. *Mammals of Victoria: Distribution, ecology and conservation.* Oxford University Press, Melbourne.

Molloy, J. 1995. *Bat (Peka Peka) recovery plan* (Mystacina, Chalinolobus). Threatened Species Recovery Plan Series No. 15. Threatened Species Unit, Department of Conservation, Wellington.

Rainey, W.E. 1998. Conservation of bats on remote Indo-Pacific islands. Pp. 326–341 *in: Bat biology and conservation* (eds. T.H. Kunz and P.A. Racey). Smithsonian Institution Press, Washington DC.

Reardon, J.B. and Flavel, S.C. 1991. *A guide to the bats of South Australia.* South Australian Museum, Adelaide.

Richards, G.C. and Hall, L.S. 1998. Conservation biology of Australian bats: Are recent advances solving our problems? Pp. 271–281 *in: Bat biology and conservation* (eds. T.H. Kunz and P.A. Racey). Smithsonian Institution Press, Washington DC.

Strahan, R. (ed.) 1983. *The Australian Museum complete book of Australian mammals.* Angus and Robertson, Sydney.

Strahan, R. (ed.) 1995. *Mammals of Australia.* Reed Books, Chatswood.

Thomson, B.G. 1991. *A field guide to the bats of the Northern Territory*. Commission of the Northern Territory, Darwin.
Tyler, M.J. (ed.) 1979. *The status of endangered Australasian wildlife*. Royal Society of South Australia, Adelaide.

5.4.3 Indomalayan Region

This account was compiled using contributions from the following: Zubaid Akbar; Paul Bates; Anne P. Brooke; John A. Burton; G.W.H. Davison; Charles M. Francis; Toni Guillen; Lawrence R. Heaney; Nina R. Ingle; the late Karl F. Koopman; Mark Robinson; Joe Walston; Gary J. Wiles; and Don E. Wilson.

Geographical boundaries of the region

The region (see Map 1) is defined by Corbet and Hill (1992) as follows: it follows Lyddeker's Line that draws the dividing line between the Moluccas and New Guinea. The islands of Weigeo and Misool, and the Aru Archipelago are excluded since they are on the New Guinea shelf . An arbitrary boundary in China is 35°N as used by Corbet (1978). Beginning in the west, the line lies between Iran and Pakistan, but crosses Afghanistan so as to include only the eastern parts draining to the Indus. From the eastern end of the Hindu Kush to central China, it follows the tree line at about 3,000m to include the forested and other lower slopes draining into Pakistan, India, Myanmar, and China. The alpine zone of the mountains is excluded along with the Tibetan plateau. This excludes the alpine fauna with Palaearctic affinities, but includes the Himalayan/Chinese montane forest fauna comprising endemic genera, as well as more widespread Indomalayan elements. Tibet (Xizang) is excluded except for small parts of the Brahmaputra, Salween, and Mekong Valleys. Nepal, Bhutan, Yunnan, and Sichuan are included except for the high alpine zones, but Qinghai is excluded. Use of 35°N as the northern boundary in China means that the southern parts of Gansu and Shaanxi are included along with most of Honan and the whole of Anhui and Jiangxu, while Shanxi, Hebei, and Shandong are excluded.

In Japan, the boundary is drawn at 30°N so that Yakushima, Tanegashima, and all the main islands are excluded, while the Ryukyu Islands are included.

In the Indian Ocean, the Laccadive, Maldive, Andaman, Nicobar, and Mentawai Islands are included, along with Christmas Island. In the Pacific, all oceanic islands, i.e., east of the Ryukyu Islands and the Philippines, are excluded.

Number of species in the region

A total of 260 species are recorded from the Indomalayan Region. Of these, one is extinct and 43 are threatened – six Critically Endangered, nine Endangered and 28 Vulnerable. A total of 189 species are listed in the Lower Risk categories – 62 as Near Threatened and 128 as Least Concern. A further 27 species are listed as Data Deficient. A full list of species is given at the end of this regional account.

Major threats to bats

As in other regions, forest loss due to increasing human population pressure is the major concern. Caves in this area can sometimes be used by millions of bats. A particular threat in this region is the harvesting of cave swiftlet nests from sites that are also used by bats. This is frequently

M. Tuttle/BCI

Lesser mouse-tailed bat, *Rhinopoma hardwickii*, a widespread species of the Indian Subcontinent westwards to North Africa and Kenya.

detrimental to both birds and bats. In Laos, it is suggested that exploitation of bats for food may be a major threat to populations. This may be true for other countries or regions.

Threats to habitats and roosts

- **Forest** Primary forest is suffering increasing rates of destruction throughout the area. Lowland forest is particularly threatened. Most endemic microchiropterans are confined to primary forest and presumably some, like megachiropterans, have restricted elevational ranges and are confined to lowland forest. In the Philippines, only 8% of the land area is now primary forest – the figure was 70% in 1900. In Malaysia also, the loss of lowland forest is of great concern. Only Taman Negara and the Krau Wildlife Reserve can be said to be secure, as they are under the control of the Federal Government. Other reserves are under State control and can be de-gazetted for other purposes at any time. In Hong Kong, mixed lowland woodlands are under threat.

  Deforestation and current forestry management practices threaten bat populations that depend upon forests for roosting sites. Older trees tend to have more hollows and crevices that provide roosting sites for bats. Management techniques may involve the removal of such trees with consequent loss of roosts. There needs to be more education of land managers about the needs of tree-roosting bats.

  Hong Kong is a particularly important area of south China in terms of its bat fauna since 40% of the land area is presently "country park" within which all mammals have a degree of protection not afforded in nearby Guandong Province, much of which has been deforested and degraded by development. Approximately 60% of Hong Kong is "countryside". Most bats roost in artificial structures, such as water tunnels, mines, and bridges. Foraging areas, particularly wetlands, are potentially more vulnerable. Bats preferring 'old buildings' are at risk due to loss of these structures. Woodland on the whole is less than 50 years old and there are few tree-hole roosting sites available for bats. There is mixed woodland bordering large reservoirs. Old country villages all possess a traditional "Fung Shui" woodland (mixed native trees) – these woodlands have traditional and spiritual importance, but many are reduced in size due to changes in land use occurring after old villagers have vacated their houses

  The isolation of roost sites has been highlighted as a particular problem in Malaysia, though this may happen throughout Southeast Asia. Isolation of roost sites, such as those in caves, can occur when immediately adjacent or nearby forested foraging areas are lost owing to agricultural and general land clearance. Similarly, in Iriomote (Ryukyu Islands, Japan), while there has been no suggestion of disturbance to caves, proposals to convert surrounding areas to agriculture will affect the amount of foraging area available, as well as the safe protected routes to and between foraging sites and roosts. Here, the endemic *Rhinolophus imaizumii* and very restricted *Hipposideros turpis* are particularly vulnerable.
- **Wetlands** Wetlands are important as feeding areas for bats and they are threatened by a variety of activities including destruction and drainage for conversion to agriculture. In Hong Kong, the threat comes from increased development including the new airport which opened in 1998. Wetlands have been highlighted as being under particular threat in Hong Kong, though undoubtedly other wetland areas throughout the region are also threatened.

  In the Philippines, there has been severe pollution and development along most major rivers, as well as extensive clearing of mangroves for fuelwood and, more recently, conversion of fresh and saline wetlands for aquaculture, particularly for fish and shrimp.
- **Caves** Many caves are used by significant aggregations of bats. Caves are threatened by a variety of activities. The guano created by these large colonies is a valuable resource for local communities. In this situation, therefore, the bats are of economic importance. Unfortunately, frequent over-harvesting of guano results in the disturbance of the bats responsible for its production. For example, in the Philippines, cave-roosting bats can be subject to high levels of disturbance by guano harvesters and by visitors to caves who seek recreation, and who often light fires inside such sites and/or use kerosene lamps. Disturbance drastically reduces bat populations in cave sites. There is a need to restrict access to caves, for example through gating. Tourism, particularly at some of the more spectacular caves, can also result in excessive disturbance. In India, some caves are used as temples and, as such, come under the management of the Antiquity Service. Inappropriate means of closure of sites may result in exclusion of bats. Throughout Southeast Asia and particularly in Malaysia, limestone caves contain substantial populations of bats and mining activities associated with limestone extraction can threaten caves and their resident bats. The loss of limestone caves is thought especially to threaten *Cheiromeles torquatus*. An additional problem in this area is that some bats share their cave roosts with cave swiftlets; in some areas, the disturbance caused during the collection of nests of these birds has been identified as a cause of decline in, for example, *C. torquatus* in Niah Caves, Borneo. Also, the species is an important source of red meat and this may additionally threaten its survival. This species occurs in Malaysia, Indonesia, and the Philippines, and is highly dependent on caves, although it is also recorded from tree hollows. The big colonies

that have disappeared are those that were in large limestone caves. Many other microchiropterans are taken as food by local people. This may, in some cases, threaten their survival, particularly if they are already under threat from other factors. There has been an apparent loss of cave bats in southwest China and only piles of guano are now left in some caves. In Laos, it is suggested that harvesting for food of species that occur in caves may be a serious threat to populations (Francis *et al.* 1999).

- **Old buildings** In Hong Kong, colonial and traditional Chinese buildings with spaces behind tiles are particularly favoured by bats, but are being lost through increased building development.

Threats to higher taxa

- **Family Craseonycteridae** The family Craseonycteridae is represented by a single species, *Craseonycteris thonglongyai*, which is known only from a restricted area around the Sai Yok National Park in western Thailand. It is the subject of a Species Action Plan presented in this volume.
- **Family Rhinolophidae** As in other areas, the family Rhinolophidae is considered particularly threatened. One species (*R. convexus*) is considered Critically Endangered and two (*R. imaizumii* and *R. keyensis*) are considered Endangered. *R. imaizumii* is found only on Iriomote Island in the Ryukyu chain of southern Japan. In the Philippines, most rhinolophids are geographically restricted and many require primary forest and/or caves for roosting and feeding. Both of these habitats are under particular threat.
- **Genus *Coelops* (Family Hipposideridae)** There are three species, *Coelops frithi*, *C. hirsutus*, and *C. robinsoni*. *C. frithi* is widespread, recorded from India, Myanmar, China, Thailand, Laos, Viet Nam, Malaysia, Indonesia, and Taiwan. *C. robinsoni* is poorly known from relatively few locations, but occurs over a wide distribution, being recorded from Malaysia, Indonesia, and Laos. *C. hirsutus* is known only from one specimen from the Philippines and its taxonomic status is uncertain.
- **Genus *Kerivoula* (Family Vespertilionidae)** Twelve species have been recorded from the Indomalayan Region – *Kerivoula agnella*, *K. atrox*, *K. flora*, *K. hardwickei*, *K. intermedia*, *K. jagori*, *K. minuta*, *K. myrella*, *K. papillosa*, *K. pellucida*, *K. picta*, and *K. whiteheadi*. *K. flora* and *K. myrella* may possibly be subspecies of *K. hardwickei*. *K. atrox* and *K. jagori* are included in the subgenus *Phoniscus*, sometimes recognised as a distinct genus. Both are only known from a few but widespread localities in Southeast Asia. A third species, *K. aerosa*, is only known from two specimens. It was originally described as being from South Africa, but is now thought to possibly be of Asian origin. Although no particular problems have been identified in this region, the genus has been highlighted as of concern in the Afrotropical and Australasian Regions, and it is possible that these concerns may also apply to the species in this region.
- **Genus *Hesperoptenus* (Family Vespertilionidae)** Five species have been recorded from this region, *Hesperoptenus blanfordi*, *H. doriae*, *H. gaskelli*, *H. tickelli*, and *H. tomesi*. Two of these, *H. doriae* and *H. gaskelli*, are poorly known; the former is only known from four specimens, while the latter is only known from the type locality. Though no specific problems have been identified, there is sufficient concern to warrant further studies.
- **Genus *Ia* (Family Vespertilionidae)** The single species of the genus *Ia*, *I. io*, is recorded from about 13 localities in China, Laos, Thailand, Viet Nam, India and Nepal. Two records represent known colonies, one in China which was destroyed in about 1960, and one current (1995) colony of about 30 in Nepal; the rest are all records of single individuals (G. Csorba *pers. comm.*). Little is known about the species and it has been considered Near Threatened. However, recent work in Viet Nam suggests that the species may not be as rare as formerly thought (J. Walston *pers. comm.*).
- **Genus *Murina* (Family Vespertilionidae)** Twelve species have been recorded from this region – *Murina aenea*, *M. aurata*, *M. cyclotis*, *M. florium*, *M. grisea*, *M. huttoni*, *M. leucogaster*, *M. puta*, *M. rozendaali*, *M. ryukyuana*, *M. suilla*, and *M. tubinaris*. Most are poorly known species of limited distribution. Although no specific problems have been identified, most of the species are sufficiently rare that the genus, which is recognized as constituting a monotypic subfamily, should be the subject of further investigation.
- **Genus *Cheiromeles* (Family Molossidae)** This is a very distinct genus of two species. The status of one species, *C. parvidens*, is uncertain; it is only known from Sulawesi and from a single, possibly conspecific, specimen from Mindoro in the Philippines. Some authorities have regarded it as a synonym of *C. torquatus*, which, although much more widespread, is reported to have suffered heavy population declines in some areas. For example, the population in Niah Caves in Borneo was reported to be 20,000 (out of a total bat population of 300,000) in 1958 (Medway 1958), but has now all but disappeared. For more information see the Species Action Plan in this volume.
- **Genus *Otomops* (Family Molossidae)** *Otomops* is a small genus of six species, most of which are poorly known. *O. wroughtoni*, described in 1913, is only known from a single cave in India, where it has been caught at least twice since. *O. formosus* (Java) and *O. johnstonei* (Alor Islands) are known from single or very few specimens. For more information see the Species Action Plan for *O. martiensseni* in this volume.

Threats to geographical areas

- **Southeast Asia** Throughout Southeast Asia there are threats to the resident bat fauna. The Philippines, in particular, is highlighted as an area with high endemicity and where there is a very high rate of forest destruction and disturbance of caves. In the Philippines, many species are very poorly known and new ones are being discovered every two to three years, and, as such, there is a need for more surveys. Harp traps have not yet been used to sample bats here and could probably greatly increase the number of captures and records. Heaney *et al.* (1987) listed 43 species of microchiropterans, nine of which were endemic. An increased survey effort could well increase these figures. Southeast Asia, as a whole, is rich with species restricted to islands that suffer severe pressure from increased disturbance and habitat loss. Many smaller islands in Southeast Asia have not been surveyed and may contain endemic species/forms.

  There is little or no recent data on bat status in Cambodia and Myanmar. In Laos, recent surveys have greatly increased the knowledge of bats in the country. In this case, it revealed a worrying threat from consumption of species, particularly cave-dwellers, for food. These surveys also suggested that a high proportion of bat species in Laos were probably at risk (Francis *et al.* 1999). In Cambodia, investigation of a problem arising from bats occupying the roof of the National Museum in Phnom Penh revealed the presence of a colony of around two million molossids (G.C. Richards *pers. comm.*). The widespread presence of land mines, political instability, and government restrictions prevent detailed bat studies. The situation is similar in Myanmar, though in Laos large-scale development projects, such as dams, power stations, and roads, have resulted in faunal studies currently being carried out as part of Environmental Impact Assessments. There is little information on threats to bats in these countries, though it is surmised that the main ones are clearing of forests, limestone mining for cement, and harvesting for human consumption (L.S. Hall *pers. comm.*).

Key areas for bat biodiversity

Hotspots at a generic level

Centres of diversity at the generic level were assessed using a WORLDMAP analysis (see Chapter 5.3 for further details). There are distinct concentrations of diversity in the northern parts of the region and in the Malaysia/Indonesia area (Map 28), but there are few areas of low diversity. The minimum set of grid-cell areas required to maintain all genera is seven (Map 29); this includes four areas that are not flexible due to the presence of genera of restricted distribution (although the diversity of some

Map 28. Generic richness per grid-cell area for genera occurring in the Indomalayan Region.
The numbers in the squares represent the number of genera per unit area.

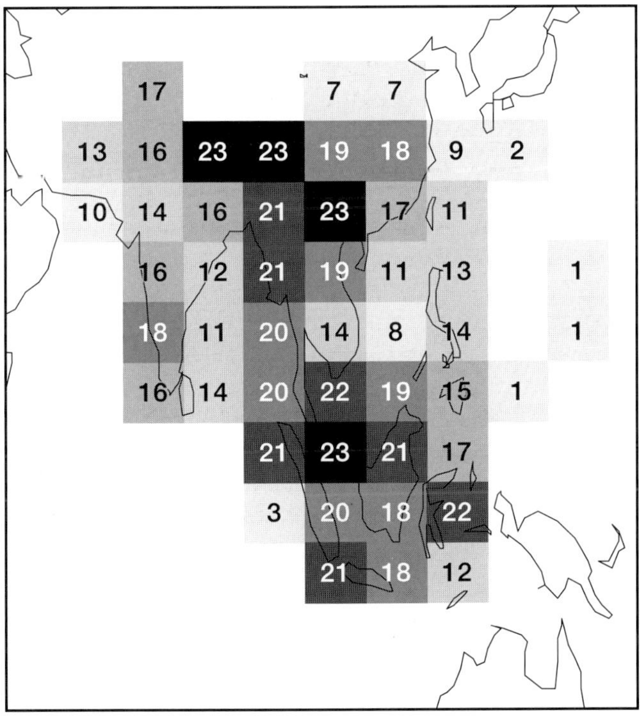

Map 29. Minimum set of grid-cell areas required to maintain all genera occurring in the Indomalayan Region.
The minimum number of squares required to conserve all genera is seven. The numbers in the squares represent the number of genera uniquely contributing to this minimum set.

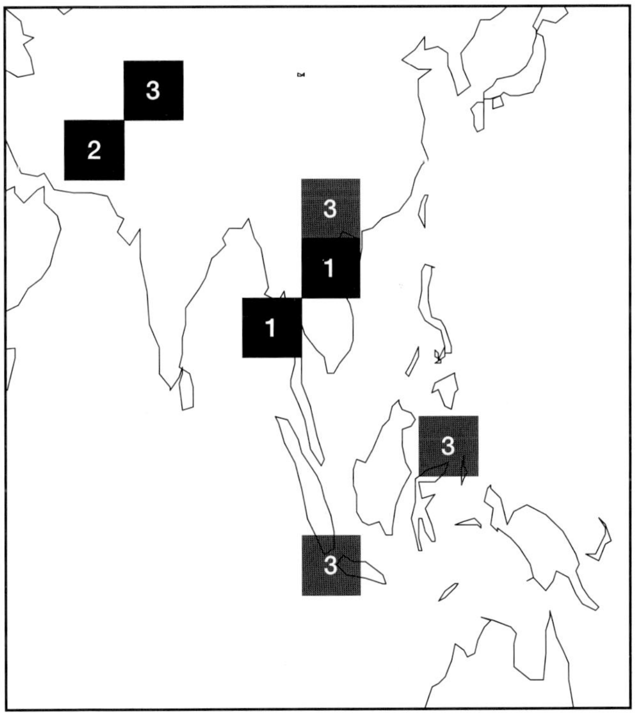

of these, e.g., the northwestern squares, may be overemphasised through containing elements of a principally Palaearctic fauna).

Malaysia

The country has a number of protected areas that are thought to be of particular importance to bats. Over 100 bat species have been recorded from Peninsular Malaysia (L.S. Hall *pers. comm.*) and several protected areas have diverse bat faunas, for example Belum Forest Reserve and Temenggor Forest Reserve in Perak State (39 species, G.W.H. Davison *pers. comm.*), and Endau Rompin Park in Johore State (22 species, G.W.H. Davison *pers. comm.*). On the island of Borneo, there are a number of large, well-known bat roosts, such as Niah Caves in Sarawak. The area around Mt. Kinabalu in Sabah provides a wide range of habitats, from lowland forest to upper montane areas. Six globally threatened species have been recorded in Malaysia – two Critically Endangered, one Endangered, and three Vulnerable.

Indonesia

The main Indonesian islands of Java, Sumatra, Borneo, and Sulawesi would all be considered of importance for bats in their own right. The province of Irian Jaya has been considered with New Guinea in the Australasian regional account. Deforestation rates on some of these islands are high; for example, on Sumatra at least a third of the natural area of montane forest on the island has already been lost and deforestation rates are probably the highest in Indonesia (Stattersfield *et al.* 1998). In Java, closed canopy forest covers less than 10% of the land area (Collins *et al.* 1991). Borneo and Sulawesi still have large tracts of undisturbed forest. A total of 18 globally threatened species have been recorded from Indonesia – four Endangered and 14 Vulnerable.

Philippines

In total, 70 species of bats have been recorded from the Philippines, 24 of them megachiropterans. The degree of endemism in the Philippines is high. There are 10–15 distinct faunal regions within the Philippines, which correspond to single islands that existed from 10,000 to 18,000 years ago during a period of low sea levels and each of these has its own endemic bats. All of these areas are threatened. The Greater Negros-Panay faunal region is the most threatened, followed by Mindoro, Greater Luzon, Greater Mindanao, Greater Palawan, Sibuyan, Greater Sulu, and the Batanes/Babuyan region (Heaney 1993). There is one globally threatened species in the Philippines. The main threat comes from habitat loss.

Viet Nam

There has been little bat research in Viet Nam until recently. A recent preliminary survey of Cuc Phuong National Park near Hanoi revealed the presence of at least 35 bat species, making it a key site in Southeast Asia (J. Walston *pers. comm.*). More intensive surveys are planned for this and other areas within Viet Nam. There are currently four globally threatened species recorded from Viet Nam – one Critically Endangered, one Endangered, and two Vulnerable.

Recommendations

The following recommendations are based upon information provided by the contributors to this section. They include both general recommendations applicable to the whole area, as well as specific ones relating to particular species, areas, or habitats.

Habitats

Particular concern has been expressed for lowland primary forests and wetlands.

Recommendations:
- make sustainable management and conservation of habitat diversity a goal of land-use policies;
- assess threat to wetland areas and possible impacts on bat populations.

Roost types

In addition to underground habitats and older trees, traditional buildings, temples, and monumental structures are widely used by a range of bat species that frequently suffer through site degradation, restoration work, and unsympathetic management of the structures.

Recommendations:
- incorporate the requirements of bats, where possible, in preservation, restoration work, and management of traditional buildings used by important bat populations;
- study effects of isolation on bat roost sites;
- study effects of guano harvesting on cave-dwelling bats;
- restrict access to vulnerable caves, where appropriate;
- assess threats to cave-dwelling bat populations from cave swiftlet nest collection;
- assess status and threats to key cave bat roosts in Borneo;
- educate land managers about needs of tree-roosting bats.

Geographical areas

Areas highlighted as of particular concern, having high levels of endemicity and current high human pressure, are the Philippines, Borneo, and Indonesia. The bat fauna of other areas, such as Cambodia, Myanmar, and many islands of Southeast Asia are still very poorly known and require more detailed survey work. The recent surveys in Laos need to be followed-up with work in other areas of the country.

Recommendations:
- adopt principles of sustainable development that will allow threatened bat species to maintain a favourable conservation status in all areas;

- survey smaller islands in Southeast Asia;
- undertake more bat survey work in the Philippines, Borneo, and Indonesia;
- assess status and threat to bat populations in Cambodia and Myanmar;
- undertake more intensive bat surveys in Viet Nam and Laos.

Taxa

Taxa of concern include Rhinolophidae, Craseonycteridae, *Otomops*, *Megaderma*, *Kerivoula*, *Murina*, and *Cheiromeles*. Species Action Plans for a number of these are presented in Chapter 5.5. The status, distribution, and threats to a wide range of other taxa are poorly known.

Recommendations:
- use the Species Action Plans provided here to develop action programmes for threatened species, especially those where higher taxa are generally at risk;
- assess threats to rhinolophid species;
- assess status of *Coelops* species;
- assess threats to *Kerivoula* species;
- assess status of *Hesperoptenus* species;
- assess status of *Ia io*;
- assess status of *Murina* species in the region;
- assess status of *Cheiromeles torquatus* populations in cave sites.

Checklist of Indomalayan bats

A total of 260 species are recorded from the Indomalayan Region. The full list of species is given below.

Species	Status
FAMILY RHINOPOMATIDAE	
Rhinopoma	
Rhinopoma hardwickei Gray 1831	LR: lc
Rhinopoma microphyllum (Brünnich 1782)	LR: lc
Rhinopoma muscatellum Thomas 1903	LR: lc
FAMILY CRASEONYCTERIDAE	
Craseonycteris	
Craseonycteris thonglongyai Hill 1974	EN: B1+2c, C2b
FAMILY EMBALLONURIDAE	
Emballonura	
Emballonura alecto (Eydoux and Gervais 1836)	LR: lc
Emballonura beccarii Peters and Doria 1881	LR: lc
Emballonura monticola Temminck 1838	LR: lc
Emballonura raffrayana Dobson 1879	LR: nt
Mosia	
Mosia nigrescens (Gray 1843)	LR: lc
Saccolaimus	
Saccolaimus saccolaimus (Temminck 1838)	LR: lc
Taphozous	
Taphozous achates Thomas 1915	VU: D2
Taphozous longimanus Hardwicke 1825	LR: lc
Taphozous melanopogon Temminck 1841	LR: lc
Taphozous nudiventris Cretzschmar 1830	LR: lc
Taphozous perforatus E. Geoffroy 1818	LR: lc
Taphozous theobaldi Dobson 1872	LR: lc
FAMILY NYCTERIDAE	
Nycteris	
Nycteris javanica E. Geoffroy 1813	VU: A1c
Nycteris tragata (K. Andersen 1912)	LR: lc
FAMILY MEGADERMATIDAE	
Megaderma	
Megaderma lyra E. Geoffroy 1810	LR: lc
Megaderma spasma (Linnaeus 1758)	LR: lc
FAMILY HIPPOSIDERIDAE	
Asellia	
Asellia tridens (E. Geoffroy 1813)	LR: lc
Aselliscus	
Aselliscus stoliczkanus (Dobson 1871)	LR: lc
Aselliscus tricuspidatus (Temminck 1835)	LR: lc
Coelops	
Coelops frithi Blyth 1848	LR: lc
Coelops hirsutus (Miller 1911)	DD
Coelops robinsoni Bonhote 1908	LR: nt
Hipposideros	
Hipposideros armiger (Hodgson 1835)	LR: lc
Hipposideros ater Templeton 1848	LR: lc
Hipposideros bicolor (Temminck 1834)	LR: lc
Hipposideros breviceps Tate 1941	VU: D2
Hipposideros calcaratus (Dobson 1877)	LR: lc
Hipposideros cervinus (Gould 1863)	LR: lc
Hipposideros cineraceus Blyth 1853	LR: lc
Hipposideros coronatus (Peters 1871)	LR: nt
Hipposideros coxi Shelford 1901	VU: D2
Hipposideros crumeniferus Lesueur and Petit 1807	DD
Hipposideros diadema (E. Geoffroy 1813)	LR: lc
Hipposideros dinops K. Andersen 1905	LR: nt
Hipposideros doriae (Peters 1871)	DD
Hipposideros durgadasi Khajuria 1970	VU: B1+2c, D2
Hipposideros dyacorum Thomas 1902	LR: lc
Hipposideros fulvus Gray 1838	LR: lc
Hipposideros galeritus Cantor 1846	LR: lc
Hipposideros halophyllus Hill and Yenbutra 1984	LR: nt
Hipposideros hypophyllus Kock and Bhat 1994	VU: B1+2c, D2
Hipposideros inexpectatus Laurie and Hill 1954	VU: A2c
Hipposideros lankadiva Kelaart 1850	LR: lc
Hipposideros larvatus (Horsfield 1823)	LR: lc
Hipposideros lekaguli Thonglongya and Hill 1974	LR: nt
Hipposideros lylei Thomas 1913	LR: nt

Species	Status
Hipposideros macrobullatus Tate 1941	LR: nt
Hipposideros madurae Kitchener and Maryanto 1993	LR: nt
Hipposideros maggietaylorae Smith and Hill 1981	LR: lc
Hipposideros nequam K. Andersen 1918	CR: B1 + 2c
Hipposideros obscurus (Peters 1861)	LR: nt
Hipposideros papua (Thomas and Doria 1886)	VU: A2c
Hipposideros pomona K. Andersen 1918	LR: lc**
Hipposideros pratti Thomas 1891	LR: nt
Hipposideros pygmaeus (Waterhouse 1843)	LR: nt
Hipposideros ridleyi Robinson and Kloss 1911	VU: B1 + 2c
Hipposideros sabanus Thomas 1898	LR: lc
Hipposideros schistaceus K. Andersen 1918	DD
Hipposideros sorenseni Kitchener and Maryanto 1993	LR: nt
Hipposideros speoris (Schneider 1800)	LR: lc
Hipposideros sumbae (Oei 1960)	LR: nt
Hipposideros turpis Bangs 1901	EN: A2c
Paracoelops	
Paracoelops megalotis Dorst 1947	CR: B1 + 2c
Triaenops	
Triaenops persicus Dobson 1871	LR: lc
FAMILY RHINOLOPHIDAE	
Rhinolophus	
Rhinolophus acuminatus Peters 1871	LR: lc
Rhinolophus affinis Horsfield 1823	LR: lc
Rhinolophus anderseni Cabrera 1909	DD
Rhinolophus arcuatus Peters 1871	LR: lc
Rhinolophus beddomei Andersen 1905	LR: nt
Rhinolophus blasii Peters 1866	LR: nt
?*Rhinolophus bocharicus* Kastschenko and Akimov 1917	LR: lc
Rhinolophus borneensis Peters 1861	LR: lc
Rhinolophus canuti Thomas and Wroughton 1909	LR: nt
Rhinolophus celebensis K. Andersen 1905	LR: nt
Rhinolophus coelophyllus Peters 1867	LR: lc
Rhinolophus cognatus K. Andersen 1906	VU: A2c, D2
Rhinolophus convexus Csorba 1997	CR: D
Rhinolophus cornutus Temminck 1835	LR: nt
Rhinolophus creaghi Thomas 1896	LR: nt
Rhinolophus euryotis Temminck 1835	LR: lc
Rhinolophus ferrumequinum (Schreber 1774)	LR: nt
Rhinolophus hipposideros (Bechstein 1800)	VU: A2c
Rhinolophus imaizumii Hill and Yoshiyuki 1980	EN: A2c, B1 + 2abcde
Rhinolophus inops K. Andersen 1905	DD
Rhinolophus keyensis Peters 1871	EN: C2a
Rhinolophus lepidus Blyth 1844	LR: lc
Rhinolophus luctus Temminck 1835	LR: lc
Rhinolophus macrotis Blyth 1844	LR: lc
Rhinolophus malayanus Bonhote 1903	LR: lc
Rhinolophus marshalli Thonglongya 1973	LR: nt
Rhinolophus megaphyllus Gray 1834	LR: lc
Rhinolophus mitratus Blyth 1844	DD
Rhinolophus monoceros K. Andersen 1905	LR: nt
Rhinolophus nereis K. Andersen 1905	LR: nt
Rhinolophus osgoodi Sanborn 1939	DD
Rhinolophus paradoxolophus (Bourret 1951)	VU: B1 + 2c
Rhinolophus pearsoni Horsfield 1851	LR: lc
Rhinolophus philippinensis Waterhouse 1843	LR: nt
Rhinolophus pusillus Temminck 1834	LR: lc
Rhinolophus rex G. M. Allen 1923	VU: B1 + 2c
Rhinolophus rouxi Temminck 1835	LR: lc
Rhinolophus rufus Eydoux and Gervais 1836	LR: nt
Rhinolophus sedulus K. Andersen 1905	LR: lc
Rhinolophus shameli Tate 1943	LR: nt
Rhinolophus sinicus K. Andersen 1905	LR: lc
Rhinolophus stheno K. Andersen 1905	LR: lc
Rhinolophus subbadius Blyth 1844	DD
Rhinolophus subrufus K. Andersen 1905	VU: A2c
Rhinolophus thomasi K. Andersen 1905	LR: nt
Rhinolophus trifoliatus Temminck 1834	LR: lc
Rhinolophus virgo K. Andersen 1905	LR: nt
Rhinolophus yunanensis Dobson 1872	LR: nt
FAMILY VESPERTILIONIDAE	
Subfamily Kerivoulinae	
Kerivoula	
Kerivoula agnella Thomas 1908	VU: D2
Kerivoula atrox Miller 1905	LR: lc
Kerivoula flora Thomas 1914	LR: lc
Kerivoula hardwickei (Horsfield 1824)	LR: lc
Kerivoula intermedia Hill and Francis 1984	LR: nt
Kerivoula jagori (Peters 1866)	LR: lc
Kerivoula minuta Miller 1898	LR: nt
Kerivoula myrella Thomas 1914	VU: A2c
Kerivoula papillosa (Temminck 1840)	LR: lc
Kerivoula pellucida (Waterhouse 1845)	LR: lc
Kerivoula picta (Pallas 1767)	LR: lc
Kerivoula whiteheadi Thomas 1894	LR: lc
Subfamily Vespertilioninae	
Arielulus	
Arielulus aureocollaris (Kock and Storch 1996)	DD
Arielulus circumdatus (Temminck 1840)	LR: lc
Arielulus cuprosus (Hill and Francis 1984)	VU: A2c
Arielulus societatis (Hill 1972)	DD
Arielulus torquatus Csorba and Lee 1999	DD
Barbastella	
Barbastella leucomelas (Cretzschmar 1826)	LR: lc
Eptesicus	
Eptesicus bottae (Peters 1869)	LR: lc
Eptesicus demissus Thomas 1916	VU: A2c
Eptesicus gobiensis Bobrinsky 1926	LR: lc
Eptesicus nasutus (Dobson 1877)	VU: A2c
Eptesicus nilssonii (Keyserling and Blasius 1839)	LR: lc
Eptesicus pachyotis (Dobson 1871)	LR: nt
Eptesicus serotinus Schreber 1774	LR: lc
Eptesicus tatei Ellerman and Morrison-Scott 1951	DD

Species	Status
Eudiscopus	
Eudiscopus denticulus (Osgood 1932)	LR: nt
Glischropus	
Glischropus javanus Chasen 1939	EN B1 + 2d
Glischropus tylopus (Dobson 1875)	LR: lc
Hesperoptenus	
Hesperoptenus blanfordi (Dobson 1877)	LR: lc
Hesperoptenus doriae (Peters 1868)	EN: B1 + 2c
Hesperoptenus gaskelli Hill 1983	VU: B1 + 2c
Hesperoptenus tickelli (Blyth 1851)	LR: lc
Hesperoptenus tomesi Thomas 1905	LR: lc
Ia	
Ia io Thomas 1902	LR: nt
Myotis	
Myotis adversus (Horsfield 1824)	LR: lc
Myotis altarium Thomas 1911	LR: lc
Myotis annectans (Dobson 1871)	LR: nt
Myotis ater (Peters 1866)	LR: lc
Myotis blythii (Tomes 1857)	LR: lc
Myotis chinensis (Tomes 1857)	LR: lc
Myotis csorbai Topal 1998	DD
Myotis daubentonii (Kuhl 1817)	LR: lc
Myotis fimbriatus (Peters 1871)	LR: nt
Myotis formosus (Hodgson 1835)	LR: lc
Myotis frater G. M. Allen 1923	LR: nt
Myotis gomatongensis Francis and Hill 1998	DD
Myotis hasseltii (Temminck 1840)	LR: lc
?*Myotis hermanni* Thomas 1923	DD
Myotis horsfieldii (Temminck 1840)	LR: lc
Myotis longipes (Dobson 1873)	VU B1 + 2c, D2
Myotis macrotarsus (Waterhouse 1845)	LR: nt
Myotis montivagus (Dobson 1874)	LR: nt
Myotis muricola (Gray 1846)	LR: lc
Myotis oreias (Temminck 1840)	DD
Myotis ricketti (Thomas 1894)	LR: nt
Myotis ridleyi Thomas 1898	LR: nt
Myotis rosseti (Oey 1951)	LR: nt
Myotis sicarius Thomas 1915	VU: A2c, D2
Myotis siligorensis (Horsfield 1855)	LR: lc
Myotis stalkeri Thomas 1910	EN: B1 + 2c
Myotis yanbarensis Maeda and Matsumara 1998	DD
Nyctalus	
Nyctalus leisleri (Kuhl 1817)	LR: nt
Nyctalus montanus (Barrett-Hamilton 1906)	LR: nt
Nyctalus noctula (Schreber 1774)	LR: lc
Nyctophilus	
Nyctophilus heran Kitchener, How, and Maharadatunkamsi 1991	EN: B1 + 2c
Otonycteris	
Otonycteris hemprichii Peters 1859	LR: lc
Philetor	
Philetor brachypterus (Temminck 1840)	LR: lc
Pipistrellus	
Pipistrellus abramus (Temminck 1840)	LR: lc
Pipistrellus affinis (Dobson 1871)	LR: lc
Pipistrellus angulatus (Peters 1880)	LR: lc
Pipistrellus anthonyi Tate 1942	CR: B1 + 2c
Pipistrellus cadornae Thomas 1916	LR: nt
Pipistrellus ceylonicus (Kelaart 1852)	LR: lc
Pipistrellus coromandra (Gray 1838)	LR: lc
Pipistrellus dormeri (Dobson 1875)	LR: lc
Pipistrellus imbricatus (Horsfield 1824)	LR: lc
Pipistrellus javanicus (Gray 1838)	LR: lc
Pipistrellus joffrei (Thomas 1915)	CR: B1 + 2c
Pipistrellus kitcheneri Thomas 1916	LR: nt
Pipistrellus kuhlii (Kuhl 1817)	LR: lc
Pipistrellus lophurus Thomas 1915	DD
Pipistrellus macrotis (Temminck 1840)	LR: nt
Pipistrellus minahassae (Meyer 1899)	DD
Pipistrellus mordax (Peters 1866)	LR: nt
Pipistrellus papuanus (Peters and Doria 1881)	LR: nt
Pipistrellus paterculus Thomas 1915	LR: nt
Pipistrellus peguensis Sinha 1969	DD
Pipistrellus petersi (Meyer 1899)	LR: lc
Pipistrellus pipistrellus (Schreber 1774)	LR: lc
Pipistrellus pulveratus (Peters 1871)	LR: nt
Pipistrellus savii (Bonaparte 1837)	LR: lc
Pipistrellus stenopterus (Dobson 1875)	LR: lc
Pipistrellus sturdeei Thomas 1915	EX
Pipistrellus tenuis (Temminck 1840)	LR: lc
Plecotus	
Plecotus auritus (Linnaeus 1758)	LR: lc
Plecotus austriacus (Fischer 1829)	LR: lc
Plecotus taivanus Yoshiyuki 1991	VU: A2c
Scotoecus	
Scotoecus pallidus Dobson 1876	LR: lc
Scotomanes	
Scotomanes emarginatus (Dobson 1871)	DD
Scotomanes ornatus (Blyth 1851)	LR: nt
Scotophilus	
Scotophilus celebensis Sody 1928	DD
Scotophilus heathi (Horsfield 1831)	LR: lc
Scotophilus kuhlii Leach 1821	LR: lc
Tylonycteris	
Tylonycteris pachypus (Temminck 1840)	LR: lc
Tylonycteris robustula Thomas 1915	LR: lc
Vespertilio	
?*Vespertilio murinus* Linnaeus 1758	LR: lc
Vespertilio superans Thomas 1899	LR: lc
Subfamily Murininae	
Harpiocephalus	
Harpiocephalus harpia (Temminck 1840)	LR: lc
Harpiocephalus mordax Thomas 1923	LR: nt
Murina	
Murina aenea Hill 1964	LR: nt
Murina aurata Milne-Edwards 1872	LR: nt
Murina cyclotis Dobson 1872	LR: lc
Murina florium Thomas 1908	LR: lc
Murina grisea Peters 1872	EN: B1 + 2c
Murina huttoni (Peters 1872)	LR: nt
Murina leucogaster Milne-Edwards 1872	LR: lc
Murina puta Kishida 1924	VU: A2c
Murina rozendaali Hill and Francis 1984	LR: nt
Murina ryukyuana Maeda and Matsumara 1998	DD
Murina suilla (Temminck,1840)	LR: lc
Murina tubinaris (Scully 1881)	LR: lc
Subfamily Miniopterinae	
Miniopterus	
Miniopterus australis Tomes 1858	LR: lc

Species	Status	Species	Status
Miniopterus fuscus Bonhote 1902	VU: A2c	*Cheiromeles torquatus* Horsfield 1824	LR: nt
Miniopterus magnater Sanborn 1931	LR: lc	***Mops***	
Miniopterus medius		*Mops mops* (de Blainville 1840)	LR: lc
Thomas and Wroughton 1909	LR: lc	*Mops sarasinorum* (Meyer 1899)	LR: nt
Miniopterus pusillus Dobson 1876	LR: lc	***Mormopterus***	
Miniopterus schreibersii (Kuhl 1817)	LR: nt	*Mormopterus beccarii* Peters 1881	LR: lc
Miniopterus tristis (Waterhouse 1845)	LR: lc	*Mormopterus doriae* K. Andersen 1907	VU: A2c
		Otomops	
FAMILY MOLOSSIDAE		*Otomops formosus* Chasen 1939	VU: A2c
Chaerephon		*Otomops johnstonei*	
Chaerephon jobensis (Miller 1902)	LR: lc	Kitchener, How, and Maryanto 1992	VU: D2
Chaerephon johorensis (Dobson 1873)	LR: nt	*Otomops wroughtoni* (Thomas 1913)	CR: B1 + 2c
Chaerephon plicata (Buchanan 1800)	LR: lc	***Tadarida***	
Cheiromeles		*Tadarida aegyptiaca* (E. Geoffroy 1818)	LR: lc
Cheiromeles parvidens		*Tadarida latouchei* Thomas 1920	DD
Miller and Hollister 1921	LR: nt	*Tadarida teniotis* (Rafinesque 1814)	LR: lc

Table 5. Number of IUCN Red List species for countries in the Indomalayan Region.

The table also includes information on numbers of endemics and the estimated size of the bat fauna. For information on the compilation of the figures for size of faunas see Chapter 6. Full lists of IUCN Red List species per country are given in the same Chapter. **Countries not included in this list do not have a recorded bat fauna.** Where a country overlaps more than one region, the fauna for the whole country is included.

	IUCN RED LIST SPECIES								ENDEMICS	TOTAL NO. OF SPECIES		
Country	**CR**	**EN**	**VU**	**LRcd**	**LRnt**	**EX**	**DD**	***Total***	***Total***	**Mega**	**Micro**	***Total***
Bangladesh	0	0	0	0	0	0	0	0	0	3	15	18
Bhutan	0	0	0	0	0	0	0	0	0	3	2	5
Brunei	0	0	0	0	1	0	0	1	0	11	11	22
Cambodia	0	0	0	0	2	0	0	2	0	10	28	38
China	0	0	2	0	20	0	3	25	6	8	82	90
India	1	1	6	0	15	0	5	28	9	13	96	109
Indonesia	0	4	14	0	25	0	4	47	24	63	112	175
Laos	0	0	1	0	18	0	2	21	0	8	82	90
Malaysia	2	1	3	0	22	0	3	31	11	17	95	112
Maldives	0	0	0	0	0	0	0	0	0	2	0	2
Myanmar	2	0	0	0	16	0	3	21	3	12	76	88
Nepal	0	0	2	0	7	0	3	12	1	4	47	51
Pakistan	0	0	2	0	5	0	0	7	0	4	43	47
Philippines	0	0	1	0	13	0	3	17	9	24	46	70
Singapore	0	0	1	0	0	0	1	2	1	5	4	9
Sri Lanka	0	0	0	0	2	0	0	2	0	4	28	32
Thailand	0	2	2	0	21	0	3	28	4	17	91	108
Viet Nam	1	1	2	0	10	0	1	15	1	11	53	64

Table 5 shows the number of IUCN Red List species recorded from each country together with information on numbers of endemics and the size of the total bat fauna.

Key references

The following is a list of important references relating to bats in the Indomalayan Region. It is by no means an exhaustive list and concentrates mainly on distributional studies at a national or regional level.

Bates, P.J.J. and Harrison, D.L. 1997. *Bats of the Indian Subcontinent.* Harrison Zoological Museum, Sevenoaks.

Bates, P.J.J., Nwe, T., Pearch, M.J., Swe, K.M., Hla Bu, S.S., and Tun, T. 2000. A review of bat research in Myanmar (Burma) and results of a recent survey. *Acta Chiropterologica*, 2(1), 53–82.

Brosset, A. 1962a. The bats of central and western India. Part 1. *Journal of the Bombay Natural History Society*, 59, 1–57.

Brosset, A. 1962b. The bats of central and western India. Part 2. *Journal of the Bombay Natural History Society*, 59, 583–642.

Brosset, A. 1962c. The bats of central and western India. Part 3. *Journal of the Bombay Natural History Society*, 59, 706–746.

Brosset, A. 1963. The bats of central and western India. Part 4. *Journal of the Bombay Natural History Society*, 60, 337–355.

Chasen, F.N. 1940. A handlist of Malaysian mammals. *Bulletin of the Raffles Museum*, 15, 1–209.

Corbet, G.B. and Hill, J. Edwards 1992. *The Mammals of the Indomalayan Region: A systematic review.* Oxford University Press, Oxford.

Csorba, G., Kruskop, S.V., and Borissenko, A.V. 1999. Recent records of bats (Chiroptera) from Nepal, with remarks on their natural history. *Mammalia*, 63, 61–78.

Dany Huy Huynh (ed.) 1994. [*Checklist of mammals of Vietnam*]. Vietnam Centre for Natural Science and Technology, Institute of Ecology and Biological Resources, Science and Technics Publishing House, Hanoi. [in Vietnamese].

Davis, D.D. 1962. Mammals of the lowland rain-forests of North Borneo. *Bulletin of the National Museum, State of Singapore*, 31, 5–129.

DeBlase, A.F. 1980. The bats of Iran: Systematics, distribution, ecology. *Fieldiana: Zoology, New Series,* 4, 1–424.

Ellerman, J.R. and Morrison-Scott, T.C.S. 1966. *Checklist of Palaearctic and Indian mammals 1758–1946,* Second edition. British Museum (Natural History), London.

Felten, H. (ed.) 1986. Contributions to the knowledge of the bats of Thailand. *Courier Forschungsinstitut Senckenberg*, 87, 1–112.

Flannery, T. 1995. *Mammals of the south-west Pacific and Moluccan Islands.* Australian Museum and Reed Books, Chatswood.

Francis, C.M., Guillen, A., and Robinson, M.F. 1999. Order Chiroptera: Bats. Pp. 225–235 *in: Wildlife in Lao PDR. 1999 status report* (compilers Duckworth, J.W., Salter, R.E., and K. Khounboline). IUCN – The World Conservation Union, Wildlife Conservation Society and Centre for Protected Areas and Watershed Management, Lao PDR.

Francis, C.M., Guillen, A., and Vonghamheng, C. 1997a. *Survey of bats and small mammals in Dong Amphan NBCA and nearby areas.* Unpublished report, Wildlife Conservation Society, New York.

Francis, C.M., Guillen, A., and Vonghamheng, C. 1997b. *Preliminary survey of bats in Dong Hua Sao NBCA.* Unpublished report, Wildlife Conservation Society, New York.

Francis, C.M., Khounboline, K., and Aspey, N. 1996. *Report on 1996 survey of bats and small mammals in the Nakai-Nam Theun NBCA and nearby areas.* Unpublished report, Wildlife Conservation Society, New York.

Francis, C.M. and Vonghamheng, C. 1998. *Report on a survey of bats in Khammouane Limestone NBCA.* Unpublished report, Wildlife Conservation Society, New York.

Heller, K. G. and Volleth, M. 1989. Fledermäuse aus Malaysia. 1. Beobachtungen zur Biologie, Morphologie und Taxonomie. *Senckenbergiana Biologica*, 69 (4/6), 243–276.

Hill, J. Edwards 1983. Bats (Mammalia: Chiroptera) from Indo-Australia. *Bulletin of the British Museum (Natural History), Zoology*, 45, 103–208.

Ingle, R.N. and Heaney, L.R. 1992. A key to the bats of the Philippine Islands. *Fieldiana: Zoology, New Series,* 69, 1–44.

Laurie, E.M.O. and Hill, J. Edwards 1954. *List of land mammals of New Guinea, Celebes and adjacent islands 1758–1952.* British Museum (Natural History), London.

Lekagul, B. and McNeely, J.A. 1977. *Mammals of Thailand.* Kuruspha Ladprao Press, Bangkok.

Medway, Lord 1977. *Mammals of Borneo: Field keys and annotated checklist.* Monograph Number 7, Royal Asiatic Society, Malaysian Branch, Kuala Lumpur.

Medway, Lord 1978. *The wild mammals of Malaya (Peninsular Malaysia) and Singapore,* Second edition. Oxford University Press, Kuala Lumpur.

Medway, Lord 1983. *The wild mammals of Malaya (Peninsular Malaysia) and Singapore,* Second edition with corrections. Oxford University Press, Kuala Lumpur.

Miller, G.S. 1902. The mammals of the Andaman and Nicobar Islands. *Proceedings of the United States National Museum,* 24, 751–795.

Payne, J., Francis, C.M., and Phillipps, K. 1985. *A field guide to the mammals of Borneo.* Sabah Society and WWF Malaysia, Kuala Lumpur.

van Peenen, P.F.D., Ryan, P.F., and Light, R.H. 1969. *Preliminary identification manual for mammals of South Vietnam.* Smithsonian Institution, Washington DC.

Phillips, W.W.A. 1986. *The manual of the mammals of Sri Lanka.* WNPS, Sri Lanka.

Roberts, T.J. 1977. *The mammals of Pakistan.* Ernest Benn, London and Tonbridge.

Roberts, T.J. 1998. *The mammals of Pakistan,* Second edition. Oxford University Press, Pakistan.

Robinson, M.F. 1997. *Chiroptera survey. Rapid biological assessment Xe Paine Protected Area, Champassak Province, Lao P.D.R.* Unpublished final report, World Wide Fund for Nature, Thailand.

Robinson, M.F. and Webber, M. 1998. *Small mammal survey. Khammouan Limestone National Biodiversity Conservation Area, Lao P.D.R.* Unpublished final report, World Wide Fund for Nature, Thailand.

Salter, R.E. (compiler) 1993. *Wildlife in Lao PDR. A status report.* IUCN, Vientiane.

Siddiqi, M.S. 1961. Checklist of mammals of Pakistan with particular reference to the mammalian collection in the British Museum (Natural History), London. *Biologia*, 7 (2), 93–225.

Taylor, E.H. 1934. *Philippine land mammals.* Monograph Number 30, Bureau of Science, Manila.

Tun Yin 1993. *Wild mammals of Myanmar.* Soe Kyi, Forest Department, Yangon.

Zhang Yongzu 1997. *Distribution of mammalian species in China.* China Forestry Publishing House, Beijing.

5.4.4 Nearctic Region

This account was compiled using contributions from the following people: John A. Burton; Brock Fenton; Barbara French; the late Karl F. Koopman; Susan Liebermann; Dixie Pierson; Steve Walker; and Don E. Wilson.

Geographical boundaries of region

The region includes Canada, the USA, and northern Mexico, including all of Baja California, extending southwards and bounded by the Sierra Madre Occidental in the west and Sierra Madre Oriental in the east (see Map 1).

Number of species in the region

A total of 73 species are recorded from the Nearctic Region. Of these, 12 are threatened – one Critically Endangered, four Endangered, and seven Vulnerable. A total of 61 species are listed in the Lower Risk categories – seven as Near Threatened and 54 as Least Concern. A full list of species is given at the end of this regional account.

Major threats to bats

Loss of forests, particularly native forests in North America, is a major concern. Deforestation rates in Mexico are also thought to be very high. Caves and mines are key roosting sites throughout the region and face a range of threats.

Threats to habitats and roosts

- **Native forests** The loss of native forests is a threat to species that rely on such habitats for roosting and feeding. It is only recently that the importance of tree cavities for Nearctic bats has been fully appreciated (Barclay and Brigham 1996). Even bats commonly associated with artificial structures, such as *Eptesicus fuscus* and *Myotis lucifugus*, or with caves (e.g., *Myotis austroriparius*) also rely on trees. Recent research (Lewis 1995; Barclay and Brigham 1996) has shown that tree-roost fidelity is directly related to roost permanency and inversely related to roost availability. Bats may not, in general, be loyal to a specific tree, but to an area containing several suitable roosts. Thus the fact that particular trees are not heavily used by bats does not imply they are not of significance. More research is required on roosting behaviour and patterns. Current silvicultural practices that favour even-aged, monospecific stands, short rotation times, and selective removal of dead and dying trees, leave little roosting habitat for bats. There should be more education of land managers about the needs of tree-roosting bats. In British Columbia, Canada, for instance, forestry operations probably have the greatest impact on bat habitat. The clear-felling of tracts of forest, removal of standing dead trees, and intensive management of young forests alters the structure and availability of roost sites. A number of species are seriously threatened by deforestation, including the hoary bat (*Lasiurus cinereus*) and silver-haired bat (*Lasionycteris noctivagans*). Keen's long-eared myotis (*Myotis keenii*) is a rare species that is restricted to the coastal forests of British Columbia. It is thought to be highly dependent on old-growth forests, although little is known of its roosting behaviour. There is increasing evidence of the importance of upland forest for *Myotis sodalis*. The big brown bat (*Eptesicus fuscus*) is a species usually closely associated with buildings, but in the Okanagan Valley in British Columbia maternity colonies are found in cavities in dead Ponderosa pines (*Pinus ponderosa*). Though little research has been carried out on the use by bats of different-age forests, it has been shown in Oregon and Washington States that bat activity is greatest in old-growth forests. Such areas provide an abundance of roosting opportunities in both live and dead trees. More research is required on the effects of management practices on bat species that use forests.

  It is likely that in certain circumstances, foraging habitat may be limiting for bats. Species vary in foraging style, habitat use, and dietary preference. The habitat structure also probably influences the composition of the bat community and partially determines what prey is available to the bats (Bradshaw 1996). For example, there is more bat activity in unlogged than logged riparian habitats (Hayes and Adam 1996) and in old rather than young or mature forest stands (Crampton and Barclay 1996).
- **Riparian habitats** Riparian habitats are of key importance to certain bat species. For example, Indiana

Hoary bat, *Lasiurus cinereus*, a widespread North American species that undertakes long seasonal migrations.

M. Tuttle/BCI

bat (*Myotis sodalis*) maternity colonies are found mostly in riparian and floodplain forest near to small or medium-sized streams. Preferred stream habitat consists of streams lined on both banks with mature trees that overhang the water by at least three metres. Streams without riparian vegetation do not appear to be suitable. Recently, there has also been increasing evidence of the importance of upland forests for the long-term survival of this species. In order to assess the impact of land-use changes, more information is needed on the habitat associations of bat prey. Thus, the disappearance of formerly abundant populations of *Myotis velifer* from the Colorado River Basin in California is correlated with the conversion of cottonwood riparian forest to agriculture (Pierson 1998).

- **Agaves** The long-nosed bats of the genus *Leptonycteris* are the main pollinators of century plants (*Agave* spp.). The two species of *Leptonycteris* in North America, *L. curasoae* and *L. nivalis*, feed not only on agaves, but also Saguaro and Organ Pipe cacti and other tropical species (Fleming 1997). Both bat species are cave-dwellers and both are declining. The relationship between the bats and plants is so close that it is thought that the one could not survive without the other. Long-nosed bats rely on a supply of food along the entirety of their migratory routes. The fermented juice of agaves is distilled to make tequila, and it is thought that the excessive harvesting of agaves may have contributed to the decline in *Leptonycteris* populations.
- **Caves** Caves are home to the largest aggregations of bats. At Bracken Cave in Texas there are thought to be around 20 million Mexican free-tailed bats (*Tadarida brasiliensis*), making it the world's largest bat colony. There are at least a dozen other colonies, most in caves, with more than one million individuals. Hubbards Cave in Tennessee ranks among the three most important hibernating sites in the USA. This and two other caves are occupied by more than 75% of the known population of the endangered gray bat (*Myotis grisescens*), and 95% of the population of this species is found in a total of nine caves. Hubbards Cave is also home to seven other bat species, including the endangered Indiana bat (*Myotis sodalis*). The big long-nosed bat, *Leptonycteris nivalis*, is restricted in the USA to a single cave in Big Bend National Park, Texas, where 1,000 bats were recorded in 1983.

The population of Mexican free-tailed bats in Carlsbad Cavern in New Mexico has suffered a dramatic decline since the 1930s. Carlsbad Cavern was once thought to be home to 8.7 million bats, but current estimates put the population at around 500,000. There have been other, more severe declines, at some caves. At Eagle Creek Cave, Arizona in 1963, the population of Mexican free-tailed bats was thought to exceed 25 million – only six years later this had fallen to 30,000, a decline of nearly 99.9%. The U-Bar Cave in southwestern New Mexico housed a large maternity colony as late as the 1970s – this had disappeared completely by 1985. Similar declines have been recorded in Mexico – a 1986 survey of nine key sites for Mexican free-tailed bats showed that five were no longer occupied. These severe declines in bat populations in caves have occurred for a variety of reasons, related mainly to human activities.

It has been suggested that pesticides may have played a role in the decline at Carlsbad Cavern. Insectivorous bats are particularly vulnerable to the use of pesticides, especially organochlorines such as DDT. Adult bats may accumulate sub-lethal amounts of these chemicals in their adipose tissue through ingesting contaminated insects. This may be released during migration and hibernation or may be passed from females to babies via milk; in the 1970s, recorded pesticide concentrations in young bats were high enough to cause poisoning during the animals first migratory flight to Mexico. The use of DDT was banned in the USA in 1972. Until 1980, Mexico was one of the world's major users of DDT, though this has declined more recently. The cotton industry was the major user of DDT and cotton is currently grown in the Pecos River Valley in southwestern Texas, where it is believed that adult bats forage. Before their arrival at Carlsbad, bats migrate through and inhabit agricultural areas in Mexico.

Bat guano is a valuable economic resource and because of the size of bat colonies that use some caves, and thus the quantity of guano produced, such sites have become important for guano miners. At Carlsbad Cavern guano mining began in 1903. In the same year, a shaft was blasted through the roof of the cave to assist in the extraction of guano. Another shaft was drilled in 1906. By 1923 some 100,000 tons of guano had been removed from the cave. These guano mining operations may have resulted initially in declines in the resident bat population; with the construction of the shaft in 1906, the internal climate of part of the cave was altered and the area was abandoned by bats for many years. Mining in the Carlsbad Cavern National Monument finally ceased in 1957. During the American Civil War, guano was extracted from nearly every substantial roost of the endangered gray bat (*Myotis grisescens*) in the southern states in order to produce nitrates for gunpowder and it is believed that gray bat colonies suffered heavy losses during this period (see also Species Action Plan for *M. sodalis*).

The increasing interest in speleology has led to some problems of disturbance. The opening of some caves to tourism has threatened the survival of the gray bat. Disturbance can result in the loss of very large numbers of bats. For example, 60,000 Indiana bats (*Myotis sodalis*) abandoned a cave which was disturbed by humans and a further 80,000 died when three caves were intentionally blocked. There have also been cases of deliberate killing of bats. For example, in 1987 four men were convicted of deliberately killing several hundred bats in Kentucky's Thornhill Cave. These included 66 Indiana bats that had been shot and crushed.

Caves can be prone to floods caused by the construction of dams or to natural flooding, and 300,000 Indiana bats were drowned when a cave flooded in 1937. Similarly, at Hubbards Cave, climatic conditions had forced bats into a low area where some were roosting only 30cm from the floor. As a result, 10,000 were killed when this area flooded.

Clearly, the tendency of bats to aggregate in large numbers in caves makes them very vulnerable. While such species as the Mexican free-tailed bat are currently very abundant, the loss of one of more of the largest colonies could have a devastating effect on the population as a whole. Some key caves have been designated as critical habitat by the US Government. As a result, the federal authorities must ensure that actions authorised, funded, or carried out by them do not result in the destruction or adverse modification of the site. The National Speleological Society has also attempted to introduce moratoria on visits to certain caves that are used by bats. Some sites, such as Carlsbad Cavern and Eckart James River Cave, have been used as sites to educate the public as to the importance of bats and their conservation (Hensley 1992). Other sites have benefited through the installation of gates that restrict access. This has often been the result of collaboration between all groups that have an interest in caves.

- **Mines** Abandoned mines have become key roost sites for bats in many areas of the USA and Canada (Tuttle and Taylor 1998). This has particularly resulted from increasing disturbance of caves along with deforestation and changes in agricultural practices that have led to fewer available alternative roost sites. More than 6,000 mines have been surveyed in Arizona, California, Colorado, and New Mexico, and between 30% and 70% have shown usage by bats, with around 10% containing important colonies. From the Great Lakes region north and eastward in the USA and Canada, up to 70% of open, subsurface mines may be used by large bat populations. In eastern Canada, aggregations of up to 15,000 hibernate in individual abandoned mines. Many mines still remain to be checked for the presence of bats. In 1992, around one million little and big brown bats (*Myotis lucifugus* and *Eptesicus fuscus*) were discovered in Millie Hill Mine, Iron Mountain, Michigan, a site scheduled for closure in 1993. This represented the second largest hibernating bat population ever discovered in a mine in North America.

Mines are key habitats for a number of threatened species. The Indiana bat (*Myotis sodalis*), listed as Endangered under the US Endangered Species Act, has been found in abandoned mines in roosts of up to 100,000. The largest known hibernating populations of the southeastern big-eared bat (*Plecotus rafinesquii*), a candidate for the Endangered Species List, live in abandoned iron and copper mines in small groups ranging from a few dozen to 500. Also, the only known roosts of the endangered lesser long-nosed bat (*Leptonycteris curasoae*) in the USA are in mines. Although the little brown bat (*Myotis lucifugus*) is a very abundant species, it is heavily reliant on abandoned mines for hibernation. Other bat species known to rely heavily on mines include the eastern small-footed myotis (*Myotis leibii*), western small-footed myotis (*M. ciliolabrum*), California myotis (*M. californicus*), eastern long-eared myotis (*M. septentrionalis*), eastern pipistrelle (*Pipistrellus subflavus*), and the big brown bat (*Eptesicus fuscus*).

Old mines are being closed at a rapid rate due to concern for public safety, reclamation, and the resurgence of open-cast mining, a common occurrence at the abandoned mines of the northern Midwest. Current mining techniques destroy old mines and create open pits as opposed to underground workings. A local mine inspector reported that, of the 12 mines already closed prior to 1993 in Iron Mountain, Michigan, some contained large numbers of bats, perhaps more than were saved in the Millie Hill Mine noted above. The largest recorded hibernating population of western big-eared bats (*Plecotus townsendii*), a species in decline, was recently destroyed in a New Mexico mine shaft when vandals set old timbers alight. In New Jersey, the state's largest hibernating population of bats was accidentally trapped in Hibernia Mine after it was capped. The bats only survived after the mine was quickly re-opened. Similarly, the Canoe Creek State Park limestone mine in Pennsylvania was re-opened in time to save its bats.

Gold mining often uses a cyanide solution to extract the gold. This can lead to the creation of large, toxin-laden ponds, which have been responsible for substantial wildlife mortality (Clark and Hothem 1991). This problem has been recognised and such ponds on public lands are required to be covered. However, so-called "heap leach pads", which use aerially applied cyanide spray, are more difficult to manage (Pierson 1998).

There have been several efforts to tackle the issue of abandoned mines and bats on a regional or national scale (Pierson 1998). The Colorado Division of Wildlife and Division of Mines and Geology, through a volunteer-based survey of abandoned mines, have identified and protected numerous previously unknown bat roosts (Navo *et al.* 1995). In New Mexico, a survey has highlighted the importance of deep shafts, while in Nevada a workshop resulted in comprehensive guidelines of how to evaluate about 300,000 abandoned mines and resolve potential conflicts (Riddle 1995). Similar projects have been carried out in Missouri and Ozark. Bat Conservation International has published guidelines on bat/mine assessment (Tuttle and Taylor 1998).

- **Buildings** Bats that roost in houses can be of concern to homeowners. Many species of bats may form colonies in buildings, sometimes numbering several hundred. Older buildings may be more frequently used, probably because of the greater number of access holes. Bats are sometimes forced to roost in buildings when their natural habitats are destroyed and, in some cases, such structures contribute to the range extension of species. The most commonly observed bats in buildings are the little brown bat (*Myotis lucifugus*), big brown bat (*Eptesicus fuscus*), and Mexican free-tailed bat (*Tadarida brasiliensis*). In many cases, homeowners may be unaware of the presence of bats. A study of roosts in Texas showed that up to 25% of homeowners did not know they had bats, and the figure was almost 85% in one Canadian village.

  Bats in houses can cause physical problems such as smell, noise, and accumulation of guano. However, homeowners may also seek to get rid of bats as a response to cultural phobias or hysteria generated by the media. The risk of transmission of diseases, especially rabies, from house-roosting bats to homeowners is very small, but the possibility has influenced how bat roosts in houses are managed. Various methods have been used to rid houses of bats and many are, at best, ineffective. In view of their generally ineffective nature and the potential dangers they pose, the use of chemical poisons in controlling bats cannot be justified. If bats do need to be excluded from properties, there are a variety of non-destructive methods that can be used and sound advice is widely available from organisations with experience in the management of bats.
- **Bridges** Bridges have only recently received attention from bat researchers, despite the fact that they are used extensively by bats as both day and night roosts. The Congress Avenue Bridge in Austin, Texas, has become a major attraction due to the presence of a large roost of *Tadarida brasiliensis*. There is further potential to develop conservation strategies for bridges in collaboration with transport authorities as has already happened in Texas and California, and Bat Conservation International has initiated a Bats in American Bridges project to assess the importance of these structures for roosting bats (Keeley and Tuttle 1999).

Threats to higher taxa

- **Genus *Leptonycteris* (Family Phyllostomidae)** The genus *Leptonycteris* includes two species, *L. curasoae* and *L. nivalis*. The former is listed as Vulnerable and the latter Endangered in *The 2000 IUCN Red List of Threatened Species*. Both species are listed as Endangered under the US Endangered Species Act. *L. curasoae* is distributed in Arizona and New Mexico, south through Mexico to El Salvador and in Venezuela, Colombia, and The Netherlands Antilles. *L. nivalis* is recorded from New Mexico and west Texas, to south Mexico and possibly Guatemala. Populations and distributions of both species have probably declined in recent decades. *L. nivalis* is discussed in a Species Action Plan in this document.
- **Genus *Macrotus* (Family Phyllostomidae)** The genus comprises two species. *M. californicus* is restricted to southwestern USA and northwestern Mexico, including Baja California, and is considered Vulnerable in *The 2000 IUCN Red List of Threatened Species*. It has rather specific requirements, including the use of particularly hot, often geothermally heated, caves and mines for roosting. *M. waterhousii* is widespread from western and central Mexico to the Yucatan Peninsula and Guatemala, through the Greater Antilles to the Bahamas.
- **Genus *Antrozous* (Family Vespertilionidae)** Many authorities regard this as a monotypic genus, separating *A. dubiaquercus* of Central America into a separate genus *Bauerus*. *A. pallidus* is discussed in a Species Action Plan in this document.
- **Genus *Lasionycteris* (Family Vespertilionidae)** The single species of the genus, *L. noctivagans*, is widespread in North America. Despite the fact that it is generally uncommon and has little association with humans, it is the species most frequently associated with human rabies incidents of supposed bat origin. In common with other tree-dwelling and woodland-feeding species, such as *Lasiurus* species, there are concerns about the effects of modern forestry management practices and forest clearance.
- **Genus *Euderma* (Family Vespertilionidae)** Though widespread in western USA and in limited parts of British Columbia and Mexico, the single species of the genus, *E. maculatum*, is considered one of the rarest and least known of North American bat species, and may have particular roosting requirements (such as rock crevices) and foraging behaviour (it has been observed landing on the ground and pursuing prey 'on foot').
- **Genus *Plecotus* (Family Vespertilionidae)** The two North American species of the genus, *P. townsendii* and *P. rafinesquii*, are regarded as threatened throughout much of their range and are discussed in a Species Action Plan. With a third species, *P. mexicanus*, found in Mexico, they are widely regarded as comprising a separate genus, *Corynorhinus*. The related genus, *Idionycteris*, is monotypic, with *I. phyllotis* restricted to mountainous regions of southwestern USA to central Mexico.

Other threats

- **Rabies** The highest incidence of rabies in North America occurs in raccoons and skunks. Of cases of rabies reported in wildlife in the USA in 1992, 55% were in raccoons, 30% in skunks, and only 8% in bats. Human rabies is an uncommon disease in the USA. Between 1960 and 1989, there was an average of less than two cases of human rabies each year. Rabies was first recorded in bats in North America in 1953, though it was probably widely distributed before that date. Since this first discovery, bat rabies has been recorded from all 48 contiguous states and has been recorded from many bat species. In Canada, bat rabies has been reported from all provinces, except Newfoundland and Prince Edward Island. Most rabid bats have been reported from Ontario and Alberta. From 1951 to 1993 a total of 23 people in the USA and Canada died from rabies believed to be of bat origin. Most of the infections have resulted from bat bites, although, in a number of cases, the source of infection is unclear.

  The risk to the general public from bat rabies is very small. Anyone finding a grounded bat is advised not to touch it – the same advice as for any inexperienced person dealing with any wild animal. The risk of contracting rabies from bats that may be present in a person's home is equally unlikely, since there is little chance of the owners coming into direct physical contact with such bats. Understandably, however, there are concerns that even a small risk of contracting rabies is too much for some, and heightened media attention can lead to over-reaction to the risk from bat rabies. Clear and factual educational programmes to make the public fully aware of the situation are vital.

  It has been suggested that bat rabies can be contracted through inhalation of the virus present in aerosol form in confined areas with extremely large numbers of bats, such as in certain caves, but there are some doubts about the very few records of human cases of this mode of transmission (see Chapter 3).
- **Distributional patterns** Pierson (1998) highlights the problem of inadequate distributional information for bats in some areas of North America. Certain areas in North America have been well researched, while others remain under-studied. For example, recent studies in British Columbia extended the range for several species (Nagorsen and Brigham 1993; Roberts and Roberts 1993; Rasheed *et al.* 1995) and the range of *Eumops perotis* was extended following bat detector surveys in California and Arizona (Pierson 1998).

  Pierson (1998) highlights how the distribution patterns of bats can affect their conservation. Current conservation policy tends to focus on species that have limited distributions. Nevertheless, species with broad distributions, though less vulnerable, can suffer severe local declines. *Myotis lucifugus* and *Eptesicus fuscus* are two of the most common and widespread species. They may be threatened by the loss of natural roosts and become reliant on buildings, but those with suitable characteristics are becomingly increasingly scarce (e.g., Neilson and Fenton 1994). The actual distribution of species may also be patchy with animals reliant, for example, on a particular roost type. *Myotis grisescens* occurs throughout much of the southeastern USA, but is reliant on a few caves in limestone karst areas (Tuttle 1976; Rabinowitz and Tuttle 1980). *Euderma maculatum* has a wide distribution from British Columbia to central Mexico, yet it appears to be limited to areas with significant rock features. There are a few examples of range contraction in North American bats – for example, *Macrotus californicus* was once distributed across southern California but is now found only in mountain ranges in the Colorado River Basin (Pierson 1998).

  Bats may also undergo seasonal movements. For some species, winter movements result in aggregation of the population into a small number of sites, increasing the risk of decline or even extinction if these sites experience a catastrophe. Thus, 95% of all known *Myotis grisescens* hibernate in nine caves (Tuttle 1986) and 87% of all known *Myotis sodalis* have been recorded from seven hibernation sites (Humphrey 1978). Some species may undergo long-distance migrations that can carry them across international borders. This in itself can cause problems for their conservation. *Tadarida brasiliensis*, *Choeronycteris*, *Lasiurus,* and *Leptonycteris* species migrate between the USA and Mexico. Concerns about conservation of such species has led to the formation of the Program for the Conservation of Migratory Bats of Mexico and the United States (PCMM). Very little is known about seasonal altitudinal migrations. Typically, bats may maintain overall distribution, but suffer from local declines or even extirpations. This is especially true for cave-dwelling species. In some species, declines of 80% or more have been recorded at some cave sites in the past few decades.
- **Taxonomy** The taxonomic status of a particular bat species can have serious implications for its conservation, particularly where conservation management is undertaken only at a species level. As an example, there are differing views as to whether *Lasiurus blossevillii* and *L. xanthinus* should be recognised as separate species. Similarly, *Myotis septentrionalis* is treated by some as a species and others as a subspecies of *M. keenii.*
- **Combined habitat and roost protection** Pierson (1998) stresses the importance of an integrated approach to bat conservation that considers the range of habitats and roost sites used by bats all year round. Though roosts may be limiting for many species (McCracken 1988), no species can survive without suitable foraging

habitat. For example, *Macrotus californicus* relies on geothermally heated mines for winter roosts. A roost in one such mine declined when renewed mining removed adjacent mine-wash vegetation, a preferred feeding habitat. At the heart of all bat conservation issues in North America, is the increasing urbanisation of the country. While such development has created features that can be used by bats as roosts (e.g., buildings, mines, and bridges), most have had a negative effect.

Key areas for bat biodiversity

Hotspots at a generic level

Centres of diversity at the generic level were assessed using a WORLDMAP analysis (see Chapter 5.3 for further details). A strong Neotropical influence in the south of the region gives a very heavy bias, both in the diversity per grid-cell area (Map 30) and in the minimum set of grid-cell areas needed to maintain all genera (Map 31). The removal

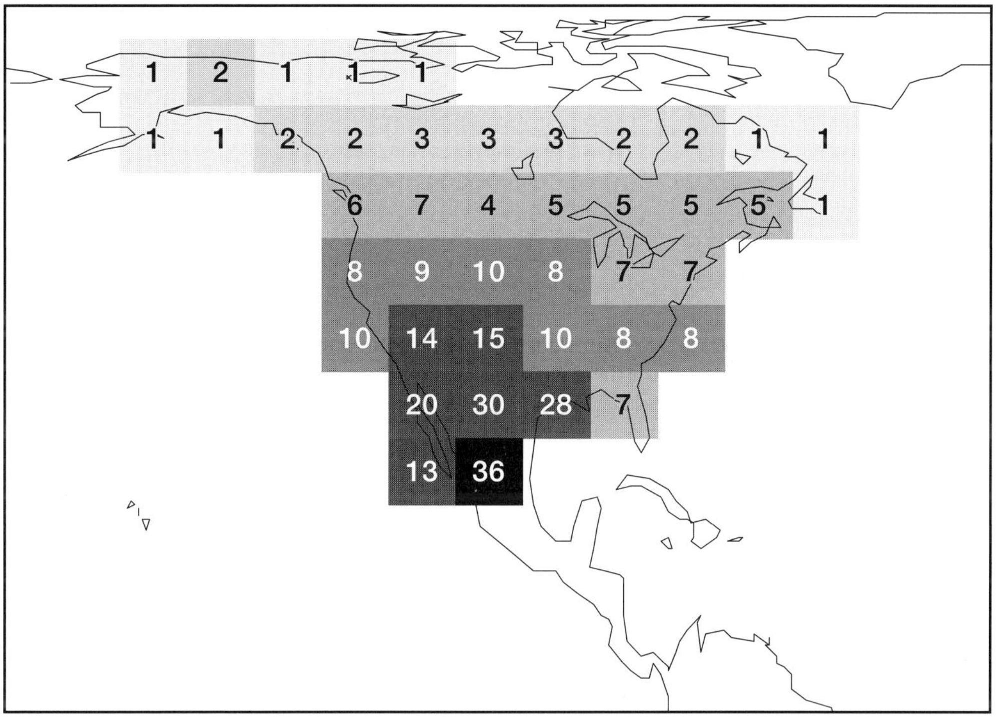

Map 30. Generic richness per grid-cell area for genera occurring in the Nearctic Region.
The numbers in the squares represent the number of genera per unit area.

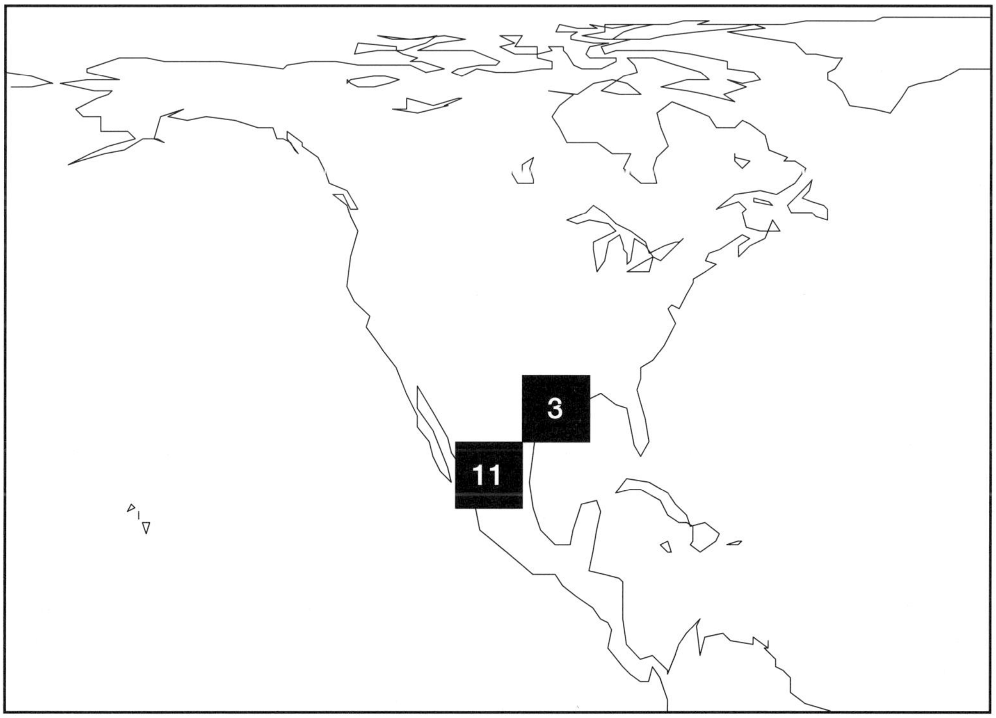

Map 31. Minimum set of grid-cell areas required to maintain all genera occurring in the Nearctic Region.
The minimum number of squares required to conserve all genera is two. The numbers in the squares represent the number of genera uniquely contributing to this minimum set.

of the Neotropical elements (particularly those that are clearly not Nearctic fauna) would leave just the family Vespertilionidae; the diversity per grid-cell area of this family for the region can be seen in Map 20 and gives a generally more even, if nevertheless southern, distribution of areas of higher diversity.

Mexico

Mexico is, by far, the most important country in this region in terms of its bat biodiversity. It is also a globally important country in terms of its overall biodiversity. Though it covers only 1% of the world's land area, it contains about 10% of all the terrestrial vertebrates and plants known to science (Harcourt and Sayer 1996). Only the northern area of the country is considered to be included in the Nearctic Region extending southwards and bounded by the Sierra Madre Occidental in the west and Sierra Madre Oriental in the east. The maps presented in Medellin *et al.* (1997) reveal that about 57 of the 137 species would fall within the area of the Nearctic Region. The richness of the bat fauna in Mexico results from this overlap between the Nearctic and the very rich Neotropical faunas. Degradation and rapid loss of forest cover is a critical issue in Mexico. Up to 60% of the loss of tropical forests can be attributed to the expansion of cattle ranching (Toledo 1990; Masera *et al.* 1992). Further deforestation has resulted from colonisation and development schemes that were promoted by the federal government (Harcourt and Sayer 1996).

Recommendations

North America has some of the best-developed bat conservation programmes, including strong links with industries whose activities affect bat populations. Bat Conservation International, in particular, has a wide range of initiatives relating to bat conservation issues in North, Central, and South America. A general problem is the risk of rabies from bats; although the risk is very small, it is important that educational programmes, which should include clear explanation of the relative risk, are maintained and enhanced. Mexico has a rich bat fauna and there is already a flourishing level of cooperation between Mexico and the USA, particularly with respect to migratory species that move between the two countries. In the USA, there are two major initiatives to establish national conservation priorities for bats, the North American Bat Conservation Plan (NABCP) and the Coalition of North American Bat Working Groups. The NABCP sets forth national level priorities and provides an umbrella document under which more specific state and regional level priorities can be set by the Coalition of Regional Working Groups. These initiatives aim to involve a wide range of interested parties, including representatives of federal agencies (Forest Service, Bureau of Land Management, Department of Defense), state agencies (fish and game departments, department of transportation, state parks, etc.), and the private sector.

The following recommendations are based upon information provided by the contributors to this section. They include both general recommendations applicable to the whole area, as well as specific ones relating to particular species, areas, or habitats.

Habitats

The management of woodland and general habitat structure is currently the subject of investigation by bat biologists, for example in western Canada, relating foraging habitat with roosting populations.

Recommendations:
- support and develop current initiatives to adapt land-use policies compatible with the conservation of bats;
- assess impact of current forestry practices on populations of tree-roosting species of bats in western Canada;
- conduct research into the use by bats of different age forests;
- carry out research on the habitat associations of bat prey;
- assess importance of riparian habitats for bats;
- research further the association between *Leptonycteris* and agaves, and threats to populations through harvesting of agaves;
- assess threats to migrating bats from pesticide residues.

Roost types

Recent initiatives have concentrated on survey and assessment of underground habitats, bridges, and the importance of older trees and standing dead wood.

Recommendations:
- support current initiatives and expand to embrace a wider geographical coverage, especially in the development of firm links with industry and land managers to ensure adequate protection of important roost sites;
- conduct research into roosting behaviour of *Myotis keenii*;
- work with speleological and other interest groups to help protect key cave roosts;
- survey abandoned mines for signs of usage by bats where this has not already been done;
- assess impact of reclamation and open-cast mining on bat species that use mines;
- conduct research on roosting behaviour for species that use trees;
- inform land managers about needs of tree-roosting bats;
- develop conservation strategies for bridges in collaboration with transport authorities.

Geographical areas

Some areas remain inadequately surveyed for bats, their status, distribution, and threats. While the migrations of some species are fairly well understood, they are still poorly understood for others. Pesticide levels may still be high in areas such as Mexico.

Recommendations:
- identify poorly surveyed areas, and plan and undertake appropriate fieldwork;

- increase collaboration in migration studies, especially for species where their migration is poorly understood; aims should include a greater understanding of altitudinal movements and of the needs of bats while on migration;
- consider the development of a programme to investigate current pesticide use and its potential impact on bat populations.

Taxa

Taxa highlighted as being of particular concern include the genera *Leptonycteris*, *Macrotus*, *Antrozous*, *Lasionycteris*, and *Plecotus*.

Recommendations:
- maintain and further develop existing bat species recovery programmes;
- develop recovery programmes for other species at risk;
- direct research on poorly known species, especially local endemics such as *Myotis keenii*;
- assess status of *Macrotus californicus*;
- assess status, biology, and ecology of *Euderma maculatum*;
- assess status, biology, and ecology of *Antrozous pallidus*;
- assess status of *Plecotus rafinesquii* and *P. townsendii*;
- assess impact of forestry management practices on *Lasionycteris noctivagans*.

Miscellaneous

Recommendations:
- ensure ready availability of clear and factual educational programmes about rabies and bats in North America;
- conduct research into seasonal altitudinal migrations;
- encourage use of the full range of systematic techniques to investigate taxa of uncertain status;
- promote an integrated approach to bat conservation looking at the range of roost sites and habitats used by bats all year round;
- support the efforts and recommendations of the Coalition of North American Bat Working Groups and the North American Bat Conservation Plan.

Checklist of Nearctic bats

A total of 73 species are recorded from the Nearctic Region. The full list is given below.

Species	Status
FAMILY EMBALLONURIDAE	
Balantiopteryx	
Balantiopteryx plicata Peters 1867	LR: lc
FAMILY NOCTILIONIDAE	
Noctilio	
Noctilio leporinus (Linnaeus 1758)	LR: lc
FAMILY MORMOOPIDAE	
Mormoops	
Mormoops megalophylla (Peters 1864)	LR: lc
Pteronotus	
Pteronotus davyi Gray 1838	LR: lc
Pteronotus parnellii (Gray 1843)	LR: lc
Pteronotus personatus (Wagner 1843)	LR: lc
FAMILY PHYLLOSTOMIDAE	
Subfamily Phyllostominae	
Macrotus	
Macrotus californicus Baird 1858	VU: A2c
Macrotus waterhousii Gray 1843	LR: lc
Subfamily Glossophaginae	
Anoura	
Anoura geoffroyi Gray 1838	LR: lc
Choeroniscus	
Choeroniscus godmani (Thomas 1903)	LR: nt
Choeronycteris	
Choeronycteris mexicana Tschudi 1844	LR: nt
Glossophaga	
Glossophaga soricina (Pallas 1766)	LR: lc
Leptonycteris	
Leptonycteris curasoae Miller 1900	VU: A1c
Leptonycteris nivalis (Saussure 1860)	EN: A1c
Subfamily Stenodermatinae	
Artibeus	
Artibeus hartii Thomas 1892	LR: lc
Artibeus hirsutus K. Andersen 1906	VU: A2c
Artibeus jamaicensis Leach 1821	LR: lc
Artibeus phaeotis (Miller 1902)	LR: lc
Artibeus toltecus (Saussure 1860)	LR: lc
Centurio	
Centurio senex Gray 1842	LR: lc
Chiroderma	
Chiroderma salvini Dobson 1878	LR: lc
Sturnira	
Sturnira lilium (E. Geoffroy 1810)	LR: lc
Sturnira ludovici Anthony 1924	LR: lc
Subfamily Desmodontinae	
Desmodus	
Desmodus rotundus (E. Geoffroy 1810)	LR: lc
Diphylla	
Diphylla ecaudata Spix 1823	LR: nt
FAMILY NATALIDAE	
Natalus	
Natalus stramineus Gray 1838	LR: lc
FAMILY VESPERTILIONIDAE	
Subfamily Vespertilioninae	
Antrozous	
Antrozous pallidus (Le Conte 1856)	LR: lc
Eptesicus	
Eptesicus fuscus (Beauvois 1796)	LR: lc
Euderma	
Euderma maculatum (J. A. Allen 1891)	LR: lc
Idionycteris	
Idionycteris phyllotis (G. M. Allen 1916)	LR: lc

Species	Status	Species	Status
Lasionycteris		*Myotis velifer* (J. A. Allen 1890)	LR: lc
Lasionycteris noctivagans (Le Conte 1831)	LR: lc	*Myotis vivesi* Menegaux 1901	VU: A2c
Lasiurus		*Myotis volans* (H. Allen 1866)	LR: lc
Lasiurus blossevillii		*Myotis yumanensis* (H. Allen 1864)	LR: lc
(Lesson and Garnet 1826)	LR: lc	***Nycticeius***	
Lasiurus borealis (Müller 1776)	LR: lc	*Nycticeius humeralis* (Rafinesque 1818)	LR: lc
Lasiurus cinereus (Beauvois 1796)	LR: lc	***Pipistrellus***	
Lasiurus ega (Gervais 1856)	LR: lc	*Pipistrellus hesperus* (H. Allen 1864)	LR: lc
Lasiurus intermedius H. Allen 1862	LR: lc	*Pipistrellus subflavus* (F. Cuvier 1832)	LR: lc
Lasiurus seminolus (Rhoads 1895)	LR: lc	***Plecotus***	
Lasiurus xanthinus (Thomas 1897)	LR: lc	*Plecotus rafinesquii* Lesson 1827	VU: A2c
Myotis		*Plecotus townsendii* Cooper 1837	VU: A2c
Myotis auriculus Baker and Stains 1955	LR: lc	***Rhogeessa***	
Myotis austroriparius (Rhoads 1897)	LR: lc	*Rhogeessa parvula* H. Allen 1866	LR: nt
Myotis californicus			
(Audubon and Bachman 1842)	LR: lc	**FAMILY MOLOSSIDAE**	
Myotis ciliolabrum (Merriam 1886)	LR: lc	***Eumops***	
Myotis evotis (H. Allen 1864)	LR: lc	*Eumops glaucinus* (Wagner 1843)	LR: lc
Myotis fortidens Miller and Allen 1928	LR: nt	*Eumops perotis* (Schinz 1821)	LR: lc
Myotis grisescens A. H. Howell 1909	EN: A1c	*Eumops underwoodi* Goodwin 1940	LR: nt
Myotis keenii (Merriam 1895)	LR: lc	***Molossus***	
Myotis leibii (Audubon and Bachman 1842)	LR: lc	*Molossus molossus* (Pallas 1766)	LR: lc
Myotis lucifugus (Le Conte 1831)	LR: lc	*Molossus sinaloae* J. A. Allen 1906	LR: lc
Myotis milleri Elliot 1903	EN: A2c	***Nyctinomops***	
Myotis peninsularis Miller 1898	VU: A1c	*Nyctinomops aurispinosus* (Peale 1848)	LR: lc
Myotis planiceps Baker 1955	CR: B1 + 2c	*Nyctinomops femorosaccus* (Merriam 1889)	LR: lc
Myotis septentrionalis (Trouessart 1897)	LR: lc	*Nyctinomops macrotis* (Gray 1840)	LR: lc
Myotis sodalis Miller and Allen 1928	EN: A1c	***Tadarida***	
Myotis thysanodes Miller 1897	LR: lc	*Tadarida brasiliensis* (I. Geoffroy 1824)	LR: nt

Table 6. Number of IUCN Red List species for countries in the Nearctic Region.
The table also includes information on numbers of endemics and the estimated size of the bat fauna. For information on the compilation of the figures for size of faunas see Chapter 6. Full lists of IUCN Red List species per country are given in the same Chapter. Where a country overlaps more than one region, the fauna for the whole country is included.

	IUCN RED LIST SPECIES								ENDEMICS	TOTAL NO. OF SPECIES		
Country	CR	EN	VU	LRcd	LRnt	EX	DD	*Total*	*Total*	Mega	Micro	*Total*
Canada	0	0	1	0	0	0	0	1	0	0	20	20
Mexico	1	4	9	0	17	0	0	31	13	0	137	137
United States	0	3	4	0	4	0	0	11	3	0	45	45

Table 6 shows the number of IUCN Red List species recorded from each country together with information on numbers of endemics and the size of the total bat fauna.

Key references

The following is a list of important references relating to bats in the Nearctic Region. It is by no means an exhaustive list and concentrates mainly on distributional studies at a national or regional level.

Arita, H.T. and Ceballos, G. 1995. *The mammals of Mexico, distribution and conservation status.* Asociación Mexicana Mastozoología, México City.

Arita, H.T. and Ortega, J. 1998. The Middle American bat fauna: conservation in the Neotropical-Nearctic border. Pp. 295–308 *in: Bat biology and conservation* (eds. Kunz, T.H. and P.A. Racey). Smithsonian Institution Press, Washington DC.

Banfield, A.W.F. 1974. *The mammals of Canada.* The University of Toronto Press, Toronto.

Barbour, R.W. and Davis, W.H. 1969. *Bats of America.* University Press of Kentucky, Lexington.

Cervantes, F.A., Castro-C, A., and Ramírez-Pulido, J. 1994. Mamíferos terrestres nativos de México. *Anales del Instituto de Biología, Universidad Nacional Autónoma de México Serie Zoología*, 65, 177–190.

Cowan, I. McT. and Guiguet, C.J. 1965. *The mammals of British Columbia*, Third edition. Handbook Number 11, British Columbia Provincial Museum.

Hall. E.R. 1981. *The mammals of North America.* J. Wiley and Sons, New York.

Harvey, M.J. 1992. *Bats of the eastern United States.* Arkansas Game and Fish Commission.

Knox Jones Jr., J., Arroyo-Cabrales, J., and Owen, D.R. 1988. Revised checklist of bats (Chiroptera) of Mexico and Central America. *Occasional Papers. The Museum, Texas Tech University,* 120, 1–34.

Medellín, R.A., Arita, H.T., and Sanchez, O. 1997. *Identificación de los murciélagos de México. Clave de campo.* Asociación Mexicana de Mastozoología, A.C. Publicaciones Especiales Núm. 2. Mexico City.

Miller, G.S. Jr. and Kellogg, R. 1955. List of North American recent mammals. *Bulletin of the United States National Museum,* 205, 1–953.

Nagorsen, D.W. and Brigham, R.M. 1993. *Bats of British Columbia.* University of British Columbia Press, Vancouver.

Pierson, E.D. 1998. Tall trees, deep holes, and scarred landscapes: Conservation biology of North American bats. Pp. 309–325 *in: Bat biology and conservation* (eds. T.H. Kunz and P.A. Racey). Smithsonian Institution Press, Washington DC.

Schmidly, D.J. 1991. *The bats of Texas.* University of Texas Press, Austin.

Tuttle, M.D. 1988. *America's neighbourhood bats.* University of Texas Press, Austin.

Villa, B. 1967. *Los Murcielagos de México.* Instituto de Biología, Universidad Nacional Autónoma de México, México City.

van Zyll de Jong, C.G. 1985. *Handbook of Canadian mammals.* National Museum of Natural Sciences, Ottawa.

5.4.5 Neotropical Region

This account was compiled using contributions from the following: Ludmilla Aguiar; Hector Arita; Keith Atkinson; Jackie Belwood; Frank Bonaccorso; Anne Brooke; John A. Burton; Nina Fascione; Brock Fenton; Ted Fleming; the late Arthur Greenhall; Timothy Gross; Roger Haagenson; Gerardo Herrera; Carlos Iudica; the late Karl F. Koopman; Tom Kunz; Ya-Fu Lee; Jader Marinho-Filho; Rodrigo Medellin; Gary McCracken; Dixie Pierson; Bill Rainey; Julieta de Samudio; Rafael Samudio Jr.; John Seyjagat; Gilberto Silva Taboada; and Don E. Wilson

Geographical boundaries of region

The region includes South America, the Caribbean, and Central America. The Galapagos Islands are also included. The region's northern continental boundary is in Mexico, running approximately from the western coast opposite the tip of Baja California to the eastern coast near the border with the USA. Inland from these points, the boundary of the region runs south, including land to the west of the Sierra Madre Occidental and east of the Sierra Madre Oriental (see Map 1).

Number of species in the region

A total of 288 species are recorded from the Neotropical Region. Of these, one is Extinct and 57 threatened – one Critically Endangered, nine Endangered, and 47 Vulnerable. A total of 223 species are listed in the Lower Risk categories – 60 as Near Threatened and 163 as Least Concern. A further seven species are listed as Data Deficient. A full list of species is given at the end of this regional account.

Major threats to bats

The Neotropical Region includes the largest area of primary lowland rainforest in the world, Amazonia. There are also significant areas of dry and montane forest. All are threatened by the activities of humans, such as agriculture, oil exploration, and mining. Caves and mines are threatened by mining activities, disturbance, and vampire control activities.

Threats to habitats and roosts

- **Forests** A range of forest habitats occur within this region.

  Lowland forests Lowland tropical moist forest is the most structurally and taxonomically diverse vegetation type in this region. The main areas are in Amazonia, the coastal region of Brazil, the Chocó, and the lower Magdalena Valley, and along the Atlantic coast of Central America to Mexico. In general, there is a strong correlation between the amount of rainfall and diversity, with wetter forests being floristically richer than drier types. The richest forests of all are the non-seasonal lowland moist and wet forests of upper Amazonia and the Chocó region. Amazonia is the single most important area of tropical rainforest in the world. More than 60% of its area is within Brazil, which alone has at least 117 species of bats.

  Dry forests This is thought, by some, to be one of the most threatened of all the Neotropical vegetation types. It is found along the Pacific side of Mexico and Central America, in northern Colombia and Venezuela, coastal Ecuador and adjacent Peru, the Velasco area (Chiquitania) of eastern Bolivia, a broad swathe from northwest Argentina to northeast Brazil encompassing chaco, cerrado, and caatinga, and with scattered smaller patches elsewhere. While dry forests are not as species-rich as moist forests, they do have many regional endemics.

  Montane forests Higher altitude or montane rainforests are divided into recognisable bands dependent on altitude: lower montane forest (900–2,000m), upper montane forest (2,000–3,200m), and subalpine forest (3,200–3,800m). Mists often engulf the forest canopy and thus these habitats are often called 'cloud forests'. Montane forests form a high percentage of total forest cover in the Andes, southern Venezuela, and Central America. These may be less damaged than other forests, but the level of bat diversity is not as high as elsewhere and there are low levels of specialism. Upland species that migrate to the lowlands may be affected by damage to lowland forests.

Forests are threatened by a variety of factors. Shifting cultivation has been identified as the principal cause of forest loss in this region. Traditionally, areas of forest were cleared by felling and burning. Crops were planted for two or three years and the area then left fallow for at least 10 years. However, fallow times have been reduced, leading to erosion and soil degradation, and permanent deforestation. Trans-migration, particularly in Brazil, has compounded the effects of shifting cultivation. Large landowners have moved in after shifting cultivators and cleared the land to convert to cattle ranches. Cattle ranching in Latin America is estimated to have occupied some 20,000km² of forest per year in the late 1970s. Up until around the 1940s, the impact of logging on forests was relatively minor. The last few decades have seen a dramatic increase in the export of tropical timbers. Improvements in technology and the building of roads and railways have greatly facilitated the exploitation of forests. Roads and railways built for initial access to forested areas can facilitate damaging follow-up occupation. The conversion of forests to pasture is a foremost cause of deforestation in the countries of Central America, and forest continues to be cleared on a large scale for plantations of oil palm, rubber, sugar cane, tea, coffee, and cacao.

Proboscis bat, *Rhynchonycteris naso*, a widespread Central and South American species commonly roosting on the trunks of trees over water.

D. Woodfall

DDT is being 'dumped' upon Third World countries. It has a half life that is dependent upon temperature so that its effects may be longer lasting in colder areas as opposed to the tropics. DDT is still regularly used in the Caribbean. Its metabolite (DDE) has powerful oestrogenic effects that can have potent effects on wildlife. Evidence from the USA and Mexico suggests that DDT may have had a role in dramatic declines in the populations of Mexican free-tailed bats (*Tadarida brasiliensis*) and spraying with DDT has caused increased mortality in bats.

The Gran Chacó is a vast area of dry forest that stretches through Brazil, Argentina, Paraguay and Bolivia. It is heavily overgrazed and the drainage system has changed. Ponds that were formally linked have become isolated. In general, agricultural change is a serious threat and it is urgent that there should be a policy on such development.

South America has rich reserves of mineral wealth. Large-scale mining operations are relatively scarce given the problems of access to sites. One of the largest mining projects is the Brazilian Grande Carajás Programme in Pará State. The area contains enormous deposits of iron ore and iron smelters have been established fuelled with charcoal produced from the rainforest. There are, however, many small-scale operations that may have locally damaging effects. In Amazonia, there are widespread deposits of gold which have been mined. Increases in the price of gold and 'improved' methods of extraction have led to gold rushes. Small-scale operations in Brazil have produced over 100 tonnes of gold per year, making the country the third or fourth largest world producer (Harcourt and Sayer 1996). The procedure for extracting gold, which requires the use of mercury, results in the production of large amounts of toxic waste, which can cause serious problems to aquatic ecosystems and soils. Mining using pressure hoses leads to the undermining of river banks. Gold mining affects many areas, including Ecuador, which has a particularly high bat biodiversity.

Oil exploration is also a major threat. In blackwater streams in Ecuador there have been problems of oil leakage. There is little control over oil companies and spillage, and the creation of sludge ponds is of particular concern, especially in dry areas. Water is used to extract oil and the resulting oil/water mixture collects in ponds. In the western USA, these ponds are especially damaging to migratory birds. The residue in these ponds can also mix with other water supplies and be transported downstream. There are large pockets of oil under the Andean rainforest. Prospecting has begun, particularly in the northern areas of this habitat.

The Panama Canal is an area of particular concern due to the effects of oil spillage from ships and high concentrations of heavy metals. Agent Orange, a potent herbicide, was used in Panama in the 1960s. There has been heavy deforestation in the area around the Canal. It is estimated that between 30 and 50km² of forest is being lost each year within the Canal's watershed.

The high rainfall in tropical South America feeds the great rivers, such as the Amazon and the Orinoco, and there is pressure to harness this capacity through the construction of dams. The Amazon has the largest hydroelectric capacity, carrying as it does 20% of the world's fresh water supply. It is estimated that the electricity that could be generated from the Amazon's tributaries is at least 100,000 megawatts. The Tucurui Dam was Brazil's first large hydroelectric project on the Amazon and flooded about 1,750km² of rainforest. Brazil has plans to build many more hydroelectric dams in Amazonia. Forests in other countries, such as Venezuela and Bolivia, have been lost because of the effects of dams.

Vampire bats may use trees as roost sites. The fear of vampires has meant that in some areas very old, hollow trees are selectively burned. In Trinidad in recent years, there has been a change of policy with regard to agriculture. Areas are now bulldozed and clear-felled, producing an open style of agriculture. Silk cotton trees (*Ceiba pentandra*) have been removed, which threatens the survival of *Vampyrum spectrum*, a species which relied on them for roost sites.

- **Deserts and arid steppe** There are a number of desert habitats within this region, mostly along the western edge of the continent from Peru to Chile, but also in northern Mexico and in the monte and Patagonian steppes of the Southern Cone of South America. The Atacama Desert of Chile and the Sechura Desert of Peru are both hyper-arid. A large semi-arid region, Patagonia, occurs in Argentina, and a smaller one, the Sertao, in northeast Brazil. Though the number of bat species found in these regions is relatively low, there are endemic species and the habitats themselves are fragile and threatened, mainly through mining activities. There is a long history of mining in the Atacama Desert in Chile. Prior to the 1800s, saltpetre was mined. After 1832, silver mines were established. Also during the 1800s, Chilean nitrates were mined on a large scale, but the industry collapsed following the production of synthetic nitrates in the early 1900s. Current mining is mainly for copper. On the western ridge of the Andean Cordillera, there is the world's largest concentration of copper ore. The largest mines were established after 1915, mainly near the Loa River and Potrerillos, in the Chanaral Basin. From 1938 to 1975, over 200 million tonnes of tailings from the Potrerillos and El Salvador copper mines were dumped in Chanaral Bay on the coast, causing dramatic changes in the beach. The contaminated area extends for 16km along the shore. A dramatic decrease in biodiversity in the area seems to be associated with copper in the sediments and pollutants in the water. Increased agriculture and loss of riverine vegetation, and additional factors may affect species such as *Platalina genovensium*, endemic to this area. These areas may also be affected by natural shifts in the climate caused by *El Niño*.
- **Caves and mines** Karstic areas, such as in southeast and central Brazil, are important to bats as they have natural caves that provide both summer and winter roost sites.

The commercialisation of caves is a serious threat in some areas. In Jamaica, caves containing large numbers of *Pteronotus* are threatened. Vampire control is a major issue in many Neotropical countries and the favoured method of control has involved the dynamiting or firing of caves thought to be roost sites for vampire bats. An estimated 900,000 bats of various species were gassed annually in Venezuela from 1964 to 1966. In Mexico, it was reported that entrances to various caves that housed populations of non-vampire bats had been barricaded with chicken wire in attempts to seal in and destroy vampire bats presumed to be inside. Localised destruction of vampires probably happens in Brazil. In Mexico, tyres are burnt inside caves rendering them unusable for bats. In Brazil and South America generally, the activities of mining companies associated with cement plants are a threat to cave systems. This is especially true in the Vale do Ribeira region of São Paulo State in southeastern Brazil. Access to this area is difficult and the human population density is low. Most of the remnants of the southeastern Atlantic Forest are in an area important for its karstic formations. In recent years, increasing levels of tourism and cave exploration have led to greater levels of disturbance to bat populations. In some cases, however, caves may be protected for cultural reasons such as their use for religious ceremonies or for parties or weddings.

Mines also may provide roost sites for bats. There are many old mines on the Pacific coast of Mexico, which are important for bats. Abandoned mines have been closed in such a way as to make them inaccessible to bats.

- **Bats in cities** Cities may provide roost sites for a variety of bat species. In Mexico City, for example, there are around 40 species of bats recorded, mainly molossids. Use is related to the prevalent architecture. As an example, tin roofs provide a climate that is very similar to that of hot caves. São Paulo in Brazil also has a rich bat fauna, including populations of *Desmodus rotundus*. Frugivorous and nectarivorous bat species may benefit from increased planting of native species. Nevertheless, development of cities may provide a threat to a range of bat species.

Threats to geographical areas

- **Caribbean** The islands of Jamaica, Hispaniola, Cuba, and Puerto Rico, and also the Lesser Antilles Islands such as Guadeloupe, are particularly important for bats. Habitat loss is a major problem throughout the Caribbean.
- **Central America** The area from Mexico to Panama harbours the richest bat fauna in the world in terms of numbers of species and genera (Arita and Ortega 1998). In this area, there are thought to be 166 bat species in 67 genera from nine families. There is also a high level of endemism, with 28 species (from 12 genera) and two genera, *Hylonycteris* and *Musonycteris*, endemic to Central America. There is much endangered habitat within this area that is of key importance for bats. The Atlantic forest areas are under increasing threat. The dry forest of the west coasts of Central America contains many endemic species. The Darien area of Panama is suffering through increasing human colonisation facilitated by extensive road construction. Cattle ranching is becoming more widespread resulting in forest habitat clearance to create pasture.
- **Amazonia** This is the largest area of tropical rainforest in the world, variously estimated to cover an area of 5–6 million km^2 Most of the Amazonian forest occurs in Brazil, with smaller areas in Bolivia, Colombia, Ecuador, Peru, Venezuela, and the Guianas. Ecuador, in particular, is noted for its high bat biodiversity. There are thought to be in excess of 117 species of bats recorded from Amazonia, 13 (about 11%) of which are endemic to this area (Marinho-Filho and Sazima 1998).
- **Atlantic forest of Brazil** This is where the initial colonisation in Brazil took place and where, for more than 300 years, almost all economic activity was concentrated (Marinho-Filho and Sazima 1998). It is the most densely populated portion of the country and includes two of the 10 largest cities in the world, São Paulo and Rio de Janeiro. The forest cover in this area has been reduced to about 5% of its original area, and only about 2% of these forest remnants are protected in federal conservation units (Marinho-Filho and Sazima 1998). The main threats come from increased growth of urban areas, expanding agriculture and cattle farming, and industrialisation with attendant pollution. Most of the remaining forest is in southeastern Brazil. In the northeastern region, the situation is even more dramatic and the largest remnant of continuous forest is the 11,500ha biological reserve of Una. The Atlantic forest still has an impressive bat fauna, with 71% of Brazil's and more than 50% of South America's species recorded there (Marinho-Filho and Sazima 1998). Five species (about 5%) are endemic.
- **Argentina** Regarded as a mostly temperate country with no 'rainforest', Argentina tends to be excluded from many of the major conservation initiatives, although 57 species of bats have been recorded there (Bárquez *et al.* 1999). The Chacó supports a rich mammal fauna and is the most species-rich area for bats in Argentina, with 44 species recorded from this region. The Paranean region, which includes the mesic tropical forests of the northeast along the border of Brazil and Paraguay, has a bat fauna of 38 species. The Yungas is the montane rainforest of northern Argentina and southern Bolivia, and has high levels of endemicity for birds; it also supports 36 species of bats.
- **Guyana** At present, the rates of deforestation in Guyana are low, estimated to be around 0.1% per year (Harcourt and Sayer 1996). The main causes of deforestation are agriculture and charcoal burning. However, large-scale logging could become a serious threat in the future. There are concerns that the road being extended from Boa Vista, Roirama, in Brazil through to the coast of Guyana at Georgetown will cause increased deforestation (Harcourt and Sayer 1996). Open-cast mining of bauxite has caused some deforestation and mining for gold is increasing rapidly. In addition to the direct effects of gold mining, some of the extraction processes, such as the use of mercury, have deleterious effects. Exploration for other minerals is taking place and could cause much more extensive deforestation. Guyana has a very rich bat fauna, with 107 species recorded.
- **Coastal deserts of northern Chile and Peru** This area has a very distinctive bat fauna. Although there are only 18 species in these desert areas, seven of them are endemics with very restricted distributions.
- **The Pampas and Patagonia** The Pampas in the extreme southern area of Brazil, and in Uruguay and Argentina, and Patagonia in Argentina and Chile have distinctive bat faunas. They do not have as many species as found in tropical areas of South America, but there is a high level of endemicity.

- **Central area of South American continent** Though they have low endemism, the Brazilian caatinga, cerrado and pantanal, and the Paraguayan Chacó harbour a large number of species (80–100). These habitats consist of open landscapes with deep soils and are thus threatened by conversion to agriculture. Because they are not covered by dense forest, they are probably excluded from major conservation initiatives.

Threats to higher taxa

- **Endemic families** A number of families are restricted to the Neotropical Region. Three are monotypic and, as such, may be deserving of particular concern. These are:
  Family Noctilionidae: genus *Noctilio*, two species;
  Family Natalidae: genus *Natalus*, five species;
  Family Thyropteridae: genus *Thyroptera*, three species
- **Family Emballonuridae** This is represented in the Neotropical Region by 18 species from eight genera that are restricted to this region. While detailed threats have not been identified, these distinctive genera with few species are considered to be of concern and their status should be watched. These are:
  Balantiopteryx: three species;
  Centronycteris: one species;
  Cormura: one species;
  Cyttarops: one species;
  Diclidurus: four species;
  Peropteryx: three species;
  Rhynchonycteris: one species;
  Saccopteryx: four species.
- **Monotypic and restricted range genera** The following genera are monotypic and have species with small and restricted distributions in the Neotropical Region. As such, they are thought to be especially vulnerable to current threats, such as habitat modification and destruction.
  Platalina: *P. genovensium* recorded only from Peru;
  Musonycteris: *M. harrisoni* recorded only from western Mexico;
  Ardops: *A. nichollsi* recorded only from the Lesser Antilles;
  Ariteus: *A. flavescens* recorded only from Jamaica;
  Phyllops: *P. falcatus* recorded only from Cuba and Hispaniola;
  Stenoderma: *S. rufum* recorded only from Puerto Rico and the Virgin Islands;
  Amorphochilus: *A. schnablii* recorded only from western Peru, western Ecuador, and northern Chile;
  Tomopeas: *T. ravus* recorded only from western Peru;

Other issues

Vampires

Wounds in cattle caused by vampire bats result in significant economic losses, particularly where they lead to infestation by screw-worms. As deforestation increases, vampire bats tend to replace native species. The effects of vampire control schemes have been discussed previously. Fear of vampires can lead to widespread and random destruction of bat populations. Insectivorous bats are important controllers of insects, while frugivorous and nectarivorous species play valuable roles in pollination, seed dispersal, and reforestation. These factors need to be considered whenever vampire control programmes are being formulated. It has been noted that the ecological aspects of rabies control should have two aims: 1) regulation of population levels of vampire bats, rather than indiscriminate destruction of individuals; and 2) protection of non-target species. Human rabies of bat origin is relatively rare with about 400 recorded cases (Brass 1994), but there have been several widely publicised incidences recently of vampire bat attacks in urban areas. The issue of vampires and rabies is discussed in more detail in Chapter 3.

Scientific collection

This is a particular problem for *Pteronotus,* which is a popular research animal especially for studies of echolocation. In certain areas, such as Jamaica, concerns have reached the point where the species is now protected from taking for research purposes. Some local universities may use them for dissection. However, some sites have very large numbers of this species, so it would be hard to argue against some collection of animals.

Molossids

These can be a problem where they occur in buildings. Problems of odour and the risk of transmission of histoplasmosis lead to colonies being exterminated.

Education

Education programmes are required, particularly in Latin America. Many areas have few bat scientists, so it is important that a list be compiled of bat biologists (including expatriates) working in the Neotropics who could contribute to the establishment of education campaigns within countries .

Migration

There is little information on the patterns of migration for Neotropical species. This includes information on altitudinal migrations.

Key areas for bat biodiversity

Hotspots at a generic level

Centres of diversity at the generic level were assessed using a WORLDMAP analysis (see Chapter 5.3 for further details) and the outstanding importance of this region for generic diversity is highlighted. The area of greatest diversity is clearly in the north of the region (Map 32), in

Central America and the Caribbean, as well as parts of northern South America. Despite the high generic diversity in the region, the minimum set of grid-cell areas required to maintain all genera is eight (Map 33), but, particularly in Central America and the Caribbean, there is a high level of local endemics, leaving little flexibility in choice of areas here.

Mexico

A total of 137 species has been recorded from Mexico (Medellin *et al.* 1997). Thirteen species are endemic. A total of 14 globally threatened species occur in Mexico – one Critically Endangered, four Endangered, and nine Vulnerable. A number of areas within Mexico have been highlighted as being of particular importance for bats. These include Baja California, the Pacific coast states (including Nayarit, Jalisco, Colima, Michoacan, and Guerrero), the central area, the Yucatan Peninsula, and the Tres Marias Islands.

Central America

The Pacific coastal area of Guatemala, El Salvador, Honduras, and Nicaragua has been highlighted as being of importance for bats. The Pacific coast and adjacent mountainous areas in Chiapas (Mexico) and Guatemala is a mosaic of diverse vegetation types, from mangroves to tropical semi-deciduous and cloud forests. Further south, there are dry tropical thorn forests and Atlantic forest. Three globally threatened species are recorded from both Honduras and Guatemala, two from El Salvador, and one from Nicaragua.

Caribbean

A total of 102 species has been recorded from the Caribbean region, 23 of which are endemic. The island of Trinidad contributes significantly to this diversity, not surprising given its proximity to the South American coast. Eleven species are globally threatened in the region and one is already extinct. Four of these threatened species are

Map 32. Generic richness per grid-cell area for genera occurring in the Neotropical Region.
The numbers in the squares represent the number of genera per unit area.

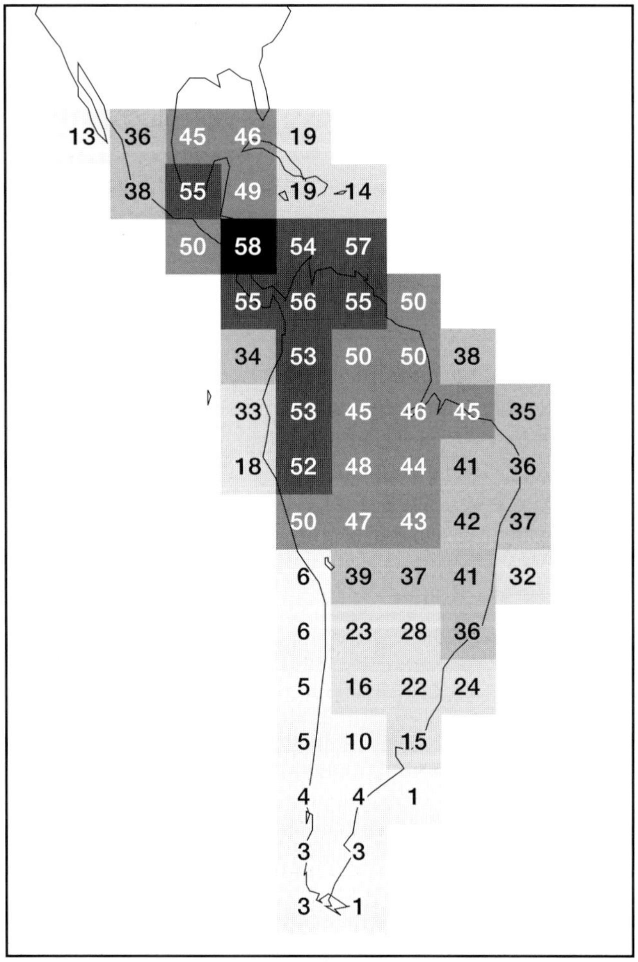

Map 33. Minimum set of grid-cell areas required to maintain all genera occurring in the Neotropical Region.
The minimum number of squares required to conserve all genera is eight. The numbers in the squares represent the number of genera uniquely contributing to this minimum set.

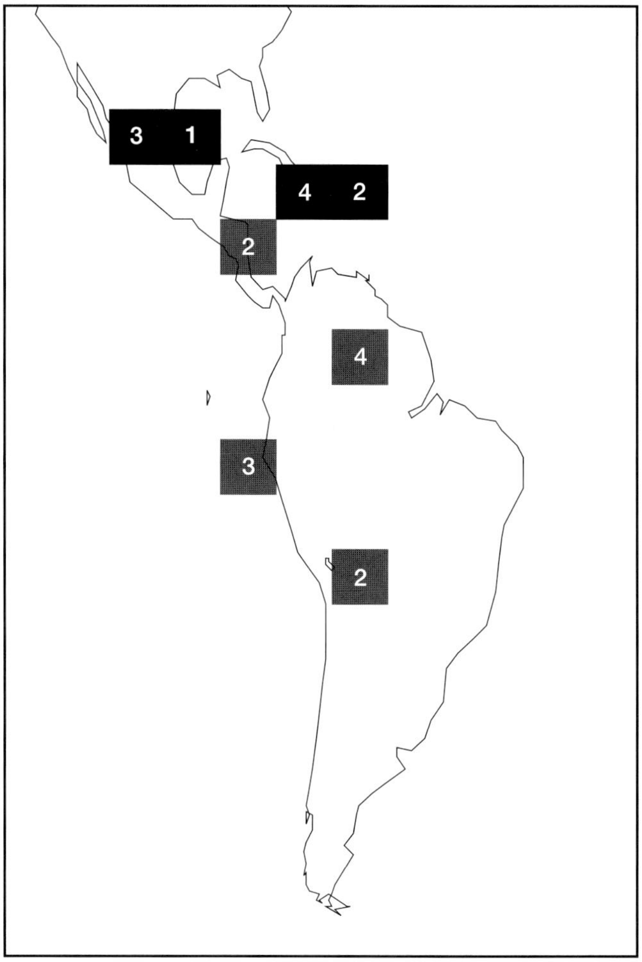

Endangered and seven Vulnerable. Several species have very restricted distributions, and Guadeloupe stands out as being of particular importance in this respect with four globally threatened species (one Endangered and three Vulnerable) recorded from this small group of islands. Two of Guadeloupe's bat species are endemic.

Brazil

The bat fauna of Brazil is thought to consist of 137 species (da Fonseca *et al.* 1996), almost 50% of the total for the whole Neotropical Region. Amazonia is the largest biome with the richest bat fauna. Though only small remnants remain, the Atlantic forest has more than half of the South American bat species. This is, by far, the most threatened habitat in Brazil. In total there are 14 globally threatened species in Brazil, all Vulnerable. Six of Brazil's bat species are endemic.

Peru

Peru has the most species-rich mammalian fauna in the Neotropical Region, including 152 bat species. Fifteen globally threatened species are present –one Endangered and 14 Vulnerable. Peru also has five endemic bat species.

Colombia

Colombia has the richest bat fauna in South America, with an estimated 170 species. Eleven globally threatened species have been recorded – one Endangered and 10 Vulnerable.

Recommendations

The following recommendations are based upon information provided by the contributors to this section. They include both general recommendations applicable to the whole area, as well as specific ones relating to particular species, areas, or habitats.

Habitats

Apart from the loss of all types of forest and riverine habitats, especially in arid areas, specific concerns have been raised about habitat damage and pollution resulting from oil and mineral extraction (particularly for gold), hydroelectric dams, and overgrazing by cattle. Karstic areas are also highlighted as being of major concern. Migration and habitat requirements during migration, including altitudinal migration, has not been investigated and may be a source of conservation problems.

Recommendations:
- develop policies for appropriate habitat management on the basis of present knowledge, but with targeted priorities for future research, including international collaboration where necessary;
- undertake Environmental Impact Assessments for major agricultural, industrial, and hydroelectric schemes within Amazonia;
- undertake Environmental Impact Assessments prior to oil exploration;
- ensure adequate protection of remaining areas of Atlantic forest in Central America, dry forest on the west coasts of Central America, forests in the Darien area of Panama, Atlantic forest in Brazil, and montane rainforests in northern Argentina and southern Bolivia;
- develop conservation plans for dry and montane forests of South America;
- assess impact of mining activities in Atacama Desert;
- assess impacts of mining and road-building activities in Guyana;
- survey important areas of karst and protect key sites identified within these areas;
- identify key cave and mine sites, and implement appropriate management schemes where required;
- survey bat populations in major cities;
- develop education programmes about importance of trees for bats.

Roost types

As elsewhere, tree holes and underground habitats, including boulder jumbles, are identified as threatened roost types. Damage to caves through vampire bat control and renewed mining operations, especially for gold, are considered particularly threatening. Some cities, such as Mexico City, have rich bat faunas where there are problems of unwelcome synanthropy and loss of available foraging habitat.

One issue within the Microchiroptera that is specific to the Neotropical Region relates to vampire bats. In this case, there is relatively little information on the level of impact (especially economic costs) of damage, and management practices and education should be improved.

Recommendations:
- consider the importance of roost sites to bats in developments affecting potential tree roosts, underground habitats, and buildings;
- develop education programmes about the importance of caves and mines for bats;
- adopt the resolution on vampire bats proposed by the 11th International Bat Research Conference (see General Recommendations, Chapter 5.2.).

Geographical areas

The Neotropical Region is extremely rich in bat species. Areas identified as of particular importance are Central America, Caribbean, Amazonia, Atlantic forests, Argentina, Bolivia, Guyanas, and Ecuador/Colombia.

Recommendations:
- support further work to identify key areas for biodiversity, assess conservation problems, and develop appropriate action;
- survey and develop conservation plans for Caribbean Islands, particularly Jamaica, Hispaniola, Cuba, Puerto Rico, and Guadeloupe;

- establish status of species in the coastal deserts in northern Chile and Peru;
- establish status of species in the Pampas in southern Brazil, Uruguay, and Argentina, and Patagonia in Argentina and Chile;
- establish status of species in the Brazilian caatinga, cerrado, and pantanal, and the Paraguayan chaco;
- survey and develop conservation plan for bats in Argentina.

Taxa

The Neotropical Region has the highest percentage of endemic families, genera, and species. There is remarkably little overlap between Old World and New World tropical bat faunas and groups highlighted as being of concern are monotypic families (such as Thyropteridae and Noctilionidae), Emballonuridae, and the genera *Platalina*, *Tonatia*, *Micronycteris*, *Mimon*, *Lonchorhina*, *Macrophyllum*, *Ectophylla*, *Musonycteris*, *Diclidurus*, and *Peropteryx*.

Recommendations:
- undertake a full review of Neotropical fauna to identify taxa at risk, with weighting for degrees of threat, endemism, systematic isolation, and biological characteristics, and develop appropriate Action Plans;
- assess status of species in the families Noctilionidae, Natalidae, Thyropteridae, and Emballonuridae;
- assess status of genera *Hylonycteris* and *Musonycteris* in Central America.

Miscellaneous

Recommendations:
- conduct studies of migration patterns of South American bat species;
- assess impacts from pesticide use;
- develop education programmes about the role of frugivorous and nectarivorous bats in pollination and seed dispersal.

Checklist of Neotropical bats

A total of 288 species are recorded from the Neotropical Region. The full list is given below.

Species	Status
FAMILY EMBALLONURIDAE	
Balantiopteryx	
Balantiopteryx infusca (Thomas 1897)	EN: B1 + 2c
Balantiopteryx io Thomas 1904	LR: nt
Balantiopteryx plicata Peters 1867	LR: lc
Centronycteris	
Centronycteris maximiliani (Fischer 1829)	LR: lc
Cormura	
Cormura brevirostris (Wagner 1843)	LR: lc
Cyttarops	
Cyttarops alecto Thomas 1913	LR: nt
Diclidurus	
Diclidurus albus Wied-Neuwied 1820	LR: lc
Diclidurus ingens Hernandez-Camacho 1955	VU: A2c
Diclidurus isabellus (Thomas 1920)	LR: nt
Diclidurus scutatus Peters 1869	LR: lc
Peropteryx	
Peropteryx kappleri Peters 1867	LR: lc
Peropteryx leucoptera Peters 1867	LR: lc
Peropteryx macrotis (Wagner 1843)	LR: lc
Rhynchonycteris	
Rhynchonycteris naso (Wied-Neuwied 1820)	LR: lc
Saccopteryx	
Saccopteryx bilineata (Temminck 1838)	LR: lc
Saccopteryx canescens Thomas 1901	LR: lc
Saccopteryx gymnura Thomas 1901	VU: A2c, D2
Saccopteryx leptura (Schreber 1774)	LR: lc
FAMILY NOCTILIONIDAE	
Noctilio	
Noctilio albiventris Desmarest 1818	LR: lc
Noctilio leporinus (Linnaeus 1758)	LR: lc
FAMILY MORMOOPIDAE	
Mormoops	
Mormoops blainvillii Leach 1821	LR: nt
Mormoops megalophylla (Peters 1864)	LR: lc
Pteronotus	
Pteronotus davyi Gray 1838	LR: lc
Pteronotus gymnonotus Natterer 1843	LR: lc
Pteronotus macleayii (Gray 1839)	VU: A2c
Pteronotus parnellii (Gray 1843)	LR: lc
Pteronotus personatus (Wagner 1843)	LR: lc
Pteronotus quadridens (Gundlach 1840)	LR: nt
FAMILY PHYLLOSTOMIDAE	
Subfamily Phyllostominae	
Chrotopterus	
Chrotopterus auritus (Peters 1856)	LR: lc
Lonchorhina	
Lonchorhina aurita Tomes 1863	LR: lc
Lonchorhina fernandezi Ochoa and Ibanez 1982	VU: A2c
Lonchorhina inusitata Handley and Ochoa 1997	DD
Lonchorhina marinkellei Hernandez-Camacho and Cadena-G. 1978	VU: A2c
Lonchorhina orinocensis Linares and Ojasti 1971	LR: nt
Macrophyllum	
Macrophyllum macrophyllum (Schinz 1821)	LR: lc
Macrotus	
Macrotus californicus Baird 1858	VU: A2c
Macrotus waterhousii Gray 1843	LR: lc
Micronycteris	
Micronycteris behnii (Peters 1865)	VU: A2c
Micronycteris brachyotis (Dobson 1879)	LR: lc

Species	Status
Micronycteris brosseti Simmons and Voss 1998	DD
Micronycteris daviesi (Hill 1964)	LR: nt
Micronycteris hirsuta (Peters 1869)	LR: lc
Micronycteris megalotis (Gray 1842)	LR: lc
Micronycteris minuta (Gervais 1856)	LR: lc
Micronycteris nicefori Sanborn 1949	LR: lc
Micronycteris pusilla Sanborn 1949	VU: A2c
Micronycteris sanborni Simmons 1996	DD
Micronycteris schmidtorum Sanborn 1935	LR: lc
Micronycteris sylvestris (Thomas 1896)	LR: nt
Mimon	
Mimon bennettii (Gray 1838)	LR: lc
Mimon crenulatum (E. Geoffroy 1810)	LR: lc
Phylloderma	
Phylloderma stenops Peters 1865	LR: lc
Phyllostomus	
Phyllostomus discolor Wagner 1843	LR: lc
Phyllostomus elongatus (E. Geoffroy 1810)	LR: lc
Phyllostomus hastatus (Pallas 1767)	LR: lc
Phyllostomus latifolius (Thomas 1901)	LR: nt
Tonatia	
Tonatia bidens (Spix 1823)	LR: lc
Tonatia brasiliense (Peters 1866)	LR: lc
Tonatia carrikeri (J. A. Allen 1910)	VU: A2c
Tonatia evotis Davis and Carter 1978	LR: nt
Tonatia saurophila Koopman and Williams 1951	LR: lc
Tonatia schulzi Genoways and Williams 1980	VU: A2c
Tonatia silvicola (d'Orbigny 1836)	LR: lc
Trachops	
Trachops cirrhosus (Spix 1823)	LR: lc
Vampyrum	
Vampyrum spectrum (Linnaeus 1758)	LR: nt
Subfamily Lonchophyllinae	
Lionycteris	
Lionycteris spurrelli Thomas 1913	LR: lc
Lonchophylla	
Lonchophylla bokermanni Sazima *et al.* 1978	VU: A2c
Lonchophylla dekeyseri Taddei *et al.* 1983	VU: A2c
Lonchophylla handleyi Hill 1980	VU: A2c, D2
Lonchophylla hesperia G. M. Allen 1908	VU: A2c, D2
Lonchophylla mordax Thomas 1903	LR: lc
Lonchophylla robusta Miller 1912	LR: lc
Lonchophylla thomasi J. A. Allen 1904	LR: lc
Platalina	
Platalina genovensium Thomas 1928	VU: D2
Subfamily Brachyphyllinae	
Brachyphylla	
Brachyphylla cavernarum Gray 1834	LR: lc
Brachyphylla nana Miller 1902	LR: nt
Subfamily Phyllonycterinae	
Erophylla	
Erophylla sezekorni (Gundlach 1860)	LR: lc
Phyllonycteris	
Phyllonycteris aphylla (Miller 1898)	EN: B1 + 2c
Phyllonycteris major Anthony 1917	EX
Phyllonycteris poeyi Gundlach 1860	LR: nt
Subfamily Glossophaginae	
Anoura	
Anoura caudifer (E. Geoffroy 1818)	LR: lc
Anoura cultrata Handley 1960	LR: lc
Anoura geoffroyi Gray 1838	LR: lc
Anoura latidens Handley 1984	LR: nt
Anoura luismanueli Molinari 1994	DD
Choeroniscus	
Choeroniscus godmani (Thomas 1903)	LR: nt
Choeroniscus intermedius (J. A. Allen and Chapman 1893)	LR: nt
Choeroniscus minor (Peters 1868)	LR: lc
Choeroniscus periosus Handley 1966	VU: D2
Choeronycteris	
Choeronycteris mexicana Tschudi 1844	LR: nt
Glossophaga	
Glossophaga commissarisi Gardner 1962	LR: lc
Glossophaga leachii Gray 1844	LR: lc
Glossophaga longirostris Miller 1898	LR: lc
Glossophaga morenoi Martinez and Villa 1938	LR: nt
Glossophaga soricina (Pallas 1766)	LR: lc
Hylonycteris	
Hylonycteris underwoodi Thomas 1903	LR: nt
Leptonycteris	
Leptonycteris curasoae Miller 1900	VU: A1c
Leptonycteris nivalis (Saussure 1860)	EN: A1c
Lichonycteris	
Lichonycteris obscura Thomas 1895	LR: lc
Monophyllus	
Monophyllus plethodon Miller 1900	LR: nt
Monophyllus redmani Leach 1821	LR: lc
Musonycteris	
Musonycteris harrisoni Schaldach and McLaughlin 1960	VU: A2c
Scleronycteris	
Scleronycteris ega Thomas 1912	VU: A2c, D2
Subfamily Carolliinae	
Carollia	
Carollia brevicauda (Schinz 1821)	LR: lc
Carollia castanea H. Allen 1890	LR: lc
Carollia perspicillata (Linnaeus 1758)	LR: lc
Carollia subrufa (Hahn 1905)	LR: lc
Rhinophylla	
Rhinophylla alethina Handley 1966	LR: nt
Rhinophylla fischerae Carter 1966	LR: nt
Rhinophylla pumilio Peters 1865	LR: lc
Subfamily Stenodermatinae	
Ametrida	
Ametrida centurio Gray 1847	LR: lc
Ardops	
Ardops nichollsi (Thomas 1891)	LR: nt
Ariteus	
Ariteus flavescens (Gray 1831)	VU: A2c, D2
Artibeus	
Artibeus amplus Handley 1987	LR: nt
Artibeus anderseni Osgood 1916	LR: lc
Artibeus aztecus K. Andersen 1906	LR: lc
Artibeus cinereus (Gervais 1856)	LR: lc
Artibeus concolor Peters 1865	LR: nt
Artibeus fimbriatus Gray 1838	LR: nt
Artibeus fraterculus Anthony 1924	VU: A2c

Species	Status	Species	Status
Artibeus glaucus Thomas 1893	LR: lc	*Sturnira magna* de la Torre 1966	LR: nt
Artibeus gnomus Handley 1987	LR: lc	*Sturnira mordax* (Goodwin 1938)	LR: nt
Artibeus hartii Thomas 1892	LR: lc	*Sturnira nana* Gardner and O'Neill 1971	VU: D2
Artibeus hirsutus K. Andersen 1906	VU: A2c	*Sturnira thomasi*	
Artibeus incomitatus		de la Torre and Schwartz 1966	EN: B1 + 2c
Kalko and Handley 1994	DD	*Sturnira tildae* de la Torre 1959	LR: lc
Artibeus inopinatus		***Uroderma***	
Davis and Carter 1964	VU: A2c	*Uroderma bilobatum* Peters 1866	LR: lc
Artibeus intermedius Allen 1897	LR: lc	*Uroderma magnirostrum* Davis 1968	LR: lc
Artibeus jamaicensis Leach 1821	LR: lc	***Vampyressa***	
Artibeus lituratus (Olfers 1818)	LR: lc	*Vampyressa bidens* (Dobson 1878)	LR: nt
Artibeus obscurus Schinz 1821	LR: nt	*Vampyressa brocki* Peterson 1968	LR: nt
Artibeus phaeotis (Miller 1902)	LR: lc	*Vampyressa melissa* Thomas 1926	LR: nt
Artibeus planirostris (Spix 1823)	LR: lc	*Vampyressa nymphaea* Thomas 1909	LR: lc
Artibeus toltecus (Saussure 1860)	LR: lc	*Vampyressa pusilla* (Wagner 1843)	LR: lc
Artibeus watsoni Thomas 1901	LR: lc	***Vampyrodes***	
Centurio		*Vampyrodes caraccioli* (Thomas 1889)	LR: lc
Centurio senex Gray 1842	LR: lc	**Subfamily Desmodontinae**	
Chiroderma		***Desmodus***	
Chiroderma doriae Thomas 1891	VU: A2c, D2	*Desmodus rotundus* (E. Geoffroy 1810)	LR: lc
Chiroderma improvisum		***Diaemus***	
Baker and Genoways 1976	EN: A2c, B1 + 2c	*Diaemus youngi* (Jentink 1893)	LR: lc
Chiroderma salvini Dobson 1878	LR: lc	***Diphylla***	
Chiroderma trinitatum Goodwin 1958	LR: lc	*Diphylla ecaudata* Spix 1823	LR: nt
Chiroderma villosum Peters 1860	LR: lc		
Ectophylla		**FAMILY NATALIDAE**	
Ectophylla alba H. Allen 1892	LR: nt	***Natalus***	
Mesophylla		*Natalus lepidus* (Gervais 1837)	LR: nt
Mesophylla macconnelli Thomas 1901	LR: lc	*Natalus micropus* Dobson 1880	LR: lc
Phyllops		*Natalus stramineus* Gray 1838	LR: lc
Phyllops falcatus (Gray 1839)	LR: nt	*Natalus tumidifrons* (Miller 1903)	VU: D2
Platyrrhinus		*Natalus tumidirostris* Miller 1900	LR: lc
Platyrrhinus aurarius			
(Handley and Ferris 1972)	LR: nt	**FAMILY FURIPTERIDAE**	
Platyrrhinus brachycephalus		***Amorphochilus***	
(Rouk and Carter 1972)	LR: lc	*Amorphochilus schnablii* Peters 1877	VU: A2c
Platyrrhinus chocoensis		***Furipterus***	
Alberico and Velasco 1991	VU: A2c, D2	*Furipterus horrens* (F. Cuvier 1828)	LR: lc
Platyrrhinus dorsalis (Thomas 1900)	LR: lc		
Platyrrhinus helleri (Peters 1866)	LR: lc	**FAMILY THYROPTERIDAE**	
Platyrrhinus infuscus (Peters 1880)	LR: nt	***Thyroptera***	
Platyrrhinus lineatus (E. Geoffroy 1810)	LR: lc	*Thyroptera discifera*	
Platyrrhinus recifinus (Thomas 1901)	VU: A2c, D2	(Lichtenstein and Peters 1855)	LR: lc
Platyrrhinus umbratus (Lyon 1902)	LR: nt	*Thyroptera lavali* Pine 1993	VU: B1 + 2c, D2
Platyrrhinus vittatus (Peters 1860)	LR: lc	*Thyroptera tricolor* Spix 1823	LR: lc
Pygoderma			
Pygoderma bilabiatum (Wagner 1843)	LR: nt	**FAMILY VESPERTILIONIDAE**	
Sphaeronycteris		**Subfamily Vespertilioninae**	
Sphaeronycteris toxophyllum		***Antrozous***	
Peters 1882	LR: lc	*Antrozous dubiaquercus*	
Stenoderma		Van Gelder 1959	VU: A2c, D2
Stenoderma rufum Desmarest 1820	VU: A1c	*Antrozous pallidus* (Le Conte 1856)	LR: lc
Sturnira		***Eptesicus***	
Sturnira aratathomasi		*Eptesicus andinus* (J. A. Allen 1914)	LR: lc
Peterson and Tamsitt 1968	LR: nt	*Eptesicus brasiliensis* (Desmarest 1819)	LR: lc
Sturnira bidens Thomas 1915	LR: nt	*Eptesicus diminutus* Osgood 1915	LR: lc
Sturnira bogotensis Shamel 1927	LR: lc	*Eptesicus furinalis* (d'Orbigny 1847)	LR: lc
Sturnira erythromos (Tschudi 1844)	LR: lc	*Eptesicus fuscus* (Beauvois 1796)	LR: lc
Sturnira lilium (E. Geoffroy 1810)	LR: lc	*Eptesicus guadeloupensis*	
Sturnira ludovici Anthony 1924	LR: lc	Genoways and Baker 1975	EN: B1 + 2c
Sturnira luisi Davis 1980	LR: lc	*Eptesicus innoxius* (Gervais 1841)	VU: A2c

Species	Status
Euderma	
Euderma maculatum (J. A. Allen 1891)	LR: lc
Histiotus	
Histiotus alienus Thomas 1916	VU: A2c
Histiotus humboldti Handley 1996	DD
Histiotus macrotus (Poeppig 1835)	LR: nt
Histiotus montanus (Philippi and Landbeck 1861)	LR: lc
Histiotus velatus (I. Geoffroy 1824)	LR: lc
Idionycteris	
Idionycteris phyllotis (G. M. Allen 1916)	LR: lc
Lasionycteris	
Lasionycteris noctivagans (Le Conte,1831)	LR: lc
Lasiurus	
Lasiurus atratus Handley,1996	DD
Lasiurus blossevillii (Lesson and Garnet 1826)	LR: lc
Lasiurus borealis (Müller 1776)	LR: lc
Lasiurus castaneus Handley 1960	VU: D2
Lasiurus cinereus (Beauvois 1796)	LR: lc
Lasiurus ebenus Fazzolari and Corrca 1994	VU: B1 + 2c, D2
Lasiurus ega (Gervais 1856)	LR: lc
Lasiurus egregius (Peters 1870)	LR: nt
Lasiurus intermedius H. Allen 1862	LR: lc
Lasiurus seminolus (Rhoads 1895)	LR: lc
Lasiurus xanthinus (Thomas 1897)	LR: lc
Myotis	
Myotis aelleni Baud 1979	VU: A2c, D2
Myotis albescens (E. Geoffroy 1806)	LR: lc
Myotis atacamensis (Lataste 1892)	VU: A2c, D2
Myotis auriculus Baker and Stains 1955	LR: lc
Myotis californicus (Audubon and Bachman 1842)	LR: lc
Myotis chiloensis (Waterhouse 1840)	LR: nt
Myotis cobanensis Goodwin 1955	CR: B1 + 2c
Myotis dominicensis Miller 1902	VU: A2c, D2
Myotis elegans Hall 1962	LR: nt
Myotis findleyi Bogan 1978	EN: B1 + 2c
Myotis fortidens Miller and Allen 1928	LR: nt
Myotis keaysi J. A. Allen 1914	LR: lc
Myotis leibii (Audubon and Bachman 1842)	LR: lc
Myotis levis (I. Geoffroy 1824)	LR: lc
Myotis lucifugus (Le Conte 1831)	LR: lc
Myotis martiniquensis LaVal 1973	LR: nt
Myotis nesopolus Miller 1900	LR: nt
Myotis nigricans (Schinz 1821)	LR: lc
Myotis oxyotus (Peters 1867)	LR: lc
Myotis riparius Handley 1960	LR: lc
Myotis ruber (E. Geoffroy 1806)	VU: A2c
Myotis simus Thomas 1901	LR: lc
Myotis thysanodes Miller 1897	LR: lc
Myotis velifer (J. A. Allen 1890)	LR: lc
Myotis volans (H. Allen 1866)	LR: lc
Myotis yumanensis (H. Allen 1864)	LR: lc
Nycticeius	
Nycticeius humeralis (Rafinesque 1818)	LR: lc
Pipistrellus	
Pipistrellus hesperus (H. Allen 1864)	LR: lc
Pipistrellus subflavus (F. Cuvier 1832)	LR: lc
Plecotus	
Plecotus mexicanus (G. M. Allen 1916)	LR: lc
Plecotus townsendii Cooper 1837	VU: A2c
Rhogeessa	
Rhogeessa alleni Thomas 1892	LR: nt
Rhogeessa genowaysi Baker 1984	VU: A2c, D2
Rhogeessa gracilis Miller 1897	LR: nt
Rhogeessa minutilla Miller 1897	LR: nt
Rhogeessa mira LaVal 1973	EN: A2c, B1 + 2cd
Rhogeessa parvula H. Allen 1866	LR: nt
Rhogeessa tumida H. Allen 1866	LR: lc
Subfamily Tomopeatinae	
Tomopeas	
Tomopeas ravus Miller 1900	VU: A2c, D2
FAMILY MOLOSSIDAE	
Eumops	
Eumops auripendulus (Shaw 1800)	LR: lc
Eumops bonariensis (Peters 1874)	LR: lc
Eumops dabbenei Thomas 1914	LR: lc
Eumops glaucinus (Wagner 1843)	LR: lc
Eumops hansae Sanborn 1932	LR: lc
Eumops maurus (Thomas 1901)	VU: A2c, D2
Eumops perotis (Schinz 1821)	LR: lc
Eumops underwoodi Goodwin 1940	LR: nt
Molossops	
Molossops abrasus (Temminck 1827)	LR: nt
Molossops aequatorianus Cabrera 1917	VU: A2c, D2
Molossops greenhalli (Goodwin 1958)	LR: lc
Molossops mattogrossensis Vieira 1942	LR: nt
Molossops neglectus Williams and Genoways 1980	LR: nt
Molossops planirostris (Peters 1865)	LR: lc
Molossops temminckii (Burmeister 1854)	LR: lc
Molossus	
Molossus ater E. Geoffroy 1805	LR: lc
Molossus aztecus Saussure 1860	LR: nt
Molossus bondae J. A. Allen 1904	LR: lc
Molossus coibensis J.A. Allen 1904	LR: nt
Molossus molossus (Pallas 1766)	LR: lc
Molossus pretiosus Miller 1902	LR: lc
Molossus sinaloae J. A. Allen 1906	LR: lc
Mormopterus	
Mormopterus kalinowskii (Thomas 1893)	VU: A2c, D2
Mormopterus minutus (Miller 1899)	VU: A2c
Mormopterus phrudus (Handley 1956)	EN: B1 + 2c
Nyctinomops	
Nyctinomops aurispinosus (Peale 1848)	LR: lc
Nyctinomops femorosaccus (Merriam 1889)	LR: lc
Nyctinomops laticaudatus (E. Geoffroy 1805)	LR: lc
Nyctinomops macrotis (Gray 1840)	LR: lc
Promops	
Promops centralis Thomas 1915	LR: lc
Promops nasutus (Spix 1823)	LR: lc
Tadarida	
Tadarida brasiliensis (I. Geoffroy 1824)	LR: nt

Table 7. Number of IUCN Red List species for countries in the Neotropical Region.
The table also includes information on numbers of endemics and the estimated size of the bat fauna. For information on the compilation of the figures for size of faunas see Chapter 6. Full lists of IUCN Red List species per country are given in the same Chapter. **Countries not listed here do not have a recorded bat fauna.** Where a country overlaps more than one region, the fauna for the whole country is included.

	IUCN RED LIST SPECIES								ENDEMICS	TOTAL NO. OF SPECIES		
Country	**CR**	**EN**	**VU**	**LRcd**	**LRnt**	**EX**	**DD**	***Total***	***Total***	**Mega**	**Micro**	***Total***
American Virgin Is.	0	0	1	0	0	0	0	1	0	0	5	5
Anguilla	0	0	0	0	1	0	0	1	0	0	5	5
Antigua and Barbuda	0	0	0	0	2	0	0	2	0	0	7	7
Argentina	0	0	3	0	7	0	0	10	1	0	57	57
Aruba	0	0	1	0	0	0	0	1	0	0	4	4
Bahamas	0	0	1	0	3	0	0	4	1	0	12	12
Barbados	0	0	0	0	2	0	0	2	0	0	6	6
Belize	0	0	1	0	8	0	0	9	0	0	69	69
Bermuda	0	0	0	0	0	0	0	0	0	0	4	4
Bolivia	0	0	1	0	9	0	0	10	0	0	107	107
Brazil	0	0	14	0	23	0	3	40	6	0	137	137
British Virgin Is.	0	0	0	0	0	0	0	0	0	0	3	3
Cayman Is.	0	0	0	0	3	0	0	3	0	0	8	8
Chile	0	0	3	0	3	0	0	6	1	0	10	10
Colombia	0	1	10	0	33	0	0	44	2	0	170	170
Costa Rica	0	0	2	0	11	0	0	13	0	0	103	103
Cuba	0	0	2	0	7	0	0	9	1	0	27	27
Dominica	0	0	1	0	3	0	0	4	0	0	12	12
Dominican Republic	0	0	0	0	6	0	0	6	0	0	18	18
Ecuador	0	1	7	0	12	0	0	20	1	0	105	105
El Salvador	0	0	2	0	6	0	1	9	0	0	58	58
Falkland Is. (1)	0	0	0	0	0	0	0	0	0	0	0	0
French Guiana	0	0	2	0	8	0	2	12	0	0	102	102
Grenada	0	0	0	0	0	0	0	0	0	0	13	13
Guadeloupe	0	1	3	0	3	0	0	7	2	0	12	12
Guatemala	1	1	1	0	11	0	0	14	1	0	94	94
Guyana	0	0	3	0	10	0	2	15	0	0	107	107
Haiti	0	0	0	0	6	0	0	6	0	0	17	17
Honduras	0	0	3	0	12	0	1	16	0	0	98	98
Jamaica	0	1	2	0	5	0	0	8	2	0	21	21
Martinique	0	0	0	0	4	0	0	4	0	0	10	10
Mexico	1	4	9	0	17	0	0	31	13	0	137	137
Montserrat	0	1	0	0	3	0	0	4	0	0	10	10
Netherlands Antilles	0	0	1	0	3	0	0	4	0	0	10	10
Nicaragua	0	0	1	0	11	0	1	13	0	0	88	88
Panama	0	0	1	0	10	0	0	11	0	0	111	111
Paraguay	0	0	1	0	4	0	0	5	0	0	49	49
Peru	0	1	14	0	21	0	1	37	5	0	152	152
Puerto Rico	0	0	1	0	3	1	0	5	1	0	13	13
St. Kitts & Nevis	0	0	0	0	1	0	0	1	0	0	4	4
St. Lucia	0	0	0	0	3	0	0	3	0	0	8	8
St. Vincent	0	0	0	0	2	0	0	2	0	0	9	9
Suriname	0	0	3	0	9	0	2	14	0	0	61	61
Trinidad and Tobago	0	0	0	0	5	0	0	5	0	0	62	62
Turks and Caicos Is.	0	0	0	0	2	0	0	2	0	0	4	4
Uruguay	0	0	1	0	1	0	0	2	0	0	15	15
Venezuela	0	0	6	0	23	0	3	32	3	0	154	154

1. Only two bats have been recorded from the Falkland Islands, both probable imports.

Table 7 shows the number of IUCN Red List species recorded from each country, together with information on numbers of endemics and the size of the total bat fauna.

Key references

The following is a list of important references relating to bats in the Neotropical Region. It is by no means an exhaustive list, and concentrates mainly on distributional studies at a national or regional level.

Acosta y Lara, E.F. 1950. Quirópteros del Uruguay. *Comunicaciones Zoologicas del Museo de Historia Natural de Montivideo*, 3 (58), 1–71.

Aellen, V. 1970. Catalogue raisonné des chiroptères de la Colombie. *Revue Suisse de Zoologie*, 77 (1), 1–37.

Albuja V.L. 1982. *Murciélagos del Ecuador.* Escuela Politecnica Nacional, Quito.

Albuja, V.L. 1999. *Murciélagos del Ecuador.* Escuela Politecnica Nacional, Quito.

Anderson, S. 1997. Mammals of Bolivia, taxonomy and distribution. *Bulletin of the American Museum of Natural History*, 231, 1-652.

Anderson, S., Koopman, K.F., and Creighton, G.K. 1982. Bats of Bolivia: An annotated checklist. *American Museum Novitates*, 2750, 1–24.

Arita, H.T. and Ceballos, G. 1995. *The mammals of Mexico, distribution and conservation status.* Asociación Mexicana Mastozoología, México City.

Arita, H.T. and Ortega, J. 1998. The Middle American bat fauna: Conservation in the Neotropical-Nearctic border. Pp. 295–308 *in: Bat biology and conservation* (eds. Kunz, T.H. and P.A. Racey). Smithsonian Institution Press, Washington DC.

Baker, R.J. and Genoways, H.H. 1978. Zoogeography of Antillean bats. *In:* Zoogeography of the Caribbean. *Special Publications. Academy of Natural Sciences of Philadelphia*, 13, 53–97.

Baker, R.J. and Knox Jones Jr., J. 1975. Additional records of bats from Nicaragua, with a revised checklist of chiroptera. *Occasional Papers. The Museum, Texas Tech University*, 32, 1–13.

Baker, R.J., Knox Jones Jr., J., and Carter, D.C. (eds.) 1976. Biology of bats of the New World family Pyllostomatidae, Part 1. *Special Publications. The Museum, Texas Tech University*, 10, 1–218.

Baker, R.J., Knox Jones Jr., J., and Carter, D.C. (eds.) 1977. Biology of bats of the New World family Pyllostomatidae, Part 2. *Special Publications. The Museum, Texas Tech University*, 13, 1–364.

Baker, R.J., Knox Jones Jr., J., and Carter, D.C. (eds.) 1979. Biology of bats of the New World family Pyllostomatidae, Part 3. *Special Publications. The Museum, Texas Tech University*, 16, 1–441.

Bárquez, R.M. 1987. *Los murciélagos de Argentina*. PhD thesis, Facultad de Ciencias Naturales e Instituto Miguel Lillo, Universidad Nacional de Tucumán.

Bárquez, R.M., Giannini, N.P., and Mares, M.A. 1993. *Guide to bats of Argentina.* Oklahoma Museum of Natural History, University of Oklahoma.

Bárquez, R.M., Mares, M.A., and Braun, J.K. 1999. The bats of Argentina. *Special Publications. Museum. Texas Tech University*, 42, 1–275.

Brosset, A. and Charles-Dominique, P. 1990. The bats from French Guiana: A taxonomic, faunistic and ecological approach. *Mammalia,* 54 (4), 509–560.

Brosset, A. and Dubost, G. 1967. Chiroptères de la Guyane française. *Mammalia*, 31 (4), 583–594.

Burt, W.H. and Stirton, R.A. 1961. The mammals of El Salvador. *Miscellaneous Publications. Museum of Zoology, University of Michigan*, 117, 1–69.

Cabrera, A. 1958. *Catálogo de los mammíferos de América del Sur,* Vol. 1. Museo Argentino de Ciencias Naturales *Bernardino Rivadavia*, Zoología, Buenos Aries.

Cervantes, F.A., Castro-C, A., and Ramírez-Pulido, J. 1994. Mamíferos terrestres nativos de México. *Anales del Instituto de Biología, Universidad Nacional Autónoma de México Serie Zoología*, 65, 177–190.

Cuervo, A., Hernández-Camacho, J., and Cadena, A. 1986. Lista actualizada de los mamíferos de Colombia. Anotaciones sobre su distribución. *Caldasia,* 25, 471–501.

Eisenberg, J.F. 1989. *Mammals of the Neotropics. Volume 1. The northern Neotropics.* The University of Chicago Press, Chicago and London.

Eisenberg, J.F. and Redford, K.H. 1999. *Mammals of the Neotropics; the Central Neotropics. Vol. 3. Ecuador, Peru, Bolivia, Brazil.* University of Chicago Press, Chicago/London. 609pp.

Felten, H. 1956a. Fledermäuse (Mammalia, Chiroptera) aus El Salvador. Teil 3, *Senckenbergiana Biologica,* 37 (3/4), 179–212.

Felten, H. 1956b. Fledermäuse (Mammalia:Chiroptera) aus El Salvador. Teil 4, *Senckenbergiana Biologica,* 37 (5/6), 341–370.

da Fonseca, G.A.B., Costa, C.M.R., Machado, R.B., and Leite, Y.L.R. 1994. *Livro vermelho dos mamíferos Brasileiros ameaçados de extinção.* Fundação Biodiversitas, Belo Horizonte.

da Fonseca, G.A.B., Costa, C.M.R., Machado, R.B., Leite, Y.L.R, and Furlani, C. (orgs.) 1994. *Mamíferos Brasileiros: uma coletâna bibliográfica.* Fundação Biodiversitas, Belo Horizonte.

da Fonseca, G.A.B., Herrmann, G., Leite, Y.L.R., Mittermeier, R.A., Rylands, A.B., and Patton, J.L. 1996. *Lista anotada dos mamíferos do Brasil.* Occasional Papers in Conservation Biology Number 4. Conservation International, Washington DC.

Goldman, E.A. 1920. Mammals of Panama. *Smithsonian Miscellaneous Collections,* 69, 1–309.

Goodwin, G.G. 1942. Mammals of Honduras. *Bulletin of the American Museum of Natural History,* 79, 107–195.

Goodwin, G.G. 1946. Mammals of Costa Rica. *Bulletin of the American Museum of Natural History,* 87, 271–474.

Goodwin, G.G. and Greenhall, A.M. 1961. A review of the bats of Trinidad and Tobago. *Bulletin of the American Museum of Natural History,* 122 (3), 191–301.

Greenhall, A.M. 1959. Bats of Guiana. *Journal of the British Guiana Museum and Zoo*, 22, 55–57.

Greenhall, A.M., Lord, R.D., and Massoia, E. 1983. *Key to the bats of Argentina.* Special Publication 5. Pan America Zoonoses Center, Buenos Aries.

Handley Jr., C.O. 1966. Checklist of the mammals of Panama. Pp. 753–795 *in: Ectoparasites of Panama* (eds. R.L. Wenzel and V.J. Tipton). Field Museum of Natural History, Chicago.

Hill, J. Edwards 1964. Notes on bats from British Guiana with a description of a new genus and species of Phyllostomidae. *Mammalia*, 28 (4), 553–572.

Husson, A.M., 1960. *De zoogdieren van de Nederlanse Antillen [Mammals of The Netherlands Antilles]*. Fauna Nederlandse Antillen, no. 2. 's-Gravenhage and Willemstad.

Husson, A.M. 1962. The bats of Suriname. *Zoologische Verhandelingen*, 58, 1–282.

Koopman, K.F. 1978. Biogeography of the bats of South America. Pp. 273–302 *in: Mammalian biology in South America* (eds. M.A. Mares and H.H. Genoways). Pymatuning Symposia in Ecology 6, Special Publication Series, Pymatuning Laboratory of Ecology, University of Pittsburgh, Pittsburgh.

Koopman, K.F. 1989. A review and analysis of the bats of the West Indies. Pp. 635–644 *in: Biogeography of the West Indies: Past, present and future* (ed. C.A. Woods). Sandhill Crane Press, Gainesville.

Knox Jones Jr., J. 1966. Bats from Guatemala. *University of Kansas Publications. Museum of Natural History*, 16, 439–472.

Knox Jones Jr., J., Arroyo-Cabrales, J., and Owen, D.R. 1988. Revised checklist of bats (Chiroptera) of Mexico and Central America. *Occasional Papers. The Museum, Texas Tech University*, 120, 1–34.

Knox Jones Jr., J. and Owen, R.D. 1986. Checklist and bibliography of Nicaraguan Chiroptera. *Occasional Papers. The Museum, Texas Tech University*, 106, 1–13.

Linares, O.J. 1986. *Murciélagos de Venezuela.* Cuardenas Lagove, Premio Nacional de Perodismo, Caracas.

Linares, O.J. 1998. *Mamíferos de Venezuela.* Sociedad Conservacionista Audubon de Venezuela and BP Venezuela, Caracas.

Marinho-Filho, J. and Sazima, I. 1998. Brazilian bats and conservation biology: A first survey. Pp. 282–294 *in: Bat biology and conservation* (eds. T.H. Kunz and P.A. Racey). Smithsonian Institution Press, Washington DC and London.

McCarthy, T. 1987. Distributional records of bats from the Caribbean lowlands of Belize and adjacent Guatemala and Mexico. *Fieldiana Zoology (new series)*, 39, 137–162.

McCarthy, T.J., Davis, W.B., Hill, J.E., Knox Jones Jr., J., and Cruz, G.A. 1993. Bats (Mammalia: Chiroptera) records, early collectors, and faunal list for northern Central America. *Annals of the Carnegie Museum*, 62 (3), 191–228.

McFarlane, D.A. 1991. The species-genus relationship in Antillean bat communities. *Mammalia*, 55 (3), 363–370.

Medellín, R.A., Arita, H.T., and Sanchez, O. 1997. *Identificación de los murciélagos de México. Clave de campo.* Asociación Mexicana de Mastozoología, A.C. Publicaciones Especiales Núm. 2. Mexico City.

Mok, W.Y., Wilson, D.E., Lacey, L.A., and Luizão, R.C.C. 1982. Lista atualizada de quirópteros da Amazônia Brasileira. *Acta Amazonica*, 12, 817–823.

Osgood, W.H. 1943. The mammals of Chile. *Field Museum of Natural History, Zoological Series*, 30, 1–268.

Owen, R.D., Knox Jones, Jr., J., and Baker, R.J. 1991. Annotated checklist of mammals of El Salvador. *Occasional Paper. The Museum, Texas Tech University*, 139, 1–17.

Pacheco, V., de Macedo, H., Vivar, E., Ascorra, C., Arana-Cardó, R., and Solari, S. 1995. *Lista Anotada de los Mamíferos Peruanos.* Occasional Papers in Conservation Biology, Number 2. Conservation International, Washington DC.

Ramírez-Pulido, J., Britton, J.M.C., Perdomo, A., and Castro, A. 1986. *Guía de los mamíferos de México.* Referencias hasta 1983. Universidad Autónoma Metropolitana Iztapalapa.

Ramírez-Pulido, J., Castro-Campillo, A., Arroyo-Cabrales, J., and Cervantes, F.A. 1996. Lista taxonómica de los mamíferos terrestes de México. *Occasional Papers, The Museum, Texas Tech University*, 158, 1–62 + Errata.

Redford, K.H. and Eisenberg, J.F. 1992. *Mammals of the Neotropics. Volume 2. The southern cone.* The University of Chicago Press, Chicago and London.

Rodriguez-H, B. and Wilson, D.E. 1999. *Lista y Distribucion de las Especies de Murcielagos de Costa Rica.* Occasional Papers in Conservation Biology No. 5. Conservation International, Washington DC.

Rodríguez-Mahecha, J.V., Hernández-Camacho, J.I., Defler, T.R., Alberico, M., Mast, R.B., Mittermeier, R.A., and Cadena, A. 1995. *Mamíferos Colombianos: Sus nombres comunes e indígenas.* Occasional Papers in Conservation Biology Number 3. Conservation International, Washington DC.

Silva Taboada, G. 1979. *Los murciélagos de Cuba.* Editorial Academia, Havana.

Tello, J. 1979. *Mamíferos de Venezuela.* Fundacion la Salle de Ciencias Naturales, Caracas.

Tirira, D. (ed.) 1999. *Mamiferos del Ecuador.* Publicacion Especial 2. Museo de Zoologia, Centro de Bioversidad y Ambiente, Pontificia Universidad Católica del Ecuador, Quito.

Tuttle, M.D. 1970. Distribution and zoogeography of Peruvian bats with comments on natural history. *University of Kansas Science Bulletin*, 49, 45–86.

Varona, L.S. 1974. *Catálogo de los mamíferos vivientes y extinguidos de las Antillas.* Instituto de Zoologia, Academia de Ciencias de Cuba, Havana.

Villa, B. 1967. *Los Murcielagos de México.* Instituto de Biología, Universidad Nacional Autónoma de México, México City.

Wilson, D.E. 1983. Checklist of mammals. Pp. 443–447 *in: Costa Rican natural history* (ed. D.H. Janzen). The University of Chicago Press, Chicago and London.

Wilson, D.E. 1996. Neotropical bats: A checklist with conservation status. Pp. 167–177 *in: Neotropical biodiversity and conservation* (ed. A.C. Gibson). Mildred E. Mathias Botanical Garden, University of California, Los Angeles.

Ximénez, A., Langguth, A., and Praderi, R. 1972. Lista sistemática de los mammíferos del Uruguay. *Anales del Museo de Historia Natural de Montivideo,* 7 (5), 1–45.

5.4.6 Palaearctic Region

This account was compiled using contributions from the following: Gary Ades; Stephane Aulagnier; Angela Bakka; Sergey Bakka; Paul Bates; Jesus Benzal; Vladimir Beshkov; John Borg; Alex Borissenko; Alexandr Botvinkin; Peter Boye; Monika Braun; Jacques Fairon; Jiri Gaisler; Felix Gonzalez-Alvarez; Green Balkans Movement, Bulgaria; Regine Grünmeier; Toni Guillen; S.S. Guitart; Marianne Haffner; Christine Harbusch; Tolibjon K. Khabilov; Tomasz Kokurewicz; Carmi Korine; the late Karl F. Koopman; Irina Kovalyova; Eugenia Kozhurina; Dorothea Krull; Sergey V. Kruskop; Boris Krystufek; Ivan. V. Kuzmin; Ralph Labes; Peter H.C. Lina; Matti Massing; Kate McAney; Jean Francois Noblet; Jorge M. Palmeirim; Rumiana Pandurska; Dainius-Haroldas Pauza; Gunars Petersons; Jacques Pir; Artiom V. Polkanov; Irina Rakhmatulina; Klaus Richarz; Luisa Rodrigues; Rolando Rodriguez-Munoz; Tamar Ron; Jens Rydell; Anthony Santana; Benny Shalmon; Friederike Spitzenberger; Peter Strelkov; Hans-Peter Stutz; Mikhail Tiunov; Zbigniew Urbanczyk; Marcel Uhrin; Aldo M. Voûte; Don E. Wilson; and Szabolcs Zavoczky.

Geographical boundaries of region

The boundaries of the Palaearctic Region follow those in Corbet (1978). They are described as follows. Beginning in the west, the islands of Spitzbergen, Iceland, Azores, Madeira, and Canaries are included, but the Cape Verde Islands are excluded. In Africa, the boundary begins in the west at 21°30'N, (i.e., between Rio de Oro and Mauritania) continues across Mauritania and Mali at the same latitude, and thereafter follows the political boundaries such as to include in their entirety Algeria, Libya, and Egypt, and to exclude the whole of Niger, Chad, and Sudan – the Hoggar Mountains are, therefore, included and the Tibesti excluded. The whole of the Arabian Peninsula is included. The boundary in Asia begins between Pakistan and Iran and cuts across Afghanistan to exclude only those eastern parts draining into the Indus. From Afghanistan to central China, it follows approximately the 3,000m contour such that the forested and other lower slopes draining into Pakistan, India, Myanmar, and China are excluded, whilst the alpine zone of the mountains is included, along with the Tibetan Plateau. As a result, Pakistan, India, Nepal, Myanmar, and the Chinese provinces of Yunnan and Szechuan are excluded, except for the alpine zones. Tibet is excluded except for the valley of the Tsangpo. In lowland China, the boundary is taken as latitude 35°N, corresponding, in part, with the Hwang-Ho. In Japan, it follows latitude 30°N so that Yakushima is the southernmost island included. In the Bering region, all territory of Russia is included, while all territory of the USA (e.g., St. Lawrence Island and the Aleutians) is excluded.

Hemprich's long-eared bat, *Otonycteris hemprichii*, is the single species of its genus occurring widely in the southern Palearctic.

I. Kuzmin

Number of species in the region

A total of 89 species are recorded from the Palaearctic Region. Of these, 24 are threatened – one Critically Endangered, five Endangered, and 18 Vulnerable. A total of 61 species are listed in the Lower Risk categories – 15 as Near Threatened, 46 as Least Concern, and four as Data Deficient. A full list of species is given at the end of this regional account.

Major threats to bats

Forests and woodlands are key sites for roosting and feeding. In the western Palaearctic much of the native forest has been lost through the impact of agriculture. Caves and mines are threatened by disturbance from human activities.

Threats to habitats and roosts

- **Forest and woodland** Deciduous forest is especially important for bats because of its diversity in both structure and insect fauna. Threats to such forests are many and varied. In Poland, pesticides are used that are considered too toxic for use in Western Europe. In Spain, woodlands are being lost through felling or the effects of fire. Woodland may also be affected by air and water pollution. In Romania, old forest is only found at higher altitudes following general deforestation for wood and paper. However, these mountain forests are very diverse and relatively unspoilt. Deforestation, especially of broad-leaved trees, is a serious threat in eastern Siberia.

Older trees tend to have more hollows and crevices that provide summer and winter roosting sites for bats. Forests are being lost or degraded through the removal of old trees and rotting wood. In general, improved management techniques can lead to the loss of old trees. Indeed, in some countries, such as Switzerland, trees with holes are systematically removed. Management techniques in many other countries, such as Germany, Spain, and Poland, involve the removal of such trees with consequent loss of roost sites. Recently, Poland has introduced a General Directorate of Forestry for the 'ecologisation' of forest management. This encourages an increase in the species diversity, more deciduous trees, and the retaining of old trees and fallen dead wood, and includes efforts for water retention and the preservation of small wetlands. The UK has a 'Veteran Tree' initiative to encourage the retention of older trees.

Semi-open woodland and parkland, especially with grazing animals, are important for a wide range of bat species. Again, intensification of agriculture and animal husbandry has often been at the expense of this habitat. Orchards are considered important habitat for bats in parts of Middle Europe (e.g., Germany and Switzerland) and threatened by loss through changes in land use. In contrast, vineyards are not widely considered important for bats. In the UK, orchards are generally subjected to very high levels of pesticide use.

The Taiga habitat in central Asia and especially the mixed broadleaf-coniferous areas of the Russian Far East are considered threatened by flooding for reservoirs and power plants, chemical plants, pollution, and general deforestation. Such problems affect particularly forest bats, such as *Eptesicus nilssonii*, *Plecotus auritus*, and *Myotis* species.

Species that rely heavily on forests as feeding habitats or that feed by gleaning are suffering through changes to forest and woodland habitat. In the most intensively cultivated areas, only species preferring open habitat (e.g., *Nyctalus*, *Pipistrellus*, *Vespertilio,* and *Eptesicus* species) are abundant. Gleaners (e.g., *Rhinolophus* species, *Myotis mystacinus*, *M. myotis, M. blythii, M. nattereri*, *M. bechsteinii*, and *Plecotus* species) are more rarely found.

Because of their preferred roosting habits, tree-dwelling bats are very difficult to study. Many species utilise trees as roosts, but there is little information on numbers that use such sites, what type of trees are preferred, or frequency of use. This lack of information threatens such species. In Cyprus, forest-dwelling species such as *Nyctalus noctula* and *Plecotus* species occur, but are rarely observed. Dense pine forests are restricted to the higher mountains, and because of the absence of woodpeckers on the island and intensive forestry, there are few available roosts for forest-dwelling species. In Ireland, areas of woodland in the vicinity of lesser horseshoe summer and winter roost sites are of special importance.

- **Wetlands** A range of wetland habitats are considered important in the Palaearctic Region. In some countries, for example Israel, springs, rivers, and pools are the major foraging habitat for bats. Rivers and their associated corridor habitats may be important as migration routes for bats. Riparian habitat is under threat in a number of countries. Marshlands are important as producers of insect biomass and hence important bat feeding habitat. In Poland such habitats are threatened by air and water pollution. In Spain, many rivers have been canalised or had associated riparian vegetation removed, and natural drought may exacerbate the loss of aquatic habitat. Many of the rivers are also polluted by agricultural pesticides and industrial wastes. This has reduced insect diversity and abundance. Similarly, in Portugal, watercourses and associated riparian vegetation in the dry southern area of the country are particularly important for bats. There are plans to build dams that would destroy large areas of this habitat. In Poland, swamps are threatened through draining. A rather unusual threat occurs in Cyprus where, since the 1950s, there have been annual anti-malarial campaigns against mosquitos involving spraying all waters with a petroleum-pesticide mixture. This is made all the more unusual since malaria has rarely, if ever, been recorded in Cyprus.
- **Cultural landscape areas** Areas where agriculture is carried out on a less intensive basis, such as Central and Eastern Europe, are important for bats because they provide a rich mosaic of habitats. Some such areas are being lost as farming techniques become more intensive and there is a greater use of agricultural pesticides. In some countries, such as Poland, the situation is made worse by the use of pesticides considered too toxic for use in Western Europe. There is sometimes illegal use of old stocks of DDT in Poland and probably other countries. However, in Romania, where the lowland plains remain subjected to long-standing intrinsic monocultural agriculture with heavy fertilisation, the plateau is re-developing smaller scale agriculture following the return of lands to local people who operate a diverse land management regimen more appropriate for bats.
- **Deserts** Deserts and semi-deserts of Central Asia are identified as threatened habitat. Cotton monoculture is the principal threat, with irrigation and the associated problem of water extraction, increased salts, and loss of associated vegetation (including drainage of large areas such as the Aral Sea). This is likely particularly to affect the arid-dwelling *Eptesicus* species (*E. bottae* and *E. bobrinskoi*).
- **Foothills and middle mountain ranges** In Russia, foothills and lower mountain regions are areas of concern for

bats. They contain many of the caves and mines that may be affected by disturbance. A similar situation exists in mountain regions of Israel. Deforestation continues, including illegal extraction from remnant forests in, for example, the Carpathians. There is little information on bat species at higher altitudes, especially in the States of the former USSR, and threats to their survival need to be more fully evaluated.

- **Pesticides and pollution** The widespread use of pesticides is still a serious environmental threat in most parts of Europe. While there have been distinct improvements both in the chemicals used and in their application, particularly in northwest Europe, changes are much slower in many Mediterranean or East European countries and the Commonwealth of Independent States. In the Canary Islands, intensive spraying was undertaken in the 1950s to control agricultural pests. High concentrations of pesticides are still used in agriculture and this may affect the endemic *Plecotus teneriffae* and *Pipistrellus maderensis*. In Morocco, regions south of the high Atlas are heavily sprayed with pesticides during locust migrations and the same occurs sometimes in parts of Spain. The use of such persistent anti-parasitic drugs as the avermectins in cattle may result in serious problems for bats that feed on the dung fauna of these animals. Radioactive and chemical pollution associated with antiquated technology and industry are considered widespread threats to bats in Russia.
- **Fire** Major fires, particularly in southern Europe, may damage local bat populations through effects on foraging habitat and insect prey.
- **Caves** Karstic areas throughout the Palaearctic Region are important to bats as they have natural caves that provide both summer and winter roost sites. France has a number of important winter hibernation sites, mostly for *Miniopterus schreibersii*, but also for *Rhinolophus ferrumequinum*, *R. euryale*, and *Myotis capaccinii*. Three sites have populations of more than 15,000 bats and one site has an estimated 70,000. France has eight globally threatened species, all of them Vulnerable. Caves are threatened by disturbance through caving and tourism, and by destruction through activities such as road building and mining. In some countries, caves are probably the most important roost sites. In Malta, for example, nine out of the 10 recorded species roost in caves, while in Israel, most microchiropteran bats use cave systems. The threats to caves revolve chiefly around disturbance. Some species that utilise cave systems, such as the horseshoe bats (*Rhinolophus* species), are especially sensitive to disturbance. Large caves are attractive both to speleologists and tourists. In Poland, most caves are not grilled and where grilles have been installed they are usually destroyed within a short space of time. This is affecting species, especially lesser horseshoe bats (*Rhinolophus hipposideros*), that are very sensitive to disturbance. In Cyprus, caves are used as store rooms or cattle shelters, and fires are lit in small caves by shepherds. The only known cave roost of a huge colony of *Miniopterus schreibersii* was visited by adventurous tourists. As a probable result of disturbance, the colony disappeared in 1989 or 1990. Teachers take school parties to the bat caves in Romania. Such internationally renowned caves are also frequently visited by speleologists at all times of year. Similarly, in Spain some caves with colonies of hundreds or thousands of cave-dwelling species (*Miniopterus schreibersii*, *Myotis myotis*, *M. blythii*) are threatened through excessive disturbance by uncontrolled visitors. A sample of 290 'important' caves in Spain demonstrated threats to all but 34 (12%). In Portugal, disturbance of underground roosts (both caves and mines) seems to be increasing and some, particularly mines, have had their entrances blocked. Caves in the Algarve area have been highlighted as particularly at risk. In Israel, caves were fumigated in an effort to reduce the populations of fruit bats that were implicated in the damage to commercial fruit orchards. Unfortunately, other species that shared caves with fruit bats suffered through these actions. This practice has been forbidden since 1989, but farmers still use it occasionally. Quarrying is identified as a threat from the UK to central Russia and, in some areas, the use of caves as weapons stores might render the sites unsuitable for bats.
- **Buildings** Buildings are of particular importance where there are few, if any, alternative roosts nearby. In Ireland, different types of buildings are important for different species. Large, old buildings are used by lesser horseshoe bats (*Rhinolophus hipposideros*). Stone buildings are of key importance for Natterer's bats (*Myotis nattereri*), while modern buildings are used by Leisler's bats (*Nyctalus leisleri*). Renovation of buildings in many countries can lead to the loss of roost sites. In Poland, for example, there is little information on what type of chemicals are used for the remedial treatment of timbers to kill wood-boring insects. There is some evidence of timber treatment operatives being poisoned by the chemicals currently in use. It is assumed that the treatments used are based on lindane or dieldrin, the use of which is already banned in a number of European countries. There is, at present, little money available for the restoration of historic buildings and, although less toxic chemicals are now available, they are mostly higher priced. Re-privatisation and renovation of old buildings in Russia are also threats to bats. In Spain, many historical buildings with bat colonies are restored and the bats excluded. In Switzerland, the number of large, undisturbed attics is declining because of the trend towards improved use of space in buildings and a change in style to an open roof situation; nevertheless, breeding colonies of *Myotis myotis* may be increasing

due to intensive conservation activity. In some countries, such as Lithuania, there is no specific legislation that protects bat roosts. Larger buildings, such as churches, are important throughout Europe, but have been a major source of conflict of interest. Such conflicts have been easier to resolve where bats are confined to the tower or steeple, but less easily resolved when bats occupy the body of the church.

The widespread occupation of buildings by bats (synanthropy) brings a range of threats including simple intolerance or a lack of understanding of their biology. While many countries can claim considerable success in educating the public to be more accepting of bats, many important roost sites continue to be lost. Occupancy of public buildings, notably churches, may be a particular problem since many such buildings are older and often house a higher proportion of rarer species. Throughout the Palaearctic Region, a very wide range of species are identified as at risk through intolerance of their occupancy of buildings. In many areas, such as Romania, where there is still a considerable amount of superstition associated with bats coupled with concerns about guano accumulation and a generally low level of respect for animals and the environment, their presence in buildings is mostly unwelcome.

- **Bridges** Bridges, particularly those made of stone, are important roost sites for a range of bat species. Maintenance work on bridges can involve the filling of any cracks or crevices which results in the loss of potential roosting sites for bats. In the worst cases, the whole bridge structure is sealed with liquid concrete.

Threats to higher taxa

- **Family Rhinolophidae** The family Rhinolophidae is represented in the Palaearctic Region by nine species of *Rhinolophus*. *R. nippon* is here included with *R. ferrumequinum*, but may be regarded as a separate species occurring to the east of Nepal (Thomas 1997). Three species (*R. euryale, R. hipposideros,* and *R. mehelyi*) are considered Vulnerable. The major threat to the family comes from disturbance to roost sites. Caves are key roosting sites for rhinolophids throughout the Palaearctic. In Spain, for example, *R. euryale* is fairly common in the east of Asturias, where it is mainly a cave-dweller. Its dependence on underground sites probably explains its rarity in the west of the region. Within caves, rhinolophids often roost in very visible situations, making them even more vulnerable to disturbance. In Hungary, *R. euryale* is a rare species found in mountainous regions. It breeds and hibernates in caves, usually forming mixed colonies with *Miniopterus schreibersii*. Breeding colonies contain between 50–200 adults. The number of undisturbed breeding and hibernating sites is falling due to increasing interest in recreational caving. Loss of feeding habitat has also been identified as a major threat in some countries (e.g., Germany, Spain, and Switzerland). This has frequently been the result of changes in agricultural practices. For example, in Switzerland the cultural landscape has been impoverished with a consequent decline in the quality of feeding areas, and this, coupled with a decline in roost sites (in this case undisturbed large attics) and an increase in tourism, has led to declines in populations of *Rhinolophus* species. Most rhinolophids are widely distributed in the Palaearctic, but dramatic declines and even extinctions have been recorded in some countries. For example, in the UK, the population decline of *R. ferrumequinum* is believed by some to be more than 90% over the past 100 years. As elsewhere, loss of roosts and decline in the quality of feeding habitat have been the major causes of decline. In Switzerland, *R. hipposideros* has suffered a drastic decline since 1940 and it has disappeared from The Netherlands and Luxembourg, although the population in the UK appears to be stable or even increasing (Schofield 1996). In other countries, some rhinolophids are now rarely recorded; for example, *R. blasii, R. euryale,* and *R. mehelyi* in Israel, *R. ferrumequinum* in Luxembourg, Ukraine, and Malta, and *R. hipposideros* in Kazakhstan.
- **Subfamily Murininae (Family Vespertilionidae)** The subfamily Murininae is represented in the Palaearctic Region by five species of *Murina*. Information on the status and distribution of these species is very limited. Most have rarely been caught. *M. leucogaster* is the species about which most is known. It has a wide distribution, but is considered common only in Tajikistan. In western Siberia, it is distributed in mountainous regions in the southeast and in the Altai Mountains. Few caves are known that contain more than 100 individuals. The species is probably limited by lack of suitable roosting sites. It is threatened by human disturbance. *M. ussuriensis* is only recorded from the Ussuri region, the Kurile Islands and Sakhalin in Russia, and from Korea. It is rarely caught and is considered Endangered.
- **Subfamily Miniopterinae (Family Vespertilionidae)** Only one member of the subfamily Miniopterinae, *Miniopterus schreibersii*, is found in the Palaearctic Region. This is probably the most widespread of all bat species and occurs from Africa, through Europe and Asia to Australia. It is, however, highly dependent on underground sites (especially caves) for breeding and hibernation. Declines have been recorded in countries throughout its range. In Austria it is considered endangered. It was formerly a breeding species, but is now only a migrant. In Bulgaria, it is recorded from caves all across the country, in some cases, in roosts of tens of thousands. There has, however, been evidence of steep declines in numbers at some roosts. In Hungary, *M. schreibersii* was once very common and abundant. It

has become rare because most large roosts have been lost. At the end of the 1980s, the largest colony in Hungary contained 2,500–3,000 bats, but there are now no colonies of that size. In Gibraltar, records of up to 5,000 in one site exist within the last 30 years – now the largest number is 150. This species is very sensitive to disturbance and the number of suitable undisturbed sites is continually decreasing. In the Slovak Republic, a rapid decline in population numbers has been recorded since 1989. This species has also become extinct in southwest Germany and the Ukraine. *M. schreibersii* is considered threatened in a number of countries or regions. It is considered endangered in Austria, Bulgaria, Israel, the Far East of Russia, and Switzerland; and considered vulnerable or potentially vulnerable in Cyprus, France, Portugal, Russia, Slovak Republic, Spain, Ukraine, and the Caucasus. It is listed as Lower Risk: Near Threatened, meaning that it has the potential to fall into the Vulnerable category if current pressures continue to operate. Recently, a collaborative international project has been set up in Central and East European countries to investigate the species and its conservation.

- **Genus *Barbastella* (Family Vespertilionidae)** The two species of *Barbastella* (*B. barbastellus* and *B. leucomelas*) both occur in the Palaearctic Region. Both species have a wide distribution, but *B. barbastellus* is considered Vulnerable. In many countries throughout its range, it is considered threatened. For example, it is considered endangered in Belgium, Germany, Luxembourg, and Switzerland, and is thought to be vulnerable or potentially vulnerable in France, Latvia, Lithuania, Poland, Russia, and Spain. There are thought to be fewer than 50 individuals in Belgium, while there have been less than 10 records in Bulgaria. In Luxembourg, there have only been two records in the last 50 years (in 1956 and 1992) and there has been no recorded breeding. In the south of Germany, there is a small winter population, but there is no information about the species' occurrence in summer. In Hungary, breeding populations are threatened by the loss of old forests. *B. barbastellus* occurs sporadically in montane regions in old forests that have caves and mines nearby. The largest hibernacula contain 300–500 bats. While the hibernating bats themselves are relatively safe, threats to the forests affect their overall status. In Poland, up to 1,400 hibernating *B. barbastellus* have been recorded from Nietoperek Bat Reserve and there has been a trend of increasing numbers in other major hibernation sites in Poland since the 1980s (G. Lesinski *pers. comm.*). It has, however, been suggested that ringing studies should be stopped because of this species' sensitivity to disturbance. Similarly, in the Slovak Republic, many hibernation sites suffer from disturbance. Little is recorded of the eastern barbastelle (*B. leucomelas*); in some areas there is concern about disturbance in winter, but generally the species is thought to be safe.

Threats to geographical areas

- **Central and eastern Europe** In many areas of central and eastern Europe, agriculture is currently undertaken in a less intensive way than is prevalent in much of western Europe. Thus, farmland areas tend to have higher bat diversities than their western counterparts. However, there is a trend towards increased efficiency in agricultural practices, which could result in dramatic changes to landscape structure in these areas. Such cultural landscape habitats should be considered both in terms of biodiversity and their importance for conservation. Poland provides a good example of the kinds of problems that affect many countries in central and eastern Europe. The Krakow-Czestochowa Upland in central Poland is a karst area with around 300 known caves important for hibernating bats. Tourist and speleological interest in these caves has increased during the last decade, and this is having an impact on bats. As far as is known, only two of the 300 caves are grilled. There are other factors contributing to a decline in bat populations in that area including deforestation and destruction of vegetation along rivers and streams. The Sudetan Mountains area in southwestern Poland is threatened by air pollution and associated acid rain from the former East Germany. It is considered by the Polish Ministry of Nature Protection as "an area specifically ecologically endangered". Almost all the coniferous woodland in that area has been destroyed.
- **Mediterranean area** The Mediterranean countries of Europe are a centre of bat diversity in the Palaearctic Region. Many of these countries contain important cave sites for bats that are threatened by disturbance. In Israel, the Mediterranean Zone is considered to be the most vulnerable since it is the most populated, and thus the most disturbed area of the country. Species that rely on Mediterranean forests and open landscapes are decreasing in numbers, while those that have adapted to the human environment, such as *Tadarida teniotis*, are increasing. Similarly, in Malta, bats are threatened through increasing urbanisation coupled with tourist development schemes. In Cyprus, the entire coastal area (both Greek and Turkish parts) is threatened by building activities and touristic development. This mainly affects rich maquis vegetation, which is the preferred hunting habitat for many bat species. Natural wetlands are in danger of drying out because of the increasing demands for drinking water along the coastal area. Creeks and rivers are being canalised, and dams and reservoirs created.
- **Central Asia** The countries of central Asia have a high level of biodiversity, but also have rapidly developing or well-developed industry and agriculture. Of particular

concern are areas such as northern Tian-Shian, Altai, Dzungharia, and deserts and semideserts of central, south, and southeast Kazakhstan. In the Caucasus, Turkmenistan, Kyrgyzstan, and Tajikistan, there are many large and easily accessible caves and abandoned mines. Thus, bats using such sites may be under severe threat. The direct and indirect effects of war are considered a considerable threat to many bats.

- **Siberia** In the Russian Far East, cave sites are used by a wide variety of species including *Myotis daubentonii*, *M. brandtii*, *M. macrodactylus*, *M. ikonnikovi*, *M. nattereri*, *Plecotus auritus*, *Eptesicus nilssonii*, and *Murina leucogaster*. In western Siberia, there are only a few sites where large numbers of bats (>100) accumulate. Such sites are threatened by tourism and speleologists. Deforestation and pollution are growing threats in eastern Siberia.
- **Lake Baikal** The area around Lake Baikal is of international importance and is less polluted, with many habitats remaining in a reasonably pristine condition. International collaboration would be valuable to set up comparative research in this area. There are caves within this area that form the only winter roost sites available to some bats. Threats include urbanisation and associated pollution near Baikalsk town on the southern bank of Lake Baikal, and in the valley of the Angara River.
- **Azores, Madeira, and the Canary Islands** The bat populations of all these small islands, including endemic species or subspecies, are fragile due to the small range. Habitat changes and use of pesticides may be affecting these small populations. However, *Nyctalus azoreum*, endemic to the Azores, is relatively abundant.
- **Morocco** In Morocco, problems are caused because areas south of the High Atlas are heavily sprayed with pesticides during locust migrations. Also, most of the major caves used by bats in the 1950s have been abandoned, as they are frequently used by shepherds as places to light fires. Bat biodiversity remains high on the southern half of the High Atlas and Anti-Atlas Mountains where Palaearctic species meet Saharan species. The northern plains are threatened by deforestation and intensive agriculture.

Other issues

The principal concerns raised here are 1) lack of adequate legislation or its implementation, and 2) educational needs, both for the general public and for authorities or professions whose activities affect bats, their roosts, or foraging activity. In many areas, concerned individuals or groups lack the resources to develop the necessary studies or conservation activity. At least most areas now have well-developed ornithological conservation groups and most of these are willing to cooperate on the conservation of other fauna.

Rabies

A recent increase in the identification of rabies-related viruses in bats in the Palaearctic, particularly western Europe, poses potential problems for the bats' image. However, the recognition of these viruses as separate from the terrestrial rabies virus and the very low public health risk, as well as well-formulated public education programmes in areas where the occurrence has been identified for the first time, has resulted in relatively minor public reaction against bats. European Bat Lyssavirus 1 is mainly associated with *Eptesicus serotinus* and EBL2 with *Myotis daubentonii* and *M. dasycneme*; an unallocated strain has been isolated from *M. blythii* in Russia.

Street lighting

In many countries, street lights are important feeding areas for bats. The type of lighting can be of particular importance – white, mercury vapour lights attract more insects than yellow, sodium lights. While street lights are widely used by bats further south, they have not been identified as significant for conservation. Their significance further north is conjectural. Areas where street lights are of importance to bats may provide good opportunities for educational campaigns. While they may be of benefit to certain aerial hawking species (*Pipistrellus*, *Eptesicus*, and *Nyctalus* species), they may be a disadvantage to bats, particularly gleaning species that avoid lit areas (*Rhinolophus*, *Myotis*, and *Plecotus* species).

Linear landscape elements

Surveys in the UK and The Netherlands have indicated that the continuity of linear landscape elements, such as hedges and tree lines, are important for bats both during feeding and larger-scale movements. It is likely that removal of these features will seriously affect bat populations.

Lack of knowledge

Bats have been studied unevenly within the Palaearctic Region. This means that no single species is known from its entire range. There is almost no data on viable population levels. The status of some species in certain regions that have not been well studied is guesswork. For example, in Slovenia, horseshoe bats (*Rhinolophus* species) are well represented in museum collections due to their highly visible roosting behaviour and their preference for caves. Consequently, *Rhinolophus ferrumequinum* and *R. hipposideros* were thought to be common in Slovenia, while *Pipistrellus pipistrellus* (represented by only one or two specimens in collections) was thought to be rare. Several years ago, *Myotis bechsteinii* was recorded for the first time in Slovenia when the use of mist nets was developed; by 1994, it appeared that this species might even be common in areas of the High Dinaric Karst.

In Spain, changes in population sizes for all bat species are unknown because there is no historical data. Distribution ranges for species for which only scattered or single records are available, such as *Nyctalus noctula*, *N. lasiopterus*, and *Pipistrellus nathusii*, are not well known.

Israel identifies lack of knowledge about the biology of most bat species in the area as one of the major threats since this prevents the authorities from directing conservation efforts in an appropriate way. Similarly, in Latvia, there are no available data to establish the conservation status of most species in wide areas of their distribution range.

While there is extensive literature on the feeding habits of bats, there is little on the specific foraging requirements of bats and the extent to which they adapt to changes in landscape. This lack of information is particularly relevant in countries in central and eastern Europe, where marked changes in the overall landscape are taking place.

There is a need for more information on the patterns of migration of bat species in the Palaearctic Region. More information is required on the key migration routes and the areas used by bats as stopping-off or resting places. Such studies would also help to identify more clearly the key winter hibernation sites for bats so that steps can be taken to protect them. This is being addressed under the Agreement on the Conservation of Bats in Europe (Bonn Convention).

There are still some uncertainties about the systematic position of some taxa.

Key areas for bat biodiversity

Hotspots at a generic level

Centres of diversity at the generic level were assessed using a WORLDMAP analysis (see Chapter 5.3 for further details). This shows a surprisingly erratic pattern (Map 34), but with the expected increased diversity towards the south. Those southern grid-cell areas of low generic

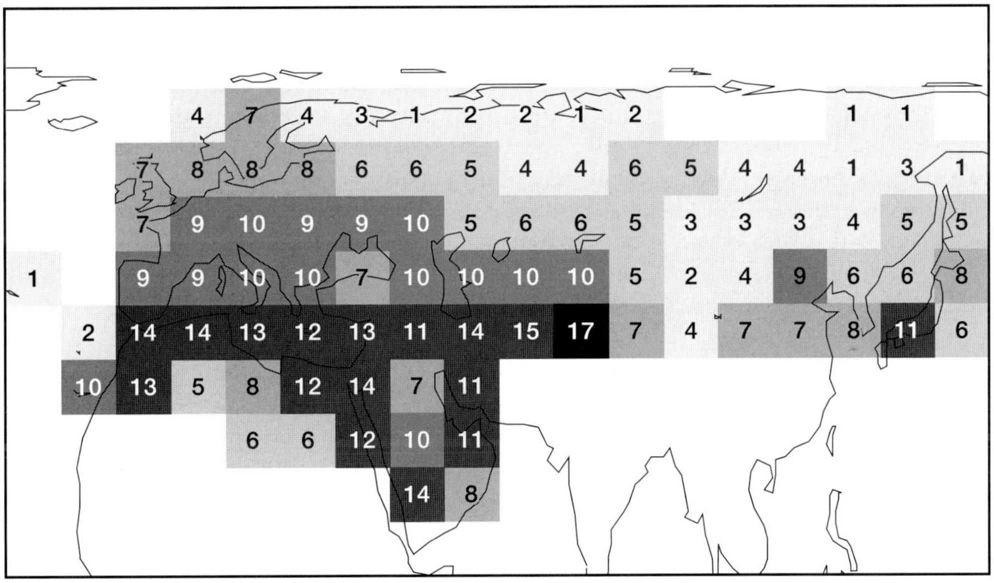

Map 34. Generic richness per grid-cell area for genera occurring in the Palaearctic Region.
The numbers in the squares represent the number of genera per unit area.

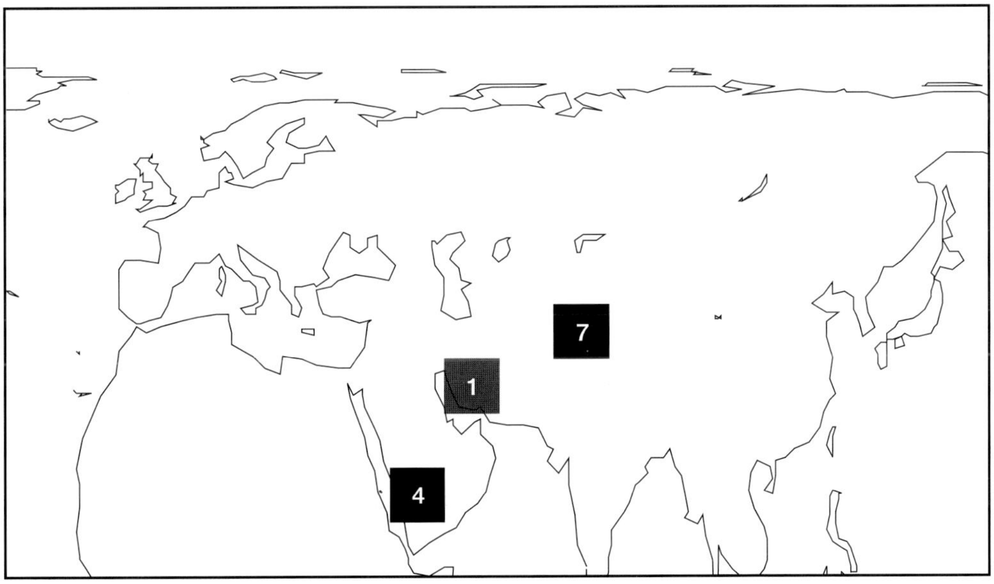

Map 35. Minimum set of grid-cell areas required to maintain all genera occurring in the Palaearctic Region.
The minimum number of squares required to conserve all genera is three. The numbers in the squares represent the number of genera uniquely contributing to this minimum set.

diversity probably consist of large areas of relatively inhospitable territory for bats. The removal of the principally tropical families represented in the fauna is unlikely to make a major difference to the pattern, as can be seen from the similarity of this map to that given just for Vespertilionidae (Map 20). The minimum set of grid-cell areas required to maintain all genera is three (Map 35), two of which contain elements that are unique for the region.

Slovakia

Slovakia has extensive areas of karst that provide important hibernacula for bats; more than 20 species have been recorded. The Slovensky kras karst area is the largest in Central Europe. An extensive system of mines in the east of the country (Dubnicke Mines, Slanske Urchy Hills) also provide important hibernation sites. Six globally threatened species are recorded from Slovakia, all of them Vulnerable.

Poland

One of the most important winter hibernation sites in northern Europe, Nietoperek in western Poland, is used by around 30,000 bats of 11 species. There are also a series of forts, tunnels, and other underground structures throughout Poland, caves in central Poland, and mines in Lower Silesia that are used by a variety of bats. Five globally threatened species are recorded from Poland, all of them Vulnerable.

Portugal

A range of underground sites are used as both breeding and hibernation sites by 13 species, including four *Rhinolophus*. One site, a natural cave, has the largest known breeding colony of *Miniopterus schreibersii*. Another site, again a natural cave, is used by 10 species during the breeding season. Eight globally threatened species are recorded from Portugal, all of them Vulnerable.

Caucasus

This is an important area as it is on the boundary between European and Asian bat faunas. It encompasses six countries, namely Armenia, Azerbaijan, Georgia, Iran, Turkey, and Russia. There are a wide variety of habitats, including broadleaf and coniferous forests, montane steppe, woodlands, subalpine and alpine meadows, and semidesert. Armenia has six globally threatened species, one Endangered and five Vulnerable. Georgia and Azerbaijan have six globally threatened species, all of them Vulnerable. Threatened species listings for the other countries are complicated by the fact that only a portion of the country falls within the Caucasus region.

Recommendations

Europe has a number of international treaties that include consideration of bats. These include the Agreement on the Conservation of Bats in Europe (Bonn Convention), EEC Habitats and Species Directive, Convention on the Conservation of European Wildlife and Natural Habitats (Bern Convention), and the Pan-European Biological and Landscape Diversity Strategy. To a varying extent, these extend to nation states of the former Soviet Union. The obligations, policies, and recommendations/resolutions of these treaties should be fully implemented by party range states and can be adopted by others. The Agreement on the Conservation of Bats in Europe has a Conservation Management Plan for the development of actions.

The following recommendations are based upon information provided by the contributors to this section. They include both general recommendations applicable to the whole area, as well as specific ones relating to particular species, areas, or habitats.

Habitats

Identified habitats of particular concern include deciduous forest, particularly in the Mediterranean area, taiga, riparian forest, wetlands, small-scale agriculture and associated cultural landscapes with continuity of landscape elements, semi-open parkland, karstic areas, and deserts. Concerns include the effects of a wide range of development and land management practices, particularly in those areas currently undergoing rapid changes. Additionally, fire in parts of the Mediterranean region is considered a threat. Large areas of monoculture (e.g., cotton) have affected areas of Central Asia.

Recommendations:

- consider bats alongside the wide range of other conservation concerns in the management and development of habitat important to bats, through activities directed by national and international treaties in collaboration with non-treaty range states where required;
- conduct research on specificity of bat feeding habits and how bats adapt to changes in landscape;
- consider the importance of cultural landscapes in conservation planning;
- assess threats to key wetland habitats and protect key sites where appropriate;
- assess threats to desert ecosystems and implement management regimens where appropriate;
- assess importance of linear landscape elements for bats in all areas of the region.

Roost types

While older trees and underground habitats still provide key roost sites, many bat species are heavily reliant on artificial structures, such as buildings and /bridges.

Recommendations:

- ensure policies that protect roost sites for bats take special account of their reliance on artificial structures.
- identify and protect key areas of karst;
- identify and protect key cave roosts;
- assess threats to cave sites from quarrying activities;

- assess threats to bats from timber treatment chemicals;
- assess importance of churches to bats;
- assess importance of bridges for bats;
- assess use of trees by bats.

Geographical areas

Areas of importance for bat biodiversity include the Caucasus, eastern and Mediterranean Europe (particularly the Balkans), Central Asia, west Siberia, and perhaps southwest China.

Recommendations:

- undertake further research to identify centres of biodiversity at the species level and develop conservation initiatives for those areas as appropriate;
- assess status of high-altitude species in Russia and the former Soviet republics;
- assess status of species in foothills and middle mountain ranges in Russia;
- assess status of species in the taiga region;
- develop conservation plan for bats in the Mediterranean region;
- assess status of bats in the Caucasus, and identify and protect key sites;
- survey cave sites in the Russian Far East and protect key roosts;
- develop cooperative international research programme in the Lake Baikal region;
- develop conservation plan for the Atlantic Islands.

Taxa

Taxa that are particularly at risk or of concern include the family Rhinolophidae, subfamilies Murininae and Miniopterinae, genus *Barbastella,* and forest-dwelling/gleaning species. Individual species are highlighted in the European treaties.

Recommendations:

- support current initiatives for the conservation of bats in Europe and ensure the issues they attempt to address recognized elsewhere in the Palaearctic. Action should include particular attention to the higher taxa identified and to individual species at risk, but should not forget the wider habitat needs to maintain other species at a favourable conservation status;
- identify gaps in knowledge of distribution of species and conduct survey work where necessary;
- assess status and distribution of *Murina* species;
- identify and protect key roosts of *Miniopterus schreibersii;*
- assess status of rhinolophid species, and identify and protect key roost sites;
- assess status of *Barbastella* species, and identify and protect key roost sites;
- assess possible impact of ringing studies on populations of *Barbastella;*
- assess threats to forest dwellers and gleaning bats.

Miscellaneous

Recommendations:

- study migration patterns of Palaearctic species;
- educate land managers about the importance of trees for bats;
- develop educational programmes where street lights are thought to be of importance to bats;
  develop educational programmes where there are conflicts between humans and bats because of use of buildings by bats;
- develop educational programmes about rabies and bats where these are required.

Checklist of Palaearctic bats

A total of 80 species are recorded from the Palaearctic Region. The full list is given below.

Species	Status
FAMILY RHINOPOMATIDAE	
Rhinopoma	
Rhinopoma hardwickei Gray 1831	LR: lc
Rhinopoma microphyllum (Brünnich 1782)	LR: lc
Rhinopoma muscatellum Thomas 1903	LR: lc
FAMILY EMBALLONURIDAE	
Coleura	
Coleura afra (Peters 1852)	LR: lc
Taphozous	
Taphozous nudiventris Cretzschmar 1830	LR: lc
Taphozous perforatus E. Geoffroy 1818	LR: lc
FAMILY NYCTERIDAE	
Nycteris	
Nycteris thebaica E. Geoffroy 1818	LR: lc
FAMILY HIPPOSIDERIDAE	
Asellia	
Asellia tridens (E. Geoffroy 1813)	LR: lc
Hipposideros	
Hipposideros caffer (Sundevall 1846)	LR: lc
Hipposideros megalotis (Heuglin 1862)	LR: nt
Triaenops	
Triaenops persicus Dobson 1871	LR: lc
FAMILY RHINOLOPHIDAE	
Rhinolophus	
Rhinolophus blasii Peters 1866	LR: nt
Rhinolophus bocharicus Kastschenko and Akimov 1917	LR: lc
Rhinolophus clivosus Cretzschmar 1828	LR: lc
Rhinolophus cornutus Temminck 1835	LR: nt

Species	Status
Rhinolophus euryale Blasius 1853	VU: A2c
Rhinolophus ferrumequinum (Schreber 1774)	LR: nt
Rhinolophus hipposideros (Bechstein 1800)	VU: A2c
Rhinolophus lepidus Blyth 1844	LR: lc
Rhinolophus mehelyi Matschie 1901	VU: A2c
FAMILY VESPERTILIONIDAE	
Subfamily Vespertilioninae	
Barbastella	
Barbastella barbastellus (Schreber 1774)	VU: A2c
Barbastella leucomelas (Cretzschmar 1826)	LR: lc
Eptesicus	
Eptesicus bobrinskoi Kuzyakin 1935	LR: lc
Eptesicus bottae (Peters 1869)	LR: lc
Eptesicus gobiensis Bobrinsky 1926	LR: lc
Eptesicus kobayashii Mori 1928	DD
Eptesicus nasutus (Dobson 1877)	VU: A2c
Eptesicus nilssonii (Keyserling and Blasius 1839)	LR: lc
Eptesicus serotinus Schreber 1774	LR: lc
Myotis	
Myotis abei Yoshikura 1944	DD
Myotis bechsteinii (Kuhl 1817)	VU: A2c
Myotis blythii (Tomes 1857)	LR: lc
Myotis bocagei (Peters 1870)	LR: lc
Myotis bombinus Thomas 1906	LR: nt
Myotis brandtii (Eversmann 1845)	LR: lc
Myotis capaccinii (Bonaparte 1837)	VU: A2c
Myotis dasycneme (Boie 1825)	VU: A2c
Myotis daubentonii (Kuhl 1817)	LR: lc
Myotis emarginatus (E.Geoffroy 1806)	VU: A2c
Myotis formosus (Hodgson 1835)	LR: lc
Myotis frater G. M. Allen 1923	LR: nt
Myotis hosonoi Imaizumi 1954	VU: A2c, B1 + 2c
Myotis ikonnikovi Ognev 1912	LR: lc
Myotis macrodactylus (Temminck 1840)	LR: lc
Myotis myotis (Borkhausen 1797)	LR: nt
Myotis mystacinus (Kuhl 1817)	LR: lc
Myotis nattereri (Kuhl 1817)	LR: lc
Myotis ozensis Imaizumi 1954	EN: A2c, B1 + 2c
Myotis pequinius Thomas 1908	LR: nt
Myotis pruinosus Yoshiyuki 1971	EN: B1 + 2c
Myotis ricketti (Thomas 1894)	LR: nt
Myotis schaubi Kormos 1934	EN: B1 + 2c, C2a, D
Myotis yanbarensis Maeda and Matsumara 1998	DD
Myotis yesoensis Yoshiyuki 1984	VU: A2c
Nyctalus	
Nyctalus aviator (Thomas 1911)	LR: nt
Nyctalus azoreum (Thomas 1901)	VU: A2c, B1 + 2c
Nyctalus lasiopterus (Schreber 1780)	LR: nt
Nyctalus leisleri (Kuhl 1817)	LR: nt
Nyctalus noctula (Schreber 1774)	LR: lc
Nycticeinops	
Nycticenops schlieffeni (Peters 1859)	LR: lc
Otonycteris	
Otonycteris hemprichii Peters 1859	LR: lc
Pipistrellus	
Pipistrellus abramus (Temminck 1840)	LR: lc
Pipistrellus aegyptius (Fischer 1829)	LR: lc
Pipistrellus arabicus Harrison 1979	VU: D2
Pipistrellus ariel Thomas 1904	VU: D2
Pipistrellus bodenheimeri Harrison 1960	LR: nt
Pipistrellus endoi Imaizumi1959	EN: B1 + 2c
Pipistrellus kuhlii (Kuhl 1817)	LR: lc
Pipistrellus maderensis (Dobson 1878)	VU: A2c, B1 + 2c
Pipistrellus nathusii (Keyserling and Blasius 1839)	LR: lc
Pipistrellus pipistrellus (Schreber 1774)	LR: lc
Pipistrellus rueppelli (Fischer 1829)	LR: lc
Pipistrellus savii (Bonaparte 1837)	LR: lc
Plecotus	
Plecotus auritus (Linnaeus 1758)	LR: lc
Plecotus austriacus (Fischer 1829)	LR: lc
Plecotus taivanus Yoshiyuki 1991	VU: A2c
Plecotus teneriffae Barret-Hamilton 1907	VU: A2c, D2
Vespertilio	
Vespertilio murinus Linnaeus 1758	LR: lc
Vespertilio superans Thomas 1899	LR: lc
Subfamily Murininae	
Murina	
Murina fusca Sowerby 1922	DD
Murina leucogaster Milne-Edwards 1872	LR: lc
Murina silvatica Yoshiyuki 1983	LR: nt
Murina tenebrosa Yoshiyuki 1970	CR: B1 + 2c, D
Murina ussuriensis Ognev 1913	EN: A2c
Subfamily Miniopterinae	
Miniopterus	
Miniopterus schreibersii (Kuhl 1817)	LR: nt
FAMILY MOLOSSIDAE	
Mops	
Mops midas (Sundevall 1843)	LR: lc
Otomops	
Otomops martiensseni (Matschie 1897)	VU: A2c
Tadarida	
Tadarida aegyptiaca (E. Geoffroy 1818)	LR: lc
Tadarida teniotis (Rafinesque 1814)	LR: lc

Table 8 shows the number of IUCN Red List species recorded from each country together with information on numbers of endemics and the size of the total bat fauna.

Key references

The following is a list of important references relating to bats in the Palaearctic Region. It is by no means an exhaustive list and concentrates mainly on distributional studies at a national or regional level.

Ablentsev, V.I. and Pidoplichko, I.G. 1956. *[Fauna of Ukraine, Volume 1, Part 1: Insectivores and bats]* Kiev. [in Ukrainian]

Allen, G.M. 1938–40. *The mammals of China and Mongolia.* Natural History of Central Asia (ed. W. Granger). Central Asiatic Expeditions of the American Museum of Natural History, New York.

Aulagnier, S. and Thevenot, M. 1986. *Catalogue des mammifères sauvages du Maroc.* Institut Scientifique Charia Ibn Batouta BP, Rabat.

Table 8. Number of IUCN Red List species for countries in the Palaearctic Region.
The table also includes information on numbers of endemics and the estimated size of the bat fauna. For information on the compilation of the figures for size of faunas see Chapter 6. Full lists of IUCN Red List species per country are given in the same Chapter. **Countries not listed here do not have a recorded bat fauna.** Where a country overlaps more than one region, the fauna for the whole country is included.

	IUCN RED LIST SPECIES								ENDEMICS	TOTAL NO. OF SPECIES		
Country	**CR**	**EN**	**VU**	**LRcd**	**LRnt**	**EX**	**DD**	***Total***	***Total***	**Mega**	**Micro**	***Total***
Afghanistan	0	0	5	0	6	0	0	11	0	0	37	37
Albania	0	0	2	0	4	0	0	6	0	0	19	19
Algeria	0	0	4	0	4	0	0	8	0	0	26	26
Andorra	0	0	2	0	2	0	0	4	0	0	11	11
Armenia	0	1	5	0	5	0	0	11	0	0	24	24
Austria	0	0	4	0	4	0	0	8	0	0	24	24
Azerbaijan	0	0	6	0	5	0	0	11	0	0	27	27
Bahrain	0	0	0	0	0	0	0	0	0	0	4	4
Belarus	0	0	3	0	3	0	0	6	0	0	17	17
Belgium	0	0	5	0	3	0	0	8	0	0	18	18
Bosnia-Herzegovina	0	0	7	0	4	0	0	11	0	0	16	16
Bulgaria	0	0	7	0	6	0	0	13	0	0	29	29
China	0	0	2	0	21	0	2	25	6	8	82	90
Croatia	0	0	7	0	4	0	0	11	0	0	26	26
Cyprus	0	0	1	0	3	0	0	4	0	1	15	16
Czech Republic	0	0	5	0	3	0	0	8	0	0	21	21
Denmark	0	0	2	0	0	0	0	2	0	0	13	13
Egypt	0	0	4	0	1	0	0	5	0	1	21	22
Estonia	0	0	1	0	0	0	0	1	0	0	11	11
Finland	0	0	0	0	0	0	0	0	0	0	8	8
France	0	0	8	0	5	0	0	13	0	0	29	29
Georgia	0	0	6	0	4	0	0	10	0	0	25	25
Germany	0	0	5	0	4	0	0	9	0	0	22	22
Gibraltar	0	0	0	0	1	0	0	1	0	0	4	4
Greece	0	0	5	0	6	0	0	11	0	0	28	28
Hungary	0	1	6	0	5	0	0	12	0	0	26	26
Iceland (1)	0	0	0	0	0	0	0	0	0	0	0	0
Iran	0	1	7	0	5	0	0	13	0	1	37	38
Iraq	0	0	5	0	2	0	0	7	0	0	19	19
Ireland	0	0	1	0	1	0	0	2	0	0	7	7
Israel	0	0	6	0	5	0	0	11	0	1	32	33
Italy	0	0	7	0	6	0	0	13	0	0	30	30
Japan	1	5	3	0	7	1	2	19	12	3	36	39
Jordan	0	0	5	0	4	0	0	9	0	0	14	14
Kazakhstan	0	0	3	0	3	0	0	6	0	0	27	27
Kuwait	0	0	0	0	0	0	0	0	0	0	1	1
Kyrgyzstan	0	0	2	0	1	0	0	3	0	0	16	16
Latvia	0	0	2	0	1	0	0	3	0	0	15	15
Lebanon	0	0	4	0	3	0	0	7	0	1	15	16
Libya	0	0	1	0	2	0	0	3	0	0	10	10
Liechtenstein	0	0	3	0	3	0	0	6	0	0	18	18
Lithuania	0	0	2	0	1	0	0	3	0	0	17	17
Luxembourg	0	0	3	0	3	0	0	6	0	0	17	17
Macedonia	0	0	7	0	4	0	0	11	0	0	23	23
Mali	0	0	0	0	3	0	0	3	0	3	15	18
Malta	0	0	1	0	3	0	0	4	0	0	10	10
Mauritania	0	0	0	0	0	0	0	0	0	0	13	13
Moldova	0	0	4	0	3	0	0	7	0	0	20	20
Monaco	0	0	0	0	0	0	0	0	0	0	5	5
Mongolia	0	0	0	0	0	0	0	0	0	0	12	12
Morocco	0	0	6	0	4	0	0	10	0	0	26	26
The Netherlands	0	0	4	0	3	0	0	7	0	0	19	19
North Korea	0	1	0	0	6	0	1	8	0	0	21	21
Norway	0	0	1	0	0	0	0	1	0	0	11	11
Oman	0	0	3	0	2	0	0	5	1	1	16	17
Poland	0	0	5	0	3	0	0	8	0	0	20	20
Portugal	0	0	8	0	5	0	0	13	1	0	24	24
Qatar	0	0	0	0	0	0	0	0	0	0	2	2
Romania	0	0	7	0	6	0	0	13	0	0	25	25

Table 8 ... continued. Number of IUCN Red List species for countries in the Palaearctic Region.

Country	IUCN RED LIST SPECIES CR	EN	VU	LRcd	LRnt	EX	DD	Total	ENDEMICS Total	TOTAL NO. OF SPECIES Mega	Micro	Total
Russia	0	1	8	0	7	0	1	17	1	0	41	41
San Marino	0	0	1	0	2	0	0	3	0	0	6	6
Saudi Arabia	0	0	4	0	4	0	0	8	0	2	21	23
Slovakia	0	0	6	0	5	0	0	11	0	0	24	24
Slovenia	0	0	7	0	5	0	0	12	0	0	27	27
South Korea	0	1	0	0	4	0	1	6	0	0	16	16
Spain	0	0	9	0	5	0	0	14	1	0	27	27
Sweden	0	0	3	0	0	0	0	3	0	0	16	16
Switzerland	0	0	4	0	5	0	0	9	0	0	26	26
Syria	0	0	1	0	4	0	0	5	0	1	10	11
Taiwan	0	0	2	0	2	0	1	5	4	0	20	20
Tajikistan	0	0	2	0	3	0	0	5	0	0	19	19
Tunisia	0	0	4	0	3	0	0	7	0	0	12	12
Turkey	0	0	7	0	6	0	0	13	0	1	30	31
Turkmenistan	0	0	3	0	3	0	0	6	0	0	21	21
Ukraine	0	0	5	0	4	0	0	9	0	0	24	24
United Arab Emirates	0	0	0	0	0	0	0	0	0	0	6	6
United Kingdom	0	0	3	0	3	0	0	6	0	0	16	16
Uzbekistan	0	0	3	0	4	0	0	7	0	0	21	21
Vatican City (2)	-	-	-	-	-	-	-	-	-	-	-	-
Yemen	0	0	2	0	3	0	0	5	0	2	22	24
Yugoslavia	0	0	8	0	5	0	0	13	0	0	26	26

Notes:
1. The only bats recorded from Iceland are vagrants.
2. As far as the authors are aware, there is no information on bats in the Vatican City.

Bate, D. 1905. On the mammals of Crete. *Proceedings of the Zoological Society of London*, 1905 (2), 315–323.

Benda, P. and Horacek, I. 1998. Bats (Mammalia: Chiroptera) of the Eastern Mediterranean. Part 1. Review of distribution and taxonomy of bats in Turkey. *Acta Societatis Zoologicae Bohemoslovenicae*, 62, 255–313.

Benzal, J. and De Paz, O. 1991. *Los murcielagos de España y Portugal.* ICONA, Spain.

Bolkay, S.J. 1926. Additions to the mammalian fauna of the Balkan peninsula. *Glasnik Zemaljskog Museja u Bosni i Hercegovini*, 38, 159–179.

Boye, P., Pott-Dorfer, B., Dorfer, K., and Demetropoulos A. 1990. New records of bats (Chiroptera) from Cyprus and notes on their biology. *Myotis*, 28, 93–100.

Corbet, G.B. 1978. *The mammals of the Palaearctic Region: A taxonomic review.* British Museum (Natural History), London and Cornell University Press, Ithaca.

Corbet, G.B. and Harris, S. (eds.) 1990. *The handbook of British mammals*, Third edition. Blackwell Science, Oxford.

Dobrosi, D. 1995. *A handbook for the conservation of bats in Hungary.* Hungarian Bat Research Society, Hungary.

Ellerman, J.R. and Morrison-Scott, T.C.S., 1966. *Checklist of Palaearctic and Indian mammals 1758–1946,* Second edition. British Museum (Natural History), London.

Fornasari, L., Violani, C., and Zava, B. 1997. *I Chirotteri Italiani.* Mediterraneo Guide naturalistiche a cura di Silvano Riggeo No. 5. L'EPOS, Palermo.

Gromov, I.M. and Baranova, G. 1981. *[Catalogue of mammals of the USSR: Pliocene to the present day]* Akademia Nauk SSSR, Leningrad. [in Russian]

Hanak, V., Benda, P., and Hanzal, V. 1995. Review of bat distribution in the Czech Republic. *Bulletin CESON*, 5, 3–15.

Harris, S., Morris, P., Wray, S., and Yalden, D. 1995. *A review of British mammals: Population estimates and conservation status of British mammals other than cetaceans.* Joint Nature Conservation Committee, Peterborough.

Harrison, D.L. and Bates, P.J.J. 1991. *The mammals of Arabia,* Second edition. Harrison Zoological Museum, Sevenoaks.

Hutson, A.M. 1993. *Action plan for the conservation of bats in the United Kingdom.* The Bat Conservation Trust, London.

Iliopoulou-Georgoudaki, J. 1977. *Systimatiki meleti kai geografiki exaplosi to Chiropteron tis Ellados [Systematic study and geographic distribution of the Chiroptera of Greece].* PhD thesis, University of Patras, Patras. [in Greek]

Isaksen, K., Syvertsen, P.O., van der Kooij, J., and Rinden, H. (eds.) 1998. Truete pattedye i Norge: Faktaark og forslag til rodliste. *Norsk Zoologisk Forening Rapport*, 5, 1–182.

Kahman, H. 1964. Contribution à l'études des Mammifères du Peloponnese. *Mammalia*, 28 (1), 109–136.

Karnellis, A. and Hatzissarantos, Ch. 1963. Ta Thilastika tis Ellados [The Mammals of Greece]. *To Vuno*, 230, 6–21.

Koopman, K.F. and Gudmundsson, F. 1966. Bats in Iceland. *American Museum Novitates*, 2262, 1–6.

Kowalski, K. and Rzebik-Kowalska, B. 1991. *Mammals of Algeria.* Zaklad Narodowy Imienia Ossolinskich Wydawnictwo Polskiej Akademii Nauk Wroclaw.

Krystufek, B. 1991. *Sesalei Slovenije [Mammals of Slovenia].* Prirodoslovni musej Slovenije, Ljubljana.

Kumerloeve, H. 1976. Die Säugetiere (Mammalia) Syriens und des Libanon. *Veröffentlichungen der Zoologischen Staatssammlung München*, 18, 159–225.

Kuzyakin, A.P. 1944. *In: Opredelitel' mlekopitayushchikh SSSR [The key to the mammals of the USSR]*, (eds. N.A. Bobrinskii, N.A., B.A. Kuznetzov, and A.P. Kuzyakin). Gosudarstvennoe Izdarelstvo [Government Publishing Office] "Sovietskaya Nauka", Moscow. [in Russian]

Kuzyakin, A.P. 1950. *Letucie Myshi (Sistematika, obraz zhizni I pol'za dlya sel'skogo I lesnogho khozyaistva). [Bats (Systematics, life history and utility for agriculture andforestry)].* Gosudarstvennoe Izdarelstvo [Government Publishing Office] "Sovietskaya Nauka", Moscow. [in Russian]

Kuzyakin, A.P. 1965. *In: Opredelitel' mlekopitayushchikh SSSR [The key to the mammals of the USSR]*, (eds. N.A. Bobrinskii, B.A. Kuznetzov, and A.P. Kuzyakin), Second edition. "Prosveshchenie", Moscow. [in Russian]

Makin, D. 1989. The status of bats in Israel. Pp. 403–408 *in: European bat research 1987* (eds. V. Hanák, I. Horácek, and J. Gaisler). Charles University Press, Prague.

Marron, D.P. 1985. The mammals of the Mongolian People's Republic. *Mammal Review*, 15 (2), 71–102.

Ognev, S.I. 1928. *[Mammals of eastern Europe and northern Asia Volume 1. Insectivora and Chiroptera].* Moscow. [in Russian]. English translation, Israel Program for Scientific Translations, Jerusalem, 1962.

O'Sullivan, P. 1994. Bats in Ireland. *Irish Naturalists Journal*, Special Zoological Supplement.

Palmeirim, J.M. 1989. Status of bats in Portugal. Pp. 565–590 *in: European bat research 1987* (eds. V. Hanák, I. Horácek, and J. Gaisler). Charles University Press, Prague.

Palmeirim, J.M. 1990. Bats of Portugal: zoogeography and systematics. *Miscellaneous Publications of the University of Kansas Museum of Natural History*, 82, 1–53.

Palmeirim, J.M. and Rodrigues, L. 1992. *Plano Nacional de Conservação dos Morcegos Cavernícolas.* Estudos de Biologia e Conservação da Natureza, Número 8. Serviço Nacional de Parques, Reservas e Conservação da Natureza, Lisbon.

Pauza, D.H. and Panziene, N. 1998. Bats of Lithuania: Distribution, status and protection. *Mammal Review*, 28, 53–67.

Pucek, Z. (ed.) 1981. *Keys to the vertebrates of Poland: mammals.* Translated and published for Smithsonian Institution and National Science Foundation, Washington DC by Polish Scientific Publishers.

Qumsiyeh, M.B. 1985. The bats of Egypt. *Special Publications. The Museum, Texas Tech University*, 23, 1–102.

Qumsiyeh, M.B., Disi, A.M., and Amr, Z.S. 1992. Systematics and distribution of the bats (Mammalia: Chiroptera) of Jordan. *Dirasat*, 19B (2), 101–118.

Rainha, A., Rodrigues, L., Bicho, S., Franco, C., and Palmeirim, J.M. 1998. *Morcegos das Areas Protegidas Portuguesas (1).* Estudos de Biologia e Conservação da Natureza, Número 26. Serviço Nacional de Parques, Reservas e Conservação da Natureza, Lisbon.

Rakhmatulina, I.K. 1996a. The bat fauna of the Caucasus and problems of its study. *Myotis*, 34, 51–57.

Rakhmatulina, I. 1996b. On the history of study and tendency of changes of the eastern transcaucasian bat fauna. *Myotis*, 34, 59–70.

Ron, T. 1995. *An action plan for the monitoring and conservation of insectivorous bats in Israel.* Division of Science and Management, Nature Reserves Authority, Jerusalem.

Rossolimo, O.L. (ed.) 1995. *[Mammals of Eurasia. II. Non-Rodentia].* Archives of Zoological Museum Moscow State University, Volume 23, Moscow. [in Russian]

Saint-Girons, M.C. 1973. *Les mammiféres de France et du Benelux.* Doin, Paris.

Schober, W. and Grimmberger, E. 1998. *Die Fledermäuse Europas.* (Revised edition). Kosmos-Naturführer, Franckh, Stuttgart.

Sokolov, V.E. and Orlov, V.N. 1980. *[Key to the mammals of the Mongolian People's Republic].* Moscow. [in Russian]

Spitzenberger, F. 1979. Die Säugetierfauna Zyperns. Teil II. Chiroptera, Lagomorpha, Carnivora und Artiodactyla. *Annalen des (K.K.) Naturhistorischen (Hof) Museums,* 82, 439–465.

Stebbings, R.E., 1988. *Conservation of European bats.* Christopher Helm, London.

Strelkov, P.P., Sosnovtseva, V.P., and Babaev, K.B. 1978. [Bats (Chiroptera) of Turkmenistan]. *Trud Zoologicheskogo Instituta. Akademiya Nauk SSSR. Leningrad*, 79, 3–71 [in Russian].

Tuinov, M.P. 1997. *The Bats of the Russian Far East.* Dalnauka, Vladivostok. 134pp (in Russian).

Vernier, E. 1997. *Manuale pratico dei Chirotteri italiana.* Second edition. Società Cooperativa Tipografica, Padova.

Yoshiyuki, M. 1989. *A systematic study of the Japanese chiroptera.* National Science Museum, Tokyo.

Zhang Yongzu 1997. *Distribution of mammalian species in China.* China Forestry Publishing House, Beijing.

5.5 Species Action Plans

5.5.1 Introduction

Sample Species Action Plans are given for 20 species that have been selected to provide a representative range of distributions, habitats and foraging types, conservation problems, existing levels of conservation activity, and potential for future activity. They are generally species for which there is sufficient knowledge to identify required action. Many of the more threatened species require further investigation before reasoned Action Plans can be developed. However, the Action Plan approach illustrated here will apply to many of the species listed in *The 2000 IUCN Red List of Threatened Species* (IUCN, 2000). Thus, it is not suggested that these species are those most deserving of attention (that should be assessed from IUCN *op. cit.*), only that they are examples of the kind of action that has been or could be carried out to improve the conservation status for many threatened species.

The format for these Action Plans is derived from others that have been published. Each plan begins with a statement of the Threats followed by a Summary statement to aid comparison with other species. Each account also ends with a statement of Wider Application, showing how conservation actions can be extended to a range of other species. For some widely distributed species, it has not been possible to assess their protected status in many range states.

The list of included species is as follows:

Craseonycteris thonglongyai
Emballonura semicaudata
Macroderma gigas
Hipposideros turpis
Rhinolophus ferrumequinum
Noctilio leporinus
Leptonycteris nivalis
Desmodus rotundus
Myzopoda aurita
Kerivoula papuensis
Antrozous pallidus
Myotis dasycneme
Myotis sodalis
Plecotus townsendii
Murina florium
Miniopterus schreibersii
Mystacina tuberculata
Cheiromeles torquatus
Otomops martiensseni
Tadarida brasiliensis

5.5.2 Species Action Plan – *Craseonycteris thonglongyai* Kitti's hog-nosed bat
(Family Craseonycteridae)

Threats
In the early days after the discovery of this species early in the 1970s, there was considerable tourist pressure from disturbance of roost caves (e.g., the Sai Yok Cave was deserted by bats, but some have now returned), scientific collection, and the sale of bats as tourist souvenirs (mounted on card or in resin). Much of this pressure was concentrated on a few known major caves, but since many small colonies exist in caves that are difficult to access, there may not have been a very serious threat to the species as a whole. The occupation of roost caves by monks during periods of meditation was also considered a potential conservation problem. Burning of forest areas near caves (especially prevalent during the breeding season) may be a more serious long-term problem, as may be the current proposal to construct a pipeline from Myanmar to Thailand.

Summary
Kitti's hog-nosed bat is arguably the smallest bat species and possibly the smallest mammal species in the world. It is the sole member of the family Craseonycteridae, with affinities to the families Rhinopomatidae and Emballonuridae, and is restricted to a small area of western Thailand.

Kitti's hog-nosed bat, *Craseonycteris thonglongyai*.

R.E. Stebbings

Soon after its description in 1974, numbers declined in the few known sites following disturbance through collecting and tourist interest, and the species was declared one of the world's rarest mammals. Further survey work has identified a number of other occupied sites and suggests that the species may be locally common, but it is still known from a very limited geographical area and is subject to a range of threats.

Protected status

The species is protected within the Sai Yok National Park, which includes the major part of its known range, but not outside the park.

- *The 2000 IUCN Red List of Threatened Species*: EN B1 + 2c, C2b

Biological assessment

Kitti's hog-nosed bat is so far known only from the area of Sai Yok National Park, Kanchanaburi Province, western Thailand. The area is dominated by limestone with numerous caves, and the forests are dominated by dry, deciduous hardwood trees and giant bamboo. Sometimes called the bumblebee bat, in reference to its size, it has a head and body length of about 30mm, forearm length of 22–26mm, no tail, and weighs about two grams. It has been recorded mainly between October and March in caves in an area that was formerly forested, but is now largely cleared. It has mainly been found in small caves with a series of chambers and close to a river (the River Kwai and related river systems). Many caves contain small numbers, 10–15, but the average group size is 100, with a maximum of 500, usually roosting high up in the walls or roof domes and well separated from each other and, hence, at low densities. There is some seasonal movement between caves. The single young is born late in the dry season (late April), with the young left in the roost during feeding; otherwise, it is attached to a false pelvic nipple.

This species has a very short activity period (30 minutes in the evening, 20 minutes at dawn), and this is readily interrupted by heavy rain and/or low temperatures. It emerges from its roosts early and has been observed foraging in open areas of cleared forest around the tops of teak trees and bamboo clumps. It has a highly manoeuvrable flight. Small flies (Diptera: Chloropidae, Agromyzidae, and Anthomyiidae) are a principal feature of the diet; Hymenoptera and Psocoptera are also recorded. Spiders have been recorded in the diet, suggesting that it may glean some prey from vegetation, but the echolocation calls indicate that gleaning is not a major feeding method. The normal foraging range seems to be limited to about 1km from the roost. Surveys of suitable areas to the north and south of the population centre have not demonstrated the presence of the species, although further survey work in this cave-rich area may show the species to be more widespread than is currently recognized.

Conservation action to date

Following the interest aroused by its original description, numbers in known sites declined. Control of pressures on the bat and its roosts has encouraged some recovery. Some ecological studies have been undertaken and recommendations for the conservation of the species identified.

Action Plan objectives

1. Establish long-term monitoring in disturbed and undisturbed habitats.
2. Establish distribution and population levels (especially in north and northeast of known range).
3. Protect key sites if appropriate.
4. Maintain suitable habitat in cave areas.
5. Manage research required to implement conservation strategies.

Conservation recommendations to meet Action Plan objectives

Policy and legislation

Recommendations:
- protect species as it is a monotypic family with a very restricted distribution, and in view of its reputation as the world's smallest mammal, including through prohibiting trade and non-essential scientific collection;
- develop policy for the sympathetic management of habitats used as flight paths and foraging areas.

Site/species safeguard and management

Recommendations:
- establish monitoring procedure to identify population change in relation to environmental factors;
- involve local people in land-use practices, including providing, as necessary, incentives that will maintain essential habitat;
- identify key cave roosts and ensure their protection with fences or grilles if necessary;
- protect the many cave roosts that are used by small numbers of bats;
- control cave use detrimental to the favourable conservation status of the species.

Advisory, communications and publicity

Recommendations:
- minimise cave disturbance to the species, which is easily visible in the evening when foraging, by promoting to interested tourists field observation of the smallest mammal in the world;
- provide interpretative material on the importance and status of the species, especially to visitors to the Sai Yok National Park;
- use funds from tourism to support the habitat protection needed for the conservation of this species.

Future research and monitoring

> **Recommendations:**
> - collect further data on diet and its relation to foraging habitat;
> - undertake further surveys to clarify the range, population levels, and ecological requirements;
> - assess whether the protection of key cave sites and surrounding habitat is appropriate;
> - investigate seasonal movements of populations and the significance to conservation;

Wider application

The careful management of caves for this species should help the conservation of other cave bats in the area. The conservation activities involving local people and tourists offers an example of education/fund-raising to help local farmers and others.

5.5.3 Species Action Plan – *Emballonura semicaudata* Pacific sheath-tailed bat

(Family Emballonuridae)

Threats

The Pacific sheath-tailed bat has disappeared or declined on a number of islands, but the reasons for this are not clear. In the Marianas, the impact of World War II, with heavy bombing directed at fortified caves, may have had an effect along with the heavy use of pesticides. Some caves were also sealed off with explosives to trap soldiers inside and other sites were attacked with flame-throwers. This may have destroyed some caves used by bats and made others, at least temporarily, uninhabitable. Caves were also fortified by the Japanese in Palau, Chuuk, and probably Pohnpei. Later mining of bat and cave swiftlet guano may have caused disturbance. On Fiji, the disturbance to caves and burning of forest near cave roosts are possible causes of decline. In American Samoa and Samoa, the species is critically endangered, possibly from the effects of cyclones (including the blocking of small sea caves by storm debris), although the populations of this species will have experienced such natural perturbations in the past. The conversion of forest to agriculture must have had some effect; other factors, such as introduced cats and rats, pesticide use, and disturbance to caves, are likely to have had a minor influence.

Pacific sheath-tailed bat, *Emballonura semicaudata*.

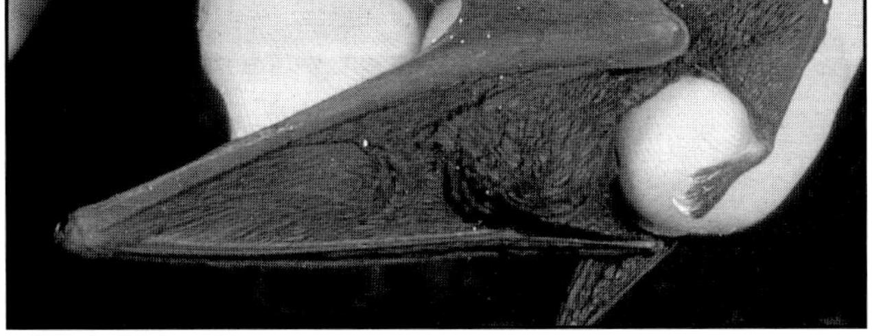

T. Lemke

Summary

E. semicaudata was once a common and widespread cave-dwelling species in Polynesia and Micronesia. Indeed, it is the only insectivorous bat recorded from a large part of this area and the only species found where it did or does occur. The only exceptions are two doubtful records from Vanuatu where other insectivorous bats occur.

A number of subspecies have been described: *E. s. semicaudata* from Samoa, Fiji, Tonga, and Vanuatu, *E. s. sulcata* from the Caroline Islands (Federated States of Micronesia), *E. s. rotensis* from the Mariana Islands, and *E. s. palauensis* from Palau. For the Mariana Islands, the last record from Guam is 1895, the last from Rota in 1932 (the origin of the subspecific description), and it was believed that this form was extinct until the recent confirmation of a population of probably less than 25 individuals in the northern Marianas. The populations of *E. s. sulcata* and *E. s. palauensis* are reported to be healthy and stable, but there are little data to support this.

Protected status

It has been fully protected in Samoa since 1993. It has also been protected on Guam (since 1981) and in the Commonwealth of the Northern Mariana Islands (since 1991) under local endangered species regulations. It is also considered a "candidate" for listing under the US Endangered Species Act in the CNMI, Guam, and American Samoa. This status means that the species will eventually be proposed for listing as endangered or threatened. However, in the meantime, the species receives protection under the Endangered Species Act. Its protected status elsewhere is uncertain.

- *The 2000 IUCN Red List of Threatened Species*: EN A1ac.

Biological assessment

This small bat (forearm length c. 45mm, weight 5.5g) is a cave-dependent species, roosting in the twilight zone of a wide range of caves, and has been found under overhanging cliffs up to 300m in Pohnpei. The caves may be shared with cave swiftlets. It has been recorded flying in daylight under forest, but normally emerges at about dusk; details of its diet are not known.

In Samoa, only five individuals were seen in a recent

two-year survey, which included visits by scientists to over 20 caves on Upolu; previously, the species occurred on both main islands. It was known from several caves in "reasonable" numbers prior to Cyclones Ofa (1990) and Val (1991), but is currently known only from a large sea cave and a lava tube at 600m. Some of the caves would have been completely flooded or entrances exposed during the cyclones, although cave swiftlets are still present in such caves. On American Samoa, there are reports of steep declines over the past 10–20 years for reasons not well understood, but perhaps related to cyclone damage. It is still present on Tau. A recent survey of caves in Tutuila in American Samoa located only two individuals. These were caves that had been reported previously as harbouring considerable numbers of bats. The bats were found in a dry part of a coastal cave that clearly is partly inundated by very high tides. Surveys of sites in Tau, Ofu, and Olosega were planned for late 1998 (R. Utzurrum *pers. comm.*).

Similarly, on Fiji, the species was abundant until the 1950s. The only recent main island record is of a group of about 100 under a bridge in 1989 and 15 collected on Viti Levu in 1979, although it is predicted to be now extinct on the latter island. All other survey efforts have produced negative results. It is, however, still found on many smaller offshore islands in the Fiji group, including Ovalau, Labeka, and there is an unsubstantiated observation in a cave on Taveuni; it is reported as common on Rotuma.

It is still present on Palau, where it is common, and on Chuuk and Pohnpei. It was commonly seen on the island of Oreor (formerly Koror) in Palau in 1991. It was locally common on the island of Moen (now called Weno) in Chuuk in 1989 and is still thought to be present there. It is believed to be extinct on Dublon, but may persist on Tol.

In the Mariana Islands, a small colony of 10 was discovered on the 7.2km² island of Aguijan (Goat Island) in 1984. A more comprehensive survey of the island in 1995 resulted in an estimate of 150–300 animals, with no immediate threats to the population identified. Bats were found in five of 84 caves searched, with group sizes ranging from two to 74 animals. Aguijan is uninhabited and its caves are rarely disturbed by people. However, about half the island was cleared of forest in the 1930s and undoubtedly resulted in loss of foraging habitat for the bats. *E. semicaudata* disappeared for unknown reasons from Rota, Guam, and Saipan sometime between the 1940s and 1970s. Archaeological evidence indicates that it occurred on Tinian prior to the arrival of European colonists, but there are no historical records for this island. It is not known to have been present on other islands in the chain.

Conservation action to date

None.

Action Plan objectives

1. Complete surveys to establish current status.
2. Develop and implement recovery programme, wherever possible, within known range

Conservation recommendations to meet Action Plan objectives

Policy and legislation

Recommendations:
- develop protective legislation in areas where the species is at risk;
- develop policies to protect caves and surrounding foraging habitat for caves that have a history of use by *E. semicaudata,* and are in use or have potential to be used.

Site/species safeguard and management

Recommendations:
- ensure adequate protection of key roosts and surrounding habitat;
- restore and enhance caves and the surrounding habitat formerly occupied by this species.

Advisory, communications, and publicity

Recommendation:
- appeal through local peoples for further information on distribution and status.

Future research and monitoring

Recommendations:
- carry out further survey work to assess current distribution and status;
- maintain monitoring of known populations;
- carry out ecological studies with a view to establishing the reasons for the recent dramatic declines;
- consider re-introduction of bats to islands formerly inhabited once probable reasons for decline are identified; this would be appropriate for Rota, Tinian, and Saipan in the Marianas, at least, and maybe elsewhere too.

Wider application

This is the only microchiropteran bat found throughout much of its range, but the establishment of the reasons for decline may have implications for other island species, as may the implementation of an appropriate recovery programme. Other species that would benefit from bat conservation measures include cave swiftlets (*Collocalia* spp.) and various invertebrates associated with caves. On Guam, for example, this would include some cave-adapted insects, amphipods, and isopods.

5.5.4 Species Action Plan – *Macroderma gigas* Ghost bat

(Family Megadermatidae)

Threats

M. gigas is very vulnerable to disturbance in its roosts in caves and mines. Cave tourism has been identified as a problem, but the most serious threat is from quarrying and reworking of old mine areas. In some cases, the collapse of disused mines may also be a threat. The species needs a wide range of roost sites for seasonal or weather-related use, and this may under-rate the importance of little-used roosts.

In some areas, habitat modification for livestock may be a problem, as may competition for prey with introduced foxes and feral cats.

Summary

The family Megadermatidae (false vampire bats) includes five species in four genera. The single species of *Macroderma* is found in northern Australia. The other species of the family occur in Asia (two species) and Africa (two species). While all are large bats and, to some extent, carnivorous, their roost patterns vary from roosting in the open in foliage (*Lavia frons*, Africa) to strict cave-dependence, as in *Megaderma*.

Ghost bat, *Macroderma gigas*.

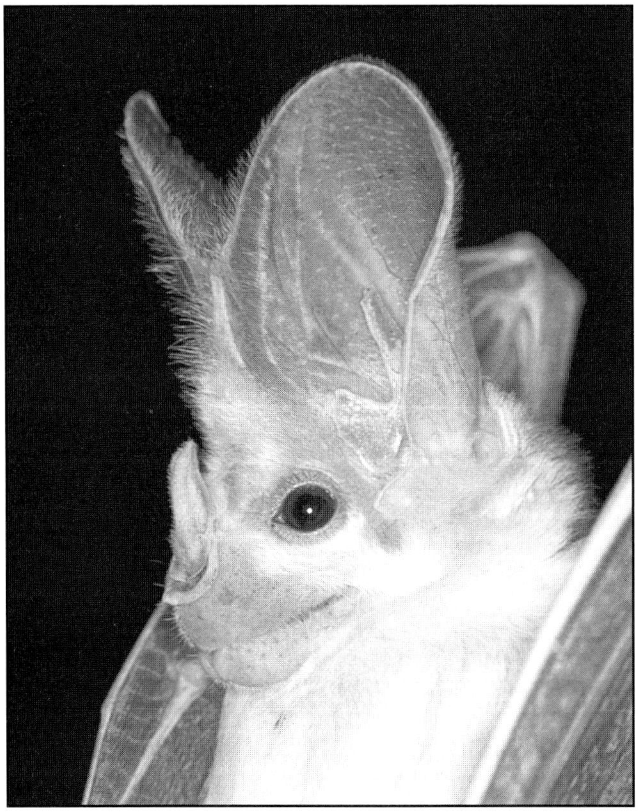

L. Lumsden

Protected status

The species is protected throughout its range in Australia, and by state legislation in Queensland, Northern Territory, and Western Australia.

- *The 2000 IUCN Red List of Threatened Species*: VU A2c
- *The Action Plan for Australian Bats:* LR: nt (near VU A2c).

Biological assessment

This is one of the largest microchiropteran species, with a forearm length of 100–112mm and weight of 140–165g. It has large eyes and ears, and very broad flight membranes. Its current distribution is coastal and up to 400km inland throughout northern Australia, more or less north of the tropic of Capricorn, with the exception of Pilbara in Western Australia. The range appears to have contracted northwards in relatively recent times, especially in central Australia. Sub-fossil evidence suggests a much wider distribution and much larger colonies in prehistoric times. The current population is estimated at 4,000–7,000 individuals in about 10 regional populations. The Queensland population is estimated at less than 1,000, with its major colony at Mount Etna having declined in the last 10 years; there may be one or two further maternity colonies to be found in Cape York or the Gulf of Carpentaria. The Northern Territory population is thought to be more or less stable at 3,000–4,000, but the main colony (800 at Kohinoor Mine, Pine Creek) is threatened by a potential mine collapse. The Western Australia population of about 1,000 is thought to be more or less stable, and there are no current threats.

Although it occurs in rainforest, the ghost bat is mostly found in the arid zone near rock outcrops, and roosts in caves, mines and rock clefts. Colonies of over 400 are recorded, but few are over 100. It mainly forages within 1–2km of the roost in individual territories, but sometimes has communal foraging areas with up to 20 individuals. Most of the prey is large invertebrates, such as beetles, Orthoptera, and cicadas, but it will also take small vertebrates, including bats, other small mammals, birds, lizards, and snakes. Such prey items may be up to 80% of the bat's body weight. Most of the prey is taken from the ground, either in flight or by 'flycatching' from a perch. Prey may be detected by listening for prey movement, although sight may also be used. Fruit has also been reported in the diet. Vertebrate prey is taken more in the cooler periods. Most prey is taken to a feeding perch in trees, rock overhangs, or cave entrances.

Ghost bats move between a number of caves seasonally or as dictated by weather changes, generally selecting very warm caves during pregnancy and lactation, but at no time able to tolerate lowered body temperature. Thus, they require a range of cave sites, including communal sites, which may be used only temporarily or under exceptional weather conditions, and their needs may involve a colony or local population dispersing over a wide area.

Conservation action to date

The species occurs in protected areas (e.g., national parks) in all areas of its distribution. Current management activities take account of the results of population genetics studies, which have shown that colonies constitute separate metapopulations. Activities include a captive breeding programme, long-term population studies and monitoring in Queensland, and population studies in Western Australia.

In the late 1980s, a massive international campaign to prevent the destruction of caves used by this bat at Mt Etna, near Rockhampton, Queensland, failed and this population has subsequently declined. Soon afterward, concerns for the largest known colony at Kohinoor Mine, Pine Creek, Northern Territory, resulted in another major conservation campaign and, although the site has not yet been damaged, there remain concerns about its naturally degrading condition.

The species is the subject of a Recovery Outline published in *The Action Plan for Australian Bats*.

Action Plan objectives

1. Improve the status such that the long-term future of the species is secure.
2. Monitor maternity colonies and take appropriate action if colonies continue to decline.
3. Identify and eliminate reasons for decline.

Conservation recommendations to meet Action Plan objectives

Policy and legislation

Recommendations:
- implement protection provided by legislation;
- develop policies for mineral extraction that ensure maintenance and enhancement of population to a favourable status.

Site/species safeguard and management

Recommendations:
- ensure that the 10 or so populations centred on maternity colonies are maintained in the protected area network;
- ensure that habitat management is sympathetic to the requirements of the bat in centres of distribution.

Advisory, communications and publicity

Recommendations:
- ensure the mining and quarrying industry is fully aware of conservation priority given to this species;
- maintain interest in the conservation of this species in caving groups and other interested parties.

Future research and monitoring

Recommendations:
- co-ordinate national monitoring of maternity colonies;
- survey for additional colonies in all range states (including Queensland: far north and around the type locality of Quilpie; Western Australia: Kimberley; Northern Territory: Arnhem Land);
- complete ongoing genetic work to clarify the status of the vulnerable arid zone regional population in Pilbara, which is geographically isolated from extant northern Australian populations;
- maintain programme of conservation-related research already initiated and as identified in *The Action Plan for Australian Bats.*

Wider application

This large and spectacular cave-dweller, with precise requirements for a range of roosts for seasonal or temporary use, provides a model for the issues relating to the conservation of many cave bats. In Australia, 75 species, or about half of the bat fauna, are more or less reliant on caves.

5.5.5 Species Action Plan – *Hipposideros turpis* Lesser great leaf-nosed bat

(Family Hipposideridae)

Threats

In Iriomote (Ryukyu Islands, Japan), the main breeding colonies are concentrated in two caves. These are used by between 5,000 and 10,000 leaf-nosed bats and about 10,000 of the endemic horseshoe bat (*Rhinolophus imaizumii*). The areas surrounding these caves are national forest, but there has been pressure to develop these areas, which would involve forest clearance. Development for agriculture and logging would remove key foraging areas and result in potential isolation of the cave roosts, causing declines of those principal populations. Similar declines and even extinctions have already been reported in other nearby islands. Publicity about the plight of these bats resulted in increased public interest, including increased tourism to the breeding caves. There is no information on status and threats to the species in Thailand and Viet Nam.

Summary

The leaf-nosed bats (family Hipposideridae) comprise 75 species, mostly in the genus *Hipposideros* (60 species), which is distributed throughout the Old World tropics and subtropics. Eight other genera comprise 15 species, some of which are extremely poorly known and with very restricted distributions. *H. turpis* has a very disjunct distribution, with one subspecies on the Ryukyu Islands (Japan) and one in southern Thailand and Viet Nam. It forms a distinct species group with *H. armiger*, a much

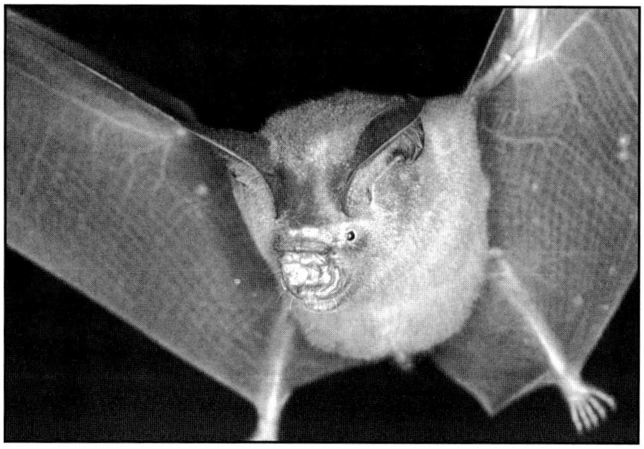

Lesser great leaf-nosed bat, *Hipposideros turpis*.

larger and widespread species in Southeast Asia. The systematic status of the two subspecies of *H. turpis* remains unclear in view of the unusual distribution. Little is known about the mainland distribution of the species, but threats to the population on Iriomote in the Ryukyu Islands (along with the endangered endemic *Rhinolophus imaizumii*), has led to surveys attempting to integrate economic development with the conservation of bats. Almost all species of *Hipposideros* are principally cave-roosting species and most rely on tropical forest, including savanna woodland, for foraging. Like members of the family Rhinolophidae, they are sensitive to disturbance of roosts and foraging habitats.

Protected status

It is protected in Japan by the Endangered Species Safety Act. It is not protected in Thailand or Viet Nam.

- *The 2000 IUCN Red List of Threatened Species*: EN A2c

Biological assessment

Hipposideros turpis is a large leaf-nosed bat (forearm 67–80mm). It is a poorly known species with two subspecies: *H. t. turpis* occurs from about 10 localities in the Ryukyu Islands (on the islands of Ishigaki, Iriomote, Yonakuni, and Yaeyama); *H. t. pendleburyi* is slightly larger, and is recorded from southern Thailand (Nakhon Si Thammarat Province and Krabi Province) and possibly also from Viet Nam. *H. turpis* is most closely related to the very large *H. armiger* (forearm 88–98mm), which is widespread in Southeast Asia from Nepal, north India and Myanmar, east through mainland Southeast Asia to Taiwan and Peninsular Malaya.

Little is known of the ecology of *H. turpis*, except that it relies on caves for roosting, and adjacent woodland for foraging and flight paths. The larger *H. armiger* feeds on large insects, such as beetles (especially scarabeids), but smaller sympatric species take softer prey such as crickets, moths, Diptera, flying termites, and Hymenoptera.

Conservation action to date

Pressure has been brought to bear to protect important roost sites and associated habitat. The Japanese Government and the Okinawa Prefecture Government responded by initiating studies to establish flight paths and foraging activity of the bats, resulting in modification to the original proposals. A monitoring strategy has been agreed. Fences were erected at the cave entrances to control tourists. In addition, a small area originally designated for development was proposed as a reserve.

Action Plan objectives

1. Ensure the maintenance of the species at a favourable conservation status.
2. Integrate development controls with the needs of the bats.
3. Ensure that the importance of the bats and their needs are recognised and understood by developers and local communities.

Conservation recommendations to meet Action Plan objectives

Policy and legislation

Recommendations:
- ensure adequate protection for key roosts, including non-breeding roosts;
- develop policies to ensure adequate protection of foraging areas and flight paths.

Site/species safeguard and management

Recomendations:
- protect key roost sites; where physical protection is required ensure that it is appropriate for the behaviour of the bats;
- manage forest and other habitat to provide adequate foraging opportunity for the bats and to maintain habitat continuity (including adjacent to the cave roosts).

Advisory, communications and publicity

Recommendations:
- develop an educational plan to encourage public, especially local, support for the conservation programme;
- provide appropriate advice for developers.

Future research and monitoring

Recommendations:
- establish status of the two forms as species or subspecies;
- identify food and foraging requirements for the species and the relationship of those requirements with roost sites;

- identify importance of non-breeding cave sites in annual cycle of bat behaviour;
- establish conservation status of species in Thailand, and identify and implement any necessary conservation measures;
- establish conservation status of species in Viet Nam.

Wider application

The Ryukyu Islands contain the best examples of subtropical fauna and flora in Japan, and Iriomote is perhaps the most important area within the island group. Every effort should be made to maintain this ecosystem, highlighting bats as an important element of Japanese biodiversity.

The leaf-nosed and horseshoe bats face similar problems of reliance on caves, e.g., the need for suitable foraging habitat close to the cave roosts and sensitivity to disturbance. Together they include 141 species (17% of all Microchiroptera). Of these, more than 50% are believed to be of conservation concern and adequate information is not available for many others. The situation in the Ryukyu Islands is probably typical for many species, although here there may be the additional problems of the fragility of island ecosystems, while elsewhere there are many additional threats to the species through exploitation of the caves or of the bats themselves.

5.5.6 Species Action Plan – *Rhinolophus ferrumequinum* Greater horseshoe bat

(Family Rhinolophidae)

Threats

Habitat change in northwest Europe is likely to have been amongst the major causes of declines, with the conversion of woodland and small-field landscapes to large-scale agricultural land being particularly damaging. While declines elsewhere, particularly in eastern Europe, may currently not be so marked, the loss of cultural landscapes in those countries as they move toward western-style economies may have significant effects in the near future.

The use of pesticides has been a recognized threat to the insect food, particularly where these have been directed against the larvae of favoured food items, such as melolonthid beetles, larvae of noctuid moths, or crane-flies. Favoured prey may be affected secondarily by pesticide use, such as the loss of dung fauna from the use of persistent anti-parasitic drugs (avermectins) on cattle.

Populations in caves and other underground habitats have suffered from increased disturbance, changes of use, and the destruction of such sites.

Where the species has occupied buildings, it requires particular features of the building itself, as well as proximity to good foraging areas and underground sites for torpor at various times of year; the latter may also be used for winter hibernation. In buildings, colonies may be affected by human intolerance, renovation work, or the application of pesticides, such as some of those used for the remedial treatment of timbers.

Summary

Rhinolophus ferrumequinum is one of 66 species in the Old World family Rhinolophidae. The family is sometimes regarded as including the Hipposideridae (75 species of Old World leaf-nosed bats). Rhinolophids are mainly cave-dwelling bats, believed to be particularly sensitive to disturbance. The family contains a high proportion of species of conservation concern. Bats of this family are generally obvious in caves, as well as in buildings and other structures, because they hang free from the roof. The two most widespread species in Europe, *R. ferrumequinum* and *R. hipposideros*, have been of particular conservation concern, and the subject of considerable research and monitoring.

R. ferrumequinum is sometimes considered conspecific with *R. clivosus* from parts of southwest Asia through to subsaharan Africa, and with *R. bocharicus* of central Asia. Several subspecies have been described.

Protected status

R. ferrumequinum is protected in most European range states. In Europe, it is included in Annex II of the EU

Greater Horseshoe bat, *Rhinolophus ferrumequinum*.

P.A. Morris

Council Directive on the Conservation of Natural Habitats and of Wild Fauna and Flora 1992 (the EEC Habitat Directive), requiring full protection and designation of Special Areas of Conservation to maintain the species and its habitats. Other international treaties of relevance are the Agreement on the Conservation of Bats in Europe (Bonn Convention, 1994), Convention on the Conservation of European Wildlife and Natural Habitats (Bern Convention, 1982), and Bern Convention Recommendation 36 (1992, Conservation of Underground Habitats) and 43 (1995, Conservation of Threatened Mammals in Europe). Most European range states are party to at least one of these treaties.

- *The 2000 IUCN Red List of Threatened Species*: LR: nt.

Biological assessment

The greater horseshoe bat has shown marked declines in its range in northwest Europe within the last 100 years (e.g., UK, The Netherlands, Belgium, Germany). Any similar declines in countries elsewhere within its range have not been documented. However, there are signs of recovery in some European countries.

The species will use caves all year, but, particularly in northern Europe, it uses buildings for summer maternity colonies. In many countries, considerable effort has been made to identify key roosts and to protect them, and it is likely that greater declines would have occurred without that effort. More recently, greater effort has been made to identify home range and important foraging habitat and landscape features. The latter includes woodland, particularly early in the year, and permanent summer-grazed pasture, particularly late in the summer. The requirements for hibernation appear to be a limited range of temperature and humidity, but these vary with age, sex, and condition of the bats. The mean temperatures in spring, at the end of hibernation, may influence the time of birth; late parturition, in turn, increases mortality rates of juveniles.

Conservation action to date

The greater horseshoe bat has been the subject of widespread conservation activity, especially in Europe. Until recently, this has concentrated on roosts in buildings and caves. Many buildings used as roosts have management agreements and many underground sites have been protected. Nevertheless, sites continue to be lost or damaged. More recently, attention has turned to identifying more precisely the food and foraging requirements. A European meeting (Germany, May 1995) discussed the status and conservation needs for the species on a pan-European scale. The Bern Convention has recently published a Europe-wide Species Action Plan under the Pan-European Biological and Landscape Diversity Strategy.

Action Plan objectives

1. Maintain populations in areas where the bats are at a favourable status and enhance populations in areas where they have declined.
2. Assess more precisely the status, distribution, and threats to populations outside Europe, and develop conservation action as appropriate.
3. Carry out research, survey work, and monitoring necessary to meet Objective 1.
4. Raise awareness in the general public, and professional and special interest groups whose activities may affect the status and protection of the species.

Conservation recommendations to meet Action Plan objectives

Policy and legislation

Recommendations:
- implement a detailed Pan-European Action Plan to meet obligations under the EEC Habitat Directive, Bonn, and Bern Conventions, and the Council of Europe's Biological and Landscape Diversity Strategy; this should involve the Co-ordinating Panel for the Conservation of Bats in Europe, a regional group of the IUCN/SSC Chiroptera Specialist Group;
- ensure that adequate legislation is in place and being implemented in all range states to protect the species and its habitats.

Site/species safeguard and management

Recommendations:
- afford the species the highest priority in decisions that may affect its roosts;
- assess and address the conservation requirements outside Europe as appropriate. The European Action Plan may help in that assessment and the identification of priorities.

Advisory, communications and publicity

Recommendation:
- encourage special interest groups, such as speleologists, and professional groups, such as those in the building industry, to operate in ways that do not threaten populations of this species.

Future research and monitoring

Recommendations:
- conduct wider investigations of food and foraging requirements to allow the development of sympathetic land management policies, especially in areas where the species is, or is likely to become, threatened; such studies should also consider the differing requirements of sympatric species;

- monitor populations through observations at maternity colonies and hibernation sites on a Europe-wide basis; this species offers good opportunity to compare the validity to long-term monitoring of counts taken pre- and post-parturition, and of reproductive success pre- and post-weaning;
- maintain and extend the exceptional long-term studies of this bat species as appropriate.

Wider application

Throughout their range, horseshoe bats demonstrate similar problems of sensitivity to disturbance in roosts, particularly in caves. The Bern Convention Recommendation 36 (1992) on the Conservation of Underground Habitats may provide a model for the development of policies to protect such habitats elsewhere.

The knowledge of this species, including the availability of data from long-term studies and from the lesser horseshoe bat (*R. hipposideros*), greatly exceeds that of other species of the family. However, within the family Rhinolophidae there would appear to be great uniformity in ecology and many of the conservation issues will apply to species other than *R. ferrumequinum*, with the notable addition of the threats encountered during hibernation in the temperate zone.

The wide-ranging concerns for cave-dwelling bats are discussed elsewhere. Since horseshoe bats are considered to be particularly sensitive, measures or policies effective for their conservation are likely to be effective for other species, but may not be suitable for all species using the cave (see, for example, notes under the action plan for *Miniopterus schreibersii*).

5.5.7 Species Action Plan – *Noctilio leporinus* Greater fishing bat

(Family Noctilionidae)

Threats

Although not of immediate concern, with no factors that at present can be clearly associated with population declines, it is widely believed that this spectacular bat will face serious threats in the future. Thus, conservation measures should be devised to prevent population declines, with immediate efforts to institute monitoring to give early warning of such population declines.

Factors affecting this species and its prey, and likely to increase in severity, are water pollution (e.g., from pesticides, oil, or other chemicals), changes to river structure, flow pattern, general water quality, and water extraction or drainage. *N. leporinus* is, however, capable of feeding over quite polluted water. In some areas, such as Cuba and Puerto Rico, the provision of new reservoirs and fish-rearing pools may be of benefit. In others, such as Ecuador, the development of open pools of oil for storage or from pipe leaks may be a hazard.

Perhaps of more importance is the damage to waterside habitats, which are relied upon to provide roost sites. Loss of or damage to waterside vegetation and associated habitats is of wide concern in many parts of the neotropics.

Summary

Noctilio leporinus is one of two species of the very distinct neotropical family Noctilionidae. While the second smaller species *N. albiventris* is principally insectivorous, *N. leporinus* preys heavily on fish, also consuming large numbers of insects. It occurs from Mexico through Central America, and on many Caribbean islands to South America as far south as Argentina. Especially within South America, the distribution is restricted mostly to non-arid lowland and coastal areas and to major river systems. While widely distributed, it occurs at low density. Its specific requirements of roost sites (caves, rock fissures, tree holes) close to suitable open, non-turbulent water of lakes and rivers and, in coastal areas, estuaries, marine bays, and lagoons, make it subject to increasing pressures. Its wide distribution means that it is not in immediate danger, but the low population density and specific habitat requirements and feeding strategy may make widespread local extinction a real possibility.

Protected status

It is probably unprotected throughout most of its range.

- *The 2000 IUCN Red List of Threatened Species*: Not listed

Biological assessment

This very distinct species is a large bat (forearm 75–88mm, weight 50–90g) with a bulldog-like muzzle, very short tight fur, large wing area with the wings attached high on the back, and greatly enlarged hind feet and claws. It takes fish from the surface of smooth water bodies, but also feeds on a variety of insects and is probably not reliant on fish. Other invertebrates, such as crabs, shrimp, and scorpions, are also taken. Much of this prey is taken by raking the water surface with the enlarged feet and claws in response to sound or ripples. The species is also an aerial insectivore, and thus shows an adaptable and opportunistic feeding ability.

Females form small stable groups, often with a single male, and other males may form separate bachelor groups. However, colonies are of mixed sex and may include up to several hundred individuals. Females from one group often forage together, but communal night roosts may include individuals from different day roosts. Both these activities may offer opportunities for the transfer of information between bats. Pregnancy may last up to nine months, probably including a delay in fertilisation or development, with a single young being born.

Many of the published studies of the ecology of this species have been carried out in Central America and the Caribbean islands, and further comparative work is needed in mainland South America.

Stephen Dalton/NHPA

Greater fishing bat, *Noctilio leporinus*.

Conservation action to date

None.

Action Plan objectives

1. Maintain this highly distinctive bat as a widespread and familiar species.
2. Monitor distribution and populations in relation to environmental factors.
3. Establish more precisely the factors affecting choice of roost site and foraging strategies.

Conservation recommendations to meet Action Plan objectives

Policy and legislation

Recommendation:
- ensure the maintenance and quality of foraging sites and associated wildlife refuges in riparian habitats; there may be the need for legislation to protect isolated populations, e.g., on some Caribbean islands.

Site/species safeguard and management

Recommendations:
- ensure the appropriate maintenance of aquatic environments and associated habitats;
- protect key roost sites in the areas where the species has a restricted distribution or limited populations.

Advisory, communications and publicity

Recommendation:
- no specific action recommended, although this species, with its unique feeding niche, size, and visibility could be highlighted in general educational activities relating to bats and their conservation.

Future research and monitoring

Recommendations:
- establish a network of sites and a protocol for long-term monitoring of distribution and populations in relation to environmental factors;
- establish more precisely factors affecting choice of roost sites and roost sharing with other species, particularly in mainland South America;
- establish more precisely the food and feeding strategies in relation to habitat and season, particularly in mainland South America.

Wider application

There are few fish-eating bats in the world and none is as specialised as *Noctilio*. Nevertheless, it is a large and obvious species that is appropriate for monitoring in relation to environmental factors. The result of monitoring will have implications for other species that rely on the aquatic environment for foraging and associated habitats for roosting. However, its adaptable feeding strategy and greater mobility than is likely for most smaller species may require careful interpretation of the monitoring data. Monitoring of many foraging sites could incorporate a multispecies approach.

5.5.8 Species Action Plan – *Leptonycteris nivalis* Greater or Mexican long-nosed bat

(Family Phyllostomidae)

Threats

These include intense harvesting of the bats' food plants, especially *Agave* species to produce liquor or quiote, loss of cave-roosting sites through destruction, recreational caving, and direct killing of bats for vampire control. One major cave roost in Mexico has been lost to road development.

Summary

L. nivalis is one of a group of nectar and pollen feeders that form the subfamily Glossophaginae. It is the main pollinator for several important *Agave* species and probably, to a lesser extent, giant saguaro and organpipe cacti. The co-evolution of these bats and plants has produced an extreme example of mutualism. The species occurs in Mexico with part of the population migrating into the USA. Its possible presence in Guatemala requires confirmation.

Protected status

It was added to the U.S. Endangered Species List (1988) and is listed as an Endangered Species in Mexico (1991).

- *The 2000 IUCN Red List of Threatened Species*: EN A1c

Biological assessment

A medium-sized species (forearm 46–59mm, weight 18–30g), it inhabits desert scrub with *Agave*, mesquite, creosote bark, and cacti. Above 5,000m in the USA, it occupies pine-oak woodland. Day roosts are mainly in caves, but are also found in mines, rock crevices, tunnels, buildings, and rarely hollow trees. It usually remains in the twilight zone of caves and is highly colonial. It may forage more than 20km from the day roost. One, sometimes two, young are born in Mexico in April to early June and, with their mothers, move north into the southern USA following the flowering of cacti and *Agave*, where they remain until August. But only part of the population migrates and the numbers that appear in the USA may be controlled by the food supply in Mexico. Examination of mitochondrial DNA from animals trapped at migratory stations has demonstrated the presence of discrete populations. Few adult males are found in the USA. *Leptonycteris* does not hibernate.

Major declines have been recorded in Mexico, such as in an abandoned mine in Nuevo Leon where numbers fell from 10,000 in 1938 to none in 1983; another mine with thousands in 1967 was used by a single individual in 1983. There is one major roost site in southwest Texas and the species has also been recorded from New Mexico, though this may have been a misidentification. Numbers have varied greatly in the Texas site (perhaps dependent on the food supply in Mexico or en route), from as high as 10,650 in 1967 to as low as zero in 1970, and a maximum of only about 1,000 between 1980 and 1984.

Greater or Mexican long-nosed bat, *Leptonycteris nivalis*.

M. Tuttle/BCI

Conservation action to date

1. The species is included in a government-supported collaborative NGO Programme for the Conservation of Migratory Bats of Mexico and the USA. This includes research on life history, habitat requirements, limiting factors, and management practices for the bats and their food plants. It supports roost surveys and education programmes in Mexico. The programme also includes *L. curasoae*, *Choeronycteris mexicana,* and *Tadarida brasiliensis.*
2. There is a US Threatened and Endangered Species Recovery Programme.
3. The Texas roost site is protected within a national park. Two caves are proposed for protection in the state of Tamaulipas in Mexico.

Action Plan objectives

1. Restore populations to 1970s levels.
2. Ensure adequate protection of roost sites, including their capacity to house increased populations.
3. Ensure adequate foraging opportunity in breeding areas and along migratory pathways.

Conservation recommendations to meet Action Plan objectives

Policy and legislation

Recommendations:
- develop policies for sympathetic management of foraging areas throughout migratory range;
- maintain full government support for international collaboration on research and conservation.

Site/species safeguard and management

Recommendations:
- protect important roost sites;
- maintain and improve continuity of food supply throughout migratory range.

Advisory, communications and publicity

> **Recommendations:**
> - maintain and enhance education programmes relating to this species;
> - encourage wider public understanding of the possible "keystone" role of this, and similar, species in the maintenance of arid zone ecology;
> - appeal for wider distributional data through, for example, observations at hummingbird feeders.

Future research and monitoring

> **Recommendations:**
> - refine knowledge of distribution, including establishing any distribution south of Mexico and identifying key sites;
> - conduct research into relationship between wide fluctuations in numbers at northern end of distribution and foraging opportunities in breeding areas, and hence, identification of appropriate population-monitoring protocols;
> - carry out further research on ecological requirements and role as possible "keystone" species in maintenance of arid zone ecology.

Wider application

It is widely believed that a breakdown in the mutualism between the bats and the plants would have major effects on desert ecology, including the range of other wildlife dependent on *Agave* and cacti.

The conservation issues affecting this species similarly affect other migratory desert nectarivores, including the related *L. curasoae*, *Choeronycteris mexicana*, as well as *Platalina genovensium* (subfamily Lonchophyllinae).

The other species of *Leptonycteris*, *L. curasoae* (including the forms *sanborni* and *yerbabuanae*), is distributed from Colombia, Venezuela, and Netherlands Antilles through El Salvador, Guatemala, and Mexico to the USA. In Curacao, there are reports of only small fractions of earlier populations remaining (800–1,000 in two caves in a 1992/93 survey). Education programmes and protection of key cave sites is proposed. Surveys in Mexico in the 1980s found one large colony of 15,000, two small groups, and unconfirmed reports from two other sites of 3,000 and 800–1,000 bats. In the USA, *L. curasoae* occupies the arid scrub of central Arizona and southwest New Mexico, where it roosts in caves, tunnels, and mines. It used to be much more common than *L. nivalis* with 20,000 recorded in one site. This site was lost when the cave was opened for tourism. A 1974 survey of all known roosts in the USA resulted in 135 individuals. A 1989 estimate suggested a population of 2,500–3,500, but a more recent survey located only about 500 in one cave in Arizona and none elsewhere. However, reports of bats feeding at hummingbird feeders in other parts of Arizona suggest two possible additional populations.

5.5.9 Species Action Plan – *Desmodus rotundus* Common vampire bat
(Family Phyllostomidae)

Threats

It is not considered that this species is in itself threatened, even by concerted vampire bat control programmes, but those control programmes can have considerable impact on bats and other fauna using caves. It has been stated that one control programme in Venezuela resulted in the destruction of 40,000 caves, and the loss of large populations of harmless or beneficial bats, as well as other cave fauna. Recent incidents of vampire bats attacking humans in Peru, Brazil, and El Salvador have attracted worldwide press interest and resulted in extensive eradication programmes. Control methods have included burning and gassing of potential roosts, as well as the dynamiting of known roosts. The impact of vampire bats on bat conservation is primarily in the negative publicity for all bats arising from vampire bat-related problems, and the unreasoned response resulting from rabies outbreaks in cattle or the incidence of vampire bat attacks on humans.

Summary

Desmodus rotundus is one of three blood-feeding bat species, which together are currently regarded as the subfamily Desmodontinae of the family Phyllostomidae. *D. rotundus* generally feeds on larger mammals, such as cattle, equids, or even seals, and may have benefited from forest clearance for the wide-scale introduction of cattle and other domestic animals. The reliance on blood-feeding has led to a range of physiological and behavioural attributes. It has also led

Common vampire bat, *Desmodus rotundus*.

M.A. Hutson

to it being regarded as a pest through the debilitating effects of its feeding on host animals; this includes direct feeding activity and the creation of wounds that result in other infestations and infections, as well as outbreaks of rabies associated with vampire bats. It occasionally feeds on humans. While most current control measures are unlikely to extirpate this species, non-specific control programmes have at times resulted in immense damage to other bats and their habitats, particularly caves.

Protected status

This species is probably not protected anywhere within its range, except under very general wildlife protection legislation (e.g., in Panama), and generally it is regarded as a pest. It is subject to a range of control measures, varying in efficacy and damage to the wider environment.

- *The 2000 IUCN Red List of Threatened Species*: Not listed

Biological assessment

The common vampire bat is a medium-sized species (forearm 52–63mm, weight 25–40g). It ranges from northern Mexico through Central America and South America to central Chile in the west and Uruguay in the east; it is probably absent from much of Amazonia at present, but that may change with changes in cattle distribution. It also occurs on Isla Margarita off the northern coast of Venezuela and on Trinidad, and formerly was recorded on Cuba and in Florida and northern California.

The blood-feeding habit is associated with many unique features of morphology, physiology, and behaviour. This includes enhanced quadrupedal ability, dentition, extended reproductive cycle (nine months pregnancy, nine months lactation), mutual grooming and food sharing, or 'community' (cross-parental) support. The feeding behaviour also has its effect on the host animals, such as cattle, where losses per annum have been estimated in millions of US dollars, though accurate figures are hard to obtain. The populations of *Desmodus* are undoubtedly unnaturally high in many areas due to the artificially high density of cattle. The effect on cattle is multifaceted, including debilitation from blood loss sustained by animals that are repeatedly visited. The anti-coagulant in a vampire bat's saliva is responsible for blood loss far beyond that taken by the bat. The opening of wounds results in fly worry and infestation by, for example, screw-worm or infection with micro-organisms. Rabies transmission is also a problem. While the economic losses may actually be a very small proportion of the total value of cattle and comparable to a range of other loss factors, vampire control has been widely practised.

The anti-coagulant characteristics of vampire bat saliva have long been the interest of medical research into the dissolution of blood clots, and modern techniques will probably allow the manufacture of a synthetic equivalent.

Conservation action to date

Efforts have been made to develop more targeted, non-chemical methods for the control of vampire bats. Immunization techniques involving oral vaccines for the localised control of rabies in vampire bats could also be considered. Other initiatives have included education programmes, such as a video programme developed by Bat Conservation International in the USA, and a range of other educational and training efforts that have been attempted locally and occasionally nationally.

The 11th International Bat Research Conference, held in Brazil, August 1998, included a symposium on vampire bats, their management, and associated conservation issues. Attended by bat researchers, public health, and veterinary officers, the meeting developed a Resolution, details of which can be found in Chapter 5.2. The following proposed actions draw upon that resolution and associated discussion.

Action Plan objectives

1. Implement mechanisms for the control of vampire bats, where and when a problem arises, that are specific to the problem being faced.
2. Provide education in the identification of vampire bats and related problems, and the means to carry out a measured response, if necessary.

Conservation recommendations to meet Action Plan objectives

Policy and legislation

Recommendations:

- apply vampire bat control activities only where there is an agreed problem, such as bites on humans or a high incidence of bites on domestic animals, and/or when there is a vampire bat-related outbreak of rabies;
- withdraw the use of environmentally damaging practices, including those that can seriously affect non-target bats and other animals;
- carry out an evaluation of control measures identified as appropriate to the incident, with the assistance of academic institutions or other appropriate non-governmental organizations;
- make pre-exposure rabies treatment available, along with subsequent monitoring of antibody levels, to all those involved in vampire bat control programmes.

Site/species safeguard and management

Recommendations:

- quantify the economic, public health, and environmental impacts (direct and indirect) of vampire bats and their control;
- carry out national assessments and monitoring of the distribution of major vampire bat-related problems;

- collaborate on sponsoring international training courses for control personnel and bat specialists on vampire bat biology and their control in Latin America, and encourage standardization of local implementation.

Advisory, communications and publicity

Recommendations:
- establish an international information exchange system to encourage the collation and exchange of information on incidents, the management of vampire bats, and related disease control; this may include a website;
- increase efforts to develop programmes of outreach and public awareness on the nature and levels of risk associated with vampire bats, on the environmental damage that can result from inappropriate control programmes, and on the intrinsic interest and unique characteristics of vampire bats;
- establish mechanisms to detect and report vampire bat bites inflicted upon people and animals using the active assistance of academic institutions and non-governmental organizations.

Future research and monitoring

Recommendations:
- increase research into the development of carefully targeted strategies based on specific behaviour of the bats, and the use of non-chemical and oral vaccines for the control of rabies and related diseases;
- develop a model to enable prediction of circumstances where vampire bat management may be required; this should include further research into the incidence and epidemiology of rabies outbreaks, and into exceptional incidents of human attacks, including unusual weather patterns, disease control in other wild and domesticated animals, and changes in land use;
- conduct further research into vampire bat ecology and behaviour both in natural habitats and those altered by human activity; this should include population dynamics, reproductive patterns, growth, longevity, roost use, movements (migration), and nocturnal behaviour;
- undertake studies of the evolution and ecology of the rabies virus and its relationship with vampire bat population biology.

Wider application

Every effort should be made to retain populations of all vampire bat species throughout their ranges. However, the above recommendations are intended primarily to protect a wide range of non-target species affected by some control programmes. Education and training programmes also offer the opportunity to emphasise the harmless or beneficial nature of the wide diversity of bats in Latin America.

5.5.10 Species Action Plan – *Myzopoda aurita* Old World or Madagascar sucker-footed bat

(Family Myzopodidae)

Threats

Loss of forest is undoubtedly a threat, but the species is poorly known and its conservation requirements remain to be established. If the species roosts in *Ravenala*, its roost sites may be secure since this plant is widespread in primary forest, but is more common in secondary forest.

Summary

This very distinct monotypic family is restricted to Madagascar. It is very poorly known. As a rare and unique species, further research is required for the development of necessary conservation action.

Protected status

It is not protected in Madagascar.

- *The 2000 IUCN Red List of Threatened Species*: VU A2c.

Biological assessment

M. aurita is a small bat (forearm length 46–50mm, weight 8–10g) and is characterized by the presence of conspicuous sucker-like pads on the thumb and soles of the feet, and characteristic ears and palate. It is recorded from less than 10 localities on the east coast and one locality on the west coast of Madagascar. It appears to be restricted mainly to the eastern rainforests. Most of these records are old. It is also recorded from a Pleistocene site in East Africa. It appears to be restricted to rainforest and *savoka* (secondary forest) and has been found roosting in the unrolled leaf of a *Ravenala madagascariensis* (Musaceae). One individual was mist-netted over a small stream, another in a vanilla plantation, and one in a sparsely forested area over a path close to a stream. The latter two individuals had radio-transmitters attached. The first immediately flew out of range of the receivers and the tag was found the following morning on the ground having been dislodged by the bat.

Old World or Madagascar sucker-footed bat, *Myzopoda aurita*.

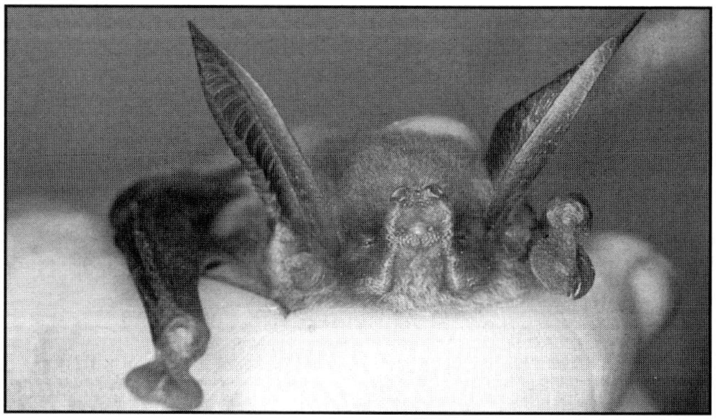

D. Bennett

The other bat was also quickly lost to the receivers. It was relocated two days later up to 1.5km from the release point, and was also tracked to close to the capture site. It was not subsequently relocated. In 1996, a single individual was captured during 20 nights of mist-netting in Tampolo Reserve north of Fenenerive-Est over a marsh containing abundant *Ravenala* near a degraded forest. Faeces from an individual captured by M.C. Gopfert and I.T. Wasserthal near Tolagnaro in 1992 comprised of Microlepidoptera. In captivity, this bat used its adhesive discs to cling to the surface of *Ravenala* leaves, the adhesion was sufficient to carry the weight of the bat. It roosted in a head-upwards position, apparently using the stiff projecting tail as a prop. Full data are not yet available for recent studies of the species, but suggest it may be widespread in parts of northeast Madagascar.

Conservation action to date

None.

Action Plan objectives

1. Improve knowledge of distribution and habitat requirements.
2. Effect any measures necessary to ensure the long-term survival of the species.

Conservation recommendations to meet Action Plan objectives

Policy and legislation

Recommendation:
- give full protection to the species and encourage research into its requirements.

Site/species safeguard and management

Recommendations:
- designate suitable areas with centres of population as reserves and manage for the benefit of the species, once details of the species' distribution and requirements are known; these may fit into the existing network of nature reserves;
- maintain *Ravenala* since the species probably roosts in its unfurled leaves; however, since *Ravenala* is one of the first colonising trees of disturbed habitats, particularly on wet ground, and is such a culturally important tree in Madagascar, its status is unlikely to become a conservation problem.

Advisory, communications and publicity

Recommendation:
- emphasise the importance of this species as the sole member of a distinct family of bats restricted to Madagascar to the authorities and people of Madagascar.

Future research and monitoring

Recommendations:
- carry out further surveys of distribution and abundance;
- radio-track individuals to establish roosting and foraging requirements, in particular the association with *Ravenala* or other roost trees;
- investigate further the flight morphology and echolocation calls to interpret feeding behaviour and foraging habitat, and help to develop field survey techniques;
- examine droppings from trapped animals to identify prey types.

Wider application

Management of natural habitats for this species is likely to benefit other bats, including a number of other endemic species.

5.5.11 Species Action Plan – *Kerivoula papuensis* Golden-tipped bat

(Family Vespertilionidae)

Threats

There are no clearly identified threats, but all species of the genus remain little known and poorly recorded. In Australia, forestry practice (including clearance and fragmentation), use of forest fires, and predation by domestic and feral cats are current potential threats. Changes in the status of the bird species providing roost sites for these bats may be important. In general, the difficulties of assessing the status and threats to species that roost singly or in small groups in forest vegetation may lead to declines going undetected.

Summary

The subfamily Kerivoulinae includes 21 species, which may all be included in the genus *Kerivoula*, occurring in subsaharan Africa and the Indian Subcontinent to Australia. Some authors separate three species (*atrox*, *jagori*, and *papuensis*) as the genus *Phoniscus*, which occurs from Thailand to Australia. All species are poorly known, although recent work on *K. papuensis* has added much to our understanding of the genus. Most species are rarely recorded, possibly by nature of their roosting and foraging behaviour; of the 21 species, three are considered Vulnerable, four Lower Risk: Near Threatened, and two Data Deficient. Most species are usually solitary, and most recorded roosts are in birds nests or amongst dead leaves.

The recent increase in records of *K. papuensis* in Australia has followed the development of novel trapping techniques, and has allowed further detailed studies through radio-tracking and other techniques. The species occurs in the coastal areas of Australia, from northern Queensland to southern New South Wales; there are about five records from Papua New Guinea and it is recorded from the island of Biak (north west of Irian Jaya).

Protected status

Protected in Australia under State legislation.

- *The 2000 IUCN Red List of Threatened Species*: LR: lc, but has more recently been considered as LR: nt in Australia and this should probably apply to the global status of the species.

Biological assessment

K. papuensis has a head and body length of 45–60mm, forearm 35.5–40.5mm, and weighs 6–10g. It is characterised by long, fine, woolly hair. Apart from its occurrence in Papua New Guinea, it was thought to be extinct in Australia until its 'rediscovery' in 1981. Now, it is thought to be probably restricted to a narrow band down the east coast of Australia, where it is proving to be most common in some areas of northern Queensland, with perhaps some other localised centres of distribution; otherwise it would appear to be sparsely distributed throughout its range. It is probably most common in various rainforest types (mesophyll vine forest to semi-evergreen vine thickets and ecotone areas), but is also found in some sclerophyll forest, riparian *Casuarina* forest, and coastal melaleuca, as well as distinctly dry areas of central Queensland (e.g., Kroombit Tops) and southeast New South Wales. It occurs to 1,300m in Papua New Guinea. The most commonly recorded roost site is in the suspended nests of yellow-throated scrub wren (*Sericornis citreogularis*) and brown gerygone (*Gerygone mouki*) at a height of 2–5m The nests may be modified to provide easy access via a basal hole. It is not found throughout the range of these birds and is also recorded in areas where they are rare or absent. It also roosts in palm fronds and thick vegetation near water courses, in tree hollows, outside of branches, and in suspended dead foliage. In Biak, it was found in a cave and buildings. Records in Papua New Guinea are of solitary or small groups of animals, in Biak a small group with one adult male, and in Australia usually singly, but up to 20 have been found in one maternity group. Little is known of breeding, but lactating adult females were trapped in temperate dry eucalypt forest of the south coast of New South Wales in March and April. With its broad wings and hovering flight, it is highly manoeuvrable and capable of foraging by gleaning or aerial hawking in cluttered environments. The echolocation calls are very quiet and are only audible on a bat detector from less than 1.5m. It feeds mainly on spiders (over 90% by volume), plus some Coleoptera, Lepidoptera, and Diptera.

In the Indomalayan Region, *K. picta* has been found roosting in the half-constructed (not completed) nests of Baya weaver (Ploceidae) in an area where suitable tree roost sites may have been scarce; it has also been found roosting in dead pendant leaves of trees and vines, in flowers, and in tall grass (including sugar cane). *K. papillosa* has been taken from the internode of bamboo, and *K. atrox* from an abandoned nest of a broadbill (Eurylaimidae).

In Africa, most species are associated with rainforest, but some also occur in savanna woodland though not in very arid areas. Various species have been recorded from the nests of a range of weaver birds and two from nests of sunbirds (Nectariniidae); in at least one instance, bats shared the nest with wasps. Otherwise, they are also recorded from dead foliage, hollow branches, lichen, on rough bark, and around houses, including in thatch. All species occur singly or in small groups of up to about six individuals and have a weak fluttering, butterfly-like flight.

Golden-tipped bat, *Kerivoula papuensis.*

L. Lumsden

Conservation action to date

Since its 'rediscovery' in Australia, the ability to catch this species in harp traps has led to increased trapping for distributional studies. Radio-telemetry, light-tagging, and dietary studies have been carried out on trapped animals. Bat biologists and ornithologists have collaborated to assess its occurrence in bird nests. This is assisting the identification of habitat and foraging requirements of the bat.

Action Plan objectives

1. Assess the status and ecological requirements of *Kerivoula* species.
2. Assess whether species of this genus have identifiable conservation problems.
3. Develop action to meet identified conservation problems.

Conservation recommendations to meet Action Plan objectives

Policy and legislation

> **Recommendation:**
> - ensure forestry management practices in Australia (New South Wales and Queensland) support the conservation of this bat species.

Site/species safeguard and management

No recommendations.

Advisory, communications and publicity

> **Recommendation:**
> - maintain communications with ornithologists to accumulate further information.

Future research and monitoring

> **Recommendations:**
> - survey to clarify distribution (including in Indonesia and Papua New Guinea);
> - assess significance of eucalypt forest in Australia;
> - investigate factors affecting roost selection, including in areas where the two principal host bird species are uncommon or absent;
> - carry out DNA analysis to assess levels of differentiation or isolation of populations throughout range.

Wider application

Four threatened bat species in Australia are recorded from bird nests, which may be important for two species; the relative importance of such roost sites for other bat species is yet to be established.

5.5.12 Species Action Plan – *Antrozous pallidus* Pallid bat

(Family Vespertilionidae)

Threats

While not considered endangered as yet, there are serious concerns about the degradation of habitat for such arid zone species, ranging from loss of riverine habitat, over-extraction of available water and, by contrast, increased irrigation for agriculture. Development of mineral extraction activities may also be a threat.

Summary

Antrozous is usually regarded as a monotypic genus, including the single species *A. pallidus.* We have included *Bauerus dubiaquercus* of Central America in this genus. *A. pallidus* occurs from central Mexico through the southern deserts and grasslands of western USA to a small area of British Columbia in Canada; a separate subspecies is recognized from Cuba (*A. p. koopmani*), but is poorly known. The pallid bat feeds on relatively large prey and has fairly specific roost requirements in caves, mines, and rock crevices.

Protected status

This species is completely protected in Canada under the Wildlife Act, but not listed under the Endangered Species Act in the USA. Information on its status in Mexico and Cuba is not available.

- *The 2000 IUCN Red List of Threatened Species*: Not listed

Biological assessment

The pallid bat is a medium-sized bat (forearm 45–50mm, weight 15–21g). It has large ears, broad flight membranes and, generally, very pale fur. It lives in areas of desert scrub, including open sagebrush and grasslands closely associated with rock outcrops or canyonland, and especially near water. It can be be found at elevations up to 2,440m. It is less abundant at the higher altitudes of evergreen or mixed forest. It generally forms small colonies, sometimes as large as 200 individuals, in rock crevices and artificial structures such as in attics of houses and outbuildings, mines, and under bridges. Occasionally hollow trees are used. Colonies are sensitive to disturbance, although in some areas roost sites are changed naturally. Thermal requirements for day roosts seem to be very precise and are a limiting factor. The colonies may include males, but most males leave the colony before parturition. Adult females usually produce twin offspring. A strong mother-young

Pallid bat, *Antrozous pallidus.*

M. Tuttle/BCI

bond and group cohesion is reported. *Antrozous* is not a deep hibernator, and is found in winter in small groups of one to four, exceptionally 20–100, sometimes remaining active in temperatures as low as 2°C. Generally, however, it is best adapted to hot, dry summers and mild winters.

Some prey is taken on the wing, but much is relatively large invertebrates (20–70mm) taken by hovering, gliding, or walking, and pouncing on the prey on the ground or on vegetation. Most foraging is carried out in uncluttered areas of sparse vegetation. Large prey, such as orthopterans, beetles, or scorpions, may be carried to a night roost, which is often communal. Small vertebrates, such as lizards (*Phrynosoma* species) or pocket mice (*Perognathus* species) form a minor part of the diet. Pallid bats also visit flowers, principally to take insects, but effectively becoming pollinators, especially of Cactaceae and Agavaceae. There are local seasonal movements, but the species is not thought to be migratory. There are no rigorous data on population trends.

Conservation action to date

No action to date except in Canada where sagebrush and grassland is being irrigated in order to cultivate orchards, and investigations are in hand to assess impact and to implement appropriate conservation action.

Action Plan objectives

1. Maintain species at a favourable conservation status.

Conservation recommendations to meet Action Plan objectives

Policy and legislation

Recommendations:
- protect the species in its centres of population and the extremes of its distribution, including disjunct populations, notably Cuba;
- develop policies to ensure that habitat modification of arid areas does not threaten this species.

Site/species safeguard and management

Recommendation:
- implement habitat preservation and restoration, where necessary.

Advisory, communications and publicity

Recommendation:
- highlight the species' rarity, its special features, and its economic importance in education programmes in parts of the range.

Future research and monitoring

Recommendations:
- conduct further research to establish whether or not breeding extends into Canada;
- survey for night roosts to establish details of distribution;
- survey and carry out research to establish status and any conservation problems for the subspecies in Cuba.

Wider application

A number of arid country insectivorous bat species may face similar problems. For example, *Otonycteris hemprichii* in the southern Palaearctic has a broadly similar morphology and behaviour, and concerns have been expressed about the same threats as have been identified for *Antrozous* applying to this species in central Asia and elsewhere. These threats have also been identified from South America, southern Africa, and Australia. Thus, to a lesser extent, some species of genera such as *Nycteris* (Africa and Asia) and *Nyctophilus* (Australasia) may be similarly affected.

5.5.13 Species Action Plan – *Myotis dasycneme* Pond bat

(Family Vespertilionidae)

Threats

The species is threatened by habitat change, such as the renovation and maintenance of buildings with roosts, including the use of chemicals for remedial timber treatment that are toxic to mammals. Few nursery roost sites are known and many of these have been lost, although numbers in hibernation sites have shown a slower decline in The Netherlands.

Water pollution may also be a threat; the species already has a relatively restricted foraging habitat of broad, open flat water of canals, rivers, and lakes with relatively open banks, and within this available habitat possibly some further seasonal (summer) restrictions. Such restrictions in summer may be opportunistic rather than enforced, and it may be that the requirements for wider dispersal in spring, and possibly autumn, are more of a conservation problem than concentration in summer in good foraging habitat close to the roost. The requirements during migration are not known and may be a constraint.

Summary

The genus *Myotis* is found worldwide and comprises 92 species. The subgenus *Leuconoe*, with about 40 species, includes *M. dasycneme* in a group of species closely associated with open water. *M. dasycneme* occurs in northern Europe, with historic or subfossil records south to Switzerland, Austria, and former Yugoslavia, and east to the River Yenisey in central Russia, with a single record from Manchuria. There are apparent centres of population where marked declines have been observed, while the species is apparently sparse in other areas. It has been considered one of the most endangered species in Europe, although recent increased survey work using bat detectors suggests it is not as rare as formerly thought.

Protected status

It is protected in all European range states and possibly in most of the rest of its range. In Europe, it is included in Annex II of the EEC Council Directive on the Conservation of Natural Habitats and of Wild Fauna and Flora 1992 (EEC Habitat Directive), requiring full protection and designation of Special Areas of Conservation to maintain it and its habitats. Other international treaties of relevance are the Agreement on the Conservation of Bats in Europe (Bonn Convention, 1994), Convention on the Conservation of European Wildlife and Natural Habitats (Bern Convention, 1982), and Bern Convention Recommendation 36 (1992, Conservation of Underground Habitats). Most European range states are party to at least one of these treaties.

- *The 2000 IUCN Red List of Threatened Species*: VU A2c.

Biological assessment

M. dasycneme is a medium-sized species (forearm 41–49mm, weight 11–23g) with large feet. It feeds principally over open, calm water, particularly canals, rivers, and lakes, on small emerging and emergent insects often taken from the water surface. It prefers water lined by open rough vegetation without trees.

Most of the known summer maternity roosts are in buildings, often in large attics and church steeples, in groups of 40–600. Some tree and bat box roosts are recorded. It frequently hibernates in underground habitats ranging from natural caves to cellars and bunkers. It is a partial migrant, with winter and summer roosts often separated by more than 100km (maximum recorded: 330km), and it may need good habitat links between summer and winter roosts.

There is a strong suggestion that within the known distribution, the summer occurrence is limited to relatively small centres of population separated by areas of very sparse populations in the western part of the range. Such data as are available for the eastern part suggest a similar pattern, and that the species is often rare in apparently suitable habitat. It is no longer found in Zeeland (Denmark). Designated centres of population include The Netherlands, Jutland, to a lesser extent eastern Germany and Poland, the Baltic States, and lowlands in parts of the former Soviet Union.

In 1986, there was a suggested population of 3,000 individuals in western Europe and a world population of 7,000, but this is regarded as an underestimate, particularly for populations outside western Europe. A recent population estimate for The Netherlands was 8–10,000.

Pond bat, *Myotis dasycneme*.

F.R. Greenaway

Conservation action to date

Numbers in underground habitats have increased following site protection. Considerable effort has been applied to the conservation of known maternity roosts, but not always with success in view of requirements for renovation and maintenance of buildings used as roosts. Particularly in The Netherlands, the use of bat detectors has more clearly demonstrated the distribution of the species, and hence allowed more precise definition of foraging habitat requirements and the need for an adequate network of protected flightpaths between roosts and foraging sites.

Under the Agreement on the Conservation of Bats in Europe, the migratory behaviour of the species will be examined. The Bern Convention has recently published a Species Action Plan under its obligations to the Pan-European Biological and Landscape Diversity Strategy.

Action Plan objectives

1. Establish more precise details of habitat, including roost requirements, and implement appropriate management.
2. Investigate distribution in relation to climatic factors.
3. Establish nature of suggested centres of population with a view to ensuring their adequate protection and enhancement of intermediate areas, where appropriate.

4. Establish co-operative measures to monitor populations, assess reasons for population change, and develop action as appropriate.

Conservation recommendations to meet Action Plan objectives

Policy and legislation

> **Recommendation:**
> - enforce protective legislation throughout its range; there may be the need for improved protective legislation which takes account of habitat requirements in the eastern part of the range.

Site/species safeguard and management

> **Recommendations:**
> - afford the species the highest priority in decisions that may affect its maternity and hibernation roost sites;
> - evaluate the importance of other roost sites and give appropriate protection;
> - ensure co-operation on protection of populations that make seasonal cross-border movements.

Advisory, communications and publicity

> **Recommendation:**
> - ensure that those managing buildings appropriate for roosts and other required habitat have knowledge of how and where to seek advice when their activities may affect the status of the species.

Future research and monitoring.

> **Recommendations:**
> - ensure implementation of detailed international Action Plan published by the Bern Convention with the involvement of the Co-ordinating Panel for the Conservation of Bats in Europe, in consideration of obligations of international treaties;
> - assess all available information, and use trained bat detector operators to establish details of distribution and to confirm centres of population;
> - assess distributional data against habitat, climatic, and other environmental factors;
> - establish long-term population monitoring procedures through as much of the range as possible; this may be accomplished by bat detector field surveys, maternity roost observations, and hibernation site counts;
> - review seasonal movement patterns, particularly in relation to cross-border movements.

Wider application

Related species in the Palaearctic, such as *M. daubentonii*, *M. capaccinii*, and *M. macrodactylus*, have similar foraging behaviour. *M. capaccinii* is regarded as vulnerable, while *M. daubentonii*, in particular, does not seem to be threatened and indeed may be undergoing population expansion. Other austro-oriental species, such as *M. adversus* and *M. hasseltii*, are widespread and common, but a number of species, including some whose validity has been questioned, such as *M. longipes* and *M. fimbriatus*, are also of restricted occurrence. A greater understanding of *M. dasycneme* in relation to the common species may help with the conservation of other rare species with similar habitat restrictions.

5.5.14 Species Action Plan – *Myotis sodalis* Indiana bat

(Family Vespertilionidae)

Threats

The species is highly dependent on a few caves for hibernation. These caves have been subject to damage such as flooding, collapse, and vandalism. Three hundred thousand bats died in a natural flooding of Bat Cave in Kentucky. There is a report of two boys killing 10,000 individuals in a cave in Kentucky in the 1960s. In 1986, there was pressure to seal a mine used by 140,000 Indiana bats following the trapping of two teenagers and their subsequent difficult rescue. Closure affecting access or changes to the internal environment has led to abandonment or reduction in numbers. In one cave used by 100,000 bats, various human disturbances reduced the population to 27, but this cave has recently been restored for bat use. Handling or other disturbance by biologists, for example for banding, has also affected populations.

Declines may also be attributed to habitat loss due, for example, to deforestation of streamside habitat, especially the removal of large dead trees for firewood and during canalisation. Pesticide use may still be a problem. It appears that upland forest habitat may be critical for this species. Despite vigorous conservation efforts, the species still seems to be declining.

Indiana bat, *Myotis sodalis.*

M. Tuttle/BCI

Summary

M. sodalis is a North American species of the most widespread genus of bats. The species occurs in the USA from eastern Oklahoma and Kansas north and east to Vermont, and south to northwestern Florida. Winter roosts are in caves where the bats form large dense clusters. Summer roosts are mainly in trees. The population is estimated at 250,000–400,000, with 85% hibernating in seven caves and 50% using just two. Thus, the loss of any one of these sites would result in a major decline in an already depleted population. The population is believed to have declined by 50% between about 1960 and 1983, and by a further 50% since 1983 and it is still declining. The continued decline of this species, despite the protection of cave roost sites, suggests that the protection of summer habitat, both foraging areas and tree roosting sites, is critical.

Many of the factors influencing this species also apply to the gray bat (*Myotis grisescens*), which is also discussed below.

Protected status

It is listed as Endangered by the US Fish and Wildlife Service (1973) and again in 1989 following the results of work on a Recovery Plan produced in 1983.

- *The 2000 IUCN Red List of Threatened Species*: EN A1c

Biological assessment

The Indiana bat is a small species (forearm 35–40mm; weight 6–9g). In summer, it is principally associated with streams and river floodplains, with maternity roosts in nearby trees, under bark, or in hollows. Some males use caves all summer. It forages in or under tree canopies to a height of about 30m, feeding mainly on moths and aquatic insects. Migrations of over 480km are recorded between summer and winter roosts. Autumn migration may be early to caves where the bats swarm during the mating period. Swarming at caves may continue into October, but hibernation is generally uninterrupted between November and March, with females leaving the cave area in April. Males leave later or may stay close to the cave. The species' distribution is particularly associated with major limestone areas, since caves are vital for hibernation. Caves with high humidity and cool temperature (4–6°C) are preferred. In Missouri, only 24 of 4,700 known caves have ever contained significant populations. Dense clusters of close to 3,000 bats per square metre are formed.

Of the winter population, 85% is concentrated into seven caves in Missouri (three caves), Kentucky (two caves), and Indiana (two caves), with 50% in two of these sites. Only occasional records in winter are noted in the north of the range and in West Virginia, for example, the maximum winter population in one site in 1995 was 6,808, with 515 in other sites. Many sites have been lost; in Connecticut and Virginia, Indiana bats were historically found in nine counties, but are now recorded from only two caves in Lee and Wise Counties. In Pennsylvania, a former population of about 5,000 was reduced to 150 in 1980. Recent extensions of known hibernation site range in Minnesota and New Jersey may be the result of greater search effort.

Conservation action to date

A Recovery Plan was produced in 1983 resulting in increased co-ordination of monitoring, improved site protection, and further ecological studies.

Action Plan objectives

1. Recover population to enable removal of species from Endangered category.
2. Protect and enhance key hibernation sites.
3. Protect and restore feeding habitat as required.

Conservation recommendations to meet Action Plan objectives

Policy and legislation

Recommendations:
- maintain and enhance protection of significant hibernation sites;
- develop policies for summer habitat management as appropriate.

Site/species safeguard and management

Recommendation:
- implement any summer habitat management policies developed.

Advisory, communications and publicity

Recommendations:
- maintain good relationships with caving groups;
- continue development and publicity for policies for the management of disused mines;
- ensure forest managers are aware of summer habitat requirements.

Future research and monitoring

Recommendations:
- conduct further surveys of abandoned mines;
- carry out further research on summer habitat requirements;
- assess effects of summer habitat loss, water pollution, siltation, and pesticide use;
- conduct further detailed surveys of distribution involving trapping along streams and at cave entrances;

- investigate non-invasive monitoring methods, for example the use of thermal infrared imaging of emergences and digital picture processing; early research suggests results within 6% of counts by experienced or skilled observers;
- use DNA gene markers to relate summer habitat use to specific winter cave colonies.

Wider application

The gray bat (*Myotis grisescens*) has an even greater reliance than *M. sodalis* on a limited number of caves; it has rarely been found roosting outside of caves and mines. It is similarly protected by the US Fish and Wildlife Service and is regarded as EN: A1c in *The 2000 IUCN Red List of Threatened Species*. It was once considered the most abundant mammal in the southeastern USA. One endangered cave fish and one species of crayfish inhabit caves used by gray bat colonies.

The gray bat has a more restricted distribution than the Indiana bat in the eastern USA, from east Kansas and Oklahoma eastwards to southwest Virginia and North Carolina; the northern limit is in southern Illinois and Indiana, and the southern limit is Florida.

Threats to the cave colonies have included excessive visits by cavers, vandalism, commercialisation, land development, closure, and the activities of biologists. Badly designed protective grilles for caves have caused desertion of sites. It is believed that the extraction of guano for saltpetre during the American Civil War was perhaps the first recorded cause of marked decline. Clearance of vegetation around cave entrances makes bats vulnerable to predators such as screech owls (*Otus asio*). Foraging habitat is not considered a limiting factor at present, although there are concerns about disruption of wooded flight lines used in migration. Migrations of over 500km are recorded between relatively warm summer caves and hibernation sites in deep vertical cold caves. Of an estimated summer population of 10,000 in Florida, only a few hundred are found in winter sites. In summer, the species forages over rivers and reservoirs, especially those with forest borders, and feeds mainly on Lepidoptera, Diptera, Coleoptera, and Trichoptera. It will travel up to 25km from the roost to feed. Maternity colonies may move between caves in a limited area, but may use as much as 70km of lakeshore for roosting and feeding. Some caves are used as transient roosts during migration.

Past populations were estimated to be many millions, with 1.5 million in one hibernaculum. A 1982 estimate put the population at 1.6 million, a decline of 50% since the 1960s. Subsequent cave protection has resulted in some increases, but overall the population is probably still in decline. Nine caves hold 95% of the winter population, with 50% in one cave in Alabama. Declines of between 60 and 90% have been recorded for caves in Kentucky, Missouri, Arkansas, Tennessee, and Alabama.

A Recovery Plan was produced in 1982 to develop cave acquisition, ensure protection, and to limit disturbance, and was coupled with public education. It considered that seasonal habitat requirements and movement patterns were well documented, but that the effects of environmental disturbance, e.g., pollution and siltation, foraging habitat and prey, and control of research, especially in hibernacula, needed further investigation. The Plan identified the need to:

1. prevent disturbance to important roosts by public education using literature, interpretative signs, and talks; control unauthorized entry using warning signs, gates, fences, and monitoring; control adverse modifications, such as inappropriate entrance protection, creation of new entrances, damage to surrounding habitat, and lack of knowledge by authorities;
2. maintain, protect, and restore foraging habitat through public education using literature and talks, and prevent adverse modification to foraging areas and travel corridors; also determine habitat requirements, preserve water quality, forest cover, and monitor changes;
3. monitor population trends in hibernation sites and maternity colonies, and investigate presence of toxic chemicals in insects, guano, and bats.

This Plan has achieved many successes in terms of direct conservation activity, public relations, and research. The co-operation of cavers has been elicited to declare bat caves off-limits. Following protection, four caves formerly housing 128,000 non-breeding bats now support expanding maternity colonies and 692,000 bats. However, the population is at most stable and may still be in decline, so clearly further work is required.

5.5.15 Species Action Plan – *Plecotus townsendii* Townsend's big-eared bat

(Family Vespertilionidae)

Threats

The principal threats seem to be disturbance to caves and loss of habitat, particularly habitat close to roost caves. The species is especially sensitive to human disturbance. The reworking of old mine areas has caused local losses, not just from the destruction of, or disturbance to, roost sites, but from other environmental damage, such as cyanide poisoning associated with expanding gold-mining operations. In the case of the Ozark big-eared bat (*Plecotus townsendii ingens*), collecting was also considered a threat, though perhaps more through disturbance than the removal of individual animals. Initial attempts at cave protection using inappropriately designed grilles were also a problem. Within the range of the Ozark big-eared bat some caves have been destroyed, and other apparently suitable caves are not used.

Summary

The two North American species of *Plecotus*, *P. townsendii* and *P. rafinesquii*, together with *P. mexicanus* (confined to Mexico), may be recognized as forming the separate genus *Corynorhinus*. Up to five subspecies of *P. townsendii* are recognized: *P. t. townsendii* (Townsend's big-eared bat), including *P. t. pallescens*, is widely distributed in the western USA, north to British Columbia in Canada, and south (as *P. t. australis*) into Mexico; *P. t. ingens* (Ozark big-eared bat) is restricted to Arkansas, Missouri, and Oklahoma; *P. t. virginianus* (Virginia big-eared bat) is restricted to Virginia, West Virginia, North Carolina, and east Kentucky. *P. rafinesquii* occurs in the southeastern USA. A fourth Nearctic big-eared bat is usually regarded as belonging to a separate genus (*Idionycteris phyllotis*).

These species are gleaning bats that mostly roost in caves. It is the eastern forms (*P. t. ingens* and *virginianus*, and *P. rafinesquii*) that are of particular concern, being reliant on caves. That part of the population of *P. townsendii* in California is also regarded as highly endangered.

Protected status

In Canada, it is included in the Blue List of potentially endangered and threatened species. In the USA, *P. t. ingens* and *virginianus* are included on the Endangered Species List (1979).

- *The 2000 IUCN Red List of Threatened Species*: VU A2c

Biological assessment

P. townsendii is a small bat (forearm 35–52mm, weight 5–13g). *Plecotus* species are characterized by the presence of ears which are as long as the body and joined at the base. Most roost sites of *P. townsendii* are in caves with maternity colonies of up to 400, though usually 75–150. Movements of up to 64km in West Virginia and 43km in California have been recorded between summer and winter roosts. Virginia big-eared bats roost in caves in limestone karst areas dominated by hardwood forests of hickory, beech, maple, and hemlock. They forage in old fields, forest, and lightly grazed pasture up to 10km from the roost. The Ozark big-eared bat uses similar habitat, foraging particularly in edge habitats of intermittent streams and on mountain slopes, with a maximum foraging distance of 7km from the roost. However, they usually remain within 1–2km of the roost during lactation. They feed mainly on small moths (3–10mm). They hibernate in well-ventilated areas near the entrance to caves, often in tight clusters from a few to 100 or more. The maternity colonies are usually in the warm parts of caves; males usually roost separately, and their behaviour and requirements are poorly known. Biological information is more readily available for *P. t. townsendii* in the west, given its much broader distribution and environmental tolerance.

In 1979, the population of *P. t. virginianus* in West Virginia was estimated to be 5,000. A survey in 1987 gave a population estimate of 8,000. West Virginia holds about 50% of the known population centred on 11 summer colonies. An additional cave colony is a bachelor roost in summer, but doubles in size when females arrive in early September. A 1994 population estimate for West Virginia

M. Tuttle/BCI

Townsend's big-eared bat, *Plecotus townsendii*.

and North Carolina was 13,000, with the increase partly attributed to cave protection. A winter census in 1995 located 7,549 individuals, of which 6,378 were in one site. Kentucky has three known colonies, one cave with 1,300 hibernating bats in 1982 and 2,600 in 1987. This was at a time when *Myotis sodalis* numbers declined by 50% in the same cave. Virginia has one known colony, which is regarded as stable. North Carolina has only one known colony, which has recently declined to about 20 individuals. Thus, there have been declines for which the reasons are not clear, but which may be due to cave intrusion, and significant recent increases perhaps due to effective cave protection and the co-operation of caving associations. The success of conservation efforts has resulted in a 1997 total population estimate of 20,000, a 350% increase since the early 1980s. Although still found throughout its recorded range, it is regarded as formerly much more abundant in the Appalachian Mountains.

In 1993, the population of *P. t. ingens* was estimated at 1,700–2,000, with about 1,400 roosting in a few caves in eastern Oklahoma and less than 300 using two caves (one for hibernation, one as a maternity roost) in Arkansas. This is an increase from about 250 estimated in 1979. In 1986, four maternity and four hibernation roost caves were known. In 1987, a summer survey located 450 in known sites and a further 260 in a new site. At that time, no winter sites with more than 100 bats were known and about 24 other sites held only isolated individuals.

Conservation action to date

More thorough and co-ordinated survey and monitoring efforts have identified key sites where improved mechanisms for site protection, including physical protection and site-use agreements, have greatly benefited the species.

A considerable amount of research on the biology and ecological requirements has been carried out and this must have helped in the remarkable recoveries of certain populations in the last 20 years. Mitigation, including encouragement of colony relocation from actively mined areas, has been successful in California. Nevertheless, there remain areas where the species is much more scarce than it was formerly.

The Western Bat Working Group in the USA has drafted a conservation plan for *Plecotus townsendii* and is in the process of seeking endorsements from various state and federal agencies.

Action Plan objectives

1. Maintain and enhance current programmes of conservation, particularly of eastern subspecies.
2. Carry out recovery actions on populations where recorded declines are still severe (e.g., Missouri, Virginia, Kentucky, California).
3. Maintain survey and monitoring activity.

Conservation recommendations to meet Action Plan objectives

Policy and legislation

Recommendations:
- maintain adequate legal protection for all populations;
- develop land-use strategies to maintain the species, especially vulnerable or discrete populations, at a favourable conservation status;
- encourage the adoption of recommendations outlined in the conservation plan produced by the Western Bat Working Group.

Site/species safeguard and management

Recommendations:
- ensure adequate protection of key roost sites;
- ensure sympathetic management of woodland foraging habitat, particularly within 2–7km of summer roost sites;
- carry out habitat enhancement at underground sites and in foraging habitats in areas where populations are still seriously threatened.

Advisory, communications and publicity

Recommendations:
- consult with caving associations and bodies involved with the closure of caves, mines, and other potential roost sites to ensure their protection;
- use species of *Plecotus,* which generally have a relatively high public appeal, in education campaigns.

Future research and monitoring

Recommendations:
- maintain and expand survey work for additional sites used by this species;
- maintain and enhance summer and winter monitoring of recorded roost sites;
- carry out further research on mating strategies and how they might affect conservation status;
- establish status and conservation requirements at northern and southern limits of distribution.

Wider application

Rafinesque's big-eared bat (*P. rafinesquii*) occurs from eastern Texas and Oklahoma to the east coast, and north to Illinois, Indiana, Ohio, West Virginia, and Virginia. Nowhere is it common and the population trends are unclear. Most maternity colonies are in abandoned buildings and other artificial structures; some are in caves. Such colonies usually contain a few to several dozen individuals. Males are mostly solitary in buildings or hollow trees. The species is less reliant on caves for hibernation in the south of the range. It forages in forested areas, mainly on large (31–57mm) moths. This species is more endangered than *P. townsendii*, but its tendency to form smaller more fragmented colonies may make it less vulnerable to major catastrophes.

5.5.16 Species Action Plan – *Murina florium* Flores tube-nosed bat
(Family Vespertilionidae)

Threats
This species is poorly known. Potential threats in Australia include clearing and fragmentation of forest, forest-harvesting operations, and predation by domestic and feral cats (since the species roosts within five metres of the ground).

Summary
M. florium is one of 16 species of a distinctive genus included with *Harpiocephalus* (two species) in the subfamily Murininae. This is a very poorly known group found in the eastern Palaearctic and Southeast Asia to Australia. Most species are rarely encountered, and almost nothing is known of their ecology and conservation requirements. *M. florium* is known from the Lesser Sunda Islands and Sulawesi in Indonesia, and from various island groups east to northern Queensland, Australia. Recent initiatives in Australia using modern survey and study techniques have identified some details of behaviour, and suggestions have been made for future work, which may be equally applicable to other lesser known species.

Protected status
It is protected in Australia, but probably not elsewhere. Of the 16 species in the genus, only five are considered as Lower Risk: Least Concern, and for even those species there is little information. One species is considered Critically Endangered: *M. tenebrosa* (Japan), two are considered Endangered: *M. grisea* (India) and *M. ussuriensis* (North Korea, Russia, and South Korea), and one Vulnerable: *M. puta* (Taiwan).

- *The 2000 IUCN Red List of Threatened Species*: Not listed

Biological assessment
Murina species are generally small bats (forearm less than 44mm, weight about 6g). The two species of the related genus *Harpiocephalus* are larger. The species have tubular nostrils similar to those found in fruit bats of the genus *Nyctimene*, but their function is unknown.

All species are poorly known; they are rarely captured in mist nets, but have recently been more frequently caught in low-set harp traps. New techniques of trapping, including the use of lures and recent advances in ultrasonic detection, have improved the ability of surveys in Australia to detect this species. In the Russian Far East, *M. leucogaster* has been caught several times in snap-traps set on the ground for rodents. *M. florium* was first recorded near Atherton, northern Queensland, Australia in 1981. Between 1981 and 1993, a further eight individuals were found. From 1993 to 1996, 32 were caught during 249 harp trap nights. Radio telemetry resulted in the discovery of three roost sites, including a group of 12 individuals in the base of a snagged frond of an *Archontophoenix* palm. Analysis of faeces shows that the bulk of the diet consists of arachnids and Coleoptera, but facial swabs reveal pollen. Apart from a low-intensity wide-band echolocation call, the species produces a distinctive, loud and audible high-pitched whistle. It roosts with the wings wrapped around the body like rhinolophids.

I. Kuzmin

The Palaearctic greater tube-nosed bat, *Murina leucogaster*.

Elsewhere, species have been found most often in hilly areas, flying low over crops or grass, or through plantations. In Borneo, they feed in the understorey of lowland forest, while in Peninsular Malaysia they are found in forests and plantations to 5,000m. In Peninsular Malaysia, *M. cyclotis* has been found roosting in dead dry leaves such as those of cardamon plants. In Australia, *M. florium* is found roosting in trees. In more temperate regions, *Murina* species sometimes roost in caves. Little is known of breeding, but some twin foetuses have been found in collected individuals.

Conservation action to date
Studies are underway in northern Australia with a view to establishing status and habitat requirements. This species is the subject of a Recovery Outline published in *The Action Plan for Australian Bats*.

Action Plan objective
1. Identify conservation requirements and develop appropriate action, especially for the threatened species of the genus.

Conservation recommendations to meet Action Plan objectives

Policy and legislation

> **Recommendations:**
> - provide adequate protection for threatened species of the genus, especially those with limited distributions;
> - implement recommendations as outlined in *The Action Plan for Australian Bats*.

Site/species safeguard and management

> **Recommendation:**
> - no action recommended until further studies completed.

Advisory, communications and publicity

> **Recommendation:**
> - no action proposed at present.

Future research and monitoring

> **Recommendation:**
> - conduct further research to identify diet, roosting, and foraging requirements.

Wider application

This distinctive genus is in great need of further study to develop conservation programmes to improve the current threatened status of the majority of the included species, and to establish the status of the one species currently regarded as Data Deficient, namely *M. fusca* (China).

5.5.17 Species Action Plan – *Miniopterus schreibersii* Schreibers' bent-winged bat

(Family Vespertilionidae)

Threats

The principal threat is human disturbance to cave-roosting sites, particularly those used as maternity roosts or for hibernation. The species is particularly sensitive to disturbance at roost sites. Traditionally designed grilles have proved unsuitable for this species, especially for maternity and other non-hibernation use.

There is also some evidence of threat due to foraging habitat loss, such as through forestry, logging, and perhaps coastal development in Australia.

Summary

Schreiber's bent-winged bat is probably the most widely distributed bat species in the world, occurring through most of the southern Palaearctic, from Portugal to Japan through much of Africa to South Africa, through Asia and the Pacific to north and eastern Australia. It is highly reliant on caves where it forms large concentrations. For this reason, it is considered highly vulnerable in the Palaearctic and Australian distribution, though there is limited knowledge of conservation concerns through much of the tropics. In more temperate regions, such as the Palaearctic, South Africa, and Australia, a range of caves are required to suit seasonal needs. Although still abundant in much of its range, the loss or significant decline of major populations is widely recorded.

There have been many attempts to separate this widely distributed species into species, subspecies, or other recognized populations, but none has been widely accepted.

Protected status

It is protected through most of its European and former Soviet Union distribution and in Australia, but protection is highly variable elsewhere.

- *The 2000 IUCN Red List of Threatened Species*: LR nt.

Biological assessment

M. schreibersii is a medium-sized species (forearm 45–48mm, weight 9–16g). It is a cave-dependent bat, often forming large concentrations (up to 300,000), where individuals may be packed to a density of about 2,000 per m^2. In temperate regions of the Palaearctic, South Africa, and Australia, it migrates between summer maternity sites and winter hibernation sites. Migrations of up to 550km have been recorded in France, 250km in South Africa, and 1,304km in Australia. Most of these populations also use transitional caves during migrations. Males are often less migratory, but their movements and summer behaviour are poorly understood.

This species forages in open areas around or above forest and woodland, and also in drier areas. It flies fast at 10–20m or more above ground, feeding on moths, small Diptera, and beetles. In temperate areas, delayed implantation of the embryo occurs between autumn mating and spring foetal development. This is in contrast to the sperm storage and delayed fertilization that has evolved in most temperate zone bats. In most tropical regions, there is no delay in embryo development. Females are highly philopatric.

Conservation action to date

International collaborative conservation programmes are in progress in southwest and southeast Europe, concentrating on identification and protection of important cave sites used for hibernation, maternity, and as migration stop-offs. This includes investigation of migration routes and requirements. Similar work is being undertaken in Australia. The species could almost be regarded as conservation dependent in parts of its European range.

Action Plan objectives

1. Restore populations to a favourable conservation status where the species is threatened or conservation dependent.
2. Confirm uniformity of populations as a single species throughout its range.

Conservation recommendations to meet Action Plan objectives

Policy and legislation

Recommendations:
- ensure adequate species protection in areas of discrete and threatened populations;
- develop policies to ensure mining development or redevelopment proposals do not harm populations of this species.

Site/species safeguard and management

Recommendation:
- give consideration to gating important underground sites, subject to the availability of suitable designs for gates; alternatively, develop fences or site use/ management agreements.

Advisory, communications and publicity

Recommendations:
- educate the public about vulnerability to disturbance of this species in caves or other underground roost sites;
- liaise with caving interest groups and others to ensure appropriate site use that does not cause unacceptable disturbance to the bats.

Future research and monitoring

Recommendations:
- conduct further research on movements/migrations and requirements en route;
- monitor major (or a random sample of) maternity and hibernation sites, in conjunction with assessment of changes in land use;
- carry out further research on mating strategies to assess implications for conservation;
- conduct further research on food and foraging requirements;
- use modern systematic techniques to investigate taxonomic status.

Wider application

The genus is subject to the same perturbations as many cave-dependent bat species. In addition, its style of flight makes it difficult for the species to negotiate cave grilles or gates of traditional design.

The genus includes 14 species, most of which are fairly widespread and abundant, but with the same concerns as apply to *M. schreibersii*. Two species are particularly at risk: *M. fuscus* (Vulnerable), restricted to the Ryukyu Islands in Japan where rapid development is in progress, and *M. robustior* (Endangered), a poorly known species restricted to the Loyalty Islands off New Caledonia.

J. Palmeirim

Schreiber's bent-winged bat, *Miniopterus schreibersii.*

5.5.18 Species Action Plan – *Mystacina tuberculata* Lesser short-tailed bat

(Family Mystacinidae)

Threats

Principal threats are predation, habitat loss, and competition with introduced animals. The terrestrial behaviour of *Mystacina*, and perhaps its tree-roosting and lek behaviour, may make it particularly vulnerable to predation by rats, stoats, and feral cats. Certainly the extinction of *Mystacina* species on Big South Cape and Solomon Islands was associated with the arrival of ship rats (*Rattus rattus*). In the past, forest clearance greatly reduced the area of suitable habitat. Replanting with non-indigenous trees has not helped. While forest clearance is now limited, some selective logging continues and this targets the larger older trees that provide favoured roost sites. The terrestrial behaviour also exposes this species to ground-laid poison baits set to kill other animals. *Mystacina* may have few direct competitors, but they may include introduced mammals such as rats and possums, which also feed on the flowers of *Dactylanthus*.

Summary

Mystacina tuberculata is the sole-surviving species of a small family of bats endemic to New Zealand. The relationship of this family to other bat families is uncertain, but it has been most frequently allied to the Neotropical family Phyllostomidae. The only other species in the family, *M. robusta*, was last seen in the 1960s. *M. tuberculata* has been separated into three subspecies. The species has been of concern for many years and is now the subject of a Recovery Plan prepared by New Zealand's Department of Conservation.

Protected status

The species is protected under the Wildlife Act 1953. New Zealand's Department of Conservation lists all three subspecies in Category A ('species of highest conservation priority').

- *The 2000 IUCN Red List of Threatened Species*: VU: A2c, C2a

Biological assessment

Historically, the nominate subspecies (southern short-tailed bat, *M.t. tuberculata*) was recorded from the extreme south of North Island, with scattered records occurring through South Island to islands off the south coast. It is currently known only from Codfish Island, fiordland, and northwest Nelson. The kauri forest short-tailed bat, *M.t. aupourica*, is known from three areas in the north of the North Island: Omahuta Kauri Forest, Warawara, and Little Barrier Island. There is a significant population on Little Barrier Island, but this subspecies appears to be rare elsewhere. The volcanic plateau short-tailed bat, *M.t. rhyacobia*, is more widespread in the central areas of North Island.

While some areas lack recent records (e.g., there is no record from Coromandel Peninsula since 1895), the use of bat detectors for widespread survey purposes is locating significant populations in other areas.

This is a medium-sized species (forearm 39–46mm, weight 12–22g). The short-tailed bat has many distinctive behavioural features. It is omnivorous, feeding on a wide range of arthropods, fruit, pollen, and nectar and may be partially carnivorous or a scavenger. It forages up to 35km from the roost. It frequently forages in leaf litter on the forest floor and by crawling on tree trunks, protecting the wing tips in special pouches. Other special features include a papillate tip to the extensile tongue (probably an adaptation for pollenivory) and basal talons on the claws of robust feet to aid in terrestrial activity, including tunnel-digging. *Mystacina* may be the principal natural pollinator of the threatened ground-dwelling parasitic wood rose, *Dactylanthus taylorii*. It is probably an important pollinator of other plants, such as *Metrosideros*, *Knightia*, and *Callospermum* species. It is also a seed disperser. Males are thought to form leks and compete for traditional song posts on trees. The species is generally associated with old-growth, indigenous forest and roosts singly or in colonies of up to 5,000 in trees. There are some records from caves and shearwater burrows; indeed, some early reports suggested cave colonies numbering thousands. The monotypic family of bat-flies, Mystacinobiidae, is only known in association with tree roosts of this species.

Conservation action to date

While concern for the species has been high for many years, action has concentrated on the conservation of the few known larger roosts. With the development of new survey and research techniques, there are opportunities to identify centres of population, and behavioural and habitat requirements. Ongoing research is discussed below. Genetic variability is also under investigation. A Recovery Plan

Lesser short-tailed bat, *Mystacina tuberculata*.

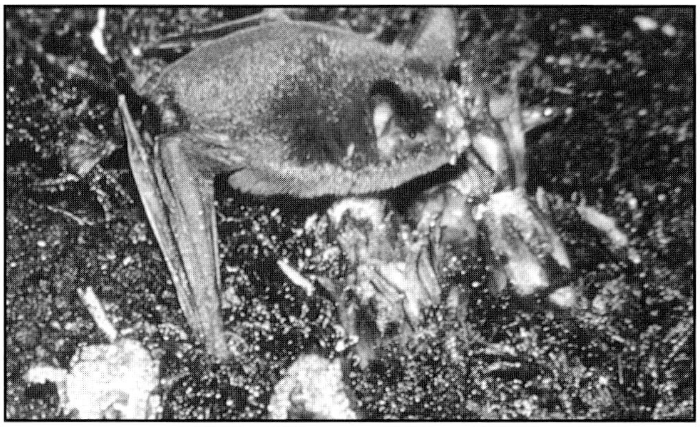

C. Ecroyd/Forest Research N. Z. and E. Anderson

was approved in 1995 and a national bat database has been established.

Action Plan objectives

The Department of Conservation (New Zealand) Recovery Plan details timetabled work plans of actions to conserve New Zealand's bats. This has the following goal: 'to ensure the perpetuation of all extant bat species and subspecies throughout their present ranges, and where feasible new populations within their historical ranges.'

With respect to *Mystacina* the objectives are to:

1. undertake or promote research that will assist in species management;
2. evaluate the species' status;
3. establish populations on suitable islands;
4. select, protect, and monitor populations throughout their geographic range;
5. raise public awareness of bats and involve the public in bat conservation.

Conservation recommendations to meet Action Plan objectives

The Recovery Plan sets out very clear proposals to meet its objectives. Elements of these are highlighted here.

Policy and legislation

Recommendation:
- develop methods for the protection of important mainland habitats; the species is protected under the Wildlife Act 1953.

Site/species safeguard and management

Recommendations:
- make efforts to protect important sites that support the species and to monitor effects of management practices;
- identify suitable rat-free islands for the establishment of populations of the three subspecies within their known ranges and undertake and monitor release programmes;
- direct survey work to search for any relict populations of the greater short-tailed bat *M. robusta*. Mainland forest sites, especially those where short-tailed bats have been recorded historically, will be surveyed and key sites identified;
- use management trials to identify effective methods to protect bats;
- consider legal protection of key forests.

Advisory, communications and publicity

Recommendation:
- prepare and implement a communication plan to meet the main objectives of publicity to promote bats (e.g., to elicit reports, stimulate survey work and encourage protection) and direct to particular target groups of people.

Future research and monitoring

Recommendations:
enhance recent and current research by:
- development of survey and monitoring techniques;
- assessment of threats affecting mainland populations, including the impact of toxins used to control rat populations;
- assessment of breeding ecology, home range size, diet, and habitat use;
- development of captive management and translocation techniques, should these prove appropriate or necessary.

Wider application

While certain aspects of the behaviour of *Mystacina* are unique (e.g., degree of terrestrial activity) or rare (e.g., lekking behaviour) among bats and result in particular threats, the general problems of the protection and management of a southern hemisphere, temperate forest species apply elsewhere. Research is already in hand and progress in meeting the objectives of the Recovery Plan will provide a valuable model for the conservation of bats in other countries.

5.5.19 Species Action Plan – *Cheiromeles torquatus* Naked bat

(Family Molossidae)

Threats

Major cave roosts have shown serious declines, partly due to disturbance during the collection of cave swiftlet nests and partly due to over-exploitation for food. The loss of forests has probably caused declines, both through loss of foraging opportunity and larger trees with hollows that are used for roosting. In Malaysia, the species has been persecuted as a result of the false impression that it is a pest of rice. Around Niah National Park in Sarawak, Borneo, there has been extensive clearing of rainforest for oil palm plantations. Though there is little information on food items selected by *Cheiromeles*, the replacement of rainforest with oil palms would have a serious deleterious effect on local insect numbers (L.S. Hall *pers. comm.*); in December 1997, cave nectar bats (*Eonycteris* species) appeared to have abandoned Niah Caves as there was no local food source available for them.

Summary

This species is one of the largest and most distinctive of insectivorous bats. *C. torquatus* is recorded from Peninsular Malaya, Borneo, Java, Sumatra, and the Philippines, including many nearby small islands. Three subspecies are recognized. Populations on Sulawesi and possibly Mindoro in the Philippines are regarded as a separate species, *C. parvidens*, by some authors, but their status remains uncertain. While large colonies are recorded in caves, the species also forms significant colonies in tree hollows. In caves, it is often associated with cave swiftlets and several other bat species.

Protected status

It is totally protected in Sarawak; protection elsewhere has not been assessed.

- *The 2000 IUCN Red List of Threatened Species*: LR nt.

Biological assessment

The naked bat is a remarkable animal and is the largest aerial, insectivorous bat (forearm 74–90mm, weight of 150–200g). It is almost hairless. The skin is dark grey or black and the bat has a very distinctive smell. There is a patch of hair in the gular pouch under the chin and a scattering of hairs elsewhere on the body. The hind feet have long bristles, typical of free-tailed bats, and a patch of short bristles on the first toe may be used for grooming. The wing tips are tucked into large pouches or folds of skin and the loose skin also forms folds elsewhere; the nipples are enclosed in these pouches. An extraordinary feature of this bat is the association with a distinct suborder of earwigs (Arexiniina), with five species included in two genera. Some of these species are principally associated with the guano, but others are more closely associated with, and frequently live on, the bats, nestling in the skin pouches, and feeding on skin debris and secretions from the animal itself. *Cheiromeles* is highly gregarious, roosting in caves, rock crevices, and trees; even colonies in tree holes may number 1,000. Colonies in caves and trees often mix with other free-tailed bats, especially *Mops mops* and *Chaerephon plicata*. *Cheiromeles* emerges early in the evening, and has a fast direct flight, hunting in clear areas or above the forest canopy, feeding on a variety of insects, including large flying ants (*Camponotus* spp.) and termites. It also feeds over open streams and rivers.

The proportion of naked bats that roost in trees is unknown, but certainly many of the traditional cave roosts have seen major declines. Niah Cave in Sarawak was estimated to hold 20–30,000 naked bats in the 1950s, with a later estimate of about 200,000 in the early 1970s. This cave was established as an "earwig sanctuary" in the 1960s, but this has not prevented excess disturbance during the collecting of cave swiftlet nests and over-exploitation of the bats themselves for food, reducing the colony to about 1,000 by 1992 with a further decline since. This was one of seven significant cave colonies known in Sarawak; five were abandoned by 1992, while the other extant colony at Mt Mulu had been reduced to 50. A large colony formerly existed in the Batu Caves of Peninsular Malaya, where it is still widespread, although not necessarily common.

Naked bat, *Cheiromeles torquatus*.

G. Jones

Conservation action to date

Apart from the designation of Niah Cave as an earwig sanctuary and its later incorporation into a national park, legislation provides for fines of up to $25,000 for killing *Cheiromeles*. However, policing of this reserve is difficult and probably ineffective. There appears to be no effective protection afforded to the species elsewhere and little interest has been paid to the conservation of this species for many years.

Action Plan objectives

1. Restore this unique species to its 1970 status.
2. Undertake further survey work and research to develop and implement a Recovery Plan that also includes management of cave swiftlet populations.
3. Take immediate steps to safeguard and enhance the known important colonies.

Conservation recommendations to meet Action Plan objectives

Policy and legislation

Recommendations:
- develop protective legislation where none currently exists;
- implement existing protective legislation to control exploitation of the species to at least a sustainable level;

- establish management policies for the control of disturbance to bats in cave colonies, and the taking of cave swiftlet nests and naked bats, to ensure their sustainability.

Site/species safeguard and management

Recommendation:
- incorporate important known roosts into national park or other protected area systems.

Advisory, communications and publicity

Recommendations:
- develop education programmes to ensure that the intrinsic interest and value of this species, and its associated fauna, is understood throughout its range both by local people and by tourists;
- ensure that it is understood that this is an insectivorous bat that is probably eating a large number of insect pests.

Future research and monitoring

Recommendations:
- carry out wider studies to assess whether recorded cave declines are matched by general, including tree roost, declines;
- carry out further basic research on autecology, including diet and foraging habitat requirements, in support of the needs for its conservation;
- establish a simple field monitoring programme for this species.

Wider application

While this is an extremely distinctive and unusual bat, and its conservation may require equally distinctive and unusual actions, the myths, prejudices, and over-exploitation for food can all be used as examples of bat conservation issues in general. The species also provides a focus of interest for visitors to the areas where it is numerous.

5.5.20 Species Action Plan – *Otomops martiensseni* Giant mastiff bat

(Family Molossidae)

Threats

This is a large, conspicuous, and widespread species, but with relatively few records and fewer colonies known. It is rarely netted, and has been recorded flying in open areas and may frequently feed high above ground level. It is a poorly-known species, although better known than its congeners. As an aerial insectivore, it is able to range widely and utilise a variety of habitats, and it is likely that food supply is not a limiting factor. However, the large and well-known colonies in Kenya, for example on Mt Suswa, have all but disappeared.

Summary

Otomops martiensseni is the most widespread species of a small, but very distinct genus of six species of free-tailed bats (family Molossidae). It is widely distributed in mainland eastern Africa; there is one record from Ghana, and it is also recorded from Madagascar and from Yemen on the Arabian Peninsula. The other species in the genus all have much more restricted ranges. *O. martiensseni* is a cave-dwelling bat that ranges widely to feed. Thus, only the most gross habitat changes are likely to affect the foraging of this species. However, there are reports of major colonies in caves either disappearing or being greatly reduced in number. Some authorities regard the population southwards from Uganda, Rwanda, and the Democratic Republic of Congo as the species *O. icarus,* and that from Madagascar as *O. madagascariensis.*

Protected status

It is presumed to lack legal protection throughout its range.
- *The 2000 IUCN Red List of Threatened Species*: VU A2c

Biological assessment

O. martiensseni is a large bat (forearm 62–72mm, weight 31–39g) with long ears that are attached along most of the

Giant mastiff bat, *Otomops martiensseni.*

A.M. Hutson

length of the head. Its wings are proportionally the longest and narrowest of all bats, having a high aspect ratio. It occupies a range of habitats from sea level to over 2,000m, and from semi-arid habitats to montane humid forest. It is recorded from Ethiopia, Central African Republic, Ghana, Democratic Republic of Congo, Kenya, Uganda, Tanzania, Rwanda, Zimbabwe, Malawi, Angola, South Africa, and Madagascar.

Relatively few colonies are known; eight small colonies (maximum 20 bats) from houses (South Africa), a small colony (10+) in a tree hole in Usumbara, Tanzania, and the others from caves. In East Africa, these colonies may number many hundreds of bats, although in countries such as Rwanda and South Africa, much smaller groups have been found. Numbers are reported to fluctuate in some caves and it has been suggested that seasonal migrations are possible during periods of food shortage. The canines are long and narrow and the species feeds almost exclusively on moths; its low echolocation frequency and rapid flight may enable it to feed on tympanate moths. Grasshoppers and beetles are also taken in small numbers. It has been seen flying out to sea at dusk in South Africa. This species produces a shrill scream when the roost site is approached. The guano from the former large colonies at Mt Suswa and Ithundu in the Chyulu Hills in Kenya have been mined for fertilizer.

Conservation action to date

No specific action is known, but at least one site in Rwanda is within national park boundaries. The colony site at Mt Suswa is believed to be protected.

Action Plan objectives

1. Assess threats, including in relation to concerns for its congeners.
2. Identify and implement necessary research and monitoring programmes.
3. Protect known key roosts.
4. Develop a more specific Recovery Plan.

Conservation recommendations to meet Action Plan objectives

Policy and legislation

> **Recommendation:**
> - protect key roost sites or at least manage so as to minimise disturbance.

Site/species safeguard and management

> **Recommendation:**
> - consider all known roosts as threatened; where guano digging is carried out, a collecting regimen that minimises disturbance to the bats should be developed.

Advisory, communications and publicity

> **Recommendation:**
> - use advisory notices at roost sites if appropriate to help limit disturbance and highlight the rarity of the species.

Future research and monitoring

> **Recommendations:**
> - reassess all known roosts to ascertain numbers and status of colonies, so that key sites can be identified;
> - use echolocation calls to assess distribution and foraging behaviour;
> - identify further research and conservation activity, depending on the results of the above.

Wider application

All species of this distinctive genus are poorly known and considered threatened. The research and conservation activity applied to *O. martiensseni* may be applicable to other species, although most are too poorly known at present to direct any conservation actions. *O. wroughtoni* is still known only from a single cave in southern India. It was described in 1913 from 30 specimens collected in 1912, and its presence was confirmed in 1961 when 12 out of about 40 individuals were collected. In 1992, at least 40 individuals were seen. It has been proposed that the cave be declared a nature reserve. *O. formosus* from western Java is known from four specimens taken from tree holes, two at one locality, two from another. The original specimen may have been from an old nest hole of a barbet or woodpecker in a decayed branch of a rubber tree. *O. johnstonei* from Alor Island, Nusa Tenggara, Indonesia is known from a single specimen collected from a hollow tree. *O. papuensis* from Papua New Guinea is known from 10 specimens from one site and one from another. *O. secundus* also from Papua New Guinea is known from four specimens from one site, one from another.

5.5.21 Species Action Plan – *Tadarida brasiliensis* Brazilian free-tailed bat

(Family Molossidae)

Threats

Most of the breeding females of the North American population of about 120–150 million are found in about 12 maternity caves. The large concentrations make the species particularly vulnerable to population loss and a range of human activities have caused such events; these have included changes in cave structure for ease of guano collection, commercialization for tourism, other uses such as archaeology, and misplaced attempts to control vampire bats in caves by destruction, burning, fumigation, and exclusion.

The introduction of DDT had been regarded as a major threat, as bats can accumulate high pesticide loads that may be metabolised during periods of stress, e.g., migration. Although no longer approved for use in the USA, DDT has been widely used in Latin America. Other pesticides may affect the bats directly or indirectly through reducing the amount of available prey.

Many of the island populations live in buildings where they may be unwelcome and subject to destructive control measures.

Summary

As currently recognized, *Tadarida* is a genus of eight species distributed through the tropics and subtropics to warm temperate areas. *T. brasiliensis* is found in drier habitats from the southern parts of the USA south (including many Caribbean islands) to Chile and Argentina, although it is unrecorded from much of central and eastern South America. It forms some of the largest aggregations of any terrestrial vertebrate, but many such colonies have been extirpated or have declined, in some cases, by as much as 99%. In the north of the range, it is a partial migrant. The larger colonies, in particular, are found in caves, but the species is frequently a house bat in much of its range. Many of the forms on Caribbean islands are recognized as separate subspecies.

Protected status

It is probably unprotected by national legislation throughout its range, except in those countries (e.g., Panama) where general legislation protects all wildlife. It is included in Appendix I of the Convention on the Conservation of Migratory Species of Wild Animals (Bonn Convention) to encourage international cooperation by formal Agreement or Memorandum of Understanding on the conservation of populations that regularly cross range state boundaries.

- *The 2000 IUCN Red List of Threatened Species*: LR nt

Biological assessment

Free-tailed bats form some of the largest colonies of bats and *T. brasiliensis* forms the largest of these. This is a medium-sized bat (forearm 36–46mm, weight 11–15g) with long, narrow wings designed for rapid long-distance travel. It feeds on insects, mainly moths, and may take more than half its body weight in food in a single night. These colonies forage over vast areas, with individuals ranging up to 50km from the roost, and to an elevation of up to 3,000m. The populations from the western half of the USA (*T. b. mexicana*, the Mexican free-tailed bat) are highly migratory, while the populations east of eastern Texas (*T. b. cynocephala*) are more or less resident. Probably most male *T. b. mexicana* remain in Mexico and so it is the females that are particularly migratory. Movements of up to 1,800km have been recorded. High-altitude foraging by large colonies may have a major impact on migrating populations of agricultural pest insects.

The largest extant colony is in Bracken Cave, Texas, with about 20 million nursing mothers, but other caves are believed to house up to 30 million or more. The large colony at Carlsbad Cavern, New Mexico, now houses about 300,000 of a former population estimated at 8.7 million. A colony at Eagle Creek Cave, Arizona, declined from more than 25 million to just 30,000 in six years, representing a fall of 99.7%. Major declines have also been recorded in other caves in the USA and Mexico. Although they roost principally in caves in much of their range, a

Brazilian free-tailed bat, *Tadarida brasiliensis*.

M. Tuttle/BCI

wide variety of other roost sites are used, including rock fissures, artificial structures such as houses and bridges (e.g., between one and 1.5 million use the Congress Avenue Bridge in Austin, Texas), and hollow trees. These bats are also known as 'guano bats' and commercial extraction of guano continues in many major roost caves. Bird, mammal, and reptile predators wait to take bats at emergence or take individuals that fall to the floor of the roost.

Conservation action to date

Much research has been directed to trying to identify reasons for the major declines recorded in recent decades in the north of the range. Here also, protection of key roost sites has been pursued, either through physical protection by the installation of grilles at cave mouths (which may be difficult for the bats to negotiate) or by local management agreements. Some sites have been used to promote public awareness by encouraging observation of the spectacular evening emergence at sites such as Carlsbad Cavern and the Congress Avenue Bridge. *T. brasiliensis* was included in Appendix I of the Bonn Convention to encourage a joint Agreement on the conservation of the species between countries that share migratory populations, such as the USA, Mexico, and Guatemala. To date, this has not been followed up, but an agreement between Bat Conservation International in the USA and other American and Mexican biologists (Program for the Conservation of Migratory Bats of Mexico and the United States) has been developed. Education plans and protection of a key site, Cueva la Boca, in Mexico are being developed, and an inventory and monitoring programme in both Mexico and the USA has been initiated. Elsewhere, little has been attempted, apart from general bat education programmes initiated in countries like Costa Rica, Venezuela, and the Cayman Islands.

Action Plan objectives

1. Ensure recovery of those populations that have shown extreme decline.
2. Maintain the bat species as one of the more familiar ones in parts of its range, and ensure that such populations continue to provide a spectacle for public enjoyment and education.
3. Establish intergovernmental co-operation in the conservation of migratory populations.
4. Assess whether declines observed in northern parts of the range have occurred elsewhere, and develop any necessary conservation programmes.

Conservation recommendations to meet Action Plan objectives

With the lack of knowledge of specific problems in the southern parts of the range, the following recommendations apply particularly to those populations in the north of the range where massive population declines have been recorded, and which are associated principally with migratory populations.

Policy and legislation

Recommendations:
- give protection to the species in those countries that are home to migratory populations;
- develop the agreement initiated by BCI between the government and people of Mexico and the USA to a firm intergovernmental Agreement or Memorandum of Understanding along the lines of those made, for example, under the Bonn Convention for other migratory animals, including bats in Europe;
- give protected status to recognised subspecies of limited distribution, especially those restricted to Caribbean islands, together with other such localised bat species.

Site/species safeguard and management

Recommendations:
- identify key roost sites, including maternity, male roosts, transitional roosts used in migration, and winter roosts; these should be gazetted and given protection through management agreements, including physical protection where appropriate;
- address the use of problem pesticides by encouraging the use of chemicals less toxic to mammals or changes in insect pest-control mechanisms; as a species that is wide-ranging in its foraging behaviour, there is little opportunity to preserve specific foraging habitat.

Advisory, communications and publicity

Recommendations:
- develop and widely implement education programmes that explain the economic value, non-pest status, and conservation needs of the species; in particular, these should provide appropriate extension to the existing facilities and materials available in the USA (such as at Carlsbad) to Latin America and should include Best Practice guidelines for the use of large cave colonies as educational resources;
- establish humane methods of exclusion of bats from buildings where they are unwelcome.

Future research and monitoring

Recommendations:
- assess ecological and economic impact of feeding behaviour;
- identify migration patterns and establish monitoring procedures;
- investigate roost-creation opportunities to replace lost sites;
- investigate changes of status and possible causes of change in populations south of Mexico;
- co-ordinate long-term monitoring of major roost sites;
- investigate migratory behaviour in the south of the range.

Wider application

The agreement on the conservation of migratory bats between Mexico and the USA is designed to help protect other migrant species, including the greater and lesser long-nosed bats (*Leptonycteris nivalis* and *L. curasoae*) and *Lasiurus* species. Efforts to protect important sites for *T. brasiliensis* will also have effects on cave-bat conservation in general, especially in Mexico, and on house bats in the Neotropics. Guidelines for the use of major bat colonies for public enjoyment and education would have worldwide implications. The role of this species in agricultural pest control may be valuable in public education campaigns.

5.6 Recent conservation and research initiatives

Many threats to bat populations worldwide have been described in this volume. This in itself can seem depressing, but there have also been many positive initiatives in the past few years. They show the breadth of what has already been achieved and what could potentially be undertaken in the coming years. Some of these initiatives are described below.

5.6.1 Survey and monitoring

National surveys and monitoring

Several countries have undertaken detailed surveys of their bat populations. In the UK, a national survey of bat habitats was conducted over three summers from 1990 to 1992 relying heavily on the involvement of volunteer batworkers (Walsh *et al.* 1995; Walsh and Harris 1996a,b). A total of 1,030 one-kilometre squares were surveyed and nearly 30,000 bat passes were counted in the 9,000km walked. The data allowed for analysis of habitat selection by bats, confirming bats' preference for broadleaved woodland and water, and the importance of linear landscape features such as hedgerows. These results are being used in the formulation of management policies for bats in the UK. Overall, the lack of continuity of the landscape, loss and fragmentation of habitat patches, plus deterioration of the quality of such patches may pose a threat to bat populations (Walsh and Harris 1996a). Following this work, a five-year National Bat Monitoring Programme was begun by The Bat Conservation Trust in 1996 with funding from the UK's Department of the Environment, Transport and the Regions. This aims to develop statistically reliable protocols for national monitoring of selected species. The programme uses counts at maternity colonies and in hibernation roosts, and field surveys with bat detectors. The wealth of information created by this survey will form the basis of an ongoing monitoring scheme to assist in determining long-term population trends for species. It hopes to relate population changes to environmental change and hence assist in the development of land management and conservation policy.

In The Netherlands, bat detectors have been widely used as a survey tool. In the 1980s, a detailed bat detector survey was undertaken to study the way in which different bat species use the landscape and to provide information on the distribution of species within the country (Limpens 1993; Limpens *et al.* 1997). As with the UK survey, much of the fieldwork was done by amateur batworkers. The survey method was based on the predictability of the behaviour of bat species and also relied on active learning of observers in the field. Thus, the skill of observers was enhanced through practising the use of bat detector survey methods in the field. The surveys revealed how bats use the landscape in terms of hunting sites, flight paths, roost sites, and mating territories. The results can be used to assist in developing landscape management policy and practice to maintain or enhance bat populations (Kapteyn 1995). As with the UK work, the results assisted in the practical protection of important landscape features. The extensive use of bat detectors as a survey tool has been further enhanced through a series of Bat Detector Workshops. The First European Bat Detector Workshop was held in The Netherlands in 1991 (Kapteyn 1993) and further workshops have been held at both international and national levels.

The intensive form of bat detector survey work described above has now been used in areas of Germany and its applicability is potentially worldwide. In Norway, the mapping of bat species has been undertaken as part of a contribution to the European Mammal Mapping Atlas. Similar bat detector surveys have been undertaken in Denmark and Sweden.

In Australia and New Zealand, large-scale bat detector surveys are being used to identify species distribution, habitat requirements, and key areas for protection. In other areas, cave surveys are the most appropriate means for survey and population monitoring and, particularly in Europe and North America, the long-term monitoring of underground habitats has been crucial to the assessment of historical population trends and in encouraging the development of wider activities.

In many countries, information on bat populations is limited. Baseline surveys have been undertaken to allow for drafting of initial management recommendations. For example, in Viet Nam, Fauna & Flora International has funded baseline survey work in Cuc Phuong National Park in the north of the country and has shown this area to be particularly rich for bats. At least 35 species, some very rare, have been recorded and the work is to be extended to other areas of Viet Nam. The survey results will assist with the development of appropriate management plans for these areas. The Solomon Islands have a rich bat fauna, with many endemic species. A six-month expedition to one of the islands, Choiseul, in 1995 rediscovered one fruit bat species (*Pteralopex anceps*) thought to be extinct and obtained a new record for another endemic species, as well as new records for a range of microchiropteran bat species (Bowen-Jones *et al.* 1997).

5.6.2 Education

Education of the general public

In North America and Europe in particular, a wide range of initiatives has been used for education of the general public and professions whose activities have particular impact on bat habitats. To varying degrees, many other countries, including Australia, Mexico, South Africa, and India, are developing educational activities. In 1986, Fauna & Flora Preservation Society (FFPS), now Fauna & Flora International (FFI), coordinated a National Bat Year in the UK. A range of events were organised including a major exhibition of bat ephemera in London. Newspaper coverage of the year's activities approached 19,000 column inches and over 4,000 enquiries were dealt with by FFPS alone (Tait 1987). As well as the exhibition in London, almost 20 other exhibitions travelled around the country. Young people were also involved in a survey of attitudes to bats. Over 5,500 interviews were conducted as a part of this survey. The success of National Bat Year has led to the organisation by The Bat Conservation Trust of a number of National Bat Weeks in the UK. In the USA, Bat Conservation International (BCI) has produced a range of educational materials including a series of sets of transparencies and videos illustrating the diversity of bat species worldwide and the threats facing them. It has also produced a major exhibition, which is currently on tour in various parts of the world. Also in the USA, the Coalition of North American Bat Working Groups is developing a "Bat Survey Week", an outreach programme for researchers to demonstrate survey techniques. The target audience is land managers who actually make the decisions on public lands. The Bat Conservation Trust has also produced a series of educational leaflets about bats, such as for individual species, bats in buildings, bats underground, bats in trees, and the construction of bat boxes. Materials targeted at children have also been produced. For example, a pack of information including teaching materials, an acoustic tape, and set of transparencies was produced specifically for use in schools in Scotland (*Bats in Scotland*). 'European Bat Night', an international event organised under the European Bats Agreement, is likely to become an annual attempt to raise public awareness of bats on a Europe-wide scale. The second European Bat Night took place in August 1998 and attracted between 15,000 and 20,000 people to a single event in Germany, as well as to events in 13 other European countries.

In a number of countries there is an extensive network of volunteers who assist in the education of the general public. These volunteers often have direct contact with the public through dealing with situations such as bats in dwellings. In the UK, many of the volunteers are organised into local bat groups or societies, of which there are currently over 90 covering the British Isles. Similar arrangements are instituted in Germany, France, The Netherlands, and North America.

Regional and national initiatives

In the USA, BCI has joined with the Bureau of Land Management (BLM), the National Fish and Wildlife Foundation (NFWF), and the Forest Service (FS) to establish the *National Bat Conservation Partnership*. This aims to conserve bats and their habitats and educate people about bats and their importance. The BLM and FS have cooperated with BCI over protection and management of abandoned mines, and the FS has developed interpretive programmes on the importance of tree snags and artificial roost boxes for bats. BCI has also initiated a series of Bat Conservation and Management Workshops involving state governmental organisations with the aim of increasing awareness of bat conservation issues, and similar workshops have been held in other countries. These workshops include lectures about bat biology and ecology, threats, habitat management for bats, education, field techniques, protection of key roost sites, and the use of artificial roosts.

In some countries or states, such as the UK, Switzerland, and the USA, 'national' bat telephone helplines have been established to enable the general public to obtain information about bats. This has followed on from, or led to regionally established helplines. Various websites have also been established.

Education about rabies and vampire bats

Educational campaigns related to bats and health have also been used in various areas of the world. In the USA, the issue of rabies and bats is a public concern. Bat Conservation International has worked with the Department of Health and Human Services, Centers for Disease Control and Prevention, and the U.S. Fish and Wildlife Service to produce information and practical guidelines for dealing with bats suspected to be rabid (B. French *pers. comm.*). In Central and South America, the threat of rabies is a constant concern for cattle owners and, as a result, eradication campaigns are undertaken to destroy bats, many of which may be of great harm to beneficial species that consume agricultural pests, disperse seeds, or pollinate vital plants. Several educational programmes have been developed to address this problem. In 1993, BCI produced a video *Control del Murcielago Vampiro y La Rabia Bovina* which was used to educate veterinarians and cattle associations across South America. In 1994, BCI, the Asociacion Mexicana de Mastozoologia, A.C., and the Instituto de Ecologia, UNAM, formed the Program for the Conservation of Migratory Bats of Mexico and the United

States (PCMM), which implemented a multi-faceted programme of research, education, and conservation action designed to reverse alarming declines in bats attributable to misguided vampire-bat control efforts. In 1998, BCI, the US Fish and Wildlife Service, and the Asociacion Venezolana para la Conservacion de Areas Naturales convened a group of biologists and rabies experts to develop a vampire control training programme that could be distributed to public health officials throughout the range of vampire bats. All of these programmes provide excellent models for countries with limited financial resources. The resolution of the 11th International Bat Research Conference included recommendations to support and expand such programmes.

5.6.3 Liaison with special interest groups

Caves

A range of initiatives have aimed at liaising with special interest groups whose activities may have impacts upon bat populations. Caves are a vital habitat for bats worldwide and the increasing popularity of speleology has led to potential conflicts. In the UK, liaison with speleologists and others led to the establishment of a code of conduct for all those visiting underground sites (Hutson *et al.* 1995). Close collaboration between all interested parties has meant that access agreements have been drawn up for important bat sites. Where grilling of sites is required, this has been done, wherever possible, with the agreement of other users of the site. As well as the code, a system was established to grade sites according to their importance for bats. Also in the UK, a Cave Conservation Handbook has been published (National Caving Association 1997), which is the result of liaison between caving groups, statutory governmental nature conservation organisations, and non-governmental organisations. It reviews the threats to caves, conservation initiatives, instruments for protection, Cave Conservation Plans, and other measures. In Portugal, a National Plan for the Conservation of Cave Bats has been published (Palmeirim and Rodrigues 1992). This reviews the status of bat species in Portugal, the conservation measures necessary to conserve species (site and habitat protection, survey, monitoring, education, and improved legislation), and an analysis of the key sites in the country. In Bulgaria, around 50 important bat roosts were surveyed in the period 1989–94. The data from this investigation were used to develop an Action Plan for Bat Protection in Bulgaria. Measures to conserve bat populations included grilling, the installation of information plaques in caves, and education programmes (Ivanova and Petrov 1994). The protection of underground habitats has been proposed under the Bern Convention (Convention on the Conservation of European Wildlife and Natural Habitats Recommendation no. 36, 1992) and a review of the current status of key cave habitats in Europe has been prepared (Juberthie 1992). This review proposes criteria for the selection of underground habitats of biological interest, establishment of a list of biologically important sites within each country (including those in need of protection), an inventory of sites of European importance, the protection of underground habitats of cave species (including bats), and methodology and implementation of underground habitat protection. It promotes collaboration with European organisations concerned with the protection of the underground environment, including the Biospeleology Society and the International Speleology Union. The European Bats Agreement is also assisting in the conservation of underground sites for bats. A set of guidelines for the protection of caves and karst worldwide has been produced by IUCN (Watson *et al.* 1997).

In the USA, BCI has initiated a management scheme, jointly with the Texas Nature Conservancy, for the Eckert James River Cave in Texas, home to approximately four million Mexican free-tailed bats (*Tadarida brasiliensis*). The most significant aspect of the plan is education and the bat emergence from the cave is used as a tool to educate local communities about bats and their importance in the ecosystem. The cave is also being used to assess the impact of human visits on bat behaviour and, if necessary, to change the visiting regimen (Hensley 1992).

Mines

As well as caves, other underground sites, particularly disused mines, are of key importance to some species. In the USA, many disused mines were sealed for safety reasons before their importance to wildlife was recognised, in some cases entombing bats. Increased awareness has led to liaison between the mining industry, public agencies, local residents, and bat researchers (Pierson 1998). Regional initiatives, for example in Colorado, New Mexico, and Nevada, as well as national programmes such as that organised by BCI, have helped to address the problem of managing disused mines (Navo *et al.* 1995; Riddle 1995; Tuttle and Taylor 1998; J.S. Altenbach *pers. comm.*). In some countries, for example the UK, policies for mine closure, usually for safety reasons, include recommendations for the conservation of bats.

Buildings

In many countries, buildings are important roosting sites for bats. In the UK, BCT and other organisations have specifically targeted the building trades in an effort to improve their awareness of the importance of buildings for bats. A series of educational leaflets has been produced including *Bats in Houses* and *Bats in Roofs,* as well as a *Bats in Buildings* video. The BCT has also attended national trade conferences to promote bat conservation. The use of timber treatment chemicals in buildings is widespread in the UK and other countries. Some of the chemicals used can be highly toxic to bats and BCT has worked closely with statutory government conservation agencies to encourage the use of less-toxic alternatives. This has included forming partnerships with timber treatment companies to spread the message from within the industry. The Ecology Building Society in the UK only provides loans for the purchase of properties where any timber treatment is carried out using less toxic chemicals.

Churches

In addition to residential buildings, bats frequently use churches. The BCT conducted a Bats in Churches survey in the early 1990s (Sargent 1995). As well as providing a nationwide assessment of the importance of churches as roosting places for bats, it was successful as an educational programme. The use of churches by bats is widespread and, in some cases, conflicts can arise between bats and those who maintain the buildings. The Bats in Churches project allowed full discussion of these issues and the instigation of effective management regimens that would not threaten the long-term survival of bat populations. Where bats may be affecting important works of art in churches, management practices have been further refined by a consortium coordinated by English Heritage. The importance of churches to bats is widely recognized in Europe and elsewhere and has resulted in many surveys and conservation initiatives.

Trees

As buildings are of importance to some bat species, so trees are to others. The importance of woodland areas to bats as both roosting and feeding habitat has long been recognised. In North America, efforts have been made to involve woodland managers in the conservation of bats. In 1995, a Bats in Forests Symposium was held in British Columbia, Canada (Barclay and Brigham 1996). A range of papers were presented detailing the importance of woodland habitats for bats and did much to raise awareness of the importance of trees to bats. In the USA and Canada, federal, state, and provincial land management agencies are moving towards ecosystem management of forests. For example, BCI has been working with the Forest Service of the United States Department of Agriculture to produce management plans that protect and enhance bat habitat (B. French *pers. comm.*). In the Interior Columbia River Basin in the USA, a study of bat species, biodiversity, and ecosystems was undertaken as part of a scientific assessment and land-use project known as the Interior Columbia River Basin Ecosystem Management Project, conducted jointly by the USDI Bureau of Land Management and the USDA Forest Service (Marcot 1996).

In the UK, BCT has produced a *Bats in Trees* leaflet aimed specifically at those who manage trees and woodland. It contains information on the importance of trees for bats, an explanation of relevant legislation, and Best Practice guidelines for planning and development, tree management, and for tree surgery. The leaflet has been widely distributed through the forestry industry. The success of this initiative is the result of close liaison with relevant industry bodies, in particular the Tree Council, a forum for the many groups interested in forest management. A set of transparencies has also been produced. Changes in forest policy in Poland have encouraged more sensitive management for conservation and a system for the designation of 'Veteran Trees' for older trees of ecological importance (as has happened in North America and the UK).

The provision of artificial roosting habitat for bats to replace that lost through the removal of trees is a rapidly expanding activity. Artificial bat boxes have been used in countries throughout the world for many years and there has been extensive experimentation with materials and designs. In 1993, BCI created the North American Bat House Research Project to learn more about the roosting needs of bats. It has produced a Handbook (Tuttle and Hensley 1993) and a twice-yearly newsletter *The Bat House Researcher,* and involves around 1,800 volunteers in its research programmes. In the USA, the Arizona Game and Fish Department has been developing and testing artificial bat bark (Siders and Sinton 1998). A large number of forest-dwelling species rely on spaces beneath loose bark of snags as primary nursery roost sites (Green *et al.* 1994, Rabe *et al.* 1998) and this research suggests that such materials may be of value to such species.

Bridges

Bridges are known to be important as bat roosts in some parts of the world. For example, in Austin, Texas, USA, the Congress Avenue Bridge is home to between one and 1.5 million Mexican free-tailed bats (*Tadarida brasiliensis*). Bat Conservation International has used the bridge as a focal point for an education programme and has itself initiated a Bats in American Bridges Project (Keeley and Tuttle 1999). This project surveyed over 2,400 structures, both bridges and culverts, and located about 4.25 million bats of 25 species in 211 structures. Keeley and Tuttle (1999) believe that providing bat habitat in bridges or culverts, either during initial construction or through retrofitting, is a highly feasible and effective way of helping bats. In the UK, a Bats in Bridges survey was undertaken with the aim of producing guidelines for those involved in the maintenance of bridges (Billington and Norman 1997). This is being further developed by the Highways Agency, together with the UK's statutory nature conservation organisations, into a guidance note on the incorporation of bat conservation into the design, construction, and after-management of roads.

Landscape features

Increased research on bats in the field since the development of portable bat detectors has greatly helped in the identification of important landscape features and foraging habitat. It is hoped that this will increasingly have influence on land management practices to benefit bats, and the Joint Nature Conservation Committee in the UK has produced a habitat management handbook specifically for land managers (Entwistle *et al.* 2001).

In Bulgaria, an educational campaign was undertaken jointly between the Bat Research and Conservation Group and the Bulgarian Birds of Prey Protection Society aimed at conserving rocky habitats for bats, birds, and flora within the country.

5.6.4 Conferences and symposia

The upsurge in interest in bats has led to a proliferation of meetings dedicated to bat conservation and research. An International Bat Research Conference (IBRC) is held every three to four years, with the 11th IBRC held in Brazil in 1998. Recent international conferences have been held in the UK (1985), Australia (1989), India (1992), and the USA (1995). A European Bat Conference is held approximately every three years with the most recent in Poland in 1999. A number of countries or regions (e.g., Australasia, USA, UK, Poland, and France) also host regular/annual bat conferences. As well as these, there are national and international mammal conferences that have a significant bat component. There have also been international workshops and symposia dedicated to particular topics. These have included the Bats and Forests Symposium mentioned above, a workshop On the Situation of the Rhinolophidae (Sachsen-Anhalt, Germany 1995), Echolocation of Bats (Geneva, Switzerland 1994), Current Problems of Bat Protection in Central and Eastern Europe (Bonn, Germany 1994), Advances in Bat Biology (London, UK 1995), Workshop on the Conservation of Brazilian Bats (Santa Teresa, Brazil, 1995), and a workshop On the Situation of the Barbastelle in Europe (Sachsen-Anhalt, Germany 1997). The increasing use of bat detectors in survey work has been accompanied by a range of international workshops, for example in The Netherlands (1991), Spain (1992), and Luxembourg (1996), and nationally throughout The Netherlands, UK, and Germany in the 1990s.

5.6.5 Regional initiatives

Extensive reviews of the bats of particular regions have taken place. The increased availability of national or regional guides, atlases, and checklists helps encourage further work; many of these are listed in the regional bibliographies given in Chapter 5.4.

A project to map the distribution of all mammals in Africa at a one-degree scale has been coordinated through the University of Copenhagen. For bats, this will be the first time the entire continent has been mapped at this scale and will allow for the pin-pointing of areas of key importance in terms of their bat biodiversity. This information, coupled with the use of the WORLDMAP package (as described in Chapter 5.3), will assist in the management of bat populations in Africa. The mammals of southern Africa were recently reviewed by Skinner and Smithers (1990) and mammals of Arabia by Harrison and Bates (1994).

The mammals of the Indomalayan Region were recently reviewed by Corbet and Hill (1992) and this complements works on New Guinea (Flannery 1995a), Australia (Churchill 1998), and the rest of the southwest Pacific and Molucca Islands (Flannery 1995b). A review of the bats of the Indian Subcontinent was published (Bates and Harrison 1997), the first for over 100 years. As well as listing all species with details of distribution, the publication gives important information on biology, ecology, and conservation. This publication is one of a number already published or planned by the Harrison Zoological Institute in the UK.

In North America, Bat Conservation International as part of its North American Bat Conservation Partnership has established a mapping programme with the aim of producing a set of detailed distribution maps for all the bat species in this area (B. French *pers. comm.*). The mammals of Europe have recently been mapped through the European Mammal Mapping Atlas coordinated by the European Mammal Society (Mitchell Jones *et al.* 1999), but large areas of the Palaearctic remain without wider assessment since Corbet (1978). Similar work is in progress in Central and South America.

Also in the USA, the Coalition of North American Working Groups has evolved as a partnership of regional working groups involving a wide range of interested parties, including representatives of federal and state agencies, and the private sector. A priority of these regional working groups is the development of state level conservation plans. The aim is that these will be consistent with the national plans put forward by the North American Bat Conservation Plan (NABCP). The involvement of state agencies is crucial since such agencies have the responsibility for managing wildlife, even on federal land. The role of federal agencies is particularly strong in the western USA, where most of the land is public land and thus under federal jurisdiction. The Forest Service, in particular, has played an important role in bat conservation and has supported research on endangered species. The Western Bat Working Group has produced a Regional Priority Matrix, which is intended to provide states, provinces, federal land management agencies, and interested organisations and individuals a better understanding of the overall status of a given bat species throughout its western North American range. The matrix will also help to focus future research and conservation actions.

In South Asia, a Chiroptera Conservation Information Network (CCINSA) has been established covering

Bangladesh, Bhutan, India, Nepal, Maldives, Pakistan, and Sri Lanka. This has focused on disseminating information collected as part of a series of ongoing PHVAs (Population and Habitat Viability Analysis) and CAMPs (Conservation Assessment and Management Plans). A CAMP workshop was held in 1997 to assess the status of 102 species of Indian bats and assessments for other species are planned (S. Walker *pers. comm.*).

5.6.6 International Action Plans

The Agreement on Conservation of Bats in Europe (Bonn Convention) and the Program for the Conservation of Migratory Bats of Mexico and the United States (PCMM) have already been discussed in Chapter 4. Under its commitments to the Pan-European Biological and Landscape Diversity Strategy, the Bern Convention has commissioned the preparation of Europe-wide Species Action Plans for the greater horseshoe bat, *Rhinolophus ferrumequinum*, (Ransome and Hutson 2000), and the pond bat *Myotis dasycneme*, (Limpens *et al.* 2000).

The EEC Habitat Directive requires the establishment of Special Areas of Conservation (SACs) by all member states for species highlighted in its Annex II, which includes 13 bat species.

The Transboundary Programme for the Protection of Bats in Western Central Europe was established in the 1990s with funding from LIFE-Nature, an environmental and nature protection programme by the EC. It worked in the border areas of France, Belgium, Luxembourg, Germany, and The Netherlands. It aimed to create a network of protected (mainly underground) sites within migration distance of endangered bat species listed on the EEC Habitat Directive. Through funding totalling ECU 1.29 million, 156 important bat sites have been protected, including several important nursery colonies of *Myotis myotis* and *Rhinolophus ferrumequinum*. It has also established education and monitoring programmes.

5.6.7 National and Local Action Plans or Recovery Plans

The Convention on Biological Diversity 1992 (Rio Convention) has been acceded to by over 170 countries. It requires *inter alia* signatories to prepare a national biodiversity strategy which allows the opportunity to include bats. The UK Government's *Biodiversity Action Plan* includes action plans for six bat species. The Bat Conservation Trust and the statutory nature conservation organisations will be working closely with a variety of other organisations to ensure these action plans achieve their objectives. An important element of this initiative is the development of partnerships between all involved parties, and the integration of bat species action plans with those of other appropriate species or habitat plans. The UK has also published *An Action Plan for the Conservation of Bats in the United Kingdom* (Hutson 1993), as well as information and recovery plans for barbastelle (*Barbastella barbastellus*) and Bechstein's bats (*Myotis bechsteinii*). *An Action Plan for the Monitoring and Conservation of Insectivorous Bats in Israel* has been published (Ron 1995), which includes detailed management measures required for the conservation of this group of species. In Hungary, *A Handbook for the Conservation of Bats in Hungary* has been published (Dobrosi 1995) and includes detailed species accounts, as well as practical methods of bat protection. The Netherlands, France, and Switzerland also have national action plans. In Australia, *The Action Plan for Australian Bats* (Duncan *et al.* 1999) was published in 1999. In New Zealand, a Bat Recovery Plan has been published (Molloy 1995) covering both extinct and extant species (*Mystacina robusta*, *M. tuberculata*, and *Chalinolobus tuberculatus*). It includes present and past distribution and abundance, threats, options for recovery, and recovery strategies.

Recovery Plans for threatened species can be successful in reversing declining population trends. An example of an integrated approach to species conservation is given by horseshoe bats (*Rhinolophus* species) in the UK (Mitchell-Jones 1995). In this case, the first strategy is to locate all significant breeding, hibernation, and other roost sites. Once sites are located, consideration should be given to means of protection. Though all roosts in the UK receive a certain degree of protection, the declaration of important roosts as SSSIs (Sites of Special Scientific Interest) allows more control of their future. However, declaration of SSSIs is a sensitive issue, particularly since many roosts are in private buildings. The protection and management of a limited number of the most important sites may help protect a significant proportion of the population. Once sites are protected, effort has been directed to identifying the key feeding habitats surrounding them, which may themselves be protected under a range of strategies to provide for sympathetic management. Finally, it is crucial to set up long-term monitoring programmes for populations in both summer and winter sites. Some species recovery plans have been in operation in the USA since the early 1980s, being extremely successful in some instances, but highlighting inadequate knowledge in others. In the USA, wildlife and conservation policy efforts are driven by the Endangered Species Act (ESA) with the result that species that are not listed receive little attention. In the mid-1990s, the Idaho Department of Fish and Game in cooperation with other agencies launched a 'proactive' conservation effort to develop conservation plans (equivalent to recovery plans) for 'at risk' species. The conservation strategy for *Corynorhinus* (in this plan included in the genus *Plecotus*) is complete and endorsements for the document are being sought.

5.6.8 Publications

In addition to the publications already cited above, there are increasing numbers of journals and newsletters devoted specifically to bat conservation and research. These include *Acta Chiropterologica* (Poland), *Bat News* (UK), *Bats* and *Bat Research News* (USA), *Myotis*, *Nyctalus*, *Mitteilungsblatt der BAG Feldermausschutz*, and *Der Flattermann* (Germany), *Chirop Echo* and *Chirop-Contact* (Belgium), *Le Rhinolophe* and *Fledermaus-Anzeiger* (Switzerland), *Czech Bat Conservation Trust Newsletter* (Czech Republic), *Vespertilio* (Slovakia), *Nieuwsbrief Vleermuiswerkgroep VZZ* (The Netherlands), *Deneverkutatas* (Hungary), *Plecotus et al.* (Russia), *The Australian Bat Society Newsletter* (Australia), *Peka Peka* (New Zealand), and *Chiroptera Neotropica* (Brazil). There are also local or regional newsletters in Norway, Germany, Spain, USA, UK, Poland, and Australia. These augment papers about bats published in a wide range of academic journals. As well as newsletters and papers, there are a wide range of publications dealing with conservation issues in a large number of countries.

5.6.9 Bat organisations

The increasing interest in bats and their conservation has led to the establishment of many organisations partially or wholly devoted to bat conservation. Some have paid staff, but rely heavily on voluntary support for their activities. In the USA, Bat Conservation International, established in the early 1980s, has grown to be an influential organisation amongst both the public and government, and has developed a number of major initiatives that have been described here. The Bat Conservation Trust in the UK developed from a bat project initially begun in 1984 by Fauna & Flora International (then Fauna & Flora Preservation Society). The Trust produces a wide range of educational materials aimed at batworkers, the general public, and special-interest groups (such as cavers, builders, and those involved in the management of trees). These include leaflets, videos, and sets of transparencies. The Trust also runs a bat helpline and coordinates national surveys. It liaises with about 90 local volunteer bat groups in the UK and organises an annual National Bat Conference. Also in the UK, the Vincent Wildlife Trust (VWT) has developed a number of projects on bats, most particularly involving greater horseshoe (*Rhinolophus ferrumequinum*) and lesser horseshoe (*R. hipposideros*) bats. The VWT has funded research into the ecology and conservation of lesser horseshoe bats, and set up reserves for both species. It has also funded work on bats in Ireland. The Lubee Foundation in the USA was established by the late Luis F. Bacardi and concentrates on the captive breeding of endangered species of bats. National or state bat conservation organisations also exist in Canada, The Netherlands, France, Germany, Poland, Czech Republic, Hungary, Bulgaria, Switzerland, Spain, Greece, Malta, Australia, New Zealand, and South Africa. In many other countries, wider interest organisations include bat conservation in their remit. Listed below are the addresses of some of organisations involved with bat conservation:

Bat Conservation International
PO Box 162603
Austin, TX 78716
USA
Tel: +(512) 327 9721
Fax: +(512) 327 9724
website: http://www.batcon.org

Fauna & Flora International
Great Eastern House
Tenison Road
Cambridge CB1 2TT
UK
Tel: +(0)1223 571 000
Fax: +(0)1223 461 481
e-mail: info@fauna-flora.org
Website: http://www.fauna-flora.org

The Bat Conservation Trust
15 Cloisters House
8 Battersea Park Road
London SW8 4BG
UK
Tel: +(0)207 627 2629
Fax: +(0)207 627 2628
e-mail: enquiries@bats.org.uk
Website: http://www.bats.org.uk

The Lubee Foundation, Inc.
1309 NW 192nd Avenue
Gainesville, FL 32609
USA
Tel: +(352) 485 1250
Fax: +(352) 485 2656
e-mail: lubeebat@aol.com
website: http://www.lubee.com

Coalition of North American Bat Working Groups
website: http://www.batworkinggroups.org

The Vincent Wildlife Trust
10 Lovat Lane
London EC3R 8DN
UK
Tel: +(0)207 283 2089
Fax: +(0)207 929 0604

Chapter 6

IUCN Red List Species Listed by Country and Threat Category

6.1 Arrangement of list

In the following list, countries are arranged alphabetically. For each country, a list of the IUCN Red List species is given, highlighting those that are endemic. It is important to note that the status assessments for each species reflect the status across the entire distribution. No attempt has been made to assess the status at a country level and, indeed, the IUCN criteria were not originally formulated for this purpose. However, guidelines for using IUCN status assessments at a regional or country level are currently under development. It is thus possible that species in this list are not considered threatened at a country level. While a species may be common within a particular country, it may be threatened globally and that country's population may play an important role in the survival of the species as a whole. Similarly, those considered threatened or listed in national Red Data Books or lists (see below) may not be shown, but are worthy of attention at a country level.

6.2 National Red Data Books and Lists

A preliminary survey has been undertaken of the occurrence of microchiropteran bat species in national Red Data Books or lists, or other national assessments. Time did not permit a comprehensive worldwide review, but the results do give an indication of the level of awareness of bat conservation issues at a national level. One of the main aims of this Action Plan is to encourage all countries to adequately assess the threats to their bat faunas. Where several such lists have been produced, only the information from the most recent publication is shown. This analysis was undertaken initially by J.A. Burton and subsequently added to by B. Smith.

6.3 Data on bat faunas

For each country, an estimate of the size of the bat fauna is given, splitting the species into megachiropterans and microchiropterans as appropriate. Citations for the basic sources of these figures given are also listed. These figures are intended to give an idea of the size of the fauna and the proportion of threatened species. It is not suggested that these are totally accurate figures, as in many countries the necessary survey work has not been carried out to produce such lists. The numbers may also include species that have been added since the quoted publications, or species that are not recognised in this volume, but time did not permit a detailed analysis at this level.

6.4 IUCN Red List species by country

Afghanistan

Species	Global status
Rhinolophus blasii	LR: nt
Rhinolophus ferrumequinum	LR: nt
Rhinolophus hipposideros	VU A2c
Rhinolophus mehelyi	VU A2c
Eptesicus nasutus	VU A2c
Myotis emarginatus	VU A2c
Myotis frater	LR: nt
Myotis longipes	VU B1 +2c, D2
Nyctalus leisleri	LR: nt
Nyctalus montanus	LR: nt
Miniopterus schreibersii	LR: nt

Summary

CR	EN	VU	LRcd	LRnt	EX	DD	Total	Endemics
0	0	5	0	6	0	0	11	0

Total number of species:	Megachiroptera	0
	Microchiroptera	37
	Total	37
Reference(s):	Corbet 1978	

Albania

Species	Global status
Rhinolophus blasii	LR: nt
Rhinolophus hipposideros	VU A2c
Myotis capaccinii	VU A2c
Myotis myotis	LR: nt
Nyctalus leisleri	LR: nt
Miniopterus schreibersii	LR: nt

Summary

CR	EN	VU	LRcd	LRnt	EX	DD	Total	Endemics
0	0	2	0	4	0	0	6	0

Total number of species:	Megachiroptera	0
	Microchiroptera	19
	Total	19
Reference(s):	Corbet 1978	

Algeria

Species	Global status
Rhinolophus blasii	LR: nt
Rhinolophus euryale	VU A2c
Rhinolophus ferrumequinum	LR: nt
Rhinolophus mehelyi	VU A2c
Myotis capaccinii	VU A2c
Myotis emarginatus	VU A2c
Nyctalus leisleri	LR: nt
Miniopterus schreibersii	LR: nt

Summary

CR	EN	VU	LRcd	LRnt	EX	DD	Total	Endemics
0	0	4	0	4	0	0	8	0

Total number of species: Megachiroptera 0; Microchiroptera 26; Total 26

Reference(s): Gaisler 1983–84, Kowalski and Rzebik-Kowalska 1991

American Samoa

Species	Global status
Emballonura semicaudata	EN A1ac
?Myotis insularum	DD

Summary

CR	EN	VU	LRcd	LRnt	EX	DD	Total	Endemics
0	1	0	0	0	0	1	2	0

Total number of species: Megachiroptera 2; Microchiroptera 2; Total 4

Reference(s): Mickleburgh *et al.* 1992, Koopman 1993, Flannery 1995b

American Virgin Islands

Species	Global status
Stenoderma rufum	VU A1c

Summary

CR	EN	VU	LRcd	LRnt	EX	DD	Total	Endemics
0	0	1	0	0	0	0	1	0

Total number of species: Megachiroptera 0; Microchiroptera 5; Total 5

Reference(s): McFarlane 1991

Andorra

Species	Global status
Rhinolophus hipposideros	VU A2c

Andorra continued

Species	Global status
Barbastella barbastellus	VU A2c
Myotis myotis	LR: nt
Nyctalus leisleri	LR: nt

Summary

CR	EN	VU	LRcd	LRnt	EX	DD	Total	Endemics
0	0	2	0	2	0	0	4	0

Total number of species: Megachiroptera 0; Microchiroptera 11; Total 11

Reference(s): S.S. Guitart, pers. comm.

Angola

Species	Global status
Saccolaimus peli	LR: nt
Nycteris intermedia	LR: nt
Rhinolophus deckenii	DD
Eptesicus flavescens	DD
Laephotis angolensis	LR: nt
Myotis seabrai	VU A2c, D2
Pipistrellus anchietai	VU A2c
Miniopterus fraterculus	LR: nt
Miniopterus schreibersii	LR: nt
Chaerephon chapini	LR: nt
Otomops martiensseni	VU A2c

Summary

CR	EN	VU	LRcd	LRnt	EX	DD	Total	Endemics
0	0	3	0	6	0	2	11	0

Total number of species: Megachiroptera 15; Microchiroptera 43; Total 58

Reference(s): Bergmans 1988, 1989, 1990, 1994, 1997, Skinner and Smithers 1990

Anguilla

Species	Global status
Monophyllus plethodon	LR: nt

Summary

CR	EN	VU	LRcd	LRnt	EX	DD	Total	Endemics
0	0	0	0	1	0	0	1	0

Total number of species: Megachiroptera 0; Microchiroptera 5; Total 5

Reference(s): Breuil and Masson 1991, McFarlane 1991

Antigua and Barbuda

Species	Global status
Monophyllus plethodon	LR: nt
Tadarida brasiliensis	LR: nt

Summary

CR	EN	VU	LRcd	LRnt	EX	DD	Total	Endemics
0	0	0	0	2	0	0	2	0

Total number of species: Megachiroptera 0; Microchiroptera 7; Total 7

Reference(s): Breuil and Masson 1991, McFarlane 1991

Argentina

Species	Global status
Artibeus fimbriatus	LR: nt
Pygoderma bilabiatum	LR: nt
Eptesicus innoxius	VU A2c
Histiotus macrotus	LR: nt
Myotis aelleni	VU A2c, D2 (Endemic)
Myotis chiloensis	LR: nt
Myotis ruber	VU A2c
Molossops abrasus	LR: nt
Molossops neglectus	LR: nt
Tadarida brasiliensis	LR: nt

Summary

CR	EN	VU	LRcd	LRnt	EX	DD	Total	Endemics
0	0	3	0	7	0	0	10	1

Total number of species: Megachiroptera 0; Microchiroptera 57; Total 57

An assessment of the status of mammals and birds in Argentina was published in 1997 (Fernández *et al.* 1997). This listed 56 bat species as threatened. Six were listed as Vulnerable, 39 as Rare, and 11 as Insufficiently Known.

Reference(s): Barquez *et al.* 1999

Armenia

Species	Global status
?*Rhinolophus blasii*	LR: nt
Rhinolophus euryale	VU A2c
Rhinolophus ferrumequinum	LR: nt
Rhinolophus hipposideros	VU A2c
Rhinolophus mehelyi	VU A2c
Barbastella barbastellus	VU A2c
Myotis emarginatus	VU A2c
Myotis schaubi	EN B1 + 2c, C2a, D
?*Nyctalus lasiopterus*	LR: nt
Nyctalus leisleri	LR: nt
Miniopterus schreibersii	LR: nt

Armenia continued

Summary

CR	EN	VU	LRcd	LRnt	EX	DD	Total	Endemics
0	1	5	0	5	0	0	11	0

Total number of species: Megachiroptera 0; Microchiroptera 24; Total 24

A Red Data Book of Animals in Armenia was published in 1987 (Movsesian 1987). Six bat species were listed in this publication.

Reference(s): E.G. Yavrovyan *pers. comm.*

Aruba

Species	Global status
Leptonycteris curasoae	VU A1c

Summary

CR	EN	VU	LRcd	LRnt	EX	DD	Total	Endemics
0	0	1	0	0	0	0	1	0

Total number of species: Megachiroptera 0; Microchiroptera 4; Total 4

Reference(s): Husson 1960

Australia

Species	Global status
Saccolaimus flaviventris	LR: nt
Saccolaimus mixtus	VU A2c
Taphozous australis	LR: nt
Taphozous kapalgensis	VU A2c (Endemic)
Taphozous troughtoni	CR A1ac, B1 + 2abcde, D (Endemic)
Macroderma gigas	VU A2c (Endemic)
Hipposideros semoni	LR: nt
Hipposideros stenotis	LR: nt (Endemic)
Rhinonicteris aurantia	VU A1c (Endemic)
Rhinolophus philippinensis	LR: nt
Chalinolobus dwyeri	VU A2c (Endemic)
Chalinolobus picatus	LR: nt (Endemic)
Eptesicus caurinus	LR: nt (Endemic)
Eptesicus douglasorum	LR: nt (Endemic)
Myotis australis	DD (Endemic)
Nycticeius rueppellii	LR: nt (Endemic)
Nyctophilus daedalus	LR: nt (Endemic)
Nyctophilus howensis	EX
Nyctophilus sherrini	LR: nt (Endemic)
Nyctophilus timoriensis	VU A2c
Nyctophilus walkeri	LR: nt (Endemic)
Pipistrellus mckenziei	VU A2c (Endemic)
Miniopterus schreibersii	LR: nt
Tadarida australis	LR: nt

Summary

CR	EN	VU	LRcd	LRnt	EX	DD	Total	Endemics
1	0	7	0	14	1	1	24	15

Australia continued

Total number of species:	Megachiroptera	12
	Microchiroptera	63
	Total	75

The Action Plan for Australian Bats (Duncan *et al.* 1999) lists eight microchiropteran bat taxa as threatened. Two are listed as Critically Endangered, three as Endangered, and three as Vulnerable. A further one is Extinct, 10 are Data Deficient, one Lower Risk: Conservation Dependent and nine Lower Risk: Near Threatened.

Reference(s): Churchill 1998

Austria

Species	Global status
Rhinolophus ferrumequinum	LR: nt
Rhinolophus hipposideros	VU A2c
Barbastella barbastellus	VU A2c
Myotis bechsteinii	VU A2c
Myotis emarginatus	VU A2c
Myotis myotis	LR: nt
Nyctalus leisleri	LR: nt
Miniopterus schreibersii	LR: nt

Summary

CR	EN	VU	LRcd	LRnt	EX	DD	Total	Endemics
0	0	4	0	4	0	0	8	0

Total number of species:	Megachiroptera	0
	Microchiroptera	24
	Total	24

A Red Data Book for Austria was published in 1988 (Anon. 1988) which listed 23 species. Fourteen were listed as Vulnerable, seven as Rare, one as Rare, possibly Extinct, and one as Indeterminate.

Reference(s): F. Spitzenberger *pers. comm.*

Azerbaijan

Species	Global status
Rhinolophus blasii	LR: nt
Rhinolophus euryale	VU A2c
Rhinolophus ferrumequinum	LR: nt
Rhinolophus hipposideros	VU A2c
Rhinolophus mehelyi	VU A2c
Barbastella barbastellus	VU A2c
Myotis bechsteinii	VU A2c
Myotis emarginatus	VU A2c
Nyctalus lasiopterus	LR: nt
Nyctalus leisleri	LR: nt
Miniopterus schreibersii	LR: nt

Summary

CR	EN	VU	LRcd	LRnt	EX	DD	Total	Endemics
0	0	6	0	5	0	0	11	0

Azerbaijan continued

Total number of species:	Megachiroptera	0
	Microchiroptera	27
	Total	27

A Red Data Book for Azerbaijan was published in 1989 (Adygezalov 1989). It listed three species of bats.

Reference(s): Rakhmatulina 1989, 1996a, 1996b

Bahamas

Species	Global status
Brachyphylla nana	LR: nt
Natalus lepidus	LR: nt
Natalus tumidifrons	VU D2 (Endemic)
Tadarida brasiliensis	LR: nt

Summary

CR	EN	VU	LRcd	LRnt	EX	DD	Total	Endemics
0	0	1	0	3	0	0	4	1

Total number of species:	Megachiroptera	0
	Microchiroptera	12
	Total	12

Reference(s): Koopman *et al.* 1957

Bahrain

No globally threatened species present.

Total number of species:	Megachiroptera	0
	Microchiroptera	4
	Total	4

Reference(s): Harrison and Bates 1994

Bangladesh

No globally threatened species present.

Total number of species:	Megachiroptera	3
	Microchiroptera	15
	Total	18

Reference(s): Bates and Harrison 1997

Barbados

Species	Global status
Monophyllus plethodon	LR: nt
Myotis martiniquensis	LR: nt

Summary

CR	EN	VU	LRcd	LRnt	EX	DD	Total	Endemics
0	0	0	0	2	0	0	2	0

Barbados continued

Total number of species:	Megachiroptera	0
	Microchiroptera	6
	Total	6
Reference(s):	McFarlane 1991	

Belarus

Species	Global status
Barbastella barbastellus	VU A2c
Myotis bechsteinii	VU A2c
Myotis dasycneme	VU A2c
Myotis myotis	LR: nt
Nyctalus lasiopterus	LR: nt
Nyctalus leisleri	LR: nt

Summary

CR	EN	VU	LRcd	LRnt	EX	DD	Total	Endemics
0	0	3	0	3	0	0	6	0

Total number of species:	Megachiroptera	0
	Microchiroptera	17
	Total	17

A Red Data Book of Belarus was published in 1993 (Darafeei *et al.* 1993). Seven species of bats were listed, all considered Rare.

Reference(s): A. Borissenko *pers. comm.*

Belgium

Species	Global status
Rhinolophus ferrumequinum	LR: nt
Rhinolophus hipposideros	VU A2c
Barbastella barbastellus	VU A2c
Myotis bechsteinii	VU A2c
Myotis dasycneme	VU A2c
Myotis emarginatus	VU A2c
Myotis myotis	LR: nt
Nyctalus leisleri	LR: nt

Summary

CR	EN	VU	LRcd	LRnt	EX	DD	Total	Endemics
0	0	5	0	3	0	0	8	0

Total number of species:	Megachiroptera	0
	Microchiroptera	18
	Total	18
Reference(s):	J. Fairon *pers. comm.*	

Belize

Species	Global status
Balantiopteryx io	LR: nt
Tonatia evotis	LR: nt
Vampyrum spectrum	LR: nt
Hylonycteris underwoodi	LR: nt
Diphylla ecaudata	LR: nt

Belize continued

Species	Global status
Antrozous dubiaquercus	VU A2c, D2
Myotis elegans	LR: nt
Eumops underwoodi	LR: nt
Tadarida brasiliensis	LR: nt

Summary

CR	EN	VU	LRcd	LRnt	EX	DD	Total	Endemics
0	0	1	0	8	0	0	9	0

Total number of species:	Megachiroptera	0
	Microchiroptera	69
	Total	69
Reference(s):	McCarthy *et al.* 1993	

Benin

Species	Global status
Nycteris major	VU A2c, D2

Summary

CR	EN	VU	LRcd	LRnt	EX	DD	Total	Endemics
0	0	1	0	0	0	0	1	0

Total number of species:	Megachiroptera	4
	Microchiroptera	21
	Total	25
Reference(s):	Bergmans 1988, 1989, 1990, 1994, 1997, Hayman and Hill 1971	

Bermuda

No globally threatened species present.

Total number of species:	Megachiroptera	0
	Microchiroptera	4
	Total	4
Reference(s):	Koopman 1993	

Bhutan

No globally threatened species present.

Total number of species:	Megachiroptera	3
	Microchiroptera	2
	Total	5
Reference(s):	Bates and Harrison 1997	

Bolivia

Species	Global status
Tonatia carrikeri	VU A2c
Artibeus obscurus	LR: nt
Platyrrhinus infuscus	LR: nt

Bolivia continued

Species	Global status
Pygoderma bilabiatum	LR: nt
Sturnira magna	LR: nt
Vampyressa bidens	LR: nt
Diphylla ecaudata	LR: nt
Histiotus macrotus	LR: nt
Molossops abrasus	LR: nt
Tadarida brasiliensis	LR: nt

Summary

CR	EN	VU	LRcd	LRnt	EX	DD	Total	Endemics
0	0	1	0	9	0	0	10	0

Total number of species: Megachiroptera 0
Microchiroptera 107
Total 107

A Red Data Book of Bolivia was published in 1996 (Ergueta and de Morales 1996). No bats were listed in this publication.

Reference(s): L.F. Aguirre *pers. comm.*

Bosnia-Herzegovina

Species	Global status
Rhinolophus euryale	VU A2c
Rhinolophus ferrumequinum	LR: nt
Rhinolophus hipposideros	VU A2c
Rhinolophus mehelyi	VU A2c
Barbastella barbastellus	VU A2c
Myotis bechsteinii	VU A2c
Myotis capaccinii	VU A2c
Myotis emarginatus	VU A2c
Nyctalus lasiopterus	LR: nt
Nyctalus leisleri	LR: nt
Miniopterus schreibersii	LR: nt

Summary

CR	EN	VU	LRcd	LRnt	EX	DD	Total	Endemics
0	0	7	0	4	0	0	11	0

Total number of species: Megachiroptera 0
Microchiroptera 16
Total 16

Reference(s): Corbet 1978

Botswana

Species	Global status
Cloeotis percivali	LR: nt
Rhinolophus deckenii	DD
Eptesicus zuluensis	LR: nt
Laephotis botswanae	LR: nt
Miniopterus schreibersii	LR: nt
Chaerephon chapini	LR: nt

Summary

CR	EN	VU	LRcd	LRnt	EX	DD	Total	Endemics
0	0	0	0	5	0	1	6	0

Botswana contimued

Total number of species: Megachiroptera 2
Microchiroptera 28
Total 30

Reference(s): Mickleburgh *et al.* 1992, Skinner and Smithers 1990, Smithers 1971, Taylor 2000

Brazil

Species	Global status
Cyttarops alecto	LR: nt
Diclidurus ingens	VU A2c
Diclidurus isabellus	LR: nt
Saccopteryx gymnura	VU A2c, D2
Micronycteris behnii	VU A2c
Diclidurus brosseti	DD
Micronycteris daviesi	LR: nt
Micronycteris pusilla	VU A2c
Micronycteris sanborni	DD (Endemic)
Micronycteris sylvestris	LR: nt
Phyllostomus latifolius	LR: nt
Tonatia carrikeri	VU A2c
Tonatia schulzi	VU A2c
Vampyrum spectrum	LR: nt
Lonchophylla bokermanni	VU A2c (Endemic)
Lonchophylla dekeyseri	VU A2c (Endemic)
Lonchorhina inusitata	DD
Choeroniscus intermedius	LR: nt
Scleronycteris ega	VU A2c, D2
Rhinophylla fischerae	LR: nt
Artibeus concolor	LR: nt
Artibeus fimbriatus	LR: nt
Artibeus obscurus	LR: nt
Chiroderma doriae	VU A2c, D2 (Endemic)
Platyrrhinus infuscus	LR: nt
Platyrrhinus recifinus	VU A2c, D2 (Endemic)
Pygoderma bilabiatum	LR: nt
?Sturnira bidens	LR: nt
Vampyressa bidens	LR: nt
Vampyressa brocki	LR: nt
Diphylla ecaudata	LR: nt
Histiotus alienus	VU A2c
Lasiurus ebenus	VU B1 + 2c, D2 (Endemic)
Laslurus egreglus	LR: nt
Myotis ruber	VU A2c
Molossops abrasus	LR: nt
Molossops mattogrossensis	LR: nt
Molossops neglectus	LR: nt
Molossus coibensis	LR: nt
Tadarida brasiliensis	LR: nt

Summary

CR	EN	VU	LRcd	LRnt	EX	DD	Total	Endemics
0	0	14	0	23	0	3	40	6

Total number of species: Megachiroptera 0
Microchiroptera 137
Total 137

A Red Data Book for Brazilian Mammals was published in 1994 (da Fonseca *et al.* 1994). No bat species were listed in this publication.

Reference(s): da Fonseca *et al.* 1996, Marinho-Filho and Sazima 1998

British Virgin Islands

No globally threatened species present.

Total number of species:	Megachiroptera	0
	Microchiroptera	3
	Total	3
Reference(s):	McFarlane 1991	

Brunei

Species	**Global status**
Pipistrellus macrotis	LR: nt

Summary

CR	EN	VU	LRcd	LRnt	EX	DD	Total	Endemics
0	0	0	0	1	0	0	1	0

Total number of species:	Megachiroptera	11
	Microchiroptera	11
	Total	22
Reference(s):	Payne *et al.* 1985	

Bulgaria

Species	**Global status**
Rhinolophus blasii	LR: nt
Rhinolophus euryale	VU A2c
Rhinolophus ferrumequinum	LR: nt
Rhinolophus hipposideros	VU A2c
Rhinolophus mehelyi	VU A2c
Barbastella barbastellus	VU A2c
Myotis bechsteinii	VU A2c
Myotis capaccinii	VU A2c
Myotis emarginatus	VU A2c
Myotis myotis	LR: nt
Nyctalus lasiopterus	LR: nt
Nyctalus leisleri	LR: nt
Miniopterus schreibersii	LR: nt

Summary

CR	EN	VU	LRcd	LRnt	EX	DD	Total	Endemics
0	0	7	0	6	0	0	13	0

Total number of species:	Megachiroptera	0
	Microchiroptera	29
	Total	29

A Red Data Book for Bulgaria was published in 1985 (Bulgarska Akadamija na Naukite 1985). Two bat species were listed in this publication, both considered rare.

Reference(s): V. Beshkov and R. Pandurska *pers. comm.*

Burkina Faso

Species	**Global status**
Hipposideros jonesi	LR: nt
Mops demonstrator	LR: nt

Burkina Faso continued

Summary

CR	EN	VU	LRcd	LRnt	EX	DD	Total	Endemics
0	0	0	0	2	0	0	2	0

Total number of species:	Megachiroptera	5
	Microchiroptera	25
	Total	30
Reference(s):	Mickleburgh *et al.* 1992, Hayman and Hill 1971	

Burundi

Species	**Global status**
Eptesicus flavescens	DD

Summary

CR	EN	VU	LRcd	LRnt	EX	DD	Total	Endemics
0	0	0	0	0	0	1	1	0

Total number of species:	Megachiroptera	5
	Microchiroptera	17
	Total	22
Reference(s):	Bergmans 1988, 1989, 1990, 1994, 1997, Hayman and Hill 1971	

Cambodia

Species	**Global status**
Rhinolophus shameli	LR: nt
Myotis rosseti	LR: nt

Summary

CR	EN	VU	LRcd	LRnt	EX	DD	Total	Endemics
0	0	0	0	2	0	0	2	0

Total number of species:	Megachiroptera	10
	Microchiroptera	28
	Total	38
Reference(s):	Corbet and Hill 1992	

Cameroon

Species	**Global status**
Saccolaimus peli	LR: nt
Nycteris intermedia	LR: nt
Nycteris major	VU A2c, D2
Nycteris woodi	LR: nt
Hipposideros camerunensis	LR: nt
Hipposideros curtus	LR: nt
Hipposideros fuliginosus	LR: nt
Rhinolophus alcyone	LR: nt
Kerivoula cuprosa	LR: nt
Kerivoula smithi	LR: nt
Chalinolobus alboguttatus	VU D2
Chalinolobus egeria	LR: nt

Cameroon continued

Species	Global status
Chalinolobus gleni	LR: nt
Eptesicus brunneus	LR: nt
Pipistrellus musciculus	LR: nt
Miniopterus schreibersii	LR: nt
Mops congicus	LR: nt
Mops petersoni	LR: nt

Summary

CR	EN	VU	LRcd	LRnt	EX	DD	Total	Endemics
0	0	2	0	16	0	0	18	0

Total number of species:	Megachiroptera	14
	Microchiroptera	57
	Total	71
Reference(s):	Mickleburgh *et al.* 1992, Hayman and Hill 1971	

Canada

Species	Global status
Plecotus townsendii	VU A2c

Summary

CR	EN	VU	LRcd	LRnt	EX	DD	Total	Endemics
0	0	1	0	0	0	0	1	0

Total number of species:	Megachiroptera	0
	Microchiroptera	20
	Total	20
Reference(s):	van Zyll de Jong 1985	

Cape Verde Islands

No globally threatened species present.

Total number of species:	Megachiroptera	0
	Microchiroptera	2
	Total	2
Reference(s):	Koopman 1993	

Cayman Islands

Species	Global status
Brachyphylla nana	LR: nt
Phyllops falcatus	LR: nt
Tadarida brasiliensis	LR: nt

Summary

CR	EN	VU	LRcd	LRnt	EX	DD	Total	Endemics
0	0	0	0	3	0	0	3	0

Total number of species:	Megachiroptera	0
	Microchiroptera	8
	Total	8
Reference(s):	McFarlane 1991	

Central African Republic

Species	Global status
Miniopterus schreibersii	LR: nt
Otomops martensseni	VU A2c

Summary

CR	EN	VU	LRcd	LRnt	EX	DD	Total	Endemics
0	0	1	0	1	0	0	2	0

Total number of species:	Megachiroptera	10
	Microchiroptera	16
	Total	26
Reference(s):	Mickleburgh *et al.* 1992, Hayman and Hill 1971	

Chad

Species	Global status
Taphozous hamiltoni	VU A2c

Summary

CR	EN	VU	LRcd	LRnt	EX	DD	Total	Endemics
0	0	1	0	0	0	0	1	0

Total number of species:	Megachiroptera	4
	Microchiroptera	17
	Total	21
Reference(s):	Mickleburgh *et al.* 1992, Hayman and Hill 1971	

Chile

Species	Global status
Amorphochilus schnablii	VU A2c
Histiotus macrotus	LR: nt
Myotis atacamensis	VU A2c, D2
Myotis chiloensis	LR: nt (Endemic)
Mormopterus kalinowskii	VU A2c, D2
Tadarida brasiliensis	LR: nt

Summary

CR	EN	VU	LRcd	LRnt	EX	DD	Total	Endemics
0	0	3	0	3	0	0	6	1

Total number of species:	Megachiroptera	0
	Microchiroptera	10
	Total	10

A Red Data Book for Chile was published in 1993 (Glade 1993). No bats were listed in this publication.

Reference(s): Redford and Eisenberg 1992

China

Species	Global status
Hipposideros pratti	LR: nt
?*Rhinolophus cornutus*	LR: nt
Rhinolophus ferrumequinum	LR: nt

China continued

Species	Global status
Rhinolophus osgoodi	DD (Endemic)
Rhinolophus rex	VU B1 + 2c (Endemic)
Rhinolophus thomasi	LR: nt
Rhinolophus yunanensis	LR: nt
Eptesicus pachyotis	LR: nt
Ia io	LR: nt
Myotis bombinus	LR: nt
Myotis dasycneme	VU A2c
Myotis fimbriatus	LR: nt (Endemic)
Myotis frater	LR: nt
Myotis montivagus	LR: nt
Myotis pequinius	LR: nt (Endemic)
Myotis ricketti	LR: nt (Endemic)
Nyctalus aviator	LR: nt
Nyctalus leisleri	LR: nt
Pipistrellus paterculus	LR: nt
Pipistrellus pulveratus	LR: nt
Scotomanes ornatus	LR: nt
Murina aurata	LR: nt
Murina fusca	DD (Endemic)
Murina huttoni	LR: nt
Miniopterus schreibersii	LR: nt

Summary

CR	EN	VU	LRcd	LRnt	EX	DD	Total	Endemics
0	0	2	0	21	0	2	25	6

Total number of species:	Megachiroptera	8
	Microchiroptera	82
	Total	90

A Red Data Book of the Endemic Mammals of China was published in 1998 (Wang 1998). This listed six microchiropteran bat species, one considered Rare, two Vulnerable, and three Indeterminate.

Reference(s): Zhang Yongzu 1997

Colombia

Species	Global status
Balantiopteryx infusca	EN B1 + 2c
Cyttarops alecto	LR: nt
Diclidurus ingens	VU A2c
Diclidurus isabellus	LR: nt
Lonchorhina marinkellei	VU A2c (Endemic)
Lonchorhina orinocensis	LR: nt
Micronycteris daviesi	LR: nt
Micronycteris pusilla	VU A2c
Micronycteris sylvestris	LR: nt
Phyllostomus latifolius	LR: nt
Tonatia carrikeri	VU A2c
Vampyrum spectrum	LR: nt
Lonchophylla handleyi	VU A2c, D2
Anoura latidens	LR: nt
Choeroniscus godmani	LR: nt
Choeroniscus intermedius	LR: nt
Choeroniscus periosus	VU D2
Leptonycteris curasoae	VU A1c
Scleronycteris ega	VU A2c, D2
Rhinophylla alethina	LR: nt

Colombia continued

Species	Global status
Rhinophylla fischerae	LR: nt
Artibeus amplus	LR: nt
Artibeus concolor	LR: nt
Artibeus obscurus	LR: nt
Ectophylla alba	LR: nt
Platyrrhinus aurarius	LR: nt
Platyrrhinus chocoensis	VU A2c, D2 (Endemic)
Platyrrhinus infuscus	LR: nt
Platyrrhinus umbratus	LR: nt
Sturnira aratathomasi	LR: nt
Sturnira bidens	LR: nt
Sturnira magna	LR: nt
Sturnira mordax	LR: nt
Vampyressa bidens	LR: nt
Vampyressa brocki	LR: nt
Vampyressa melissa	LR: nt
Diphylla ecaudata	LR: nt
Lasiurus castaneus	VU D2
Lasiurus egregius	LR: nt
Myotis nesopolus	LR: nt
Rhogeessa minutilla	LR: nt
Molossops abrasus	LR: nt
Molossops mattogrossensis	LR: nt
Tadarida brasiliensis	LR: nt

Summary

CR	EN	VU	LRcd	LRnt	EX	DD	Total	Endemics
0	1	10	0	33	0	0	44	2

Total number of species:	Megachiroptera	0
	Microchiroptera	170
	Total	170

Reference(s): Rodríguez-Mahecha *et al.* 1995

Commonwealth of the Northern Mariana Islands

Species	Global status
Emballonura semicaudata	EN A1ac

Summary

CR	EN	VU	LRcd	LRnt	EX	DD	Total	Endemics
0	1	0	0	0	0	0	1	0

Total number of species:	Megachiroptera	1
	Microchiroptera	1
	Total	2

Reference(s): Mickleburgh *et al.* 1992, Flannery 1995b

Comoros

Species	Global status
Myotis goudoti	LR: nt
Miniopterus minor	LR: nt

Comoros continued

Summary

CR	EN	VU	LRcd	LRnt	EX	DD	Total	Endemics
0	0	0	0	2	0	0	2	0

Total number of species:	Megachiroptera	3
	Microchiroptera	2
	Total	5
Reference(s):	Cheke and Dahl 1981, Mickleburgh *et al.* 1992	

Congo Republic

Species	Global status
Saccolaimus peli	LR: nt
Nycteris major	VU A2c, D2
Hipposideros fuliginosus	LR: nt
Rhinolophus adami	DD (Endemic)
Rhinolophus alcyone	LR: nt
Rhinolophus silvestris	LR: nt
Chalinolobus beatrix	LR: nt
Scotophilus nigrita	LR: nt
Miniopterus minor	LR: nt

Summary

CR	EN	VU	LRcd	LRnt	EX	DD	Total	Endemics
0	0	1	0	7	0	1	9	1

Total number of species:	Megachiroptera	12
	Microchiroptera	36
	Total	48
Reference(s):	Bergmans 1988, 1989, 1990, 1994, 1997, Hayman and Hill 1971	

Cook Islands

No microchiropteran bats present.

Total number of species:	Megachiroptera	1
	Microchiroptera	0
	Total	1
Reference(s):	Mickleburgh *et al.* 1992	

Costa Rica

Species	Global status
Cyttarops alecto	LR: nt
Micronycteris daviesi	LR: nt
Micronycteris sylvestris	LR: nt
Vampyrum spectrum	LR: nt
Choeroniscus godmani	LR: nt
Ectophylla alba	LR: nt
Sturnira mordax	LR: nt
Diphylla ecaudata	LR: nt
Antrozous dubiaquercus	VU A2c, D2
Lasiurus castaneus	VU D2
Myotis elegans	LR: nt
Molossus coibensis	LR: nt
Tadarida brasiliensis	LR: nt

Costa Rica continued

Summary

CR	EN	VU	LRcd	LRnt	EX	DD	Total	Endemics
0	0	2	0	11	0	0	13	0

Total number of species:	Megachiroptera	0
	Microchiroptera	103
	Total	103
Reference(s):	Wilson 1983	

Côte d'Ivoire

Species	Global status
Nycteris intermedia	LR: nt
Nycteris major	VU A2c, D2
Hipposideros marisae	VU A2c
Kerivoula smithi	LR: nt
Chalinolobus beatrix	LR: nt
Chalinolobus poensis	LR: nt
Chalinolobus superbus	VU D2
Myopterus daubentonii	DD

Summary

CR	EN	VU	LRcd	LRnt	EX	DD	Total	Endemics
0	0	3	0	4	0	1	8	0

Total number of species:	Megachiroptera	12
	Microchiroptera	34
	Total	46
Reference(s):	Mickleburgh *et al.* 1992, Hayman and Hill 1971	

Croatia

Species	Global status
Rhinolophus euryale	VU A2c
Rhinolophus ferrumequinum	LR: nt
Rhinolophus hipposideros	VU A2c
Rhinolophus mehelyi	VU A2c
Barbastella barbastellus	VU A2c
Myotis bechsteinii	VU A2c
Myotis capaccinii	VU A2c
Myotis emarginatus	VU A2c
Nyctalus lasiopterus	LR: nt
Nyctalus leisleri	LR: nt
Miniopterus schreibersii	LR: nt

Summary

CR	EN	VU	LRcd	LRnt	EX	DD	Total	Endemics
0	0	7	0	4	0	0	11	0

Total number of species:	Megachiroptera	0
	Microchiroptera	26
	Total	26

A Red Data Book for Croatia was published in 1994 (Draganovic 1994). Twenty-seven species of bats were listed. Two were considered Extinct, seven Endangered, three Vulnerable, seven Rare, and eight Indeterminate.

Reference(s): Dulic 1989

Cuba

Species	Global status
Mormoops blainvillii	LR: nt
Pteronotus macleayii	VU A2c
Pteronotus quadridens	LR: nt
Brachyphylla nana	LR: nt
Phyllonycteris poeyi	LR: nt
Phyllops falcatus	LR: nt
Natalus lepidus	LR: nt
Mormopterus minutus	VU A2c (Endemic)
Tadarida brasiliensis	LR: nt

Summary

CR	EN	VU	LRcd	LRnt	EX	DD	Total	Endemics
0	0	2	0	7	0	0	9	1

Total number of species: Megachiroptera 0, Microchiroptera 27, Total 27

Reference(s): G. Silva-Taboada *pers. comm.*

Cyprus

Species	Global status
Rhinolophus blasii	LR: nt
Rhinolophus euryale	VU A2c
Rhinolophus ferrumequinum	LR: nt
Myotis myotis	LR: nt

Summary

CR	EN	VU	LRcd	LRnt	EX	DD	Total	Endemics
0	0	1	0	3	0	0	4	0

Total number of species: Megachiroptera 1, Microchiroptera 15, Total 16

Reference(s): Mickleburgh *et al.* 1992, Boye *et al.* 1990

Czech Republic

Species	Global status
Rhinolophus ferrumequinum	LR: nt
Rhinolophus hipposideros	VU A2c
Barbastella barbastellus	VU A2c
Myotis bechsteinii	VU A2c
Myotis dasycneme	VU A2c
Myotis emarginatus	VU A2c
Myotis myotis	LR: nt
Nyctalus leisleri	LR: nt

Summary

CR	EN	VU	LRcd	LRnt	EX	DD	Total	Endemics
0	0	5	0	3	0	0	8	0

Total number of species: Megachiroptera 0, Microchiroptera 21, Total 21

A Red Data Book for the whole of Czechoslovakia was published in 1989 (Baruš 1989). Twenty-four species of bats were listed. Six were listed as Endangered, 13 as Vulnerable, and five as Rare.

Reference(s): Hanak *et al.* 1995

Democratic Republic of Congo (formerly Zaire)

Species	Global status
Saccolaimus peli	LR: nt
Nycteris intermedia	LR: nt
Nycteris major	VU A2c, D2
Cloeotis percivali	LR: nt
Hipposideros camerunensis	LR: nt
Hipposideros fuliginosus	LR: nt
Rhinolophus alcyone	LR: nt
Rhinolophus blasii	LR: nt
Rhinolophus maclaudi	LR: nt
Kerivoula cuprosa	LR: nt
Kerivoula smithi	LR: nt
Chalinolobus alboguttatus	VU D2
Chalinolobus poensis	LR: nt
Chalinolobus superbus	VU D2
Eptesicus brunneus	LR: nt
Eptesicus guineensis	LR: nt
Laephotis angolensis	LR: nt
Laephotis botswanae	LR: nt
Pipistrellus anchietai	VU A2c
Pipistrellus musciculus	LR: nt
Scotophilus nigrita	LR: nt
Miniopterus minor	LR: nt
Miniopterus schreibersii	LR: nt
Chaerephon chapini	LR: nt
Chaerephon gallagheri	CR B1 + 2c (Endemic)
Mops congicus	LR: nt
Mops demonstrator	LR: nt
Mops niangarae	CR B1 + 2c (Endemic)
Mops trevori	LR: nt
Myopterus daubentonii	DD
Otomops martiensseni	VU A2c
Tadarida fulminans	LR: nt
Tadarida ventralis	LR: nt

Summary

CR	EN	VU	LRcd	LRnt	EX	DD	Total	Endemics
2	0	5	0	25	0	1	33	2

Total number of species: Megachiroptera 17, Microchiroptera 78, Total 95

Reference(s): Bergmans 1988, 1989, 1990, 1994, 1997, Hayman and Hill 1971

Denmark

Species	Global status
Barbastella barbastellus	VU A2c
Myotis dasycneme	VU A2c

Summary

CR	EN	VU	LRcd	LRnt	EX	DD	Total	Endemics
0	0	2	0	0	0	0	2	0

Total number of species: Megachiroptera 0, Microchiroptera 13, Total 13

A list of threatened animal and plants of the Nordic countries, including Denmark, was published in 1995 (Nordiska Ministerrådet 1995). This included six species of bats, one considered Endangered, three Vulnerable, and two Rare.

Reference(s): Stebbings 1988

Djibouti

Species	Global status
Hipposideros megalotis	LR: nt
Otomops martiensseni	VU A2c

Summary

CR	EN	VU	LRcd	LRnt	EX	DD	Total	Endemics
0	0	1	0	1	0	0	2	0

Total number of species:	Megachiroptera	0
	Microchiroptera	2
	Total	2
Reference(s):	Hayman and Hill 1971	

Dominica

Species	Global status
Monophyllus plethodon	LR: nt
Ardops nichollsi	LR: nt
Myotis dominicensis	VU A2c, D2
Tadarida brasiliensis	LR: nt

Summary

CR	EN	VU	LRcd	LRnt	EX	DD	Total	Endemics
0	0	1	0	3	0	0	4	0

Total number of species:	Megachiroptera	0
	Microchiroptera	12
	Total	12
Reference(s):	McFarlane 1991	

Dominican Republic

Species	Global status
Mormoops blainvillii	LR: nt
Pteronotus quadridens	LR: nt
Brachyphylla nana	LR: nt
Phyllonycteris poeyi	LR: nt
Phyllops falcatus	LR: nt
Tadarida brasiliensis	LR: nt

Summary

CR	EN	VU	LRcd	LRnt	EX	DD	Total	Endemics
0	0	0	0	6	0	0	6	0

Total number of species:	Megachiroptera	0
	Microchiroptera	18
	Total	18
Reference(s):	McFarlane 1991	

Ecuador (including Galapagos Islands)

Species	Global status
Balantiopteryx infusca	EN B1 + 2c
Micronycteris daviesi	LR: nt
Micronycteris sylvestris	LR: nt
Vampyrum spectrum	LR: nt

Ecuador continued

Species	Global status
Lonchophylla handleyi	VU A2c, D2
Lonchophylla hesperia	VU A2c, D2
Choeroniscus periosus	VU D2
Rhinophylla alethina	LR: nt
Rhinophylla fischerae	LR: nt
Artibeus fraterculus	VU A2c
Artibeus obscurus	LR: nt
Platyrrhinus infuscus	LR: nt
Sturnira aratathomasi	LR: nt
Sturnira bidens	LR: nt
Sturnira magna	LR: nt
Diphylla ecaudata	LR: nt
Amorphochilus schnablii	VU A2c
Eptesicus innoxius	VU A2c
Molossops aequatorianus	VU A2c, D2 (Endemic)
Tadarida brasiliensis	LR: nt

Summary

CR	EN	VU	LRcd	LRnt	EX	DD	Total	Endemics
0	1	7	0	12	0	0	20	1

Total number of species:	Megachiroptera	0
	Microchiroptera	105
	Total	105

A Red Data Book of Threatened Animals of Ecuador was published in 1986 (Suarez and Garcia 1986). No species of bats were listed in this publication.

Reference(s): Albuja 1982

Egypt

Species	Global status
Rhinolophus euryale	VU A2c
Rhinolophus hipposideros	VU A2c
Rhinolophus mehelyi	VU A2c
Pipistrellus ariel	VU D2
Pipistrellus bodenheimeri	LR: nt

Summary

CR	EN	VU	LRcd	LRnt	EX	DD	Total	Endemics
0	0	4	0	1	0	0	5	0

Total number of species:	Megachiroptera	1
	Microchiroptera	21
	Total	22
Reference(s):	Qumsiyeh 1985	

El Salvador

Species	Global status
Choeroniscus godmani	LR: nt
Choeronycteris mexicana	LR: nt
Leptonycteris curasoae	VU A1c
Artibeus incomitatus	DD
Artibeus inopinatus	VU A2c
Diphylla ecaudata	LR: nt
Eumops underwoodi	LR: nt

El Salvador continued

Species	Global status
Molossus coibensis	LR: nt
Tadarida brasiliensis	LR: nt

Summary

CR	EN	VU	LRcd	LRnt	EX	DD	Total	Endemics
0	0	2	0	6	0	1	9	0

Total number of species: Megachiroptera 0
Microchiroptera 58
Total 58

Reference(s): McCarthy *et al.* 1991

Equatorial Guinea

Species	Global status
Hipposideros curtus	LR: nt
Hipposideros fuliginosus	LR: nt
Hipposideros jonesi	LR: nt
Rhinolophus alcyone	LR: nt
Chalinolobus poensis	LR: nt
Eptesicus brunneus	LR: nt
Eptesicus platyops	VU D2
Scotoecus albofuscus	LR: nt
Scotophilus nigrita	LR: nt

Summary

CR	EN	VU	LRcd	LRnt	EX	DD	Total	Endemics
0	0	1	0	8	0	0	9	0

Total number of species: Megachiroptera 9
Microchiroptera 39
Total 48

Reference(s): Bergmans 1988, 1989, 1990, 1994, 1997,
J. Juste *pers. comm.*

Eritrea

Species	Global status
Asellia patrizii	VU A2c, D2
Rhinolophus hipposideros	VU A2c

Summary

CR	EN	VU	LRcd	LRnt	EX	DD	Total	Endemics
0	0	2	0	0	0	0	2	0

Total number of species: Megachiroptera 0
Microchiroptera 11
Total 11

Reference(s): Hayman and Hill 1971

Estonia

Species	Global status
Myotis dasycneme	VU A2c

Estonia continued

Summary

CR	EN	VU	LRcd	LRnt	EX	DD	Total	Endemics
0	0	1	0	0	0	0	1	0

Total number of species: Megachiroptera 0
Microchiroptera 11
Total 11

A list of species in the Estonian Red Data Book was published in 1993 (Ingelög *et al.* 1993). Six bat species were listed, all considered Rare.

Reference(s): M. Masing *pers. comm.*

Ethiopia

Species	Global status
Rhinopoma macinnesi	VU A2c, D2
Nycteris aurita	LR: nt
Nycteris woodi	LR: nt
Cardioderma cor	LR: nt
Asellia patrizii	VU A2c, D2
Hipposideros fuliginosus	LR: nt
Hipposideros megalotis	LR: nt
Rhinolophus blasii	LR: nt
Rhinolophus hipposideros	VU A2c
Eptesicus guineensis	LR: nt
Laephotis wintoni	LR: nt
Myotis morrisi	VU D2
Myotis scotti	VU A2c, D2 (Endemic)
?Pipistrellus aero	DD
Scotophilus nigrita	LR: nt
Miniopterus schreibersii	LR: nt
Chaerephon chapini	LR: nt
Mormopterus acetabulosus	VU B1 + 2c
Otomops martiensseni	VU A2c
Tadarida ventralis	LR: nt

Summary

CR	EN	VU	LRcd	LRnt	EX	DD	Total	Endemics
0	0	7	0	12	0	1	20	1

Total number of species: Megachiroptera 8
Microchiroptera 58
Total 66

Reference(s): Bergmans 1988, 1989, 1990, 1994, 1997,
D. Yalden *pers. comm.*

Falkland Islands

A bat recorded from the Falkland Islands was a female *Tadarida brasiliensis* found mummified in 1985. It is thought that this may have arrived from mainland South America having been blown off course, or it may have been accidentally transported by sea or air. Another of the same species was found alive in 1998. There are not thought to be any resident populations of bats on the Falkland Islands.

Reference(s): Hill 1988,
A.M. Hutson *pers. comm.*

Federated States of Micronesia

Species	Global status
Emballonura semicaudata	EN A1ac

Summary

CR	EN	VU	LRcd	LRnt	EX	DD	Total	Endemics
0	1	0	0	0	0	0	1	0

Total number of species:	Megachiroptera	4
	Microchiroptera	1
	Total	5
Reference(s):	Mickleburgh *et al.* 1992, Flannery 1995b	

Fiji

Species	Global status
Emballonura semicaudata	EN A1ac
Chaerephon bregullae	LR: nt

Summary

CR	EN	VU	LRcd	LRnt	EX	DD	Total	Endemics
0	1	0	0	1	0	0	2	0

Total number of species:	Megachiroptera	4
	Microchiroptera	2
	Total	6
Reference(s):	Mickleburgh *et al.* 1992, Flannery 1995b	

Finland

No globally threatened species present.

Total number of species:	Megachiroptera	0
	Microchiroptera	8
	Total	8

A list of the threatened animals and plants of the Nordic countries, including Finland, was published in 1995 (Nordiska Ministerrådet 1995). One bat species listed was considered Endangered.

Reference(s): T. Stjernberg *pers. comm.*

France

Species	Global status
Rhinolophus euryale	VU A2c
Rhinolophus ferrumequinum	LR: nt
Rhinolophus hipposideros	VU A2c
Rhinolophus mehelyi	VU A2c
Barbastella barbastellus	VU A2c
Myotis bechsteinii	VU A2c
Myotis capaccinii	VU A2c
Myotis dasycneme	VU A2c
Myotis emarginatus	VU A2c
Myotis myotis	LR: nt
Nyctalus lasiopterus	LR: nt

France continued

Species	Global status
Nyctalus leisleri	LR: nt
Miniopterus schreibersii	LR: nt

Summary

CR	EN	VU	LRcd	LRnt	EX	DD	Total	Endemics
0	0	8	0	5	0	0	13	0

Total number of species:	Megachiroptera	0
	Microchiroptera	29
	Total	29

A Red Data Book of mammals in France was published in 1994 (Maurin, 1994). This listed 20 bat species, three of which were considered Endangered, 12 Vulnerable, four Rare and one Indeterminate.

Reference(s): J.F. Noblet *pers. comm.*

French Guiana

Species	Global status
Lonchorhina inusitata	DD
Micronycteris brosseti	DD
Micronycteris daviesi	LR: nt
Phyllostomus latifolius	LR: nt
Tonatia schulzi	VU A2c
Vampyrum spectrum	LR: nt
Choeroniscus intermedius	LR: nt
Artibeus concolor	LR: nt
Artibeus obscurus	LR: nt
Vampyressa melissa	LR: nt
Lasiurus castaneus	VU D2
Lasiurus egregius	LR: nt

Summary

CR	EN	VU	LRcd	LRnt	EX	DD	Total	Endemics
0	0	2	0	8	0	2	12	0

Total number of species:	Megachiroptera	0
	Microchiroptera	102
	Total	102
Reference(s):	Simmons *et al.* 2000	

Gabon

Species	Global status
Saccolaimus peli	LR: nt
Nycteris intermedia	LR: nt
?Nycteris major	VU A2c, D2
Rhinolophus alcyone	LR: nt
Rhinolophus silvestris	LR: nt
Pipistrellus musciculus	LR: nt

Summary

CR	EN	VU	LRcd	LRnt	EX	DD	Total	Endemics
0	0	1	0	5	0	0	6	0

Total number of species:	Megachiroptera	9
	Microchiroptera	23
	Total	32
Reference(s):	Bergmans 1988, 1989, 1990, 1994, 1997, Hayman and Hill 1971	

Gambia

Species	Global status
Scotoecus albofuscus	LR: nt

Summary

CR	EN	VU	LRcd	LRnt	EX	DD	Total	Endemics
0	0	0	0	1	0	0	1	0

Total number of species:	Megachiroptera	4
	Microchiroptera	23
	Total	27
Reference(s):	Grubb *et al.* 1998	

Georgia

Species	Global status
Rhinolophus euryale	VU A2c
Rhinolophus ferrumequinum	LR: nt
Rhinolophus hipposideros	VU A2c
Rhinolophus mehelyi	VU A2c
Barbastella barbastellus	VU A2c
Myotis bechsteinii	VU A2c
Myotis emarginatus	VU A2c
Nyctalus lasiopterus	LR: nt
Nyctalus leisleri	LR: nt
Miniopterus schreibersii	LR: nt

Summary

CR	EN	VU	LRcd	LRnt	EX	DD	Total	Endemics
0	0	6	0	4	0	0	10	0

Total number of species:	Megachiroptera	0
	Microchiroptera	25
	Total	25
Reference(s):	I. Rakhmatulina *pers. comm.*	

Germany

Species	Global status
Rhinolophus ferrumequinum	LR: nt
Rhinolophus hipposideros	VU A2c
Barbastella barbastellus	VU A2c
Myotis bechsteinii	VU A2c
Myotis dasycneme	VU A2c
Myotis emarginatus	VU A2c
Myotis myotis	LR: nt
Nyctalus lasiopterus	LR: nt
Nyctalus leisleri	LR: nt

Summary

CR	EN	VU	LRcd	LRnt	EX	DD	Total	Endemics
0	0	5	0	4	0	0	9	0

Total number of species:	Megachiroptera	0
	Microchiroptera	22
	Total	22

A Red Data Book for Germany was published in 1997 (Jedicke, 1997). This listed 21 bat species, one of which was considered Extinct, six Endangered, and 14 Vulnerable.

Reference(s): Stebbings 1988, Schober and Grimmberger 1998

Ghana

Species	Global status
Saccolaimus peli	LR: nt
Nycteris intermedia	LR: nt
Hipposideros fuliginosus	LR: nt
Hipposideros jonesi	LR: nt
Hipposideros lamottei	DD
Rhinolophus alcyone	LR: nt
Chalinolobus beatrix	LR: nt
Chalinolobus poensis	LR: nt
Chalinolobus superbus	VU D2
Eptesicus brunneus	LR: nt
Eptesicus guineensis	LR: nt
Pipistrellus musciculus	LR: nt
Scotoecus albofuscus	LR: nt
Scotophilus nigrita	LR: nt
Chaerephon chapini	LR: nt
Mops congicus	LR: nt
Mops demonstrator	LR: nt
Mops petersoni	LR: nt
Otomops martiensseni	VU A2c

Summary

CR	EN	VU	LRcd	LRnt	EX	DD	Total	Endemics
0	0	2	0	16	0	1	19	0

Total number of species:	Megachiroptera	13
	Microchiroptera	71
	Total	84
Reference(s):	Grubb *et al.* 1998	

Gibraltar

Species	Global status
Miniopterus schreibersii	LR: nt

Summary

CR	EN	VU	LRcd	LRnt	EX	DD	Total	Endemics
0	0	0	0	1	0	0	1	0

Total number of species:	Megachiroptera	0
	Microchiroptera	4
	Total	4
Reference(s):	Stebbings 1988	

Greece

Species	Global status
Rhinolophus blasii	LR: nt
Rhinolophus euryale	VU A2c
Rhinolophus ferrumequinum	LR: nt
Rhinolophus hipposideros	VU A2c
Rhinolophus mehelyi	VU A2c
Myotis capaccinii	VU A2c
Myotis emarginatus	VU A2c
Myotis myotis	LR: nt
Nyctalus lasiopterus	LR: nt
Nyctalus leisleri	LR: nt
Miniopterus schreibersii	LR: nt

Greece continued

Summary

CR	EN	VU	LRcd	LRnt	EX	DD	Total	Endemics
0	0	5	0	6	0	0	11	0

Total number of species: Megachiroptera 0
Microchiroptera 28
Total 28

A Red Data Book of the threatened vertebrates of Greece was published in 1992 (Karandinos and Paraschi, 1992). It listed 28 species of bats, 21 of which were considered Endangered, four Vulnerable and three Rare.

Reference(s): Karandinos and Paraschi 1992

Grenada

No globally threatened species present.

Total number of species: Megachiroptera 0
Microchiroptera 13
Total 13

Reference(s): Breuil and Masson 1991

Guadeloupe

Species	Global status
Monophyllus plethodon	LR: nt
Ardops nichollsi	LR: nt
Chiroderma improvisum	EN A2c, B1 + 2c
Sturnira thomasi	EN B1 + 2c (Endemic)
Eptesicus guadeloupensis	EN B1 + 2c (Endemic)
Myotis dominicensis	VU A2c, D2
Tadarida brasiliensis	LR: nt

Summary

CR	EN	VU	LRcd	LRnt	EX	DD	Total	Endemics
0	3	1	0	3	0	0	7	2

Total number of species: Megachiroptera 0
Microchiroptera 12
Total 12

Reference(s): Breuil and Masson 1991

Guam

Species	Global status
Emballonura semicaudata (ex)	EN A1cd

Summary

CR	EN	VU	LRcd	LRnt	EX	DD	Total	Endemics
0	1	0	0	0	0	0	1	0

Total number of species: Megachiroptera 1
Microchiroptera 1
Total 2

Reference(s): Mickleburgh *et al.* 1992, Flannery 1995a

Guatemala

Species	Global status
Balantiopteryx io	LR: nt
Tonatia evotis	LR: nt
Vampyrum spectrum	LR: nt
Choeroniscus godmani	LR: nt
Choeronycteris mexicana	LR: nt
Hylonycteris underwoodi	LR: nt
Leptonycteris curasoae	VU A1c
?Leptonycteris nivalis	EN A1c
Diphylla ecaudata	LR: nt
Myotis cobanensis	CR B1 + 2c (Endemic)
Myotis elegans	LR: nt
Myotis fortidens	LR: nt
Molossus aztecus	LR: nt
Tadarida brasiliensis	LR: nt

Summary

CR	EN	VU	LRcd	LRnt	EX	DD	Total	Endemics
1	1	1	0	11	0	0	14	1

Total number of species: Megachiroptera 0
Microchiroptera 94
Total 94

Reference(s): McCarthy *et al.* 1993

Guinea

Species	Global status
Hipposideros jonesi	LR: nt
Hipposideros lamottei	DD (Endemic)
Hipposideros marisae	VU A2c
Rhinolophus guineensis	LR: nt
Rhinolophus maclaudi	LR: nt
Eptesicus guineensis	LR: nt
Scotophilus nigrita	LR: nt
Miniopterus schreibersii	LR: nt

Summary

CR	EN	VU	LRcd	LRnt	EX	DD	Total	Endemics
0	0	1	0	6	0	1	8	1

Total number of species: Megachiroptera 9
Microchiroptera 28
Total 37

Reference(s): Barnett and Prangley 1997

Guinea-Bissau

Species	Global status
Rhinolophus alcyone	LR: nt
?Hipposideros fuliginosus	LR: nt
Eptesicus somalicus	LR: nt
?Chalinolobus beatrix	LR: nt
Chalinolobus poensis	LR: nt

Summary

CR	EN	VU	LRcd	LRnt	EX	DD	Total	Endemics
0	0	0	0	5	0	0	5	0

Guinea-Bissau continued

Total number of species:	Megachiroptera	7
	Microchiroptera	28
	Total	35
Reference(s):	A. Rainho *pers. comm.*	

Guyana

Species	Global status
Cyttarops alecto	LR: nt
Diclidurus ingens	VU A2c
Diclidurus isabellus	LR: nt
Micronycteris brosseti	DD
Micronycteris daviesi	LR: nt
Tonatia carrikeri	VU A2c
Vampyrum spectrum	LR: nt
Choeroniscus godmani	LR: nt
Artibeus amplus	LR: nt
Vampyressa bidens	LR: nt
Vampyressa brocki	LR: nt
Lasiurus atratus	DD
Eumops maurus	VU A2c, D2
Molossops abrasus	LR: nt
Molossops mattogrossensis	LR: nt

Summary

CR	EN	VU	LRcd	LRnt	EX	DD	Total	Endemics
0	0	3	0	10	0	2	15	0

Total number of species:	Megachiroptera	0
	Microchiroptera	107
	Total	107
Reference(s):	Smith and Kerry 1996, Lim *et al.* 1999	

Haiti

Species	Global status
Mormoops blainvillii	LR: nt
Pteronotus quadridens	LR: nt
Brachyphylla nana	LR: nt
Phyllonycteris poeyi	LR: nt
Phyllops falcatus	LR: nt
Tadarida brasiliensis	LR: nt

Summary

CR	EN	VU	LRcd	LRnt	EX	DD	Total	Endemics
0	0	0	0	6	0	0	6	0

Total number of species:	Megachiroptera	0
	Microchiroptera	17
	Total	17
Reference(s):	Klingener *et al.* 1978, McFarlane 1991	

Honduras

Species	Global status
Micronycteris daviesi	LR: nt
Micronycteris sylvestris	LR: nt

Honduras continued

Species	Global status
Tonatia evotis	LR: nt
Vampyrum spectrum	LR: nt
Choeroniscus godmani	LR: nt
Choeronycteris mexicana	LR: nt
Leptonycteris curasoae	VU A1cd
Artibeus incomitatus	DD
Artibeus inopinatus	VU A2c
Ectophylla alba	LR: nt
Diphylla ecaudata	LR: nt
Antrozous dubiaquercus	VU A2c, D2
Myotis elegans	LR: nt
Eumops underwoodi	LR: nt
Molossus aztecus	LR: nt
Tadarida brasiliensis	LR: nt

Summary

CR	EN	VU	LRcd	LRnt	EX	DD	Total	Endemics
0	0	3	0	12	0	1	16	0

Total number of species:	Megachiroptera	0
	Microchiroptera	98
	Total	98
Reference(s):	McCarthy *et al.* 1993	

Hungary

Species	Global status
Rhinolophus euryale	VU A2c
Rhinolophus ferrumequinum	LR: nt
Rhinolophus hipposideros	VU A2c
Barbastella barbastellus	VU A2c
Myotis bechsteinii	VU A2c
Myotis dasycneme	VU A2c
Myotis emarginatus	VU A2c
Myotis myotis	LR: nt
Myotis schaubi (ex.)	EN B1 + 2c, C2a, D
Nyctalus lasiopterus	LR: nt
Nyctalus leisleri	LR: nt
Miniopterus schreibersii	LR: nt

Summary

CR	EN	VU	LRcd	LRnt	EX	DD	Total	Endemics
0	1	6	0	5	0	0	12	0

Total number of species:	Megachiroptera	0
	Microchiroptera	26
	Total	26

A Red Data Book for Hungary was published in 1989 (Rakonczay, 1989). Five species of bats were listed in this publication.

Reference(s): Dobrosi 1995

Iceland

No globally threatened species present.
The only bats recorded in Iceland are vagrants.

Reference(s): Petersen 1994

India (including Andaman and Nicobar Islands)

Species	Global status
Hipposideros durgadasi	VU B1 + 2c, D2 (Endemic)
Hipposideros hypophyllus	VU B1 + 2c, D2 (Endemic)
Hipposideros schistaceus	DD (Endemic)
Rhinolophus beddomei	LR: nt
Rhinolophus cognatus	VU A2c, D2 (Endemic)
Rhinolophus ferrumequinum	LR: nt
Rhinolophus hipposideros	VU A2c
Rhinolophus mitratus	DD (Endemic)
Rhinolophus subbadius	DD
Rhinolophus yunanensis	LR: nt
Eptesicus pachyotis	LR: nt
Eptesicus tatei	DD (Endemic)
Ia io	LR: nt
Myotis annectans	LR: nt
Myotis longipes	VU B1 + 2c, D2
Myotis montivagus	LR: nt
Myotis sicarius	VU A2c, D2
Nyctalus leisleri	LR: nt
Nyctalus montanus	LR: nt
Pipistrellus cadornae	LR: nt
Pipistrellus paterculus	LR: nt
?Scotomanes emarginatus	DD (Endemic)
Scotomanes ornatus	LR: nt
Murina aurata	LR: nt
Murina grisea	EN B1 + 2c (Endemic)
Murina huttoni	LR: nt
Miniopterus schreibersii	LR: nt
Otomops wroughtoni	CR B1 + 2c (Endemic)

Summary

CR	EN	VU	LRcd	LRnt	EX	DD	Total	Endemics
1	1	6	0	15	0	5	28	9

Total number of species:	Megachiroptera	13
	Microchiroptera	96
	Total	109

A Red Data Book on Indian Animals was published in 1994 (Ghosh 1994). No species of bats were listed in this publication.

Reference(s): Bates and Harrison 1997

Indonesia

Species	Global status
Emballonura furax	VU A2c, D2
Emballonura raffrayana	LR: nt
Taphozous achates	VU D2 (Endemic)
Nycteris javanica	VU A1c (Endemic)
Coelops robinsoni	LR: nt
Hipposideros breviceps	VU D2 (Endemic)
Hipposideros corynophyllus	VU A2c, D2
Hipposideros crumeniferus	DD (Endemic)
Hipposideros dinops	LR: nt
Hipposideros inexpectatus	VU A2c (Endemic)
Hipposideros macrobullatus	LR: nt (Endemic)
Hipposideros madurae	LR: nt (Endemic)

Indonesia continued

Species	Global status
Hipposideros muscinus	VU D2
Hipposideros papua	VU A2c (Endemic)
Hipposideros sorenseni	LR: nt (Endemic)
Hipposideros sumbae	LR: nt (Endemic)
Hipposideros wollastoni	LR: nt
Rhinolophus canuti	LR: nt (Endemic)
Rhinolophus celebensis	LR: nt (Endemic)
Rhinolophus creaghi	LR: nt
Rhinolophus keyensis	EN C2a (Endemic)
Rhinolophus nereis	LR: nt (Endemic)
Rhinolophus philippinensis	LR: nt
Kerivoula myrella	VU A2c
Glischropus javanus	EN B1 + 2d (Endemic)
Hesperoptenus gaskelli	VU B1 + 2c (Endemic)
Myotis annectans	LR: nt
?Myotis hermanni	DD (Endemic)
Myotis ridleyi	LR: nt
Myotis stalkeri	EN B1 + 2c (Endemic)
Nyctophilus heran	EN B1 + 2c (Endemic)
Nyctophilus timoriensis	VU A2c
Pipistrellus kitcheneri	LR: nt
Pipistrellus macrotis	LR: nt
Pipistrellus minahassae	DD (Endemic)
Pipistrellus mordax	LR: nt
Pipistrellus papuanus	LR: nt
Scotophilus celebensis	DD (Endemic)
Miniopterus schreibersii	LR: nt
Chaerephon johorensis	LR: nt
Cheiromeles parvidens	LR: nt
Cheiromeles torquatus	LR: nt
Mops sarasinorum	LR: nt
Mormopterus doriae	VU A2c (Endemic)
Otomops formosus	VU A2c (Endemic)
Otomops johnstonei	VU D2 (Endemic)
Tadarida australis	LR: nt

Summary

CR	EN	VU	LRcd	LRnt	EX	DD	Total	Endemics
0	4	14	0	25	0	4	47	24

Total number of species:	Megachiroptera	63
	Microchiroptera	112
	Total	175

Reference(s): Mickleburgh *et al.* 1992, Corbet and Hill 1992, Koopman 1993

Iran

Species	Global status
Rhinolophus blasii	LR: nt
Rhinolophus euryale	VU A2c
Rhinolophus ferrumequinum	LR: nt
Rhinolophus hipposideros	VU A2c
Rhinolophus mehelyi	VU A2c
Eptesicus nasutus	VU A2c
Myotis bechsteinii	VU A2c
Myotis capaccinii	VU A2c
Myotis emarginatus	VU A2c

Iran continued

Species	Global status
Myotis schaubi	EN B1 + 2c, C2a, D
Nyctalus lasiopterus	LR: nt
Nyctalus leisleri	LR: nt
Miniopterus schreibersii	LR: nt

Summary

CR	EN	VU	LRcd	LRnt	EX	DD	Total	Endemics
0	1	7	0	5	0	0	13	0

Total number of species: Megachiroptera 1
Microchiroptera 37
Total 38

Reference(s): DeBlase 1980

Iraq

Species	Global status
Rhinolophus euryale	VU A2c
Rhinolophus ferrumequinum	LR: nt
Rhinolophus hipposideros	VU A2c
Rhinolophus mehelyi	VU A2c
Eptesicus nasutus	VU A2c
Myotis capaccinii	VU A2c
Miniopterus schreibersii	LR: nt

Summary

CR	EN	VU	LRcd	LRnt	EX	DD	Total	Endemics
0	0	5	0	2	0	0	7	0

Total number of species: Megachiroptera 0
Microchiroptera 19
Total 19

Reference(s): Harrison and Bates 1991

Ireland

Species	Global status
Rhinolophus hipposideros	VU A2c
Nyctalus leisleri	LR: nt

Summary

CR	EN	VU	LRcd	LRnt	EX	DD	Total	Endemics
0	0	1	0	1	0	0	2	0

Total number of species: Megachiroptera 0
Microchiroptera 7
Total 7

A list of threatened mammals, birds, amphibians, and fish was published in 1993 (Whilde 1993). Two species of bats were listed in this publication, with a status of Indeterminate. The remaining five species are listed as Internationally Important.

Reference(s): O'Sullivan 1994

Israel

Species	Global status
Rhinolophus blasii	LR: nt
Rhinolophus euryale	VU A2c

Israel continued

Species	Global status
Rhinolophus ferrumequinum	LR: nt
Rhinolophus hipposideros	VU A2c
Rhinolophus mehelyi	VU A2c
Myotis capaccinii	VU A2c
Myotis emarginatus	VU A2c
Myotis myotis	LR: nt
Pipistrellus ariel	VU D2
Pipistrellus bodenheimeri	LR: nt
Miniopterus schreibersii	LR: nt

Summary

CR	EN	VU	LRcd	LRnt	EX	DD	Total	Endemics
0	0	6	0	5	0	0	11	0

Total number of species: Megachiroptera 1
Microchiroptera 32
Total 33

The Action Plan for Israeli Bats published in 1995 (Ron 1995) lists five species as Extinct?, 12 as Endangered, and three as Rare.

Reference(s): Ron 1995

Italy

Species	Global status
Rhinolophus blasii	LR: nt
Rhinolophus euryale	VU A2c
Rhinolophus ferrumequinum	LR: nt
Rhinolophus hipposideros	VU A2c
Rhinolophus mehelyi	VU A2c
Barbastella barbastellus	VU A2c
Myotis bechsteinii	VU A2c
Myotis capaccinii	VU A2c
Myotis emarginatus	VU A2c
Myotis myotis	LR: nt
Nyctalus lasiopterus	LR: nt
Nyctalus leisleri	LR: nt
Miniopterus schreibersii	LR: nt

Summary

CR	EN	VU	LRcd	LRnt	EX	DD	Total	Endemics
0	0	7	0	6	0	0	13	0

Total number of species: Megachiroptera 0
Microchiroptera 30
Total 30

A list of threatened terrestrial vertebrates of Italy published in 1997 (Pinchera and Boitani 1997) includes two bat species, both considered Vulnerable.

Reference(s): Vernier 1997

Jamaica

Species	Global status
Mormoops blainvillii	LR: nt
Pteronotus macleayii	VU A2c

Jamaica continued

Species	Global status
Pteronotus quadridens	LR: nt
Vampyrum spectrum	LR: nt
Brachyphylla nana (ex)	LR: nt
Phyllonycteris aphylla	EN B1 + 2c (Endemic)
Ariteus flavescens	VU A2c, D2 (Endemic)
Tadarida brasiliensis	LR: nt

Summary

CR	EN	VU	LRcd	LRnt	EX	DD	Total	Endemics
0	1	2	0	5	0	0	8	2

Total number of species: Megachiroptera 0
Microchiroptera 21
Total 21

Reference(s): McFarlane 1991

Japan

Species	Global status
Hipposideros turpis	EN A2c
Rhinolophus cornutus	LR: nt
Rhinolophus ferrumequinum	LR: nt
Rhinolophus imaizumii	EN A2c, B1 + 2abcde (Endemic)
Myotis bombinus	LR: nt
Myotis frater	LR: nt
Myotis hosonoi	VU A2c, B1 + 2c (Endemic)
Myotis ozensis	EN A2c, B1 + 2c (Endemic)
Myotis pruinosus	EN B1 + 2c (Endemic)
Myotis yesoensis	VU A2c (Endemic)
Myotis yonbarensis	DD (Endemic)
Nyctalus aviator	LR: nt
Pipistrellus endoi	EN: B1 + 2c (Endemic)
Pipistrellus sturdeei	EX (Endemic)
Murina ryukyuana	DD (Endemic)
Murina silvatica	LR: nt (Endemic)
Murina tenebrosa	CR B1 + 2c, D (Endemic)
Miniopterus fuscus	VU A2c (Endemic)
Miniopterus schreibersii	LR: nt

Summary

CR	EN	VU	LRcd	LRnt	EX	DD	Total	Endemics
1	5	3	0	7	1	2	19	12

Total number of species: Megachiroptera 3
Microchiroptera 36
Total 39

The Red Data Book of Japan published in 1991 (Anon. 1991a) lists 14 species and subspecies of bats. One of these is considered Extinct and the remaining 13 Rare.

Reference(s): Yoshiyuki 1989

Jordan

Species	Global status
Rhinolophus blasii	LR: nt
Rhinolophus euryale	VU A2c

Jordan continued

Species	Global status
Rhinolophus ferrumequinum	LR: nt
Rhinolophus hipposideros	VU A2c
Myotis capaccinii	VU A2c
Myotis emarginatus	VU A2c
Myotis myotis	LR: nt
Pipistrellus ariel	VU D2
Miniopterus schreibersii	LR: nt

Summary

CR	EN	VU	LRcd	LRnt	EX	DD	Total	Endemics
0	0	5	0	4	0	0	9	0

Total number of species: Megachiroptera 0
Microchiroptera 14
Total 14

Reference(s): Harrison and Bates 1991

Kazakhstan

Species	Global status
Rhinolophus ferrumequinum	LR: nt
Rhinolophus hipposideros	VU A2c
Myotis dasycneme	VU A2c
Myotis emarginatus	VU A2c
Nyctalus lasiopterus	LR: nt
Nyctalus leisleri	LR: nt

Summary

CR	EN	VU	LRcd	LRnt	EX	DD	Total	Endemics
0	0	3	0	3	0	0	6	0

Total number of species: Megachiroptera 0
Microchiroptera 27
Total 27

The list of threatened animals and plants in the Red Data Book of Kazakhstan (see Krever *et al.* 1998) includes five bat species.

Reference(s): A.V. Polkanov *pers. comm.*

Kenya

Species	Global status
Rhinopoma macinnesi	VU A2c, D2
Saccolaimus peli	LR: nt
Taphozous hamiltoni	VU A2c
Taphozous hildegardeae	VU A2c
Nycteris aurita	LR: nt
Cardioderma cor	LR: nt
Cloeotis percivali	LR: nt
Hipposideros camerunensis	LR: nt
Hipposideros megalotis	LR: nt
Kerivoula cuprosa	LR: nt
Kerivoula smithi	LR: nt
Chalinolobus beatrix	LR: nt
Chalinolobus kenyacola	DD (Endemic)
Laephotis wintoni	LR: nt
Pipistrellus aero	DD

Kenya continued

Species	Global status
Scotoecus albofuscus	LR: nt
Scotophilus nigrita	LR: nt
Miniopterus fraterculus	LR: nt
Miniopterus minor	LR: nt
Miniopterus schreibersii	LR: nt
Otomops martiensseni	VU A2c
Tadarida fulminans	LR: nt
Tadarida lobata	VU D2
Tadarida ventralis	LR: nt

Summary

CR	EN	VU	LRcd	LRnt	EX	DD	Total	Endemics
0	0	5	0	17	0	2	24	1

Total number of species: Megachiroptera 10
Microchiroptera 72
Total 82

Reference(s): Mickleburgh *et al.* 1992, I. Aggundey *pers. comm.*

Kuwait

No globally threatened species present.

Total number of species: Megachiroptera 0
Microchiroptera 1
Total 1

Reference(s): Harrison and Bates 1991

Kyrgyzstan

Species	Global status
Rhinolophus ferrumequinum	LR: nt
Rhinolophus hipposideros	VU A2c
Myotis emarginatus	VU A2c

Summary

CR	EN	VU	LRcd	LRnt	EX	DD	Total	Endemics
0	0	2	0	1	0	0	3	0

Total number of species: Megachiroptera 0
Microchiroptera 16
Total 16

The list of threatened animals and plants in the Red Data Book of Kyrgyzstan (see Krever *et al.* 1998) includes two species of bats.

Reference(s): Rybin *et al.* 1989

Laos

Species	Global status
?Coelops robinsoni	LR: nt
Hipposideros lylei	LR: nt
Rhinolophus marshalli	LR: nt
Rhinolophus paradoxolophus	VU B1 + 2c

Laos continued

Species	Global status
Rhinolophus shameli	LR: nt
?Rhinolophus subbadius	DD
Rhinolophus thomasi	LR: nt
Arielulus aureocollaris	DD
Eudiscopus denticulus	LR: nt
Ia io	LR: nt
Myotis annectans	LR: nt
Myotis montivagus	LR: nt
Myotis ricketti	LR: nt
Myotis rossetti	LR: nt
Pipistrellus cadornae	LR: nt
Pipistrellus pulveratus	LR: nt
Scotomanes ornatus	LR: nt
Miniopterus schreibersii	LR: nt
Harpiocepahlus mordax	LR: nt
Murina aurata	LR: nt
Murina huttoni	LR: nt

Summary

CR	EN	VU	LRcd	LRnt	EX	DD	Total	Endemics
0	0	1	0	18	0	2	21	0

Total number of species: Megachiroptera 8
Microchiroptera 82
Total 90

Francis *et al.* 1999 notes that one species in Laos is at risk, 32 are potentially at risk, and 10 are little known in the country.

Reference(s): Francis *et al.* 1999

Latvia

Species	Global status
Barbastella barbastellus	VU A2c
Myotis dasycneme	VU A2c
Nyctalus leisleri	LR: nt

Summary

CR	EN	VU	LRcd	LRnt	EX	DD	Total	Endemics
0	0	2	0	1	0	0	3	0

Total number of species: Megachiroptera 0
Microchiroptera 15
Total 15

The Red Data Book of Latvia published in 1985 (Andrusaitis 1985) lists 11 species of bats, six of which are Vulnerable and five Rare.

Reference(s): G. Petersons *pers. comm.*

Lebanon

Species	Global status
Rhinolophus euryale	VU A2c
Rhinolophus ferrumequinum	LR: nt
Rhinolophus hipposideros	VU A2c
Myotis capaccinii	VU A2c

Lebanon continued

Species	Global status
Myotis emarginatus	VU A2c
Myotis myotis	LR: nt
Miniopterus schreibersii	LR: nt

Summary

CR	EN	VU	LRcd	LRnt	EX	DD	Total	Endemics
0	0	4	0	3	0	0	7	0

Total number of species:	Megachiroptera	1
	Microchiroptera	15
	Total	16

A report on the biological diversity of Lebanon published in 1992 (Ministry of Agriculture of Lebanon 1992) lists 14 species and subspecies of bats considered threatened. Three species are listed as Vulnerable, nine as Rare, and one as Diminishing.

Reference(s): Harrison and Bates 1991

Lesotho

No globally threatened species present.

Total number of species:	Megachiroptera	0
	Microchiroptera	4
	Total	4

Reference(s): Hayman and Hill 1971, Taylor 2000

Liberia

Species	Global status
Saccolaimus peli	LR: nt
Nycteris intermedia	LR: nt
Nycteris major	VU A2c, D2
Hipposideros fuliginosus	LR: nt
?Hipposideros lamottei	DD
Hipposideros marisae	VU A2c
Rhinolophus guineensis	LR: nt
Rhinolophus maclaudi	LR: nt
Kerivoula smithi	LR: nt
?Chalinolobus poensis	LR: nt
Eptesicus brunneus	LR: nt

Summary

CR	EN	VU	LRcd	LRnt	EX	DD	Total	Endemics
0	0	2	0	8	0	1	11	0

Total number of species:	Megachiroptera	12
	Microchiroptera	35
	Total	47

Reference(s): Mickleburgh *et al.* 1992, Hayman and Hill 1971

Libya

Species	Global status
Rhinolophus mehelyi	VU A2c

Libya continued

Species	Global status
Nyctalus lasiopterus	LR: nt
Nyctalus leisleri	LR: nt

Summary

CR	EN	VU	LRcd	LRnt	EX	DD	Total	Endemics
0	0	1	0	2	0	0	3	0

Total number of species:	Megachiroptera	0
	Microchiroptera	10
	Total	10

Reference(s): Hayman and Hill 1971

Liechtenstein

Species	Global status
Rhinolophus ferrumequinum	LR: nt
Rhinolophus hipposideros (ex)	VU A2c
Barbastella barbastellus	VU A2c
Myotis bechsteinii	VU A2c
Myotis myotis	LR: nt
Nyctalus leisleri	LR: nt

Summary

CR	EN	VU	LRcd	LRnt	EX	DD	Total	Endemics
0	0	3	0	3	0	0	6	0

Total number of species:	Megachiroptera	0
	Microchiroptera	18
	Total	18

Reference(s): S. Hoch *pers. comm.*

Lithuania

Species	Global status
Barbastella barbastellus	VU A2c
Myotis dasycneme	VU A2c
Nyctalus leisleri	LR: nt

Summary

CR	EN	VU	LRcd	LRnt	EX	DD	Total	Endemics
0	0	2	0	1	0	0	3	0

Total number of species:	Megachiroptera	0
	Microchiroptera	17
	Total	17

The Red Data Book of Lithuania published in 1992 (Lapele and Vaicunaite 1992) lists nine species of bats. The status of all species is given as Indeterminate.

Reference(s): Pauza and Panziene 1998

Luxembourg

Species	Global status
Rhinolophus ferrumequinum	LR: nt
Rhinolophus hipposideros (ex?)	VU A2c

Luxembourg continued

Species	Global status
Barbastella barbastellus	VU A2c
Myotis dasycneme	VU A2c
Myotis myotis	LR: nt
Nyctalus leisleri	LR: nt

Summary

CR	EN	VU	LRcd	LRnt	EX	DD	Total	Endemics
0	0	3	0	3	0	0	6	0

Total number of species:	Megachiroptera	0
	Microchiroptera	17
	Total	17
Reference(s):	J. Pir *pers. comm.*	

Macedonia

Species	Global status
Rhinolophus euryale	VU A2c
Rhinolophus ferrumequinum	LR: nt
Rhinolophus hipposideros	VU A2c
Rhinolophus mehelyi	VU A2c
Barbastella barbastellus	VU A2c
Myotis bechsteinii	VU A2c
Myotis capaccinii	VU A2c
Myotis emarginatus	VU A2c
Nyctalus lasiopterus	LR: nt
Nyctalus leisleri	LR: nt
Miniopterus schreibersii	LR: nt

Summary

CR	EN	VU	LRcd	LRnt	EX	DD	Total	Endemics
0	0	7	0	4	0	0	11	0

Total number of species:	Megachiroptera	0
	Microchiroptera	23
	Total	23
Reference(s):	Krystufek *et al.* 1992	

Madagascar

Species	Global status
Emballonura atrata	VU A2c (Endemic)
Nycteris madagascariensis	DD (Endemic)
Triaenops auritus	DD (Endemic)
Triaenops furculus	VU A2c (Endemic)
Triaenops rufus	DD (Endemic)
Myzopoda aurita	VU A2c (Endemic)
Eptesicus matroka	DD (Endemic)
Myotis goudoti	LR: nt
Scotophilus borbonicus	CR A1c
Scotophilus robustus	LR: nt (Endemic)
Miniopterus fraterculus	LR: nt
Miniopterus gleni	LR: nt (Endemic)
Miniopterus majori	DD (Endemic)
Miniopterus menavi	DD (Endemic)
Miniopterus minor	LR: nt
Miniopterus schreibersii	LR: nt

Madagascar continued

Species	Global status
Chaerephon leucogaster	DD (Endemic)
Mops leucostigma	DD (Endemic)
Mormopterus acetabulosus	VU B1 + 2c
Mormopterus jugularis	VU A2c (Endemic)
Otomops martiensseni	VU A2c
Tadarida fulminans	LR: nt

Summary

CR	EN	VU	LRcd	LRnt	EX	DD	Total	Endemics
1	0	6	0	7	0	8	22	14

Total number of species:	Megachiroptera	3
	Microchiroptera	25
	Total	28
Reference(s):	Mickleburgh *et al.* 1992, Peterson *et al.* 1995, Garbutt 1999	

Malawi

Species	Global status
Nycteris woodi	LR: nt
Rhinolophus deckenii	DD
Laephotis botswanae	LR: nt
Scotoecus albofuscus	LR: nt
Scotophilus nigrita	LR: nt
Miniopterus fraterculus	LR: nt
Miniopterus schreibersii	LR: nt
Tadarida fulminans	LR: nt
Tadarida ventralis	LR: nt

Summary

CR	EN	VU	LRcd	LRnt	EX	DD	Total	Endemics
0	0	0	0	8	0	1	9	0

Total number of species:	Megachiroptera	6
	Microchiroptera	51
	Total	57
Reference(s):	Happold *et al.* 1987, D.C.D. and M. Happold *pers. comms.*	

Malaysia

Species	Global status
Coelops robinsoni	LR: nt
Hipposideros coxi	VU D2 (Endemic)
Hipposideros doriae	DD (Endemic)
Hipposideros lekaguli	LR: nt
Hipposideros lylei	LR: nt
Hipposideros nequam	CR B1 + 2c (Endemic)
Hipposideros pratti	LR: nt
Hipposideros ridleyi	VU B1 + 2c
Rhinolophus convexus	CR D (Endemic)
Rhinolophus creaghi	LR: nt
Rhinolophus marshalli	LR: nt
Rhinolophus philippinensis	LR: nt
Rhinolophus shameli	LR: nt

Malaysia continued

Species	Global status
Kerivoula intermedia	LR: nt (Endemic)
Kerivoula minuta	LR: nt
Arielulus cuprosus	VU A2c (Endemic)
Arielulus societatis	DD (Endemic)
Hesperoptenus doriae	EN B1 + 2c (Endemic)
Myotis gomatongensis	DD (Endemic)
Myotis macrotarsus	LR: nt
Myotis montivagus	LR: nt
Myotis ridleyi	LR: nt
?Pipistrellus kitcheneri	LR: nt
Pipistrellus macrotis	LR: nt
Harpiocephalus mordax	LR: nt
Murina aenea	LR: nt (Endemic)
Murina huttoni	LR: nt
Murina rozendaali	LR: nt (Endemic)
Miniopterus schreibersii	LR: nt
Chaerephon johorensis	LR: nt
Cheiromeles torquatus	LR: nt

Summary

CR	EN	VU	LRcd	LRnt	EX	DD	Total	Endemics
2	1	3	0	22	0	3	31	11

Total number of species: Megachiroptera 17
Microchiroptera 95
Total 112

Reference(s): Corbet and Hill 1992

Maldives

No microchiropteran bats present.

Total number of species: Megachiroptera 2
Microchiroptera 0
Total 2

Reference(s): Mickleburgh *et al.* 1992

Mali

Species	Global status
Hipposideros jonesi	LR: nt
Eptesicus floweri	LR: nt
Scotophilus nigrita	LR: nt

Summary

CR	EN	VU	LRcd	LRnt	EX	DD	Total	Endemics
0	0	0	0	3	0	0	3	0

Total number of species: Megachiroptera 3
Microchiroptera 15
Total 18

Reference(s): Mickleburgh *et al.* 1992, Hayman and Hill 1971

Malta

Species	Global status
?Rhinolophus ferrumequinum	LR: nt
Rhinolophus hipposideros	VU A2c

Malta continued

Species	Global status
Myotis myotis	LR: nt
Miniopterus schreibersii	LR: nt

Summary

CR	EN	VU	LRcd	LRnt	EX	DD	Total	Endemics
0	0	1	0	3	0	0	4	0

Total number of species: Megachiroptera 0
Microchiroptera 10
Total 10

A Red Data Book for the Maltese Islands published in 1989 (Schembri and Sultana 1989) lists 10 species of bats. Three are considered Very Rare, five Vulnerable, and two Rare.

Reference(s): Borg *et al.* 1997

Martinique

Species	Global status
Monophyllus plethodon	LR: nt
Ardops nichollsi	LR: nt
Myotis martiniquensis	LR: nt
Tadarida brasiliensis	LR: nt

Summary

CR	EN	VU	LRcd	LRnt	EX	DD	Total	Endemics
0	0	0	0	4	0	0	4	0

Total number of species: Megachiroptera 0
Microchiroptera 10
Total 10

Reference(s): Breuil and Masson 1991, McFarlane 1991

Mauritania

No globally threatened species present.

Total number of species: Megachiroptera 0
Microchiroptera 13
Total 13

Reference(s): Hayman and Hill 1971

Mauritius

Species	Global status
Mormopterus acetabulosus	VU B1 + 2c

Summary

CR	EN	VU	LRcd	LRnt	EX	DD	Total	Endemics
0	0	1	0	0	0	0	1	0

Total number of species: Megachiroptera 1
Microchiroptera 2
Total 3

Reference(s): Mickleburgh *et al.* 1992, Cheke and Dahl 1981

Mayotte

No globally threatened bats present.

Total number of species:	Megachiroptera	1
	Microchiroptera	1
	Total	2
Reference(s):	Mickleburgh *et al.* 1992, Cheke and Dahl 1981	

Mexico

Species	Global status
Balantiopteryx io	LR: nt
Macrotus californicus	VU A2c
Micronycteris sylvestris	LR: nt
Tonatia evotis	LR: nt
Vampyrum spectrum	LR: nt
Choeroniscus godmani	LR: nt
Choeronycteris mexicana	LR: nt
Glossophaga morenoi	LR: nt (Endemic)
Hylonycteris underwoodi	LR: nt
Leptonycteris curasoae	VU A1c
Leptonycteris nivalis	EN A1c
Musonycteris harrisoni	VU A2c (Endemic)
Artibeus hirsutus	VU A2c (Endemic)
Diphylla ecaudata	LR: nt
Antrozous dubiaquercus	VU A2c, D2
Myotis elegans	LR: nt
Myotis findleyi	EN B1 + 2c (Endemic)
Myotis fortidens	LR: nt
Myotis milleri	EN A2c (Endemic)
Myotis peninsularis	VU A1c (Endemic)
Myotis planiceps	CR B1 + 2c (Endemic)
Myotis vivesi	VU A2c (Endemic)
Plecotus townsendii	VU A2c
Rhogeessa alleni	LR: nt (Endemic)
Rhogeessa genowaysi	VU A2c, D2 (Endemic)
Rhogeessa gracilis	LR: nt (Endemic)
Rhogeessa mira	EN A2c, B1 + 2cd (Endemic)
Rhogeessa parvula	LR: nt (Endemic)
Molossus aztecus	LR: nt
Molossus coibensis	LR: nt
Tadarida brasiliensis	LR: nt

Summary

CR	EN	VU	LRcd	LRnt	EX	DD	Total	Endemics
1	4	9	0	17	0	0	31	13

Total number of species:	Megachiroptera	0
	Microchiroptera	137
	Total	137

A publication on Biodiversity and Conservation in Mexico published in 1994 (Villela and Gerez 1994) does not list any threatened bat species.

Reference(s): Medellin *et al.* 1997

Moldova

Species	Global status
Rhinolophus ferrumequinum	LR: nt
Rhinolophus hipposideros	VU A2c

Moldova continued

Species	Global status
Barbastella barbastellus	VU A2c
Myotis bechsteinii	VU A2c
Myotis dasycneme	VU A2c
Nyctalus lasiopterus	LR: nt
Nyctalus leisleri	LR: nt

Summary

CR	EN	VU	LRcd	LRnt	EX	DD	Total	Endemics
0	0	4	0	3	0	0	7	0

Total number of species:	Megachiroptera	0
	Microchiroptera	20
	Total	20
Reference(s):	S. Andreev *pers. comm.*	

Monaco

No globally threatened species present

Total number of species:	Megachiroptera	0
	Microchiroptera	5
	Total	5
Reference(s):	C. Joulot *pers. comm.*	

Mongolia

No globally threatened species present.

Total number of species:	Megachiroptera	0
	Microchiroptera	12
	Total	12

A publication on the Rare Vertebrate Species of Mongolia produced in 1996 (Sokolov 1996) does not list any bat species.

Reference(s): Mallon 1985

Montserrat

Species	Global status
Monophyllus plethodon	LR: nt
Ardops nichollsi	LR: nt
Chiroderma improvisum	EN A2c, B1 + 2c
Tadarida brasiliensis	LR: nt

Summary

CR	EN	VU	LRcd	LRnt	EX	DD	Total	Endemics
0	1	0	0	3	0	0	4	0

Total number of species:	Megachiroptera	0
	Microchiroptera	10
	Total	10
Reference(s):	Breuil and Masson 1991, McFarlane 1991	

Morocco

Species	Global status
Rhinolophus blasii	LR: nt
Rhinolophus euryale	VU A2c

Morocco continued

Species	Global status
Rhinolophus ferrumequinum	LR: nt
Rhinolophus hipposideros	VU A2c
Rhinolophus mehelyi	VU A2c
Barbastella barbastellus	VU A2c
Myotis capaccinii	VU A2c
Myotis emarginatus	VU A2c
Nyctalus lasiopterus	LR: nt
Miniopterus schreibersii	LR: nt

Summary

CR	EN	VU	LRcd	LRnt	EX	DD	Total	Endemics
0	0	6	0	4	0	0	10	0

Total number of species: Megachiroptera 0
Microchiroptera 26
Total 26

Reference(s): Aulagnier and Thevenot 1986

Mozambique

Species	Global status
Nycteris woodi	LR: nt
Cloeotis percivali	LR: nt
Rhinolophus deckenii	DD
Scotoecus albofuscus	LR: nt
Scotophilus nigrita	LR: nt
Miniopterus fraterculus	LR: nt
Miniopterus schreibersii	LR: nt
Tadarida ventralis	LR: nt

Summary

CR	EN	VU	LRcd	LRnt	EX	DD	Total	Endemics
0	0	0	0	7	0	1	8	0

Total number of species: Megachiroptera 5
Microchiroptera 41
Total 46

Reference(s): Mickleburgh *et al.* 1992, Smithers and Tello 1976

Myanmar

Species	Global status
Hipposideros lylei	LR: nt
Hipposideros pratti	LR: nt
Rhinolophus shameli	LR: nt
Rhinolophus subbadius	DD
Rhinolophus thomasi	LR: nt
Rhinolophus yunanensis	LR: nt
Eptesicus pachyotis	LR: nt
Eudiscopus denticulus	LR: nt
Myotis annectans	LR: nt
Myotis montivagus	LR: nt
Pipistrellus anthonyi	CR B1 + 2c (Endemic)
Pipistrellus cadornae	LR: nt
Pipistrellus joffrei	CR B1 + 2c (Endemic)
Pipistrellus lophurus	DD

Myanmar continued

Species	Global status
Pipistrellus paterculus	LR: nt
Pipistrellus peguensis	DD (Endemic)
Scotomanes ornatus	LR: nt
Harpiocephalus mordax	LR: nt
Murina aurata	LR: nt
Murina huttoni	LR: nt
Miniopterus schreibersii	LR: nt

Summary

CR	EN	VU	LRcd	LRnt	EX	DD	Total	Endemics
2	0	0	0	16	0	3	21	3

Total number of species: Megachiroptera 12
Microchiroptera 76
Total 88

Reference(s): Bates *et al.* 2000

Namibia

Species	Global status
Rhinolophus deckenii	DD
Eptesicus zuluensis	LR: nt
Laephotis namibensis	EN A2c (Endemic)
Myotis seabrai	VU A2c, D2
Miniopterus schreibersii	LR: nt
Chaerephon chapini	LR: nt

Summary

CR	EN	VU	LRcd	LRnt	EX	DD	Total	Endemics
0	1	1	0	3	0	1	6	1

Total number of species: Megachiroptera 3
Microchiroptera 23
Total 26

Reference(s): Bergmans 1988, 1989, 1990, 1994, 1997, Hayman and Hill 1971, Taylor 2000

Nepal

Species	Global status
Hipposideros pomona	DD
Rhinolophus ferrumequinum	LR: nt
Rhinolophus subbadius	DD
Ia io	LR: nt
Myotis csorbai	DD (Endemic)
Myotis longipes	VU B1 + 2c, D2
Myotis sicarius	VU A2c, D2
Nyctalus montanus	LR: nt
Scotomanes ornatus	LR: nt
Murina aurata	LR: nt
Murina huttoni	LR: nt
Miniopterus schreibersii	LR: nt

Summary

CR	EN	VU	LRcd	LRnt	EX	DD	Total	Endemics
0	0	2	0	7	0	3	12	1

Nepal continued

Total number of species: Megachiroptera 4
Microchiroptera 47
Total 51

The Red Data Book of Nepal published in 1995 (Keeling and Verheught, 1995) lists no species of bats.

Reference(s): Bates and Harrison 1997, Csorba *et al.* 1999

The Netherlands

Species	Global status
?Rhinolophus ferrumequinum	LR: nt
Barbastella barbastellus	VU A2c
Myotis bechsteinii	VU A2c
Myotis dasycneme	VU A2c
Myotis emarginatus	VU A2c
Myotis myotis	LR: nt
Nyctalus leisleri	LR: nt

Summary

CR	EN	VU	LRcd	LRnt	EX	DD	Total	Endemics
0	0	4	0	3	0	0	7	0

Total number of species: Megachiroptera 0
Microchiroptera 19
Total 19

The Red Data Book of Threatened Mammals of The Netherlands published in 1994 (Hollander and van der Reest 1994) lists 13 species of bats. Two are considered Extinct, two Endangered, one Vulnerable, five Susceptible, and three Insufficiently Known.

Reference(s): Limpens *et al.* 1997

Netherlands Antilles

Species	Global status
Leptonycteris curasoae	VU A1c
Ardops nichollsi	LR: nt
Myotis nesopolus	LR: nt
Tadarida brasiliensis	LR: nt

Summary

CR	EN	VU	LRcd	LRnt	EX	DD	Total	Endemics
0	0	1	0	3	0	0	4	0

Total number of species: Megachiroptera 0
Microchiroptera 10
Total 10

Reference(s): Husson 1960

New Caledonia

Species	Global status
Chalinolobus neocaledonicus	EN B1 + 2c (Endemic)
Nyctophilus howensis	EX
Miniopterus robustior	EN B1 + 2c (Endemic)

New Caledonia continued

Summary

CR	EN	VU	LRcd	LRnt	EX	DD	Total	Endemics
0	2	0	0	0	1	0	3	2

Total number of species: Megachiroptera 4
Microchiroptera 4
Total 8

Reference(s): Mickleburgh *et al.* 1992, Flannery 1995b

New Zealand

Species	Global status
Chalinolobus tuberculatus	VU A2b,c (Endemic)
Mystacina robusta	EX (Endemic)
Mystacina tuberculata	VU A2c, C2a (Endemic)

Summary

CR	EN	VU	LRcd	LRnt	EX	DD	Total	Endemics
0	0	2	0	0	1	0	3	3

Total number of species: Megachiroptera 0
Microchiroptera 3
Total 3

The assessment of the conservation status of New Zealand wildlife published in 1986 (Bell 1986) listed one of the three bat species as Extinct and the other two as Threatened.

Reference(s): King 1995

Nicaragua

Species	Global status
Cyttarops alecto	LR: nt
Micronycteris sylvestris	LR: nt
Vampyrum spectrum	LR: nt
Choeroniscus godmani	LR: nt
Hylonycteris underwoodi	LR: nt
Artibeus incomitatus	DD
Artibeus inopinatus	VU A2c
Ectophylla alba	LR: nt
Diphylla ecaudata	LR: nt
Myotis elegans	LR: nt
Eumops underwoodi	LR: nt
Molossus aztecus	LR: nt
Tadarida brasiliensis	LR: nt

Summary

CR	EN	VU	LRcd	LRnt	EX	DD	Total	Endemics
0	0	1	0	11	0	1	13	0

Total number of species: Megachiroptera 0
Microchiroptera 88
Total 88

Reference(s): McCarthy *et al.* 1993

Niger

No globally threatened species present.

Niger continued

Total number of species:	Megachiroptera	2
	Microchiroptera	19
	Total	21
Reference(s):	Mickleburgh *et al.* 1992, Hayman and Hill 1971	

Nigeria

Species	Global status
Saccolaimus peli	LR: nt
?Hipposideros curtus	LR: nt
Hipposideros jonesi	LR: nt
Rhinolophus alcyone	LR: nt
Rhinolophus maclaudi	LR: nt
Kerivoula smithi	LR: nt
Chalinolobus poensis	LR: nt
Eptesicus brunneus	LR: nt
Eptesicus platyops	VU D2
Myotis morrisi	VU D2
Scotoecus albofuscus	LR: nt
Scotophilus nigrita	LR: nt
Mops congicus	LR: nt

Summary

CR	EN	VU	LRcd	LRnt	EX	DD	Total	Endemics
0	0	2	0	11	0	0	13	0

Total number of species:	Megachiroptera	12
	Microchiroptera	59
	Total	71
Reference(s):	Happold 1987	

Niue

No microchiropteran bats present.

Total number of species:	Megachiroptera	1
	Microchiroptera	0
	Total	1
Reference(s):	Mickleburgh *et al.* 1992	

North Korea

Species	Global status
Rhinolophus ferrumequinum	LR: nt
Eptesicus kobayashii	DD
Myotis bombinus	LR: nt
Myotis frater	LR: nt
Nyctalus aviator	LR: nt
Murina aurata	LR: nt
Murina ussuriensis	EN A2c
Miniopterus schreibersii	LR: nt

Summary

CR	EN	VU	LRcd	LRnt	EX	DD	Total	Endemics
0	1	0	0	6	0	1	8	0

North Korea continued

Total number of species:	Megachiroptera	0
	Microchiroptera	21
	Total	21
Reference(s):	G. Csorba *pers. comm.*	

Norway

Species	Global status
Barbastella barbastellus	VU A2c

Summary

CR	EN	VU	LRcd	LRnt	EX	DD	Total	Endemics
0	0	1	0	0	0	0	1	0

Total number of species:	Megachiroptera	0
	Microchiroptera	11
	Total	11

The Norwegian Red List was published in 1999 (Direktoratet fur naturforvaltning 1999). Eight species were listed as DM (Declining, monitoring species) and one as Rare.

Reference(s): Isaksen *et al.* 1998

Oman

Species	Global status
Rhinolophus blasii	LR: nt
Eptesicus nasutus	VU A2c
Myotis emarginatus	VU A2c
Pipistrellus arabicus	VU D2 (Endemic)
Pipistrellus bodenheimeri	LR: nt

Summary

CR	EN	VU	LRcd	LRnt	EX	DD	Total	Endemics
0	0	3	0	2	0	0	5	1

Total number of species:	Megachiroptera	1
	Microchiroptera	16
	Total	17
Reference(s):	Harrison and Bates 1991	

Pakistan

Species	Global status
Rhinolophus blasii	LR: nt
Rhinolophus ferrumequinum	LR: nt
Rhinolophus hipposideros	VU A2c
Eptesicus nasutus	VU A2c
Nyctalus leisleri	LR: nt
Nyctalus montanus	LR: nt
Murina huttoni	LR: nt

Summary

CR	EN	VU	LRcd	LRnt	EX	DD	Total	Endemics
0	0	2	0	5	0	0	7	0

Total number of species:	Megachiroptera	4
	Microchiroptera	43
	Total	47
Reference(s):	Bates and Harrison 1997	

Palau

Species	Global status
Emballonura semicaudata	EN A1ac

Summary

CR	EN	VU	LRcd	LRnt	EX	DD	Total	Endemics
0	1	0	0	0	0	0	1	0

Total number of species: Megachiroptera 2 (1 Extinct)
Microchiroptera 1
Total 3

Reference(s): Mickleburgh *et al.* 1992, Flannery 1995a

Panama

Species	Global status
Micronycteris daviesi	LR: nt
Micronycteris sylvestris	LR: nt
Hylonycteris underwoodi	LR: nt
Ectophylla alba	LR: nt
Platyrrhinus umbratus	LR: nt
Sturnira mordax	LR: nt
Diphylla ecaudata	LR: nt
Lasiurus castaneus	VU D2
Lasiurus egregius	LR: nt
Molossus coibensis	LR: nt
Tadarida brasiliensis	LR: nt

Summary

CR	EN	VU	LRcd	LRnt	EX	DD	Total	Endemics
0	0	1	0	10	0	0	11	0

Total number of species: Megachiroptera 0
Microchiroptera 111
Total 111

Reference(s): Eisenberg 1989, Reid 1997

Papua New Guinea

Species	Global status
Emballonura dianae	VU A2c
Emballonura furax	VU A2c, D2
Emballonura raffrayana	LR: nt
Emballonura serii	DD (Endemic)
Saccolaimus flaviventris	LR: nt
Saccolaimus mixtus	VU A2c
Taphozous australis	LR: nt
Anthops ornatus	VU A2c, D2
Hipposideros corynophyllus	VU A2c, D2 (Endemic)
Hipposideros dinops	LR: nt
Hipposideros edwardshilli	LR: nt (Endemic)
Hipposideros muscinus	VU D2
Hipposideros semoni	LR: nt
Hipposideros wollastoni	LR: nt
Rhinolophus philippinensis	LR: nt
Kerivoula agnella	VU D2 (Endemic)
Kerivoula muscina	VU D2 (Endemic)
Kerivoula myrella	VU A2c

Papua New Guinea continued

Species	Global status
Nyctophilus microdon	VU D2 (Endemic)
Nyctophilus timoriensis	VU A2c
Pharotis imogene	CR B1 + 2c, C2b (Endemic)
Pipistrellus papuanus	LR: nt
Pipistrellus wattsi	LR: nt (Endemic)
Otomops papuensis	VU D2 (Endemic)
Otomops secundus	VU D2 (Endemic)
Miniopterus schreibersii	LR: nt
Tadarida australis	LR: nt

Summary

CR	EN	VU	LRcd	LRnt	EX	DD	Total	Endemics
1	0	13	0	12	0	1	27	10

Total number of species: Megachiroptera 34
Microchiroptera 57
Total 91

A country study on the biological diversity of Papua New Guinea published in 1995 (Sekhran and Miller 1995) listed three species of bats, all considered Rare.

Reference(s): Bonaccorso 1998

Paraguay

Species	Global status
Artibeus fimbriatus	LR: nt
Pygoderma bilabiatum	LR: nt
Myotis ruber	VU A2c
Molossops abrasus	LR: nt
Tadarida brasiliensis	LR: nt

Summary

CR	EN	VU	LRcd	LRnt	EX	DD	Total	Endemics
0	0	1	0	4	0	0	5	0

Total number of species: Megachiroptera 0
Microchiroptera 49
Total 49

Reference(s): Redford and Eisenberg 1992

Peru

Species	Global status
Diclidurus ingens	VU A2c
Micronycteris behnii	VU A2c
Micronycteris brosseti	DD
Micronycteris daviesi	LR: nt
Micronycteris sylvestris	LR: nt
Tonatia carrikeri	VU A2c
Vampyrum spectrum	LR: nt
Lonchophylla handleyi	VU A2c, D2
Lonchophylla hesperia	VU A2c, D2
Platalina genovensium	VU D2 (Endemic)
Anoura latidens	LR: nt
Choeroniscus intermedius	LR: nt
Rhinophylla fischerae	LR: nt

Peru continued

Species	Global status
Artibeus concolor	LR: nt
Artibeus fraterculus	VU A2c
Artibeus obscurus	LR: nt
Platyrrhinus infuscus	LR: nt
Sturnira aratathomasi	LR: nt
Sturnira bidens	LR: nt
Sturnira magna	LR: nt
Sturnira nana	VU D2 (Endemic)
Vampyressa bidens	LR: nt
Vampyressa brocki	LR: nt
Vampyressa melissa	LR: nt
Diphylla ecaudata	LR: nt
Amorphochilus schnablii	VU A2c
Thyroptera lavali	VU B1 + 2c, D2 (Endemic)
Eptesicus innoxius	VU A2c
Histiotus macrotus	LR: nt
Myotis atacamensis	VU A2c, D2
Tomopeas ravus	VU A2c, D2 (Endemic)
Molossops abrasus	LR: nt
Molossops neglectus	LR: nt
Mormopterus kalinowskii	VU A2c, D2
Mormopterus phrudus	EN B1 + 2c (Endemic)
Molossus coibensis	LR: nt
Tadarida brasiliensis	LR: nt

Summary

CR	EN	VU	LRcd	LRnt	EX	DD	Total	Endemics
0	1	14	0	21	0	1	37	5

Total number of species: Megachiroptera 0
Microchiroptera 152
Total 152

A Red Data Book of Peru published in 1991 (Pulido 1991) lists no species of bats.

Reference(s): Pacheco *et al.* 1995

Philippines

Species	Global status
Coelops hirsutus	DD (Endemic)
Hipposideros coronatus	LR: nt (Endemic)
Hipposideros lekaguli	LR: nt
Hipposideros obscurus	LR: nt (Endemic)
Hipposideros pygmaeus	LR: nt (Endemic)
Rhinolophus anderseni	DD (Endemic)
Rhinolophus inops	DD (Endemic)
Rhinolophus philippinensis	LR: nt
Rhinolophus rufus	LR: nt (Endemic)
Rhinolophus subrufus	VU A2c (Endemic)
Rhinolophus virgo	LR: nt (Endemic)
Myotis macrotarsus	LR: nt
?Pipistrellus mordax	LR: nt
Miniopterus schreibersii	LR: nt
Cheiromeles parvidens	LR: nt
Cheiromeles torquatus	LR: nt
Mops sarasinorum	LR: nt

Summary

CR	EN	VU	LRcd	LRnt	EX	DD	Total	Endemics
0	0	1	0	13	0	3	17	9

Philippines continued

Total number of species: Megachiroptera 24
Microchiroptera 46
Total 70

The Red Data Book of the Philippines published in 1997 (Wildlife Conservation Society of the Philippines 1997) lists three species of bats, one considered Rare and two Indeterminate.

Reference(s): Heaney *et al.* 1987, Ingle and Heaney 1992

Poland

Species	Global status
Rhinolophus ferrumequinum	LR: nt
Rhinolophus hipposideros	VU A2c
Barbastella barbastellus	VU A2c
Myotis bechsteinii	VU A2c
Myotis dasycneme	VU A2c
Myotis emarginatus	VU A2c
Myotis myotis	LR: nt
Nyctalus leisleri	LR: nt

Summary

CR	EN	VU	LRcd	LRnt	EX	DD	Total	Endemics
0	0	5	0	3	0	0	8	0

Total number of species: Megachiroptera 0
Microchiroptera 20
Total 20

The Red List of threatened animals in Poland published in 1992 (Glowacinski 1992) includes 11 species of bats. Two are considered Endangered, one Vulnerable, and eight Rare.

Reference(s): Pucek 1981, T. Kokurewicz *pers. comm.*

Portugal (including Azores and Madeira)

Species	Global status
Rhinolophus euryale	VU A2c
Rhinolophus ferrumequinum	LR: nt
Rhinolophus hipposideros	VU A2c
Rhinolophus mehelyi	VU A2c
Barbastella barbastellus	VU A2c
Myotis bechsteinii	VU A2c
Myotis emarginatus	VU A2c
Myotis myotis	LR: nt
Nyctalus azoreum	VU A2c, B1 + 2c (Endemic)
Nyctalus lasiopterus	LR: nt
Nyctalus leisleri	LR: nt
Pipistrellus maderensis	VU A2c, B1 + 2c
Miniopterus schreibersii	LR: nt

Summary

CR	EN	VU	LRcd	LRnt	EX	DD	Total	Endemics
0	0	8	0	5	0	0	13	1

Portugal continued

Total number of species: Megachiroptera 0
Microchiroptera 24
Total 24

The Red List of vertebrates of Portugal published in 1990 (SNPRCN 1990) lists 19 species of bats. Nine are considered Endangered, two Vulnerable, one Rare, five Indeterminate, and two Insufficiently Known.

Reference(s): Palmeirim 1989

Puerto Rico

Species	Global status
Mormoops blainvillii	LR: nt
Pteronotus quadridens	LR: nt
Phyllonycteris major	EX (Endemic)
Stenoderma rufum	VU A1c
Tadarida brasiliensis	LR: nt

Summary

CR	EN	VU	LRcd	LRnt	EX	DD	Total	Endemics
0	0	1	0	3	1	0	5	1

Total number of species: Megachiroptera 0
Microchiroptera 13
Total 13

Reference(s): McFarlane 1991

Qatar

No globally threatened species present.

Total number of species: Megachiroptera 0
Microchiroptera 2
Total 2

Reference(s): Harrison and Bates 1991

Réunion

Species	Global status
Scotophilus borbonicus	CR A1c
Mormopterus acetabulosus	VU B1 + 2c

Summary

CR	EN	VU	LRcd	LRnt	EX	DD	Total	Endemics
1	0	1	0	0	0	0	2	0

Total number of species: Megachiroptera 2 (Extinct)
Microchiroptera 3
Total 5

Reference(s): Cheke and Dahl 1981

Romania

Species	Global status
Rhinolophus blasii	LR: nt

Romania continued

Species	Global status
Rhinolophus euryale	VU A2c
Rhinolophus ferrumequinum	LR: nt
Rhinolophus hipposideros	VU A2c
Rhinolophus mehelyi	VU A2c
Barbastella barbastellus	VU A2c
Myotis bechsteinii	VU A2c
Myotis capaccinii	VU A2c
Myotis emarginatus	VU A2c
Myotis myotis	LR: nt
Nyctalus lasiopterus	LR: nt
Nyctalus leisleri	LR: nt
Miniopterus schreibersii	LR: nt

Summary

CR	EN	VU	LRcd	LRnt	EX	DD	Total	Endemics
0	0	7	0	6	0	0	13	0

Total number of species: Megachiroptera 0
Microchiroptera 25
Total 25

Reference(s): Corbet 1978

Russia

Species	Global status
Rhinolophus euryale	VU A2c
Rhinolophus ferrumequinum	LR: nt
Rhinolophus hipposideros	VU A2c
Rhinolophus mehelyi	VU A2c
Barbastella barbastellus	VU A2c
Myotis abei	DD (Endemic)
Myotis bechsteinii	VU A2c
Myotis bombinus	LR: nt
Myotis capaccinii	VU A2c
Myotis dasycneme	VU A2c
Myotis emarginatus	VU A2c
Myotis frater	LR: nt
Nyctalus aviator	LR: nt
Nyctalus lasiopterus	LR: nt
Nyctalus leisleri	LR: nt
Murina ussuriensis	EN A2c
Miniopterus schreibersii	LR: nt

Summary

CR	EN	VU	LRcd	LRnt	EX	DD	Total	Endemics
0	1	8	0	7	0	1	17	1

Total number of species: Megachiroptera 0
Microchiroptera 41
Total 41

Reference(s): A. Borissenko and S.V. Kruskop *pers. comm.*

Rwanda

Species	Global status
Rhinolophus maclaudi	LR: nt

Rwanda continued

Species	Global status
?*Miniopterus schreibersii*	LR: nt
Otomops martiensseni	VU A2c
Tadarida fulminans	LR: nt

Summary

CR	EN	VU	LRcd	LRnt	EX	DD	Total	Endemics
0	0	1	0	3	0	0	4	0

Total number of species: Megachiroptera 8
Microchiroptera 33
Total 41

Reference(s): Mickleburgh *et al.* 1992, Baeten *et al* 1984

St. Kitts and Nevis

Species	Global status
Tadarida brasiliensis	LR:nt

Summary

CR	EN	VU	LRcd	LRnt	EX	DD	Total	Endemics
0	0	0	0	1	0	0	1	0

Total number of species: Megachiroptera 0
Microchiroptera 4
Total 4

Reference(s): McFarlane 1991

St. Lucia

Species	Global status
Monophyllus plethodon	LR: nt
Ardops nichollsi	LR: nt
Tadarida brasiliensis	LR: nt

Summary

CR	EN	VU	LRcd	LRnt	EX	DD	Total	Endemics
0	0	0	0	3	0	0	3	0

Total number of species: Megachiroptera 0
Microchiroptera 8
Total 8

Reference(s): Breuil and Masson 1991, McFarlane 1991

St. Vincent

Species	Global status
Monophyllus plethodon	LR: nt
Ardops nichollsi	LR: nt

Summary

CR	EN	VU	LRcd	LRnt	EX	DD	Total	Endemics
0	0	0	0	2	0	0	2	0

St Vincent continued

Total number of species: Megachiroptera 0
Microchiroptera 9
Total 9

Reference(s): Breuil and Masson 1991, McFarlane 1991

Samoa

Species	Global status
Emballonura semicaudata	EN A1ac
?*Myotis insularum*	DD

Summary

CR	EN	VU	LRcd	LRnt	EX	DD	Total	Endemics
0	1	0	0	0	0	1	2	0

Total number of species: Megachiroptera 2
Microchiroptera 2
Total 4

Reference(s): Mickleburgh *et al.* 1992, Flannery 1995b

San Marino

Species	Global status
Rhinolophus ferrumequinum	LR: nt
Rhinolophus hipposideros	VU A2c
Miniopterus schreibersii	LR: nt

Summary

CR	EN	VU	LRcd	LRnt	EX	DD	Total	Endemics
0	0	1	0	2	0	0	3	0

Total number of species: Megachiroptera 0
Microchiroptera 6
Total 6

Reference(s): D. Scaravelli *pers. comm.*

São Tomé and Príncipe

Species	Global status
Miniopterus minor	LR: nt
Chaerephon tomensis	VU A2c, D2 (Endemic)

Summary

CR	EN	VU	LRcd	LRnt	EX	DD	Total	Endemics
0	0	1	0	1	0	0	2	1

Total number of species: Megachiroptera 3
Microchiroptera 6
Total 9

The Red List of threatened animals of São Tomé and Príncipe published in 1995 (Gascoigne 1995) lists three species of bats, one considered Vulnerable and two Indeterminate.

Reference(s): Juste and Ibanez 1993

Saudi Arabia

Species	Global status
Asellia patrizii	VU A2c, D2
Hipposideros megalotis	LR: nt
Rhinolophus ferrumequinum	LR: nt
Rhinolophus hipposideros	VU A2c
Eptesicus nasutus	VU A2c
Myotis emarginatus	VU A2c
Pipistrellus bodenheimeri	LR: nt
Miniopterus schreibersii	LR: nt

Summary

CR	EN	VU	LRcd	LRnt	EX	DD	Total	Endemics
0	0	4	0	4	0	0	8	0

Total number of species: Megachiroptera 2
Microchiroptera 21
Total 23

Reference(s): Harrison and Bates 1991

Senegal

Species	Global status
Rhinolophus alcyone	LR: nt
Chalinolobus poensis	LR: nt
?Barbastella barbastellus	VU A2c
Eptesicus guineensis	LR: nt
Eptesicus platyops	VU D2
Scotoecus albofuscus	LR: nt
Scotophilus nigrita	LR: nt
Myopterus daubentonii	DD

Summary

CR	EN	VU	LRcd	LRnt	EX	DD	Total	Endemics
0	0	2	0	5	0	1	8	0

Total number of species: Megachiroptera 5
Microchiroptera 36
Total 41

Reference(s): Mickleburgh *et al.* 1992, Hayman and Hill 1971, Koopman 1993

Seychelles

Species	Global status
Coleura seychellensis	CR B1 + 2cde, C2b, D (Endemic)
Triaenops furculus	VU A2c
Chaerephon pusilla	VU D1 + 2 (Endemic)

Summary

CR	EN	VU	LRcd	LRnt	EX	DD	Total	Endemics
1	0	2	0	0	0	0	3	2

Total number of species: Megachiroptera 1
Microchiroptera 3
Total 4

The Red Data Book of the Seychelles published in 1997 (Gerlach 1997) lists one bat species as Critically Endangered.

Reference(s): Hill 1971, Mickleburgh *et al.* 1992, Gerlach 1997

Sierra Leone

Species	Global status
Hipposideros fuliginosus	LR: nt
Hipposideros jonesi	LR: nt
Hipposideros lamottei	DD
?Rhinolophus alcyone	LR: nt
Rhinolophus guineensis	LR: nt
Chalinolobus poensis	LR: nt
Eptesicus brunneus	LR: nt
Pipistrellus musciculus	LR: nt
Scotoecus albofuscus	LR: nt
Miniopterus schreibersii	LR: nt

Summary

CR	EN	VU	LRcd	LRnt	EX	DD	Total	Endemics
0	0	0	0	9	0	1	10	0

Total number of species: Megachiroptera 10
Microchiroptera 46
Total 56

Reference(s): Grubb *et al.* 1998

Singapore

Species	Global status
Hipposideros ridleyi	VU B1 + 2c
Myotis oreias	DD (Endemic)

Summary

CR	EN	VU	LRcd	LRnt	EX	DD	Total	Endemics
0	0	1	0	0	0	1	2	1

Total number of species: Megachiroptera 5
Microchiroptera 4
Total 9

The Red Data Book of Singapore published in 1994 (Ng and Wee 1994) lists three species of microchiropteran bats, two listed as Endangered and one Vulnerable.

Reference(s): Mickleburgh *et al.* 1992, Corbet and Hill 1992

Slovakia

Species	Global status
Rhinolophus euryale	VU A2c
Rhinolophus ferrumequinum	LR: nt
Rhinolophus hipposideros	VU A2c
Barbastella barbastellus	VU A2c
Myotis bechsteinii	VU A2c
Myotis dasycneme	VU A2c
Myotis emarginatus	VU A2c
Myotis myotis	LR: nt
Nyctalus lasiopterus	LR: nt
Nyctalus leisleri	LR: nt
Miniopterus schreibersii	LR: nt

Summary

CR	EN	VU	LRcd	LRnt	EX	DD	Total	Endemics
0	0	6	0	5	0	0	11	0

Slovakia continued

Total number of species: Megachiroptera 0
Microchiroptera 24
Total 24

A Red Data Book for the whole of Czechoslovakia was published in 1989 (Baruš 1989). Twenty-four species of bats were listed. Six were listed as Endangered, 13 as Vulnerable, one as Rare (Vulnerable), and four as Rare.

Reference(s): M. Uhrin *pers. comm.*

Slovenia

Species	Global status
Rhinolophus euryale	VU A2c
Rhinolophus ferrumequinum	LR: nt
Rhinolophus hipposideros	VU A2c
Rhinolophus mehelyi	VU A2c
Barbastella barbastellus	VU A2c
Myotis bechsteinii	VU A2c
Myotis capaccinii	VU A2c
Myotis emarginatus	VU A2c
Myotis myotis	LR: nt
Nyctalus lasiopterus	LR: nt
Nyctalus leisleri	LR: nt
Miniopterus schreibersii	LR: nt

Summary

CR	EN	VU	LRcd	LRnt	EX	DD	Total	Endemics
0	0	7	0	5	0	0	12	0

Total number of species: Megachiroptera 0
Microchiroptera 27
Total 27

A Red List for Slovenia published in 1992 (Krystufek 1992) lists 25 species of bats. Two are considered Extinct?, two Endangered, and 21 Vulnerable.

Reference(s): Krystufek 1991,
Krystufek and Cerveny 1997

Solomon Islands

Species	Global status
Emballonura raffrayana	LR: nt
Emballonura dianae	VU A2c
Anthops ornatus	VU A2c, D2 (Endemic)
Hipposideros demissus	VU A2c, D2 (Endemic)
Hipposideros dinops	LR: nt
Chaerephon solomonis	LR: nt (Endemic)
Miniopterus schreibersii	LR: nt

Summary

CR	EN	VU	LRcd	LRnt	EX	DD	Total	Endemics
0	0	3	0	4	0	0	7	3

Total number of species: Megachiroptera 20
Microchiroptera 13
Total 33

Reference(s): Mickleburgh *et al.* 1992,
Flannery 1995b

Somalia

Species	Global status
Rhinopoma macinnesi	VU A2c, D2
Nycteris aurita	LR: nt
Nycteris woodi	LR: nt
Cardioderma cor	LR: nt
Hipposideros megalotis	LR: nt
Rhinolophus blasii	LR: nt
?Miniopterus schreibersii	LR: nt

Summary

CR	EN	VU	LRcd	LRnt	EX	DD	Total	Endemics
0	0	1	0	6	0	0	7	0

Total number of species: Megachiroptera 2
Microchiroptera 35
Total 37

Reference(s): Bergmans 1988, 1989, 1990, 1994, 1997,
Hayman and Hill 1971

South Africa

Species	Global status
Nycteris woodi	LR: nt
Cloeotis percivali	LR: nt
Rhinolophus blasii	LR: nt
Rhinolophus capensis	VU A2c, D2 (Endemic)
Rhinolophus deckenii	DD
?Kerivoula aerosa	DD (Endemic)
Eptesicus zuluensis	LR: nt
Laephotis botswanae	LR: nt
Laephotis wintoni	LR: nt
Myotis lesueuri	VU A2c, D2 (Endemic)
Myotis seabrai	VU A2c, D2
Miniopterus fraterculus	LR: nt
Miniopterus schreibersii	LR: nt
Mormopterus acetabulosus	VU B1 + 2c
Otomops martiensseni	VU A2c
Tadarida fulminans	LR: nt
Tadarida ventralis	LR: nt

Summary

CR	EN	VU	LRcd	LRnt	EX	DD	Total	Endemics
0	0	5	0	10	0	2	17	3

Total number of species: Megachiroptera 4
Microchiroptera 47
Total 51

The Red Data Book for South Africa published in 1986 (Smithers 1986) lists 27 species and subspecies of bats, all considered Indeterminate.

Reference(s): Skinner and Smithers 1990,
Mickleburgh *et al.* 1992,
Taylor 2000

South Korea

Species	Global status
Rhinolophus ferrumequinum	LR: nt
Eptesicus kobayashii	DD

South Korea continued

Species	Global status
Myotis frater	LR: nt
Nyctalus aviator	LR: nt
Murina ussuriensis	EN A2c
Miniopterus schreibersii	LR: nt

Summary

CR	EN	VU	LRcd	LRnt	EX	DD	Total	Endemics
0	1	0	0	4	0	1	6	0

Total number of species: Megachiroptera 0
Microchiroptera 16
Total 16

The Red Data Book for Korea published in 1981 (Pyong-oh 1981) lists four species of bats. Three are considered Vulnerable and one Rare.

Reference(s): G. Csorba *pers. comm.*

Spain (including Balearics and Canary Islands)

Species	Global status
Rhinolophus euryale	VU A2c
Rhinolophus ferrumequinum	LR: nt
Rhinolophus hipposideros	VU A2c
Rhinolophus mehelyi	VU A2c
Barbastella barbastellus	VU A2c
Myotis bechsteinii	VU A2c
Myotis capaccinii	VU A2c
Myotis emarginatus	VU A2c
Myotis myotis	LR: nt
Nyctalus lasiopterus	LR: nt
Nyctalus leisleri	LR: nt
Pipistrellus maderensis	VU A2c, B1 + 2c
Plecotus teneriffae	VU A2c, D2 (Endemic)
Miniopterus schreibersii	LR: nt

Summary

CR	EN	VU	LRcd	LRnt	EX	DD	Total	Endemics
0	0	9	0	5	0	0	14	1

Total number of species: Megachiroptera 0
Microchiroptera 27
Total 27

The Red List of Vertebrates of Spain published in 1992 (Blanco and González 1992) lists 24 species of bats. One is considered Extinct, three Endangered, seven Vulnerable, one Rare, eight Indeterminate, and four Insufficiently Known.

Reference(s): Benzal and de Paz 1991

Sri Lanka

Species	Global status
Rhinolophus beddomei	LR: nt
Miniopterus schreibersii	LR: nt

Summary

CR	EN	VU	LRcd	LRnt	EX	DD	Total	Endemics
0	0	0	0	2	0	0	2	0

Sri Lanka continued

Total number of species: Megachiroptera 4
Microchiroptera 28
Total 32

Reference(s): Bates and Harrison 1997

Sudan

Species	Global status
Taphozous hamiltoni	VU A2c
Cardioderma cor	LR: nt
Hipposideros jonesi	LR: nt
Rhinolophus alcyone	LR: nt
Rhinolophus hipposideros	VU A2c
Eptesicus floweri	LR: nt
Eptesicus guineensis	LR: nt
Pipistrellus ariel	VU D2
Scotoecus albofuscus	LR: nt
Scotophilus nigrita	LR: nt
Miniopterus schreibersii	LR: nt
Mops demonstrator	LR: nt
Tadarida ventralis	LR: nt

Summary

CR	EN	VU	LRcd	LRnt	EX	DD	Total	Endemics
0	0	3	0	10	0	0	13	0

Total number of species: Megachiroptera 9
Microchiroptera 58
Total 67

Reference(s): Bergmans 1988, 1989, 1990, 1994, 1997,
Kock 1969, Koopman 1975

Suriname

Species	Global status
Lonchorhina inusitata	DD
Micronycteris daviesi	LR: nt
Tonatia carrikeri	VU A2c
Tonatia schulzi	VU A2c
Vampyrum spectrum	LR: nt
Choeroniscus godmani	LR: nt
Platyrrhinus aurarius	LR: nt
Pygoderma bilabiatum	LR: nt
Vampyressa bidens	LR: nt
Vampyressa brocki	LR: nt
Lasiurus atratus	DD
Eumops maurus	VU A2c, D2
Molossops abrasus	LR: nt
Molossops neglectus	LR: nt

Summary

CR	EN	VU	LRcd	LRnt	EX	DD	Total	Endemics
0	0	3	0	9	0	2	14	0

Total number of species: Megachiroptera 0
Microchiroptera 61
Total 61

Reference(s): Husson 1962

Swaziland

Species	Global status
Cloeotis percivali	LR: nt

Summary

CR	EN	VU	LRcd	LRnt	EX	DD	Total	Endemics
0	0	0	0	1	0	0	1	0

Total number of species: Megachiroptera 1, Microchiroptera 10, Total 11

Reference(s): Mickleburgh *et al.* 1992, Skinner and Smithers 1990, Taylor 2000

Sweden

Species	Global status
Barbastella barbastellus	VU A2c
Myotis bechsteinii	VU A2c
Myotis dasycneme	VU A2c

Summary

CR	EN	VU	LRcd	LRnt	EX	DD	Total	Endemics
0	0	3	0	0	0	0	3	0

Total number of species: Megachiroptera 0, Microchiroptera 16, Total 16

The list of threatened animals of the Nordic countries, including Sweden, published in 1995 (Nordiska Ministerrådet 1995) lists six species of bats. Two are considered Endangered, two Vulnerable, one Rare, and one in need of monitoring.

Reference(s): Ahlen and Gerrell 1989

Switzerland

Species	Global status
Rhinolophus ferrumequinum	LR: nt
Rhinolophus hipposideros	VU A2c
Barbastella barbastellus	VU A2c
Myotis bechsteinii	VU A2c
Myotis emarginatus	VU A2c
Myotis myotis	LR: nt
Nyctalus lasiopterus	LR: nt
Nyctalus leisleri	LR: nt
Miniopterus schreibersii	LR: nt

Summary

CR	EN	VU	LRcd	LRnt	EX	DD	Total	Endemics
0	0	4	0	5	0	0	9	0

Total number of species: Megachiroptera 0, Microchiroptera 26, Total 26

The Red List for Switzerland published in 1994 (Duelli 1994) includes 24 species of bats. One is considered Extinct, three Endangered, eight Vulnerable, 10 Rare, and one Indeterminate.

Reference(s): Moeschler 1991

Syria

Species	Global status
Rhinolophus blasii	LR: nt
Rhinolophus euryale	VU A2c
Rhinolophus ferrumequinum	LR: nt
Myotis myotis	LR: nt
Miniopterus schreibersii	LR: nt

Summary

CR	EN	VU	LRcd	LRnt	EX	DD	Total	Endemics
0	0	1	0	4	0	0	5	0

Total number of species: Megachiroptera 1, Microchiroptera 10, Total 11

Reference(s): Harrison and Bates 1994

Taiwan

Species	Global status
Rhinolophus monoceros	LR: nt (Endemic)
Arielulus torquatus	DD (Endemic)
Plecotus taivanus	VU A2c (Endemic)
Murina puta	VU A2c (Endemic)
Miniopterus schreibersii	LR: nt

Summary

CR	EN	VU	LRcd	LRnt	EX	DD	Total	Endemics
0	0	2	0	2	0	1	5	4

Total number of species: Megachiroptera 0, Microchiroptera 20, Total 20

Reference(s): Hsu 1997

Tajikistan

Species	Global status
Rhinolophus ferrumequinum	LR: nt
Rhinolophus hipposideros	VU A2c
Myotis emarginatus	VU A2c
Myotis frater	LR: nt
Miniopterus schreibersii	LR: nt

Summary

CR	EN	VU	LRcd	LRnt	EX	DD	Total	Endemics
0	0	2	0	3	0	0	5	0

Total number of species: Megachiroptera 0, Microchiroptera 19, Total 19

The list of rare and endangered animals and plants included in the Red Data Book of Tajikistan (see Krever *et al.* 1998) includes five species and subspecies of bats, all considered Rare.

Reference(s): Khabilov 1989

Tanzania (including Zanzibar and Pemba)

Species	Global status
Taphozous hildegardeae	VU A2c

Tanzania continued

Species	Global status
Nycteris aurita	LR: nt
Nycteris intermedia	LR: nt
Nycteris woodi	LR: nt
Cardioderma cor	LR: nt
Cloeotis percivali	LR: nt
Rhinolophus deckenii	DD
Kerivoula africana	DD (Endemic)
?Eptesicus guineensis	LR: nt
Laephotis botswanae	LR: nt
Laephotis wintoni	LR: nt
Pipistrellus permixtus	DD (Endemic)
Scotophilus nigrita	LR: nt
Miniopterus minor	LR: nt
Miniopterus schreibersii	LR: nt
Otomops martiensseni	VU A2c
Tadarida fulminans	LR: nt
Tadarida ventralis	LR: nt

Summary

CR	EN	VU	LRcd	LRnt	EX	DD	Total	Endemics
0	0	2	0	13	0	3	18	2

Total number of species:	Megachiroptera	13
	Microchiroptera	66
	Total	79
Reference(s):	Mickleburgh *et al.* 1992, Bauer 1992	

Thailand

Species	Global status
Craseonycteris thonglongyai	EN B1 + 2c, C2b (Endemic)
Hipposideros halophyllus	LR: nt (Endemic)
Hipposideros lekaguli	LR: nt
Hipposideros lylei	LR: nt
Hipposideros pratti	LR: nt
Hipposideros turpis	EN A2c
Rhinolophus marshalli	LR: nt
Rhinolophus paradoxolophus	VU B1 + 2c
Rhinolophus shameli	LR: nt
Rhinolophus thomasi	LR: nt
Rhinolophus yunanensis	LR: nt
Kerivoula minuta	LR: nt
Arielulus aureocollaris	DD
Eptesicus demissus	VU A2c (Endemic)
Eptesicus pachyotis	LR: nt
Ia io	LR: nt
Myotis annectans	LR: nt
Myotis montivagus	LR: nt
Myotis rosseti	LR: nt
Pipistrellus cadornae	LR: nt
Pipistrellus lophurus	DD
Pipistrellus paterculus	LR: nt
Pipistrellus pulveratus	LR: nt
Scotomanes ornatus	LR: nt
Harpiocephalus mordax	LR: nt
Murina huttoni	LR: nt
Miniopterus schreibersii	LR: nt
Tadarida latouschei	DD (Endemic)

Thailand continued

Summary

CR	EN	VU	LRcd	LRnt	EX	DD	Total	Endemics
0	2	2	0	21	0	3	28	4

Total number of species:	Megachiroptera	17
	Microchiroptera	91
	Total	108
Reference(s):	Lekagul and McNeely 1977, B. Stewart-Cox *pers. comm.*	

Togo

Species	Global status
Hipposideros fuliginosus	LR: nt
Chalinolobus poensis	LR: nt
Scotophilus nigrita	LR: nt

Summary

CR	EN	VU	LRcd	LRnt	EX	DD	Total	Endemics
0	0	0	0	3	0	0	3	0

Total number of species:	Megachiroptera	9
	Microchiroptera	31
	Total	40
Reference(s):	Bergmans 1988, 1989, 1990, 1994, 1997, Grubb *et al.* 1998	

Tonga

Species	Global status
Emballonura semicaudata	EN A1ac

Summary

CR	EN	VU	LRcd	LRnt	EX	DD	Total	Endemics
0	1	0	0	0	0	0	1	0

Total number of species:	Megachiroptera	1
	Microchiroptera	1
	Total	2
Reference(s):	Mickleburgh *et al.* 1992, Flannery 1995b	

Trinidad and Tobago

Species	Global status
Micronycteris daviesi	LR: nt
Micronycteris sylvestris	LR: nt
Vampyrum spectrum	LR: nt
Choeroniscus intermedius	LR: nt
Tadarida brasiliensis	LR: nt

Summary

CR	EN	VU	LRcd	LRnt	EX	DD	Total	Endemics
0	0	0	0	5	0	0	5	0

Total number of species:	Megachiroptera	0
	Microchiroptera	62
	Total	62
Reference(s):	Breuil and Masson 1991	

Tunisia

Species	Global status
Rhinolophus blasii	LR: nt
Rhinolophus euryale	VU A2c
Rhinolophus ferrumequinum	LR: nt
Rhinolophus mehelyi	VU A2c
Myotis capaccinii	VU A2c
Myotis emarginatus	VU A2c
Miniopterus schreibersii	LR: nt

Summary

CR	EN	VU	LRcd	LRnt	EX	DD	Total	Endemics
0	0	4	0	3	0	0	7	0

Total number of species: Megachiroptera 0
Microchiroptera 12
Total 12

Reference(s): Hayman and Hill 1971, Koopman 1993

Turkey

Species	Global status
Rhinolophus blasii	LR: nt
Rhinolophus euryale	VU A2c
Rhinolophus ferrumequinum	LR: nt
Rhinolophus hipposideros	VU A2c
Rhinolophus mehelyi	VU A2c
Barbastella barbastellus	VU A2c
Myotis bechsteinii	VU A2c
Myotis capaccinii	VU A2c
Myotis emarginatus	VU A2c
Myotis myotis	LR: nt
Nyctalus lasiopterus	LR: nt
Nyctalus leisleri	LR: nt
Miniopterus schreibersii	LR: nt

Summary

CR	EN	VU	LRcd	LRnt	EX	DD	Total	Endemics
0	0	7	0	6	0	0	13	0

Total number of species: Megachiroptera 1
Microchiroptera 30
Total 31

A draft Red List of threatened animals of Turkey published in 1991 (Anon. 1991) includes 29 species of bats. Three are listed as Endangered, 10 Vulnerable, 13 Rare, two Indeterminate, and one Insufficiently Known.

Reference(s): Benda and Horacek 1998

Turkmenistan

Species	Global status
Rhinolophus blasii	LR: nt
Rhinolophus euryale	VU A2c
Rhinolophus ferrumequinum	LR: nt
Rhinolophus hipposideros	VU A2c
Myotis emarginatus	VU A2c
Miniopterus schreibersii	LR: nt

Turkmenistan continued

Summary

CR	EN	VU	LRcd	LRnt	EX	DD	Total	Endemics
0	0	3	0	3	0	0	6	0

Total number of species: Megachiroptera 0
Microchiroptera 21
Total 21

The list of rare and endangered animals and plants included in the Red Data Book of Turkmenistan (see Krever *et al.* 1998) includes seven species of bats.

Reference(s): T. Khabilov and A. Borissenko *pers. comm.*

Turks and Caicos Islands

Species	Global status
Brachyphylla nana	LR: nt

Summary

CR	EN	VU	LRcd	LRnt	EX	DD	Total	Endemics
0	0	0	0	1	0	0	1	0

Total number of species: Megachiroptera 0
Microchiroptera 4
Total 4

Reference(s): Hill 1985

Uganda

Species	Global status
Saccolaimus peli	LR: nt
Cardioderma cor	LR: nt
Rhinolophus alcyone	LR: nt
Rhinolophus maclaudi	LR: nt
Chalinolobus egeria	LR: nt
Chalinolobus gleni	LR: nt
Chalinolobus poensis	LR: nt
Scotophilus nigrita	LR: nt
Miniopterus schreibersii	LR: nt
Chaerephon chapini	LR: nt
Mops congicus	LR: nt
Mops demonstrator	LR: nt
Mops trevori	LR: nt
Otomops martiensseni	VU A2c

Summary

CR	EN	VU	LRcd	LRnt	EX	DD	Total	Endemics
0	0	1	0	13	0	0	14	0

Total number of species: Megachiroptera 11
Microchiroptera 51
Total 62

Reference(s): Bergmans 1988, 1989, 1990, 1994, 1997, Kingdon 1974

Ukraine

Species	Global status
Rhinolophus ferrumequinum	LR: nt
Rhinolophus hipposideros	VU A2c

Ukraine continued

Species	Global status
Barbastella barbastellus	VU A2c
Myotis bechsteinii	VU A2c
Myotis dasycneme	VU A2c
Myotis emarginatus	VU A2c
Myotis myotis	LR: nt
Nyctalus lasiopterus	LR: nt
Nyctalus leisleri	LR: nt

Summary

CR	EN	VU	LRcd	LRnt	EX	DD	Total	Endemics
0	0	5	0	4	0	0	9	0

Total number of species: Megachiroptera 0
Microchiroptera 24
Total 24

Reference(s): I. Kovalyova *pers. comm.*

United Arab Emirates

No globally threatened species present.

Total number of species: Megachiroptera 0
Microchiroptera 6
Total 6

Reference(s): Harrison and Bates 1991

United Kingdom (including Channel Islands and Isle of Man)

Species	Global status
Rhinolophus ferrumequinum	LR: nt
Rhinolophus hipposideros	VU A2c
Barbastella barbastellus	VU A2c
Myotis bechsteinii	VU A2c
Myotis myotis (ex?)	LR: nt
Nyctalus leisleri	LR: nt

Summary

CR	EN	VU	LRcd	LRnt	EX	DD	Total	Endemics
0	0	3	0	3	0	0	6	0

Total number of species: Megachiroptera 0
Microchiroptera 16
Total 16

The Action Plan for the Conservation of Bats in the UK published in 1993 (Hutson 1993) lists eight bat species considered threatened. One is considered Endangered, six Rare, and one Scarce.

Reference(s): Harris *et al.* 1995

United States

Species	Global status
Macrotus californicus	VU A2c
Choeronycteris mexicana	LR: nt
Leptonycteris curasoae	VU A1c

United States continued

Species	Global status
Leptonycteris nivalis	EN A1c
Diphylla ecaudata	LR: nt
Myotis grisescens	EN A1c (Endemic)
Myotis sodalis	EN A1c (Endemic)
Plecotus rafinesquii	VU A2c (Endemic)
Plecotus townsendii	VU A2c
Eumops underwoodi	LR: nt
Tadarida brasiliensis	LR: nt

Summary

CR	EN	VU	LRcd	LRnt	EX	DD	Total	Endemics
0	3	4	0	4	0	0	11	3

Total number of species: Megachiroptera 0
Microchiroptera 45
Total 45

Reference(s): Pierson 1998

Uruguay

Species	Global status
Histiotus alienus	VU A2c
Tadarida brasiliensis	LR:nt

Summary

CR	EN	VU	LRcd	LRnt	EX	DD	Total	Endemics
0	0	1	0	1	0	0	2	0

Total number of species: Megachiroptera 0
Microchiroptera 15
Total 15

Reference(s): Redford and Eisenberg 1992

Uzbekistan

Species	Global status
Rhinolophus ferrumequinum	LR: nt
Rhinolophus hipposideros	VU A2c
Myotis capaccinii	VU A2c
Myotis emarginatus	VU A2c
Myotis frater	LR: nt
Nyctalus lasiopterus	LR: nt
?*Nyctalus leisleri*	LR: nt

Summary

CR	EN	VU	LRcd	LRnt	EX	DD	Total	Endemics
0	0	3	0	4	0	0	7	0

Total number of species: Megachiroptera 0
Microchiroptera 21
Total 21

The list of rare and endangered animals and plants included in the Red Data Book of Uzbekistan (see Krever *et al.* 1998) includes three species of bats.

Reference(s): T. Khabilov *pers. comm.*

Vanuatu

Species	Global status
Emballonura semicaudata	EN A1a,c
Chaerephon bregullae	LR: nt

Summary

CR	EN	VU	LRcd	LRnt	EX	DD	Total	Endemics
0	1	0	0	1	0	0	2	0

Total number of species:	Megachiroptera	4
	Microchiroptera	7
	Total	11
Reference(s):	Mickleburgh *et al.* 1992, Flannery 1995a	

Vatican City

As far as the authors are aware, there is no available information on bats in the Vatican City.

Venezuela

Species	Global status
Diclidurus ingens	VU A2c
Diclidurus isabellus	LR: nt
?*Saccopteryx gymnura*	VU A2c, D2
Lonchorhina fernandezi	VU A2c (Endemic)
Lonchorhina inusitata	DD
Lonchorhina orinocensis	LR: nt
Micronycteris daviesi	LR: nt
Micronycteris sylvestris	LR: nt
Tonatia carrikeri	VU A2c
Vampyrum spectrum	LR: nt
Anoura latidens	LR: nt
Anoura luismanueli	DD (Endemic)
Choeroniscus godmani	LR: nt
Leptonycteris curasoae	VU A1c
Scleronycteris ega	VU A2c, D2
Artibeus amplus	LR: nt
Artibeus concolor	LR: nt
Artibeus obscurus	LR: nt
Platyrrhinus aurarius	LR: nt
Platyrrhinus umbratus	LR: nt
Sturnira aratathomasi	LR: nt
Sturnira bidens	LR: nt
Vampyressa bidens	LR: nt
Diphylla ecaudata	LR: nt
Histiotus humboldti	DD (Endemic)
Myotis nesopolus	LR: nt
Rhogeessa minutilla	LR: nt
Molossops abrasus	LR: nt
Molossops mattogrossensis	LR: nt
Molossops neglectus	LR: nt
Molossus coibensis	LR: nt
Tadarida brasiliensis	LR: nt

Summary

CR	EN	VU	LRcd	LRnt	EX	DD	Total	Endemics
0	0	6	0	23	0	3	32	3

Venezuela continued

Total number of species:	Megachiroptera	0
	Microchiroptera	154
	Total	154

The Red Data Book of Venezuela published in 1995 (Rodriguez and Rojas-Suarez, 1995) includes 20 species of bats. One is considered Endangered, one Vulnerable, seven Insufficiently Known, and 11 Lower Risk.

Reference(s): Linares 1998

Viet Nam

Species	Global status
Hipposideros pratti	LR: nt
Hipposideros turpis	EN A2c
Paracoelops megalotis	CR B1 + 2c (Endemic)
Rhinolophus marshalli	LR: nt
Rhinolophus paradoxolophus	VU B1 + 2c
Rhinolophus subbadius	DD
Rhinolophus thomasi	LR: nt
Ia io	LR: nt
?*Myotis longipes*	VU B1 + 2c, D2
Pipistrellus cadornae	LR: nt
Pipistrellus paterculus	LR: nt
Pipistrellus pulveratus	LR: nt
Scotomanes ornatus	LR: nt
Murina huttoni	LR: nt
Miniopterus schreibersii	LR: nt

Summary

CR	EN	VU	LRcd	LRnt	EX	DD	Total	Endemics
1	1	2	0	10	0	1	15	1

Total number of species:	Megachiroptera	11
	Microchiroptera	53
	Total	64

The Red Data Book of Viet Nam published in 1992 (Ministry of Science, Technology and Environment 1992) lists eight species of microchiropteran bats, all considered Rare.

Reference(s): Corbet and Hill 1992, Bates *et al.* 1997

Wallis and Futuna Islands

No microchiropteran bats present.

Total number of species:	Megachiroptera	1
	Microchiroptera	0
	Total	1
Reference(s):	Mickleburgh *et al.* 1992	

Yemen

Species	Global status
Rhinolophus blasii	LR: nt
Eptesicus nasutus	VU A2c
Pipistrellus bodenheimeri	LR: nt

Yemen continued

Species	Global status
Miniopterus schreibersii	LR: nt
Otomops martiensseni	VU A2c

Summary

CR	EN	VU	LRcd	LRnt	EX	DD	Total	Endemics
0	0	2	0	3	0	0	5	0

Total number of species:	Megachiroptera	2
	Microchiroptera	22
	Total	24
Reference(s):	Harrison and Bates 1991	

Yugoslavia

Species	Global status
Rhinolophus blasii	LR: nt
Rhinolophus euryale	VU A2c
Rhinolophus ferrumequinum	LR: nt
Rhinolophus hipposideros	VU A2c
Rhinolophus mehelyi	VU A2c
Barbastella barbastellus	VU A2c
Myotis bechsteinii	VU A2c
Myotis capaccinii	VU A2c
Myotis dasycneme	VU A2c
Myotis emarginatus	VU A2c
Myotis myotis	LR: nt
Nyctalus leisleri	LR: nt
Miniopterus schreibersii	LR: nt

Summary

CR	EN	VU	LRcd	LRnt	EX	DD	Total	Endemics
0	0	8	0	5	0	0	13	0

Total number of species:	Megachiroptera	0
	Microchiroptera	26
	Total	26
Reference(s):	Savic *et al.* 1995, Paunovic *et al.* 1998	

Zambia

Species	Global status
Nycteris woodi	LR: nt
Cloeotis percivali	LR: nt
Eptesicus zuluensis	LR: nt
Laephotis botswanae	LR: nt
Pipistrellus anchietai	VU A2c
Miniopterus fraterculus	LR: nt
Miniopterus schreibersii	LR: nt
Chaerephon chapini	LR: nt
Otomops martiensseni	VU A2c
Tadarida fulminans	LR: nt

Summary

CR	EN	VU	LRcd	LRnt	EX	DD	Total	Endemics
0	0	2	0	8	0	0	10	0

Zambia continued

Total number of species:	Megachiroptera	11
	Microchiroptera	54
	Total	65
Reference(s):	Mickleburgh *et al.* 1992, Ansell 1978	

Zimbabwe

Species	Global status
Nycteris woodi	LR: nt
Cloeotis percivali	LR: nt
Rhinolophus deckenii	DD
Laephotis botswanae	LR: nt
Scotophilus nigrita	LR: nt
Miniopterus fraterculus	LR: nt
Miniopterus schreibersii	LR: nt
Chaerephon chapini	LR: nt
Otomops martiensseni	VU A2c
Tadarida fulminans	LR: nt
Tadarida lobata	VU D2

Summary

CR	EN	VU	LRcd	LRnt	EX	DD	Total	Endemics
0	0	2	0	8	0	1	11	0

Total number of species:	Megachiroptera	6
	Microchiroptera	41
	Total	47
Reference(s):	Mickleburgh *et al.* 1992, Fenton 1975, Taylor 2000	

6.5 IUCN Red List species in order of threat status and including distribution by country

Extinct (4 species)

PHYLLOSTOMIDAE

Phyllonycteris major EX
Puerto Rico

VESPERTILIONIDAE

Pipistrellus sturdeei EX
Japan

Nyctophilus howensis EX
Australia, New Caledonia

MYSTACINIDAE

Mystacina robusta EX
New Zealand

Critically Endangered (15 species)

EMBALLONURIDAE

Coleura seychellensis CR B1 + 2cde, C2b, D
Seychelles

Taphozous troughtoni CR A1ac, B1 + 2abcde, D
Australia

HIPPOSIDERIDAE

Hipposideros nequam CR B1 + 2c
Malaysia

Paracoelops megalotis CR B1 + 2c
Viet Nam
RHINOLOPHIDAE
Rhinolophus convexus CR D
Malaysia
VESPERTILIONIDAE
Myotis cobanensis CR B1 + 2c
Guatemala
Myotis planiceps CR B1 + 2c
Mexico
Pharotis imogene CR B1 + 2c, C2b
Papua New Guinea
Pipistrellus anthonyi CR B1 + 2c
Myanmar
Pipistrellus joffrei CR B1 + 2c
Myanmar
Scotophilus borbonicus CR A1c
Madagascar, Réunion
Murina tenebrosa CR B1 + 2c, D
Japan
MOLOSSIDAE
Chaerephon gallagheri CR B1 + 2c
Democratic Republic of Congo
Mops niangarae CR B1 + 2c
Democratic Republic of Congo
Otomops wroughtoni CR B1 + 2c
India

Endangered (30 species)

CRASEONYCTERIDAE
Craseonycteris thonglongyai EN B1 + 2c, C2b
Thailand
EMBALLONURIDAE
Balantiopteryx infusca EN B1 + 2c
Colombia, Ecuador
Emballonura semicaudata EN A1ac
American Samoa, Commonwealth of the Northern Mariana Islands, Federated States of Micronesia, Fiji, Guam (ex), Palau, Samoa, Tonga, Vanuatu
HIPPOSIDERIDAE
Hipposideros turpis EN A2c
Japan, Thailand, Viet Nam
RHINOLOPHIDAE
Rhinolophus imaizumii EN A2c, B1 + 2abcde
Japan
Rhinolophus keyensis EN C2a
Indonesia
PHYLLOSTOMIDAE
Phyllonycteris aphylla EN B1 + 2c
Jamaica
Leptonycteris nivalis EN A1c
Guatemala?, Mexico, United States
Chiroderma improvisum EN A2c, B1 + 2c
Guadeloupe, Montserrat
Sturnira thomasi EN B1 + 2c
Guadeloupe
VESPERTILIONIDAE
Chalinolobus neocaledonicus EN B1 + 2c
New Caledonia
Eptesicus guadeloupensis EN B1 + 2c
Guadeloupe
Glischropus javanus EN B1 + 2d
Indonesia
Hesperoptenus doriae EN B1 + 2c
Malaysia
Laephotis namibensis EN A2c
Namibia
Myotis findleyi EN B1 + 2c
Mexico
Myotis grisescens EN A1c
United States
Myotis milleri EN A2c
Mexico
Myotis ozensis EN A2c, B1 + 2c
Japan
Myotis pruinosus EN B1 + 2c
Japan
Myotis schaubi EN B1 + 2c, C2a, D
Armenia, Hungary (ex), Iran
Myotis sodalis EN A1c
United States
Myotis stalkeri EN B1 + 2c
Indonesia
Nyctophilus heran EN B1 + 2c
Indonesia
Pipistrellus endoi EN B1 + 2c
Japan
Rhogeessa mira EN A2c, B1 + 2c,d
Mexico
Murina grisea EN B1 + 2c
India
Murina ussuriensis EN A2c
North Korea, Russia, South Korea
Miniopterus robustior EN B1 + 2c
New Caledonia
MOLOSSIDAE
Mormopterus phrudus EN B1 + 2c
Peru

Vulnerable (135 species)

RHINOPOMATIDAE
Rhinopoma macinnesi VU A2c, D2
Ethiopia, Kenya, Somalia
EMBALLONURIDAE
Diclidurus ingens VU A2c
Brazil, Colombia, Guyana, Peru, Venezuela
Emballonura atrata VU A2c
Madagascar

Emballonura dianae VU A2c
Papua New Guinea, Solomon Islands
Emballonura furax VU A2c, D2
Indonesia, Papua New Guinea
Saccolaimus mixtus VU A2c
Australia, Papua New Guinea
Saccopteryx gymnura VU A2c, D2
Brazil, Venezuela?
Taphozous achates VU D2
Indonesia
Taphozous hamiltoni VU A2c
Chad, Kenya, Sudan
Taphozous hildegardeae VU A2c
Kenya, Tanzania
Taphozous kapalgensis VU A2c
Australia
NYCTERIDAE
Nycteris javanica VU A1c
Indonesia
Nycteris major VU A2c, D2
Benin, Cameroon, Congo Republic, Democratic Republic of Congo, Gabon?, Ivory Coast, Liberia
MEGADERMATIDAE
Macroderma gigas VU A2c
Australia
HIPPOSIDERIDAE
Anthops ornatus VU A2c, D2
Papua New Guinea, Solomon Islands
Asellia patrizii VU A2c, D2
Eritrea, Ethiopia, Saudi Arabia
Hipposideros breviceps VU D2
Indonesia
Hipposideros corynophyllus VU A2c, D2
Indonesia, Papua New Guinea
Hipposideros coxi VU D2
Malaysia
Hipposideros demissus VU A2c, D2
Solomon Islands
Hipposideros durgadasi VU B1 + 2c, D2
India
Hipposideros hypophyllus VU B1 + 2c, D2
India
Hipposideros inexpectatus VU A2c
Indonesia
Hipposideros marisae VU A2c
Côte d'Ivoire, Guinea, Liberia
Hipposideros muscinus VU D2
Indonesia, Papua New Guinea
Hipposideros papua VU A2c
Indonesia
Hipposideros ridleyi VU B1 + 2c
Malaysia, Singapore
Rhinonicteris aurantia VU A1c
Australia
Triaenops furculus VU A2c
Madagascar, Seychelles
RHINOLOPHIDAE
Rhinolophus capensis VU A2c, D2
South Africa
Rhinolophus cognatus VU A2c, D2
India (Andaman and Nicobar Islands)
Rhinolophus euryale VU A2c
Algeria, Armenia, Azerbaijan, Bosnia-Herzegovina, Bulgaria, Croatia, Cyprus, Egypt, France, Georgia, Greece, Hungary, Iran, Iraq, Israel, Italy, Jordan, Lebanon, Macedonia, Morocco, Portugal, Romania, Russia, Slovakia, Slovenia, Spain, Syria, Tunisia, Turkey, Turkmenistan, Yugoslavia
Rhinolophus hipposideros VU A2c
Afghanistan, Albania, Andorra, Armenia, Austria, Azerbaijan, Belgium, Bosnia-Herzegovina, Bulgaria, Croatia, Czech Republic, Egypt, Eritrea, Ethiopia, France, Georgia, Germany, Greece, Hungary, India, Iran, Iraq, Ireland, Israel, Italy, Jordan, Kazakhstan, Kyrgyzstan, Lebanon, Liechtenstein (ex), Luxembourg (ex?), Macedonia, Malta, Moldova, Morocco, Pakistan, Poland, Portugal, Romania, Russia, San Marino, Saudi Arabia, Slovakia, Slovenia, Spain, Sudan, Switzerland, Tajikistan, Turkey, Turkmenistan, Ukraine, United Kingdom, Uzbekistan, Yugoslavia
Rhinolophus mehelyi VU A2c
Afghanistan, Algeria, Armenia, Azerbaijan, Bosnia-Herzegovina, Bulgaria, Croatia, Egypt, France, Georgia, Greece, Iran, Iraq, Israel, Italy, Libya, Macedonia, Morocco, Portugal, Romania, Russia, Slovenia, Spain, Tunisia, Turkey, Yugoslavia
Rhinolophus paradoxolophus VU B1 + 2c
Laos, Thailand, Viet Nam
Rhinolophus rex VU B1 + 2c
China
Rhinolophus subrufus VU A2c
Philippines
MORMOOPIDAE
Pteronotus macleayii VU A2c
Cuba, Jamaica
PHYLLOSTOMIDAE
Lonchorhina fernandezi VU A2c
Venezuela
Lonchorhina marinkellei VU A2c
Colombia
Macrotus californicus VU A2c
Mexico, United States
Micronycteris behnii VU A2c
Brazil, Peru
Micronycteris pusilla VU A2c
Brazil, Colombia
Tonatia carrikeri VU A2c
Bolivia, Brazil, Colombia, Guyana, Peru, Suriname, Venezuela

Tonatia schulzi VU A2c
Brazil, French Guiana, Suriname
Lonchophylla bokermanni VU A2c
Brazil
Lonchophylla dekeyseri VU A2c
Brazil
Lonchophylla handleyi VU A2c, D2
Colombia, Ecuador, Peru
Lonchophylla hesperia VU A2c, D2
Ecuador, Peru
Platalina genovensium VU D2
Peru
Choeroniscus periosus VU D2
Colombia, Ecuador
Leptonycteris curasoae VU A1c
Aruba, Colombia, El Salvador, Guatemala, Honduras, Mexico, Netherlands Antilles, United States, Venezuela
Musonycteris harrisoni VU A2c
Mexico
Scleronycteris ega VU A2c, D2
Brazil, Colombia, Venezuela
Ariteus flavescens VU A2c, D2
Jamaica
Artibeus fraterculus VU A2c
Ecuador, Peru
Artibeus hirsutus VU A2c
Mexico
Artibeus inopinatus VU A2c
El Salvador, Honduras, Nicaragua
Chiroderma doriae VU A2c, D2
Brazil
Platyrrhinus chocoensis VU A2c, D2
Colombia
Platyrrhinus recifinus VU A2c, D2
Brazil
Stenoderma rufum VU A1c
American Virgin Islands, Puerto Rico
Sturnira nana VU D2
Peru
NATALIDAE
Natalus tumidifrons VU D2
Bahamas
FURIPTERIDAE
Amorphochilus schnablii VU A2c
Chile, Ecuador, Peru
THYROPTERIDAE
Thyroptera lavali VU B1 + 2c, D2
Peru
MYZOPODIDAE
Myzopoda aurita VU A2c
Madagascar
VESPERTILIONIDAE
Kerivoula agnella VU D2
Papua New Guinea
Kerivoula muscina VU D2
Papua New Guinea
Kerivoula myrella VU A2c
Indonesia, Papua New Guinea
Antrozous dubiaquercus VU A2c, D2
Belize, Costa Rica, Honduras, Mexico
Arielulus cuprosus VU A2c
Malaysia
Barbastella barbastellus VU A2c
Andorra, Armenia, Austria, Azerbaijan, Belarus, Belgium, Bosnia-Herzegovina, Bulgaria, Croatia, Czech Republic, Denmark, France, Georgia, Germany, Hungary, Italy, Latvia, Liechtenstein, Lithuania, Luxembourg, Macedonia, Moldova, Morocco, The Netherlands, Norway, Poland, Portugal, Romania, Russia, Senegal?, Slovakia, Slovenia, Spain (mainland and Canary Islands), Sweden, Switzerland, Turkey, Ukraine, United Kingdom, Yugoslavia
Chalinolobus alboguttatus VU D2
Cameroon, Democratic Republic of Congo
Chalinolobus dwyeri VU A2c
Australia
Chalinolobus superbus VU D2
Côte d'Ivoire, Democratic Republic of Congo, Ghana
Chalinolobus tuberculatus VU A2bc
New Zealand
Eptesicus demissus VU A2c
Thailand
Eptesicus innoxius VU A2c
Argentina, Ecuador (Galápagos Islands), Peru
Eptesicus nasutus VU A2c
Afghanistan, Iran, Iraq, Oman, Pakistan, Saudi Arabia, Yemen
Eptesicus platyops VU D2
Equatorial Guinea, Nigeria, Senegal
Hesperoptenus gaskelli VU B1 + 2c
Indonesia
Histiotus alienus VU A2c
Brazil, Uruguay
Lasiurus castaneus VU D2
Colombia, Costa Rica, French Guiana, Panama
Lasiurus ebenus VU B1 + 2c, D2
Brazil
Myotis aelleni VU A2c, D2
Argentina
Myotis atacamensis VU A2c, D2
Chile, Peru
Myotis bechsteinii VU A2c
Austria, Azerbaijan, Belarus, Belgium, Bosnia-Herzegovina, Bulgaria, Croatia, Czech Republic, France, Georgia, Germany, Hungary, Iran, Italy, Liechtenstein, Macedonia, Moldova, The Netherlands, Poland, Portugal, Romania, Russia, Slovakia, Slovenia, Spain, Sweden, Switzerland, Turkey, Ukraine, United Kingdom, Yugoslavia

Myotis capaccinii VU A2c
Albania, Algeria, Andorra?, Bosnia-Herzegovina, Bulgaria, Croatia, France, Greece, Iran, Iraq, Israel, Italy, Jordan, Lebanon, Macedonia, Morocco, Romania, Russia, Slovenia, Spain, Tunisia, Turkey, Uzbekistan, Yugoslavia
Myotis dasycneme VU A2c
Belarus, Belgium, China, Czech Republic, Denmark, Estonia, France, Germany, Hungary, Kazakhstan, Latvia, Lithuania, Luxembourg, Moldova, The Netherlands, Poland, Russia, Slovakia, Sweden, Ukraine, Yugoslavia
Myotis dominicensis VU A2c, D2
Dominica, Guadeloupe
Myotis emarginatus VU A2c
Afghanistan, Algeria, Andorra, Armenia, Austria, Azerbaijan, Belgium, Bosnia-Herzegovina, Bulgaria, Croatia, Czech Republic, France, Georgia, Germany, Greece, Hungary, Iran, Israel, Italy, Jordan, Kazakhstan, Kyrgyzstan, Lebanon, Macedonia, Morocco, The Netherlands, Oman, Poland, Portugal, Romania, Russia, Saudi Arabia, Slovakia, Slovenia, Spain, Switzerland, Tajikistan, Tunisia, Turkey, Turkmenistan, Ukraine, Uzbekistan, Yugoslavia
Myotis hosonoi VU A2c, B1 + 2c
Japan
Myotis lesueuri VU A2c, D2
South Africa
Myotis longipes VU B1 + 2c, D2
Afghanistan, India, Nepal, Viet Nam?
Myotis morrisi VU D2
Ethiopia, Nigeria
Myotis peninsularis VU A1c
Mexico
Myotis ruber VU A2c
Argentina, Brazil, Paraguay
Myotis scotti VU A2c, D2
Ethiopia
Myotis seabrai VU A2c, D2
Angola, Namibia, South Africa
Myotis sicarius VU A2c, D2
India, Nepal
Myotis vivesi VU A2c
Mexico
Myotis yesoensis VU A2c
Japan
Nyctalus azoreum VU A2c, B1 + 2c
Portugal (Azores)
Nyctophilus microdon VU D2
Papua New Guinea
Nyctophilus timoriensis VU A2c
Australia, Indonesia, Papua New Guinea
Pipistrellus anchietai VU A2c
Angola, Democratic Republic of Congo, Zambia
Pipistrellus arabicus VU D2
Oman
Pipistrellus ariel VU D2
Egypt, Israel, Jordan, Sudan
Pipistrellus maderensis VU A2c, B1 + 2c
Portugal (Madeira), Spain (Canary Islands)
Pipistrellus mckenziei VU A2c
Australia
Plecotus rafinesquii VU A2c
United States
Plecotus taivanus VU A2c
Taiwan
Plecotus teneriffae VU A2c, D2
Spain (Canary Islands)
Plecotus townsendii VU A2c
Canada, Mexico, United States
Rhogeessa genowaysi VU A2c, D2
Mexico
Murina puta VU A2c
Taiwan
Miniopterus fuscus VU A2c
Japan
Tomopeas ravus VU A2c, D2
Peru
MYSTACINIDAE
Mystacina tuberculata VU A2c, C2a
New Zealand
MOLOSSIDAE
Chaerephon pusilla VU D1 + 2
Seychelles
Chaerephon tomensis VU A2c, D2
São Tomé and Príncipe
Eumops maurus VU A2c, D2
Guyana, Suriname
Molossops aequatorianus VU A2c, D2
Ecuador
Mormopterus acetabulosus VU B1 + 2c
Ethiopia, Madagascar, Mauritius, Réunion, South Africa
Mormopterus doriae VU A2c
Indonesia
Mormopterus jugularis VU A2c
Madagascar
Mormopterus kalinowskii VU A2c, D2
Chile, Peru
Mormopterus minutus VU A2c
Cuba
Otomops formosus VU A2c
Indonesia
Otomops johnstonei VU D2
Indonesia
Otomops martiensseni VU A2c
Angola, Central African Republic, Democratic Republic of Congo, Djibouti, Ghana, Ethiopia, Kenya, Madagascar, Rwanda, South Africa, Tanzania, Uganda, Yemen, Zambia, Zimbabwe

Otomops papuensis VU D2
Papua New Guinea
Otomops secundus VU D2
Papua New Guinea
Tadarida lobata VU D2
Kenya, Zimbabwe

Data Deficient (56 species)

EMBALLONURIDAE
Emballonura serii DD
Papua New Guinea
NYCTERIDAE
Nycteris madagascariensis DD
Madagascar
HIPPOSIDERIDAE
Coelops hirsutus DD
Philippines
Hipposideros crumeniferus DD
Indonesia
Hipposideros doriae DD
Malaysia
Hipposideros lamottei DD
Ghana, Guinea, Liberia?, Sierra Leone
Hipposideros schistaceus DD
India
Triaenops auritus DD
Madagascar
Triaenops rufus DD
Madagascar
RHINOLOPHIDAE
Rhinolophus adami DD
Congo Republic
Rhinolophus anderseni DD
Philippines
Rhinolophus deckenii DD
Angola, Botswana, Malawi, Mozambique, Namibia, South Africa, Tanzania, Zimbabwe
Rhinolophus inops DD
Philippines
Rhinolophus mitratus DD
India
Rhinolophus osgoodi DD
China
Rhinolophus subbadius DD
India, Laos?, Myanmar, Nepal, Viet Nam
PHYLLOSTOMIDAE
Lonchorhina inusitata DD
Brazil, French Guiana, Suriname, Venezuela
Micronycteris brosseti DD
Brazil, French Guiana, Guyana, Peru
Micronycteris sanborni DD
Brazil
Anoura luismanueli DD
Venezuela
Artibeus incomitatus DD
El Salvador, Honduras, Nicaragua
VESPERTILIONIDAE
Kerivoula aerosa DD
South Africa?
Kerivoula africana DD
Tanzania
Arielulus aureocollaris DD
Laos, Thailand
Arielulus societatis DD
Malaysia
Arielulus torquatus DD
Taiwan
Chalinolobus kenyacola DD
Kenya
Eptesicus flavescens DD
Angola, Burundi
Eptesicus kobayashii DD
North Korea, South Korea
Eptesicus matroka DD
Madagascar
Eptesicus tatei DD
India
Histiotus humboldti DD
Venezuela
Lasiurus atratus DD
Guyana, Suriname
Myotis abei DD
Russia
Myotis australis DD
Australia
Myotis csorbai DD
Nepal
Myotis gomatongensis DD
Malaysia
Myotis hermanni DD
Indonesia?
Myotis insularum DD
American Samoa?, Samoa?
Myotis oreias DD
Singapore
Myotis yanbarensis DD
Japan
Pipistrellus aero DD
Ethiopia?, Kenya
Pipistrellus lophurus DD
Myanmar, Thailand
Pipistrellus minahassae DD
Indonesia
Pipistrellus peguensis DD
Myanmar
Pipistrellus permixtus DD
Tanzania
Scotomanes emarginatus DD
India?

Scotophilus celebensis DD
Indonesia
Murina fusca DD
China
Murina ryukyuana DD
Japan
Miniopterus majori DD
Madagascar
Miniopterus menavi DD
Madagascar
MOLOSSIDAE
Chaerephon leucogaster DD
Madagascar
Mops leucostigma DD
Madagascar
Myopterus daubentonii DD
Côte d'Ivoire, Democratic Republic of Congo, Senegal
Tadarida latouschei DD
Thailand

Lower Risk: Near Threatened (190 species)

EMBALLONURIDAE
Balantiopteryx io LR: nt
Belize, Guatemala, Mexico
Cyttarops alecto LR: nt
Brazil, Colombia, Costa Rica, Guyana, Nicaragua
Diclidurus isabellus LR: nt
Brazil, Colombia, Guyana, Venezuela
Emballonura raffrayana LR: nt
Indonesia, Papua New Guinea, Solomon Islands
Saccolaimus flaviventris LR: nt
Australia, Papua New Guinea
Saccolaimus peli LR: nt
Angola, Cameroon, Congo Republic, Democratic Republic of Congo, Gabon, Ghana, Kenya, Liberia, Nigeria, Uganda
Taphozous australis LR: nt
Australia, Papua New Guinea
NYCTERIDAE
Nycteris aurita LR: nt
Ethiopia, Kenya, Somalia, Tanzania
Nycteris intermedia LR: nt
Angola, Cameroon, Côte d'Ivoire, Democratic Republic of Congo, Gabon, Ghana, Liberia, Tanzania
Nycteris woodi LR: nt
Cameroon, Ethiopia, Malawi, Mozambique, Somalia, South Africa, Tanzania, Zambia, Zimbabwe
MEGADERMATIDAE
Cardioderma cor LR: nt
Ethiopia, Kenya, Somalia, Sudan, Tanzania, Uganda
HIPPOSIDERIDAE
Cloeotis percivali LR: nt
Botswana, Democratic Republic of Congo, Kenya, Mozambique, South Africa, Swaziland, Tanzania, Zambia, Zimbabwe
Coelops robinsoni LR: nt
Indonesia, Laos?, Malaysia
Hipposideros camerunensis LR: nt
Cameroon, Democratic Republic of Congo, Kenya
Hipposideros coronatus LR: nt
Philippines
Hipposideros curtus LR: nt
Cameroon, Equatorial Guinea, Nigeria?
Hipposideros dinops LR: nt
Indonesia, Papua New Guinea, Solomon Islands
Hipposideros edwardshilli LR: nt
Papua New Guinea
Hipposideros fuliginosus LR: nt
Cameroon, Congo Republic, Democratic Republic of Congo, Equatorial Guinea, Ethiopia, Ghana, Guinea-Bissau?, Liberia, Sierra Leone, Togo
Hipposideros halophyllus LR: nt
Thailand
Hipposideros jonesi LR: nt
Burkina Faso, Equatorial Guinea, Ghana, Guinea, Mali, Nigeria, Sierra Leone, Sudan
Hipposideros lekaguli LR: nt
Malaysia, Philippines, Thailand
Hipposideros lylei LR: nt
Malaysia, Myanmar, Thailand
Hipposideros macrobullatus LR: nt
Indonesia
Hipposideros madurae LR: nt
Indonesia
Hipposideros megalotis LR: nt
Djibouti, Ethiopia, Kenya, Saudi Arabia, Somalia
Hipposideros obscurus LR: nt
Philippines
Hipposideros pratti LR: nt
China, Malaysia, Myanmar, Thailand, Viet Nam
Hipposideros pygmaeus LR: nt
Philippines
Hipposideros semoni LR: nt
Australia, Papua New Guinea
Hipposideros sorenseni LR: nt
Indonesia
Hipposideros stenotis LR: nt
Australia
Hipposideros sumbae LR: nt
Indonesia
Hipposideros wollastoni LR: nt
Indonesia, Papua New Guinea
RHINOLOPHIDAE
Rhinolophus alcyone LR: nt
Cameroon, Congo Republic, Democratic Republic of Congo, Equatorial Guinea, Gabon, Ghana, Guinea-Bissau, Nigeria, Senegal, Sierra Leone?, Sudan, Uganda

Rhinolophus beddomei LR: nt
India, Sri Lanka
Rhinolophus blasii LR: nt
Afghanistan, Albania, Algeria, Armenia?, Azerbaijan, Bulgaria, Cyprus, Democratic Republic of Congo, Ethiopia, Greece, Iran, Israel, Italy, Jordan, Morocco, Oman, Pakistan, Romania, Somalia, South Africa, Syria, Tunisia, Turkey, Turkmenistan, Yemen, Yugoslavia
Rhinolophus canuti LR: nt
Indonesia
Rhinolophus celebensis LR: nt
Indonesia
Rhinolophus cornutus LR: nt
China?, Japan
Rhinolophus creaghi LR: nt
Indonesia, Malaysia
Rhinolophus ferrumequinum LR: nt
Afghanistan, Algeria, Andorra?, Armenia, Austria, Azerbaijan, Belgium, Bosnia-Herzegovina, Bulgaria, China, Croatia, Cyprus, Czech Republic, France, Georgia, Germany, Greece, Hungary, India, Iran, Iraq, Israel, Italy, Japan, Jordan, Kazakhstan, Kyrgyzstan, Lebanon, Liechtenstein, Luxembourg, Macedonia, Malta?, Moldova, Morocco, Nepal, The Netherlands?, North Korea, Pakistan, Poland, Portugal, Romania, Russia, San Marino, Saudi Arabia, Slovakia, Slovenia, South Korea, Spain, Switzerland, Syria, Tajikistan, Tunisia, Turkey, Turkmenistan, Ukraine, United Kingdom, Uzbekistan, Yugoslavia
Rhinolophus guineensis LR: nt
Guinea, Guinea Bissau, Liberia, Sierra Leone
Rhinolophus maclaudi LR: nt
Democratic Republic of Congo, Guinea, Liberia, Nigeria, Rwanda, Uganda
Rhinolophus marshalli LR: nt
Laos, Malaysia, Thailand, Viet Nam
Rhinolophus monoceros LR: nt
Taiwan
Rhinolophus nereis LR: nt
Indonesia
Rhinolophus philippinensis LR: nt
Australia, Indonesia, Malaysia, Papua New Guinea, Philippines
Rhinolophus rufus LR: nt
Philippines
Rhinolophus shameli LR: nt
Cambodia, Malaysia, Myanmar, Thailand
Rhinolophus silvestris LR: nt
Congo Republic, Gabon
Rhinolophus thomasi LR: nt
China, Laos, Myanmar, Thailand, Viet Nam
Rhinolophus virgo LR: nt
Philippines
Rhinolophus yunanensis LR: nt
China, India, Myanmar, Thailand
MORMOOPIDAE
Mormoops blainvillii LR: nt
Cuba, Dominican Republic, Haiti, Jamaica, Puerto Rico
Pteronotus quadridens LR: nt
Cuba, Dominican Republic, Haiti, Jamaica, Puerto Rico
PHYLLOSTOMIDAE
Lonchorhina orinocensis LR: nt
Colombia, Venezuela
Micronycteris daviesi LR: nt
Brazil, Colombia, Costa Rica, Ecuador, French Guiana, Guyana, Honduras, Panama, Peru, Suriname, Trinidad and Tobago, Venezuela
Micronycteris sylvestris LR: nt
Brazil, Colombia, Costa Rica, Ecuador, Honduras, Mexico, Nicaragua, Panama, Peru, Trinidad and Tobago, Venezuela
Phyllostomus latifolius LR: nt
Brazil, Colombia, French Guiana
Tonatia evotis LR: nt
Belize, Guatemala, Honduras, Mexico
Vampyrum spectrum LR: nt
Belize, Brazil, Colombia, Costa Rica, Ecuador, French Guiana, Guatemala, Guyana, Honduras, Jamaica, Mexico, Nicaragua, Peru, Suriname, Trinidad and Tobago, Venezuela
Brachyphylla nana LR: nt
Bahamas, Cayman Islands, Cuba, Dominican Republic, Haiti, Jamaica (ex), Turks and Caicos Islands
Phyllonycteris poeyi LR: nt
Cuba, Dominican Republic, Haiti
Anoura latidens LR: nt
Colombia, Peru, Venezuela
Choeroniscus godmani LR: nt
Colombia, Costa Rica, El Salvador, Guatemala, Guyana, Honduras, Mexico, Nicaragua, Suriname, Venezuela
Choeroniscus intermedius LR: nt
Brazil, Colombia, French Guiana, Peru, Trinidad and Tobago
Choeronycteris mexicana LR: nt
El Salvador, Guatemala, Honduras, Mexico, United States
Glossophaga morenoi LR: nt
Mexico
Hylonycteris underwoodi LR: nt
Belize, Guatemala, Mexico, Nicaragua, Panama
Monophyllus plethodon LR: nt
Anguilla, Antigua and Barbuda, Barbados, Dominica, Guadeloupe, Martinique, Montserrat, St. Lucia, St. Vincent
Rhinophylla alethina LR: nt
Colombia, Ecuador

Rhinophylla fischerae LR: nt
Brazil, Colombia, Ecuador, Peru
Ardops nichollsi LR: nt
Dominica, Guadeloupe, Martinique, Montserrat, Netherlands Antilles, St. Lucia, St. Vincent
Artibeus amplus LR: nt
Colombia, Guyana, Venezuela
Artibeus concolor LR: nt
Brazil, Colombia, French Guiana, Peru, Venezuela
Artibeus fimbriatus LR: nt
Argentina, Brazil, Paraguay
Artibeus obscurus LR: nt
Bolivia, Brazil, Colombia, Ecuador, French Guiana, Peru, Venezuela
Ectophylla alba LR: nt
Colombia, Costa Rica, Honduras, Nicaragua, Panama
Phyllops falcatus LR: nt
Cayman Islands, Cuba, Dominican Republic, Haiti
Platyrrhinus aurarius LR: nt
Colombia, Suriname, Venezuela
Platyrrhinus infuscus LR: nt
Bolivia, Brazil, Colombia, Ecuador, Peru
Platyrrhinus umbratus LR: nt
Colombia, Panama, Venezuela
Pygoderma bilabiatum LR: nt
Argentina, Bolivia, Brazil, Paraguay, Suriname
Sturnira aratathomasi LR: nt
Colombia, Ecuador, Peru, Venezuela
Sturnira bidens LR: nt
Brazil?, Colombia, Ecuador, Peru, Venezuela
Sturnira magna LR: nt
Bolivia, Colombia, Ecuador, Peru
Sturnira mordax LR: nt
Colombia, Costa Rica, Panama
Vampyressa bidens LR: nt
Bolivia, Brazil, Colombia, Guyana, Peru, Suriname, Venezuela
Vampyressa brocki LR: nt
Brazil, Colombia, Guyana, Peru, Suriname
Vampyressa melissa LR: nt
Colombia, French Guiana, Peru
Diphylla ecaudata LR: nt
Belize, Bolivia, Brazil, Colombia, Costa Rica, Ecuador, El Salvador, Guatemala, Honduras, Mexico, Nicaragua, Panama, Peru, United States, Venezuela
NATALIDAE
Natalus lepidus LR: nt
Bahamas, Cuba
VESPERTILIONIDAE
Kerivoula cuprosa LR: nt
Cameroon, Democratic Republic of Congo, Kenya
Kerivoula intermedia LR: nt
Malaysia
Kerivoula minuta LR: nt
Malaysia, Thailand
Kerivoula smithi LR: nt
Cameroon, Côte d'Ivoire, Democratic Republic of Congo, Kenya, Liberia, Nigeria
Chalinolobus beatrix LR: nt
Congo Republic, Côte d'Ivoire, Ghana, Guinea-Bissau?, Kenya
Chalinolobus egeria LR: nt
Cameroon, Uganda
Chalinolobus gleni LR: nt
Cameroon, Uganda
Chalinolobus picatus LR: nt
Australia
Chalinolobus poensis LR: nt
Côte d'Ivoire, Democratic Republic of Congo, Equatorial Guinea, Ghana, Guinea-Bissau, Liberia?, Nigeria, Senegal, Sierra Leone, Togo, Uganda
Eptesicus brunneus LR: nt
Cameroon, Democratic Republic of Congo, Equatorial Guinea (Bioko), Ghana, Liberia, Nigeria, Sierra Leone
Eptesicus caurinus LR: nt
Australia
Eptesicus douglasorum LR: nt
Australia
Eptesicus floweri LR: nt
Mali, Sudan
Eptesicus guineensis LR: nt
Democratic Republic of Congo, Ethiopia, Ghana, Guinea, Guinea-Bissau, Senegal, Sudan, Tanzania?
Eptesicus pachyotis LR: nt
China, India, Myanmar, Thailand
Eptesicus zuluensis LR: nt
Botswana, Namibia, South Africa, Zambia
Eudiscopus denticulus LR: nt
Laos, Myanmar
Histiotus macrotus LR: nt
Argentina, Bolivia, Chile, Peru
Ia io LR: nt
China, India, Laos, Nepal, Thailand, Viet Nam
Laephotis angolensis LR: nt
Angola, Democratic Republic of Congo
Laephotis botswanae LR: nt
Botswana, Democratic Republic of Congo, Malawi, South Africa, Tanzania, Zambia, Zimbabwe
Laephotis wintoni LR: nt
Ethiopia, Kenya, South Africa, Tanzania
Lasiurus egregius LR: nt
Brazil, Colombia, French Guiana, Panama
Myotis annectans LR: nt
India, Indonesia, Laos, Myanmar, Thailand
Myotis bombinus LR: nt
China, Japan, North Korea, Russia

Myotis chiloensis LR: nt
Chile
Myotis elegans LR: nt
Belize, Costa Rica, Guatemala, Honduras, Mexico, Nicaragua
Myotis fimbriatus LR: nt
China
Myotis fortidens LR: nt
Guatemala, Mexico
Myotis frater LR: nt
Afghanistan, China, Japan, North Korea, Russia, South Korea, Tajikistan, Uzbekistan
Myotis goudoti LR: nt
Comoros, Madagascar
Myotis macrotarsus LR: nt
Malaysia, Philippines
Myotis martiniquensis LR: nt
Barbados, Martinique
Myotis montivagus LR: nt
China, India, Malaysia, Myanmar, Thailand
Myotis myotis LR: nt
Albania, Andorra, Austria, Belarus, Belgium, Bulgaria, Cyprus, Czech Republic, France, Germany, Greece, Hungary, Israel, Italy, Jordan, Lebanon, Liechtenstein, Luxembourg, Malta, The Netherlands, Poland, Portugal (mainland and Azores), Romania, Slovakia, Slovenia, Spain, Switzerland, Syria, Turkey, Ukraine, United Kingdom (ex?), Yugoslavia
Myotis nesopolus LR: nt
Colombia, Netherlands Antilles, Venezuela
Myotis pequinius LR: nt
China
Myotis ricketti LR: nt
China, Laos
Myotis ridleyi LR: nt
Indonesia, Malaysia
Myotis rosseti LR: nt
Cambodia, Thailand
Nyctalus aviator LR: nt
China, Japan, North Korea, Russia, South Korea
Nyctalus lasiopterus LR: nt
Armenia?, Azerbaijan, Belarus, Bosnia-Herzegovina, Bulgaria, Croatia, France, Georgia, Germany, Greece, Hungary, Iran, Italy, Kazakhstan, Libya, Macedonia, Moldova, Morocco, Portugal, Romania, Russia, Slovakia, Slovenia, Spain, Switzerland, Turkey, Ukraine, Uzbekistan
Nyctalus leisleri LR: nt
Afghanistan, Albania, Algeria, Andorra, Armenia, Austria, Azerbaijan, Belarus, Belgium, Bosnia-Herzegovina, Bulgaria, China, Croatia, Czech Republic, France, Georgia, Germany, Greece, Hungary, India, Iran, Ireland, Italy, Kazakhstan, Latvia, Libya, Liechtenstein, Lithuania, Luxembourg, Macedonia, Moldova, The Netherlands, Pakistan, Poland, Portugal (mainland and Madeira), Romania, Russia, Slovakia, Slovenia, Spain (mainland and Canary Islands), Switzerland, Turkey, Ukraine, United Kingdom, Uzbekistan?, Yugoslavia
Nyctalus montanus LR: nt
Afghanistan, India, Nepal, Pakistan
Nycticeius rueppellii LR: nt
Australia
Nyctophilus daedalus LR: nt
Australia
Nyctophilus sherrini LR: nt
Australia
Nyctophilus walkeri LR: nt
Australia
Pipistrellus bodenheimeri LR: nt
Egypt, Israel, Oman, Saudi Arabia, Yemen
Pipistrellus cadornae LR: nt
India, Myanmar, Thailand, Viet Nam
Pipistrellus kitcheneri LR: nt
Indonesia, Malaysia?
Pipistrellus macrotis LR: nt
Brunei, Indonesia, Malaysia
Pipistrellus mordax LR: nt
Indonesia, Philippines?
Pipistrellus musciculus LR: nt
Cameroon, Democratic Republic of Congo, Gabon, Ghana, Sierra Leone
Pipistrellus papuanus LR: nt
Indonesia, Papua New Guinea
Pipistrellus paterculus LR: nt
China, India, Myanmar, Thailand, Viet Nam
Pipistrellus pulveratus LR: nt
China, Laos, Thailand, Viet Nam
Pipistrellus wattsi LR: nt
Papua New Guinea
Rhogeessa alleni LR: nt
Mexico
Rhogeessa gracilis LR: nt
Mexico
Rhogeessa minutilla LR: nt
Colombia, Venezuela
Rhogeessa parvula LR: nt
Mexico
Scotoecus albofuscus LR: nt
Equatorial Guinea, Gambia, Ghana, Kenya, Malawi, Mozambique, Nigeria, Senegal, Sierra Leone, Sudan
Scotomanes ornatus LR: nt
China, India, Laos, Myanmar, Nepal, Thailand, Viet Nam
Scotophilus nigrita LR: nt
Congo Republic, Democratic Republic of Congo, Equatorial Guinea, Ethiopia, Ghana, Guinea,

Kenya, Malawi, Mali, Mozambique, Nigeria, Senegal, Sierra Leone, Sudan, Tanzania, Togo, Uganda, Zimbabwe

Scotophilus robustus LR: nt
Madagascar

Harpiocephalus mordax LR: nt
Laos, Malaysia, Myanmar, Thailand

Murina aenea LR: nt
Malaysia

Murina aurata LR: nt
China, India, Myanmar, Nepal, North Korea

Murina huttoni LR: nt
China, India, Malaysia, Myanmar, Nepal, Pakistan, Thailand, Viet Nam

Murina rozendaali LR: nt
Malaysia

Murina silvatica LR: nt
Japan

Miniopterus fraterculus LR: nt
Angola, Kenya, Madagascar, Malawi, Mozambique, South Africa, Zambia, Zimbabwe

Miniopterus gleni LR: nt
Madagascar

Miniopterus minor LR: nt
Comoros, Congo Republic, Democratic Republic of Congo, Kenya, Madagascar, São Tomé and Príncipe, Tanzania

Miniopterus schreibersii LR: nt
Afghanistan, Albania, Algeria, Angola, Armenia, Australia, Austria, Azerbaijan, Bosnia-Herzegovina, Botswana, Bulgaria, Cameroon, Central African Republic, China, Croatia, Democratic Republic of Congo, Ethiopia, France, Ghana, Georgia, Gibraltar, Greece, Guinea, Hungary, India, Indonesia, Iran, Iraq, Israel, Italy, Japan, Jordan, Kenya, Laos, Lebanon, Macedonia, Malawi, Malaysia, Malta, Morocco, Mozambique, Myanmar, Namibia, Nepal, North Korea, Papua New Guinea, Philippines, Portugal, Romania, Russia, Rwanda?, San Marino, Saudi Arabia, Sierra Leone, Slovakia, Slovenia, Solomon Islands, Somalia?, South Africa, South Korea, Spain, Sri Lanka, Sudan, Switzerland, Syria, Taiwan, Tajikistan, Tanzania, Thailand, Tunisia, Turkey, Turkmenistan, Uganda, Viet Nam, Yemen, Yugoslavia, Zambia, Zimbabwe

MOLOSSIDAE

Chaerephon bregullae LR:nt
Fiji, Vanuatu

Chaerephon chapini LR: nt
Angola, Botswana, Democratic Republic of Congo, Ghana, Ethiopia, Namibia, Uganda, Zambia, Zimbabwe

Chaerephon johorensis LR: nt
Indonesia, Malaysia

Chaerephon solomonis LR: nt
Solomon Islands

Cheiromeles parvidens LR: nt
Indonesia, Philippines

Cheiromeles torquatus LR: nt
Indonesia, Malaysia, Philippines

Eumops underwoodi LR: nt
Belize, El Salvador, Honduras, Nicaragua, United States

Molossops abrasus LR: nt
Argentina, Bolivia, Brazil, Colombia, Guyana, Paraguay, Peru, Suriname, Venezuela

Molossops mattogrossensis LR: nt
Brazil, Colombia, Guyana, Venezuela

Molossops neglectus LR: nt
Argentina, Brazil, Peru, Suriname, Venezuela

Molossus aztecus LR: nt
Guatemala, Honduras, Mexico, Nicaragua

Molossus coibensis LR: nt
Brazil, Costa Rica, El Salvador, Mexico, Panama, Peru, Venezuela

Mops congicus LR:nt
Cameroon, Democratic Republic of Congo, Ghana, Nigeria, Uganda

Mops demonstrator LR:nt
Burkina Faso, Democratic Republic of Congo, Ghana, Sudan, Uganda

Mops petersoni LR:nt
Cameroon, Ghana

Mops sarasinorum LR:nt
Indonesia, Philippines

Mops trevori LR:nt
Democratic Republic of Congo, Uganda

Tadarida australis LR:nt
Australia, Indonesia, Papua New Guinea

Tadarida brasiliensis LR:nt
Antigua and Barbuda, Argentina, Bahamas, Belize, Bolivia, Brazil,Cayman Islands, Chile, Colombia, Costa Rica, Cuba, Dominica, Dominican Republic, Ecuador, El Salvador, Falkland Islands (vagrant), Guadeloupe, Guatemala, Haiti, Honduras, Jamaica, Martinique, Mexico, Montserrat, Netherlands Antilles, Nicaragua, Panama, Paraguay, Peru, Puerto Rico, St. Kitts and Nevis, St. Lucia, Trinidad and Tobago, Turks and Caicos Islands, United States, Uruguay, Venezuela

Tadarida fulminans LR:nt
Democratic Republic of Congo, Kenya, Madagascar, Malawi, Rwanda, South Africa, Tanzania, Zambia, Zimbabwe

Tadarida ventralis LR:nt
Democratic Republic of Congo, Ethiopia, Kenya, Malawi, Mozambique, South Africa, Sudan, Tanzania

6.6 Microchiropteran bats – changes in threat status from *The 1996 IUCN Red List of Threatened Animals*

Taxon	Status 1996 Red List	New Status	Citation
Rhinopoma hadithaensis	VU: B1 +2c, D2	Removed	Synonym of *R. hardwickei* (D. Kock *pers. comm.*)
Emballonura raffrayana	LR: cd	LR: nt	Not conservation dependent
Emballonura semicaudata	EN: A2c	EN: A1ac	G. Wiles *pers. comm.*
Saccopteryx gymnura	LR: nt	VU: A2c, D2	Brazil Workshop, 1995
Nycteris madagascariensis	Not listed	DD	Recognised as full species (Peterson *et al.* 1995)
Nycteris vinsoni	CR: B1 + 2c	Removed	Synonym of *N. macrotis* (D. Kock *pers. comm.*)
Hipposideros hypophyllus	LR: nt	VU: B1+2c, D2	P.J.J. Bates *pers. comm.*
Hipposideros megalotis	Not listed	LR: nt	I. Aggundey, D. Yalden & J. Kingdon *pers. comms.*
Hipposideros pomona	DD	LR: lc	P. J.J. Bates *pers. comm.*
Hipposideros schistaceus	LR: nt	DD	Only one locality (P.J.J. Bates *pers. comm.*)
Triaenops auritus	Not listed	DD	Recognised as full species (Peterson *et al.* 1995)
Triaenops rufus	Not listed	DD	Recognised as full species (Peterson *et al.* 1995)
Rhinolophus beddomei	Not listed	LR: nt	Valid species (P.J.J. Bates *pers. comm.*)
Rhinolophus convexus	Not listed	CR: D	New species, type only
Rhinolophus ferrumequinum	LR: cd	LR: nt	Not conservation dependent
Rhinolophus marshalli	Not listed	LR: nt	P.J.J. Bates *pers. comm.*
Rhinolophus sinicus	Not listed	LR: lc	Thomas 1997
Lonchorhina inusitata	Not listed	DD	New species
Micronycteris brosseti	Not listed	DD	New species
Micronycteris sanborni	Not listed	DD	New species
Hylonycteris underwoodi	Not listed	LR: nt	H. Arita and D. Ortega *pers. comms.*
Leptonycteris curasoae	VU: A1cd	VU: A1c	Not exploited (K. Koopman *pers. comm.*)
Leptonycteris nivalis	EN: A1cd	EN: A1c	Not exploited (K. Koopman *pers. comm.*)
Artibeus hirsutus	VU: A2cd	VU: A2c	Not exploited (H. Arita, D. Ortega, and K. Koopman *pers. comms.*)
Artibeus inopinatus	LR: nt	VU: A2c	Arita and Ortega 1998
Ectophylla alba	Not listed	LR: nt	Arita and Ortega 1998
Pygoderma bilabiatum	Not listed	LR: nt	Brazil Workshop 1995
Stenoderma rufum	VU: A1cd	VU: A1c	K. Koopman *pers. comm.*
Vampyressa brocki	VU: D2	LR: nt	Extensive distribution in northern South America (K. Koopman *pers. comm.*)
Kerivoula eriophora	VU: D2	Removed	Synonym of *K. lanosa* (D. Kock *pers. comm.*)
Arielulus aureocollaris	Not listed	DD	New species
Arielulus torquatus	Not listed	DD	New species
Chalinolobus tuberculatus	LR: nt	VU: A2bc	Evidence of recent significant declines (C. O'Donnell *pers. comm.*)
Eptesicus bobrinskoi	LR: nt	LR: lc	V. Iljin *pers. comm.*
Eptesicus matroka	Not listed	DD	Recognised as full species (Peterson *et al.* 1995)
Eptesicus zuluensis	Not listed	LR: nt	Recognised as full species (I. Aggundey *pers. comm.*)
Glischropus javanus	LR: nt	EN B1 + 2d	L. Lumsden *pers. comm.*
Histiotus humboldti	Not listed	DD	New species
Histiotus velatus	LR: nt	LR: lc	Brazil Workshop, 1995
Lasiurus atratus	Not listed	DD	New species
Myotis csorbai	Not listed	DD	New species
Myotis elegans	Not listed	LR: nt	Arita and Ortega 1998
Myotis fimbriatus	DD	LR: nt	Corbet and Hill 1992, Ades 1993
Myotis gomatongensis	Not listed	DD	New species
Myotis hosonoi	LR: nt	VU: A2c, B1 + 2c	Yoshiyuki 1989
Myotis longipes	DD	VU: B1+2c, D2	Few large colonies in only nine localities (P.J.J. Bates *pers. comm.*)
Myotis macrodactylus	LR: nt	LR: lc	Yoshiyuki 1989
Myotis milleri	EX	EN: A2c	Not extinct (Arita and Ortega 1998, K. Koopman *pers. comm.*)
Myotis ozensis	DD	EN: A2c, B1 + 2c	Yoshiyuki 1989
Myotis peninsularis	VU: A1cd	VU: A1c	Not exploited (K. Koopman *pers. comm.*)
Myotis planiceps	EX	CR: B1 + 2c	Not extinct (Arita and Ortega 1998, K. Koopman *pers. comm.*)
Myotis schaubi	DD	EN: B1 + 2c, C2a, D	This is a valid species – I. Horacek, J. Gaisler, and A.M. Hutson *pers. comms.*

Taxon	Status 1996 Red List	New Status	Citation
Myotis yanbarensis	Not listed	DD	New species
Nyctalus azoreum	VU: A2c, B1 + 2c, D2	VU: A2c, B1 + 2c	J. Palmeirim *pers. comm.*
Pipistrellus ariel	LR: nt	VU: D2	B. Shalmon *pers. comm.*
Pipistrellus endoi	DD	EN: B1 + 2c	After consultation with Japanese colleagues
Pipistrellus sturdeei	DD	EX	After consultation with Japanese colleagues
Rhogeessa genowaysi	LR: nt	VU: A2c, D2	Arita and Ortega 1998
Rhogeessa mira	LR: nt	EN: A2c, B1 +2cd	Arita and Ortega 1998
Vespertilio orientalis	VU: A2c, D2	Removed	Synonym of *V. superans* (E. Kozhurina *pers. comm.*)
Murina ryukyuana	Not listed	DD	New species
Murina tenebrosa	DD	CR: B1 + 2c, D	Yoshiyuki 1989
Miniopterus gleni	Not listed	LR: nt	Recognised as full species (P.J.J. Bates *pers. comm.*)
Miniopterus majori	Not listed	DD	Recognised as full species (Peterson *et al.* 1995)
Miniopterus manavi	Not listed	DD	Recognised as full species (Peterson *et al.* 1995)
Chaerephon leucogster	Not listed	DD	Recognised as full species (Peterson *et al.* 1995)
Molossops neglectus	EN: B1 + 2c	LR: nt	Widely distributed in eastern South America (K. Koopman *pers. comm.*)
Mops leucostigma	Not listed	DD	Recognised as full species (Peterson *et al.* 1995)
Tadarida espiritosantensis	LR: nt	Removed	Synonym of *Nyctinomops laticaudatus* (Zortea and Taddei 1995)
Tadarida latouchei	Not listed	DD	Recognised as full species (D. Kock 1999)

References

Note: The following reference list includes not only those publications cited in this Plan but also other groups of publications considered to be of importance. References that are marked with an asterisk (*) are key works on bat taxonomy, biology and conservation and will provide the reader with a broad grounding in these issues. References marked with a cross (+) are individual species accounts published by the American Society of Mammalogists in their series *Mammalian Species*. Each of these accounts provides details of the biology and ecology of species and, in more recent accounts, conservation. This series is constantly expanding and as of mid-2000, there were over 140 accounts on bats, mostly microchiropterans. References marked with an 'R' are those that have been highlighted in the regional accounts as being of importance. They are also annotated with Af (for Afrotropical), As (Australasian), In (Indomalayan), Ne (Nearctic), No (Neotropical), and Pa (Palaearctic).

Abello-Fernandez, C. 1966. Intento de erradicacion de murcielagos hematophagos. *5th Cong. Panamer. Med. Vet. Zootec.*, 1966, Doc. 51.

Ablentsev, V.I. and Pidoplichko, I.G. 1956. [*Fauna of Ukraine, Volume 1, Part 1: Insectivores and bats*] Kiev. [in Ukrainian] (RPa)

Acha, P.N. 1986. Informacion epidemiologica sobre rabia bovina en Latinoamerica, anos 1983–1984, segun pais. Unpublished data.

Acha, P.N. and Arambulo III, P.V. 1985. Rabies in the tropics – history and current status. P. 343 *in: Rabies in the tropics* (eds. Kuwert, E., Merieux, C., Koprowski, H., and K. Bogel). Springer-Verlag, Heidelberg.

Acosta y Lara, E.F. 1950. Quirópteros del Uruguay. *Comunicaciones Zoologicas del Museo de Historia Natural de Montivideo*, 3 (58), 1–71. (RNo)

Adams, J.K. 1989. *Pteronotus davyi. Mammalian Species*, 346, 1–5. (+)

Ades, G. 1990. *The bats of Hong Kong.* WWF, Hong Kong.

Adygezalov, B.M. (ed.) 1989. *[Red data book of the Republic of Azerbaijan].* [in Russian]

Aellen, V. 1952. Contribution à l'étude des chiroptères du Cameroun. *Mémoires de la Société des Sciences Naturelles de Neuchâtel*, 8, 1–121. (RAf)

Aellen, V. 1970. Catalogue raisonné des chiroptères de la Colombie. *Revue Suisse de Zoologie*, 77 (1), 1–37. (RNo)

Aggundey, I.R. and Schlitter, D.A. 1985. Annotated checklist of the mammals of Kenya. I. Chiroptera. *Annals of the Carnegie Museum*, 53 (5), 119–158. (RAf)

Ahlen, I. and Gerell, R. 1989. Distribution and status of bats in Sweden. Pp. 319–325 *in: European bat research 1987* (eds. Hanak, V., Horacek, I., and J. Gaisler). Charles University Press, Prague.

Albuja V.L. 1982. *Murciélagos de Ecuador.* Escuela Politechnica Nacional, Quito. (RNo)

Albuja, V.L. 1999. *Murciélagos del Ecuador.* Escuela Politechnica Nacional, Quito. (RNo)

Allen, G.M. 1938–40. *The mammals of China and Mongolia.* Natural History of Central Asia (ed. W. Granger). Central Asiatic Expeditions of the American Museum of Natural History, New York. (RPa)

Allen, G.M. 1939a. A checklist of African mammals. *Bulletin of the Museum of Comparative Zoology, Harvard College*, 83, 1–763. (RAf)

Allen, G.M. 1939b. *Bats.* Harvard University Press, Cambridge, USA.

Allen, G.M. and Coolidge, H.J. 1930. Mammals of Liberia. *In: The African Republic of Liberia and the Belgian Congo. Based on observations made and material collected during the Harvard East African Expedition 1926–1927.* (ed. R.P. Strong). Harvard University Press, Cambridge, USA. (RAf)

Alonso-Mejia, A. and Medellin, R.A. 1991. *Micronycteris megalotis. Mammalian Species*, 376, 1–6. (+)

*Altringham, J.D. 1996. *Bats – biology and behaviour.* Oxford University Press, Oxford.

Alvarez, J., Willig, M.R., Knox Jones Jr., J., and Webster, W.D. 1991. *Glossophaga soricina. Mammalian Species*, 379, 1–7. (+)

Alvarez-Castaneda, S.T. and Bogan, M.A. 1997. *Myotis milleri. Mammalian Species*, 561, 1–3. (+)

Alvarez-Castaneda, S.T. and Bogan, M.A. 1998. *Myotis peninsularis. Mammalian Species*, 573, 1–2. (+)

Anderson, S. 1969. *Macrotus waterhousii. Mammalian Species*, 1, 1–4. (+)

Anderson, S. 1997. Mammals of Bolivia, taxonomy and distribution. *Bulletin of the American Museum of Natural History*, 231, 1-652. (RNo)

Anderson, S., Koopman, K.F., and Creighton, G.K. 1982. Bats of Bolivia: An annotated checklist. *American Museum Novitates*, 2750, 1–24. (RNo)

Andrusaitis, G., 1985. (ed.) *Red data book of the Latvian SSR.* Zinatne Publishing House, Riga [in Latvian].

Anon. 1988. *Rote listen der gefahrdeten vogel und saugetiere Osterreichs.* Naturhistoriches Museum Wien, Vienna.

Anon. 1991a. *Red data book of Japan.* Two volumes: Vertebrates and invertebrates. Japanese Wildlife Research Centre.

Anon. 1991b. *Draft red list of threatened animals of Turkey*. Prime Ministry Undersecretariat for Environment. Unpublished.

Anon. 1998. Doñana in trouble. *Oryx*, 32(3), 179.

Ansell, W.F.H. 1960. *Mammals of Northern Rhodesia.* Lusaka, Northern Rhodesia. (RAf)

Ansell, W.F.H. 1978. *The mammals of Zambia.* National Parks and Wildlife Service, Chilanga, Zambia.(RAf)

Ansell, W.F.H. and Dowsett, R.J. 1988. *The mammals of Malawi.* The Trendrine Press, Trendrine, UK. (RAf)

Anthony, E.L.P. and Kunz, T.H. 1977. Feeding strategies of the little brown bat, *Myotis lucifugus*, in southern New Hampshire. *Ecology*, 58, 755–786.

Arellano-Sota, C. 1988. Vampire bat-transmitted rabies in cattle. *Rev. Infect. Dis.*, 10(Suppl. 4), S707.

Arita, H.T. and Ceballos, G. 1995. *The mammals of Mexico, distribution and conservation status.* Asociación Mexicana Mastozoología, México City. (RNe) (RNo)

Arita, H.T. and Ortega, J. 1998. The Middle American bat fauna: conservation in the Neotropical-Nearctic border. Pp. 295–308 *in: Bat biology and conservation* (eds Kunz, T.H. and P.A. Racey), Smithsonian Institution Press, Washington DC. (RNe) (RNo)

Arita, H.T. and Wilson, D.E. 1987. Long-nosed bats and agaves: the tequila connection. *Bats*, 5(4), 3–5.

Arroyo-Cabrales, J., Hollander, R.R., and Knox Jones Jr., J. 1987. *Choeronycteris mexicana. Mammalian Species*, 291, 1–5. (+)

Arroyo-Cabrales, J. and Knox Jones Jr., J. 1988a. *Balatiopteryx plicata. Mammalian Species*, 301, 1–4. (+)

Arroyo-Cabrales, J. and Knox Jones Jr., J. 1988b. *Balantiopteryx io* and *Balatiopteryx infusca. Mammalian Species*, 313, 1–3. (+)

Arroyo-Cabrales, J. and Owen, R.D. 1997. *Enchisthenes hartii. Mammalian Species*, 546, 1–4. (+)

Arroyo-Cabrales, J. and Polaco, O.J. 1997. *Rhogeessa mira. Mammalian Species*, 550, 1–2. (+)

Aulagnier, S. and Thevenot, M. 1986. *Catalogue des mammifères sauvages du Maroc.* Institut Scientifique Charia Ibn Batouta BP, Rabat, Morocco. (RPa)

Baeten, B., van Cakenberghe, V., and de Vree, F. 1984. An annotated inventory of a collection of bats from Rwanda. *Revue de Zoologie et de Botanique Africaines*, 98, 183–196. (RAf)

Baker, R.J., August, P.V., and Steuter, A.A. 1978. *Erophylla sezekeorni. Mammalian Species*, 115, 1–5. (+)

Baker, R.J. and Clark, C.L. 1987. *Uroderma bilobatum. Mammalian Species*, 279, 1–4. (+)

Baker, R.J. and Genoways, H.H. 1978. Zoogeography of Antillean bats. Pp. 53–97 *in:* Zoogeography of the Caribbean. *Special Publications. Academy of Natural Sciences of Philadelphia*, 13. (RNo)

Baker, R.J. and Knox Jones Jr., J. 1975. Additional records of bats from Nicaragua, with a revised checklist of chiroptera. *Occasional Papers. The Museum, Texas Tech University*, 32, 1–13. (RNo)

*Baker, R.J., Knox Jones Jr., J., and Carter, D.C. (eds) 1976. Biology of bats of the New World family Pyllostomatidae, part 1. *Special Publications. The Museum, Texas Tech University*, 10, 1–218. (RNo)

*Baker, R.J., Knox Jones Jr., J., and Carter, D.C. (eds.) 1977. Biology of bats of the New World family Pyllostomatidae, part 2. *Special Publications. The Museum, Texas Tech University*, 13, 1–364. (RNo)

*Baker, R.J., Knox Jones Jr., J., and Carter, D.C. (eds.) 1979. Biology of bats of the New World family Pyllostomatidae, part 3. *Special Publications. The Museum, Texas Tech University*, 16, 1–441.(RNo)

Banfield, A.W.F. 1974. *The mammals of Canada.* The University of Toronto Press, Toronto. (RNe)

Barbour, M.G. and Christensen, N.L. 1993. Vegetation. Pp. 97–131 *in: Flora of North America north of Mexico. Vol. 1. Introduction* (eds. Flora of North America Editorial Committee). Oxford University Press, New York.

Barbour, R.W. and Davis, W.H. 1969. *Bats of America.* University Press of Kentucky, Lexington,. (RNe)

Barclay, R.M.R. and Brigham, R.M. (eds.) 1996. *Bats and forests symposium, October 19–21, 1995, Victoria, British Columbia, Canada.* Working Paper 23/1996, Research Branch, BC Ministry of Forests, Victoria.

Barlow, K. 1999. *Expedition Field Techniques – Bats.* Expedition Advisory Centre (Royal Geographical Society), London. 69 pp.

Barnett, A.A. and Prangley, M.L. 1997. Mammalogy in the Republic of Guinea: an overview of research from 1946 to 1996, a preliminary check-list and a summary of research recommendations for the future. *Mammal Review*, 27 (3), 115–164. (RAf)

Barratt, E.M., Deaville, R., Burland, T.M., Bruford, M.W, Jones, G., Racey, P.A., and Wayne, R.K. 1997. DNA answers the call of pipistrelle bat species. *Nature*, 387, 138–139.

Bárquez, R.M. 1987. *Los murciélagos de Argentina.* PhD thesis, Facultad de Ciencias Naturales e Instituto Miguel Lillo, Universidad Nacional de Tucumán, Argentina. (RNo)

Bárquez, R.M., Giannini, N.P., and Mares, M.A. 1993. *Guide to bats of Argentina.* Oklahoma Museum of Natural History, University of Oklahoma, USA. (RNo)

Bárquez, R.M., Mares, M.A., and Braun, J.K. 1999. The bats of Argentina. *Special Publications. Museum. Texas Tech University*, 42, 1–275. (RNo)

Baruš, V. (ed.) 1989. *Red data book for Czechoslovakia SSR. Vol. 2. Vertebrates.* Stani Zemedelske Nakladatelsvi, Prague.

Bate, D. 1905. On the mammals of Crete. *Proceedings of the Zoological Society of London*, 1905 (2), 315–323. (RPa)

Bates, P.J.J. and Harrison, D. 1997 *Bats of the Indian Subcontinent.* Harrison Zoological Museum, Sevenoaks, UK. (RIn)

Bates, P.J.J., Harrison, D.L., Jenkins, P.D., and Walston, J.L. 1997. Three rare species of *Pipistrellus* (Chiroptera: Vespertilionidae) new to Vietnam. *Acta Zoologica Academiae Scientiarum Hungaricae*, 43(4), 359–374.

Bates, P.J.J., Nwe, T., Pearch, M.J., Swe, K.M., Hla Bu, S.S., and Tun, T. 2000. A review of bat research in Myanmar (Burma) and results of a recent survey. *Acta Chiropterologica*, 2(1), 53–82. (RIn).

Bauer, K. 1992. *Laephotis botswanae* – a bat new for Tanzania. Pp. 13–15 *in: Prague studies in mammalogy* (eds. Horacek, I. and V. Vohralik). Charles University Press, Prague.

Bayliss, J. and Hayes, B. 1999. *The status and distribution of bats, primates and butterflies from the Makira Plateau, Madagascar.* Unpublished report to Fauna & Flora International, Cambridge, UK.

de Beer, J.H. and McDermott, M.J. 1989. *The economic value of non-timber forest products in Southeast Asia.* Netherlands Committee for IUCN, Amsterdam.

Bell, B.D. 1986. *The conservation status of New Zealand wildlife.* New Zealand Wildlife Service, Department of Internal Affairs, Wellington.

Benda, P. and Horacek, I. 1998. Bats (Mammalia: Chiroptera) of the Eastern Mediterranean. Part 1. Review of distribution and taxonomy of bats in Turkey. *Acta Societatis Zoologicae Bohemoslovenicae*, 62, 255–313. (RPa)

Benzal, J. and De Paz, O. 1991. *Los murcielagos de España y Portugal.* ICONA, Spain. (RPa)

Bennett, A.F., Lumsden, L.F., and Nicholls, A.O. 1994. Tree hollows as a resource for wildlife in remnant woodlands: Spatial and temporal patterns across the northern plains of Victoria. *Pacific Conservation Biology*, 1, 222–235.

Bergmans, W. 1988. Taxonomy and biogeography of African fruit bats (Mammalia, Megachiroptera). 1. General introduction; material and methods; results: The genus *Epomophorus* Bennett, 1836. *Beaufortia*, 38(5), 75–146.

Bergmans, W. 1989. Taxonomy and biogeography of African fruit bats (Mammalia, Megachiroptera). 2. The genera *Micropteropus* Matschie, 1899, *Epomops* Gray, 1870, *Hypsignathus* H. Allen, 1861, *Nanonycteris* Matschie, 1899, and *Plerotes* Andersen, 1910. *Beaufortia*, 39(4), 89–153.

Bergmans, W. 1990. Taxonomy and biogeography of African fruit bats (Mammalia, Megachiroptera). 3. The genera *Scotonycteris* Matschie, 1894, *Casinycteris* Thomas, 1910, *Pteropus* Brisson, 1762, and *Eidolon* Rafinesque, 1815. *Beaufortia*, 40 (7), 111–177.

Bergmans, W. 1994. Taxonomy and biogeography of African fruit bats (Mammalia, Megachiroptera). 4. The genus *Rousettus* Gray, 1821. *Beaufortia*, 44(4), 79–126.

Bergmans, W. 1997. Taxonomy and biogeography of African fruit bats (Mammalia, Megachiroptera). 5. The genera *Lissonycteris* Andersen, 1912, *Myonycteris* Matschie, 1899 and *Megaloglossus* Pagenstecher, 1885; general remarks and conclusions; Annex: Key to all species. *Beaufortia*, 47(2), 11–90.

Best, T.L. and Jennings, J.B. 1997. *Myotis leibii. Mammalian Species*, 547, 1–6. (+)

Best, T.L., Kiser, W.M., and Freeman, P.W. 1996. *Eumops perotis. Mammalian Species*, 534, 1–8. (+)

Best, T.L., Kiser, W.M., and Rainey, J.C. 1997. *Eumops glaucinus. Mammalian Species*, 551, 1–6. (+)

Billington, G. and Norman, G. 1997. *The conservation of bats in bridges project. A report on the survey and conservation of bat roosts in Cumbria, England.* Lake District National Park, Cumbria, UK.

Black, H.L. 1974. A north temperate bat community: Structure and prey populations. *Journal of Mammalogy*, 55, 138–157.

Blanco, J.C. and González, J.L. (eds.) 1992. *Libro rojo de los vertebrados de España.* Ministerio de Agricultura Pesca y Alimentacion (ICONA), Madrid.

Blood, B.R. and Clark, M.K. 1998. *Myotis vivesi. Mammalian Species*, 588, pp 1–5. (+)

Bolkay, S.J. 1926. Additions to the mammalian fauna of the Balkan peninsula. *Glasnik Zemaljskog Museja u Bosni i Hercegovini*, 38, 159–179. (RPa)

Bogdanowicz, W. 1994. *Myotis daubentonii. Mammalian Species*, 475, pp 1–9. (+)

Bonaccorso, F. 1998. *Bats of Papua New Guinea.* Conservation International, Washington DC. (RAs)

Borg, J.J., Violani, C., and Zava, B. 1997. The bat fauna of the Maltese Islands. *Myotis*, 35, 49–65.

Bouchard, S. 1998. *Chaerephon pumilis. Mammalian Species*, 574, 1–6. (+)

Boulay, M.C. and Robbins, C.B. 1989. *Epomophorus gambianus. Mammalian Species*, 344, 1–5. (+)

Bowen-Jones E., Abrutat, D., Markham, B., and Bowe, S. 1997. Flying foxes on Choiseul (Solomon Islands) – the need for conservation action. *Oryx*, 31(3), 209–217.

Boye, P., Pott-Dorfer, B., Dorfer, K., and Demetropoulos A. 1990. New records of bats (Chiroptera) from Cyprus and notes on their biology. *Myotis*, 28, 93–100. (RPa)

Bradshaw, P.A. 1996. The physical nature of vertical forest habitat and its importance in shaping bat species assemblages. Pp 199–212 *in: Bats and forests symposium, October 19–21, 1995, Victoria, British Columbia, Canada* (eds R.M.R. Barclay and R.M. Brigham). Working Paper 23/1996, Research Branch, BC Ministry of Forests, Victoria.

Brass, D.A. 1994. *Rabies in bats, natural history, and public health implications.* Livia Press, Connecticut.

Brenner, F.J. 1968. A three-year study of two breeding colonies of the big brown bat, *Eptesicus fuscus*. *Journal of Mammalogy*, 49, 775–778.

Breuil, M. and Masson, D. 1991. Quelques remarques sur la biogeographie des chauves-souris des Petites Antilles. *Compte Rendu de la Société de Biogéographie. Paris*, 67(1), 25–39.

Brosset, A. 1962a. The bats of central and western India. Part 1. *Journal of the Bombay Natural History Society*, 59, 1–57. (RIn)

Brosset, A. 1962b. The bats of central and western India. Part 2. *Journal of the Bombay Natural History Society*, 59, 583–642. (RIn)

Brosset, A. 1962c. The bats of central and western India. Part 3. *Journal of the Bombay Natural History Society*, 59, 706–746. (RIn)

Brosset, A. 1963. The bats of central and western India. Part 4. *Journal of the Bombay Natural History Society*, 60, 337–355. (RIn)

*Brosset, A. 1966. *La biologie des chiroptères.* Masson et Cie, Paris.

Brosset, A. and Charles-Dominique, P. 1990. The bats from French Guiana: A taxonomic, faunistic and ecological approach. *Mammalia,* 54 (4), 509–560. (RNo)

Brosset, A. and Dubost, G. 1967. Chiroptères de la Guyane française. *Mammalia*, 31 (4), 583–594. (RNo)

Brown Jr. , K.S. and Brown G.G., 1992. Habitat alteration and species loss in Brazilian forests. Pp. 119–142 *in: Tropical deforestation and species extinction* (eds. T.C. Whitmore and J.A. Sayer). Chapman and Hall, London.

Brown, K.M. and Dunlop, J. 1997. *Rhinolophus landeri. Mammalian Species*, 567, 1–4. (+)

Bulgarska Akadamija na Naukite 1985. *Red data book of the People's Republic of Bulgaria.* Izd.vo na Bulgarskata na Naukite, Bulgaria.

Burt, W.H. and Stirton, R.A. 1961. The mammals of El Salvador. *Miscellaneous Publications. Museum of Zoology, University of Michigan*, 117, 1–69. (RNo)

Busby, D.G., White, L.M., and Pearce, P.A. 1990. Effects of aerial spraying of Fenitrothion on breeding white-throated sparrows. *Journal of Applied Ecology*, 27, 743–755.

Cabrera, A. 1929. Catalogo descriptivo de los mammiferos de la Guinea Espanola. *Memorias de la Real Sociedad Espãnola de Historia Natural*, 16, 1–121. (RAf)

Cabrera, A. 1958. *Catálogo de los mammíferos de América del Sur,* Vol. 1. Museo Argentino de Ciencias Naturales Bernardino Rivadavia, Zoología, Buenos Aries. (RNo)

Cansdale, G.S. 1948. *Provisional checklist of Gold Coast Mammals.* Government Printing Department, Accra, Gold Coast. (RAf)

Ceballos, G. and Medellin, R.A. 1988. *Diclidurus albus. Mammalian Species*, 316, 1–4. (+)

Cervantes, F.A., Castro-C, A., and Ramírez-Pulido, J. 1994. Mamíferos terrestres nativos de México. *Anales del Instituto de Biología, Universidad Nacional Autónoma de México Serie Zoología*, 65, 177–190. (RNe) (RNo)

Chasen, F.N. 1940. A handlist of Malaysian mammals. *Bulletin of the Raffles Museum*, 15, 1–209. (RIn)

Cheke, A.S. and Dahl, J.F. 1981. The status of bats on Western Indian Ocean islands, with special reference to *Pteropus. Mammalia*, 45, 205–238. (RAf)

Churchill, S. 1998. *Australian bats.* New Holland Publishers, Sydney. (RAs)

Clark, D.R. Jr. 1981. Bats and environmental contaminants: A review. *US Fish and Wildlife Service, Special Scientific Report*, 235, 1–27.

Clark, D.R. Jr. 1988. Environmental contaminants and the management of bat populations in the United States. Pp. 409–413 *in: Management of amphibians, reptiles and small mammals in North America. Proceedings of the symposium* (eds. R.C. Szaro *et al.*). General Technical Report, RM-166. US Forest Service, Fort Collins.

Clark, D.R., Jr. and Hothem, R.L. 1991. Mammal mortality at Arizona, California, and Nevada gold mines using cyanide extraction. *California Fish and Game*, 77, 61–69.

Clark, D.R., Jr., LaVal, R.K., and Krynitsky, A.J. 1980. Dieldrin and heptachlor residues in dead gray bats, Franklin County, Missouri – 1976 versus 1977. *Pesticide Monitoring Journal*, 13, 137–140.

Clark, D.R., Jr., LaVal, R.K and Swinford, D.N. 1978. Dieldrin-induced mortality in an endangered species, the gray bat (*Myotis grisescens*). *Science*, 199, 1359–1367.

Clawson, R.L. and Clark, Jr., D.R. 1989. Pesticide contamination of endangered gray bats and their food base in Boone County, Missouri, 1982. *Bulletin of Environmental Contamination and Toxicology,* 42, 431–437.

Cloutier, D. and Thomas, D.W. 1992. *Carollia perspicillata. Mammalian Species*, 417, 1–9. (+)

Cockrum, E.L. 1955. Reproduction in North American bats. *Transactions of the Kansas Academy of Sciences,* 58, 487–511.

Cockrum, E.L. 1969. Insecticides and Arizona bat populations – Editorial. *Journal of the Arizona Academy of Sciences*, 5(4), 1.

Cockrum, E.L. 1970. Insecticides and guano bats. *Ecology*, 51, 761–762.

Collins, N.M, Sayer, J.A., and Whitmore, T.C. (eds.) 1991. *The conservation atlas of tropical forests. Asia and the Pacific.* IUCN. Macmillan Press, London.

Conservation International 1990. *The rainforest imperative. A ten-year strategy to save earth's most threatened ecosystems.* Conservation International, Washington DC.

Corbet, G.B. 1970. Vagrant bats in Shetland and the North Sea. *Journal of Zoology*, 161, 281–282.

Corbet, G.B. 1971. Provisional distribution maps of British mammals. *Mammal Review*, 1, 95–142.

Corbet, G.B. 1978. *The mammals of the Palaearctic Region: A taxonomic review*. British Museum (Natural History), London and Cornell University Press, Ithaca, USA. (RPa)

Corbet, G.B. and Harris, S. (eds.) 1990. *The handbook of British mammals*, 3rd edition. Blackwell Science, Oxford. (RPa)

Corbet, G.B. and Hill, J. Edwards 1991. *A world list of mammalian species*. Third Edition. Oxford University Press, Oxford.

Corbet, G.B. and Hill, J. Edwards 1992. *The mammals of the Indomalayan Region: A systematic review*. Oxford University Press, Oxford. (RIn)

Cowan, I. McT. and Guiguet, C.J. 1965. *The mammals of British Columbia*, 3rd edition. Handbook Number 11, British Columbia Provincial Museum, Canada. (RNe)

Crampton, L.H. and Barclay, R.M.R. 1996. Habitat selection by bats in fragmented and unfragmented aspen mixedwood stands of different ages. Pp. 238–259 *in: Bats and forests symposium, October 19–21, 1995, Victoria, British Columbia, Canada* (eds. R.M.R. Barclay and R.M. Brigham). Working Paper 23/1996, Research Branch, BC Ministry of Forests, Victoria.

Crick, H.Q.P. 1986. Effects of Fenitrothion applications to control pine beauty moth on non-target animals in Scotland. Pp. 101–107 *in: Trees and wildlife in the Scottish Uplands* (ed. Jenkins, D.). ITE Symposium 17, Natural Environment Research Council, Institute of Terrestrial Ecology, Banchory, UK.

Crome, F.H.J., Moore, L.A., and Richards, G.C. 1991. A study of logging damage in upland rainforest in north Queensland. *Forest Ecology and Management*, 49, 1–29.

Crome, F.H.J. and Richards, G.C. 1988. Bats and gaps: Microchiropteran community structure in a Queensland rain forest. *Ecology*, 69, 1960–1969.

Csada, R. 1996. *Cardioderma cor*. *Mammalian Species*, 519, 1–4. (+)

Csorba, G., Kruskop, S.V., and Borissenko, A.V. 1999. Recent records of bats (Chiroptera) from Nepal, with remarks on their natural history. *Mammalia*, 63, 61–78. (RIn)

Cuervo, A., Hernández-Camacho, J., and Cadena, A. 1986. Lista actualizada de los mamíferos de Colombia. Anotaciones sobre su distribución. *Caldasia*, 25, 471–501. (RNo)

Cumming, D.H.M. 1991. Wildlife products and the market place: a view from southern Africa. Pp. 11–25 in: *Wildlife production: conservation and sustainable development* (eds. L.A. Renecker and R.J. Hudson). AFES Miscellaneous Publications 91–96. University of Alaska, Fairbanks.

Czaplewski, N.J. 1983. *Idionycteris phyllotis*. *Mammalian Species*, 208, 1–4. (+)

Dalton, V.M., Brack Jr., V., and McTeer, P.M. 1986. Food habits of the big-eared bat, *Plecotus townsendii virginianus*, in Virginia. *Virginia Journal of Science*, 37, 248–254.

Dang Huy Huynh (ed.) 1994. [*Checklist of mammals of Vietnam*]. Vietnam Centre for Natural Science and Technology, Institute of Ecology and Biological Resources, Science and Technics Publishing House, Hanoi. [in Vietnamese]. (RIn)

Daniel, M.J. 1976. Feeding by the short-tailed bat (*Mystacina tuberculata*) on fruit and possibly nectar. *New Zealand Journal of Zoology*, 3, 391–398.

Daniel, M.J. 1990. Bats: order Chiroptera. Pp. 114–137 *in: The handbook of New Zealand mammals*, (ed. C.M. King). Oxford University Press, Auckland.

Daniel, M.J. and Williams, G.R. 1984. A survey of the distribution, seasonal activity and roost sites of New Zealand bats. *New Zealand Journal of Ecology*, 7, 9–25.

Darafeei, M., Sushchenya, L.M., and Parafenai, V.I. (eds.) 1993. *[Red data book of the Republic of Belarus]*. Belaruskaya Entsyklapedia im. Petrus Broik, Minsk. [in Russian].

Davis, D.D. 1962. Mammals of the lowland rain-forests of North Borneo. *Bulletin of the National Museum, State of Singapore*, 31, 5–129. (RIn)

De Beaux, O. 1924. Mammiferi della Somalia Italiana. *Atti della Societá Ligustica di Scienze Naturali e Geograpfiche*, 1, 149–168. (RAf)

DeBlase, A.F. 1980. The bats of Iran: Systematics, distribution, ecology. *Fieldiana: Zoology, New Series*, 4, 1–424. (RIn)

Decher, J. and Choate, J.R. 1995. *Myotis grisescens*. 510, 1–7.

Dekeyser, P.L. 1955. *Les mammifères de l'Afrique Française*. Dakar, Senegal. (RAf)

Delpietro, H.A., Marchevsky, N., and Simonetti, E. 1992. Relative population densities and predation of the common vampire bat (*Desmodus rotundus*) in natural and cattle-raising areas in north-east Argentina. *Prev. Vet. Med.*, 14, 13–20.

Dengis, C.A. 1996. *Taphozous mauritianus*. *Mammalian Species*, 522, 1–5. (+)

Dias, B.F. de S., 1990. Conservação da natureza no cerrado brasiliero. Pp. 583–640 *in: Cerrado: Caracterização ocupação e perspectivas* (ed. M. Novaes Pinto). Editora Universidade de Brasília, Brasília.

Direktoratet for naturforvaltning 1999. Nasjonal rødkiste for teuete arter i Norge 1998. [Norweigan red list 1998]. *DN-rapport*, 1999–3, 1–161. Direktoratet for naturforvaltning, Trondheim. [In Norweigan].

Dinerstein, E., Olson, D.M., Graham, D.J., Webster, A.L., Primm, S.A., Bookbinder, M.P., and Ledec, G. 1995. *A conservation assessment of the terrestrial ecoregions of Latin America and the Caribbean*. World Bank, Washington DC.

*Dobat, K. and Peikert-Holle, T. 1985. *Blüten und Fledermäuse; Bestäubung durch Fledermäuse und Flughunde.* Waldemar Kramer, Frankfurt am Main.

Dobrosi, D. 1995. *A handbook for the conservation of bats in Hungary.* Hungarian Bat Research Society. (RPa)

*Dobson, G.E. 1878. *Catalogue of the chiroptera in the collection of the British Museum.* British Museum, London.

Dowsett, R.J. and Granjon, L. 1991. Liste préliminaire des mammifères du Congo. *Tauraco Research Report*, 4, 297–310. (RAf)

Draganovic, E. 1994. *Red data book of mammals of the Republic of Croatia.* Department of Nature Protection, Zagreb.

Duelli, P. (ed.) 1994. *Rote Listen der gefährdeten Tierarten in der Schweiz.* Bundesamt für Umwelt, Wald und Landschaft (BUWAL), Bern.

Dulic, B. 1989. Bats in the Red Data List of Croatia (Yugoslavia). Pp 389–392 *in: European bat research 1987* (eds. Hanak, V., Horacek, I., and J. Gaisler). Charles University Press, Prague.

Duncan, A., Baker, G.B., and Montgomery, N. (eds.) 1999. *The action plan for Australian bats.* Environment Australia, Canberra. (RAs)

Dunlop, J. 1997. *Coleura afra. Mammalian Species*, 566, 1–4. (+)

Dunlop, J. 1999. *Mops midas. Mammalian Species*, 615, 1–4. (+)

Duvergé, P.L. and Jones, G. 1994. Greater horseshoe bats – activity, foraging behaviour and habitat use. *British Wildlife,* 6, 69–77.

Dwyer, P.D. 1964. Fox predation on cave bats. *Australian Journal of Science*, 26, 397.

Dwyer, P.D. 1969. Population ranges of *Miniopterus schreibersii* (Chiroptera) in south-eastern Australia. *Australian Journal of Zoology*, 17, 665–686.

Eisenberg, J.F. 1989. *Mammals of the Neotropics. Volume 1. The northern Neotropics.* University of Chicago Press, Chicago and London. (RNo)

Eisenberg, J.F. and Redford, K.H. 1999. *Mammals of the Neotropics; the Central Neotropics. Vol. 3. Ecuador, Peru, Bolivia, Brazil.* University of Chicago Press, Chicago/London. 609 pp. (RNo)

Eisentraut, M. 1964. La faune de chiroptères de Fernando-Po. *Mammalia*, 28, 529–552. (RAf)

Ellerman, J.R. and Morrison-Scott, T.C.S. 1966. *Checklist of Palaearctic and Indian mammals 1758–1946,* 2nd edition. British Museum (Natural History), London. (RIn) (RPa)

Ellerman, J.R., Morrison-Scott, T.C.S., and Hayman, R.W. 1953. *Southern African mammals 1758 to 1951: A reclassification.* British Museum (Natural History), London. (RAf)

Engstrom, M.D., Lee, T.E., and Wilson, D.E. 1987. *Bauerus dubiaquercus. Mammalian Species*, 282, 1–3. (+)

Entwistle, A.C., Harris, S., Hutson, A.M., Racey, P.A., and Walsh, A., Gibson, S., Hepburn, I., Johnson, J., Larkin, B., and Bennett, N. In press. *Habitat management for bats.* Joint Nature Conservation Committee, Peterborough, UK.

Entwistle, A.C., Racey, P.A., and Speakman, J.R. 1997. Roost selection by the brown long-eared bat (*Plecotus auritus*). *Journal of Applied Ecology,* 34, 399–408.

Ergueta, S.P. and de Morales, C. (eds.) 1996. *Libro rojo de los vertebrados de Bolivia.* Centro de datos para la conservacion, La Paz.

Europa Publications 1987. *The Far East and Australasia 1988.* 19th Edition, Europa, London.

Faegri, K. and Pijl, L. van der 1971. *The principles of pollination ecology.* Pergamon Press, Oxford.

Fairon, J., Busch, E., Petit, T., and Schuiten, M. 1996. Contribution à l'étude du problème de la cohabitation Effroies-Chiroptères. *Documents de Travail. Institut Royal des Sciences naturelles de Belgique*, 84, 1–37.

FAO 1988. *Second interim report on the state of tropical forests.* Report to the 10th World Forestry Congress, Paris, France. Forest Resources Assessment Project, FAO, Rome.

FAO 1991. *FAO Yearbook of Forest Products 1978–1989.* FAO Forestry Series No. 24 and FAO Statistics Series No. 97. FAO, Rome.

Fascione, N., Marceron, T., and Fenton, M.B. 1991. Evidence for mosquito consumption in *M. lucifugus. Bat Research News*, 32(1), 2–3.

Fayard, A. (coord.) 1994. *Atlas des mammifères sauvages de France.* Société Française pour l'Étude et la Protection des Mammifères, Paris.

Fearnside, P.M. 1990. The rate and extent of deforestation in Brazilian Amazonia. *Environmental Conservation*, 17(3), 213–226.

Fearnside, P.M., Tardin, A.T., and Meira, L.G.M. 1990. *Deforestation rate in Brazilian Amazonia.* National Secretariat of Science and Technology, Brasília.

Felten, H. 1956a. Fledermäuse (Mammalia:Chiroptera) aus El Salvador. Teil 3. *Senckenbergiana Biologica,* 37 (3/4), 179–212. (RNo)

Felten, H. 1956b. Fledermäuse (Mammalia:Chiroptera) aus El Salvador. Teil 4. *Senckenbergiana Biologica,* 37 (5/6), 341–370. (RNo)

Felten, H. (ed.) 1986. Contributions to the knowledge of the bats of Thailand. *Courier Forschungsinstitut Senckenberg*, 87, 1–112. (RIn)

Fenton, M.B. 1975. Observations on the biology of some Rhodesian bats, including a key to the Chiroptera of Rhodesia. *Life Sciences Contributions, Royal Ontario Museum*, 104, 1–27. (RAf)

Fenton, M.B. 1982. Echolocation, insect hearing, and feeding ecology of insectivorous bats. Pp. 261–285 *in: Ecology of bats* (ed. T.H. Kunz). Plenum, New York.

*Fenton, M.B. 1983. *Just bats.* University of Toronto Press, Toronto.

*Fenton, M.B. 1985. *Communication in the chiroptera.* University of Indiana Press, Bloomington.

Fenton, M.B. 1992. *Bats.* Facts on File, New York.

Fenton, M.B. 1997. Science and the conservation of bats. *Journal of Mammalogy*, 78, 1–14.

Fenton, M.B. and Barclay, R.M.R. 1980. *Myotis lucifugus. Mammalian Species*, 142, 1–8. (+)

*Fenton, M.B., Racey, P.A., and Rayner, J.M.V. 1987. *Recent advances in the study of bats.* Cambridge University Press, Cambridge.

Fenton, M.B. and Rautenbach, I.L. 1986. A comparison of the roosting and foraging behaviour of three species of African insectivorous bats. *Canadian Journal of Zoology*, 64, 2860–2867.

Fenton, M.B. and Rautenbach, I.L. 1998. Impacts of ignorance and human and elephant populations on the conservation of bats in African woodlands. Pp. 261–270 *in: Bat biology and conservation* (eds. T.H. Kunz and P.A. Racey). Smithsonian Institution Press, Washington DC. (RAf)

Fernández, J.J.C, Ojeda, R.A, Fraga, R.M, Díaz, G.B., and Baigun R.J. 1997 *Mamíferos y aves amenazados de la Argentina.* Fundación Para la Conservación de las Especies y el Medio, Buenos Aries.

Ferrell, C.S. and Wilson, D.E. 1991. *Platyrrhinus helleri. Mammalian Species*, 373, 1–5. (+)

*Findley, J.S. 1993. *Bats – a community perspective.* Cambridge University Press, Cambridge.

Fitch, J.H. and Shump Jr., K.A. 1979. *Myotis keenii. Mammalian Species*, 121, 1–3. (+)

Fitch, J.H., Shump Jr., K.A., and Shump, A.U. 1981. *Myotis velifer. Mammalian Species*, 149, 1–5. (+)

Flannery, T. 1990. *The mammals of New Guinea.* Robert Brown and Associates, Carina, Australia. (RAs)

Flannery, T. 1995a. *Mammals of New Guinea.* Revised and expanded edition. Reed Books, Chatswood, Australia. (RAs)

Flannery, T. 1995b. *Mammals of the south-west Pacific and Moluccan Islands.* Australian Museum and Reed Books, Chatswood, Australia. (RAs) (RIn)

Fleming, T.H. 1982. Foraging strategies of plant-visiting bats. In *Ecology of bats* (ed. T.H. Kunz), pp 287–326. Plenum, New York.

Fleming, T.H. 1988. *The short-tailed fruit bat. A study in plant-animal interaction.* University of Chicago Press, Chicago and London.

Fleming, T.H. 1989. Climb every cactus. *Bats*, 7(3), 3–6.

Fleming, T.H. 1991. Following the nectar trail. *Bats*, 9, 4–7.

Fleming, T.H. 1997. The long and the short of it – comparative ecology of two plant-visiting phyllostomid bats. *Bat Research News*, 38(2), 40.

Fleming, T.H., Nuñez, R.A., and Sternberg, L. 1993. Seasonal changes in the diets of migrant and non-migrant nectarivorous bats as revealed by carbon stable isotope analysis. *Oecologia*, 94, 72–75.

Flores-Crespo, R. and Arellano-Sota, C. 1991. Biology and control of the vampire bat. *In: The natural history of rabies* (ed. G.M. Baer), 2nd edition. CRC Press Inc., Boca Raton, USA.

da Fonseca, G.A.B., Costa, C.M.R., Machado, R.B., and Leite, Y.L.R. 1994. *Livro Vermelho dos mamíferos Brasilieros ameaçados de extinção.* Fundação Biodiversitas, Belo Horizonte, Brazil. (RNo)

da Fonseca, G.A.B., Costa, C.M.R., Machado, R.B., Leite, Y.L.R., and Furlani, C. (orgs) 1994. *Mamíferos Brasileiros: Uma coletânea bibliográfica.* Fundação Biodiversitas, Belo Horizonte, Brazil. (RNo)

da Fonseca, G.A.B., Herrmann, G., Leite, Y.L.R., Mittermeier, R.A., Rylands, A.B., and Patton, J.L. 1996. *Lista anotada dos mamíferos do Brasil.* Occasional Papers in Conservation Biology Number 4. Conservation International, Washington DC. (RNo)

Fornasari, L., Violani, C., and Zava, B. 1997. *I Chirotteri Italiani.* Mediterraneo Guide naturalistiche a cura di Silvano Riggeo No. 5. L'EPOS, Palermo. (RPa)

Francis, C.M., 1987. *The management of edible birds nest caves in Sabah.* Wildlife Section, Sabah Forestry Department, Malaysia.

Francis, C.M., Guillen, A., and Robinson, M.F. 1999. Order Chiroptera: Bats. Pp. 225–235 *in: Wildlife in Lao PDR. 1999 status report* (compilers Duckworth, J.W., Salter, R.E., and K. Khounboline). IUCN – The World Conservation Union, Wildlife Conservation Society and Centre for Protected Areas and Watershed Management, Lao PDR. (RIn)

Francis, C.M., Guillen, A., and Vonghamheng, C. 1997a. *Survey of bats and small mammals in Dong Amphan NBCA and nearby areas.* Unpublished report, Wildlife Conservation Society, New York. (RIn)

Francis, C.M., Guillen, A., and Vonghamheng, C. 1997b. *Preliminary survey of bats in Dong Hua Sao NBCA.* Unpublished report, Wildlife Conservation Society, New York. (RIn)

Francis, C.M., Khounboline, K., and Aspey, N. 1996. *Report on 1996 survey of bats and small mammals in the Nakai-Nam Theun NBCA and nearby areas.* Unpublished report, Wildlife Conservation Society, New York. (RIn)

Francis, C.M. and Vonghamheng, C. 1998. *Report on a survey of bats in Khammouane Limestone NBCA.* Unpublished report, Wildlife Conservation Society, New York. (RIn)

Fraser, G., Gleeson, L., and Hooper, P. 1996. *Lyssavirus* encephalitis in the black flying fox (*Pteropus alecto*). *Animal Health Survey Quarterly* 1(2), 4.

Fujita, M.S. and Kunz, T.H. 1984. *Pipistrellus subflavus. Mammalian Species*, 228, 1–6. (+)

Fujita, M.S. and Tuttle, M.D. 1991. Flying foxes (Chiroptera: Pteropodidae): Threatened animals of key economic importance. *Conservation Biology*, 5, 455–463.

Funaioli, G. and Simonetta, A.M. 1966. The mammalian fauna of the Somali Republic: Status and conservation problems. *Monitore Zoologico Italiano (Supplement)*, 74, 285–347. (RAf)

Gaisler, J. 1983–84. Bats of northern Algeria and their winter activity. *Myotis*, 21–22, 89–95.

Gaisler, J. and Kolibac, J.1992. Summer occurrence of bats in agrocoenoses. *Folia Zoologica*, 41, 19–27.

Gannon, M.R., Willig, M.R., and Knox Jones Jr., J. 1989. *Sturnira lilium. Mammalian Species*, 333, 1–5. (+)

Garbutt, N. 1999. *Mammals of Madagascar.* Pica Press, East Sussex. (RAf)

Gardner, A.L. 1977. Feeding habits. Pp. 293–350 *in: Biology of bats of the New World family Phyllostomatidae. Part II.* (eds. R.J. Baker, J. K. Jones Jr., and D.C. Carter). Special Publication No. 13. The Museum, Texas Tech University, Lubbock.

Gascoigne, A. 1995. *A lista vermelha de animais ameaçados São Tomé e Principe [The red data list of threatened animals of São Tomé e Principe].* ECOFAC.

Geluso, K.N., Altenbach, J.S., and Kerbo, R.C. 1987. *Bats of Carlsbad Caverns National Park.* Carlsbad Caverns Natural History Association, Carlsbad.

Genoways, H.H. and Baker, R.J. 1972. *Stenoderma rufum. Mammalian Species*, 18, 1–4. (+)

Gerlach, J. (ed.) 1997. *Seychelles red data book – 1997.* The Nature Protection Trust of Seychelles, Victoria, Mahé, Seychelles. (RAf)

Gharaibeh, B.M. and Qumsiyeh, M.B. 1995. *Otonycteris hemprichii. Mammalian Species*, 514, 1–4. (+)

Ghosh, A.K. (ed.) 1994. *The red data book of Indian animals. Part 1. Vertebrates. (Mammalia, Aves, Reptilia and Amphibia.* Zoological Survey of India, Calcutta.

Gillette, D.D. and Kimborough, J.D. 1970. Chiropteran mortality. Pp. 262–283 *in: About bats* (eds. B.H. Slaughter and D.W. Walton). Southern Methodist University Press, Dallas.

Glade, A.A. (ed.) 1993. *Red list of Chilean terrestrial vertebrates* (Second edition). Proceedings of the Symposium "Conservation Status of Chilean Terrestrial Vertebrate Fauna. Chilean Forest Service (CONAF), Santiago.

Glowacinski, Z. 1992. *Red List of Threatened Animals in Poland.* Nature Protection Research Centre of the Polish Academy of Sciences, Kracow.

Goldman, E.A. 1920. Mammals of Panama. *Smithsonian Miscellaneous Collections,* 69, 1–309. (RNo)

Goodwin, G.G. 1942. Mammals of Honduras. *Bulletin of the American Museum of Natural History,* 79, 107–195. (RNo)

Goodwin, G.G. 1946. Mammals of Costa Rica. *Bulletin of the American Museum of Natural History,* 87, 271–474. (RNo)

Goodwin, G.G. and Greenhall, A.M. 1961. A review of the bats of Trinidad and Tobago. *Bulletin of the American Museum of Natural History*, 122(3), 191–301. (RNo)

Gore, J.A. and Hovis, J.A. 1992. The southeastern bat: Another cave-roosting species in peril. *Bats*, 10, 10–12.

Gould, A.R., Hyatt, A.D., Lunt, R.A., Kattenbelt, J.A., Hengstberger, S., and Blacksell, S.D. 1998. A characterisation of a novel lyssavirus isolated from a pteropodid bat in Australia. *Virus Research* 54(2), 165–187.

Graetz, R.D., Fisher, R.P., and Wilson, M.A. 1992. *Looking back. The changing face of the Australian continent, 1972–1992.* CSIRO, Canberra.

Gray, P.A., Fenton, M.B., and van Cakenberghe, V. 1999. *Nycteris thebaica. Mammalian Species*, 612, 1–8. (+)

Green, H., Morrell, T., and Grantges, J.B. 1994. Roost sites used by forest dwelling bats. Regional Meeting of the Wildlife Society, February 4 1994, Sierra Vista, USA.

Green, G.M. and Sussman, R.W. 1990. Deforestation history of the eastern rain forests of Madagascar from satellite images. *Science*, 248, 212–215.

Greenhall, A.M. 1956. The food of some Trinidad fruit bats (*Artibeus* and *Carollia*). *Journal of the Agricultural Society of Trinidad and Tobago*, 869, 1–23.

Greenhall, A.M. 1959. Bats of Guiana. *Journal of the British Guiana Museum and Zoo*, 22, 55–57. (RNo)

Greenhall, A.M. 1963. Use of mist nets and strychnine for vampire control in Trinidad. *Journal of Mammalogy*, 44(3), 396–399.

Greenhall, A.M. 1965. Sapucaia nut dispersal by greater spear-nosed bats in Trinidad. *Caribbean Journal of Science*, 5, 167–171.

Greenhall, A.M. 1968a. Notes on the behavior of the false vampire bat. *Journal of Mammalogy*, 49, 337–340.

Greenhall, A.M. 1968b. Bats, rabies and control problems. *Oryx*, 9, 263–266.

Greenhall, A.M. 1970. Vampire bat control: A review and proposed programme for Latin America. Pp. 41–54 *in: Proceedings of the Fourth Vertebrate Pest Conference* (ed. R.H. Dana). California Vertebrate Pest Committee, West Sacramento, USA. March 3–5, 1970.

Greenhall, A.M. 1974. Vampire bat control in the Americas: A review an proposed program for action. *Bulletin of the Pan American Health Organisation*, 8(1), 30.

Greenhall, A.M. 1985. Effects of vampire bats and paralytic rabies on livestock production. P. 537 *in: Parasites, pests and predators* (eds. Gaafar, S.M., Howard, W.E., and R.E. Marsh). Elsevier Science Publishing Co., Inc., New York.

Greenhall, A.M., Joermann, G., and Schmidt, U. 1983. *Desmodus rotundus. Mammalian Species*, 202 ,1–6. (+)

Greenhall, A.M., Lord, R.D., and Massoia, E. 1983. *Key to the bats of Argentina.* Special Publication 5. Pan America Zoonoses Center, Buenos Aries. (RNo)

Greenhall, A.M. and Schmidt, U. (eds.) 1988. *Natural history of vampire bats.* CRC Press, Boca Raton, USA.

Greenhall, A.M., Schmidt, U., and Joermann, G. 1984. *Diphylla ecaudata. Mammalian Species*, 227, 1–3. (+)

Greenhall, A.M. and Schutt Jr., W.A. 1996. *Diaemus youngi. Mammalian Species*, 533, 1–7. (+)

*Griffin, D.R. 1958. *Listening in the dark: the acoustic orientation of bats and men.* Yale University Press, New Haven.

Gromov, I.M. and Baranova, G. 1981. [*Catalogue of mammals of the USSR: Pliocene to the present day*] Akademia Nauk SSSR, Leningrad. [in Russian]. (RPa)

Grubb, P., Jones, T.S., Davies, A.G., Edberg, E., Starin, A.D., and Hill, J.E. 1998. *Mammals of Ghana, Sierra Leone and The Gambia.* Trendrine Press, Zennor. (RAf)

Hall, E.R. 1981. *The mammals of North America.* J. Wiley and Sons, New York. (RNe)

Hall, L.S. and Richards, G.C. 1979. *The bats of eastern Australia.* Queensland Museum Booklet Number 12, Brisbane. (RAs)

Hanak, V., Benda, P., and Hanzal, V. 1995. Review of bat distribution in the Czech Republic. *Bulletin CESON*, 5, 3–15. (RPa)

*Hanak, V., Horacek, I., and Gaisler, J. 1989. *European bat research 1987.* Charles University Press, Prague.

Handley, Jr., C.O. 1966. Checklist of the mammals of Panama. Pp. 753–795 *in: Ectoparasites of Panama* (eds. R.L. Wenzel and V.J. Tipton). Field Museum of Natural History, Chicago. (RNo)

Happold, D.C.D. 1987. *The mammals of Nigeria.* Clarendon Press, Oxford. (RAf)

Happold, D.C.D, Happold, M., and Hill, J. Edwards, 1987. The bats of Malawi. *Mammalia*, 51 (3), 337–414. (RAf)

Harcourt, C.S. and Sayer, J.A. (eds.) 1996. *The conservation atlas of tropical forests. The Americas.* IUCN – The World Conservation Union. Simon and Schuster/ Macmillan, London and Basingstoke.

Harris, S., Morris, P., Wray, S., and Yalden, D. 1995. *A review of British mammals: Population estimates and conservation status of British mammals other than cetaceans.* Joint Nature Conservation Committee, Peterborough. (RPa)

Harrison, D.L. 1960. A checklist of the bats (Chiroptera) of Kenya Colony. *Journal of the East African Natural History Society and National Museum*, 23 (7), 286–295. (RAf)

Harrison, D.L. 1975. *Macrophyllum macrophyllum. Mammalian Species*, 62, 1–3. (+)

Harrison, D.L. and Bates, P.J.J. 1991. *The mammals of Arabia,* 2nd edition. Harrison Zoological Museum, Sevenoaks. (RPa)

Harvey, M.J. 1980. Status of the endangered bats, *Myotis sodalis, M. grisescens* and *Plecotus townsendii ingens*, in the southern Ozarks.) Pp. 221–223 *in: Proceedings of Fifth International Bat Research Conference* (eds. D.E. Wilson and A.L. Gardner. Texas Tech Press, Lubbock, USA.

Harvey, M.J. 1992. *Bats of the eastern United States.* Arkansas Game and Fish Commission, USA. (RNe)

Hayes, J.P., and Adam, M.D. 1996. The influence of logging riparian areas on habitat utilization by bats in western Oregon. Pp. 228–237 *in: Bats and forests symposium, October 19–21, 1995, Victoria, British Columbia, Canada* (eds. R.M.R. Barclay and R.M. Brigham). Working Paper 23/1996, Research Branch, BC Ministry of Forests, Victoria.

Hayman, R.W. 1967. *Preliminary identification manual for African mammals. 2. Chiroptera.* U.S. National Museum, Washington DC. (RAf)

Hayman, R.W. and Hill, J. Edwards 1971. Order Chiroptera. Pp. 1–73 *in: The mammals of Africa. An identification manual. Part 2.* (eds. J. Meester and H.W. Setzer). Smithsonian Institution Press, Washington DC. (RAf)

Hayman, R.W., Misonne, X., and Verheyen, W. 1966. The bats of the Congo and of Rwanda and Burundi. *Annales Musée Royal de l'Afrique Centrale*, 154, 1–105. (RAf)

Heaney, L.R. 1993 Biodiversity patterns and the conservation of mammals in the Philippines. *Asia Life Sciences,* 2 (2), 261–274.

Heaney, L.R., Gonzales, P.C., and Alcala, A.C. 1987. An annotated checklist of the taxonomic and conservation status of land mammals in the Philippines. *Siliman Journal*, 34, 32–66.

van Heijnsbergen, P. 1997. *International legal protection of wild fauna and flora.* IOS Press, Amsterdam.

Heller, K-G. and Volleth, M. 1989. Fledermäuse aus Malaysia. 1. Beobachtungen zur Biologie, Morphologie und Taxonomie. *Senckenbergiana Biologica*, 69 (4/6), 243–276. (RIn)

Hensley, A.P. and Wilkins, K.T. 1988. *Leptoycteris nivalis. Mammalian Species*, 307, 1–4. (+)

Hensley, D. 1992. The James River bat cave. *Bats*, 10(2), 17.

Hensley, S. and Scott, C. 1995. *Ozark big-eared bat,* Plecotus townsendii ingens *(Handley), revised recovery plan.* U.S. Fish and Wildlife Service, Region 2, Albuquerque.

Herd, R.M. 1983. *Pteronotus parnellii. Mammalian Species*, 209, 1–5. (+)

Hermanson, J.W. and O'Shea, T.J. 1983. *Antrozous pallidus. Mammalian Species*, 213, 1–8. (+)

Hill, J. Edwards 1964. Notes on bats from British Guiana with a description of a new genus and species of Phyllostomidae. *Mammalia*, 28 (4), 553–572. (RNo)

Hill, J. Edwards 1971. The bats of Aldabra Atoll, western Indian Ocean. *Philosophical Transactions of the Royal Society London B* 260, 573–576. (RAf)

Hill, J. Edwards 1983. Bats (Mammalia: Chiroptera) from Indo-Australia. *Bulletin of the British Museum (Natural History), Zoology*, 45, 103–208. (RAs) (RIn)

Hill, J. Edwards 1985. Bats from the Bahamas. *Scientific Exploration Society Newsletter*, 16(1), 11–13.

Hill, J. Edwards 1988. A bat from the Falkland Islands. *Bat News*, 15, 6.

Hill, J. Edwards and Smith, S.E. 1981. *Craseonycteris thonglongyai. Mammalian Species*, 160, 1–4. (+)

*Hill, J. Edwards and Smith, J.D. 1984. *Bats: A natural history*. British Museum (Natural History), London.

Hill, J. Eric and Carter, T.D. 1941. The mammals of Angola, Africa. *Bulletin of the American Museum of Natural History*, 78 (1), 1–212. (RAf)

Hollander, H. and van der Reest, P. 1994. *Rode lijst van bedreigde zoodieren in Nederland. Vereniging voor Zoodierkunde en Zoodierbescherming*. Utrecht, The Netherlands.

Homan, J.A. and Knox Jones Jr., J. 1975a. *Monophyllus redmani. Mammalian Species*, 57, 1–3. (+)

Homan, J.A. and Knox Jones Jr., J. 1975b. *Monophyllus plethodon. Mammalian Species*, 58, 1–2. (+)

*Honacki, J.H., Kinman, K.E., and Koeppl, J.W. (eds.) 1982. *Mammal species of the world.* Allen Press and Association of Systematics Collections, Lawrence, USA.

Hood, C.S. and Knox Jones Jr., J. 1984. *Noctilio leporinus. Mammalian Species*, 216, 1–7. (+)

Hood, C.S. and Pitocchelli, J. 1983. *Noctilio albiventris. Mammalian Species*, 197, 1–5. (+)

Hooper, P.T., Lunt, R.A., Gould, A.R., Samaratunga, H., Hyatt, A.D., Gleeson, L.J., Rodwell, B.J., Ruprecht, C.E., Smith, J.S., and Murray, P.K. 1997. A new lyssavirus, the first endemic rabies-related virus recognised in Australia. *Bulletin de l'Institut Pasteur*, 95(4), 209–218.

Hoyt, R.A. and Baker, R.J. 1980. *Natalus major. Mammalian Species*, 130, 1–3. (+)

Hsu, M.J. 1997. Population status and conservation of bats (Chiroptera) in Kenting National Park, Taiwan. *Oryx*, 31(4), 295–301.

Hudson, W.S. and Wilson, D.E. 1986. *Macroderma gigas. Mammalian Species*, 260, 1–4. (+)

Humphrey, S.R. 1978. Status, winter habitat, and management of the endangered Indiana bat, *Myotis sodalis. Florida Scientist,* 41, 65–76.

Humphrey, S.R. and Bonaccorso, F.J. 1979. Population and community ecology. Pp. 409–441 *in: Biology of the bats of the New World family Phyllostomatidae. Part III* (eds. R.J. Baker, J. Knox Jones Jr., and D.C. Carter). Special Publications of the Texas Tech University No. 16.

Husson, A.M. 1960. *De zoogdieren van de Nederlanse Antillen [Mammals of The Netherlands Antilles]*. Fauna Nederlandse Antillen, no. 2. 's-Gravenhage and Willemstad, The Netherlands. (RNo)

Husson, A.M. 1962. The bats of Suriname. *Zoologische Verhandelingen* , 58, 1–282. (RNo)

Hutson, A.M. 1993. *Action plan for the conservation of bats in the United Kingdom.* The Bat Conservation Trust, London. (RPa)

Hutson, A.M., Mickleburgh, S., and Mitchell-Jones, A.J. 1995. *Bats underground: A conservation code,* 2nd edition. The Bat Conservation Trust, London.

Hutton, J.M. 1986. The status and distribution of bats in Zimbabwe. *Cimbebasia, (Series A)*, 8 (26), 219–236. (RAf)

Iliopoulou-Georgoudaki, J. 1977. *Systimatiki meleti kai geografiki exaplosi to Chiropteron tis Ellados [Systematic study and geographic distribution of the Chiroptera of Greece*]. PhD thesis, University of Patras, Patras, Greece [in Greek]. (RPa)

Ingelög, T, Andersson, R., and Tjernberg, M. (eds.) 1993. *Red data book of the Baltic Region*. Swedish Threatened Species Unit, Uppsala.

Ingle, R.N. and Heaney, L.R. 1992. A key to the bats of the Philippine Islands. *Fieldiana: Zoology, New Series,* 69, 1–44. (RIn)

INPE, 1992. *Deforestation in the Brazilian Amazon*. Instituto Nacional de Pesquisas Espaciaias, São José Dos Campos.

Isaksen, K., Syvertsen, P.O., van der Kooij, J., and Rinden, H. (eds.) 1998. Truete pattedye i Norge: Faktaark og forslag til rodliste. *Norsk Zoologisk Forening Rapport*, 5, 1–182. (RPa)

IUCN 1994. *IUCN red list categories.* Prepared by IUCN Species Survival Commission. IUCN, Gland, Switzerland.

IUCN 1996. *The 1996 IUCN red list of threatened animals.* IUCN, Gland, Switzerland.

IUCN 2000. *The 2000 IUCN red list of threatened species.* IUCN, Gland, Switzerland.

Ivanova, T. and Petrov, B. 1994. Bulgarian project for mapping and protecting bat colonies in caves. Abstract of paper present at Symposium on *Current Problems of Bat Protection in Central and Eastern Europe*, held in Bonn, Germany, July 1994.

Jedicke, E. 1997. *Die roten listen: Gefahrdete Pflanzen, Tiere, Pflanzengesellschaften and Biotope in Bund und Landern.* Ulmer, Stuttgart.

Jones, C. 1977. *Plecotus rafinesquii. Mammalian Species*, 69, 1–4. (+)

Jones, C. and Manning, R.W. 1989. *Myotis austroriparius. Mammalian Species*, 332, 1–3. (+)

Jones, G. and Barrett, E. 1999. Case 3073. *Vespertilio pipistrellus* Schreber, 1774 and *V. pgymaeus* Leach, 1825 (Currently *Pipistrellus pipistrellus* and *P. pygmaeus*; Mammalia, Chiroptera): Proposed assignment of neotypes. *Bulletin of Zoological Nomenclature*, 56(3), 182–186.

Juberthie, C. 1992. *Underground habitats and their protection*. Convention on the Conservation of European Wildlife and Natural Habitats, Standing Committee, T-PVS (92) 46. Council of Europe, Strasbourg, France.

Juste, J. and Ibanez, C. 1993. Bats of the Gulf of Guinea islands: Faunal composition and origins. *Biodiversity and Conservation,* 3 (9), 837–850. (RAf)

Kahman, H. 1964. Contribution à l'études des Mammifères du Peloponnese. *Mammalia*, 28 (1), 109–136. (RPa)

Kalko, E.K.V. and Schnitzler, H.-U. 1998. How echolocating bats approach and acquire food. Pp. 197–204 *in: Bat biology and conservation* (eds. T.H. Kunz and P.A. Racey). Smithsonian Institution Press, Washington DC.

Kapteyn, K. (ed.) 1993. *Proceedings of the first European bat detector workshop*. Netherlands Bat Research Foundation, Amsterdam.

Kapteyn, K. 1995. *Vleermuizen in het landschap.* Schuyt and Co., Haarlem, The Netherlands.

Karandinos, M. and Paraschi, L. 1992. *The red data book of threatened vertebrates of Greece*. Hellenic Zoological Society, Athens.

Karnellis, A. and Hatzissarantos, Ch. 1963. Ta Thilastika tis Ellados [The Mammals of Greece]. *To Vuno*, 230, 6–21. (RPa)

Keeley, B.W. and Tuttle, M.D. 1999. *Bats in American bridges*. Bat Conservation International, Austin, USA.

Keeling, S.J. and Verheught, W.J.M. (eds.) 1995. *Biodiversity Profiles Project 1995. Red data book of the fauna of Nepal.* Biodiversity Profiles Project Technical Publication No. 4. Department of National Parks and Wildlife Conservation, Ministry of Forests and Soil Conservation, His Majesty's Government of Nepal, Kathmandu.

Kennedy, C.E.J. and Southwood, T.R.E. 1984. The numbers of species of insects associated with British trees. A re-analysis. *Journal of Animal Ecology*, 53, 455–478.

Kerridge, D.C. and Baker, R.J. 1978. *Natalus micropus. Mammalian Species*, 114, 1–3. (+)

Khabilov, T. K. 1989. The bats of Tajikistan: their species composition, distribution and protection. Pp. 415–419 *in: European bat research 1987* (eds. Hanak, V., Horacek, I., and J. Gaisler). Charles University Press, Prague.

King, C.M. (ed.) 1995. *The handbook of New Zealand mammals.* Oxford University Press, Oxford. (RAs)

Kingdon, J. 1974. *East African mammals. An atlas of evolution in Africa, Volume 2A (Insectivores and bats).* Academic Press, New York and London. (RAf)

Kingdon, J. 1997. *The Kingdon field guide to African mammals.* Academic Press, London. (RAf)

Kiser, W.M. 1995. *Eumops underwoodi. Mammalian Species*, 516, 1–4. (+)

Klingener, D., Genoways, H.H., and Baker, R.J. 1978. Bats from southern Haiti. *Annals of the Carnegie Museum*, 47, 81–99.

Knox Jones, Jr., J. 1966. Bats from Guatemala. *University of Kansas Publications. Museum of Natural History*, 16, 439–472. (RNo)

Knox Jones Jr., J. 1977. *Rhogeessa gracilis. Mammalian Species*, 76, 1–2. (+)

Knox Jones Jr., J. and Arroyo-Cabrales, J. 1990. *Nyctinomops aurispinosus. Mammalian Species*, 350, 1–3. (+)

Knox Jones, Jr., J., Arroyo-Cabrales, J., and Owen, D.R. 1988. Revised checklist of bats (Chiroptera) of Mexico and Central America. *Occasional Papers. The Museum, Texas Tech University,* 120, 1–34. (RNe) (RNo)

Knox Jones Jr., J. and Baker, R.J. 1980. *Chiroderma improvisum. Mammalian Species*, 134, 1–2. (+)

Knox Jones Jr., J. and Genoways, H.H. 1975. *Sturnira thomasi. Mammalian Species*, 68, 1–2. (+)

Knox Jones Jr., J. and Genoways, H.H. 1973. *Ardops nicholsi. Mammalian Species*, 24, 1–2. (+)

Knox Jones Jr., J. and Homan, J.A. 1974. *Hylonycteris underwoodi. Mammalian Species*, 32, 1–2. (+)

Knox Jones, Jr., J. and Owen, R.D. 1986. Checklist and bibliography of Nicaraguan Chiroptera. *Occasional Papers. The Museum, Texas Tech University,* 106, 1–13. (RNo)

Koch-Weser, S. 1984. Fledermäuse aus Obervolta, W-Afrika. *Senckenbergiana Biologica,* 64 (4/6), 255–311. (RAf)

Kock, D. 1969. Die Fledermaus-Fauna des Sudan. *Abhandlungen der Senckenbergischen Naturforschenden Gesellschaft*, 521, 1–238. (RAf)

Kock, D. 1981. Zur Chiropteren-fauna von Burundi (Mammalia). *Senckenbergiana Biologica,* 61 (5/6), 329–336. (RAf)

Kock, D. 1999. Tadarida (Tadarida) latouchei, a separate species recorded from Thailand with remarks on related Asian taxa (Mammalia, Chiroptera, Molossidae). *Senckenbergiana biologica* 78, 237-240

Kokurewicz, T. 1995. Increased population of Daubenton's bat (*Myotis daubentonii* (Kuhl, 1819)) (Chiroptera: Vespertilionidae) in Poland. *Myotis*, 32–33, 155–161.

Koopman, K.F. 1967. The southernmost bats. *Journal of Mammalogy*, 48, 487–488.

Koopman, K.F. 1972. *Eudiscopus denticulus. Mammalian Species*, 19, 1–2. (+)

Koopman, K.F. 1975. Bats of the Sudan. *Bulletin of the American Museum of Natural History,* 154 (4), 353–444. (RAf)

Koopman, K.F. 1978. Biogeography of the bats of South America. Pp. 273–302 *in: Mammalian biology in South America* (eds. M.A. Mares and H.H. Genoways). Pymatuning Symposia in Ecology 6, Special Publication Series, Pymatuning Laboratory of Ecology, University of Pittsburgh, Pittsburgh. (RNo)

Koopman, K.F. 1989. A review and analysis of the bats of the West Indies. Pp. 635–644 *in: Biogeography of the West Indies: past, present and future* (ed. C.A. Woods). Sandhill Crane Press, Gainesville, USA.

*Koopman, K.F. 1993. Order Chiroptera. Pp. 137–232 *in: Mammal species of the world* (eds. D.E. Wilson and D.M. Reeder). Smithsonian Institution Press, Washington DC.

*Koopman, K.F. 1994. Chiroptera: Systematics. *Handbuch der Zoologie*, 8 (60), 1–217.

Koopman, K.F. and Gudmundsson, F. 1966. Bats in Iceland. *American Museum Novitates*, 2262, 1–6. (RPa)

Koopman, K.F., Hecht, M.K., and Lidecky-Janacek, E. 1957. Notes on the mammals of the Bahamas with special reference to bats. *Journal of Mammalogy*, 38, 164–174.

Koopman, K.F., Kofron, C.P., and Chapman, A. 1995. The bats of Liberia: Systematics, ecology and distribution. *American Museum Novitates*, 3148, 1–24. (RAf)

Kowalski, M. and Lesinski, G. 1990. The food of the tawny owl (*Strix aluco* L.) from near a bat cave in Poland. *Bonner Zoologische Beiträge*, 41, 23–26.

Kowalski, K. and Rzebik-Kowalska, B. 1991. *Mammals of Algeria.* Zaklad Narodowy Imienia Ossolinskich Wydawnictwo Polskiej Akademii Nauk Wroclaw, Poland. (RPa)

Krever, V., Pereladova, O., Williams, M., and Jungius, H. 1998. *Biodiversity conservation in Central Asia. An analysis of biodiversity and current threats and initial investment portfolio.* World Wide Fund for Nature, Almaty, Ashgabad, Bishkek, Dushanbe, Tashkent, Gland, Moscow and Washington DC.

Krystufek, B. 1991. *Sesalei Slovenije [Mammals of Slovenia].* Prirodoslovni musej Slovenije, Ljubljana. (RPa)

Krystufek, B. 1992. The red list of endangered mammals in Slovenia. *Varstvo Narave*, 17, 1–224.

Krystufek, B. and Cerveny, J. 1997. New and noteworthy records of bats in Slovenia. *Myotis*, 35, 89–93.

Krystufek, B., Vohralik, V., Flousek, J., and Petkowski, S. 1992. Bats (Mammalia: Chiroptera) of Macedonia, Yugoslavia. Pp. 93–111 *in: Prague studies in Mammalogy* (eds. Horacek, I and V. Vohralik). Charles University Press, Prague.

Krzanoswki, A. 1973. Numerical comparison of Vespertilionidae and Rhinolophidae (Chiroptera: Mammalia) in the owl pellets. *Acta Zoologica Cracoviensia*, 18, 133–140.

Kuhn, H.J. 1965. A provisional check-list of the mammals of Liberia. *Senckenbergiana Biologica,* 46 (5), 321–340. (RAf)

Kulzer, E. 1962. Fledermäuse aus Tanganyika. *Zeitschrift für Säugetierkunde,* 27 (2), 164–181. (RAf)

Kumerloeve, H. 1976. Die Säugetiere (Mammalia) Syriens und des Libanon. *Veröffentlichungen der Zoologischen Staatssammlung München*, 18, 159–225. (RPa)

Kumirai, A. and Knox Jones Jr., J. 1990. *Nyctinomops femorosaccus. Mammalian Species*, 349, 1–5. (+)

Kunz, T.H. 1974a. Feeding ecology of a temperate insectivorous bat, *Myotis velifer*. *Ecology*, 55, 693–711.

Kunz, T.H. 1974b. Reproduction, growth and mortality of the vespertilionid bat, *Eptesicus fuscus*, in Kansas. *Journal of Mammalogy,* 55, 1–13.

Kunz, T.H. 1982a. *Lasionycteris noctivagans. Mammalian Species*, 172, 1–5. (+)

*Kunz, T.H. 1982b. *Ecology of bats.* Plenum, New York.

Kunz, T.H. 1982c. Roosting ecology. Pp. 1–55 *in: Ecology of bats* (ed. T.H. Kunz). Plenum, New York.

*Kunz, T.H. 1988. *Ecological and behavioural methods for the study of bats.* Smithsonian Institution Press, Washington DC.

Kunz, T.H. and Martin, R.A. 1982. *Plecotus townsendii. Mammalian Species*, 175, 1–6. (+)

Kunz, T.H. and Pena, I.M. 1992. *Mesophylla macconnelli. Mammalian Species*, 405, 1–5. (+)

*Kunz, T.H. and Pierson, E.D. 1994. Introduction. Pp. 1–46 *in: Walker's bats of the world* (ed. R.W. Nowak). John Hopkins University Press, Baltimore.

*Kunz, T.H. and Racey, P.A. (eds.) 1998. *Bat biology and conservation.* Smithsonian Institution Press, Washington DC.

Kunz, T.H., Whitaker Jr., J.O., and Wadanoli, M.D. 1995. Dietary energetics of the insectivorous Mexican free-tailed bat (*Tadarida brasiliensis*) during pregnancy and lactation. *Oecologia (Berlin)*, 101, 407–415.

Kurta, A. and Baker, R.H. 1990. *Eptesicus fuscus. Mammalian Species*, 356, 1–10. (+)

Kurta, A., Bell, G.P., Nagy, K.A., and Kunz, T.H. 1989. Energetics of pregnancy and lactation in free-ranging little brown bats (*Myotis lucifugus*). *Physiological Zoology*, 62, 804–818.

Kurta, A. and Lehr, G.C. 1995. *Lasiurus ega. Mammalian Species*, 515, 1–7. (+)

Kuzyakin, A.P. 1944. *In: Opredelitel' mlekopitayushchikh SSSR [The key to the mammals of the USSR]*, (eds. N.A. Bobrinskii, B.A. Kuznetzov, and A.P. Kuzyakin). Gosudarstvennoe Izdarelstvo [Government Publishing Office] "Sovietskaya Nauka", Moscow. [In Russian]. (RPa)

Kuzyakin, A.P. 1950. *Letucie Myshi (Sistematika, obraz zhizni I pol'za dlya sel'skogo I lesnogho khozyaistva). [Bats (Systematics, life history and utility for agriculture and forestry)].* Gosudarstvennoe Izdarelstvo [Government Publishing Office] "Sovietskaya Nauka", Moscow. [in Russian] (RPa)

Kuzyakin, A.P. 1965. *In: Opredelitel' mlekopitayushchikh SSSR [The key to the mammals of the USSR]*, (eds. N.A. Bobrinskii, B.A. Kuznetzov, and A.P. Kuzyakin), 2nd edition. "Prosveshchenie", Moscow. [in Russian] (RPa)

Lancaster, W.C. and Kalko, E.K.V. 1996. *Mormoops blainvillii. Mammalian Species*, 544, 1–5. (+)

Langevin, P. and Barclay, R.M.R. 1990. *Hypsignathus monstrosus. Mammalian Species*, 357, 1–4. (+)
Lapele, M. and Vaicunaite, R. 1992. *The Lithuanian red data book.* Lithuanian Republic Environmental Protection Department, Vilnius.
Largen, M.J., Kock, D., and Yalden, D.W. 1974. Catalogue of the mammals of Ethiopia. 1. Chiroptera. *Monitore Zoologico Italiano, (Supplement V)*, 16, 221–298. (RAf)
Lassieur, S. and Wilson, D.E. 1989. *Lonchorhina aurita. Mammalian Species*, 347, 1–4. (+)
Laurie, E.M.O. and Hill, J. Edwards 1954. *List of land mammals of New Guinea, Celebes and adjacent islands 1758–1952.* British Museum (Natural History), London. (RIn)
Lccuwangh, P. and Voûte, A.M. 1985. Bats and wood preservatives. Pesticide residues in Dutch pond bats (*Myotis dasycneme*) and its implication. *Mammalia*, 49, 417–424.
Lehmann, J., Jenni, L.K., and Maumary, L. 1992. A new longevity record for the long-eared bat (*Plecotus auritus*, Chiroptera). *Mammalia*, 56 (2), 316–318.
Lekagul, B. and McNeely, J.A. 1977. *Mammals of Thailand.* Kuruspha Ladprao Press, Bangkok. (RIn)
Lewis, S.E. 1995. Roost fidelity of bats – a review. *Journal of Mammalogy*, 76, 481–496.
Lewis, S.E. and Wilson, D.E. 1987. *Vampyressa pusilla. Mammalian Species*, 292, 1–5. (+)
Lim, B.K., Engstom, R.M., Anderson, R.P., and Watson, L.C. 1999. First records of 10 species and comments on diversity of bats in Iwokrama Forest. *Acta Chiropterologica*, 1(2), 179–190.
Limpens, H.J.G.A. 1993. Bat-detectors in a detailed bat survey: a method. Pp. 79–90 *in: Proceedings of the first European bat detector workshop* (ed. K. Kapteyn). Netherlands Bat Research Foundation, Amsterdam.
Limpens, H.J.G.A., Helmer, W., van Winden, A., and Mostert, K. 1989. Vleermuizen (Chiroptera) en Lintvormige landschapselementen; Een overzicht van de huidige kennis van het belang van lintvormige landschapselementen voor vleermuizen. *Lutra*, 32, 1–20.
Limpens, H.J.G.A. and Kapteyn, K. 1991. Bats, their behaviour and linear landscape elements. *Myotis*, 29, 39–48.
Limpens, H.G.J.A., Lina, P.H.C., and Hutson, A.M. 2000. *Action Plan for the Conservation of the Pond Bat in Europe (Myotis dasycneme).* Nature and Environment, No.108. Council of Europe Publishing, Strasbourg. 50 pp.
Limpens, H.J.G.A., Mostert, K., and Bongers, W. (eds.) 1997. *Atlas van de Nederlandse vleermuizen.* KNNV Uitgeverij, Utrecht, The Netherlands.
Linares, O.J. 1986. *Murciélagos de Venezuela.* Cuardenas Lagove, Premio Nacional de Perodismo, Caracas. (RNo)
Linares, O.J. 1998. *Mamíferos de Venezuela.* Sociedad Conservacionista Audubon de Venezuela and BP Venezuela, Caracas. (RNo)
Linhart, S.B. 1975. The biology and control of vampire bats. P. 221 *in: The natural history of rabies* (ed. G.M. Baer). Vol. II. Academic Press, New York.
Lipej, L. and Gjerkes, H. 1992. Bats in the diet of owls in NW Istra. *Myotis*, 30, 133–138.
Long, J.K. 1995. *Otomops martiensseni. Mammalian Species*, 493, 1–5. (+)
Lopez-Gonzalez, C. 1998. *Micronycteris minuta. Mammalian Species*, 583, 1–4. (+)
Lord, R. 1988. Control of vampire bats. Pp. 215–226 *in: Natural history of vampire bats* (eds. A.M. Greenhall, and U. Schmidt). CRC Press, Florida.
Lunney, D. 1991. The future of Australia's forest fauna. Pp. 1–24 *in: Conservation of Australia's forest fauna* (ed. D. Lunney). Royal Zoological Society of New South Wales, Mosman.
MacKinnon, K., Hatta. G., Halim. H., and Mangalik, A. 1996. *The ecology of Kalimantan. Indonesian Borneo.* The ecology of Indonesia series, Volume III. Periplus Editions (HK) Ltd., Republic of Singapore.
Makin, D. 1989. The status of bats in Israel. Pp. 403–408 *in: European bat research 1987* (eds. V. Hanák, I. Horácek and J. Gaisler). Charles University Press, Prague. (RPa)
Makin, D. and Mendelssohn, H. 1986. Israel wipes out its bats. *Ecologist*, 16 (1), 46–47.
Makin, D. and Mendelssohn, H. 1987. The fruit-bat issue in Israel. *Bat News*, 11, 4–5.
Malbrant, R. and Maclatchy, A. 1949. *Faune de l'équateur Africain Français. Tome II. Mammifères.* Lechevalier, Paris. (RAf)
Mallon, D.P. 1985. The mammals of the Mongolian People's Republic. *Mammal Review*, 15(2), 71–102. (RPa)
Manning, R.W. and Knox Jones Jr., J. 1989. *Myotis evotis. Mammalian Species*, 329, 1–5. (+)
Marcot, B.G. 1996. An ecosystem context for bat management: A case study of the interior Colombia River Basin, USA. Pp. 19–36 *in: Bats and forests symposium, October 19–21 1995, Victoria, British Columbia, Canada* (eds. R.M.R. Barclay and R.M.Brigham).Working Paper 23/1996, Research Branch, BC Ministry of Forests, Victoria, Canada.
Marinho-Filho, J. and Sazima, I. 1998. Brazilian bats and conservation biology: a first survey. Pp. 282–294 *in: Bat biology and conservation* (eds. T.H. Kunz and P.A. Racey). Smithsonian Institution Press, Washington DC. (RNo)
Masera, O., Ordoñez, M.J., and Dirzo, R. 1992. *Carbon emissions from deforestation in Mexico: Current situation and long-term scenarios.* Internal Report, Environmental Protection Agency.
Matson, J.O. 1975. *Myotis planiceps. Mammalian Species*, 60, 1–2. (+)

Maurin, H. 1994. *Le Livre Rouge: Inventaire de la faune menace en France*. Museum National d'Histoire Naturelle, Paris.

McCarthy, T.J. 1978. *Comments on paralytic rabies in Belize*. Contribution of the Vampire Bat Education and Control Program, Belize. Unpublished document.

McCarthy, T. 1987. Distributional records of bats from the Caribbean lowlands of Belize and adjacent Guatemala and Mexico. *Fieldiana Zoology (new series)*, 39, 137–162. (RNo)

McCarthy, T.J., Davis, W.B., Hill, J. Edwards, Knox Jones Jr., J., and Cruz, G.A. 1993. Bat (Mammalia: Chiroptera) records, early collectors, and faunal lists for northern Central America. *Annals of the Carnegie Museum*, 62 (3), 191–228. (RNo)

McCarthy, T.J., Gardner, A.L., and Handley Jr., C.O. 1992. *Tonatia carrikeri*. *Mammalian Species*, 407, 1–4. (+)

McCracken, G.F. 1986. Why are we losing our Mexican free-tailed bats? *Bats*, 3(3), 1–4.

McCracken, G.F. 1988. Who's endangered and what can we do? *Bats*, 6, 5–9.

McCracken, G.F. 1989. Cave conservation: Special problems of bats. *National Speleological Society Bulletin*, 51, 47–51.

McCracken, G.F. 1996. Bats Aloft: A study of high-altitude feeding. *Bats*, 14(3), 7–10.

McCracken, G.F., Hayes, J.P., Cevallos, J., Guffey, S.Z., and Carlos Romero, F. 1997. Observations on the distribution, ecology, and behaviour of bats on the Galapagos Islands. *Journal of Zoology London*, 243, 757–770.

McFarlane, D.A. 1991. The species-genus relationship in Antillean bat communities. *Mammalia*, 55(3), 363–370. (RNo)

McWilliam, A.N. 1994. Nocturnal animals. Pp. 103–133 *in: DDT in the tropics, the impact on wildlife in Zimbabwe of ground-spraying for tsetse fly control* (eds. J.R. Douthwaite and C.C.D. Tingle). Natural Resources Institute, Chatham, UK.

Medellin, R.A. 1989. *Chrotopterus auritus*. *Mammalian Species*, 343, 1–5. (+)

Medellin, R.A. and Arita, H.T. 1989. *Tonatia evotis* and *Tonatia silvicola*. *Mammalian Species*, 34, 1–5. (+)

Medellín, R.A., Arita, H.T., and Sanchez, O. 1997. *Identificación de los murciélagos de México. Clave de campo*. Asociación Mexicana de Mastozoología, A.C. Publicaciones Especiales Núm. 2. Mexico City. (RNe) (RNo)

Medellin, R.A., Wilson, D.E., and Navarro L.D. 1985. *Micronycteris brachyotis*. *Mammalian Species*, 251, 1–4. (+)

Medway, Lord 1957. Bird nest collecting. *Sarawak Museum Journal*, 8(10), 252–260.

Medway, Lord 1958. 300,000 bats. *Sarawak Museum Journal*, 8(12), 667–679.

Medway, Lord 1960. Cave swiftlets. *In: The birds of Borneo* (ed. B.E. Smythies). Oliver and Boyd, Edinburgh.

Medway, Lord 1977. *Mammals of Borneo: Field keys and annotated checklist*. Monograph Number 7, Royal Asiatic Society, Malaysian Branch, Kuala Lumpur. (RIn)

Medway, Lord 1978. *The wild mammals of Malaya (Peninsular Malaysia) and Singapore*, 2nd edition. Oxford University Press, Kuala Lumpur. (RIn)

Medway, Lord 1983. *The wild mammals of Malaya (Peninsular Malaysia) and Singapore*, 2nd edition with corrections. Oxford University Press, Kuala Lumpur. (RIn)

Meester, J. and Setzer, H.W. (eds.) 1971. *The mammals of Africa: an identification manual*. Smithsonian Institution Press, Washington DC. (RAf)

Meester, J.A.J., Rautenbach, I.L., Dippenaar, N.J., and Baker, C.M. 1986. Classification of southern African mammals. *Transvaal Museum Monographs*, 5, 1–359. (RAf)

Meirte, D. 1984. De vleermuizen van de Comoren. *Africa-Tervuren*, 30 (1–4), 49–57. (RAf)

Menkhorst, P. (ed) 1995. *Mammals of Victoria: Distribution, ecology and conservation*. Oxford University Press, Melbourne, Australia. (RAs)

van der Merwe, M. 1973. Aspects of hibernation and winter activity of the Natal clinging bat (*Miniopterus schreibersi natalensis* (A. Smith, 1834) on the Transvaal Highveld. *South African Journal of Science*, 69, 116–118.

van der Merwe, M. 1975. Preliminary study on the annual movements of the Natal clinging bat. *South African Journal of Science*, 71, 237–241.

van der Merwe, M. 1978. Postnatal development and mother-infant relationships in the Natal clinging bat, *Miniopterus schreibersi natalensis* (A. Smith, 1834). Pp. 309–322 *in: Proceedings of the Fourth International Bat Research Conference* (eds. R.J. Olembo, J.B. Castelino, and F.A. Mutere). Kenya Literature Bureau, Nairobi.

*Mickleburgh, S.P., Hutson, A.M., and Racey, P.A. (eds.) 1992. *Old World fruit bats. An action plan for their conservation*. IUCN, Gland, Switzerland.

Mies, R., Kurta, A., and King, D.G. 1996. *Eptesicus furinalis*. *Mammalian Species*, 526, 1–7. (+)

Miller, G.S. 1902. The mammals of the Andaman and Nicobar Islands. *Proceedings of the United States National Museum*, 24, 751–795. (RIn)

*Miller, G.S. 1905. The families and genera of bats. *Bulletin of the United States National Museum*, 57, 1–282.

Miller, G.S. Jr. and Kellogg, R. 1955. List of North American recent mammals. *Bulletin of the United States National Museum*, 205, 1–953. (RNe)

Milner, J., Jones, C., and Knox Jones Jr., J. 1990. *Nyctinomops macrotis*. *Mammalian Species*, 351, 1–4. (+)
Ministry of Agriculture of Lebanon 1992. *Biological diversity of Lebanon*. Ministry of Agriculture of Lebanon and United Nations Environment Programme.
Ministry of Science, Technology and Environment 1992. *Red data book of Vietnam, Vol. 1: Animals* 1992. Science and Technics Publishing House, Hanoi.
Mitchell-Jones, A.J. 1995. The status and conservation of horseshoe bats in Britain. *Myotis*, 32–33, 271–284.
Mitchell-Jones, A.J., Amori, G., Bogdanowicz, W., Krystufek, B., Reijnders, P.J.H., Spitzenberger, F., Stubbe, M., Thissen, J.B.M., Vohralik, V., and Zima, J. 1999. *The Atlas of European Mammals*. T & AD Poyser Natural History, London.
Mittermeier, R.A. 1988. Primate diversity and the tropical forest; case studies from Brazil and Madagascar and the importance of the megadiversity countries. Pp. 145–154 *in: Biodiversity* (ed. E.O. Wilson). National Academy Press, Washington DC.
Mittermeier, R.A., Gil, P.R., and Mittermeier, C.G. 1997. *Megadiversity. Earth's biologically wealthiest nations*. Cemex, Mexico.
Mittermeier, R.A., Myers, N., Thomsen, J.B., da Fonseca, G.A.B., and Olivieri, S., 1998. Biodiversity hotspots and major tropical wilderness areas: Approaches to setting conservation priorities. *Conservation Biology*, 12(3), 516–520.
Moeschler, P. 1991. Concept national pour la protection et l'Etude des chauves-souris. *Publications Speciale de Rhinolophe*, 1, 1–102.
Mohr, C.E. 1952. A survey of bat banding in North America, 1932–1951. *National Speleological Society Bulletin*, 14, 3–13.
Mohr, C.E. 1953. Possible causes of an apparent decline in wintering populations of cave bats. *National Speleological Society News*, 4–5.
Mohr, C.E. 1972. The status of threatened species of cave-dwelling bats. *National Speleological Society Bulletin*, 34, 33–47.
*Mohr, C.E. 1976. *The world of the bat.* J.B. Lippincott Co., Philadelphia and New York.
Mok, W.Y., Wilson, D.E., Lacey, L.A., and Luizão, R.C.C. 1982. Lista atualizada de quirópteros da Amazônia Brasileira. *Acta Amazonica*, 12, 817–823. (RNo)
Molinari, J. and Soriano, P.J. 1987. *Sturnira bidens*. *Mammalian Species*, 276, 1–4. (+)
Molloy, J. 1995. *Bat (Peka Peka) recovery plan* (Mystacina, Chalinolobus). Threatened Species Recovery Plan Series No. 15. Threatened Species Unit, Department of Conservation, Wellington, New Zealand. (RAs)
Morton, P.A. 1990. Habitat for free-tailed bats protected. *Bats*, 8(2), 17.
Movsesian, S.O. (ed.), 1987. *Krasnaia kniga Armianskoi SSR: Redkie i nakhodiashchiesia pod ugrozoi ischeznoveniia vidy zhivotnykh [Animal red data book of Armenian SSR]*. Aiastan, Erevan, Armenia. [in Armenian].
Murphy, M. 1987a. India's Samanar Hill caves saved. *Bats*, 5(3), 6.
Murphy, M. 1987b. Thornhill cave bat killers convicted. *Bats*, 5(4), 2.
Mutere, F.A. 1973. A comparative study of reproduction in two populations of the insectivorous bats, *Otomops martiensseni*, at latitudes 1°5' S and 2°30' S. *Journal of Zoology London*, 171, 79–92.
Myers, P. 1964. Sexual dimorphism in size of vespertilionid bats. *American Naturalist*, 112, 701–711.
Myers, N. 1988. Threatened biotas: 'Hot spots' in tropical forests. *The Environmentalist*, 8, 187–208.
Myers, N. 1990. The biodiversity challenge: Expanded hot-spots analysis. *The Environmentalist*, 10, 243–256.
Nagorsen, D.W. and Brigham, R.M. 1993. *Bats of British Columbia.* University of British Columbia Press, Vancouver, Canada. (RNe)
National Caving Association 1997. *Cave conservation handbook*. National Caving Association, London.
Navarro, L., Arroyo, J., and Medellín, R. 1996. Bat awareness in Mexico begins with children. *Bats*, 14(3), 3–6.
Navarro, D. and Wilson, D.E. 1982. Vampyrum spectrum. *Mammalian Species*, 184, 1–4. (+)
Navo, K., Sheppard, J., and Ingersoll, T. 1995. Colorado's bats/inactive mines project: the use of volunteers in bat conservation. Pp. 49–54 *in: Inactive mines as bat habitat: guidelines for research, survey, monitoring and mine management in Nevada* (ed. B.R. Riddle). Biological Resources Research Center, University of Nevada, Reno.
Neilson, A.L. and Fenton, M.B. 1994. Responses of little brown myotis to exclusion and to bat houses. *Wildlife Society Bulletin*, 22, 8–14.
Nellis, D. 1971. Additions to the natural history of *Brachyphylla* (Chiroptera). *Caribbean Journal of Science*, 11, 91.
*Neuweiler, G. 2000. *The biology of bats*. Oxford University Press, London and New York.
Ng, P.K.L. and Wee, Y.C. 1994. *Red data book: Threatened plants and animals of Singapore*. The Nature Society, Singapore.
Nordiska Ministerrådet 1995. Threatened animals and plants of the Nordic countries. *Tema Nord*, 520, 1.
*Novick, A. and Leen, N. 1969. *The world of bats.* Holt, Rinehart and Winston, New York.
*Nowak, R.M. 1992. *Walker's mammals of the world.* John Hopkins University Press, Baltimore.
*Nowak, R.M. 1995. *Walker's bats of the world.* John Hopkins University Press, Baltimore.

ODA (Overseas Development Agency) 1992a. *Environmental synopsis of Uganda.* International Institute for Environment and Development, London.

ODA (Overseas Development Agency) 1992b. *Environmental synopsis of Ghana.* International Institute for Environment and Development, London.

Ognev, S.I. 1928. [*Mammals of eastern Europe and northern Asia Volume 1. Insectivora and Chiroptera*]. Moscow, USSR. [in Russian]. English translation, Israel Program for Scientific Translations, Jerusalem, 1962. (RPa)

Olson, D.M. and Dinerstein, E. 1998. The Global 200: A representation approach to conserving the earth's most biologically valuable ecoregions. *Conservation Biology*, 12(3), 502–515.

Ortega, J. and Arita, H.T. 1997. *Mimon bennettii. Mammalian Species*, 549, 1–4. (+)

Osborne, L. and Krebs, J. 1981. Replanting after Dutch elm disease. *New Scientist*, 29 April 1981, 212–215.

Osgood, W.H. 1943. The mammals of Chile. *Field Museum of Natural History, Zoological Series,* 30, 1–268. (RNo)

Owen, R.D., Knox Jones, Jr., J., and Baker, R.J. 1991. Annotated checklist of mammals of El Salvador. *Occasional Papers. The Museum, Texas Tech University*, 139, 1–17. (RNo)

Owen-Ashley, N.T. and Wilson, D.E. 1998. *Micropteropus pusillus. Mammalian Species*, 577, 1–5.(+)

O'Farrell, M.J. and Studier, E.H. 1980. *Myotis thysanodes. Mammalian Species*, 137, 1–5. (+)

O'Sullivan, P. 1994. Bats in Ireland. *Irish Naturalists Journal*, Special Zoological Supplement. (RPa)

Pacheco, V., de Macedo, H., Vivar, E., Ascorra, C., Arana-Cardó, R., and Solari, S. 1995. *Lista Anotada de los Mamíferos Peruanos.* Occasional Papers in Conservation Biology, Number 2. Conservation International, Washington DC. (RNo)

PAHO/WHO 1991. Expert consultation on the care of persons exposed to rabies transmitted by vampire bats – Final report. *In: Expert consultation on the care of persons exposed to rabies transmitted by vampire bats.* PAHO/ WHO. Programs for Veterinary Public Health. Washington DC, April 1–5, 1991.

Pakenham, R.H.W. 1984. *The mammals of Zanzibar and Pemba Islands.* Privately published, Harpenden, UK. (RAf)

Palmeirim, J.M. 1989. Status of bats in Portugal. Pp. 373–379 *in: European bat research 1987* (eds. V. Hanak, I. Horacek, and J. Gaisler). Charles University Press, Prague. (RPa)

Palmeirim, J.M. 1990. Bats of Portugal: Zoogeography and systematics. *Miscellaneous Publications of the University of Kansas Museum of Natural History*, 82, 1–53. (RPa)

Palmeirim J.M. and Rodrigues, L. 1992. *Plano nacional de Conservação dos Morcegos Cavernícolas.* Estudos de Biologia e Conservação da Natureza, Número 8. Serviço Nacional de Parques, Reservas e Conservação da Natureza, Lisbon. (RPa)

Panouse, J.B. 1951. Les chauves-souris du Maroc. *Travaux de l'Institut Scientifique Chérifan,* 1, 1–120. (RAf)

Parker, D.I., Cook, J.A., and Lewis, S.W. 1995. Effects of timber harvest on bat activity in southeastern Alaska's temperate rainforests. Pp. 277–292 *in: Bats and Forests Symposium October 19–21, 1995, Victoria, British Columbia, Canada* (eds. R.M.R. Barclay and R.M. Brigham). British Columbia Ministry of Forests, Victoria, British Columbia, Working Paper 23/1996.

Parnaby, H. 1991. A sound species taxonomy is crucial to the conservation of forest bats. Pp. 101–112 *in: Conservation of Australia's forest fauna* (ed. D. Lunney). Royal Zoological Society of New South Wales, Mosman.

Paunovic, M., Paunovic, A., and Ivovic, M. 1998. Mehely's horseshoe bat *Rhinolophus mehelyi* Matschie, 1901 – New to the Yugoslavian bat fauna. *Myotis*, 36, 115–119.

Pauza, D.H. and Panziene, N. 1998. Bats of Lithuania: Distribution, status and protection. *Mammal Review*, 28, 53–67. (RPa)

Payne, J., Francis, C.M., and Phillipps, K. 1985. *A field guide to the mammals of Borneo.* Sabah Society and WWF Malaysia, Kuala Lumpur. (RIn)

Pearl, D.L. 1994. *Rhinolophus hildebrandti. Mammalian Species*, 486, 1–3. (+)

van Peenen, P.F.D., Ryan, P.F., and Light, R.H. 1969. *Preliminary identification manual for mammals of South Vietnam.* Smithsonian Institution, Washington DC. (RIn)

Petersen, A. 1994. Leðurblökur á Íslandi. *Náttúrufræðingurinn*, 64 (1), 3–12. [In Icelandic].

Peterson, R.L., Eger, J.L., and Mitchell, L. 1995. Chiroptères. *Faune de Madagascar* , 84, 1–204. (RAf)

Phillips, W.R. 1990. *Priorities for ghost bat (*Macroderma gigas*) conservation and management.* Australian National Parks and Wildlife Service, Canberra.

Phillips, W.W.A. 1986. *The manual of the mammals of Sri Lanka.* WNPS, Sri Lanka. (RIn)

Pierson, E.D. 1998. Tall trees, deep holes, and scarred landscapes: Conservation biology of North American bats. Pp. 309–325 *in: Bat biology and conservation* (eds. T.H. Kunz and P.A. Racey). Smithsonian Institution Press, Washington DC. (RNe)

Pierson, E.D., Sarich, V.M., Lowenstein, J.M., Daniel, M.J., and Rainey, W.E. 1986. A molecular link between the bats of New Zealand and South America. *Nature*, 323, 60–63.

van der Pijl, L. 1972. *Principles of dispersal in higher plants.* 2nd edition. Springer-Verlag, Berlin.

Pinchera, F. and Boitani, L. 1997. Application to the terrestrial Vertebrates of Italy of a system proposed by IUCN for a new classification of national red list categories. *Biodiversity & Conservation,* 6, 959–978.

Pint, J.J. 1994. Who cares about Mexican bats? *National Speleological Society News*, 52(3), 94.

Plumpton, D.L. and Knox Jones Jr., J. 1992. *Rhynchonycteris naso. Mammalian Species*, 413, 1–5. (+)

Pucek, Z. (ed) 1981. *Keys to the vertebrates of Poland: Mammals.* Translated and published for Smithsonian Institution and National Science Foundation, Washington DC by Polish Scientific Publishers. (RPa)

Pulido, V. 1991. *El libro rojo de la faune silvestre del Perú.* INIAA, WWF and USFWS, Lima.

Pyong-Oh, W. 1981. *Red data book of the Republic of Korea.* Korean Association for Conservation of Nature, Republic of Korea.

Qumsiyeh, M.B. 1985. The bats of Egypt. *Special Publications. The Museum, Texas Tech University*, 23, 1–102. (RPa)

Qumsiyeh, M.B., Disi, A.M., and Amr, Z.S. 1992. Systematics and distribution of the bats (Mammalia: Chiroptera) of Jordan. *Dirasat*, 19B (2), 101–118. (RPa)

Qumsiyeh, M.B. and Knox Jones Jr., J. 1986. *Rhinopoma hardwickii* and *Rhinopoma muscatellum. Mammalian Species*, 263, 1–5. (+)

Rabe, M.J., Morrel, T.E., Green, H., and Miller, C.R. 1998. Characteristics of ponderosa pine snag roosts used by reproductive bats in North America. *Journal of Wildlife Management*, 62(2), 612–621.

Rabinowitz, A. and Tuttle, M.D. 1980. Status of summer colonies of the endangered gray bat in Kentucky. *Journal of Wildlife Management,* 44, 955–960.

Racey, P.A. 1982. Ecology of bat reproduction. Pp. 57–104 *in: Ecology of bats* (ed. T.H. Kunz). Plenum Press, New York and London.

Racey, P.A. 1998a. Ecology of European bats in relation to their conservation. Pp. 249–260 *in: Bat biology and conservation* (eds. T.H. Kunz and P.A. Racey). Smithsonian Institution Press, Washington DC.

Racey, P.A. 1998b. The importance of the riparian environment as a habitat for British bats. Pp. 69–91 *in: Behaviour and ecology of riparian mammals* (eds. N. Dunstone and M.L. Gorman). Zoological Society of London Symposium Volume No. 71. Cambridge University Press, Cambridge.

Racey, P.A. 2000. Does legislation conserve and does research drive policy? The case of bats in the UK. Pp. 159–173 *in: Priorities for the conservation of mammalian diversity – Has the panda had its day?* (eds. A.C. Entwistle and N. Dunstone). Cambridge University Press, Cambridge.

Racey, P.A. and Entwistle, A.C. 2000. Life history and reproductive strategies of bats. Pp. 363–414 *in: Reproductive biology of bats* (eds. E. Crighton and P.H. Krutzsch). Academic Press, Cambridge.

Racey, P.A. and Entwistle, A.C. In press. Conservation ecology of bats. *In: Ecology of bats* (ed. T. Kunz).

Racey, P.A. and Nicoll, M.E. 1984. Mammals of the Seychelles. Pp. 607–626 *in: Biogeography and ecology of the Seychelles Islands* (ed. D.R. Stoddart). Junk, Den Haag. (RAf)

Racey, P.A. and Swift, S.M. 1986. The residual effects of remedial timber treatments on bats. *Biological Conservation,* 35, 205–214.

*Racey, P.A. and Swift, S.M. (eds.) 1995. *Ecology, behaviour and evolution of bats.* Zoological Society of London Symposium Volume No. 67. Oxford University Press, Oxford.

Racey, P.A., Swift, S.M., Rydell, J., and Brodie, C. 1998. Bats and insects over two Scottish rivers with contrasting nitrate status. *Animal Conservation*, 1, 195–202.

Rainey, W.E. 1998. Conservation of bats on remote Indo-Pacific islands. Pp. 326–341 *in: Bat biology and conservation* (eds. T.H. Kunz and P.A. Racey). Smithsonian Insitution Press, Washington DC. (RAs)

Rainha, A., Rodrigues, L., Bicho, S., Franco, C., and Palmeirim, J.M. 1998. *Morcegos das Areas Protegidas Portuguesas (1).* Estudos de Biologia e Conservação da Natureza, Número 26. Serviço Nacional de Parques, Reservas e Conservação da Natureza, Lisbon. (RPa)

Rakhmatulina, I.K. 1989. The peculiarity of the bat fauna of Azerbaijan. Pp. 409–414 *in: European bat research 1987* (eds. V. Hanak, I. Horacek and J. Gaisler). Charles University Press, Prague.

Rakhmatulina, I.K. 1996a. The bat fauna of the Caucasus and problems of its study. *Myotis*, 34, 51–57. (RPa)

Rakhmatulina, I. 1996b. On the history of study and tendency of changes of the eastern transcaucasian bat fauna. *Myotis*, 34, 59–70. (RPa)

Rakonczay, Z. 1989. *Voroskonyv: A Magyororszagon kipusztult es veszelyeztetett noveny-es allatfajok.* Akademiai Kaido, Budapest. [in Hungarian].

Ramírez-Pulido, J., Britton, J.M.C., Perdomo, A., and Castro, A. 1986. *Guía de los mamíferos de México.* Referencias hasta 1983. Universidad Autónoma Metropolitana Iztapalapa, México. (RNo)

Ramírez-Pulido, J., Castro-Campillo, A., Arroyo-Cabrales, J., and Cervantes, F.A. 1996. Lista taxonómica de los mamíferos terrestes de México. *Occasional Papers. The Museum, Texas Tech University*, 158, 1–62 + Errata. (RNo)

*Ransome, R.D. 1990. *The natural history of hibernating bats.* Christopher Helm, London.

Ransome, R.D. and Hutson, A.M. 2000. *Action Plan for the Conservation of the Greater Horseshoe Bat in Europe (Rhinolophus ferrumequinum).* Nature and Environment, No. 109. Council of Europe Publishing, Strasbourg. 53 pp.

Rasheed, S.A., Garcia, P.F.J., and Holroyd, S.L. 1995. *Status of the fringed myotis in British Columbia.* Wildlife Working Report WR–73, Ministry of Environment, Lands and Parks, Victoria.

Reardon, J.B. and Flavel, S.C. 1991. *A guide to the bats of South Australia*. South Australian Museum, Adelaide. (RAs)

Redford, K.H. and Eisenberg, J.F. 1992. *Mammals of the Neotropics. Volume 2. The southern cone.* University of Chicago Press, Chicago and London. (RNo)

Reid, F. 1997. *A field guide to the mammals of southeast Mexico and Central America*. Oxford University Press, Oxford.

Reidinger Jr., R.F. and Cockrum, E.L. 1978. Organochlorine residues in free-tailed bats (*Tadarida brasiliensis*) at Eagle Creek Cave, Greenlee County, Arizona. Pp. 85–96 *in: Proceedings of the Fourth International Bat Research Conference* (eds. R.J. Olembo, J.B. Castelino, and F.A. Mutere). Kenya Literature Bureau, Nairobi.

Reijnders, P.J.H. 1986. Reproductive failure in common seals feeding on fish from polluted coastal waters. *Nature*, 324, 456–457.

Resource Assessment Commission 1991. *Forest timber inquiry. Draft report,* volumes 1 and 2. Australian Government Publishing Service, Canberra.

Rezsutek, M. and Cameron, G.N. 1993. *Mormoops megalophylla. Mammalian Species*, 448, 1–5. (+)

Richards, G.C. 1994. Relationships of forest bats with habitat structure and foliage nutrients in south-eastern Australia. Abstracts of the *Sixth Australasian bat research conference*, Southern Cross University, Lismore.

Richards, G.C. and Hall, L.S. 1998. Conservation biology of Australian bats: Are recent advances solving our problems? Pp. 271–281 *in: Bat biology and conservation* (eds. T.H. Kunz and P.A. Racey). Smithsonian Insitution Press, Washington DC. (RAs)

*Richardson, P. 1985. *Bats.* Whittet Books, London.

Richarz, K. and Limbrunner, A. 1992. *Fledermäuse – flieginde Kobolde der Nacht.* Franckh-Kosmos Verlags-GmbH & Co., Stuttgart. [English translation, 1993, TFH Publications, New Jersey].

Riddle, B.R. (ed.) 1995. *Inactive mines as bat habitat: Guidelines for research, survey, monitoring and mine management in Nevada*. Biological Resources Research Center, University of Nevada, Reno, USA.

Robbins, C.B. 1980. Small mammals of Togo and Benin. I. Chiroptera. *Mammalia*, 44 (1), 83–88. (RAf)

Roberts, A. 1951. *The mammals of South Africa.* Trustees of the Mammals of South Africa Bookfund, Johannesburg. (RAf)

Roberts, G. and Roberts, A. 1993. *Biodiversity in the Caribo-Chilcotin grasslands*. Report to the Ministry of Environment, Lands and Parks, Wildlife Branch, Williams Lake, Canada.

Roberts, T.J. 1977. *The mammals of Pakistan.* Ernest Benn, London and Tonbridge. (RIn)

Roberts, T.J. 1998. *The mammals of Pakistan, 2nd edition.* Oxford University Press, Pakistan. (RIn)

Robinson, M.F. 1997. *Chiroptera survey. Rapid biological assessment Xe Paine Protected Area, Champassak Province, Lao P.D.R.* Unpublished final report, World Wide Fund for Nature, Thailand. (RIn)

Robinson, M.F. and Webber, M. 1998. *Small mammal survey. Khammouan Limestone National Biodiversity Conservation Area, Lao P.D.R.* Unpublished final report, World Wide Fund for Nature, Thailand. (RIn)

Rodrigues, M.L.S.V. 1996. *Utilizacao de grades para proteccao de abrigos de morcegos cavernicolas.* Dissertation of Faculty of Sciences, University of Lisbon, Portugal.

Rodríguez, J.P. and Rojas-Suárez, F. 1995. *Red book of the fauna of Venezuela*. PROVITA, Caracas.

Rodriguez-Duran, A. and Kunz, T.H. 1992. *Pteronotus quadridens. Mammalian Species*, 395, 1–4. (+)

Rodriguez-H, B. and Wilson, D.E. 1999. *Lista y Distribucion de las Especies de Murcielagos de Costa Rica.* Occasional Papers in Conservation Biology No. 5. Conservation International, Washington DC. (RNo)

Rodríguez-Mahecha, J.V., Hernández-Camacho, J.I., Defler, T.R., Alberico, M., Mast, R.B., Mittermeier, R.A., and Cadena, A. 1995. *Mamíferos Colombianos: Sus nombres comunes e indigenas.* Occasional Papers in Conservation Biology Number 3. Conservation International, Washington DC. (RNo)

Romanowski, J. and Lesinski, G. 1991. A note on the diet of stone marten in southeastern Romania. *Acta Theriologica*, 36 (1–2), 201–204.

Ron, T. 1995. *An action plan for the monitoring and conservation of insectivorous bats in Israel.* Division of Science and Management, Nature Reserves Authority, Jerusalem. (RPa)

Roots, E.H. and Baker, R.J. 1998. *Rhogeessa genowaysi. Mammalian Species*, 589, 1–3. (+)

Rosevear, D. 1953. *Checklist and atlas of Nigerian mammals, with a foreword on vegetation.* Government Printer, Lagos. (RAf)

Rosevear, D. 1965. *Bats of West Africa.* British Museum (Natural History), London. (RAf)

Ross, A. 1967. Ecological aspects of food habits of insectivorous bats. *Proceedings of the Western Foundation of Vertebrate Zoology*, 1, 205–263.

Rossolimo, O.L. (ed.) 1995. [*Mammals of Eurasia. II. Non-Rodentia*]. Archives of Zoological Museum Moscow State University, Volume 23, Moscow [in Russian]. (RPa)

Ruiz, A. and Diaz, A.M. 1990. *Epidemiology of rabies transmitted by vampire bats.* Subject 3.8. Pan American Health Organization, Pan American Sanitary Bureau, Regional Office of the World Health Organization, WHO Seminar on Wildlife Rabies Control, Geneva, July 2–5, 1990.

Rybin, S.N., Horacek, I., and Cerveny, J. 1989. The bats of southern Kirghizia: Distribution and faunal status. Pp. 421–441 *in: European bat research 1987* (eds. V. Hanak, I. Horacek and J. Gaisler). Charles University Press, Prague.

Rydell, J. 1986. Foraging and diet of the northern bat *Eptesicus nilssoni* in Sweden. *Holarctic Ecology*, 9, 272–276.

Rydell, J. 1993. *Eptesicus nilssonii. Mammalian Species*, 430, 1–7. (+)

Rydell, J. and Baagoe, H.J. 1994. *Vespertilio murinus. Mammalian Species*, 467, 1–6. (+)

Rydell, J. and Bogdanowicz, W. 1997. *Barbastella barbastellus. Mammalian Species*, 557, 1–8. (+)

Rydell, J., Straun, K-B., and Speakman, J.R. 1994. First record of breeding bats above the Arctic Circle: Northern bats at 68°N in Norway. *Journal of Zoology London*, 233(2), 335–339.

Sacks, J.J., Ajello, L., and Crockett, L.K., 1986. An outbreak and review of cave-associated *Histoplasmosis capsulati. Journal of Medical and Veterinary Mycology*, 24, 313–327.

Saint-Girons, M-C. 1973. *Les mammiféres de France et du Benelux.* Doin, Paris. (RPa)

Salter, R.E. (compiler) 1993. *Wildlife in Lao PDR. A status report.* IUCN, Vientiane. (RIn)

Sanborn, C.C. and Crespo, J.A. 1957. El murcielago blanquizco (*Lasiurus cinereus*) y sus subspecies. *Boletín del Museo Argentino de Ciencias Naturales "Bernardino Rivadavia" e Instituto Nacional de Investigacion de las Ciencias Naturales*, 4, 1–13.

Sargent, G. 1995. *The bats in churches project.* The Bat Conservation Trust, London.

Savic, I.R., Paunovic, M., Milenkovic, M., and Stamenkovic, S. 1995. [Diversity of mammal fauna of Yugoslavia, with review of the species of international importance. *In: Biodiversity of Yugoslavia with review of species of international importance* (eds. V. Stevanovic, and V. Vasic)]. Biological Faculty and Ecolibri, Belgrade. [in Serbian].

Sayer, J.A., Harcourt, C.S., and Collins, N.M. 1992. *The conservation atlas of tropical forests: Africa* Macmillan, Basingstoke, UK.

Schembri, P.J. and Sultana, J. (eds.) 1989. *Red data book for the Maltese Islands.* Environment Department, Ministry of Education, Malta.

Schliemann, H. and Maas, B. 1978. *Myzopoda aurita. Mammalian Species*, 116, 1–2. (+)

Schlitter, D.A. and Qumsiyeh, M.B. 1996. *Rhinopoma microphyllum. Mammalian Species*, 542, 1–5. (+)

Schlitter, D.A., Robbins, L.W., and Buchanan, S.A. 1983. Bats of the Central African Republic (Mammalia: Chiroptera). *Annals of the Carnegie Museum,* 51 (8), 133–155. (RAf)

Schmidly, D.J. 1991. *The bats of Texas.* University of Texas Press, Austin, USA. (RNe)

Schneider, M.C. 1991. Epidemiological situation of human rabies transmitted by bats in Brazil. *In: Expert consultation on the care of persons exposed to rabies transmitted by vampire bats.* PAHO/WHO. Programs for Veterinary Public Health. Washington DC, April 1–5, 1991.

Schneider, M.C. and Uieda, W. 1998. *Ecology and epidemiology of attacks upon humans by the common vampire bat.* Abstract of paper presented at 11th International Bat Research Conference, Pierenopolis, Brazil, 2–6 August 1998. Abstracts prepared by Departamento de Zoologia, Universidade de Brasília.

Schnitzler, H.-U. and Kalko, E.K.V. 1998. How echo-locating bats search and find food. Pp. 183–196. *in: Bat biology and conservation* (eds. T.H. Kunz and P.A. Racey) Smithsonian Institution Press, Washington DC.

*Schober, W. 1984. *The lives of bats.* Croom Helm, London.

Schober, W. and Grimmberger, E. 1998. *Die Fledermäuse Europas.* (Revised edition). Kosmos-Naturfuhrer, Stuttgart. (RPa)

Schofield, H.W. 1996. *The ecology and conservation biology of* Rhinolophus hipposideros, *the lesser horseshoe bat.* PhD thesis, University of Aberdeen, Aberdeen, UK.

Schwarz, J. 1981. *Histoplasmosis.* Praeger Special Studies, Praeger Publishers, New York.

Sclater, W.L. 1900. *The mammals of South Africa.* I and II. Trustees of the British Museum (Natural History), London. (RAf)

Sekhran, N. and Miller, S. E. (eds.) 1995. *Papua New Guinea country study on biological diversity.* The Department of the Environment and Conservation, Waigani, Papua New Guinea.

Shortridge, G.C. 1934. *The mammals of South West Africa.* Heinemann, London. (RAf)

Shump Jr., K.A. and Shump, A.U. 1982a. *Lasiurus borealis. Mammalian Species*, 183, 1–6. (+)

Shump Jr., K.A. and Shump, A.U. 1982b. *Lasiurus cinereus. Mammalian Species*, 185, 1–5. (+)

Siddiqi, M.S. 1961. Checklist of mammals of Pakistan with particular reference to the mammalian collection in the British Museum (Natural History), London. *Biologia*, 7 (2), 93–225. (RIn)

Siders, M.S. and Sinton, D. 1998. *Artificial bat bark development and testing.* Final Report for Arizona Game and Fish Department, IIPAM Heritage Grant I996004, North Kaibab Ranger District, Kaibab National Forest, Fredonia, USA.

Silva Taboada, G. 1979. *Los murciélagos de Cuba.* Editorial Academia, Havana. (RNo)

Simmons, N.B., Voss, R.S., and Pecham, H.C. 2000. The bat fauna of the Saül region, French Guiana. *Acta Chiropterologica*, 2(1), 23–36.

Simpson, M.R. 1993. *Myotis californicus. Mammalian Species*, 428, 1–4. (+)

Skinner, J.D. and Smithers, R.H.N. 1990. *Mammals of the southern African subregion,* 2nd edition. University of Pretoria Press, Pretoria. (RAf)

*Slaughter, B.H. and Walton, D.W. 1970. *About bats: A chiropteran symposium.* Southern Methodist University Press, Dallas.

Sluiter, J.W. and Heerdt, P.F. van 1966. Seasonal habits of the noctule bat (*Nyctalus noctula*) *Archives Neerlanaises de Zoologie*, 16, 423–439.

Smith, J.S., Orciari, L.A., and Yager, P.A. 1995. Molecular epidemiology of rabies in the United States. *Seminars in Virology* 6, 387–400.

Smith, P.G. and Kerry, S.M. 1996. The Iwokrama Rain Forest Programme for sustainable development: How much of Guyana's bat (Chiroptera) diversity does it encompass? *Biodiversity and Conservation*, 5, 921–942.

Smithers, R.H.N. 1971. *The mammals of Botswana.* Museum Memoir 4. Trustees National Museum Rhodesia, Salisbury, Rhodesia. (RAf)

Smithers, R.H.N. 1983. *Mammals of the southern African subregion.* University of Pretoria Press, Pretoria. (RAf)

Smithers, R.H.N. 1986. *Red data book – terrestrial mammals.* South African National Scientific Programmes Report No. 125. A Report of the Committee for Nature Conservation Research, National Programme for Ecosystem Research, Pretoria.

Smithers, R.H.N. and Tello, J.L.P.L. 1976. *Checklist and atlas of the mammals of Mocambique.* Museum Memoir No. 8. Trustees National Museums and Monuments, Salisbury, Rhodesia. (RAf)

Smithers, R.H.N. and Wilson, V.J. 1979. *Checklist and atlas of the mammals of Zimbabwe Rhodesia.* Trustees National Museums and Monuments, Salisbury, Zimbabwe Rhodesia. (RAf)

Snow, J.L., Knox Jones Jr., J., and Webster, W.D. 1980. *Centurio senex. Mammalian Species*, 138, 1–3. (+)

SNPRCN 1990. *Livro Vermelho dos Vertebrados de Portugal. Vol. 1 – Mamiferos, Aves, Repteis e Anfibios.* SNPRCN, Lisbon.

Sokolov, V.E. and Orlov, V.N. 1980. [*Key to the mammals of the Mongolian People's Republic*]. Moscow. [in Russian]. (RPa)

Sokolov, V.E. 1996. [*Rare species of Mongolia: Animals*]. Institut Problem Ekologii I Evolyutsii imeni A.N.Severtzova, Moscow. [in Russian].

Soriano, P.J. and Molinari, J. 1987. *Sturnira aratathomasi. Mammalian Species*, 284, 1–4. (+)

Spitzenberger, F. 1979. Die säugetierfauna Zyperns. Teil II. Chiroptera, Lagomorpha, Carnivora und Artiodactyla. *Annalen des (K.K.) Naturhistorischen (Hof) Museums,* 82, 439–465. (RPa)

Stager, K.E. 1943. Remarks on *Myotis occultus* in California. *Journal of Mammalogy*, 24, 197–199.

Starrett, A. 1972. *Cyttarops alecto. Mammalian Species*, 13, 1–2. (+)

State of the Environment Advisory Council 1996. *Australia, state of the environment 1996.* Report to the Commonwealth Minister for the Environment, CSIRO, Canberra.

Stattersfield, A.J., Crosby, M.J., Long, A.J., and Wege, D.C. 1998. *Endemic bird areas of the world. Priorities for biodiversity conservation.* BirdLife Conservation Series No. 7, BirdLife International, Cambridge, UK.

Stebbings, R.E. 1988. *Conservation of European Bats.* Christopher Helm, London. (RPa)

Storz, J.F. and Kunz, T.E. 1999. *Cynopterus sphinx. Mammalian Species*, 613, 1–8. (+)

Strahan, R. (ed.) 1983. *The Australian Museum complete book of Australian mammals.* Angus and Robertson, Sydney. (RAs)

Strahan, R. (ed.) 1995. *Mammals of Australia.* Reed Books, Chatswood, Australia

Strelkov, P.P. 1969. Migratory and stationary bats (Chiroptera) of the European part of the Soviet Union. *Acta Zoologica Cracoviensia*, 14, 393–439.

Strelkov, P.P. 1997. Nursing area and its position within the range in migratory bats (Chiroptera: Vespertilionidae) from Eastern Europe and neighbouring regions. *Russian Journal of Zoology*, 1(4), 545–553.

Strelkov, P.P., Sosnovtseva, V.P., and Babaev, K.B. 1978. [Bats (Chiroptera) of Turkmenistan]. *Trud Zoologicheskogo Instituta. Akademiya Nauk SSSR. Leningrad*, 79, 3–71 [in Russian]. (RPa)

Strong, L. 1992. Avermectins: A review of their impact on insects in cattle dung. *Bulletin of Entomological Research*, 82, 265–274.

Suarez, L. and Garcia, M. 1986. *Extinción de Animales en el Ecuador*. Fundación Natura, Quito.

Swanepoel, P. and Genoways, H.H. 1983a. *Brachypylla cavernarum. Mammalian Species*, 205, 1–6. (+)

Swanepoel, P. and Genoways, H.H. 1983b. *Brachypylla nana. Mammalian Species*, 206, 1–3. (+)

Swanepoel, R.E., Racey, P.A., Shore, R.F., and Speakman, J.R. 1999. Energetic effects of sublethal exposure to lindane on pipistrelle bats (*Pipistrellus pipistrellus*). *Environmental Pollution*, 104, 169–177.

Sweeney, R.C.H. 1959. *A preliminary annotated checklist of the mammals of Nyasaland.* The Nyasaland Society, Blantyre, Nyasaland. (RAf)

Swift, S.M., Racey, P.A., and Avery, M.I. 1985. Feeding ecology of *Pipistrellus pipistrellus* (Chiroptera: Vespertilionidae) during pregnancy and lactation. II. Diet. *Journal of Animal Ecology*, 54, 217–225.

Swynnerton, G.H. and Hayman, R.W. 1951. Checklist of the land mammals of the Tanganyika Territory and the Zanzibar Protectorate. *Journal of the East African Natural History Society,* 20 (6–7), 274–392. (RAf)

Tait, J. 1987. National Bat Year – the end. *Bat News*, 10, 2–3.

Tamsit, J.R. and Hauser, C. 1985. *Sturnira magna. Mammalian Species*, 240, 1–4. (+)
Tamsitt, J.R. and Nagorsen, D. 1982. *Anoura cultrata. Mammalian Species*, 179, 1–5. (+)
Taylor, D.A.R. 1995. North American Bats and Mines Project makes major progress. *Bats*, 13(2), 3–4.
Taylor, E.H. 1934. *Philippine land mammals.* Monograph Number 30, Bureau of Science, Manila. (RIn)
Taylor, P.J. 2000. *Bats of Southern Africa; Guide to biology, identification, and conservation.* University of Natal Press, Pietermaritzburg. 206 pp. (RAf)
Tello, J. 1979. *Mamíferos de Venezuela.* Fundacion la Salle de Ciencias Naturales, Caracas. (RNo)
The Nature Conservancy 1997. *Designing geography of hope: Guidelines for ecoregion-based conservation in The Nature Conservancy.* The Nature Conservancy, Arlington, USA.
Thomas, N.T. 1997. *A systematic review of selected Afro-Asiatic Rhinolophidae (Mammalia: Chiroptera). An evaluation of taxonomic methodologies.* PhD thesis, University of Aberdeen/Harrison Zoological Museum, Sevenoaks, UK.
Thomson, B.G. 1991. *A field guide to the bats of the Northern Territory.* Commission of the Northern Territory, Darwin, Australia. (RAs)
Thomson, C.E. 1982. *Myotis sodalis. Mammalian Species*, 163, 1–5. (+)
Timm, R.M. 1982. *Ectophylla alba. Mammalian Species*, 166, 1–4. (+)
Timm, R.M. 1985. *Artibeus phaeotis. Mammalian Species*, 235, 1–6. (+)
Tirira, D. (ed.) 1999. *Mamíferos del Ecuador.* Publicacion Especial 2. Museo de Zoologia, Centro de Bioversidad y Ambiente, Pontificia Universidad Católica del Ecuador, Quito. (RNo)
Toledo, V. 1990. El Proceso de Ganaderización y la Destrucción Biologica y Ecologica de México. Pp. 191–227 *in: Medio Ambiente y Dessarollo en México, Vol. 1* (ed. E. Leff). Centro de Investigaciones Interdisciplinarias en Humanidades, UNAM, Mexico.
Tryjanowski, P. 1997. Food of the stone marten (*Martes foina*) in Nietoperek Bat Reserve. *Zeitschrift für Säugetierkunde*, 67, 318–320.
Tuinov, M.P. 1997. *The Bats of the Russian Far East.* Dalnauka, Vladivostok. 134 pp (in Russian). (RPa)
Tumlinson, R. 1992. *Plecotus mexicanus. Mammalian Species*, 401, 1–3. (+)
Tun Yin 1993. *Wild mammals of Myanmar.* Soe Kyi, Forest Department, Yangon. (RIn).
*Tupinier, D. 1989. *La chauve-souris et l'homme.* Editions L'Harmattan, Paris.
Turner, D.C. 1975. *The vampire bat: A field study in behavior and ecology.* The John Hopkins University Press, Baltimore.
Tuttle, M.D. 1970. Distribution and zoogeography of Peruvian bats with comments on natural history. *University of Kansas Science Bulletin*, 49, 45–86. (RNo)
Tuttle, M.D. 1976. Population ecology of the gray bat (*Myotis grisescens*): Philopatry, timing and patterns of movement, weight loss during migration, and seasonal adaptive strategies. *Occasional Papers of the Museum of Natural History, University of Kansas*, 54, 1–38.
Tuttle, M.D. 1979. Status, causes of decline, and management of endangered gray bats. *Journal of Wildlife Management*. 43, 1–17.
Tuttle, M.D. 1986. Endangered gray bat benefits from protection. *Bats*, 4 (4), 1–4.
Tuttle, M.D. 1988. *America's neighbourhood bats.* University of Texas Press, Austin.
Tuttle, M.D. and Hensley, D.L. 1993. *The bat house builder's handbook.* Bat Conservation International, Austin.
Tuttle, M.D. and Stevenson, D. 1982. Growth and survival of bats. Pp. 105–150 *in: Ecology of bats* (ed. T.H. Kunz). Plenum, New York.
Tuttle, M.D. and Taylor, D.A.R. 1998. *Bats and mines.* Revised edition. Resource Publication Number 3, Bat Conservation International, Austin.
Tyler, M.J. (ed.) 1979. *The status of endangered Australasian wildlife.* Royal Society of South Australia, Adelaide. (RAs)
Uhl, C. and Viera, I.C.G. 1989. Ecological impacts of selective logging in the Brazilian Amazon: A case study from the Paragominas region of the state of Pará. *Biotropica*, 21, 98–106.
UN Department of International Economic and Social Affairs 1989. *World population prospects.* United Nations, New York.
United States Department of Agriculture 1991. Environmental effects, in Tongass land management plan revision, supplement to the draft environmental impact statement. R10-MB-146. *U.S. Department of Agriculture, Forest Service, Juneau, Alaska*, 1–765.
United States Department of Agriculture 1993. Timber supply and demand 1992. Report number 12. September 1993. *U.S. Department of Agriculture, Forest Service, Juneau, Alaska.*
Valdivieso, D. 1964. La fauna quiroptera del Departamento de Cundinamarca, Colombia. *Revista de Biologia Tropical*, 12, 19–45.
Vane-Wright, R.I., Humphries, C.J., and Williams, P.H. 1991. What to protect? Systematics and the agony of choice. *Biological Conservation*, 55, 235–254.
Varona, L.S. 1974. *Catálogo de los mamíferos vivientes y extinguidos de las Antillas.* Instituto de Zoologia, Academia de Ciencias de Cuba, Havana. (RNo)
Verboom, B. 1998. *The use of edge habitats by commuting and foraging bats.* IBN Scientific Contributions 10. DLO Institute for Forestry and Nature Research (IBN-DLO), Wageningen, The Netherlands.

Vernier, E. 1997. *Manuale pratico dei Chirotteri italiana.* 2nd edition. Società Cooperativa Tipografica, Padova, Italy. (RPa)

de Verteuil, E. and Urich, F.W. 1936. The study and control of paralytic rabies transmitted by bats in Trinidad, British West Indies. *Trans. Roy. Soc. Trop. Med. Hyg.*, 29, 317–347.

Vielliard, J. 1974. Les Cheiroptères du Tchad. *Revue Suisse de Zoologie,* 81 (4), 975–991. (RAf)

Villa, B. 1967. *Los Murcielagos de México.* Instituto de Biología, Universidad Nacional Autónoma de México, México City. (RNe) (RNo)

Villela O.F. and Gerez, P. 1994. *Biodiversidad y conservacion en Mexico: Vertebrados, vegetacion y uso del suelo.* Universidad National Autonoma de Mexico, Mexico.

Vogel, S. 1969. Chiropterophilie in der neotropischen Flora. *Neue Mitteilungen III. Flora, Abt. B.*, 158, 289–323.

Vonhoff, M.J. and Kalcounis, M.C. 1999. *Lavia frons. Mammalian Species*, 614, 1–4. (+)

Walker, S. 1995. Mexico-U.S. partnership makes gains for migratory bats. *Bats*, 13(3), 3–5.

Walker, S. 1997. Murciélagos de Nuevo León. *Bats*, 15(1), 16.

Walsh, A.L. and Harris, S. 1996a. Foraging habitat preferences of vespertilionid bats in Britain. *Journal of Applied Ecology*, 33, 508–518.

Walsh, A.L. and Harris, S. 1996b. Factors determining the abundance of vespertilionid bats in Britain: Geographical, land class and local habitat relationships. *Journal of Applied Ecology*, 33, 519–529.

Walsh, A.L., Harris, S., and Hutson, A.M. 1995. Abundance and habitat selection of foraging vespertilionid bats in Britain: A landscape-scale approach. Pp. 325–344 *in: Ecology, behaviour and evolution of bats* (eds. P.A. Racey and S.M. Swift). Zoological Society of London Symposium Volume No. 67. Oxford University Press, Oxford.

Wang, S. 1998. *China red data book of endangered animals: Mammalia.* Science Press, Beijing.

Warner, R.M. 1982. *Myotis auriculus. Mammalian Species*, 191, 1–3. (+)

Warner, R.M. 1984. Interspecific and temporal dietary variation in an Arizona bat community. *Journal of Mammalogy*, 66, 45–51.

Warner, R.M. and Czaplewski, N.J. 1984. *Myotis volans. Mammalian Species*, 224, 1–4. (+)

Watkins, L.C. 1972. *Nycticeius humeralis. Mammalian Species*, 23, 1–4. (+)

Watkins, L.C. 1977. *Euderma maculatum. Mammalian Species*, 77, 1–4. (+)

Watson, J, Hamilton-Smith, E, Gillieson and Kiernan, K. (eds.) 1997. *Guidelines for cave and karst protection.* IUCN, Gland, Switzerland and Cambridge, UK.

Webster, W.D., Handley Jr., C.O., and Soriano, P.J. 1998. *Glossophaga longirostris. Mammalian Species*, 576, 1–5. (+)

Webster, W.D. and Knox Jones Jr., J. 1982a. *Artibeus aztecus. Mammalian Species*, 177, 1–3. (+)

Webster, W.D. and Knox Jones Jr., J. 1982b. *Artibeus toltecus. Mammalian Species*, 178, 1–3. (+)

Webster, W.D. and Knox Jones Jr., J. 1983. *Artibeus hirsutus* and *Artibeus inopinatus. Mammalian Species*, 199, 1–3. (+)

Webster, W.D. and Knox Jones Jr., J. 1984. *Glossophaga leachii. Mammalian Species*, 226, 1–3. (+)

Webster, W.D. and Knox Jones Jr., J. 1985. *Glossophaga mexicana. Mammalian Species*, 245, 1–2. (+)

Webster, W.D. and Knox Jones Jr., J. 1993. *Glossophaga commissarisi. Mammalian Species*, 446, 1–4. (+)

Webster, W.D., Knox Jones Jr., J., and Baker, R.J. 1980. *Lasiurus intermedius. Mammalian Species*, 132, 1–3. (+)

Webster, W.D. and Owen, R.D. 1984. *Pygoderma bilabiatum. Mammalian Species*, 220, 1–3. (+)

Wetmore, A. and Swales, B.H. 1931. The birds of Haiti and the Dominican Republic. *Bulletin of the U.S. National Museum*, 155, 1–483.

Whilde, A. (ed.) 1993. *Threatened mammals, birds, amphibians and fish in Ireland: Irish red data book 2: Vertebrates.* Her Majesty's Stationary Office, Belfast.

Whitaker Jr., J.O. 1993. Bats, beetles and bugs. *Bats*, 11, 23.

Whitaker, Jr., J.O. and Black, H.L. 1976. Food habits of cave bats from Sabia, Africa. *Journal of Mammalogy*, 57, 56–65.

Whitaker, Jr., J.O., Maser, C., and Keller, L.E. 1977. Food habits of bats of western Oregon. *Northwest Science*, 51, 46–55.

Wildlife Conservation Society of the Philippines 1997. *Philippine red data book.* Bookmark, Inc., Makati, Philippines.

Williams, P.H. 1994. *WORLDMAP. Priority areas for biodiversity: Using version 3.* Privately distributed by the author, The Natural History Museum, London.

Wilkins, K.T. 1987. *Lasiurus seminolus. Mammalian Species*, 280, 1–5. (+)

Wilkins, K.T. 1989. *Tadarida brasiliensis. Mammalian Species*, 331, 1–10. (+)

Willig, M.R. and Hollander, R.R. 1987. *Vampyrops lineatus. Mammalian Species*, 275, 1–4. (+)

Willig, M.R. and Knox Jones Jr., J. 1985. *Neoplatymops mattogrossensis. Mammalian Species*, 244, 1–3. (+)

Willis, K.B., Willig, M.R., and Knox Jones Jr., J. 1990. *Vampyrodes caraccioli. Mammalian Species*, 359, 1–4. (+)

Wilson, D.E. 1978. *Thyroptera discifera. Mammalian Species*, 104, 1–3. (+)

Wilson, D.E. 1983. Checklist of mammals. Pp. 443–447 *in: Costa Rican natural history* (ed. D.H. Janzen). University of Chicago Press, Chicago. (RNo)

Wilson, D.E. 1996. Neotropical bats: A checklist with conservation status. Pp. 167–177 *in: Neotropical biodiversity and conservation* (ed. A.C. Gibson). Mildred E. Mathias Botanical Garden, University of California, Los Angeles.

Wilson, D.E. and Findley, J.S. 1977. *Thyroptera tricolor. Mammalian Species*, 71, 1–3. (+)

Wilson, D.E. and LaVal, R.K. 1974. *Myotis nigricans. Mammalian Species*, 39, 1–3. (+)

*Wilson, D.E. and Reeder, D.M. 1993. *Mammal species of the world: A taxonomic and geographic reference.* Smithsonian Institution Press, Washington DC.

*Wimsatt, W.A. 1970a. *Biology of bats*, Volume 1. Academic Press, New York.

*Wimsatt, W.A., 1970b. *Biology of bats*, Volume 2. Academic Press, New York.

*Wimsatt, W.A., 1977. *Biology of bats*, Volume 3. Academic Press, New York.

World Bank 1988. *Staff Appraisal Report: Ghana Forest Resources Management Project (No. 7295–GH).* World Bank, Washington DC.

World Conservation Monitoring Centre 1988. *Directory of protected areas. Afghanistan. Draft.* WCMC, Protected Areas Data Unit, Cambridge, UK. (Unpublished draft document).

World Resources Institute 1992. *World resources 1992–93: A guide to the global environment.* Oxford University Press, New York.

WWF and IUCN 1994. *Centres of plant diversity. A guide and strategy for their conservation.* 3 volumes. IUCN Publications Unit, Cambridge, UK.

Ximénez, A., Langguth, A., and Praderi, R. 1972. Lista sistemática de los mammíferos del Uruguay. *Anales del Museo de Historia Natural de Montivideo,* 7 (5), 1–45. (RNo)

Yalden, D.W., Largen, M.J., Kock, D., and Hillman, J.C. 1996. Catalogue of the mammals of Ethiopia and Eritrea. 7. Revised checklist, zoogeography and conservation. *Tropical Ecology*, 9, 73–164. (RAf)

*Yalden, D.W. and Morris, P.A. 1975. *The lives of bats.* David and Charles, Newton Abbott, UK.

Yancey II, F.D., Goetze, J.R., and Jones, C. 1998a. *Saccopteryx bilineata. Mammalian Species*, 581, 1–5. (+)

Yancey II, F.D., Goetze, J.R., and Jones, C. 1998b. *Saccopteryx leptura. Mammalian Species*, 582, 1–3. (+)

Yoshiyuki, M. 1989. *A systematic study of the Japanese Chiroptera.* National Science Museum, Tokyo. (RPa)

Zhang Yongzu 1997. *Distribution of mammalian species in China.* China Forestry Publishing House, Beijing. (RIn) (RPa)

Zortea, M. and Taddei, V.A. 1995. Taxonomic status of *Tadarida espiritosantensis* Ruschi, 1951 (Chiroptera: Molossidae). *Boletim de Museu de Biologia Mello Leitao,* 2, 15–21.

van Zyll de Jong, C.G. 1985. *Handbook of Canadian mammals.* National Museum of Natural Sciences, Ottawa. (RNe)

Appendix 1

IUCN Red List Categories

From Craig Hilton-Taylor, 2000. *2000 Red List of Threatened Species*. The IUCN Species Survival Commission, Gland

Extinct (EX)

A taxon is Extinct when there is no reasonable doubt that the last individual has died.

Extinct in the Wild (EW)

A taxon is Extinct in the Wild when it is known only to survive in cultivation, in captivity, or as a naturalised population (or populations) well outside the past range. A taxon is presumed Extinct in the Wild when exhaustive surveys in known and/or expected habitat, at appropriate times (diurnal, seasonal, annual) throughout its historic range have failed to record an individual. Surveys should be over a time frame appropriate to the taxon's life cycle and life form.

Critically Endangered (CR)

A taxon is Critically Endangered when it is facing an extremely high risk of extinction in the wild in the immediate future, as defined by any of the following criteria (A to E):

A. Population reduction in the form of either of the following:
   1. An observed, estimated, inferred, or suspected reduction of at least 80% over the last 10 years or three generations, whichever is the longer, based on (and specifying) any of the following:
      (a) direct observation
      (b) an index of abundance appropriate for the taxon
      (c) a decline in the area of occupancy, extent of occurrence, and/or quality of habitat
      (d) actual or potential levels of exploitation
      (e) the effects of introduced taxa, hybridisation, pathogens, pollutants, competitors, or parasites.
   2. A reduction of at least 80%, projected or suspected to be met within the next 10 years or three generations, whichever is the longer, based on (and specifying) any of (b), (c), (d), or (e) above.

B. Extent of occurrence estimated to be less than 100km^2 or area of occupancy estimated to be less than 10km^2, and estimates indicating any two of the following:
   1. Severely fragmented or known to exist at only a single location.
   2. Continuing decline, inferred, observed, or projected, in any of the following:
      (a) extent of occurrence
      (b) area of occupancy
      (c) area, extent, and/or quality of habitat
      (d) number of locations or subpopulations
      (e) number of mature individuals.
   3. Extreme fluctuations in any of the following:
      (a) extent of occurrence
      (b) area of occupancy
      (c) number of locations or subpopulations
      (d) number of mature individuals.

C. Population estimated to number less than 250 mature individuals and either:
   1. An estimated continuing decline of at least 25% within three years or one generation, whichever is the longer, or
   2. A continuing decline, observed, projected, or inferred, in numbers of mature individuals and population structure in the form of either:
      (a) severely fragmented (i.e., no subpopulation estimated to contain more than 50 mature individuals) or
      (b) all individuals are in a single subpopulation.

D. Population estimated to be less than 50 mature individuals.

E. Quantitative analysis showing the probability of extinction in the wild is at least 50% within 10 years or three generations, whichever is the longer.

Endangered (EN)

A taxon is Endangered when it is not Critically Endangered, but is facing a very high risk of extinction in the wild in the near future, as defined by any of the following criteria (A to E):

A. Population reduction in the form of either of the following:
   1. An observed, estimated, inferred, or suspected reduction of at least 50% over the last 10 years or three generations, whichever is the longer, based on (and specifying) any of the following:
      (a) direct observation
      (b) an index of abundance appropriate for the taxon

(c) a decline in the area of occupancy, extent of occurrence, and/or quality of habitat
(d) actual or potential levels of exploitation
(e) the effects of introduced taxa, hybridisation, pathogens, pollutants, competitors, or parasites.
2. A reduction of at least 50%, projected or suspected to be met within the next 10 years or three generations, whichever is the longer, based on (and specifying) any of (b), (c), (d), or (e) above.

B. Extent of occurrence estimated to be less than 5,000km^2 or area of occupancy estimated to be less than 500km^2, and estimates indicating any two of the following:
1. Severely fragmented or known to exist at no more than five locations.
2. Continuing decline, inferred, observed, or projected, in any of the following:
(a) extent of occurrence
(b) area of occupancy
(c) area, extent, and/or quality of habitat
(d) number of locations or subpopulations
(e) number of mature individuals.
3. Extreme fluctuations in any of the following:
(a) extent of occurrence
(b) area of occupancy
(c) number of locations or subpopulations
(d) number of mature individuals.

C. Population estimated to number less than 2,500 mature individuals and either:
1. An estimated continuing decline of at least 20% within five years or two generations, whichever is the longer, or
2. A continuing decline, observed, projected, or inferred, in numbers of mature individuals and population structure in the form of either:
(a) severely fragmented (i.e., no subpopulation estimated to contain more than 250 mature individuals) or
(b) all individuals are in a single subpopulation.

D. Population estimated to number less than 250 mature individuals.

E. Quantitative analysis showing the probability of extinction in the wild is at least 20% within 20 years or five generations, whichever is the longer.

Vulnerable (VU)

A taxon is Vulnerable when it is not Critically Endangered or Endangered, but is facing a high risk of extinction in the wild in the medium-term future, as defined by any of the following criteria (A to E):

A. Population reduction in the form of either of the following:
1. An observed, estimated, inferred, or suspected reduction of at least 20% over the last 10 years or three generations, whichever is the longer, based on (and specifying) any of the following:
(a) direct observation
(b) an index of abundance appropriate for the taxon
(c) a decline in the area of occupancy, extent of occurrence, and/or quality of habitat
(d) actual or potential levels of exploitation
(e) the effects of introduced taxa, hybridisation, pathogens, pollutants, competitors, or parasites.
2. A reduction of at least 20%, projected or suspected to be met within the next 10 years or three generations, whichever is the longer, based on (and specifying) any of (b), (c), (d), or (e) above.

B. Extent of occurrence estimated to be less than 20,000km^2 or area of occupancy estimated to be less than 2,000km^2, and estimates indicating any two of the following:
1. Severely fragmented or known to exist at no more than 10 locations.
2. Continuing decline, inferred, observed, or projected, in any of the following:
(a) extent of occurrence
(b) area of occupancy
(c) area, extent, and/or quality of habitat
(d) number of locations or subpopulations
(e) number of mature individuals.
3. Extreme fluctuations in any of the following:
(a) extent of occurrence
(b) area of occupancy
(c) number of locations or subpopulations
(d) number of mature individuals.

C. Population estimated to number less than 10,000 mature individuals and either:
1. An estimated continuing decline of at least 10% within 10 years or three generations, whichever is the longer, or
2. A continuing decline, observed, projected, or inferred, in numbers of mature individuals and population structure in the form of either:
(a) severely fragmented (i.e., no subpopulation estimated to contain more than 1,000 mature individuals) or
(b) all individuals are in a single subpopulation.

D. Population very small or restricted in the form of either of the following:
1. Population estimated to be less than 1,000 mature individuals.
2. Population is characterised by an acute restriction in its area of occupancy (typically less than 100km^2)

or in the number of locations (typically less than five). Such a taxon would thus be prone to the effects of human activities (or stochastic events whose impact is increased by human activities) within a very short period of time in an unforeseeable future, and is thus capable of becoming Critically Endangered or even Extinct in a very short period.

E. Quantitative analysis showing the probability of extinction in the wild is at least 10% within 100 years.

Lower Risk (LR)

A taxon is Lower Risk when it has been evaluated and does not satisfy the criteria for any of the categories Critically Endangered, Endangered, or Vulnerable. Taxa included in the Lower Risk Category can be separated into three subcategories:

1. **Conservation Dependent (cd).** Taxa which are the focus of a continuing taxon-specific or habitat-specific conservation programme targeted towards the taxon in question, the cessation of which would result in the taxon qualifying for one of the threatened categories above within a period of five years;

2. **Near Threatened (nt).** Taxa which do not qualify for Conservation Dependent, but which are close to qualifying for Vulnerable;

3. **Least Concern (lc).** Taxa which do not qualify for Conservation Dependent or Near Threatened.

Data Deficient (DD)

A taxon is Data Deficient when there is inadequate information to make a direct or indirect assessment of its risk of extinction based on its distribution and/or population status. A taxon in this category may be well studied and its biology well known, but appropriate data on abundance and/or distribution is lacking. Data Deficient is, therefore, not a category of threat or Lower Risk. Listing of taxa in this category indicates that more information is required and acknowledges the possibility that future research will show that threatened classification is appropriate. It is important to make positive use of whatever data are available. In many cases, great care should be exercised in choosing between Data Deficient and threatened status. If the range of the taxon is suspected to be relatively circumscribed, if a considerable period of time has elapsed since the last record of the taxon, threatened status may well be justified.

Not Evaluated (NE)

A taxon is Not Evaluated when it has not yet been assessed against the criteria.

IUCN/SSC Action Plans for the Conservation of Biological Diversity

Action Plan for African Primate Conservation 1986-1990. Compiled by J.F. Oates. IUCN/SSC Primate Specialist Group, 1986, 41 pp. (out of print)

Action Plan for Asian Primate Conservation 1987–1991. Compiled by A.A. Eudey. IUCN/SSC Primate Specialist Group, 1987, 65 pp. (out of print)

Antelopes. Global Survey and Regional Action Plans. Part 1. East and Northeast Africa. Compiled by R. East. IUCN/SSC Antelope Specialist Group, 1988, 96 pp. (out of print)

Dolphins, Porpoises and Whales. An Action Plan for the Conservation of Biological Diversity 1987–1991. Second Edition. Compiled by W.F. Perrin. IUCN/SSC Cetacean Specialist Group, 1989, 27 pp. (out of print)

The Kouprey. An Action Plan for its Conservation. Edited by J.R. MacKinnon and S.N. Stuart. IUCN/SSC Asian Wild Cattle Specialist Group, 1988, 19 pp. (out of print)

Weasels, Civets, Mongooses and their Relatives. An Action Plan for the Conservation of Mustelids and Viverrids. Compiled by A. Schreiber, R. Wirth, M. Riffel, and H. van Rompaey. IUCN/SSC Mustelid and Viverrid Specialist Group, 1989, 99 pp. (out of print)

Antelopes. Global Survey and Regional Action Plans. Part 2. Southern and South-central Africa. Compiled by R. East. IUCN/SSC Antelope Specialist Group, 1989, 96 pp. (out of print)

Asian Rhinos. An Action Plan for their Conservation. Compiled by Mohd Khan bin Momin Khan. IUCN/SSC Asian Rhino Specialist Group, 1989, 23 pp. (out of print)

Tortoises and Freshwater Turtles. An Action Plan for their Conservation. Compiled by the IUCN/SSC Tortoise and Freshwater Turtle Specialist Group, 1989, 47 pp.

African Elephants and Rhinos. Status Survey and Conservation Action Plan. Compiled by D.H.M. Cumming, R.F. du Toit, and S.N. Stuart. IUCN/SSC African Elephant and Rhino Specialist Group, 1990, 73 pp. (out of print)

Foxes, Wolves, Jackals, and Dogs. An Action Plan for the Conservation of Canids. Compiled by J.R. Ginsberg and D.W. Macdonald. IUCN/SSC Canid and Wolf Specialist Groups, 1990, 116 pp. (out of print)

The Asian Elephant. An Action Plan for its Conservation. Compiled by C. Santiapillai and P. Jackson. IUCN/SSC Asian Elephant Specialist Group, 1990, 79 pp.

Antelopes. Global Survey and Regional Action Plans. Part 3. West and Central Africa. Compiled by R. East. IUCN/SSC Antelope Specialist Group, 1990, 171 pp.

Otters. An Action Plan for their Conservation. Edited by P. Foster-Turley, S. Macdonald, and C. Maso. IUCN/SSC Otter Specialist Group, 1990, 126 pp. (out of print)

Rabbits, Hares and Pikas. Status Survey and Conservation Action Plan. Compiled and edited by J.A. Chapman and J.E.C. Flux. IUCN/SSC Lagomorph Specialist Group, 1990, 168 pp.

African Insectivora and Elephant-Shrews. An Action Plan for their Conservation. Compiled by M.E. Nicoll and G.B. Rathbun. IUCN/SSC Insectivore, Tree-Shrew, and Elephant-Shrew Specialist Group, 1990, 53 pp.

Swallowtail Butterflies. An Action Plan for their Conservation. Compiled by T.R. New and N.M. Collins. IUCN/SSC Lepidoptera Specialist Group, 1991, 36 pp.

Crocodiles. An Action Plan for their Conservation. Compiled by J. Thorbjarnarson and edited by H. Messel, F.W. King, and J.P. Ross. IUCN/SSC Crocodile Specialist Group, 1992, 136 pp.

South American Camelids. An Action Plan for their Conservation. Compiled and edited by H. Torres. IUCN/SSC South American Camelid Specialist Group, 1992, 58 pp.

Australasian Marsupials and Monotremes. An Action Plan for their Conservation. Compiled by M. Kennedy. IUCN/SSC Australasian Marsupial and Monotreme Specialist Group, 1992, 103 pp.

Lemurs of Madagascar. An Action Plan for their Conservation 1993–1999. Compiled by R.A. Mittermeier, W.R. Konstant, M.E. Nicoll, and O. Langrand. IUCN/SSC Primate Specialist Group, 1992, 58 pp. (out of print)

Zebras, Asses and Horses. An Action Plan for the Conservation of Wild Equids. Edited by P. Duncan. IUCN/SSC Equid Specialist Group, 1992, 36 pp.

Old World Fruit Bats. An Action Plan for their Conservation. Compiled by S. Mickleburgh, A.M. Hutson, and P.A. Racey. IUCN/SSC Chiroptera Specialist Group, 1992, 252 pp. (out of print)

Seals, Fur Seals, Sea Lions, and Walrus. Status Survey and Conservation Action Plan. Peter Reijnders, Sophie Brasseur, Jaap van der Toorn, Peter van der Wolf, Ian Boyd, John Harwood, David Lavigne, and Lloyd Lowry. IUCN/SSC Seal Specialist Group, 1993, 88 pp.

Pigs, Peccaries, and Hippos. Status Survey and Conservation Action Plan. Edited by William L.R. Oliver. IUCN/SSC Pigs and Peccaries Specialist Group. IUCN/SSC Hippo Specialist Group, 1993, 202 pp.

Pecaries. Extraido de *Pigs, Peccaries, and Hippos. Status Survey and Conservation Action Plan (1993).* Editado por William L.R. Oliver. IUCN/CSE Groupo de Especialistas en Puercos y Pecaries, 1996, 58 pp.

The Red Panda, Olingos, Coatis, Raccoons, and their Relatives. Status Survey and Conservation Action Plan for Procyonids and Ailurids. In English and Spanish. Compiled by Angela R. Glatston. IUCN/SSC Mustelid, Viverrid, and Procyonid Specialist Group, 1994, 103 pp.

Dolphins, Porpoises, and Whales. 1994–1998 Action Plan for the Conservation of Cetaceans. Compiled by Randall R. Reeves and Stephen Leatherwood. IUCN/SSC Cetacean Specialist Group, 1994, 91 pp.

Megapodes. An Action Plan for their Conservation 1995–1999. Compiled by René W.R.J. Dekker and Philip J.K. McGowan, and the WPA/Birdlife/SSC Megapode Specialist Group, 1995, 41 pp.

Partridges, Quails, Francolins, Snowcocks and Guineafowl. Status Survey and Conservation Action Plan 1995–1999. Compiled by Philip J.K. McGowan, Simon D. Dowell, John P. Carroll, and Nicholas J.A. Aebischer, and the WPA/BirdLife/SSC Partridge, Quail, and Francolin Specialist Group, 1995, 102 pp.

Pheasants. Status Survey and Conservation Action Plan 1995–1999. Compiled by Philip J.K. McGowan and Peter J. Garson on behalf of the WPA/BirdLife/SSC Pheasant Specialist Group, 1995, 116 pp.

Wild Cats. Status Survey and Conservation Action Plan. Compiled and edited by Kristin Nowell and Peter Jackson. IUCN/SSC Cat Specialist Group, 1996, 406 pp.

Eurasian Insectivores and Tree Shrews. Status Survey and Conservation Action Plan. Compiled by David Stone. IUCN/SSC Insectivore, Tree Shrew, and Elephant Shrew Specialist Group, 1996, 108 pp.

African Primates. Status Survey and Conservation Action Plan (Revised Edition). Compiled by John F. Oates. IUCN/SSC Primate Specialist Group, 1996, 80 pp.

The Cranes. Status Survey and Conservation Action Plan. Compiled by Curt D. Meine and George W. Archibald. IUCN/SSC Crane Specialist Group, 1996, 401 pp.

Orchids. Status Survey and Conservation Action Plan. Edited by Eric Hágsater and Vinciane Dumont. Compiled by Alec Pridgeon. IUCN/SSC Orchid Specialist Group, 1996, 153 pp.

Palms. Their Conservation and Sustained Utilization. Status Survey and Conservation Action Plan. Edited by Dennis Johnson. IUCN/SSC Palm Specialist Group, 1996, 116 pp.

Conservation of Mediterranean Island Plants. 1. Strategy for Action. Compiled by O. Delanoë, B. de Montmollin, and L. Olivier. IUCN/SSC Mediterranean Islands Plant Specialist Group, 1996, 106 pp.

Wild Sheep and Goats and their Relatives. Status Survey and Conservation Action Plan for Caprinae. Edited and compiled by David M. Shackleton. IUCN/SSC Caprinae Specialist Group, 1997, vii + 390 pp.

Asian Rhinos. Status Survey and Conservation Action Plan (New Edition). Edited by Thomas J. Foose and Nico van Strien. IUCN/SSC Asian Rhino Specialist Group, 1997, v + 112 pp.

The Ethiopian Wolf. Status Survey and Conservation Action Plan. Compiled and edited by Claudio Sillero-Zubiri and David Macdonald. IUCN/SSC Canid Specialist Group, 1997, 123 pp. (out of print)

Cactus and Succulent Plants. Status Survey and Conservation Action Plan. Compiled by Sara Oldfield. IUCN/SSC Cactus and Succulent Specialist Group, 1997, x + 212 pp.

Dragonflies. Status Survey and Conservation Action Plan. Compiled by Norman W. Moore. IUCN/SSC Odonata Specialist Group, 1997, v + 28 pp.

Tapirs. Status Survey and Conservation Action Plan. Edited by Daniel M. Brooks, Richard E. Bodmer, and Sharon Matola. IUCN/SSC Tapir Specialist Group, 1997, viii + 164 pp.

The African Wild Dog. Status Survey and Conservation Action Plan. Compiled and edited by Rosie Woodroffe, Joshua Ginsberg, and David Macdonald. IUCN/SSC Canid Specialist Group, 1997, 166 pp.